WILLARD MULLIN'S
GOLDEN AGE OF BASEBALL

By WILLARD MULLIN, HAL BOCK, and MICHAEL POWERS

For Michael and Sara, who make me smile each day the way
Willard Mullin did so many years ago.

—Hal Bock

Designer: JACOB COVEY
Editorial Supervisor: GARY GROTH
Copy Desk: J. MICHAEL CATRON
Production: PAUL BARESH
Proofreader: JANICE LEE
Editorial Assistance: TOM GRAHAM and KRISTY VALENTI
Associate Publisher: ERIC REYNOLDS
Publishers: GARY GROTH and KIM THOMPSON

Fantagraphics Books, Inc. | 7563 Lake City Way NE | Seattle WA 98115

To receive a free catalogue of more books like this as well as a variety of cutting-edge graphic novels, classic comic book and newspaper strip collections, eclectic prose novels, uniquely insightful cultural criticism, and other fine works of artistry, call (800) 657-1100 or visit Fantagraphics.com. Follow us on Twitter at @fantagraphics and on Facebook at facebook.com/fantagraphics.

Images on pages 11, 15 (bottom), 65, 105, 106, 116, 120, 137, 139, 140, 144, 146, 154, 156, 162, 163, 167, 173, 177, 184, 189, 193, 194, 210–213, 219–222, 225 (bottom left and right), and 228–231 courtesy Warren Bernard. Images from 1972 Red Sox TV schedule, page 187, courtesy Richard Stover.

Special thanks to: The National Baseball Hall of Fame, The Estate of Willard Mullin, Shirley Mullin Rhodes, Lee Sullivan, Jason Powers Photography, Seppala Photography, Finkbeiner Photography, Bruce Stark, National Art Museum of Sport (NAMOS), David Kaplan, Tim Wiles, Jake Elwell, and the Yogi Berra Museum & Learning Center.

First Fantagraphics printing: July 2013
ISBN 978-1-60699-639-3
Printed in China

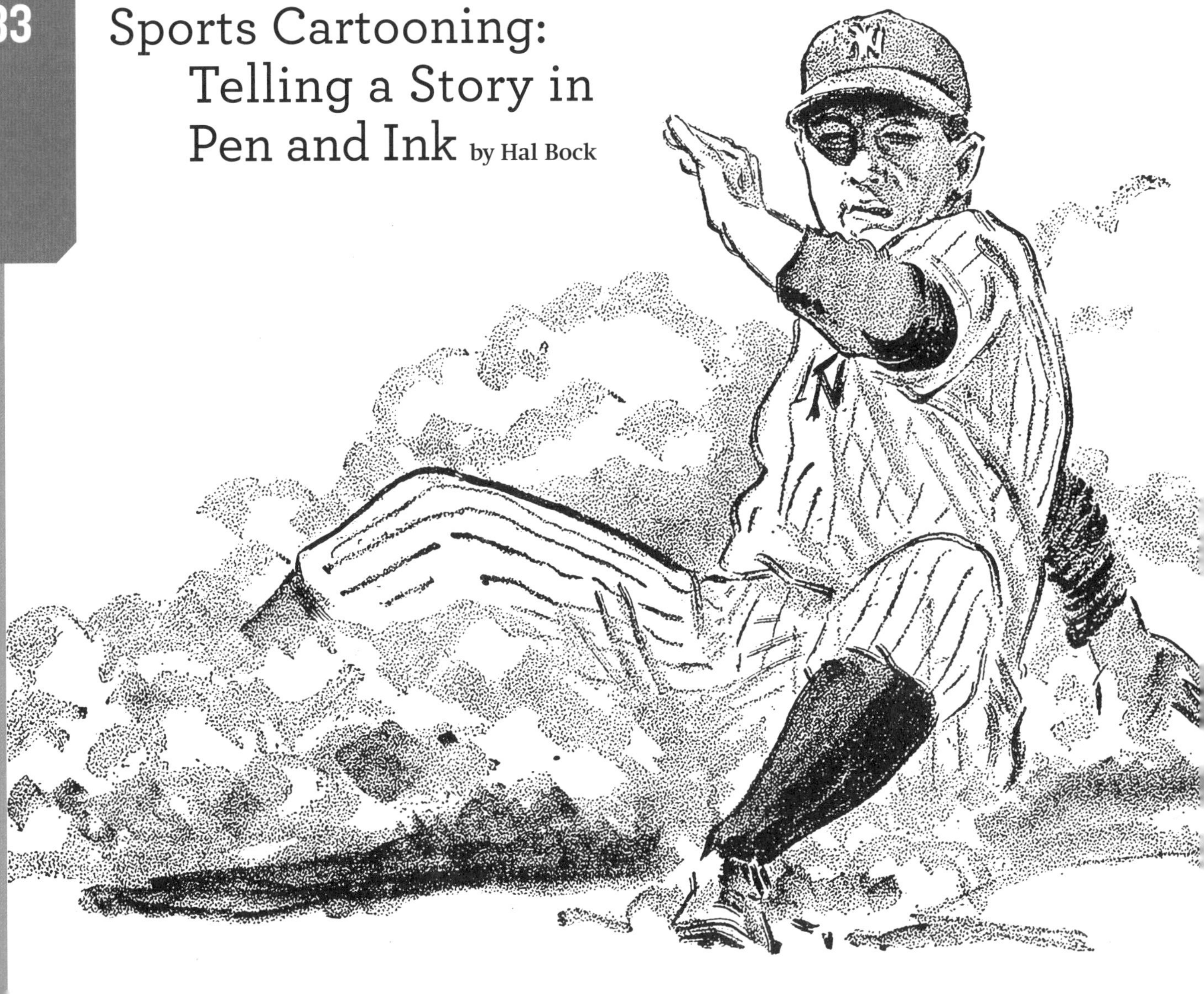

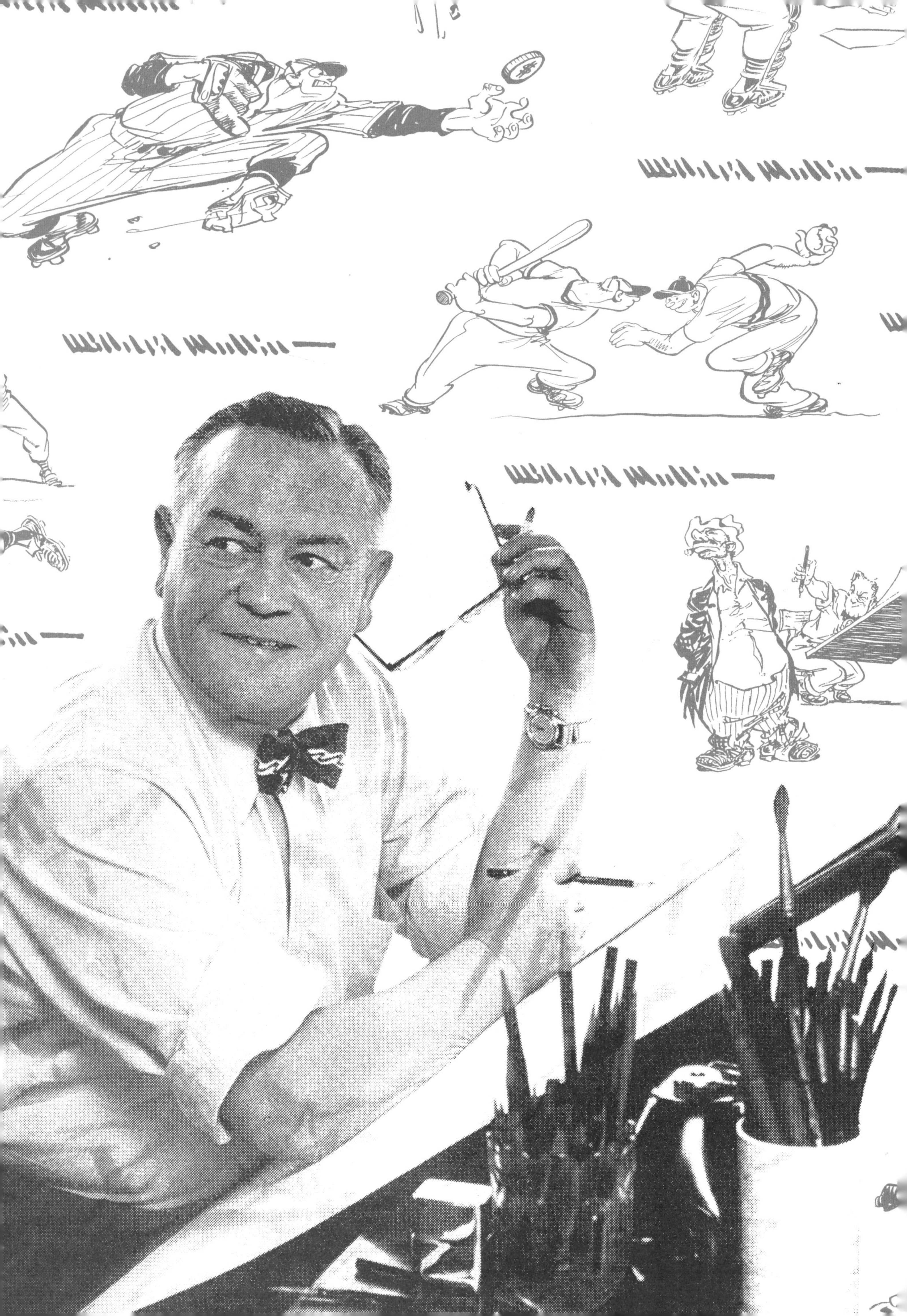

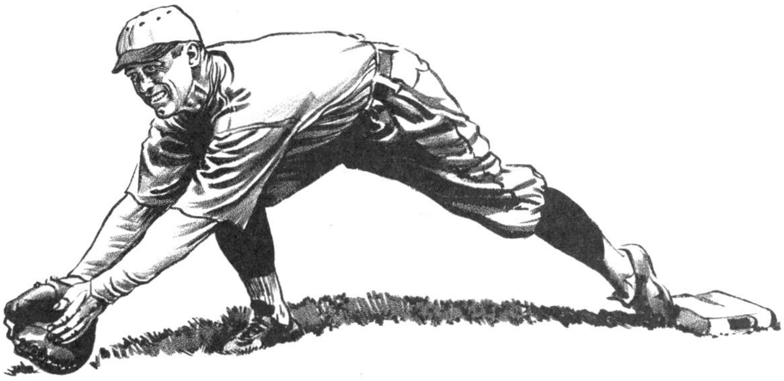

Mulling Over Willard

Bob Staake

I'D NEVER STOLEN A THING in my life — until I came across Willard Mullin.

I was a 14-year-old boy growing up in Los Angeles when I stumbled on a copy of Mullin's *Junior Encyclopedia Of Sport* at the Torrance Public Library. I was floored — and the book would come to change my life. His fluidity of line, his command of anatomy, his stunning sense of composition within the most impossible dimensions, I *had* to steal the thing and make it mine, so I carefully tucked it into my Hang Ten shirt, nervously slithered past the clueless librarians at the checkout desk, triumphantly rode off on my root beer-colored Schwinn and took the book home to ogle the drawings like any normal boy would drool over a 1971 *Playboy* centerfold.

For me, Mullin was cartoon porn.

How did he get his pen nib to effortlessly bite into Bristol board like that? *How* could he have such an understanding of an athlete's body while caricaturing the staccato movements with utter perfection? *How* could he mix his thick-to-thin strokes in a way that his two-dimensional characters quite literally performed, ballet-like, on a printed page? To a stupid teenage boy hopelessly committed to one day becoming a cartoonist himself, it was all a huge mystery, but I was bound and determined to figure out Willard Mullin's secret.

Mom, however, was my frigid shower.

She found the dog-eared Mullin book tucked into a shelf in my bedroom, shrewdly noticed that I had tried to remove the 'Torrance Public Library' rubber stamp from the spine with both ink eradicator *and* belt sander, made me confess to the petty crime, and unceremoniously escorted me to the library where she made me come clean that I had indeed stolen the book to a blue-haired librarian.

My German, always-by-the-book mother probably did the right thing, but I was humiliated.

Still, I'd devoured the book for a good six months before being busted, so I learned what I'd needed — each night opening the book, obsessively studying Mullin's ethereal drawings, doing my damnedest through mimicked idolatry to replicate them line-for-line. The swirl of a crowquill, the grease pencil shading on pebble board, the occassional brushstrokes of black to pop his characters.

OPPOSITE: Mullin at his drawing board in 1957.

Mullin simply confounded and infuriated me with his artistic aplomb, but with enough practice, I was soon able to create my own passable sports cartoons, even seeing them published in the local newspaper.

As chance would have it, many years later, in 2012, a woman in Colorado whose father worked with Mullin's publisher, Bobbs-Merrill, sent me an email stating she had 66 Mullin original drawings from a book called *Junior Encyclopedia Of Sport* and wondered if I might be interested in buying them.

Of course I bought them — and immediately, via PayPal.

There's not a lot for me to learn by studying Mullin today. He drew his breathless sports cartoons from the 1940s right into the early 1970s, and I eventually grew up to find my own "style" by illustrating children's books and animation and *New Yorker* covers — but owning those 66 personally important drawings (along with another dozen of Mullin's cartoons for the *New York World-Telegram*), one really couldn't come more "full-circle" than that.

I once stole the drawings in book form, but now I *owned* them — in all their original pen-and-ink glory.

Willard Mullin was a maestro. Any discriminating artist would determine that by looking at his printed work, yet when you scrutinize his original drawings, you're left slack-jawed, envious, and utterly blown away by his uncommon prowess. In these drawings, there's *very* little penciling and when you notice it at all, it's loose, natural, the artist slashing playfully like a jazz musician wielding nothing more than a hint of 2B clarinet on a stage of 3-ply Bristol.

That sort of spontaneity and Mullin's linear flow would always be the sketchy pre-product of a man obviously saddled with tons of deadlines breathing down his neck, an uncommon confidence in his inking skills, and simply no time or patience at all to do anything other than follow his aesthetic instincts to crunch out drawings awash in the scent of 5 p.m. deadline. He'd almost completely avoid the brush, but adopted a soft-touch-to-hard-pressed pen technique that made his line vary from delicate and lyrical to fat and juicy.

His giant-format drawings may have routinely been grounded in the sports cartoon standard of the large, central, semi-realist grease penciled visage of the main subject's head, but my eye was always drawn to Mullin's accompanying three or four gestural drawings (most loosely caricatured) showing the lead subject sliding into home, stretching to snag a fly, watching a grounder trickle, Bill Buckner-style, between the ankles of an opposing first baseman. Granted, the "gags" were usually pedestrian, but you never gazed at a Mullin for the writing — you sucked them in for their dance; the stretch of a pin-striped leg, the sweep of an outstretched arm, the ripple of a toned 20-something's deltoid — and Mullin understood the rhythmic play of an elite athlete's body like nobody else.

The sports cartoon has been dead for years, traditional newspapers themselves doing their best to cling on for dear life. But Willard Mullin remains the high benchmark of the art form, a historical touchstone, the standard bearer of one of print journalism's most esoteric niche features — and as a historical record of his uncommon artistic achievements, which alone makes this Fantagraphics book both long overdue and necessary.

In Willard Mullin's drawings, you smell the lukewarm beer being burped out of the Brooklyn Bum, you hear the roar of the crowd when a ball short-smacks the center field wall, you taste the salt of the peanut shells crunched beneath the well-worn heels of the proletariat in the bleachers of Ebbets Field.

Me, I may have once stole a Mullin book — but not even my mother could make me return his original drawings.

They're mine now — forever and always. ❖

BOB STAAKE is an illustrator and author. His work appears in the *New Yorker*, *The Washington Post*, *The New York Times*, and many other publications. He is also the creator of over 60 children's books published by Random House, Little Brown, Simon & Schuster, and HarperCollins. He lives and works on Cape Cod.

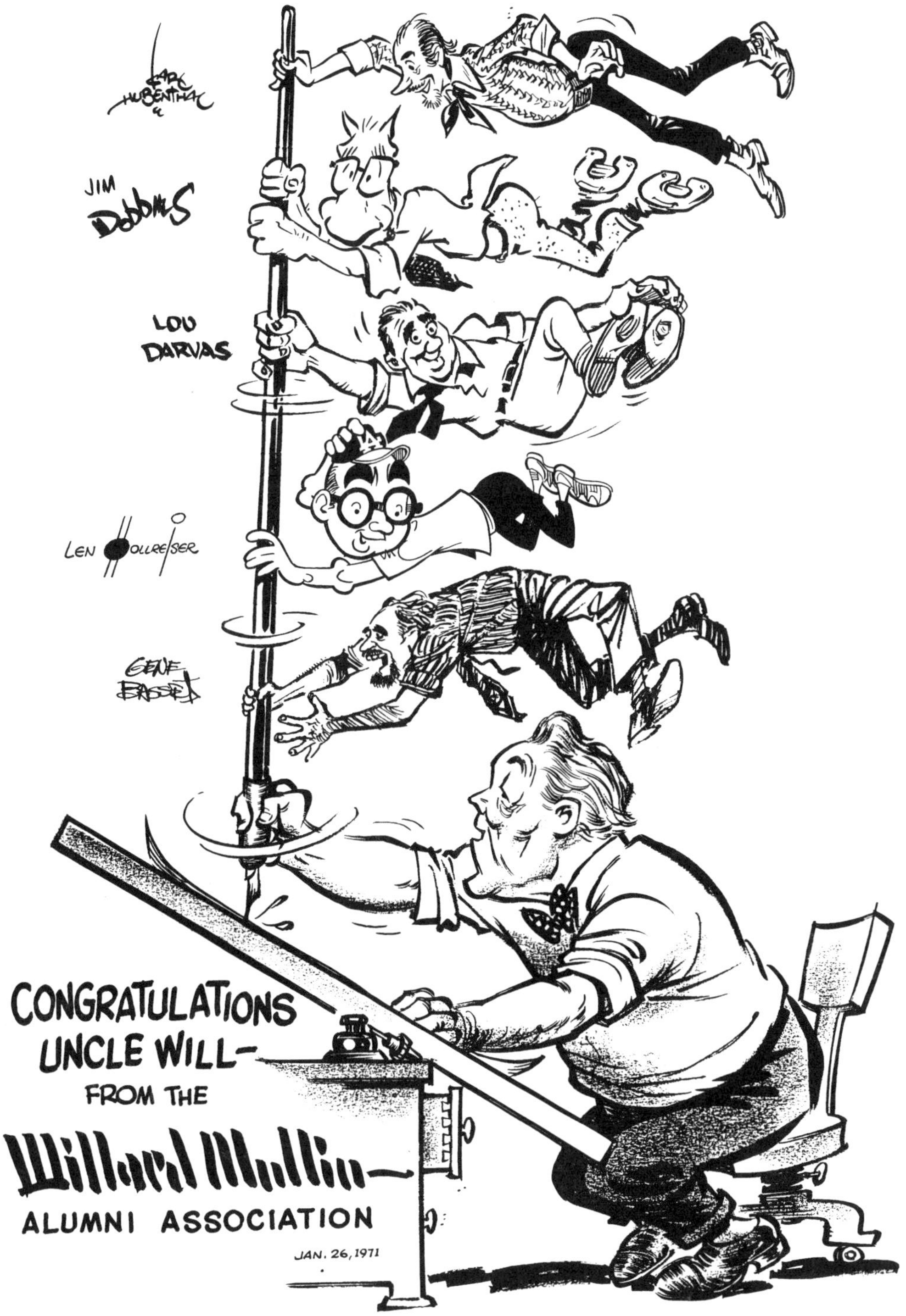
JIM
LOU DARVAS
CONGRATULATIONS
UNCLE WILL—
FROM THE
Willard Mullin
ALUMNI ASSOCIATION
JAN. 26, 1971

LEFT: When Mullin retired in 1970, Karl Hubenthal, a famed cartoonist in his own right, did this drawing of the unofficial Willard Mullin Alumni Association.

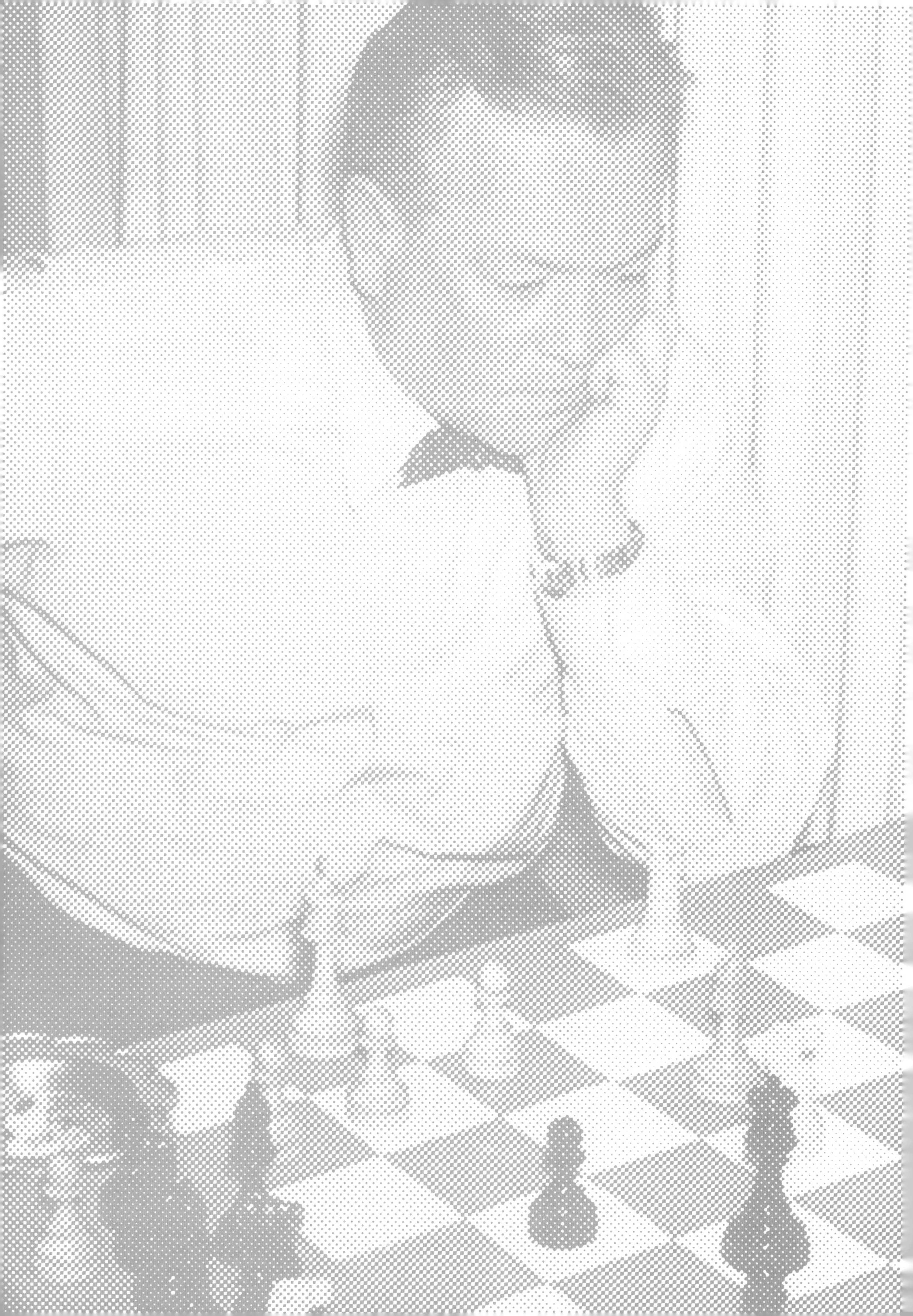

Willard Mullin Through the Eyes of His Daughter

Shirley Mullin Rhodes

ABOVE: A young Mullin and his lifelong friend, Gil Wheat.

OPPOSITE: Mullin engages in a favorite pastime.

HE WAS KIND, gentle, and generous. And he was my father. Was I ever lucky!

Pop was also about having fun. Simple errands with him were adventures. If there were any bystanders, he charmed them and they had fun, too.

A self-made man, Pop assumed that everyone could pull himself up Horatio Alger-style, as he had done. On this subject, as on others, you could say that Pop was strongly opinionated. But how nice when the opinion fell your way. While Pop and my mom expected me to toe the line (and I did), he was consistently and lovingly on my side.

Pop was a terrific competitor and an incorrigible gamester. Any daily activity became a contest or a wager. "How far do you think it is from here to that stop sign over there?" It was, of course, a distance he had already figured out before offering a bet and happily pocketing the dollar bill you were saving for a week's worth of ice cream. He was always up for checkers, chess, or any board game. Once at age 10 or so, I beat him at Five-in-a-Row. He was delighted at my prowess and I knew I had really earned his respect as he never threw a game or played down to a youngster. Sometimes a shared chore, like peeling potatoes, didn't lend itself to a game and he'd say, "Let's get this job done fast so we have more time to play!"

Pop loved his work and called it the best job in the world. Imagine being paid to cover a Yankees-Dodgers World Series or a Joe Louis fight in the Garden! He loved living in New York and mixing with the greats of the sports world and the writers who covered them. Many of these sportswriters became his close friends who would gather at places like Mama Leone's, Toots Shor's, or Al Schacht's.

Of course, viewing games from the press box was fun — turning out a witty, interesting, well-drawn cartoon was the real work. To this day I think it's awesome that he produced six cartoons a week for thirty years for the sports page of the *New York World-Telegram & Sun*.

After television began broadcasting baseball and football, Pop would draw his cartoons from home. Often, friends would drop over while he would be in his office working on his cartoon for Monday. Once the drawing, text, and balloons were penciled in, some friends would go into his office and watch the drawing come to life in ink. As he progressed from idea to execution, he joined the party and at this point usually poured himself a Scotch.

He never demanded quiet, or even privacy, when he was working. As for those unexpected guests, my mother was a miracle worker. No matter how many showed up, she would stretch whatever was in the fridge to feed them all.

After starting to work from home, Pop still had to get his drawings to the paper. We lived on the north shore of Long Island, a short block from the Plandome Station where the Long Island Rail Road commuter trains run every hour or so. When the ink had dried on a finished cartoon and the pencil marks were erased, Pop would roll it up, secure it with a rubber band, slip three one-dollar bills under the rubber band, and walk down to the station.

When the westbound train rolled in, a happy conductor took custody of the drawing — and the tip — and delivered it to Western Union in Penn Station. Then a WU messenger would take it to the *World-Telegram* offices. It sounds like a fragile plan, but in fifteen years he lost exactly one cartoon.

I never saw my Pop worry about getting an idea for a cartoon, even with a short deadline hanging over him. If he did feel pressure, he never showed it. He had a fertile mind and the ability to bring up a lifetime of observations that he could set to paper in a way that no other sports cartoonist has ever equaled.

I never really thought about Pop's fame or how great he was when I was young. He was just my Pop. But one time as a teenager I had been in New York City and I boarded the train to go home. The car was filled with commuters. I climbed on at the rear of the car. Every single newspaper was opened to the Mullin cartoon.

I was so proud! I wanted to shout "That's my Pop!" ❖

ABOVE, RIGHT: Mullin and his daughter, Shirley, at her wedding.

OPPOSITE: The cover for the first New York Mets yearbook. Mullin's grandson, Ted Rhodes, served as the model.

NEW YORK NATIONAL LEAGUE BASEBALL CLUB

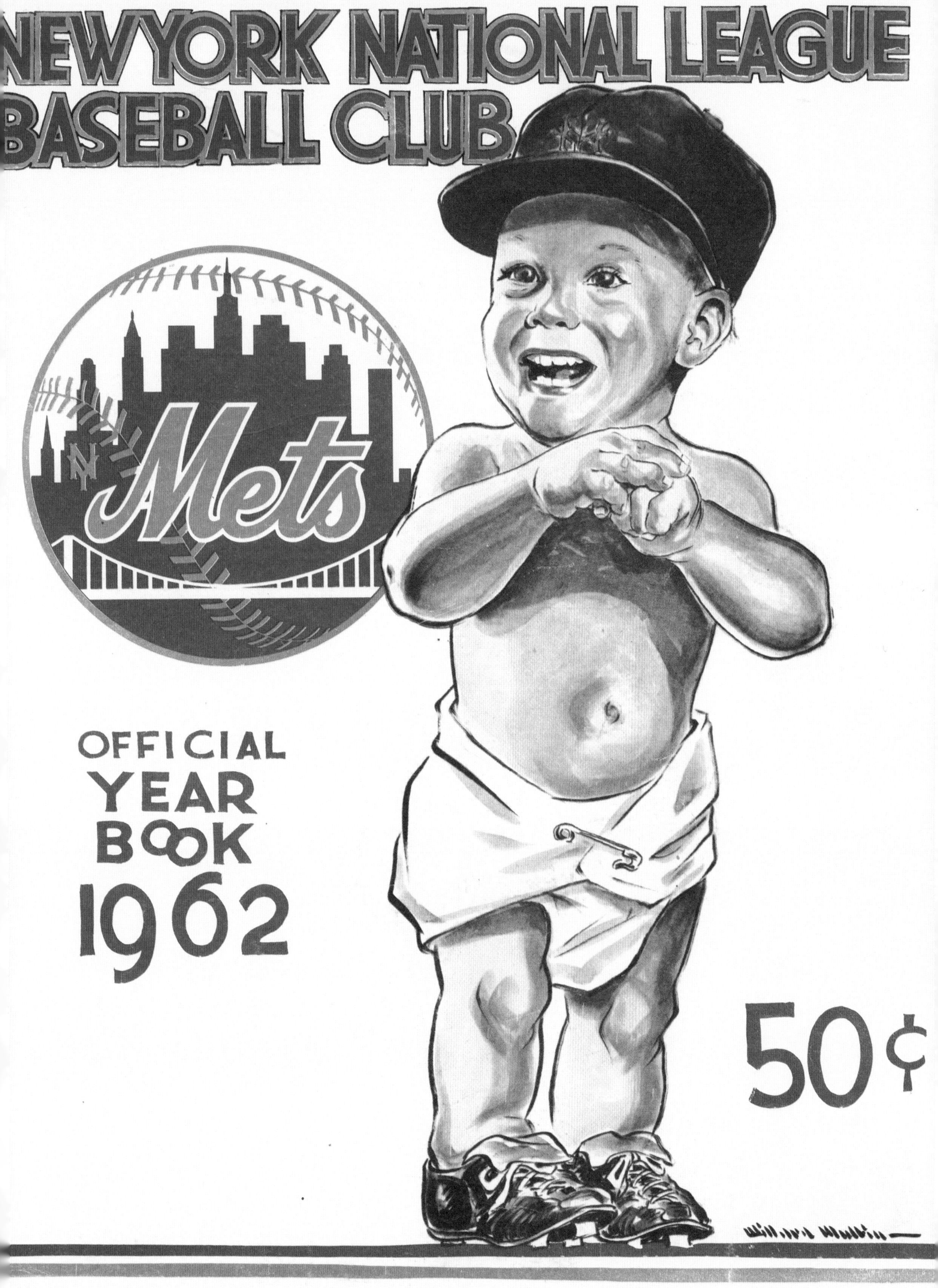

OFFICIAL
YEAR
BOOK
1962

50¢

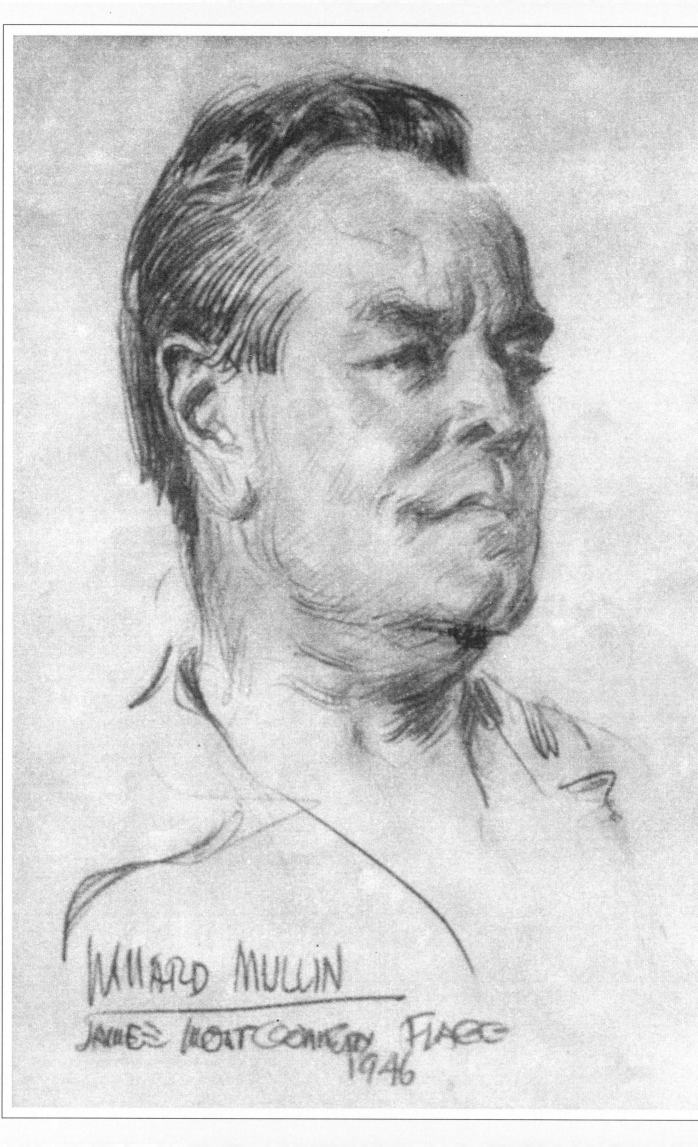

WILLARD MULLIN

JAMES MONTGOMERY FLAGG
1946

Gallo on Mullin

• • •

BILL GALLO

WHEN I THINK ABOUT the perfect boxer, I think of Sugar Ray Robinson. When I think of the perfect artist, I think of Willard Mullin.

Just as Robinson was in a class by himself as a fighter, Mullin was incomparable with pen and ink. Sugar Ray was an artistic fighter. Mullin was an expert at the easel.

My friend Willard Mullin created the most wonderful newspaper art ever put on paper. Mullin would bristle when people called him an artist. "I am not an artist," he once said. "I am a cartoonist."

No one ever did it better.

This man was born with a great talent for drawing, but it's what he did with that talent that made him a giant in his field. He brought a wry sense of humor to his work, a lighthearted approach to the world of sports. The Brooklyn Bum

OPPOSITE: One of Mullin's mentors was the famed illustrator James Montgomery Flagg. Flagg made this portrait of Mullin one morning while they were visiting West Point, as guests of legendary Army Football coach Earl "Red" Blaik.

BELOW: In 1954, Mullin won the Reuben Award for Outstanding Cartoonist of the Year from the National Cartoonists Society. There followed an appearance on the Ed Sullivan Show with Rube Goldberg, famed cartoonist and founder of the NCS. Right to left: Mullin, Goldberg, Sullivan.

EDITOR'S NOTE: *Award-winning New York Daily News cartoonist Bill Gallo had agreed to write the introduction to this book of Willard Mullin's cartoons but died, in May 2011, before* *he could do so. Nonetheless, Gallo had written previously about his old friend. These are some of Bill Gallo's thoughts on the man he considered to be the best sports cartoonist in history.*

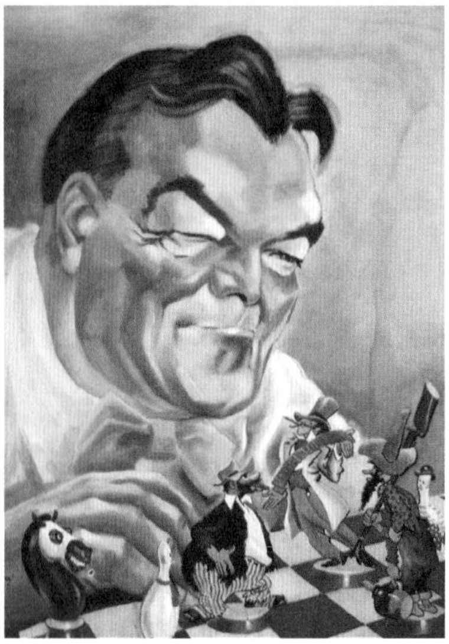

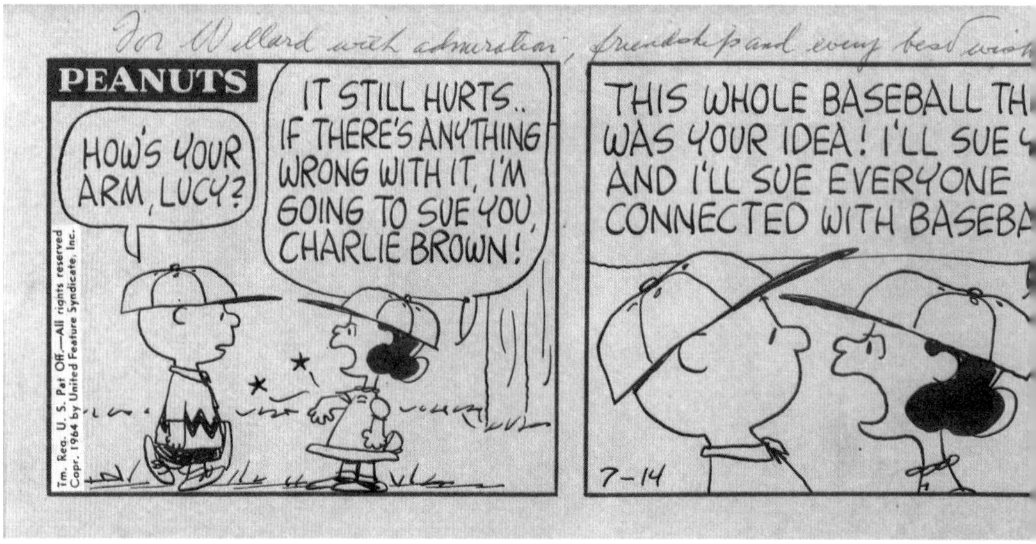
PEANUTS
HOW'S YOUR ARM, LUCY?
IT STILL HURTS.. IF THERE'S ANYTHING WRONG WITH IT, I'M GOING TO SUE YOU, CHARLIE BROWN!
Tm. Reg. U. S. Pat. Off.—All rights reserved
Copr. 1964 by United Feature Syndicate, Inc.
THIS WHOLE BASEBALL TH
WAS YOUR IDEA! I'LL SUE
AND I'LL SUE EVERYONE
CONNECTED WITH BASEB
7-14

was his signature character, but only one of the stable of images that Mullin drew six times a week with insight and ingenuity.

As a young kid, the idea of being a newspaperman captured me. It was going to be my life's goal and I always knew I'd get there. I tell you all this only to let you know of my great love of newspapers. Picking up a newspaper daily and reading it from back to front (I'd start with the sports, of course) was as natural to me as brushing my teeth in the morning and tying my shoelaces. There were plenty of newspapers in New York City while I was growing up — the *Daily News,* the *Mirror,* the *Sun,* the *Post,* the *Journal-American,* the *World-Telegram,* the *Herald Tribune,* and the *Brooklyn Eagle* — and each of these sheets carried a sports cartoon.

The first thing I'd turn to on all the papers was the lead sports page where the sports cartoon was displayed. There was Paprocki on the *Sun,* Burris Jenkins Jr. on the *Journal,* Johnny Pierotti at the *Post,* and a host of others.

These were all formidable artists who knew sports and also had a facility to write. Yes, they were good and I admired them so. But, when I opened the *World-Telegram,* there was Mullin, the Rembrandt of the bunch, the greatest sports cartoonist of all time. He was marvelous in his portraying of the big sports stars of the day.

Mullin's spot on the paper was so well drawn, so well explained that there was hardly any need to read the accompanying stories.

Mullin lived his life to the fullest and he always was proud to make that statement. He took his talent and stretched it as far as it could go. He loved doing what he did and had the utmost respect for the pen-and-ink line drawing. "I look for the perfect line," he'd say.

That's why it was fascinating to listen to the conversation one day at a drinking oasis called The Fourth Estate, where newspaper people hung out. A handful of cartoonists were there, admiring Mullin's work in the *World-Telegram* and singing his praises.

"As far as newspapers go, this guy Mullin is the greatest of all draftsmen," said one.

They all agreed except a guy with thick horn-rimmed glasses at the end of the bar. This fellow, seemingly in his cups, tore the newspaper out of the guy's

ABOVE, LEFT: This drawing of Mullin playing chess is by "Mullin alumnus" Karl Hubenthal.

ABOVE, RIGHT: Charles Schulz loved baseball and, starting in the early 1950s, had something of a friendly rivalry with Mullin. This strip from 1964 pays homage to Mullin and is still in the possession of Mullin's daughter, Shirley.

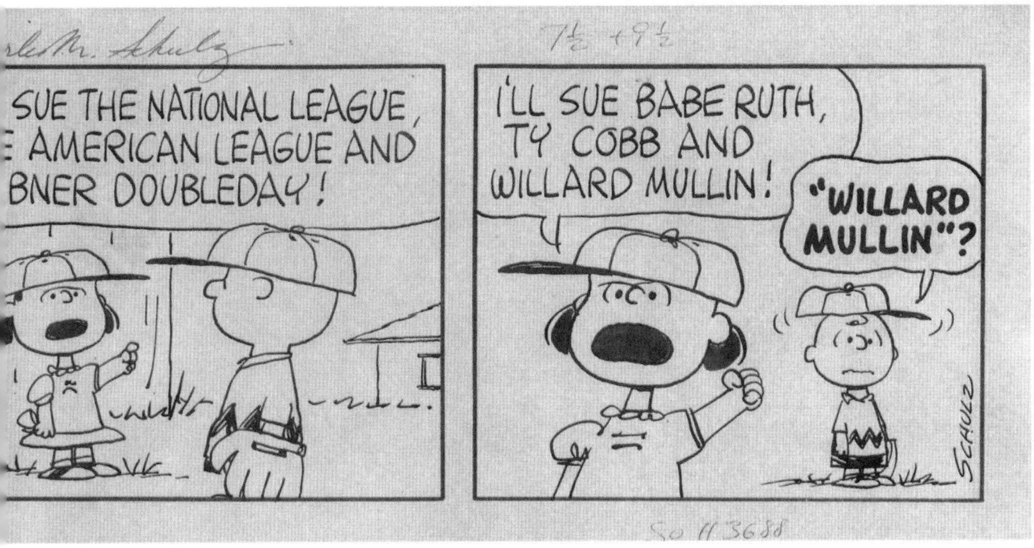
SUE THE NATIONAL LEAGUE,
E AMERICAN LEAGUE AND
BNER DOUBLEDAY!
I'LL SUE BABE RUTH, TY COBB AND WILLARD MULLIN!
"WILLARD MULLIN"?
SCHULZ

hands and said, "Let me show you how this guy you are all applauding is not the best."

With pen in hand, the critic started going over Mullin's drawing and nit-picking it. "Look at this arm … too long for that body. And how about his badly drawn legs?" he said.

He went on with his scratching and critique of the drawing until a Mullin fan took back the newspaper. "Mullin's not here but I'm taking this to him because he should know what you think of his work," the man said.

His pal told Mullin how his cartoon had been manhandled at the bar. Mullin looked at his drawing, which now looked like mass doodling, and said, "What son of a bitch did this? This man can't draw a lick!"

The critic, Mullin was told, was Walt Kelly, creator of *Pogo.*

"Walt Kelly?" Mullin blustered. "Never heard of the bum." And he followed that with a genuine Mullin belly laugh.

It was as if nobody could put down a Mullin work. He knew how good he was. And by the way, so did Walt Kelly. ❖

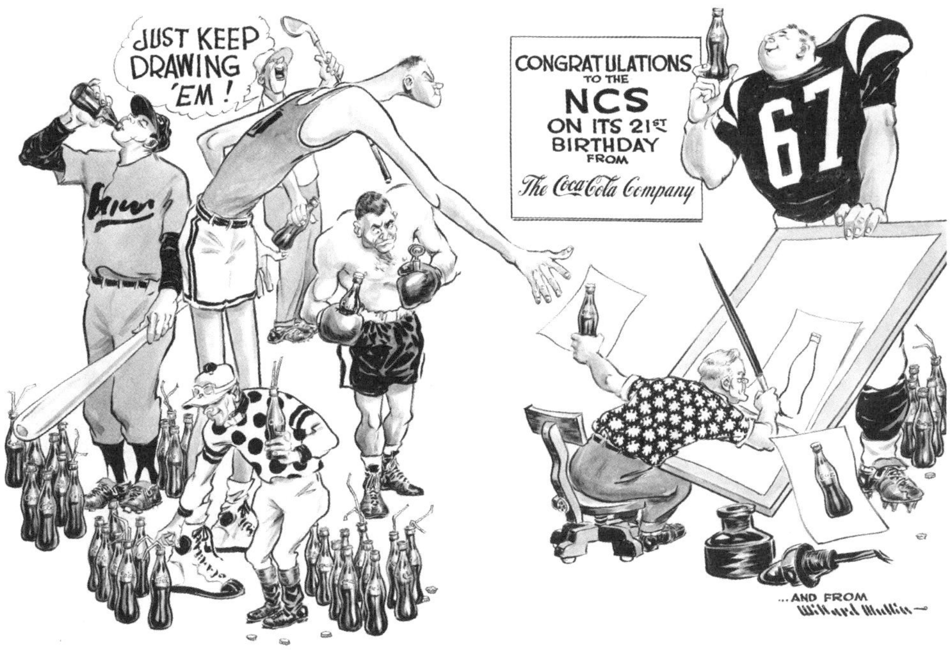
JUST KEEP DRAWING 'EM!
CONGRATULATIONS TO THE NCS ON ITS 21ST BIRTHDAY FROM The Coca-Cola Company
67
...AND FROM Willard Mullin

LEFT: A Mullin drawing of Mullin drawing for the National Cartoonists Society.

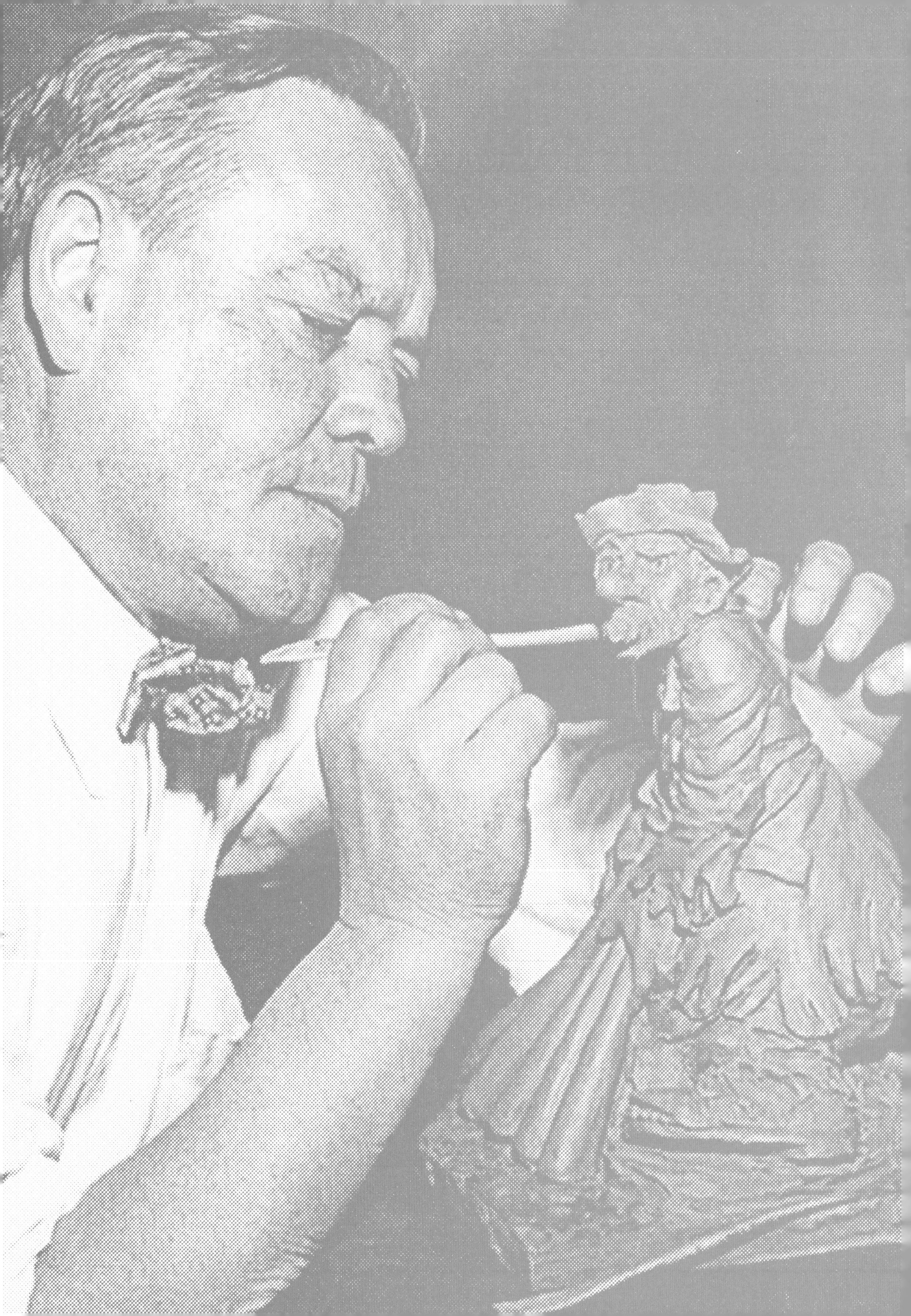

The Baseball World of Willard Mullin

• • •

Hal Bock

WILLARD MULLIN'S WORLD WAS HOME to a community of characters born of his whimsical view of sports. They were pen- or brush-and-ink creations that made him the Sports Cartoonist of the Century and a model for many who followed him.

Mullin's easel sat at a corner of the newsroom at the *New York World-Telegram & Sun,* adjacent to a window where he easily could watch the passing scene. From there, he captured the people and passions of sports each day.

Mullin would climb up onto his chair, hook his feet around the legs, and begin to draw. The lettering always came first because that was a greater challenge to him than the characters. He sketched his drawing and then filled out the image with brush or pen and ink. The lettering was vital, though, because the first cartoon he ever created at his first job with the *Los Angeles Herald* included 13 misspelled words. After that unpleasant affair, he learned to work with a dictionary nearby for the rest of his career.

He knew early in life that he wanted to become a cartoonist, becoming intrigued by the craft by his mother's first cousin, Clare Victor Dwiggins, who detoured from a career as an architect when the *St. Louis Post-Dispatch* and *New York World* published his artwork in 1897. He signed his works "Dwig" and had the rights to draw Tom Sawyer and Huckleberry Finn. He did a strip based on the Mark Twain characters beginning in 1918. "When I was 10 years old," Mullin once told an interviewer, "I knew it would be my career forever."

But Mullin recognized that he would have to print clearly if he was to succeed. That's why, after high school, he went to work first in the sign shop and then in the luggage department of Bullock's Department Store in Los Angeles. He used his time at Bullock's to work on lettering (the weakest part of his craft), by hand-lettering the suitcases of celebrities to practice his printing. Although it did occur to him, he resisted the urge to spell out the first name "Thomas" when one of Tom Mix's bags needed to be lettered. That was just as well. The cowboy star might not have been amused.

One of his sketches in the department store's golf shop caught the eye of Clyde Victor Forsythe, a syndicated cartoonist. Forsythe invited Mullin to his studio, encouraged him, and left an indelible mark on the young man. When Mullin became the most prominent sports cartoonist in America, he always remembered Forsythe's support and tried to help other young, aspiring artists.

ABOVE: Mullin created a number of iconic characters to represent teams, including the Brooklyn Bum.

OPPOSITE: In the mid 1950s, Mullin was commissioned to create a three-dimensional image of the "Bum" for use by a company that was going to produce and sell "Brooklyn Bum" table lamps. Unfortunately, the company went under before production could begin. Only two copies of this Mullin "statute" are known to exist today.

It was his way of passing the torch to the next generation, much the way Forsythe had done with him.

Like most people involved in sports journalism, Mullin was a frustrated athlete. He was born in 1902 on a farm in Ohio. It was there that young Willard had his first brush with sports when, at age 4, his pinky was crushed as he tried to snatch back a croquet ball before his brother smacked it. It was, Mullin reflected later in life, the first of 15 breaks or dislocations that he endured. "I was always careless with myself," he wrote in his autobiography.

Some of the injuries were more serious than others. Working on a dam in Oregon after graduation from high school, Mullin broke his right arm, wrist, and several ribs in a 40-foot drop. On a fishing trip in the Sierras, he tore some cartilage in his knee when he stepped into a hole in the ground. Then there was the time he nearly lost the middle finger of his left hand in a bit of hijinks with Stanley Woodward, then sports editor of the *New York Herald Tribune*. They were amusing themselves by finger wrestling one night, each using his right hand, elbows resting on a table. They hooked fingers and twisted. First hand down loses. Mullin was on a winning streak, greatly frustrating Woodward. Finally, they decided to switch hands. This time, Woodward twisted hard and sent Mullin's hand to the deck, his finger dangling limply. "I was the luckiest guy in the world," Mullin reflected later. "If I hadn't switched hands, I would have been out of business."

That was a magical time in New York sports sections. Pulitzer Prize winners Red Smith and Arthur Daley were rival columnists for the *Herald Tribune* and the *Times.* Dan Daniel, so well known that he used the single name Daniel in his byline, was covering the Yankees for the *World-Telegram,* writing against John Drebinger of the *Times.* Some of the other heavyweights included Damon Runyon, Bill Corum, Frank Graham, John Kiernan, Jimmy Powers, and Jimmy Cannon. It was a who's who of sports journalism. And into this mix moved Mullin, hired after drifting back and forth between papers in Texas and Los Angeles.

His first assignment was to cover a Babe Ruth press conference. Mullin's Babe looked nothing like the slugger and his boss suggested that the only part of the cartoon that worked were the slugger's feet, propped up on a desk. It was a daunting beginning to what would become a brilliant New York career.

Mullin looked at things a little differently. When the paper he was working on in Fort Worth went out of business, the city room was awash in self-pity. Mullin tried to cheer up his colleagues. He consoled society editor Leila Rogers, telling her, "Well, you can always put your kid in the movies." That suggestion worked out because Leila's kid was named Ginger.

ABOVE: Mullin's St. Louis Swiftie and New York Yankee.

ABOVE, RIGHT: In the spring of 1956, "The Mick" (Mickey Mantle) watches Mullin render one of his creations.

It may have been his own troubling history of injuries that made Mullin's treatment of the 1949 Yankees so sensitive. The team had one player after another sidelined by a series of breaks and bruises, supplying Mullin with a summer's worth of material. One of his best creations had a tattered Casey Stengel leading a contingent of his bandaged and battered players — a takeoff on the famous Revolutionary War painting.

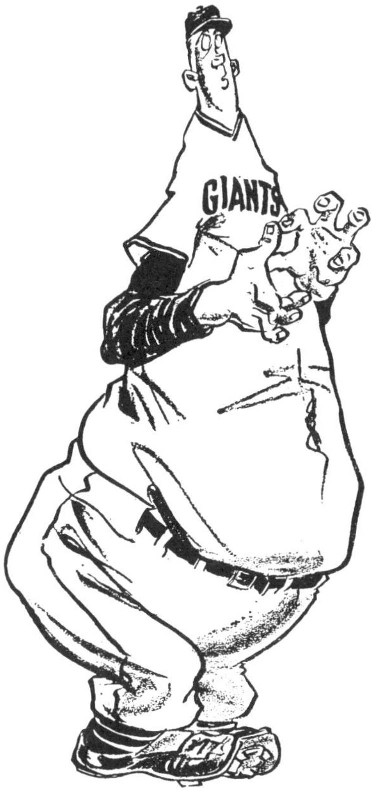

GIANTS

Mullin was proud of his craft. He once told an interviewer, "I'm not an artist. I'm a cartoonist." He followed a proud heritage. At the turn of the 20th century, cartooning became an important editorial instrument for newspapers. In New York, Pulitzer's *World* and Hearst's *Journal* conducted a spirited battle over a yellow-clad urchin who looked like a ragamuffin and became the centerpiece of tabloid style that became known as yellow journalism. The Yellow Kid never met Mullin's Brooklyn Bum, but they probably would have been comfortable together, examining society's underclass.

The Bum, symbol of the bedraggled Dodgers, would have been perfect in that era. He was Mullin's most enduring character. Like so many memorable creations, The Bum came about quite by accident. Mullin had journeyed to Ebbets Field, shopping for an idea. He left the ballpark and hopped into a cab when the driver asked offhandedly, "How'd our bums do today?" That planted the seed for one of the most memorable characters in sports cartooning history. Mullin took care of the rest.

His imagination created a proud but down-on-his-luck character, poor but independent, unshaven with the stump of a cigar stuck in his mouth. Mullin positioned a worn hat on the character's head and gave him a tattered coat and baggy pants. The only parts that matched were the plaid patches that adorned each of the elbows and knees. The Bum was always cobbler challenged, one shoe held together by a neatly tied bandana, the other with a hole in the sole.

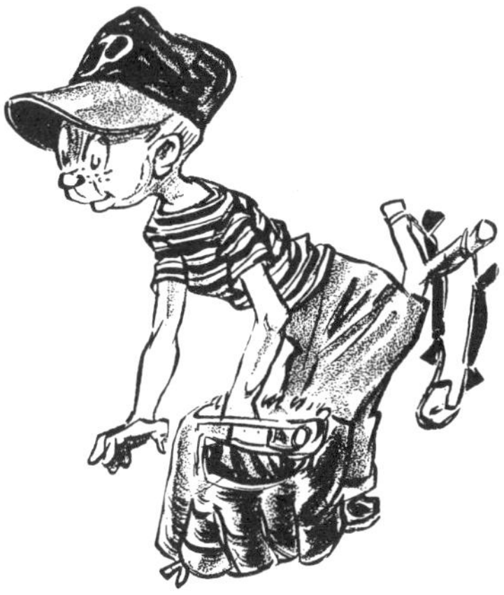

Mullin brought a different view of the world to his work. To his fertile mind, the nicknames of baseball teams translated easily. Instead of the logical redbird for the St. Louis Cardinals, Mullin chose a riverboat gambler, looking appropriately sly, shuffling cards and rolling dice. The St. Louis Swifty wore a top hat, handlebar mustache, ascot, checkered vest, and sinister look as he confronted other teams, who would invariably be woefully overmatched dealing with this slick character.

The Philadelphia Phillies Whiz Kids, a team composed of young players, became Mullin's juvenile delinquent, a Dead End kid wearing a polo shirt and dungarees, a slingshot sticking casually out of his back pocket. When the New York Mets were born in 1962, Mullin used his grandson, Ted, as inspiration for the new kid on the block.

Mullin's beloved New York Giants were captured in an oversized character named Willy, who had a tiny head sitting atop a bulbous body. Why Willy? Mullin never said, although it seemed to fit.

For the New York Yankees, Mullin created an aristocratic character who strode around his cartoons with chest thrust out, proud of the dynasty that ruled baseball at the time.

Classic Native Americans leaped off Mullin's easel, representing the Milwaukee Braves and Cleveland Indians in a time before political correctness might have frowned on those caricatures.

ABOVE: Mullin's Willy the Giant and the Whiz Kid.

From 1947 to 1956, New York was the baseball capital of the country with seven of ten World Series involving the three New York teams. Mullin called those intra-city showdowns "The Subway Series." In 1951, when the Giants overtook the Dodgers, wiping out a 13-1/2 game deficit and then winning the pennant on Bobby Thomson's home run in the ninth inning of the last playoff game, Mullin had another name for it — "The Little Miracle of Coogan's Bluff."

Mullin's work was unique because he combined traditional art — dramatic portraits of sports icons like Lou Gehrig, Joe Louis, Joe DiMaggio, Casey Stengel, and Ted Williams are among his most compelling works — and playful line drawings that regularly captured the essence of his subjects. It was Mullin who gave Gehrig his nickname, "The Iron Horse." And when Gehrig gave his emotional farewell speech at Yankee Stadium on July 4, 1939, it was Mullin who turned from cartooning to the written word, composing a touching poem to salute the great slugger. He often incorporated poetry in his cartoons.

Mullin's approach was whimsical but his cartoons always carried a message. His affection for his craft and subjects always shone through. His work was often stark, lacking a busy background that might distract his audience. Even his signature was special. He used a combination of 26 pen strokes, all but two of them vertical, to create the unique Willard Mullin label at the bottom of his works.

Remembering the impact Forsythe had had on him early in his own career, Mullin was generous with his time and advice for younger cartoonists. Among those he counseled were Karl Hubenthal, Jim Dobbins, Lou Darvas, Len Hollreiser, and Bob Staake. They called him "Uncle Will," and Staake maintains a Mullin homepage on the internet to keep his mentor's name and work alive.

When he completed his newspaper career, his peers named Mullin "Sports Cartoonist of the Century." A major exhibition of his work was on display in the summer of 2003 at the Museum of Illustration in New York City and another was part of the 2004 expansion of the Yogi Berra Museum on the campus of Montclair State University. His cartoons are on display at New York's Metropolitan Museum of Art, the National Art Museum of Sport in Indianapolis, the Smithsonian in Washington, D.C., and, of course, the Baseball Hall of Fame in Cooperstown, N.Y. He is a recent inductee in the Planet Cartoonist Hall of Fame.

Now, through the generosity of his daughter Shirley Mullin Rhodes, the Mullin Estate, and attorney Michael Powers, this coffee table collection presents many of Mullin's cartoons, accompanied with text by Hal Bock, the award-winning Associated Press sports writer, columnist, and George Polk Journalist-in-Residence at Long Island University.

Some of the cartoons are colorized, adding to the depth and drama of the works. They offer a peek into another era of baseball history. They represent The Baseball World of Willard Mullin. ❖

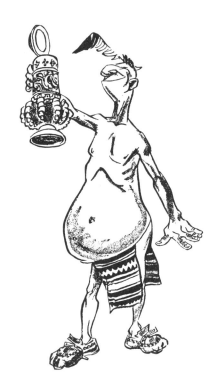

ABOVE: Mullin's beer-drinking, German-speaking Milwaukee Brave and the St. Louis Brown Hillbilly.

OPPOSITE: Mullin's printed images were often irregular in shape because they had to be fitted among columns of type. This is the front page of the *Sporting News*, May 14, 1958.

HAL BOCK wrote sports for 40 years at The Associated Press, covering every major event from the Kentucky Derby to the Indy 500, from Wimbledon to the Masters, from the Stanley Cup to the Davis Cup. Over his career, he covered more World Series and more Super Bowls than any other AP reporter. He has written scores of magazine articles and written or edited 13 sports books including *The Associated Press Pictorial History of Baseball* and has been Adjunct Professor of Journalism and Journalist-in-Residence at Long Island University's Brooklyn campus. He lives on Long Island with his wife, a retired psychologist, and their cat.

Individual Fielding in All Major Box Scores

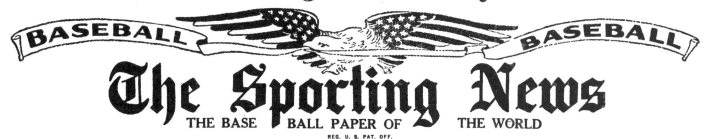

BASEBALL BASEBALL

The Sporting News

THE BASE BALL PAPER OF THE WORLD

REG. U. S. PAT. OFF.

VOLUMNE 145, NUMBER 16 | ST. LOUIS, MAY 14, 1958 | PRICE: TWENTY-FIVE CENTS

STAN SHOOTS FOR MOON IN N. L. MARKS

Speeding Toward New Records .·. *By Mullin*

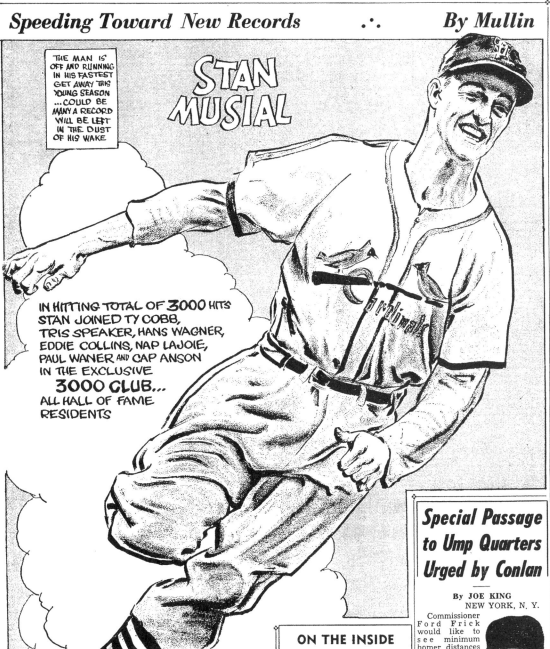

STAN MUSIAL
THE MAN IS OFF AND RUNNING IN HIS FASTEST GET AWAY THIS YOUNG SEASON ...COULD BE MANY A RECORD WILL BE LEFT IN THE DUST OF HIS WAKE
IN HITTING TOTAL OF 3000 HITS STAN JOINED TY COBB, TRIS SPEAKER, HANS WAGNER, EDDIE COLLINS, NAP LAJOIE, PAUL WANER AND CAP ANSON IN THE EXCLUSIVE 3000 CLUB... ALL HALL OF FAME RESIDENTS

Eyes Loop's All-Time High Total of Hits

Quickest in Reaching 3,000, He Could Finish Second Only to Cobb in Big Time

By BOB BROEG

ST. LOUIS, Mo.

As Stan Musial entered the exclusive 3,000-Hit Club, the Cardinal star turned his sharp brown eyes on becoming the National League's No. 1 record-holder and, barring injury, perhaps finishing second only to Ty Cobb on the all-time hit parade.

Reaching the golden 3,000-hit plateau in fewer seasons than Cobb as well as his six other predecessors in the select circle, Musial at 37 has found his second wind, athletically speaking, and can be expected—again barring crippling injury—to play two and possibly three more seasons.

"The way I feel now," chuckled the Cardinals' veteran star, glowing with satisfaction as he reached the 3,000 figure, "I honestly believe that if I hadn't missed the one season (1945 in the Navy), I might have an outside shot at 4,000 hits. Back in those days I was good for more than 200 a season."

Although except for that year away he might have approached mid-May beyond the 3,200-hit mark, an amazingly durable and physically sound Musial still could wind up past Tris Speaker, whose 3,515 safeties in 21 years rank the Grey Eagle second only to Georgia Peach Cobb. Ty compiled a terrific 4,191 total in 24 years before he hung up his spikes at the age of 42 in 1928.

Five Others Still Ahead of Stan

Still ahead of Stan the Man, too, are Honus Wagner, Eddie Collins, Nap Lajoie, Paul Waner and Cap Anson. Wagner had 3,430 hits in 21 years, Collins 3,311 in 25, Lajoie 3,251 in 21, Waner 3,152 in 19-plus and Anson 3,081 in 22.

Of all the members of the 3,000-Hit Club, however, Musial got to the portals more quickly than any other, as demonstrated by research conducted by James L. Toomey, publicity director of the Cardinals. Toomey's efforts showed that whereas The Man closed in on his goal early in his sixteenth full season, Cobb didn't get the 3,000 until late in his sixteenth year. Ty, in addition, had the benefit of 41 games in 1905, a fragmentary season Toomey didn't count against him, compared with only 12 contests Musial played with the Cardinals in the fall of 1941.

The way Stan looked physically—and counting his confidence, desire, determination and concentration—it seemed quite likely he would finish this season with approximately 3,125 hits and maybe as many as 3,150.

To illustrate the importance of Musial's consistency and the endurance that has permitted him to miss few games in his colorful career, Cobb stood at 3,055 hits after his sixteenth full year, Waner had 2,956, Speaker 2,961, Wagner 2,951, Collins 2,753, Lajoie 2,736 and Anson 2,736. Cobb, as mentioned, also had played 41 games before his first full season, Speaker seven and 31 contests in each of two campaigns, Wagner 61, Collins 14 and Lajoie 39. And even if Anson's years

(CONTINUED ON PAGE 2, COL. 1)

Special Passage to Ump Quarters Urged by Conlan

By JOE KING

NEW YORK, N. Y.

Jocko Conlan

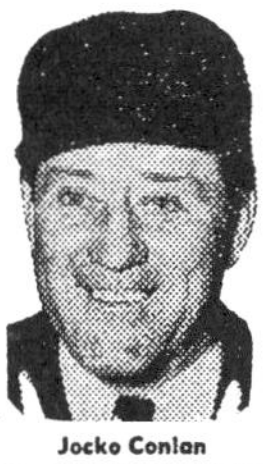

Commissioner Ford Frick would like to see minimum homer distances established for ball parks of the future, but Jocko Conlan is more perturbed about decent facilities for umpires to guard their privacy and independence in touchy circumstances.

"Let's have a special passage for umpires right behind home plate in these new parks," the crack N. L. arbiter demanded, "to permit us to leave the field without being forced

(CONTINUED ON PAGE 6, COL. 1)

ON THE INSIDE

MAJOR LEAGUE REPORTS

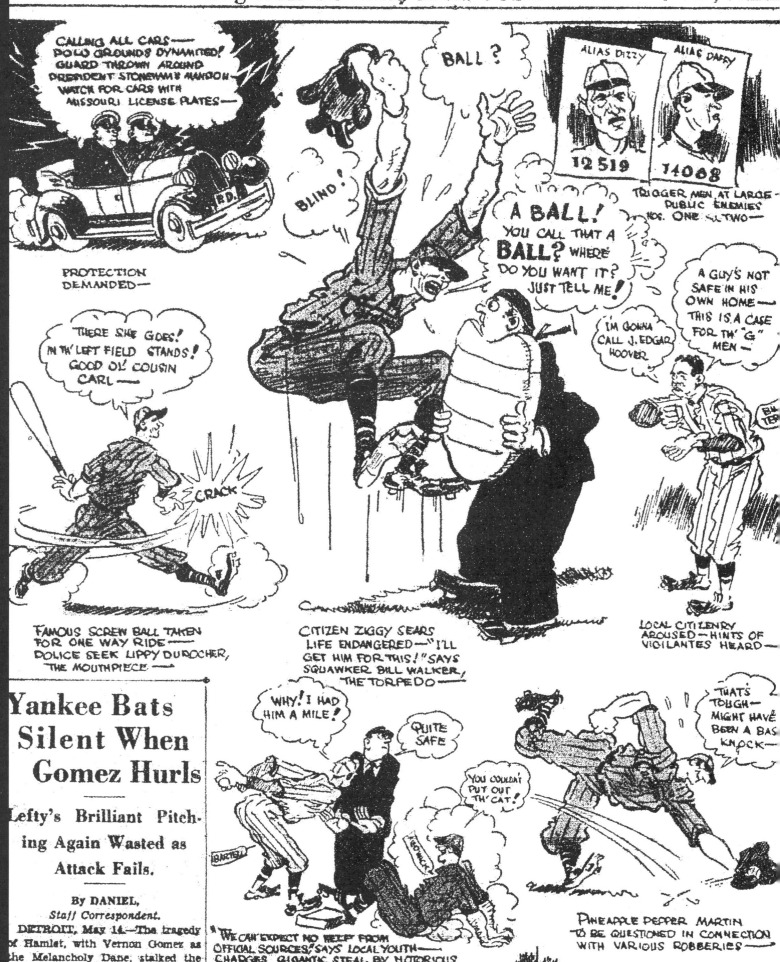

Giants and Cardinals Staging Be

The Gas House Gang from St. Looey Is In Town. . . . . By Mulli

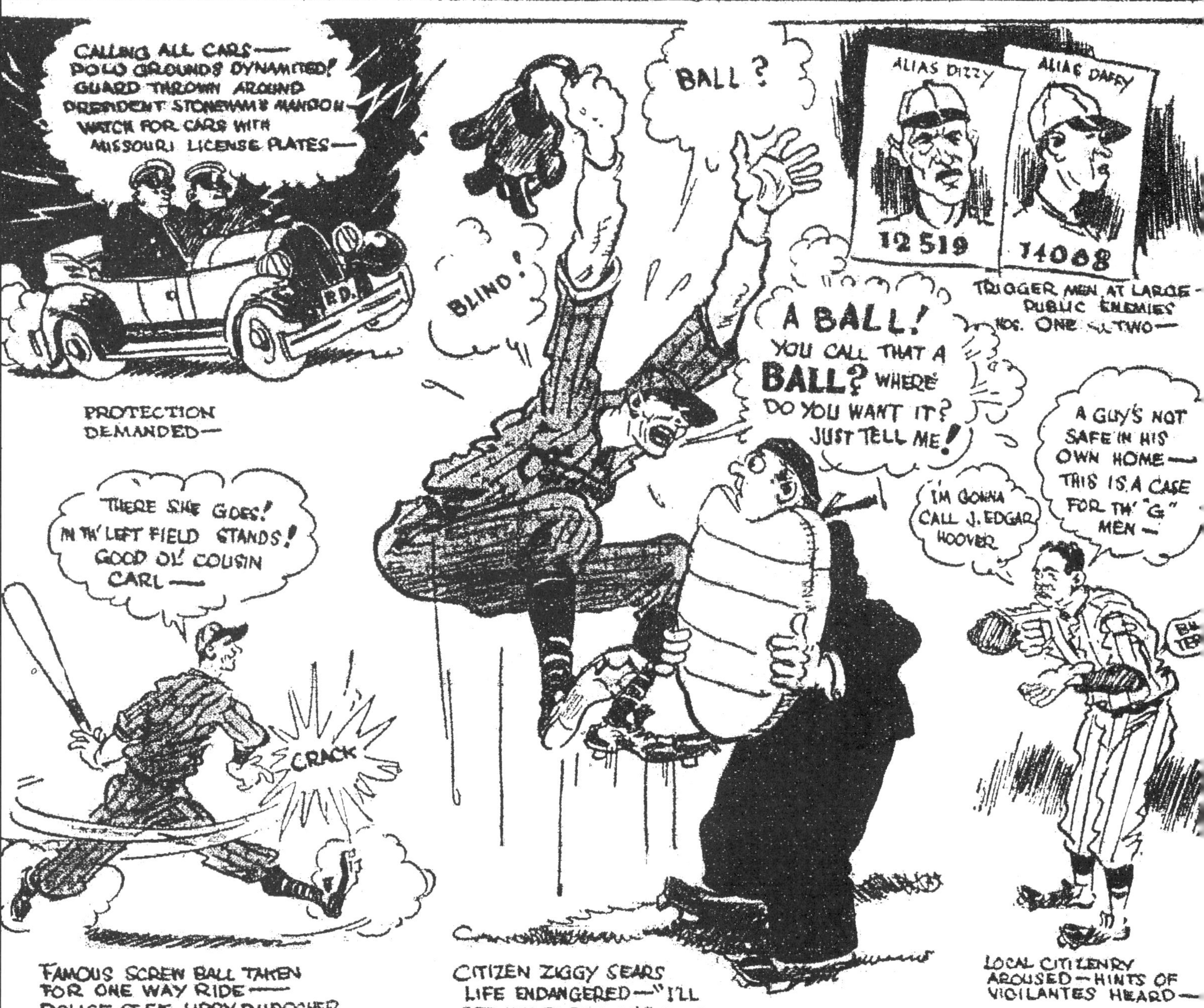

CALLING ALL CARS— POLO GROUNDS DYNAMITED! GUARD THROWN AROUND PRESIDENT STONEHAM'S MANSION— WATCH FOR CARS WITH MISSOURI LICENSE PLATES—
P.D.
PROTECTION DEMANDED—
BALL ?
BLIND!
ALIAS DIZZY
12519
ALIAS DAFFY
14088
TRIGGER MEN AT LARGE PUBLIC ENEMIES NOS. ONE & TWO—
A BALL! YOU CALL THAT A BALL? WHERE DO YOU WANT IT? JUST TELL ME!
A GUY'S NOT SAFE IN HIS OWN HOME— THIS IS A CASE FOR TH' "G" MEN—
I'M GONNA CALL J. EDGAR HOOVER
THERE SHE GOES! IN TH' LEFT FIELD STANDS! GOOD OL' COUSIN CARL—
CRACK
FAMOUS SCREW BALL TAKEN FOR ONE WAY RIDE— POLICE SEEK LIPPY DUROCHER, THE MOUTHPIECE—
CITIZEN ZIGGY SEARS LIFE ENDANGERED—"I'LL GET HIM FOR THIS!" SAYS SQUAWKER BILL WALKER, THE TORPEDO—
LOCAL CITIZENRY AROUSED—HINTS OF VIGILANTES HEARD—

Yankee Bats Silent When Gomez Hurls

Lefty's Brilliant Pitching Again Wasted as Attack Fails.

By DANIEL,
Staff Correspondent.

DETROIT, May 14.—The tragedy of Hamlet, with Vernon Gomez as the Melancholy Dane, stalked the baseball stage today. The Yankee southpaw made a more convincing Sourpuss than Sothern, Hampden or any of the other exponents that

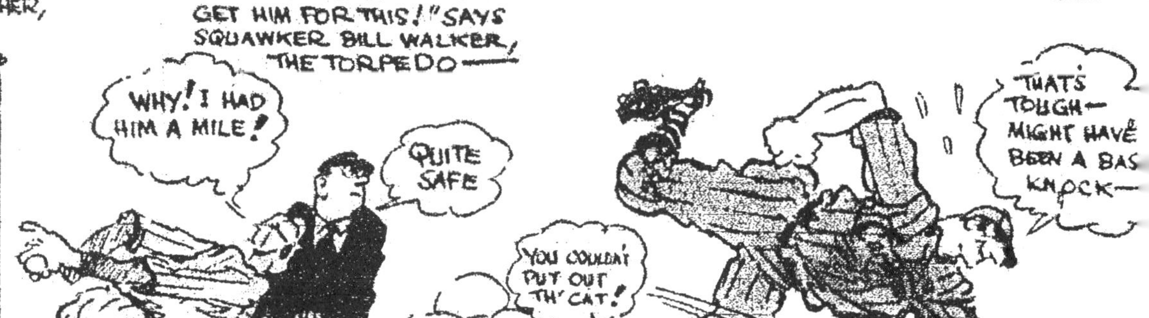

WHY! I HAD HIM A MILE!
QUITE SAFE
YOU COULDN'T PUT OUT TH' CAT!
BARTELL
MEDWICK
"WE CAN EXPECT NO HELP FROM OFFICIAL SOURCES," SAYS LOCAL YOUTH— CHARGES GIGANTIC STEAL BY NOTORIOUS VEGETABLE BARON—
THAT'S TOUGH— MIGHT HAVE BEEN A BAS KNOCK—
PINEAPPLE PEPPER MARTIN TO BE QUESTIONED IN CONNECTION WITH VARIOUS ROBBERIES—

N. J. Assembly

Grimm Praises Successo

The 1930s

• • •

If the Golden Age of Sports occurred in the 1920s

with Babe Ruth, Jack Dempsey, Bobby Jones, Red Grange, and Big Bill Tilden dominating the landscape, then the Golden Age of Baseball came in the 1930s. No period in the history of the game had a greater galaxy of stars — men who helped distract attention from the struggles of the Great Depression and, for a few hours each day, focused it instead on the Great American Pastime.

Ruth, of course, was still around, placing his personal punctuation mark on America's favorite pastime with his "called shot" home run in the 1932 World Series and his decisive two-run homer in the first All-Star Game a year later. But he had plenty of company in an era jammed with larger-than-life characters.

American League sluggers like Jimmie Foxx and Hank Greenberg made runs at Ruth's record of 60 home runs in a single season, each finishing with 58. Bill Terry became the National League's last .400 hitter in 1930, the same year pint-sized Hack Wilson hit 56 home runs and drove in 190. Lefty Grove had a 30-win season on the road to 300 victories. Dizzy Dean became the National League's last 30-game winner. Carl Hubbell struck out five Hall of Famers in succession in another All-Star Game, and Rogers Hornsby finished off a 23-year career in which he batted .358.

Right in the middle of the convention of great players, a cartoonist with a whimsical sense of humor arrived in New York. Willard Mullin had two stints in Los Angeles and two others in Texas before settling in a city that would provide him with material for the next four decades.

Mullin's New York included three baseball teams: the lordly Yankees of Ruth and Lou Gehrig, the storied Giants of Terry and Hubbell, and the daffy Dodgers of Van Lingle Mungo and Frenchy Bordagaray. The Yankees were about to launch a dynasty. The Giants had history on their side. The Dodgers occasionally encountered basepath buffoonery that once led to three of them converging at third base at the same moment. It was a palette overflowing with material for an aspiring sports cartoonist.

At the *Los Angeles Herald,* Mullin had stepped in on short notice to produce four political cartoons. He scrambled to complete the job on time, and when he was paid a paltry $30 for the hurry-up effort, he decided his future lay elsewhere. He learned that the *World-Telegram* in New York was shopping for a cartoonist. Mullin shipped some samples, got invited to Florida to interview with columnist Joe Williams, and was hired.

This was a major step for Mullin, moving clear across the country to a new job in the nation's largest city. He was warming up for the assignment, working with Williams in Florida when word came from New York that the managing editor of the *World-Telegram,* a barrel-chested, imposing bear of a man named Lee B. Wood, was unhappy with some of the cartoons and wanted to see his new employee in person.

Meanwhile, despite landmark moments like his "called shot" home run in the 1932 World Series and the decisive home run in the first All-Star Game a year later, Ruth had become increasingly disenchanted with his situation. There had been a nasty holdout at the start of the decade and when the team laughed off his bid to become manager of the Yankees, the Babe was on his way out the door.

OPPOSITE: Leo Durocher credited Mullin with dubbing the 1934 Cardinals "The Gashouse Gang." This is one of the earliest representations of that Cardinals team.

.625

One reason the Yankees were unhappy with Ruth was an incident that occurred at the start of the decade. With his career soaring, highlighted by heroics that bordered on storybook stuff, the Babe signed an $80,000 contract that was brokered by sports writer Dan Daniel, who would become a colleague of Mullin's at the *World-Telegram*.

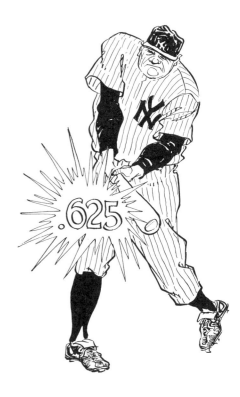

Daniel was a pal of Ruth's, and when the slugger decided to stage a holdout at a difficult time in American history — the country's economy was struggling through the Great Depression, the stock market was in free fall, and millions of people were unemployed — the writer counseled common sense.

Ruth claimed ignorance of the situation. "Why didn't somebody tell me?" he asked. When Daniel did, an agreement was put in place, and the writer had a front-page scoop. But then, Yankees owner Jacob Ruppert and general manager Ed Barrow decided to balk at the contract. Now Daniel had to calm ownership down to get the deal done and protect his story.

Peace prevailed but not before a critic noted the circumstances and pointed out to Ruth that with his fancy new contract, the Babe would be making more than the president.

Ruth chomped down on his trademark cigar, and his round face lit up with laughter. "Well," he chortled, "I had a better year."

Ruth was an iconic figure and Mullin knew it. When the Babe drew a sellout crowd playing in a benefit for the children of World War I veterans, Mullin drew the packed stands and sent a copy to the Babe with an inscription. "This was a cinch," it read. "You drew the crowd."

It's not as if baseball was immune from the dreary economic climate of the country. Connie Mack's Philadelphia Athletics won American League pennants in 1929, 1930, and 1931, but the team was forced to sell off its star players — Al Simmons, Jimmy Dykes, Lefty Grove, Jimmie Foxx, and Mickey Cochrane — after that, in order to raise revenue. Each of them, except Dykes, was headed to the Hall of Fame. The A's would never win another pennant in Philadelphia, moving first to Kansas City and then to Oakland before reaching the World Series again.

The Triple Crown — leading the league in batting average, home runs, and runs batted in — is no small feat. But in 1933, Philadelphia had two winners, Foxx (.356, 48, 163) with the American League's Athletics and Chuck Klein (.368, 28, 120) with the National League's Phillies.

Hack Wilson had his own milestone season in 1930 with 56 home runs and 190 runs batted in. Wilson was short and squat, built like a human fire hydrant. He also enjoyed the nightlife, which occasionally interfered with his baseball responsibilities. He had drifted to Brooklyn late in his career and was still recovering after a night on the town while patrolling right field on one particularly hot afternoon in Philadelphia. Balls kept coming his way, banging off the wall behind him and sending him on a merry chase. Finally, manager Casey Stengel had seen enough of pitcher Walter "Boom-Boom" Beck and decided on a change.

ABOVE, RIGHT: Babe Ruth from *The World Series Encyclopedia*, 1961.

Wilson, grateful for a break in the action, bent over for a breather, huffing and puffing, staring at the grass, his hands on his knees. On the mound, though, the

unhappy Beck punctuated his departure by heaving the baseball. It clanked off the tin-plated Baker Bowl wall behind Wilson, like so many others before it had, and the right fielder, aroused by the sound, took off after it, corralled the ball, and unleashed a perfect throw to second base. Unfortunately for him, there was no runner to gun down. "It was his best throw all season," Stengel noted.

By the middle of the decade, age was beginning to catch up with Ruth. Relations with the Yankees had deteriorated, and the team decided to release him. No problem. The Babe had a standing offer from the Boston Braves to become assistant vice president, assistant manager, and, by the way, gate attraction in the twilight of his career for a franchise that had difficulty selling tickets.

A press conference was arranged at Ruppert's Brewery, where the divorce from the Yankees would be announced. On his first day in New York, February 26, 1935, Mullin was dispatched to Ruth's farewell. He drew a cartoon of the departure scene, further annoying his boss because any resemblance to Ruth in the drawing was purely coincidental. The Babe bordered on mythical. Mullin's rendering of him that day fell well short of that target. Mullin drew Ruth with his feet up on a desk and had the Babe ordering an underling around. The managing editor, already critical, took one look at Mullin's effort and suggested the only part of the Babe that Mullin had captured were his feet. Mullin agreed that the cartoon left something to be desired, but his work improved quickly. Later renderings of Ruth looked much more like the Babe and, eventually, the crisis ended.

Ruth's pit stop with the Braves was brief. Age had caught up with the Babe, and by mid-season, he was done as a player. But he went out with one last moment of glory. On May 25, 1935, he hit three home runs at Pittsburgh, giving him a mathematically symmetrical total of 714. A week later, on June 2, he retired. That was the same day Judge Emil Fuchs, owner of the Braves, decided Ruth was no longer needed as assistant manager or assistant vice president and fired the Babe. Mullin, determined he could do a better reckoning of Ruth, drew him that winter lugging golf clubs and fishing pole, heading jauntily for St. Petersburg, Fla., because old habits are hard to break, and Florida is where baseball players head in the dead of winter.

Later, Ruth made a cameo appearance as a first base coach for the Brooklyn Dodgers and then drifted out of baseball, never to get the offer to manage that he wanted so badly. Stricken with throat cancer, the Babe died in 1948. Mullin's farewell was a drawing of a fan, his head in his hands as he read the news and realized that the symbol of his youth was gone.

Just months after Ruth left the Yankees, baseball changed forever with the introduction of night games. The Cincinnati Reds were the first team to install lights and the first night game was played May 24, 1935. How big a deal was it? Well, President Franklin Delano Roosevelt threw a remote control switch in Washington, D.C. that illuminated Crosley Field in Cincinnati for the game.

Not everyone was in favor of this dramatic change. In an editorial, the *Sporting News,* considered the bible of baseball, wrote: "The night air is not like the day air; The man who goes to baseball after he has eaten a hearty meal is apt to have indigestion if he is nervous and excited; the disturbed and misanthropic fan will not sleep well after a night game. Who wants to go home in the dark when it is twice as pleasant to drive leisurely in the approaching twilight and sniff a good meal cooking on the range when the front door is opened and the aroma of a sputtering steak spreads all through the house?"

Of course, in the middle of the Great Depression, not too many fans could afford cars or steaks. Mullin noted that condition with a 1937 cartoon of an out-of-work man down on his luck, sitting on a park bench, surrounded by newspapers with headlines of baseball stars seeking fat contracts. Baseball pressed ahead with the move to night games, a change that would eventually revolutionize the game. It was around that same time that Mullin came upon the St. Louis Cardinals and the Gashouse Gang.

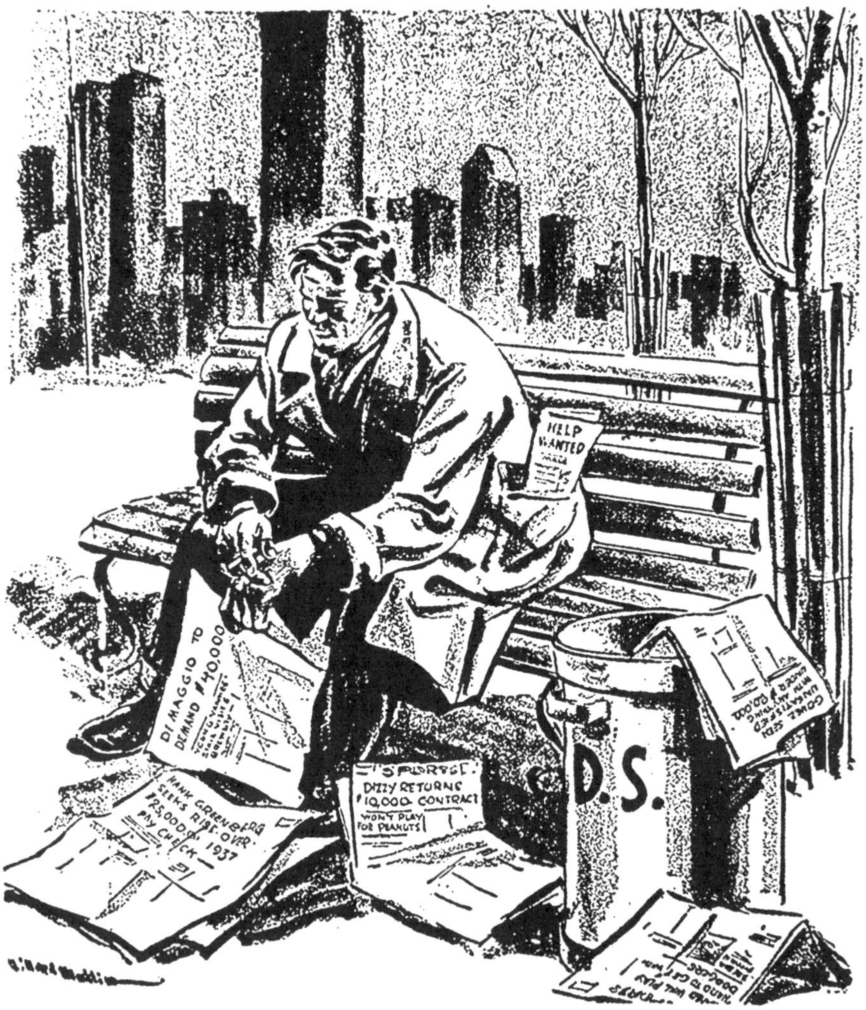
HELP WANTED
DI MAGGIO TO DEMAND $40,000
HANK GREENBERG SEEKS RISE OVER $25,000.00 1937 PAY CHECK
SPORTS
DIZZY RETURNS $10,000 CONTRACT
WON'T PLAY FOR PEANUTS
D.S.

In the early part of the decade, the Cardinals began assembling a roster of roustabouts, a gritty group that played hard on and off the field. Thirty-game winner Dizzy Dean was the centerpiece of this rowdy bunch, a folksy, homespun hurler from the hills of Arkansas who boasted about what he would do to opponents and then went out and did it. Dean called himself "The Great One" a generation before Muhammad Ali took the label "The Greatest." When the Cardinals added Dean's brother, Paul, to their pitching staff, it gave Dizzy added incentive. "Me and Paul will win 50 games," he boasted before the 1934 season. They came close, Dizzy winning 30, and his brother, nicknamed Daffy, adding 19. They each won two games in the World Series against Detroit.

Dizzy was a character. Once inserted as a pinch runner in the World Series, he failed to duck on a double-play relay. The ball knocked him unconscious, and he was carried off the field and sent to the hospital. Dizzy returned to start the next day, reporting in perfect Deanese to all concerned, "They X-rayed my head and didn't find nuthin'."

In his post-playing career, Dean was hired to broadcast baseball. It was an intriguing network decision, especially when the master of malaprops tossed around phrases like "Who'da thunk it?" and "He slud into the base." When umpire Bill McKinley made a controversial call, Dean dug into American presidential history and observed, "They shot the wrong McKinley."

The Gashouse Gang was managed by Frankie Frisch, who in 1931 was the National League's first Most Valuable Player. Lefty Grove, a 31-game winner that year in Philadelphia, won the American League trophy. It wasn't until 25 years later that a separate prize, the Cy Young Award, was created for pitchers.

ABOVE, RIGHT: Mullin's drawings were not limited to the sports page. Here, he makes a point about the greed of professional athletes in the face of a nation buried in the Great Depression.

ABOVE: In game 4 of the 1934 World Series, Dizzy Dean was hit in the head while trying to break up a double play. The headline the next day famously read, "X-ray of Dean's head reveals nothing."

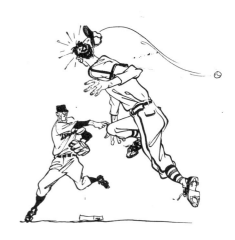

Frisch's Cardinals team included Joe Medwick, Rip Collins, Pepper Martin, and a cast of characters who weren't afraid of getting their uniforms dirty. They didn't always get along with each other, either. One day, Dean, who wasn't always careful with his words, said something in the dugout that offended Medwick, who responded by decking the pitcher.

Medwick was in the middle of another celebrated brawl in the 1934 World Series. His hard slide into Detroit third baseman Marv Owen in the seventh game touched off a near riot, with Tiger fans throwing so much debris on the field that commissioner Kenesaw Mountain Landis ordered Medwick out of the game. The Cardinals were winning 9-0 at the time.

It was typical Gashouse Gang brand of baseball during a time when the game bordered on the bawdy. In Chicago, Cubs catcher Gabby Hartnett was photographed signing an autograph for mobster Al Capone. Landis was livid and called Hartnett on the carpet. The catcher shrugged off the episode, saying, "I go to his place of business. Why shouldn't he come to mine?"

There are various accounts of how the Gashouse Gang nickname began, including one that traces its roots to a day when the Cardinals showed up for a game in New York looking slightly disheveled in uniforms caked with mud and sweat that made them resemble a team from the other side of the railroad tracks. *World-Telegram* columnist Joe Williams took one look at the raggedy Redbirds and wrote, "Here comes the Gas House Gang. They looked like a bunch of boys from the gas house district who had crossed the railroad tracks for a game of ball with the nice kids."

Mullin seized the image, drawing a cartoon that showed two gas tanks on the wrong side of the railroad tracks and a platoon of ballplayers crossing the tracks, carrying clubs slung over their shoulders instead of baseball bats. After that, the ragtag Redbirds of that era would forever be known as the Gashouse Gang.

When age caught up with the Cardinals and, one by one, they faded away, Mullin drew a cartoon of manager Frankie Frisch pining for the good old days and singing sadly, "Gee but I'd give the world to have that old gang of mine."

Rogers Hornsby, who starred with the Cardinals from 1915 to 1926, made a brief return to the team in 1933 for a cameo appearance with the Gashousers, before moving across town to join the St. Louis Browns. When Hornsby was elected to the Hall of Fame in 1942, Mullin saluted him with a portrait and the declaration that he was the greatest right-handed hitter of all time. There were no arguments about that, not with Hornsby's resume that included a lifetime average of .358 in 23 years and three seasons in which he batted over .400.

Ruth would have fit in perfectly with that Gashouse crew. He was a fun-loving free spirit, who sometimes seemed like an overgrown kid blessed with remarkable baseball ability and a flair for the dramatic. He batted .342 for his career and once noted, "If I just tried for them dinky singles, I could've batted .600."

Ruth's "called shot" during the 1932 World Series was the kind of moment that helped build his legend. Some who were there swore it happened. Some who were there swore it didn't. The Babe, not one to spoil a good story, never confirmed that he called his homer against Chicago Cubs pitcher Charlie Root. But he never denied it, either.

The moment came in the middle of some vicious bench jockeying between the Yankees and Cubs. The Yankees were angry at the Cubs for shortchanging ex-teammate Mark Koenig on World Series shares. Ruth, of course, was the main man in the heckling, giving as good as he got. His answer to the Chicago bench came when he seemed to point to the bleachers at Wrigley Field and then hit Root's next pitch to that very spot. Then he circled the bases, grinning widely and pointing at the Cubs players in their dugout.

So did he really call his shot? His explanation left as many questions as it provided answers.

"Right now, I want to settle all the arguments," Ruth told Chicago sportswriter John P. Carmichael. "I didn't exactly point to any spot, like the flagpole. Anyway, I didn't mean to. I just sorta waved at the whole fence, but that was foolish enough. All I wanted to do was give that thing a ride ... outta the park ... anywhere."

The "called shot" was typical of the Babe, master of the moment. During another World Series, he took time out to visit an ailing youngster in a local hospital. The boy asked Ruth to hit a home run for him. No problem. Ruth didn't hit one that day. He hit three.

The Yankees' divorce from Ruth was not as painful as it might have been because they had the perfect replacement part waiting in the wings. Joe DiMaggio arrived in 1936, fresh from hitting .398 including a 61-game hitting streak the year before in the Pacific Coast League. DiMaggio patrolled center field effortlessly, displaying a grace and style that would be hard to duplicate. His arrival touched off the first great Yankees dynasty, a stretch of six World Championships and seven American League titles in the next eight years.

When the team broke open the race one year with a 12-1/2 game lead by July 4, Mullin celebrated their dominance with the proud Yankee strutting around, surrounded by rockets as the team marched towards a fourth straight pennant.

But DiMaggio was hounded by an annoying string of injuries, and Mullin reminded him — and World-Telegram readers — of them after DiMaggio staged a cantankerous holdout in 1938.

Players demanding fat salaries for the part they played in the Yankees dynasty bedeviled the front office. Mullin expressed his sympathies to Col. Ruppert with a cartoon of the Yankees owner in an expensive restaurant, thinking about those contracts and deciding he had no appetite.

There were other great stars who arrived during the decade. Among the most notable were Bob Feller, a teenaged pitcher from Van Meter, Iowa, and Ted Williams, a slender outfielder from San Diego.

Feller joined the Cleveland Indians on July 6, 1936 and immediately turned heads when he struck out eight of the nine batters he faced in an exhibition game against the St. Louis Cardinals. The first batter he faced was Leo Durocher. "I got two strikes over and he went to the dugout," Feller recalled. "The umpire said, 'Get back here. You have another strike coming.' And he said, 'You take it for me. I'm going to get a drink of water.'" Later, Feller struck out 15 St. Louis Browns and 17 Philadelphia A's, launching a Hall of Fame career that produced 266 victories.

Williams joined the Boston Red Sox, equipped with baseball's sweetest swing, a slugger who would replace Lou Gehrig as the game's best left-handed hitter. As a rookie in 1939, he led the league with 145 runs batted in. His first hit that season was a double on April 20 at Yankee Stadium. As he turned first and headed for second, Williams passed Gehrig, a shell of himself, already stricken with what would be a fatal illness.

Midway through the 1930s, baseball decided it would be smart to establish a Hall of Fame, a place where the history and greats of the game could be celebrated for eternity. There were plenty of candidates for the first class of inductees but there could be little argument with the list of charter members — Babe Ruth, Ty Cobb, Honus Wagner, Walter Johnson, and Christy Mathewson.

The location of the baseball shrine would be simple. It would be built in the little hamlet of Cooperstown, N.Y., the home of General Abner Doubleday. Years earlier, baseball had launched a search for the origins of the game. The Mills Commission announced that Doubleday, a native of Cooperstown, was at the heart of the game's roots. That conclusion was not universally embraced. There was, for example, the opinion of baseball executive Branch Rickey, who would play a major role in the evolution of the game. Noting the general's military service at Fort Sumter in 1861, Rickey observed, "The only thing Abner Doubleday ever started was the Civil War."

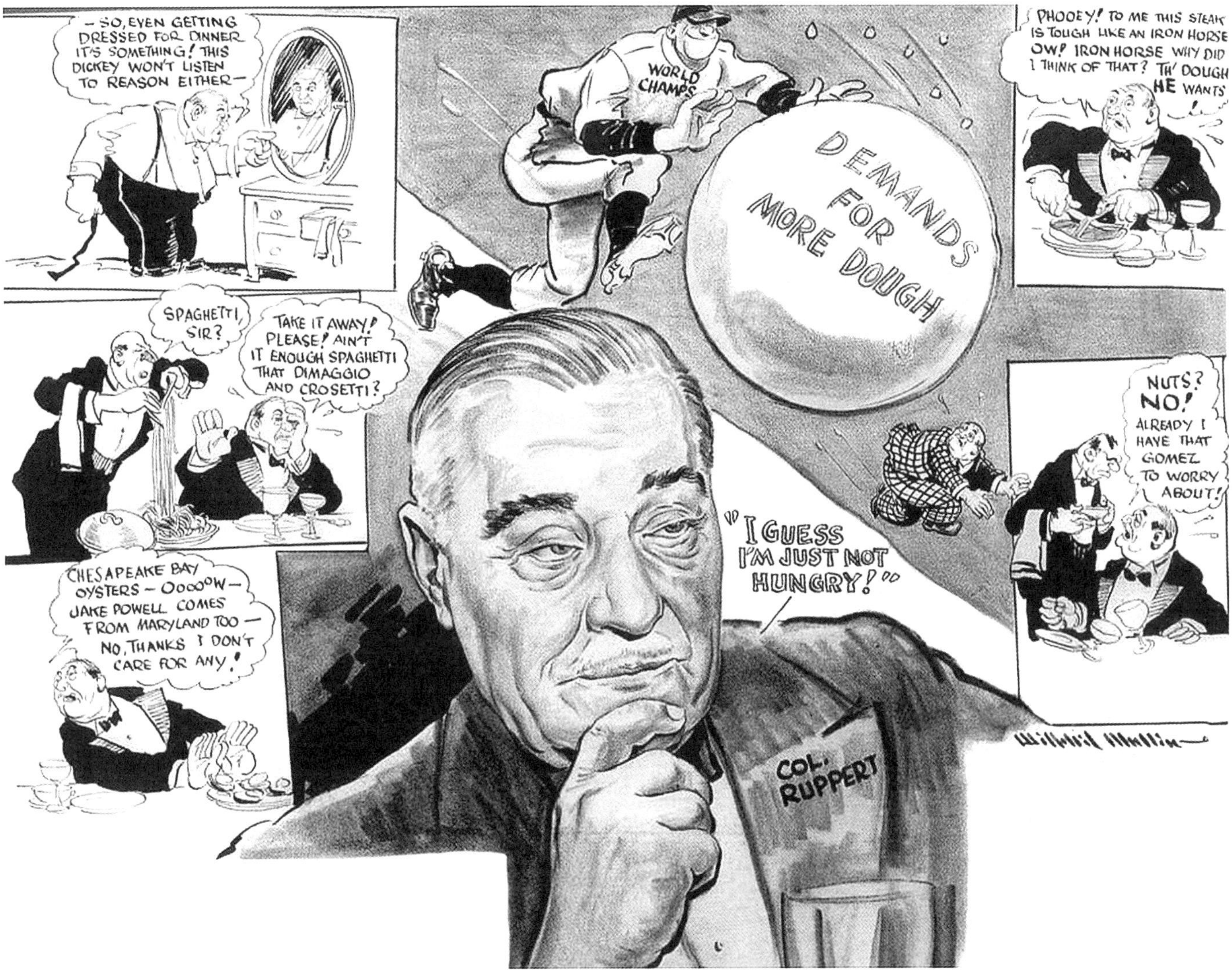
— SO, EVEN GETTING DRESSED FOR DINNER IT'S SOMETHING! THIS DICKEY WON'T LISTEN TO REASON EITHER —
WORLD CHAMPS
DEMANDS FOR MORE DOUGH
PHOOEY! TO ME THIS STEAK IS TOUGH LIKE AN IRON HORSE OW! IRON HORSE WHY DID I THINK OF THAT? TH' DOUGH HE WANTS!
SPAGHETTI, SIR?
TAKE IT AWAY! PLEASE! AIN'T IT ENOUGH SPAGHETTI THAT DIMAGGIO AND CROSETTI?
NUTS? NO! ALREADY I HAVE THAT GOMEZ TO WORRY ABOUT!
"I GUESS I'M JUST NOT HUNGRY!"
CHESAPEAKE BAY OYSTERS — OOOOOW — JAKE POWELL COMES FROM MARYLAND TOO — NO, THANKS I DON'T CARE FOR ANY!
COL. RUPPERT

Ruth's partner in the middle of the Yankees' Murderers' Row lineup had been first baseman Lou Gehrig, who was still a productive hitter when DiMaggio joined the team. Gehrig was the exact opposite of the boisterous Babe, a low-key, understated player. Gehrig drove in 184 runs in 1931, but that was six short of Hack Wilson's record of 190 set the year before. One day in 1932, Gehrig hit four home runs in one game, something Ruth never accomplished.

The achievement should have earned Gehrig banner headlines. Instead, those headlines belonged to John McGraw, who picked that same day to resign as manager of the Giants, a job he had held since the beginning of the century.

McGraw's replacement would be Bill Terry, the Giants' slugging first baseman and the last National League player to hit over .400. Terry led the team to the World Series Championship in 1933, the same year *Chicago Tribune* sports editor Arch Ward came up with the idea of an All-Star Game between the American and National Leagues, played for charity.

McGraw returned to manage the National League against Connie Mack of the Philadelphia Athletics. The rosters were crammed with future Hall of Famers: Al Simmons, Charlie Gehringer, and Mickey Cochrane for the American League; and Chuck Klein, Paul Waner, and Pie Traynor for the National League. Ruth, always the master of the moment, put an exclamation point on the event with a two-run homer that sealed a 4-2 American League victory. It was typical Babe, grabbing the spotlight, standing center stage.

ABOVE: In 1936, the Yankees won the first of four World Series Championships in a row, due in large part to their rookie center fielder, Joe DiMaggio. As happens with all Championship teams, the players wanted to be rewarded for their efforts. Apparently, the thought of having to compensate the newly crowned World Champs put Col. Ruppert, the owner of the Yankees, off his "feed."

A year later, Hubbell had his signature moment in the second All-Star Game. Equipped with a screwball that baffled batters, the left-hander struck out Ruth, Gehrig, Jimmie Foxx, Al Simmons, and Joe Cronin in succession, a monumental achievement against five of baseball's greatest sluggers. After giving up a single to Bill Dickey, Hubbell struck out notoriously weak hitting pitcher Lefty Gomez. Hubbell left the game after those two innings, leading 4-0. The American League sluggers did measurably better against his successors and won the game 9-7.

It was Gomez who earned the nickname "Goofy," for antics like standing on the mound during a World Series game and staring at an airplane flying over Yankee Stadium. He was obviously fascinated by the phenomenon of flight. He could pitch, though, and Mullin saluted his streak of five straight World Series wins with an image that included Jack Coombs and Herb Pennock, who had similar streaks. And when Gomez won 21 games including six shutouts and led the league in ERA in 1937, Mullin drew him wearing a king's crown, celebrating his achievements.

That spring, Terry held court as manager of the World Champions and was asked about the rest of the National League. He talked about each team except the Giants' intracity rivals, the Brooklyn Dodgers. When the omission was pointed out, Terry delivered one of baseball's eternal quotes. "Brooklyn?" he said. "Is Brooklyn still in the league?"

It might have seemed a fair question at the time. The Dodgers were in the doldrums, rarely in contention after winning the pennant in 1920, sixth-place finishers in six of the previous nine seasons. They seemed hopeless but their fans were hopeful. One Mullin cartoon had a fan dreaming about winning the pennant and beating the Yankees in the World Series in four straight games. That would never happen but it was a nice dream.

Terry's putdown stuck in the craw of the struggling Dodgers, and even though they were headed for another sixth place finish in 1934, they rose up on the final weekend of the season and beat the Giants two straight games, allowing the Cardinals' Gashouse Gang to finish in first place.

It was satisfying payback in the rivalry that would become one of baseball's most heated in the years to come. It did not, however, light any kind of spark for the Dodgers. They were still drifting aimlessly near the bottom of the National League standings in 1938 when cartoonist Mullin, looking for some inspiration, headed out to Ebbets Field one day.

Until then, the most significant event at the home of the Dodgers came when, in the first night game at the ballpark, June 15, 1938, Cincinnati pitcher Johnny Vander Meer established what might be baseball's most unbreakable record.

Vander Meer had pitched a no-hitter against the Boston Braves on the afternoon of June 11 and then, four days later, pitching under the lights in the first night game in Brooklyn, threw another one against the Dodgers. The achievement is widely considered baseball's most unbreakable record. That's because to top it, somebody would have to throw three no-hitters in a row.

Mullin, hoping to beat the crowd that night, ducked out of the ballpark in the seventh inning and hopped in a cab. The driver turned and innocently asked a question that is right up there with Bill Terry's inquiry about Brooklyn. "Well," the cabbie said, "how'd our bums do today?"

For Mullin, it was an epiphany.

"He couldn't have scored a more direct hit if he had hit me over the head with a bat," Mullin said in his autobiography. "Notice that he didn't say 'the Bums.' He said 'our Bums.' That was the key to whatever personality I could create. He had to have a certain warmth coupled with a happy ignorance and a downright arrogance that would make him lovable to a lot of people — Brooklyn people primarily."

And so, Mullin set pen and brush to ink and came up with his most famous character, the iconic down-on-his-luck Brooklyn Bum. At first, Mullin had used a clown

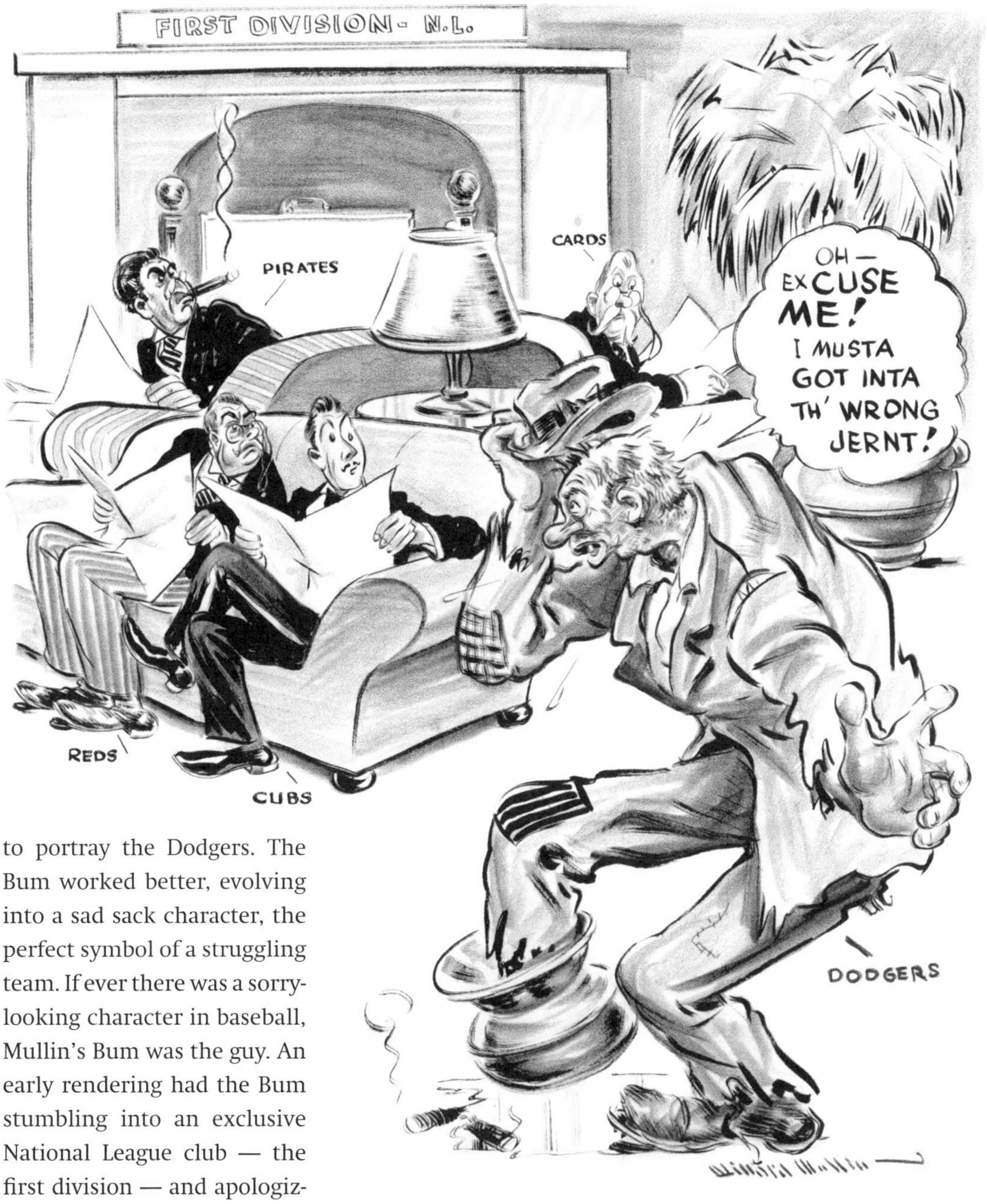
FIRST DIVISION - N.L.
PIRATES
CARDS
OH — EXCUSE ME! I MUSTA GOT INTA TH' WRONG JERNT!
REDS
CUBS
DODGERS

to portray the Dodgers. The Bum worked better, evolving into a sad sack character, the perfect symbol of a struggling team. If ever there was a sorry-looking character in baseball, Mullin's Bum was the guy. An early rendering had the Bum stumbling into an exclusive National League club — the first division — and apologizing profusely for the mistake. But Mullin's character wore his ragtag wardrobe proudly and never wavered from his optimistic view of the Dodgers. Their mantra, following failed season after failed season, became "Wait 'til Next Year." And for a long time, the Dodgers fit the image. Even when they improved to win six pennants over 10 years beginning in 1947, the iconic Bum spoke volumes about who and what they were.

If there was one constant in New York during the 1930s, it was Lou Gehrig at first base for the Yankees. He quickly became one of Mullin's favorite subjects, a man who played day after day and was one of baseball's top sluggers. From the time he took over for Wally Pipp in 1925, he was a great run producer, leading the league in runs batted in five times and in home runs three times. That was no small trick in a lineup that included Babe Ruth.

When Ruth left, there was a seamless transition with the arrival of Joe DiMaggio in 1936 as the Yankees dominated the American League. Gehrig was still positioned in the middle of the Yankees' lineup and Mullin was fascinated not only by the first baseman's offensive production (493 home runs and 1,995 runs batted in) but also by his appearance day after day in the Yankees lineup.

ABOVE: In 1939, under new manager Leo Durocher, the Dodgers, long the doormat of the National League, ended up finishing third overall out of eight teams . This is the first known drawing of the Brooklyn Bum by Willard Mullin.

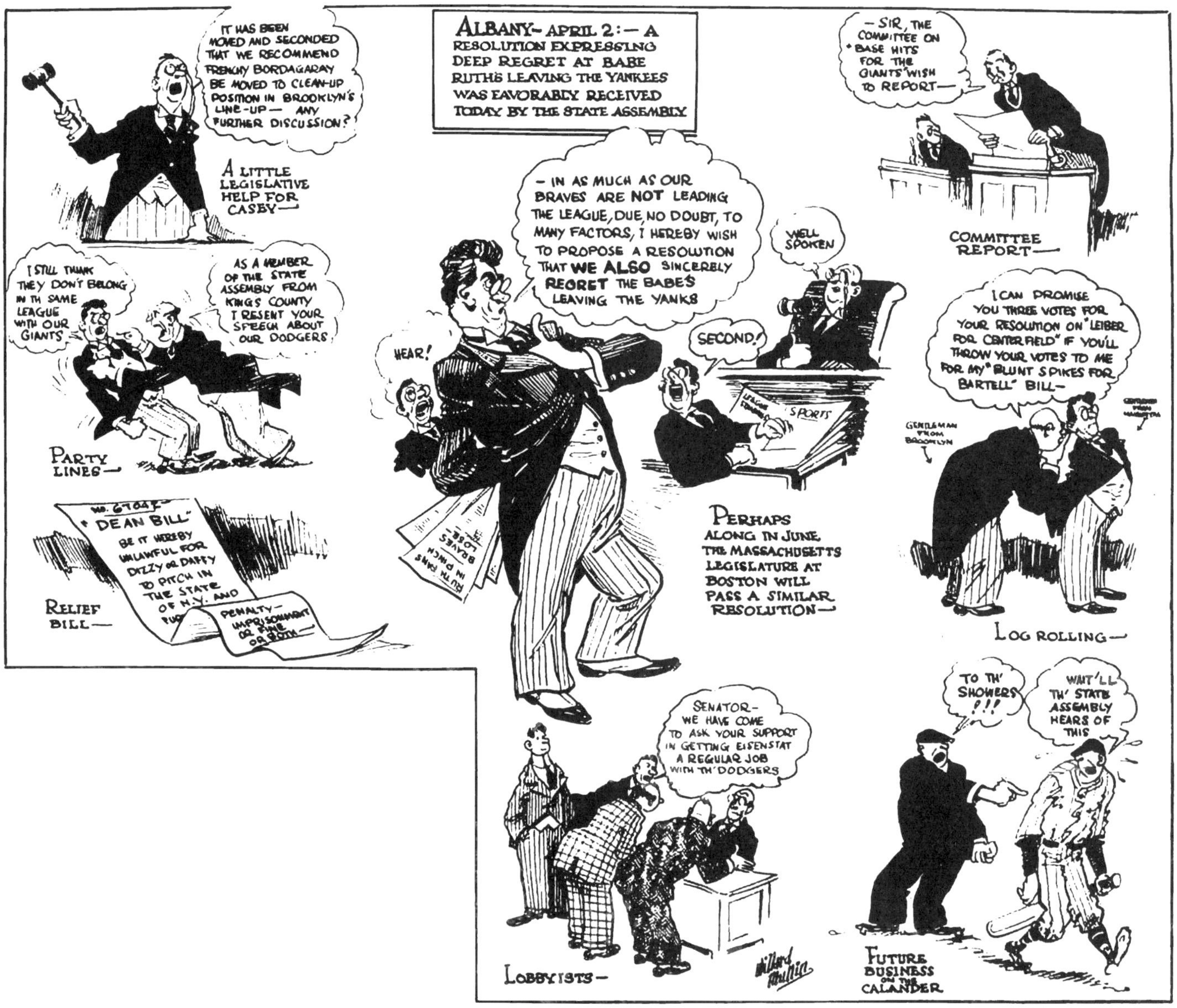
IT HAS BEEN MOVED AND SECONDED THAT WE RECOMMEND FRENCHY BORDAGARAY BE MOVED TO CLEAN-UP POSITION IN BROOKLYN'S LINE-UP — ANY FURTHER DISCUSSION?
A LITTLE LEGISLATIVE HELP FOR CASBY—
I STILL THINK THEY DON'T BELONG IN TH SAME LEAGUE WITH OUR GIANTS
AS A MEMBER OF THE STATE ASSEMBLY FROM KINGS COUNTY I RESENT YOUR SPEECH ABOUT OUR DODGERS
PARTY LINES—
"DEAN BILL" BE IT HEREBY UNLAWFUL FOR DIZZY OR DAFFY TO PITCH IN THE STATE OF N.Y. AND
PENALTY— IMPRISONMENT OR FINE OR BOTH—
RELIEF BILL—
ALBANY— APRIL 2:— A RESOLUTION EXPRESSING DEEP REGRET AT BABE RUTH'S LEAVING THE YANKEES WAS FAVORABLY RECEIVED TODAY BY THE STATE ASSEMBLY
— IN AS MUCH AS OUR BRAVES ARE NOT LEADING THE LEAGUE, DUE, NO DOUBT, TO MANY FACTORS, I HEREBY WISH TO PROPOSE A RESOLUTION THAT WE ALSO SINCERELY REGRET THE BABE'S LEAVING THE YANKS
HEAR!
RUTH FANS IN PINCH BRAVES LOSE
WELL SPOKEN
SECOND!
SPORTS
PERHAPS ALONG IN JUNE THE MASSACHUSETTS LEGISLATURE AT BOSTON WILL PASS A SIMILAR RESOLUTION—
— SIR, THE COMMITTEE ON "BASE HITS FOR THE GIANTS" WISH TO REPORT—
COMMITTEE REPORT—
I CAN PROMISE YOU THREE VOTES FOR YOUR RESOLUTION ON "LEIBER FOR CENTER FIELD" IF YOU'LL THROW YOUR VOTES TO ME FOR MY "BLUNT SPIKES FOR BARTELL" BILL—
GENTLEMAN FROM BROOKLYN
LOG ROLLING—
SENATOR— WE HAVE COME TO ASK YOUR SUPPORT IN GETTING EISENSTAT A REGULAR JOB WITH TH' DODGERS
LOBBYISTS—
Willard Mullin
TO TH' SHOWERS !!!
WAIT'LL TH' STATE ASSEMBLY HEARS OF THIS
FUTURE BUSINESS ON THE CALANDER

The cartoonist labeled the slugger "The Iron Horse," a tribute to his streak of 2,130 consecutive games and paid homage to him in a cartoon that portrayed Gehrig as the classical Casey at the Bat. The difference was the original Casey struck out. In Mullin's cartoon version, Gehrig homered.

When Gehrig balked at his 1937 contract, Mullin drew the horse kicking wildly as GM Ed Barrow, owner Jacob Ruppert, and manager Joe McCarthy try to corral him. When Gehrig signed, leaving Dizzy Dean as baseball's most prominent holdout, Mullin drew Dean surrounded by picket signs, protesting Gehrig's contract. Dean's contract demand was $50,000, tip money for today's players.

But in 1939, when DiMaggio batted a career-high .381 and won the Most Valuable Player award, there was a pall around the Yankees. Gehrig was failing, his body ravaged by amyotrophic lateral sclerosis, an incurable disease that attacks the motor neurons and saps strength, eventually killing its victim. On May 2, Gehrig removed himself from the lineup, ending his streak. Two months later, on July 4, 1939, Yankee Stadium was packed for Lou Gehrig Appreciation Day when Gehrig, in an emotional speech, declared himself "the luckiest man on the face of the earth."

Mullin saluted Gehrig with a lyrical ode, a full-page poem that captured the emotions of the cartoonist and the whole city of New York. There was also a drawing of Gehrig, a broad smile on his face as he crossed home plate.

Two years later, Lou Gehrig was dead. ❖

ABOVE: In February 1935, after 15 years, Babe Ruth left the Yankees. It was still a story for several months afterward. Mullin, having just arrived in New York, drew this commentary about the Babe's departure in April 1935.

OPPOSITE: On May 1, 1939, Lou Gehrig's consecutive games streak ended, and Gehrig never played another game. Mullin wrote this homage, which appeared in the *New York World-Telegram* the next day, May 2. Over the years, this poem has remained popular. Every year on the Fourth of July, the date of Gehrig's famous "luckiest man on the face of the Earth" speech, there are multiple requests for permission to use this poem to commemorate the legacy of Lou Gehrig.

Iron Horse Lou

You've heard of the wonderful
Iron Horse Lou,
Who looked as if he would
never be through
For fourteen years as good
as new,
And then of a sudden, he —
ah, its true! —
I'll tell you what happened
without ado,
Scaring McCarthy into fits,
Frightening Yank fans out of
their wits, —
Did you ever think it could
happen to Lou?

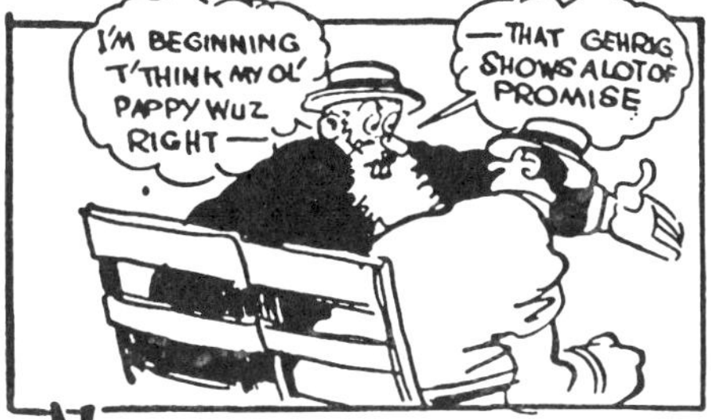
I'M BEGINNING T'THINK MY OL' PAPPY WUZ RIGHT —
— THAT GEHRIG SHOWS A LOT OF PROMISE

Now in building a player,
I tell you what,
There is always *somewhere*
a weakest spot; —
In arm, foot, elbow, in thigh
or slat;
In body, or shoulder, or neck
or at bat,
In fielding, or hitting, or feet
that are flat,
Something someplace will fold
like a hat.

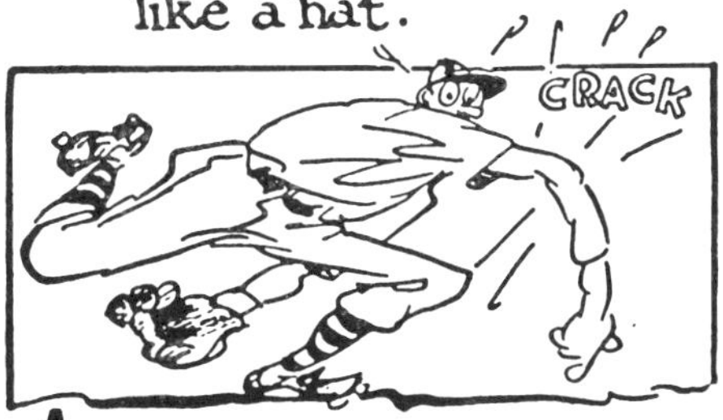
CRACK

And thats the reason, beyond
a doubt,
That a player *breaks down*
but doesn't *wear out!*

But Gehrig was not like the
common folk;
Created, was he, like the
strongest oak;
Seemed nothing could crack
on this hardy bloke!

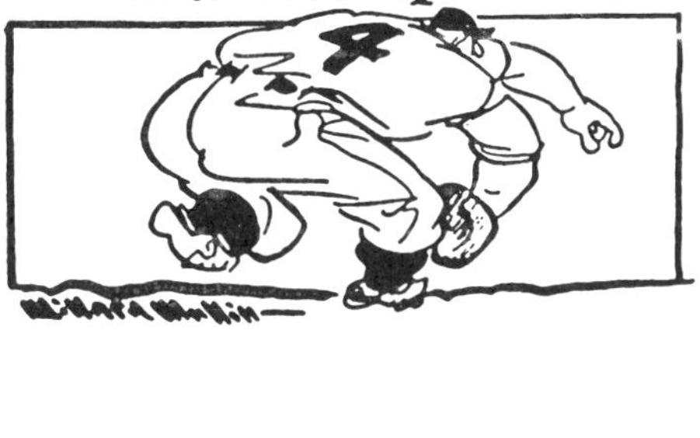

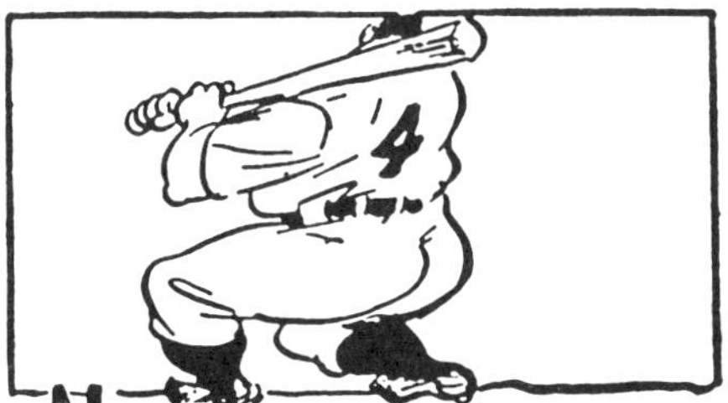

No flaw to be found, no
use to try
With hand as good and sure
as his eye,
His arm was just as strong
as his knee;
His back and shoulders enough
for three;
And his legs the best you
ever did see.

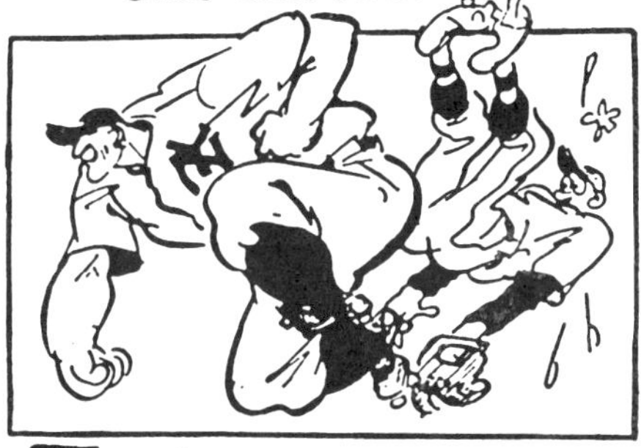

Tops! I tell you, I rather
guess
He was a wonder and nothing
less!

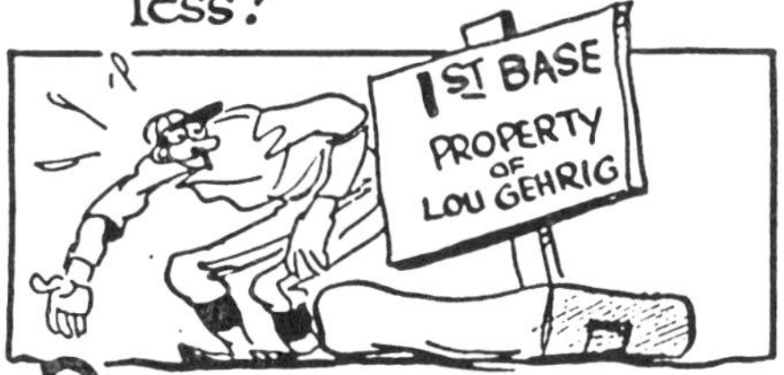
1ST BASE
PROPERTY OF LOU GEHRIG

Players they came for a
year or two,
Stayed a while --- were re-
placed by new.
Dugan, Ruth, Meusel, all are
through
But there stood the stout, old
Iron Horse Lou
Playing the bag as the best
could do!

A thousand ball games
passed and found
Gehrig at first base strong
and sound.
Fifteen hundred came and
went;
Eighteen hundred - and still
unbent.
And then the two-thousand
twenty first game
Playing as usual, much the
same.

Piling a record gol-darn
purty,
Came two thousand one hundred
and thirty.

Nineteen thirtynine, the first
day of May —
About the Oak's temples the
hair had turned gray,
A general flavor of mild decay,
But nothing local as one
may say.

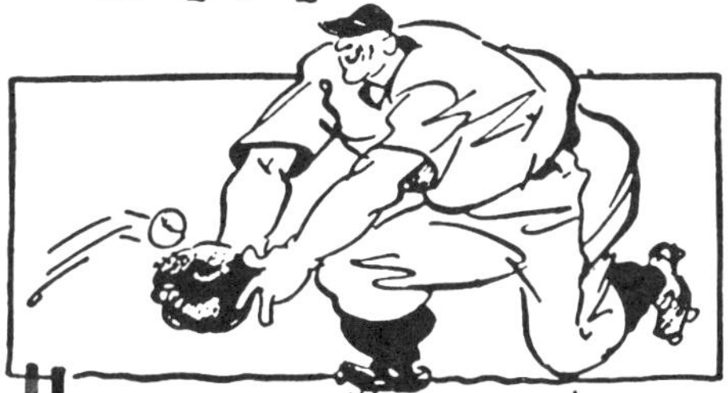

His body was sturdy - just like
at the start;
His lungs were still as strong
as his heart,
He was sound all over as any
part, —
And yet, as *a whole*, it is past
a doubt
In one more game he will
be *worn out!*

The second of May, Thirty
nine!
McCarthy was naming his
men down the line —
And what do you think the
people found?
Dahlgren on first to the right
of the mound!
And off in the dugout with
head going round
Was the man who had played
himself into the ground.

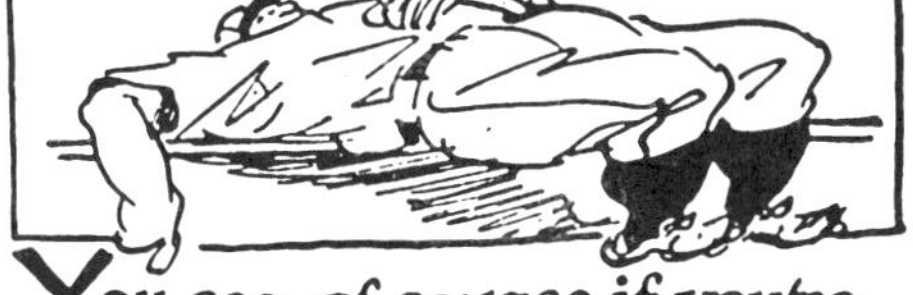

You see, of course, if you're
not a dunce
How he went to pieces all
at once, —
All at once, and nothing first, —
Just as bubbles do when
they burst.

End of the wonderful Iron
Horse Lou.
Flesh is flesh - and Lou is
through.

APOLOGIES TO OLIVER WENDELL HOLMES – AND HIS "THE DEACON'S MASTERPIECE"

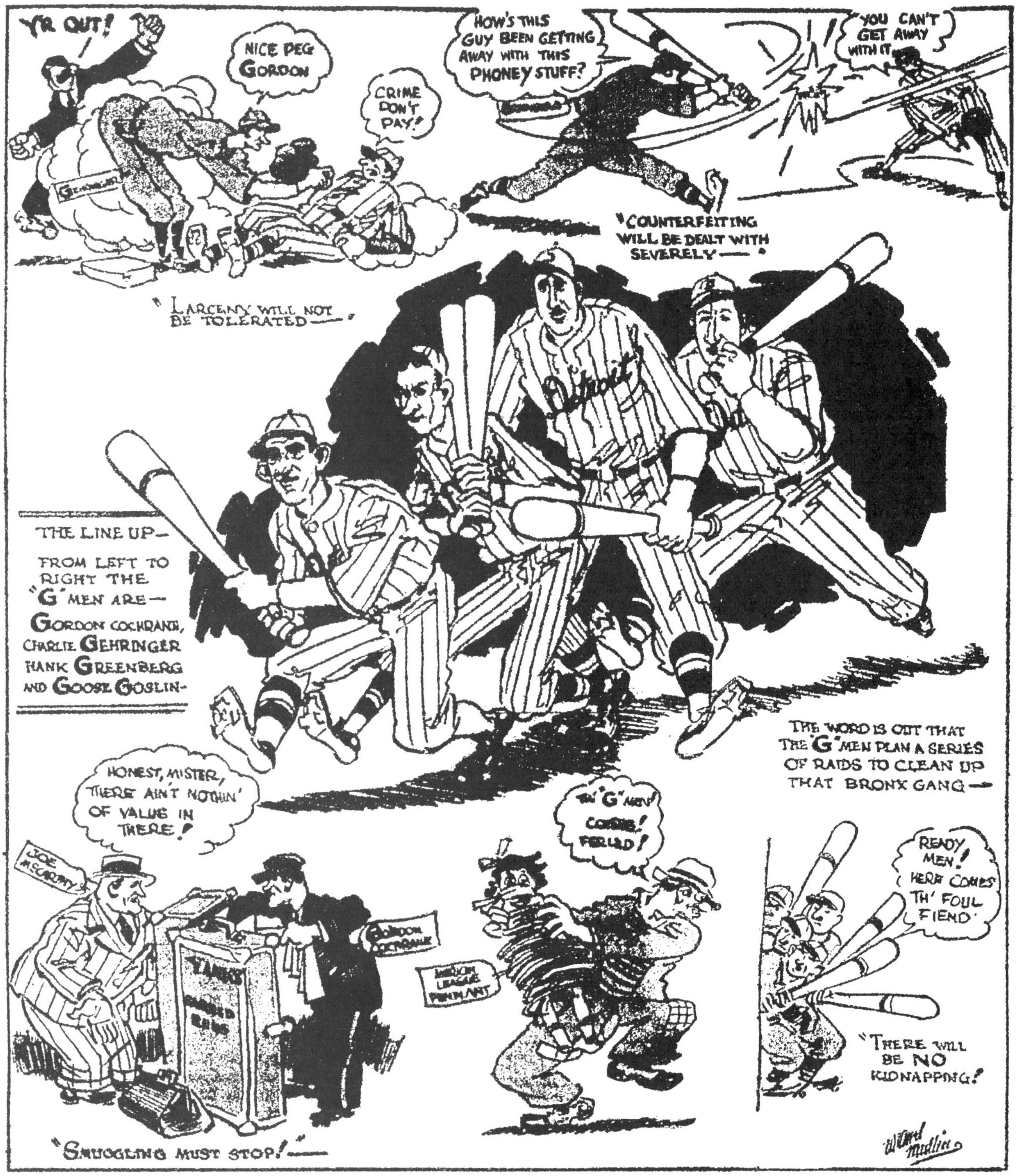
YR OUT!
NICE PEG GORDON
CRIME DON'T PAY!
HOW'S THIS GUY BEEN GETTING AWAY WITH THIS PHONEY STUFF?
YOU CAN'T GET AWAY WITH IT
"COUNTERFEITING WILL BE DEALT WITH SEVERELY—"
"LARCENY WILL NOT BE TOLERATED—"
THE LINE UP— FROM LEFT TO RIGHT THE "G" MEN ARE— GORDON COCHRANE, CHARLIE GEHRINGER HANK GREENBERG AND GOOSE GOSLIN-
THE WORD IS OUT THAT THE "G" MEN PLAN A SERIES OF RAIDS TO CLEAN UP THAT BRONX GANG—
HONEST, MISTER, THERE AIN'T NOTHIN' OF VALUE IN THERE!
JOE McCARTHY
GORDON COCHRANE
AMERICAN LEAGUE PENNANT
READY MEN! HERE COMES TH' FOUL FIEND
"THERE WILL BE NO KIDNAPPING!"
"SMUGGLING MUST STOP!—"

Equally as fierce as the Cardinals were the 1934–1935 Detroit Tigers. This drawing from 1935 shows the Tigers team that had just lost the Series in game 7 to the Cardinals in 1934 and would win their own World Championship in 1935.

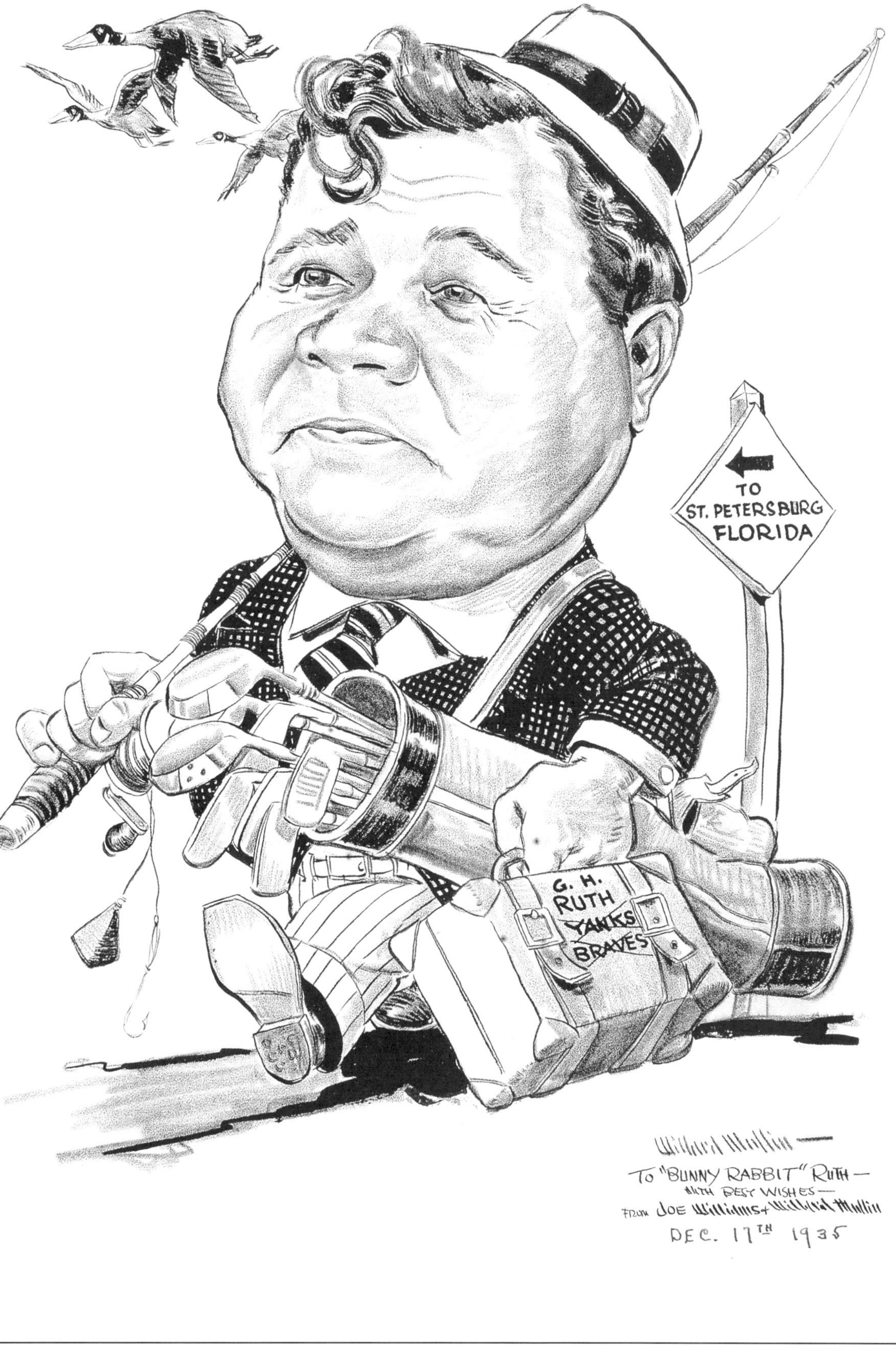
TO
ST. PETERSBURG
FLORIDA
G. H.
RUTH
YANKS
BRAVES
Willard Mullin —
To "BUNNY RABBIT" RUTH —
WITH BEST WISHES —
FROM JOE WILLIAMS + WILLARD MULLIN
DEC. 17TH 1935

ABOVE: Even though he had retired after the 1935 season after 20 years in baseball, old habits die hard, and the Babe was off to spring training in February of 1936. This is the first appearance of Mullin's iconic signature.

FOLLOWING: On October 18, 1935, the recently retired Babe Ruth played in a charity game to benefit the children of World War I veterans. Mullin, a personal friend of the Babe's, drew this crowd scene. Note the signature. It wasn't until 1936 that he solidified his unique 26-stroke signature (above).

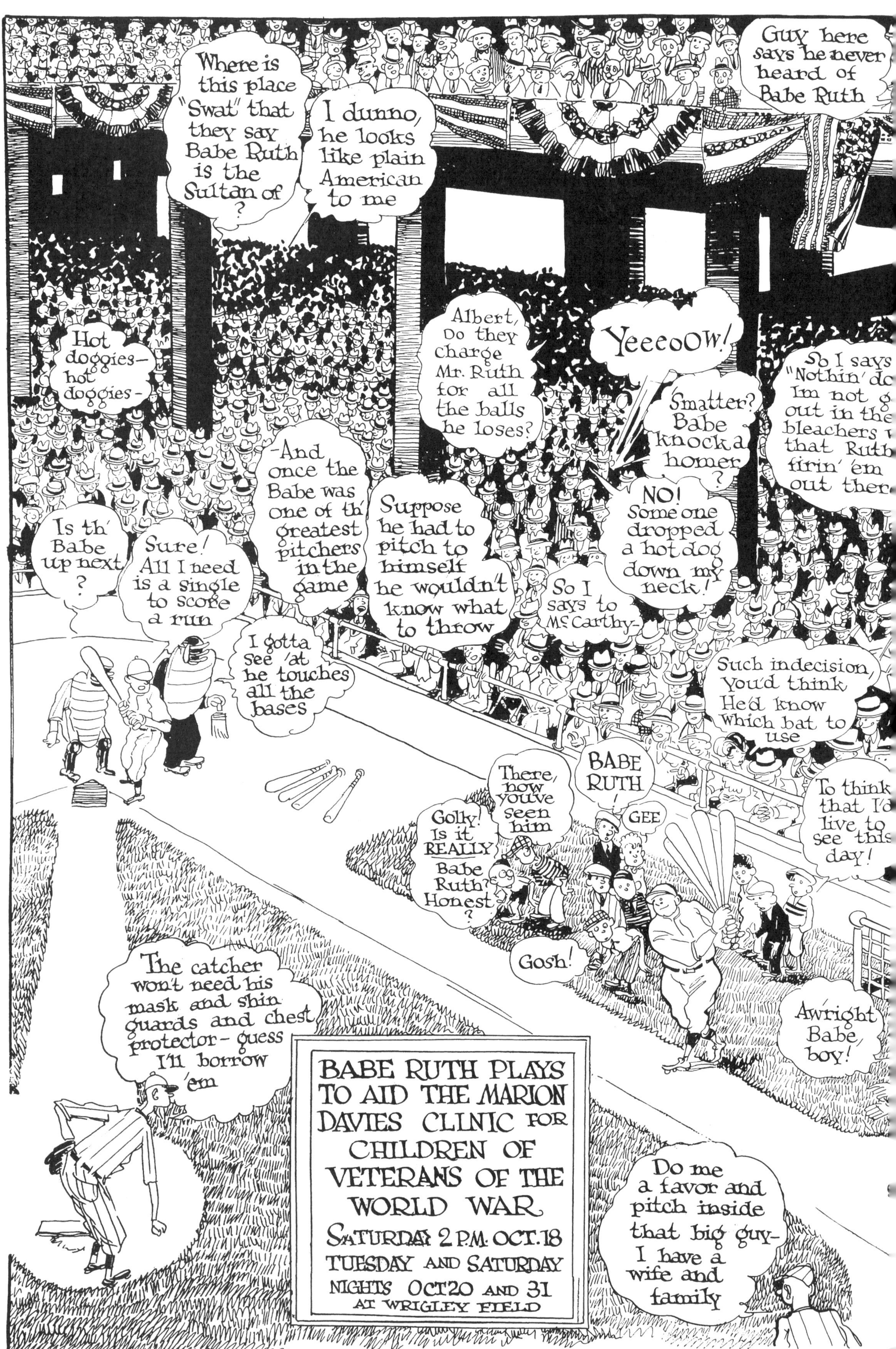
Where is this place "Swat" that they say Babe Ruth is the Sultan of ?
I dunno, he looks like plain American to me
Guy here says he never heard of Babe Ruth
Hot doggies- hot doggies-
Albert, Do they charge Mr. Ruth for all the balls he loses?
Yeeeoow!
So I says "Nothin' do Im not g out in the bleachers that Ruth firin' 'em out ther
Smatter? Babe knock a homer ?
NO! Some one dropped a hot dog down my neck!
-And once the Babe was one of th' greatest pitchers in the game
Suppose he had to pitch to himself he wouldn't know what to throw
Is th' Babe up next ?
Sure! All I need is a single to score a run
So I says to McCarthy-
I gotta see 'at he touches all the bases
Such indecision, You'd think He'd know Which bat to use
There, now you've seen him
BABE RUTH !
GEE
Golly! Is it REALLY Babe Ruth? Honest ?
To think that I' live to see this day!
Gosh!
Awright Babe, boy!
The catcher won't need his mask and shin guards and chest protector- guess I'll borrow 'em
BABE RUTH PLAYS TO AID THE MARION DAVIES CLINIC FOR CHILDREN OF VETERANS OF THE WORLD WAR
SATURDAY 2 P.M. OCT. 18 TUESDAY AND SATURDAY NIGHTS OCT 20 AND 31 AT WRIGLEY FIELD
Do me a favor and pitch inside that big guy- I have a wife and family

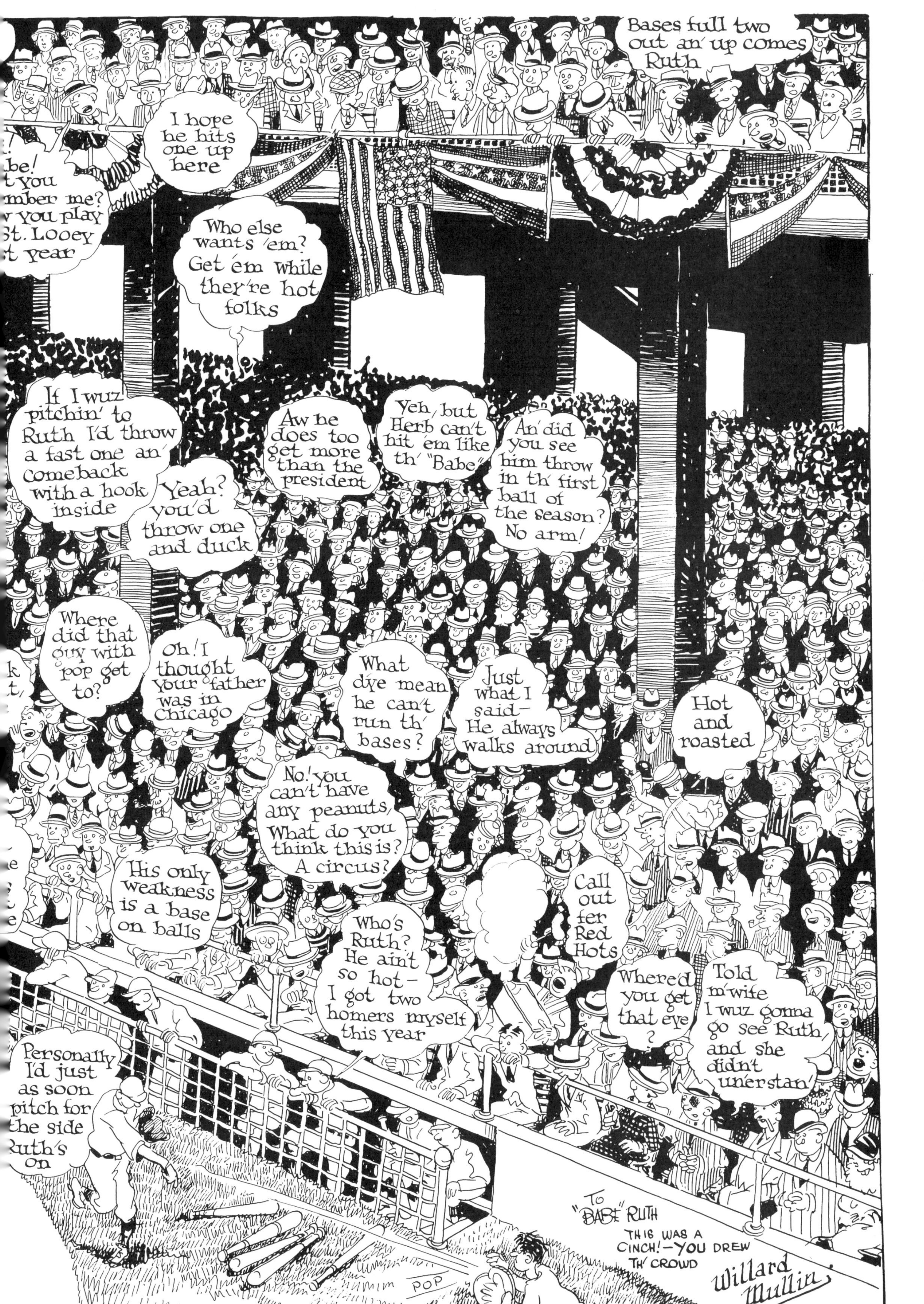
Bases full two out an' up comes Ruth
I hope he hits one up here
Who else wants 'em? Get 'em while they're hot folks
If I wuz pitchin' to Ruth I'd throw a fast one an' comeback with a hook inside
Yeah? you'd throw one and duck
Aw he does too get more than the president
Yeh, but Herb can't hit 'em like th' "Babe"
An' did you see him throw in th' first ball of the season? No arm!
Where did that guy with pop get to?
Oh! I thought your father was in Chicago
What d'ye mean he can't run th' bases?
Just what I said— He always walks around
Hot and roasted
No! you can't have any peanuts, What do you think this is? A circus?
His only weakness is a base on balls
Call out fer Red Hots
Who's Ruth? He ain't so hot— I got two homers myself this year
Where'd you get that eye?
Told m'wife I wuz gonna go see Ruth, and she didn't unerstan'
Personally I'd just as soon pitch for the side Ruth's on
POP
To "Babe" Ruth
This was a cinch! —You drew th' crowd
Willard Mullin

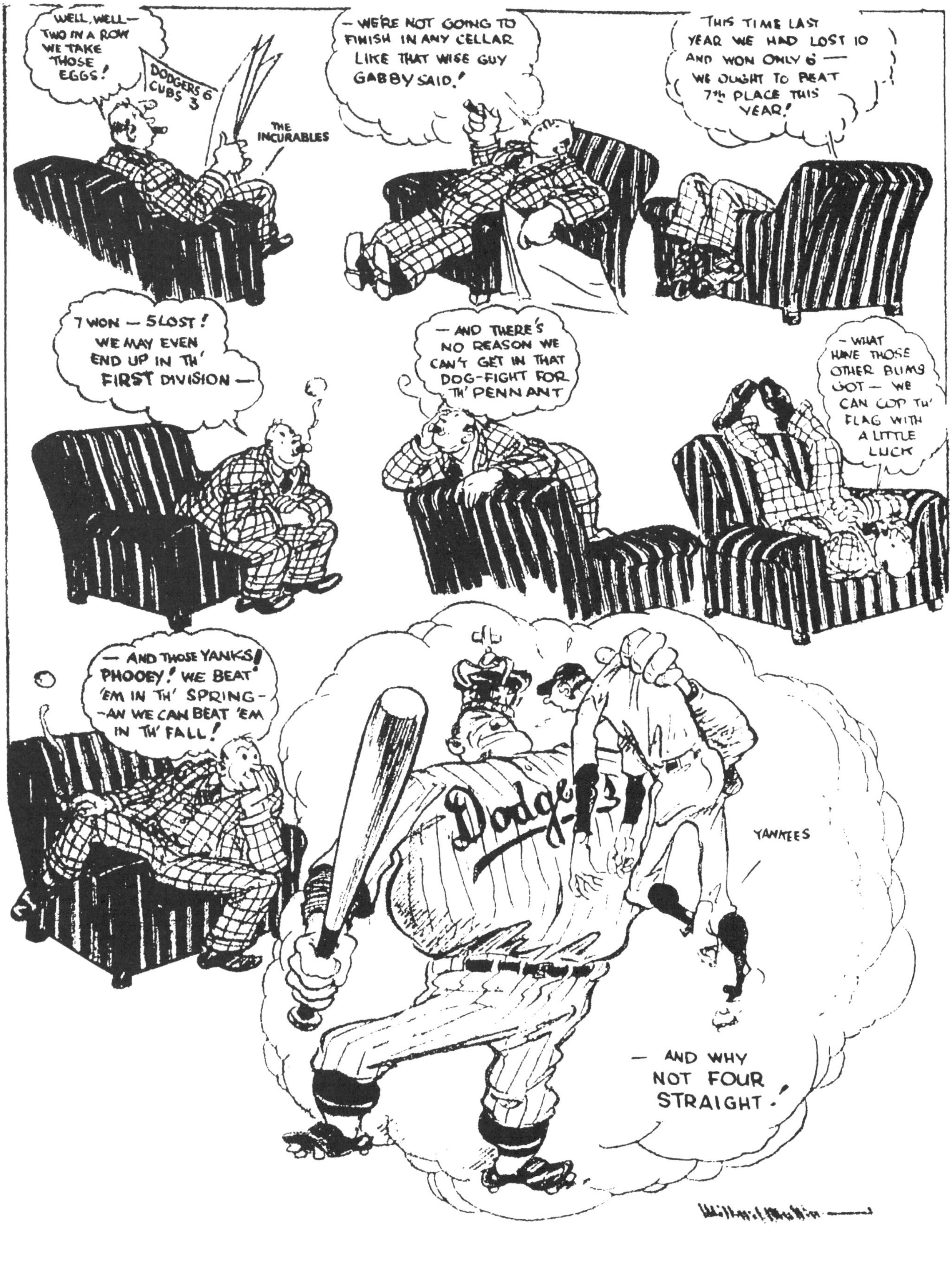
WELL, WELL— TWO IN A ROW WE TAKE THOSE EGGS!
DODGERS 6 CUBS 3
THE INCURABLES
— WE'RE NOT GOING TO FINISH IN ANY CELLAR LIKE THAT WISE GUY GABBY SAID!
THIS TIME LAST YEAR WE HAD LOST 10 AND WON ONLY 6 — WE OUGHT TO BEAT 7th PLACE THIS YEAR!
7 WON — 5 LOST! WE MAY EVEN END UP IN TH' FIRST DIVISION —
— AND THERE'S NO REASON WE CAN'T GET IN THAT DOG-FIGHT FOR TH' PENNANT
— WHAT HAVE THOSE OTHER BUMS GOT — WE CAN COP TH' FLAG WITH A LITTLE LUCK
— AND THOSE YANKS! PHOOEY! WE BEAT 'EM IN TH' SPRING- -AN WE CAN BEAT 'EM IN TH' FALL!
Dodgers
YANKEES
— AND WHY NOT FOUR STRAIGHT!

In the first few weeks of the 1936 season, the usually hapless Brooklyn Dodgers, managed by Casey Stengel, played .500 baseball. Mullin's cartoon portrays not only the always-optimistic Brooklyn fan, but also represents the Dodgers team as a single, if still oversized, player. It wasn't until 1938 that Mullin came up with his most iconic character, the Brooklyn Bum.

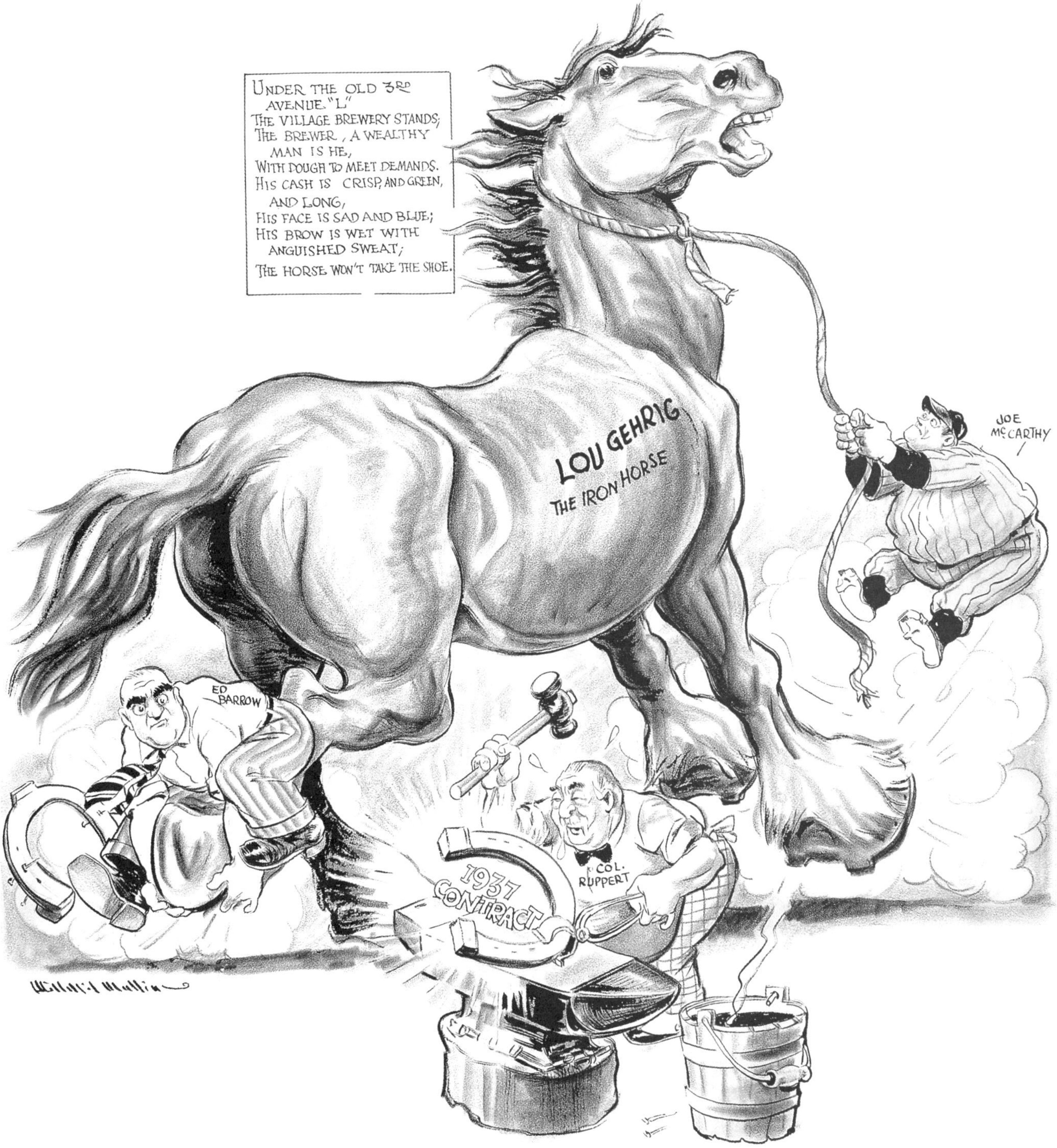
UNDER THE OLD 3RD AVENUE "L"
THE VILLAGE BREWERY STANDS;
THE BREWER, A WEALTHY MAN IS HE,
WITH DOUGH TO MEET DEMANDS.
HIS CASH IS CRISP, AND GREEN, AND LONG,
HIS FACE IS SAD AND BLUE;
HIS BROW IS WET WITH ANGUISHED SWEAT;
THE HORSE WON'T TAKE THE SHOE.
LOU GEHRIG
THE IRON HORSE
JOE McCARTHY
ED BARROW
COL. RUPPERT
1937 CONTRACT

This drawing is from the winter of 1936, when the Yankees were attempting to sign Lou Gehrig to a new contract. In addition to Mullin's parody of Longfellow's "The Village Blacksmith," this cartoon contains the first known reference to Lou Gehrig as the "Iron Horse."

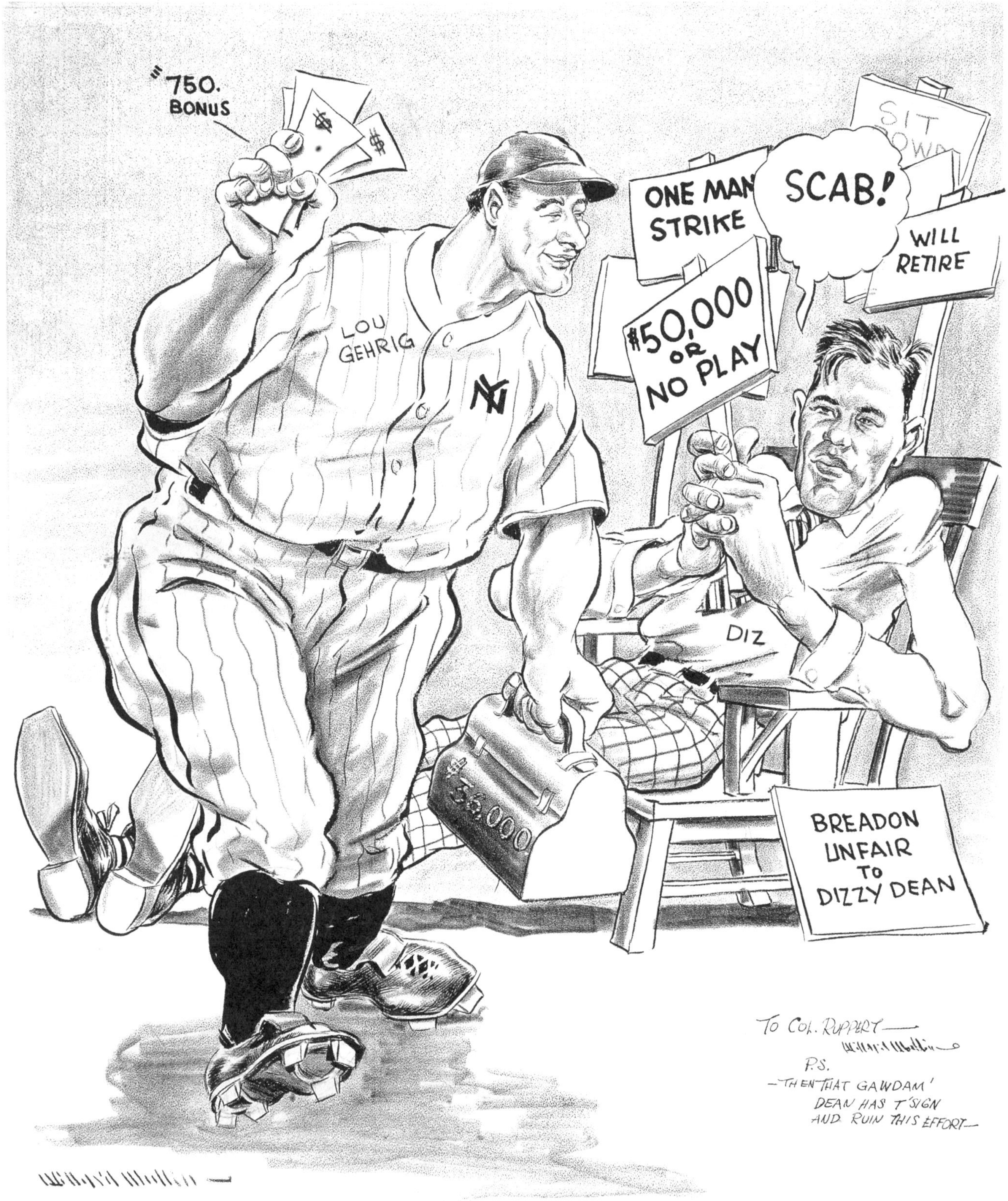
$750.
BONUS
LOU
GEHRIG
ONE MAN
STRIKE
SCAB!
SIT
WILL
RETIRE
$50,000
OR
NO PLAY
DIZ
$36,000
BREADON
UNFAIR
TO
DIZZY DEAN
TO COL. RUPPERT—
P.S.
—THEN THAT GAWDAM'
DEAN HAS T'SIGN
AND RUIN THIS EFFORT—

Before the start of the 1937 season, Lou Gehrig signed a contract for $36,000 and received a $750 bonus from the Yankees. Dizzy Dean, coming off his fourth straight 20-plus-win season, felt he was entitled to more and held out during the first part of spring training. He eventually signed for $25,500.

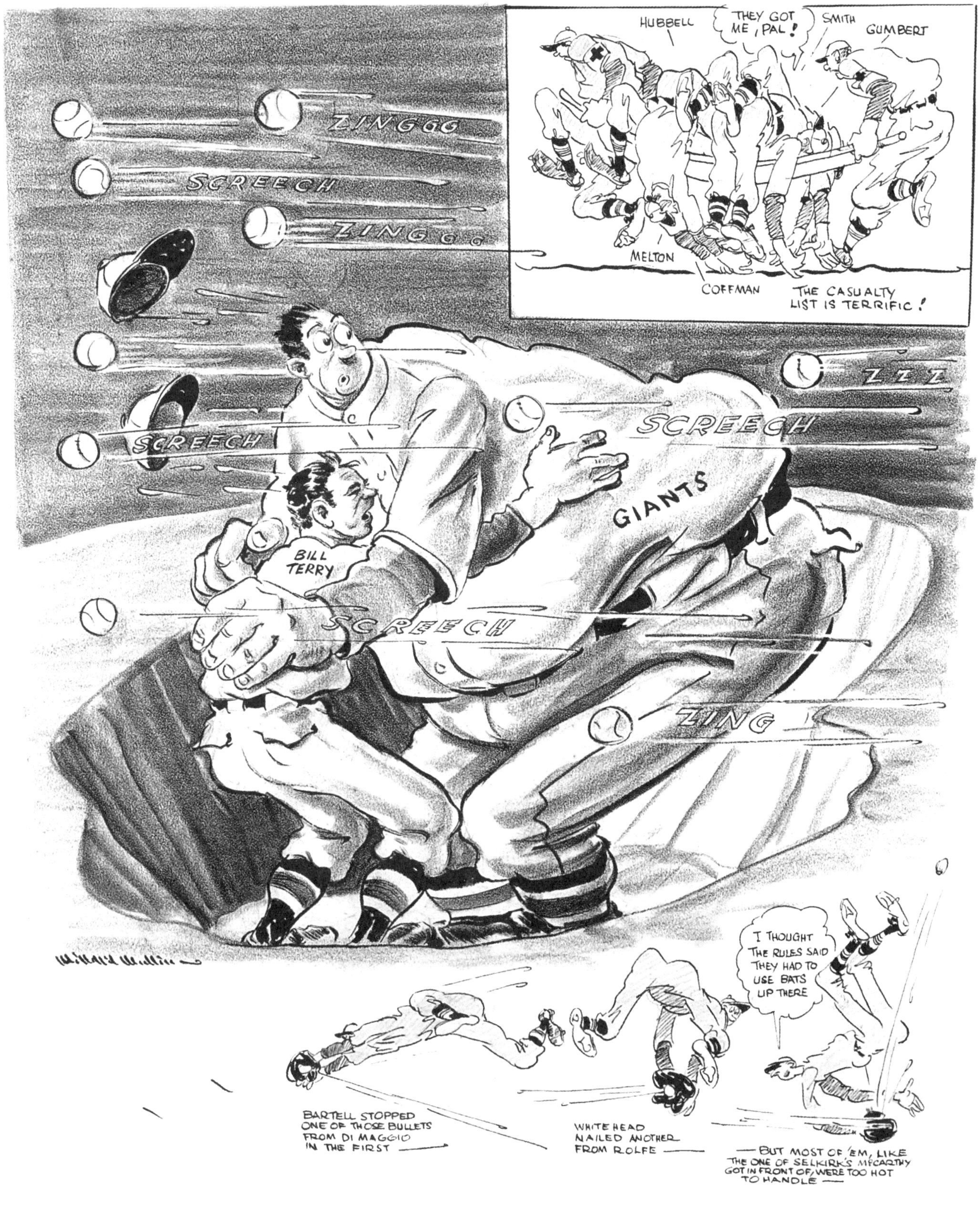

HUBBELL
THEY GOT ME, PAL!
SMITH
GUMBERT
MELTON
COFFMAN
THE CASUALTY LIST IS TERRIFIC!
ZINGGG
SCREECH
ZINGGG
ZZZ
SCREECH
SCREECH
GIANTS
BILL TERRY
SCREECH
ZING
I THOUGHT THE RULES SAID THEY HAD TO USE BATS UP THERE
BARTELL STOPPED ONE OF THOSE BULLETS FROM DI MAGGIO IN THE FIRST
WHITEHEAD NAILED ANOTHER FROM ROLFE
BUT MOST OF 'EM, LIKE THE ONE OF SELKIRK'S McCARTHY GOT IN FRONT OF, WERE TOO HOT TO HANDLE

In 1937, the New York Yankees played Bill Terry's New York Giants. In the first two games, the Yankees scored 16 runs to the Giants' two. The Yankees were on the way to their second World Championship in as many years.

JACK COOMBS - WITH THE A'S IN 1910 AND '11 AND THE DODGERS IN 1916 WON FIVE WORLD SERIES TILTS WITHOUT A LOSS!

HERB PENNOCK HAS A RECORD OF FIVE FALL CLASSIC WINS AND NO DEFEATS - WITH THE YANKEES IN 1923, '26 AND '27 —

—AND LEFTY GOMEZ ALSO HAS A PERFECT SCORE THROUGH THE 1932, 1936 AND 1937 SERIES WITH FIVE VICTORIES—

SMART GUY, MC CARTHY PITCHES ME IN THE TIMER — WEDNESDAY —

AN' THEN WE ONLY NEED THREE MORE

GOOFY

THE WAY IT LOOKS NOW LEFTY WILL GET HIS FIRST CHANCE TO MAKE IT 6 IN A ROW THIS WEDNESDAY —

WITH BEST WISHES AND CONGRATULATIONS TO LEFTY GOMEZ from

Going into the 1938 World Series, Lefty Gomez had pitched five straight World Series games with no losses (one in 1932 and two each in 1936 and 1937). At that point, he was tied with Jack Coombs and Yankees great Herb Pennock. In game 2 in the 1938 Fall Classic, Gomez would win his sixth World Series game with no defeats, a record that still stands.

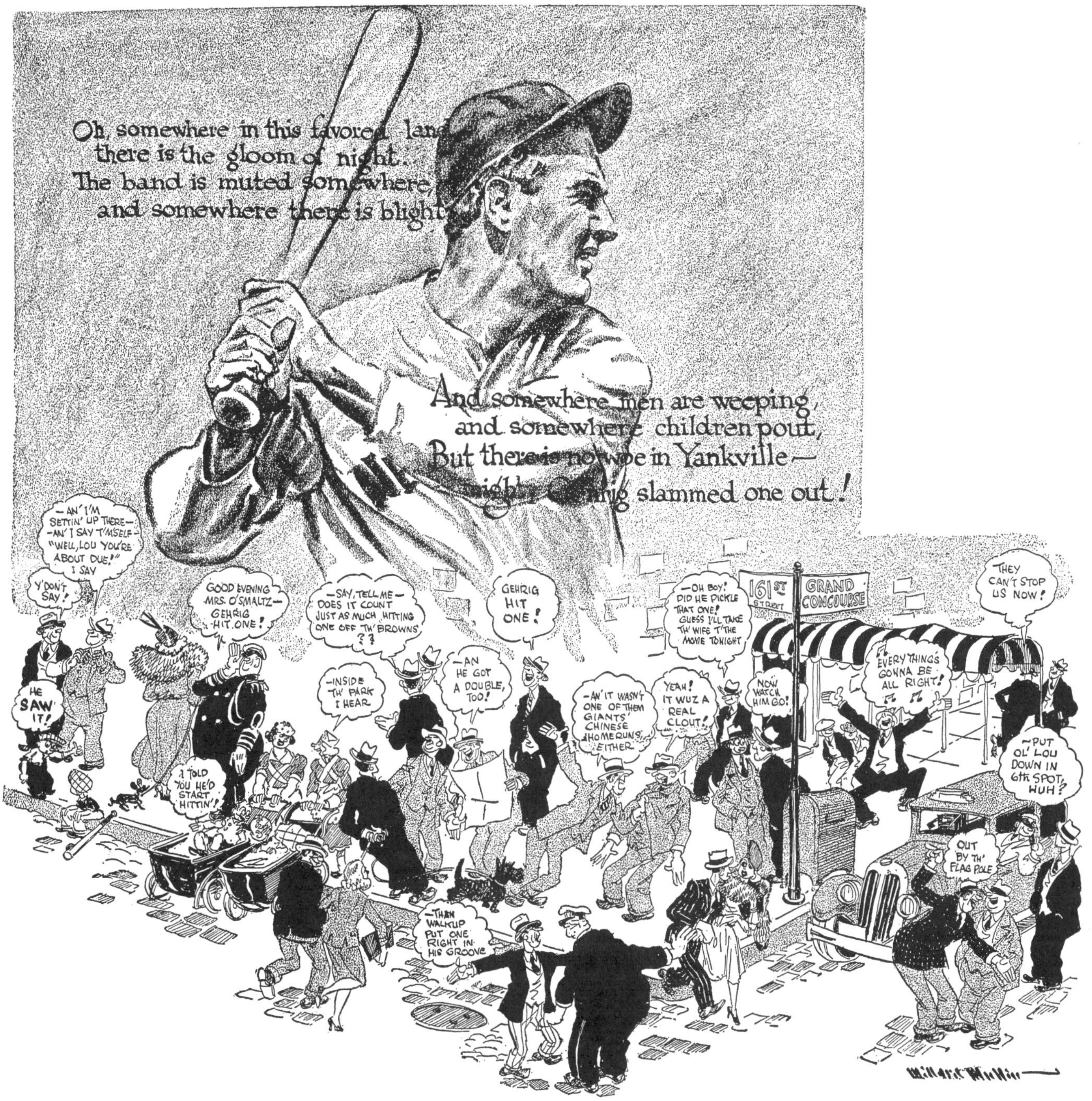
Oh, somewhere in this favored lan
there is the gloom of night...
The band is muted somewhere,
and somewhere there is blight;
And somewhere men are weeping,
and somewhere children pout,
But there is no woe in Yankville —
slammed one out!
— AN' I'M SETTIN' UP THERE — — AN' I SAY T'M'SELF — "WELL, LOU YOU'RE ABOUT DUE!" I SAY
Y'DON'T SAY!
HE SAW IT!
GOOD EVENING MRS. O'SMALTZ — GEHRIG HIT ONE!
I TOLD YOU HE'D START HITTIN'!
— SAY, TELL ME — DOES IT COUNT JUST AS MUCH HITTING ONE OFF TH' BROWNS ??
— INSIDE TH' PARK I HEAR
— AN HE GOT A DOUBLE, TOO!
GEHRIG HIT ONE!
— AN' IT WASN'T ONE OF THEM GIANTS' CHINESE HOMERUNS, EITHER
YEAH! IT WUZ A REAL CLOUT!
— OH BOY! DID HE PICKLE THAT ONE! GUESS I'LL TAKE TH' WIFE T' THE MOVIE TONIGHT
161ST STREET
GRAND CONCOURSE
NOW WATCH HIM GO!
EVERY THING'S GONNA BE ALL RIGHT!
THEY CAN'T STOP US NOW!
— PUT OL' LOU DOWN IN 6th SPOT, HUH?
OUT BY TH' FLAG POLE
— THEN WALK UP PUT ONE RIGHT IN HIS GROOVE

1938 saw Lou Gehrig's batting average fall below .300 for the first time since his rookie season. Gehrig didn't hit his first home run until the 16th game of the season, and Mullin celebrated it with a parody of "Casey at the Bat." It wasn't until 1939, when he was diagnosed with amyotrophic lateral sclerosis (ALS), that the reason for Gehrig's decline became apparent. Gehrig was dead by 1941.

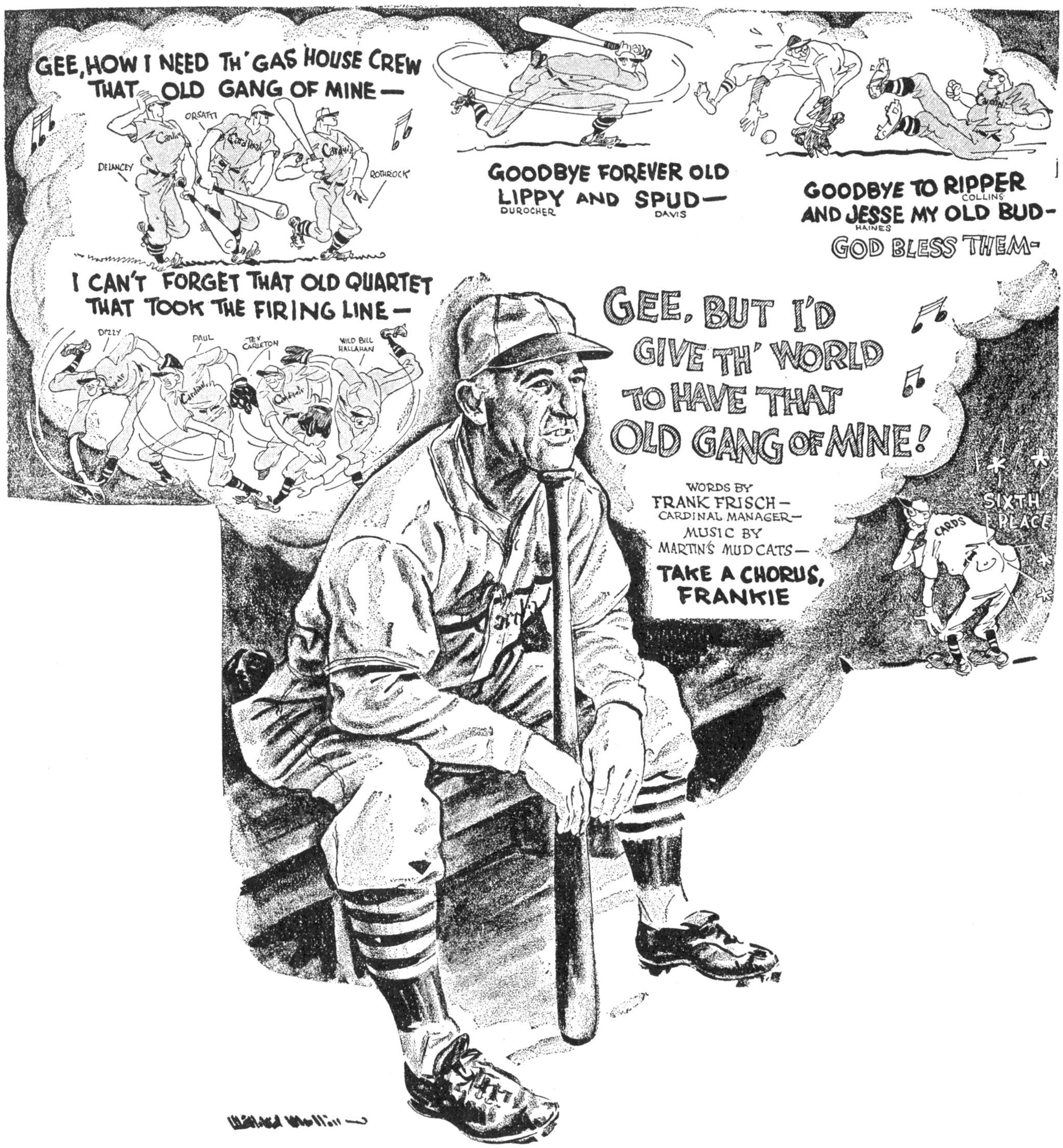
GEE, HOW I NEED TH' GAS HOUSE CREW
THAT OLD GANG OF MINE—
DELANCEY
ORSATTI
ROTHROCK
GOODBYE FOREVER OLD
LIPPY AND SPUD—
DUROCHER
DAVIS
GOODBYE TO RIPPER
COLLINS
AND JESSE MY OLD BUD-
HAINES
GOD BLESS THEM-
I CAN'T FORGET THAT OLD QUARTET
THAT TOOK THE FIRING LINE—
DIZZY
PAUL
TEX CARLETON
WILD BILL HALLAHAN
GEE, BUT I'D
GIVE TH' WORLD
TO HAVE THAT
OLD GANG OF MINE!
WORDS BY
FRANK FRISCH—
CARDINAL MANAGER—
MUSIC BY
MARTIN'S MUD CATS—
TAKE A CHORUS,
FRANKIE
CARDS
SIXTH PLACE

Frankie Frisch was player-manager for the St. Louis Cardinals from 1933 until 1937. In 1934, the Cardinals beat the Detroit Tigers to win the World Series. By 1938, Frisch had retired as a player but continued to manage the Cards; however, the stars of his 1934 team were gone, most notably Dizzy Dean and Leo Durocher. Frisch apparently couldn't take the mediocrity and quit with 16 games remaining in the season and St. Louis firmly in sixth place.

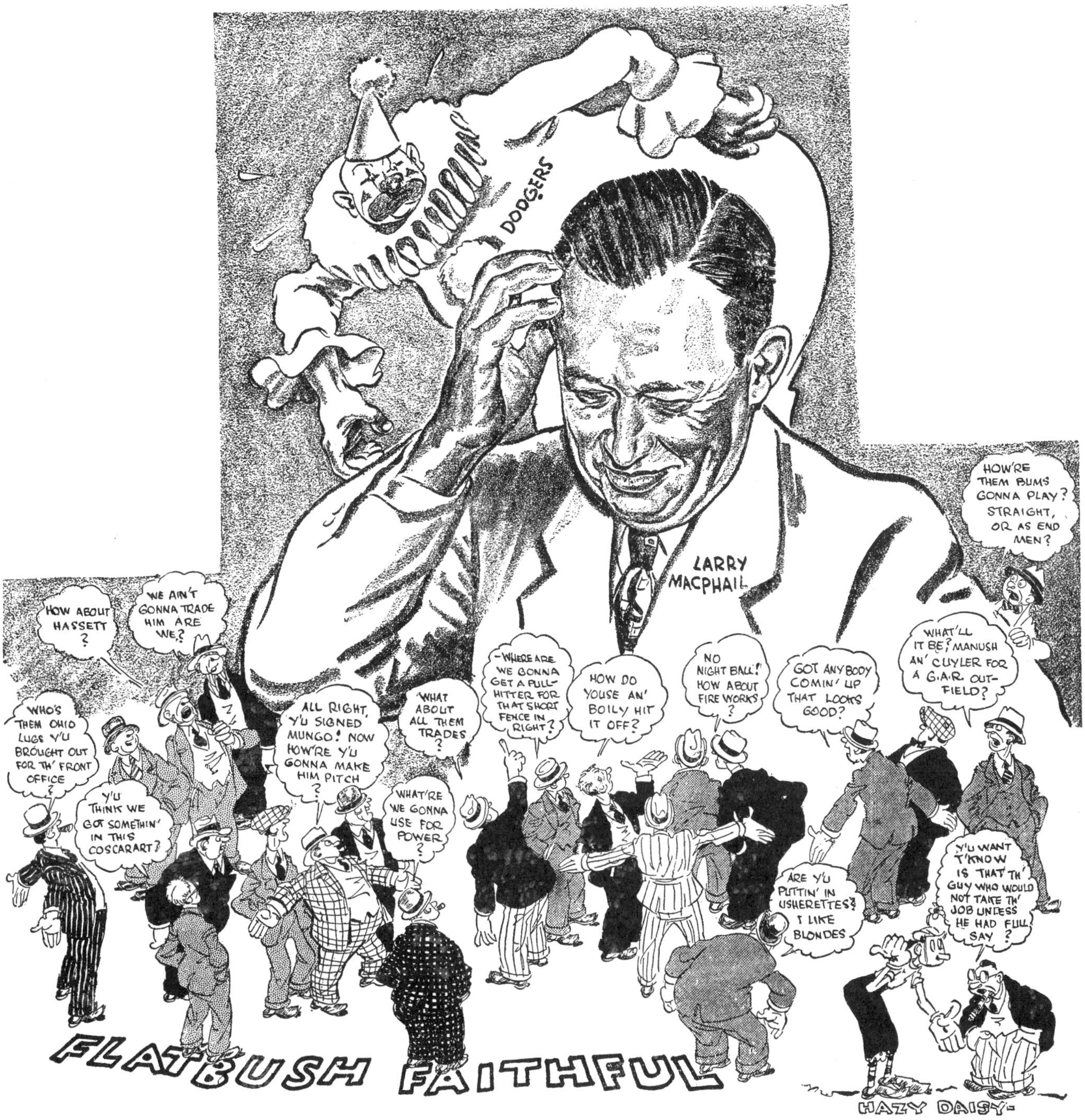
DODGERS
LARRY MACPHAIL
HOW ABOUT HASSETT ?
WE AIN'T GONNA TRADE HIM ARE WE?
WHO'S THEM OHIO LUGS Y'U BROUGHT OUT FOR TH' FRONT OFFICE ?
Y'U THINK WE GOT SOMETHIN' IN THIS COSCARART?
ALL RIGHT, Y'U SIGNED MUNGO! NOW HOW'RE Y'U GONNA MAKE HIM PITCH ?
WHAT ABOUT ALL THEM TRADES ?
WHAT'RE WE GONNA USE FOR POWER ?
-WHERE ARE WE GONNA GET A PULL-HITTER FOR THAT SHORT FENCE IN RIGHT?
HOW DO YOUSE AN' BOILY HIT IT OFF?
NO NIGHT BALL! HOW ABOUT FIRE WORKS ?
GOT ANYBODY COMIN' UP THAT LOOKS GOOD?
WHAT'LL IT BE? MANUSH AN' CUYLER FOR A G.A.R. OUT-FIELD?
HOW'RE THEM BUMS GONNA PLAY? STRAIGHT, OR AS END MEN?
ARE Y'U PUTTIN' IN USHERETTES? I LIKE BLONDES
Y'U WANT T'KNOW IS THAT TH' GUY WHO WOULD NOT TAKE TH' JOB UNLESS HE HAD FULL SAY ?
FLATBUSH FAITHFUL
HAZY DAISY-

It wasn't until the middle of the 1938 season that Mullin created his quintessential character, the Brooklyn Bum. The Bum was inspired by a question from a cabbie driving Mullin home from Ebbets Field. "Well, how did our bums do today?" he asked. This cartoon from early 1938 was one of several personifications Mullin applied to the Dodgers before coming up with The Bum. As the previous year's 1937 Dodgers had lost 91 games, the clown, at least at the time, seemed appropriate.

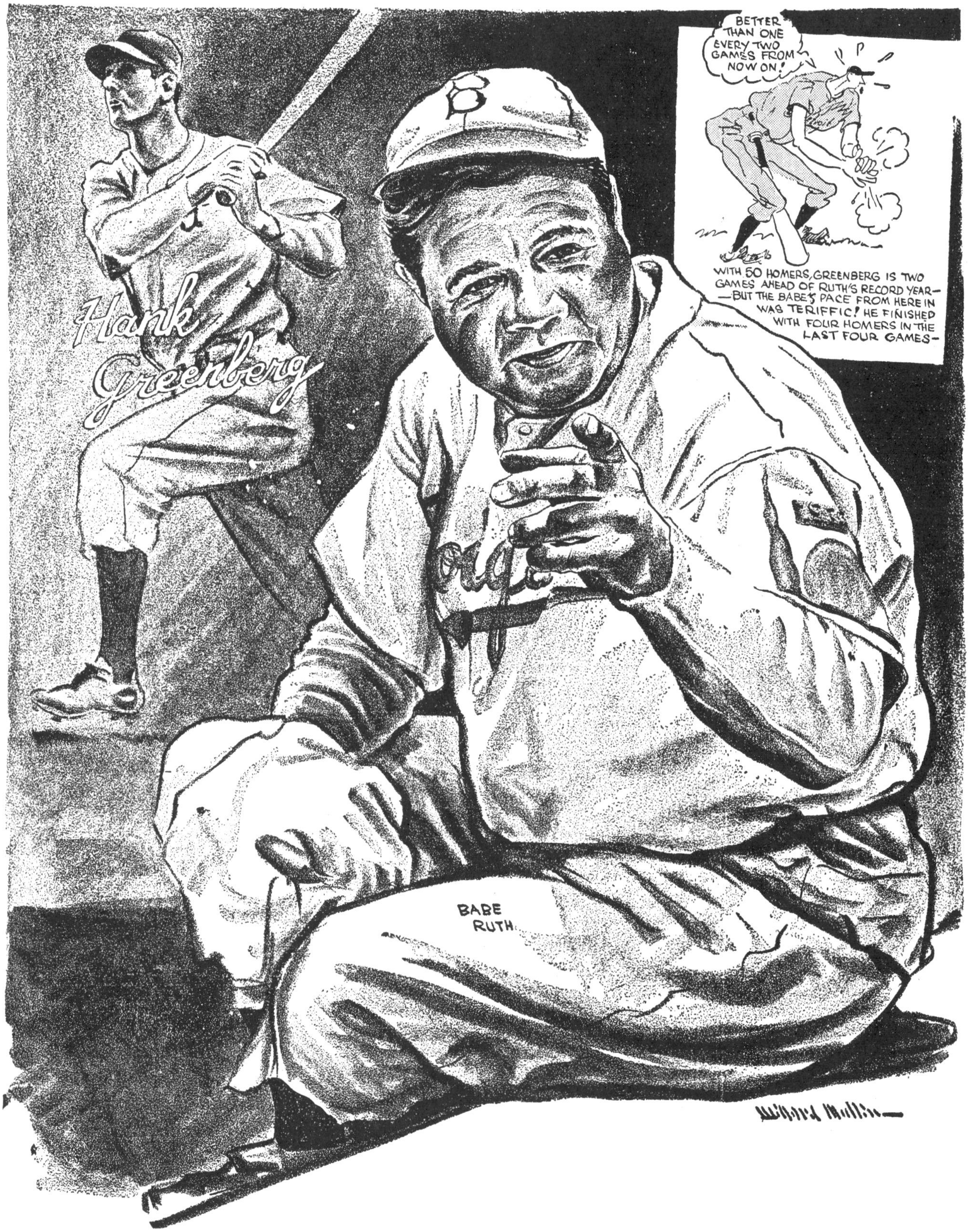
Hank Greenberg
BETTER THAN ONE EVERY TWO GAMES FROM NOW ON!
WITH 50 HOMERS, GREENBERG IS TWO GAMES AHEAD OF RUTH'S RECORD YEAR— —BUT THE BABE'S PACE FROM HERE IN WAS TERIFFIC! HE FINISHED WITH FOUR HOMERS IN THE LAST FOUR GAMES—
BABE RUTH

In 1938 Hank Greenberg challenged the most hallowed record in baseball, Babe Ruth's 60 home runs in a single season. He fell just short, with 58. Babe, by that time, was a third-base coach for the Brooklyn Dodgers and Mullin, who was a personal friend of the Babe's, drew this portrait, which was more about the greatness of the Babe than the accomplishments of Greenberg.

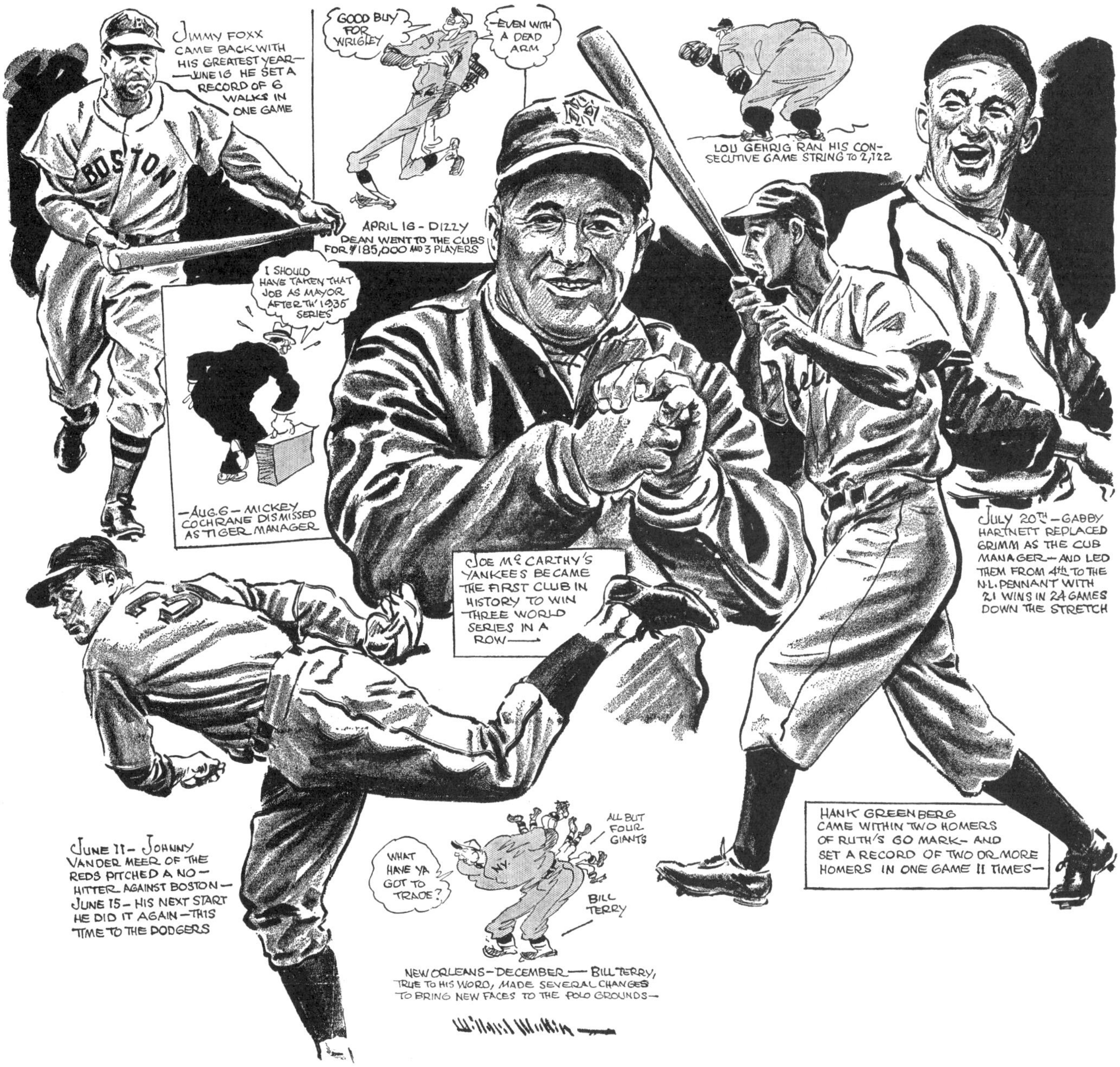
JIMMY FOXX CAME BACK WITH HIS GREATEST YEAR— —JUNE 16 HE SET A RECORD OF 6 WALKS IN ONE GAME
GOOD BUY FOR WRIGLEY
—EVEN WITH A DEAD ARM
APRIL 16 - DIZZY DEAN WENT TO THE CUBS FOR $185,000 AND 3 PLAYERS
LOU GEHRIG RAN HIS CONSECUTIVE GAME STRING TO 2,122
I SHOULD HAVE TAKEN THAT JOB AS MAYOR AFTER TH' 1935 SERIES
—AUG. 6 — MICKEY COCHRANE DISMISSED AS TIGER MANAGER
JOE MCCARTHY'S YANKEES BECAME THE FIRST CLUB IN HISTORY TO WIN THREE WORLD SERIES IN A ROW
JULY 20TH — GABBY HARTNETT REPLACED GRIMM AS THE CUB MANAGER — AND LED THEM FROM 4TH TO THE N.L. PENNANT WITH 21 WINS IN 24 GAMES DOWN THE STRETCH
JUNE 11 - JOHNNY VANDER MEER OF THE REDS PITCHED A NO-HITTER AGAINST BOSTON— JUNE 15 - HIS NEXT START HE DID IT AGAIN — THIS TIME TO THE DODGERS
WHAT HAVE YA GOT TO TRADE?
ALL BUT FOUR GIANTS
BILL TERRY
HANK GREENBERG CAME WITHIN TWO HOMERS OF RUTH'S 60 MARK — AND SET A RECORD OF TWO OR MORE HOMERS IN ONE GAME 11 TIMES—
NEW ORLEANS — DECEMBER — BILL TERRY, TRUE TO HIS WORD, MADE SEVERAL CHANGES TO BRING NEW FACES TO THE POLO GROUNDS—

This piece, done in 1938, represented a changing of the guard. Mickey Cochrane, who had led the Tigers to the World Series Championship just three years before in 1935, was fired. Dizzy Dean, who had injured his arm in 1937, was traded in April 1938 to the Cubs. Joe McCarthy became the first manager to win three World Series in a row, and Lou Gehrig extended his consecutive streak of games played in a row to 2,122. Gehrig would only play eight more games in his career; he retired on May 1, 1939, after having been diagnosed with ALS, which became known as "Lou Gehrig's Disease."

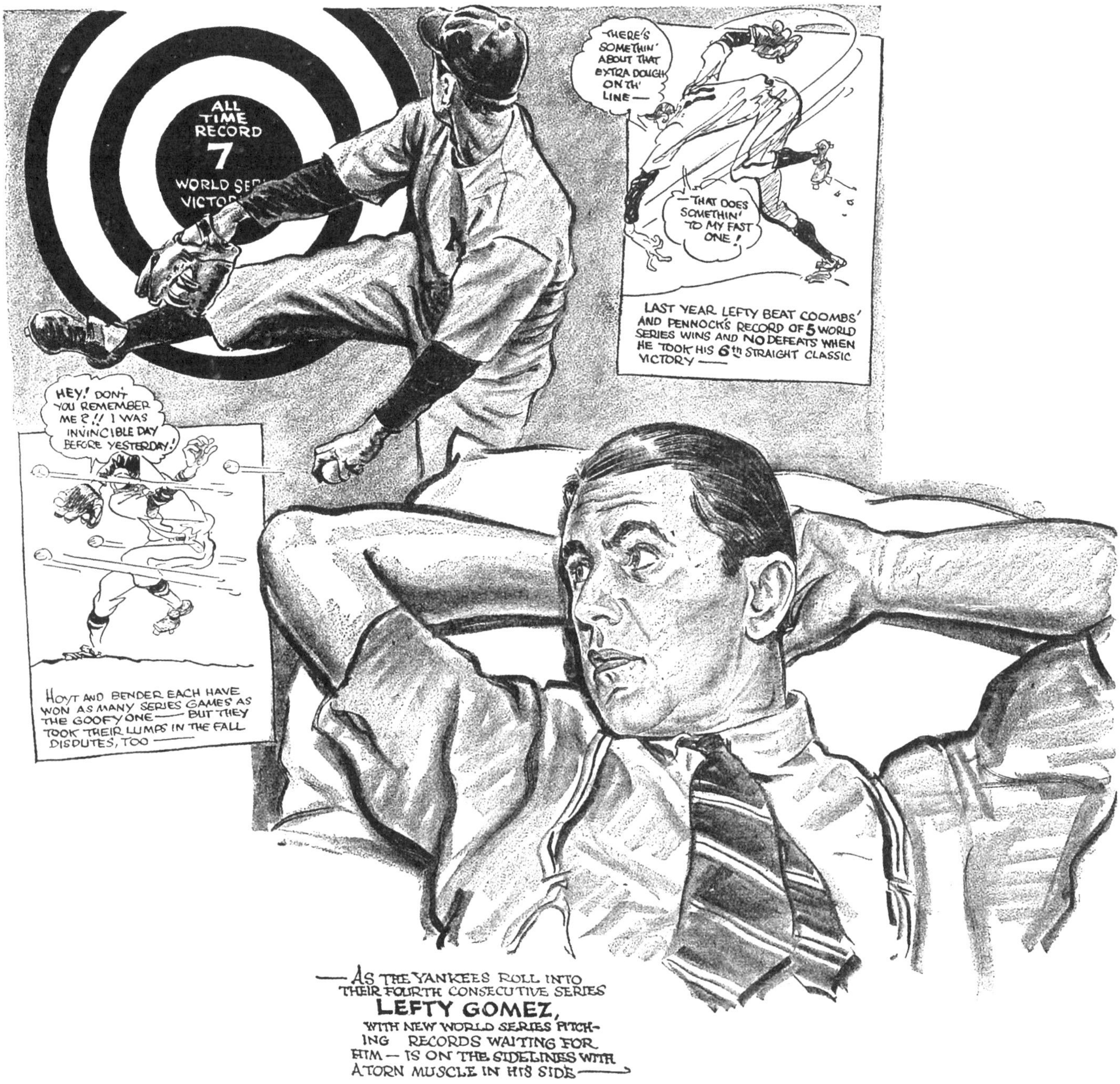
ALL TIME RECORD 7 WORLD SERIES VICTORIES
THERE'S SOMETHIN' ABOUT THAT EXTRA DOUGH ON TH' LINE —
— THAT DOES SOMETHIN' TO MY FAST ONE!
LAST YEAR LEFTY BEAT COOMBS' AND PENNOCK'S RECORD OF 5 WORLD SERIES WINS AND NO DEFEATS WHEN HE TOOK HIS 6th STRAIGHT CLASSIC VICTORY —
HEY! DON'T YOU REMEMBER ME?!! I WAS INVINCIBLE DAY BEFORE YESTERDAY!
HOYT AND BENDER EACH HAVE WON AS MANY SERIES GAMES AS THE GOOFY ONE — BUT THEY TOOK THEIR LUMPS IN THE FALL DISPUTES, TOO —
— AS THE YANKEES ROLL INTO THEIR FOURTH CONSECUTIVE SERIES LEFTY GOMEZ, WITH NEW WORLD SERIES PITCHING RECORDS WAITING FOR HIM — IS ON THE SIDELINES WITH A TORN MUSCLE IN HIS SIDE —

By 1939, Yankees pitcher Lefty Gomez was a perfect 6–0 in World Series play. As the Series against the Reds approached, Lefty was hoping for one more chance. As the Series started, Lefty was on the sidelines with a torn muscle in his side. He got that chance in game 3, but only lasted one inning before being relieved by Bump Hadley, who got the victory in a game the Yankees won, 7-3.

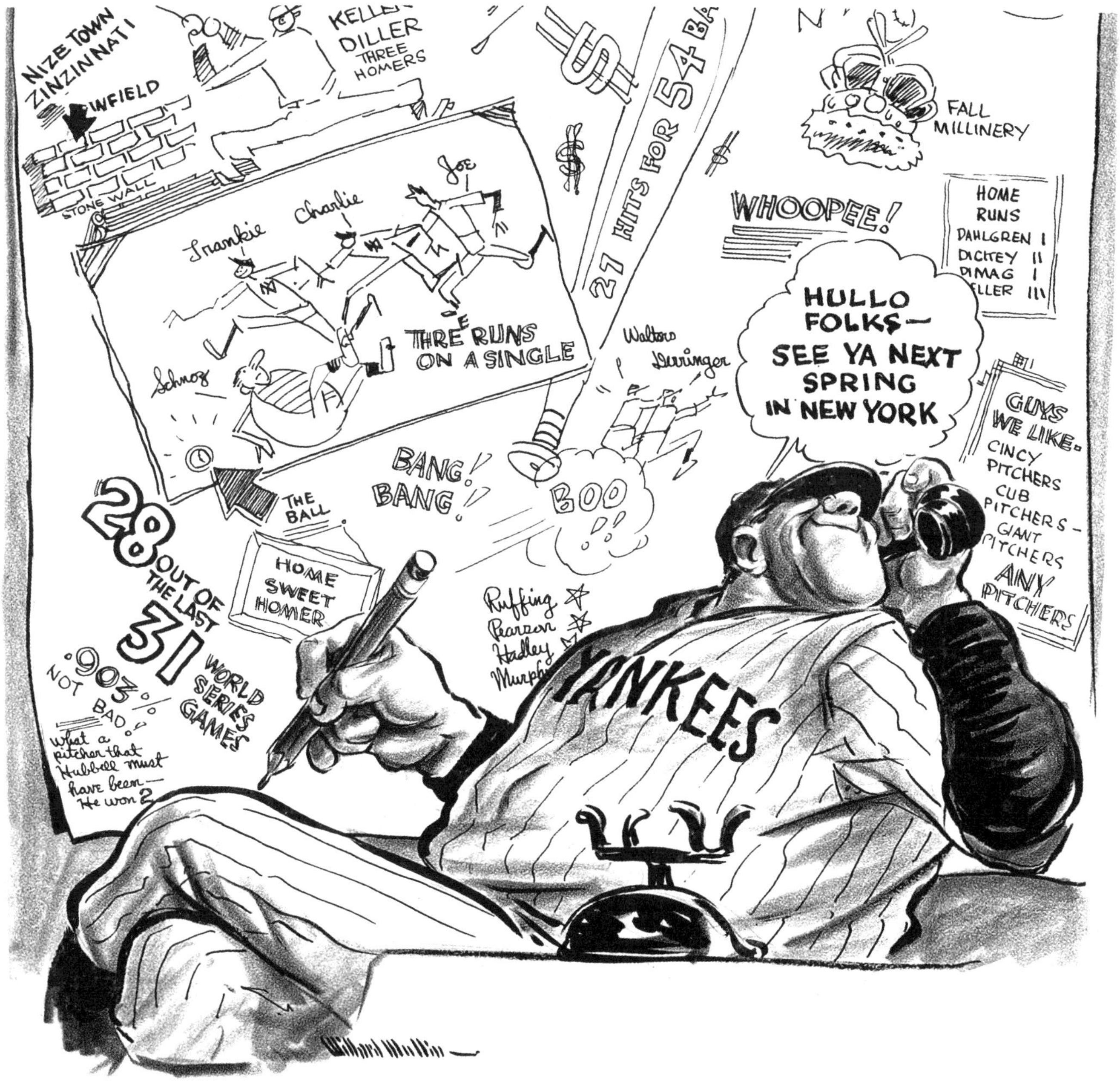
NIZE TOWN ZINZINNATI
STONE WALL
DILLER
THREE HOMERS
Frankie
Charlie
Joe
THREE RUNS ON A SINGLE
Schnoz
THE BALL
27 HITS FOR 54
WHOOPEE!
FALL MILLINERY
HOME RUNS
DAHLGREN I
DICKEY II
DIMAG I
HULLO FOLKS—
SEE YA NEXT SPRING IN NEW YORK
Walters
Derringer
GUYS WE LIKE.
CINCY PITCHERS
CUB PITCHERS -
GIANT PITCHERS
ANY PITCHERS
BANG! BANG!
BOO
HOME SWEET HOMER
28 OUT OF THE LAST 31 WORLD SERIES GAMES
.903% NOT BAD!
What a pitcher that Hubbell must have been— He won 2
Ruffing
Pearson
Hadley
YANKEES

By the end of 1939, the Yankees were the kings of the baseball world, having won four straight World Championships, including their four-game sweep of the Reds that year. The Yankees' World Series record for 1936–1939 was 16–3, including two four-game sweeps in 1938 and 1939.

Brooklyn, My Brooklyn

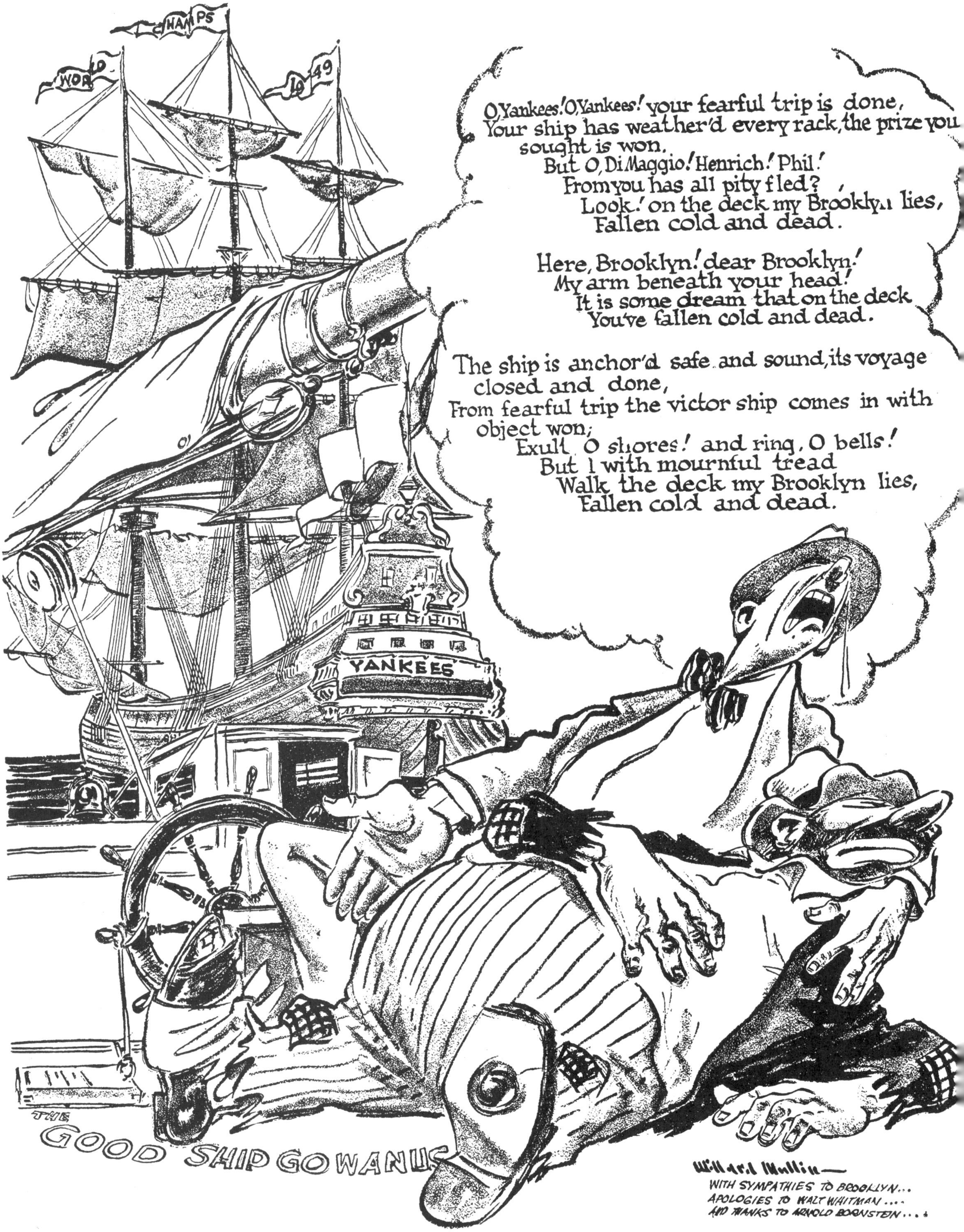
WORLD
CHAMPS
1949
O Yankees! O Yankees! your fearful trip is done,
Your ship has weather'd every rack, the prize you sought is won.
But O, DiMaggio! Henrich! Phil!
From you has all pity fled?
Look! on the deck my Brooklyn lies,
Fallen cold and dead.
Here, Brooklyn! dear Brooklyn!
My arm beneath your head!
It is some dream that on the deck
You've fallen cold and dead.
The ship is anchor'd safe and sound, its voyage closed and done,
From fearful trip the victor ship comes in with object won;
Exult, O shores! and ring, O bells!
But I with mournful tread
Walk the deck my Brooklyn lies,
Fallen cold and dead.
YANKEES
THE GOOD SHIP GOWANUS
Willard Mullin
WITH SYMPATHIES TO BROOKLYN...
APOLOGIES TO WALT WHITMAN....
AND THANKS TO ARNOLD BORNSTEIN....

The 1940s

• • •

As baseball turned into a new decade,

the winds of war were spreading over Europe. Armies of Germany's Third Reich were on the march throughout the continent, and in the Far East, Japan was flexing its military muscle. It seemed that sooner or later, the world would be plunged into a full-fledged war, and that eventually, the United States would be drawn into the conflict.

But on Opening Day of the 1940 season, America was not yet involved, and the country's attention was diverted by Cleveland's high-kicking right-hander Bob Feller, who put an exclamation point on the start of the season by throwing a no-hitter at Chicago.

Feller, 21 years old and in his fifth big league season, won 27 games and led the league in earned run average, strikeouts, shutouts, innings pitched, and complete games that year. He was blessed with a fastball that pushed 100 miles per hour, and he simply overwhelmed batters. In the final game of the 1938 season, with Detroit's Hank Greenberg just two homers short of Babe Ruth's single season record of 60, Feller shut the slugger down and set a record with 18 strikeouts.

Ruth was well aware of Greenberg's pursuit of the record and Willard Mullin took note of that in a cartoon with the pensive Babe asking, "How'd that kid do today?" The likeness of Ruth, then 43 and wearing a Dodgers uniform as their trophy first base coach, was a great improvement on Mullin's first Ruth cartoon years earlier, the one that raised the ire of his boss, Lee B. Wood. When Ruth died in 1948, Mullin drew a dramatic portrait of the man who changed the face of baseball.

As Ruth passed from the scene, Feller was emerging as baseball's best young pitcher. He dominated the White Sox on Opening Day in 1940, and with his no-hitter, took the minds of Americans off world politics, at least for one day. The 1-0 victory remains the only no-hitter ever thrown on Opening Day.

Cincinnati defeated Detroit in the 1940 World Series, but the two best hitters in the game were not involved. Joe DiMaggio of the New York Yankees won two straight batting titles, hitting .381 in 1939 and .352 in 1940. Boston's Ted Williams led the league with 145 RBIs in 1939 and finished right behind DiMaggio, batting .344 in 1940.

That set the stage for a season never to be forgotten, one of the most remarkable years for batting achievement in the history of the game.

As the shadows of war lengthened over Europe and the world, there were signs everywhere that the conflict would inevitably involve this country. There was a fore-boding sense that this might be America's last summer of innocence. The nation searched desperately for relief from the flames of a world on fire, and baseball sup-plied the antidote with two remarkable individual accomplishments — the 56-game hitting streak of Joe DiMaggio and the .406 season of Ted Williams.

They remain the barometers for batters — the longest hitting streak in Major League Baseball history and the game's last .400 season. They have occasionally been threatened but never come close to being broken. They are the magical reminders of the summer of 1941, a time of innocence and accomplishment, a time for heroes.

OPPOSITE: In 1949, the Yankees, under Casey Stengel, beat their perennial opponent, the Brooklyn Dodgers, to win the first of five consecutive World Series Championships. Between 1941 and 1956, the Yankees and the Dodgers met seven times in the World Series, with the Yankees triumphing six of those times. Mullin lamented the Dodgers' 1949 defeat in verse with his parody of Walt Whitman's "Oh Captain, My Captain."

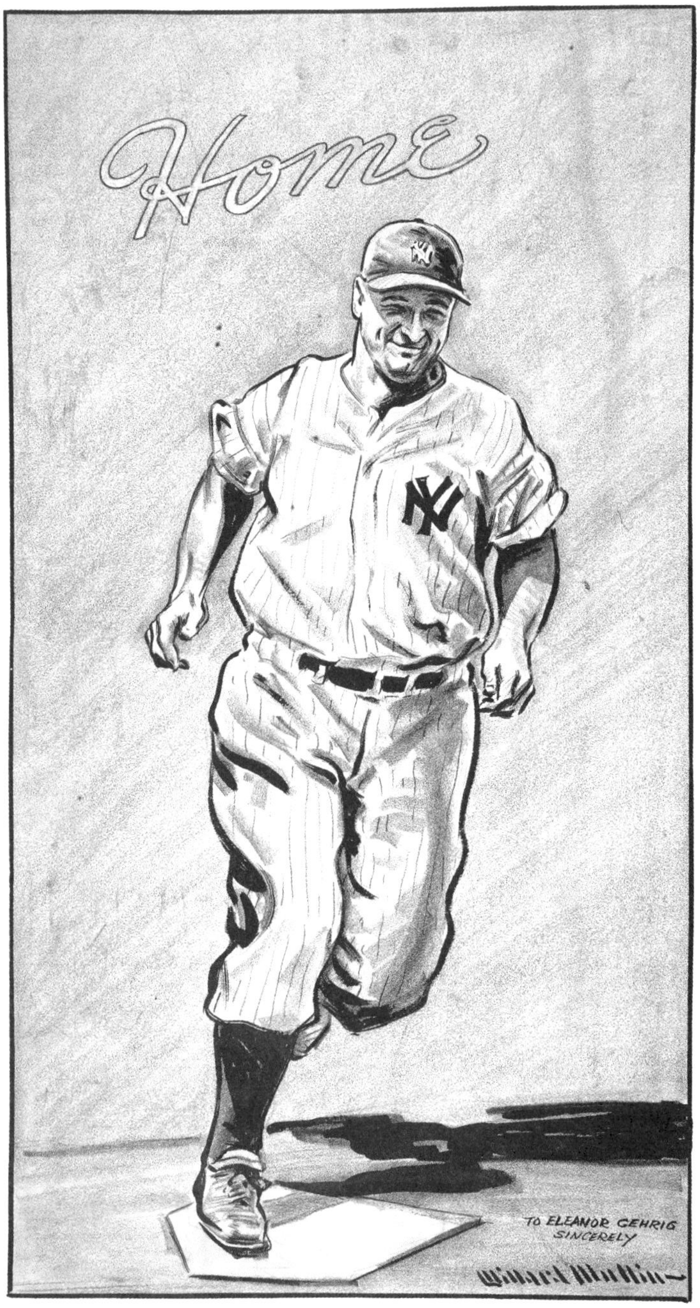
Home
TO ELEANOR GEHRIG
SINCERELY
Willard Mullin

ABOVE: This drawing was done shortly after Lou Gehrig's passing in June 1941. It never appeared in the paper. Mullin gave it personally to Gehrig's widow, Eleanor.

The 1941 season began badly for the New York Yankees. The team drifted at 14-13, stuck in fourth place in the American League. Their best hitter, DiMaggio, was in the worst slump of his career, batting just .194 over three weeks.

On May 15, the Yankees were battered by the Chicago White Sox 13-1. Their only run was driven in by DiMaggio with an otherwise innocuous first-inning single. He had been hitless in the previous two games, and the RBI single against Edgar Smith was his only hit that day. But it would be two months and two days before he had another game *without* a hit.

On the same day that DiMaggio's streak began, Ted Williams stretched his own hitting streak to 17 games and was hitting .429 for the season. Now, with DiMaggio hitting again, America was riveted on DiMaggio and Williams and their parallel marches through the American League. It would turn out to be a magical summer of baseball.

DiMaggio's streak took on a life of its own. There were peaks and valleys and milestones throughout. One day against Boston, DiMaggio made outs in his first two swings, then had an extra base hit robbed by his brother, Dom, in center field. Dom was saddened that his play might have ended his brother's streak. No problem. In his next swing, Joe hit a home run, keeping the streak alive.

Two weeks after the streak started, DiMaggio was credited with a hit when Boston's Pete Fox lost his fly ball in the sun. On June 2, Lou Gehrig died. The next day, in Detroit, the city where Gehrig's 2,130-consecutive game streak had ended two years before, DiMaggio kept his streak alive in a 4-2 loss, as the team grieved the loss of a Yankees icon. DiMaggio scored three home runs in a doubleheader June 8, the same day Williams's 18-game hitting streak ended.

Mullin was devastated by Gehrig's death. He drew an iconic cartoon of the Iron Horse scoring a run and labeled it "Home." He dedicated it to Gehrig's widow, Eleanor. Another Mullin tribute showed Gehrig swinging and the message "Lou Gehrig didn't take the last strike with the bat on his shoulder."

The DiMaggio streak reached 30 games when official scorer Dan Daniel, a colleague of Willard Mullin's and a pal of the Yankees slugger, credited a hit when a ball bounced off the shoulder of Chicago's Luke Appling. The next day, Daniel credited DiMaggio with another hit on a grounder muffed by Appling. There was no debate at the time about Daniel's calls but those were the only hits DiMaggio had in those games.

The streak was in danger again in Game 38. Hitless in his first three at-bats against St. Louis pitcher Elden Auker, DiMaggio was scheduled to be the fourth batter in the bottom of the eighth inning in a game the Yankees led 3-1. He might not have another swing. With one out, Red Rolfe walked. The next hitter, Tommy Henrich, knew that if he hit into a double play, DiMaggio's streak would be over. So he effectively saved a swing for his teammate by bunting Rolfe to second. DiMaggio followed with a double. The streak remained intact.

The next day, an obscure Philadelphia pitcher named Johnny Babich swore he'd stop DiMaggio. The strategy would be to walk the Yankees slugger every time he batted.

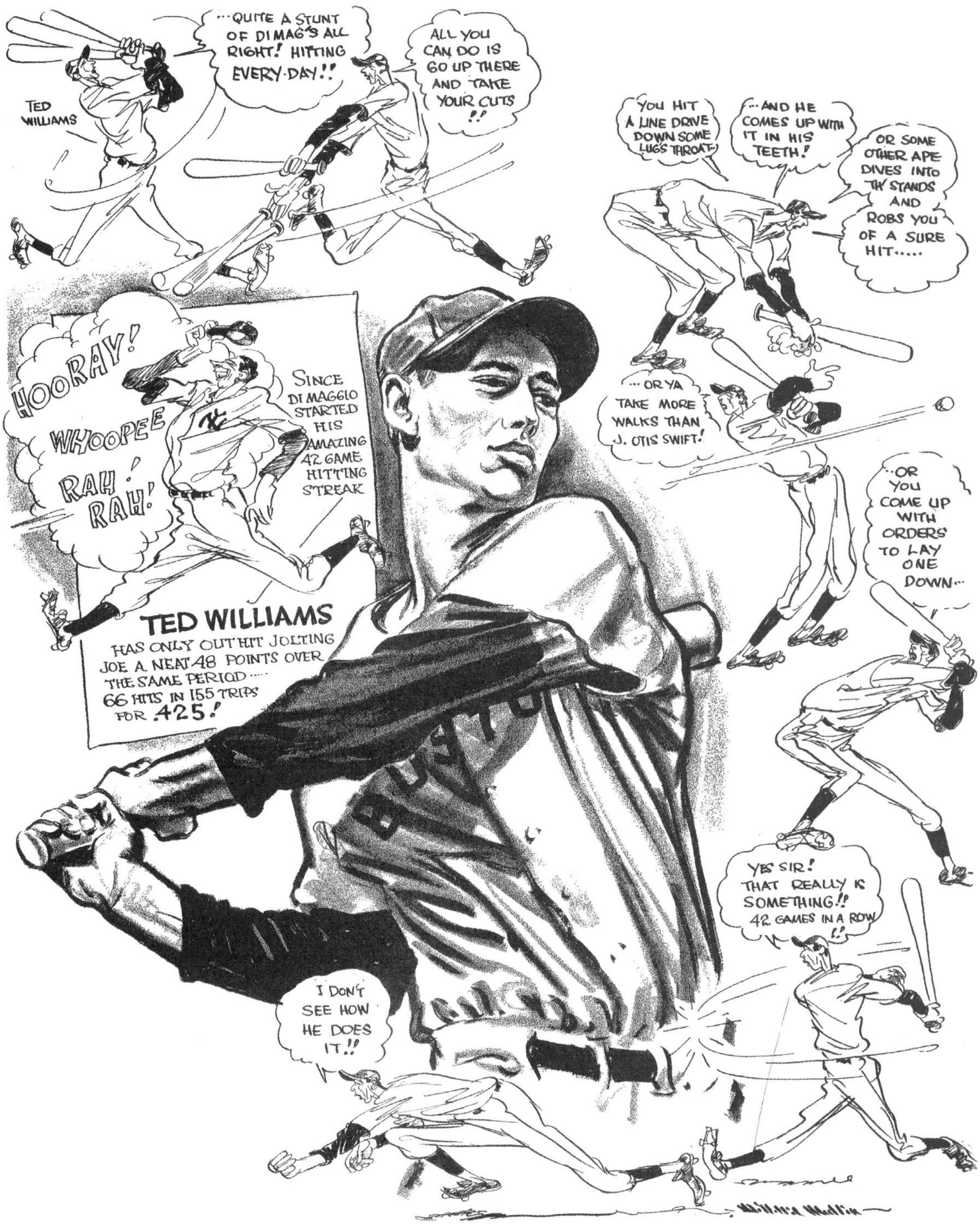
TED WILLIAMS
···QUITE A STUNT OF DIMAG'S ALL RIGHT! HITTING EVERY·DAY!!
ALL YOU CAN DO IS GO UP THERE AND TAKE YOUR CUTS !!
YOU HIT A LINE DRIVE DOWN SOME LUGS THROAT·
···AND HE COMES UP WITH IT IN HIS TEETH!
OR SOME OTHER APE DIVES INTO TH' STANDS AND ROBS YOU OF A SURE HIT.....
HOORAY!
WHOOPEE
RAH! RAH!
SINCE DI MAGGIO STARTED HIS AMAZING 42 GAME HITTING STREAK
TED WILLIAMS
HAS ONLY OUTHIT JOLTING JOE A NEAT 48 POINTS OVER THE SAME PERIOD····
66 HITS IN 155 TRIPS FOR .425!
··· OR YA TAKE MORE WALKS THAN J. OTIS SWIFT!
··OR YOU COME UP WITH ORDERS TO LAY ONE DOWN···
YES SIR! THAT REALLY IS SOMETHING!! 42 GAMES IN A ROW!!
I DON'T SEE HOW HE DOES IT.!!

Four walks would end the streak, according to the rules in those days. DiMaggio remembered Game No. 40 vividly.

"My first time up, the count went to 3-and-0," he said. "I got the hit sign but the pitch was way outside." The pattern was the same for his second swing — four straight balls. "The third at-bat was the same," DiMaggio said. "Three straight balls. They gave me the hit sign again. This time Babich got the pitch not quite as far outside." DiMaggio swung and sent a shot right up the middle, through the pitcher's legs for a base hit. "Babich went down flat on his back," DiMaggio said. "When he came up, he was ashen."

Now DiMaggio was one game short of George Sisler's modern record of 41 straight games with a doubleheader coming up at Washington. He tied Sisler with a hit

ABOVE: This drawing was done on or around June 29, 1941, when Joe DiMaggio was 42 games into what would ultimately become a 56-game hitting streak. Ted Williams ended up hitting .406 that year, the last player to hit .400 or better. Even so, Williams lost the 1941 MVP award to DiMaggio — by a single vote.

against knuckleballer Dutch Leonard in the opener. Then, between games of the doubleheader, DiMaggio's bat was stolen out of the Yankees' dugout. Disrupted, DiMaggio was hitless in his first three at-bats in the nightcap. For his fourth swing, he borrowed a bat from Tommy Henrich and delivered a last-chance hit. The record was his.

Meanwhile, Williams was staying hot as well and Mullin saluted the Boston star. When DiMaggio reached 42 games, Mullin drew a cartoon reminding readers that Williams was hitting .425 during the Yankees star's streak. During the 56-game streak, Williams batted .412 on the road to baseball's last .400 season.

Next up for DiMaggio was Wee Willie Keeler's 44-game mark set before the turn of the century. In a rain-shortened five-inning game, DiMaggio singled to tie the mark, then broke Keeler's mark the next day, hitting his 18th home run of the season. Mullin saluted the accomplishment with a cartoon of Keeler, complete in his 19th-century uniform.

DiMaggio's stolen bat, missing in action for a week, was returned before Game 46 of the streak. He celebrated by hitting a home run on the first pitch he saw that day.

The streak finally ended in Cleveland on July 14 with Indians third baseman Ken Keltner making a pair of sharp backhanded stops to foil DiMaggio. When it was over, DiMaggio had 91 hits in 223 at-bats with 15 home runs, 55 runs batted in, and a .408 batting average.

The 56-game streak was the centerpiece of DiMaggio's brilliant career. And he expected to be paid well for his contribution to the Yankees' success. That set up a frequent tug of war with Yankees general manager George Weiss, not the most generous fellow.

In one Mullin cartoon, Weiss is pictured as an umpire dusting off home plate, labeled the DiMaggio contract. Over him stands Joe D, who scribbled on the cartoon, "Nice dustin' George." Another time, Mullin positioned Weiss on a treasure chest after DiMaggio got $100,000. He is fighting off the rest of the Yankees, protecting the payroll from the marauding players.

Williams, in his third season, was a slender slugger blessed with a sweet swing. He quickly challenged DiMaggio as the league's most dominant hitter. He wanted to be remembered as baseball's greatest hitter, and he began to lay claim to that title in 1941. Typical of his season was the All-Star Game in Detroit.

DiMaggio's streak was at 48 games, and the Yankees slugger slammed a double, drove in one run, and scored three times.

Pretty good but the headlines that day belonged to Williams, who doubled and then won the game for the American League with a three-run homer in the bottom of the ninth inning. He all but flew around the bases in celebration. Waiting at home plate to congratulate him was DiMaggio. The image is captured in an iconic Mullin cartoon.

DiMaggio was a favorite subject of Mullin's through the slugger's ups and downs. In spring training of 1949, the cartoonist reminded Yankees fans that DiMaggio's frequent ailments could spell trouble and had a devil aiming his pitchfork at Joe D's Achilles' heel.

As consistent as DiMaggio was in the summer of 1941, Williams kept pace with him. The Boston slugger was batting .435 in mid-June and was still around .400 as the season steamed in to September. He told an interviewer he was becoming a smarter hitter.

"Hell, I've been up here three years now," he said, "and if a fellow can't learn to hit in three years he ought to throw his bat away. And another thing's helping me. I'm all full of confidence. I keep on saying to myself, 'Williams, even if nobody else thinks you can hit, you know you can, so go out there and do your stuff.'"

On the last day of the season, with Boston out of the race and set for a doubleheader against Philadelphia, Williams's average stood at .3995. Rounded off, that would be .400, the first Major Leaguer to reach that figure in 11 years.

OPPOSITE: In 1949, George Weiss signed Joe DiMaggio to a contract worth $100,000, making DiMaggio the highest-paid player in baseball history up to that time. This drawing, which DiMaggio inscribed to Weiss in appreciation, is in the Baseball Hall of Fame.

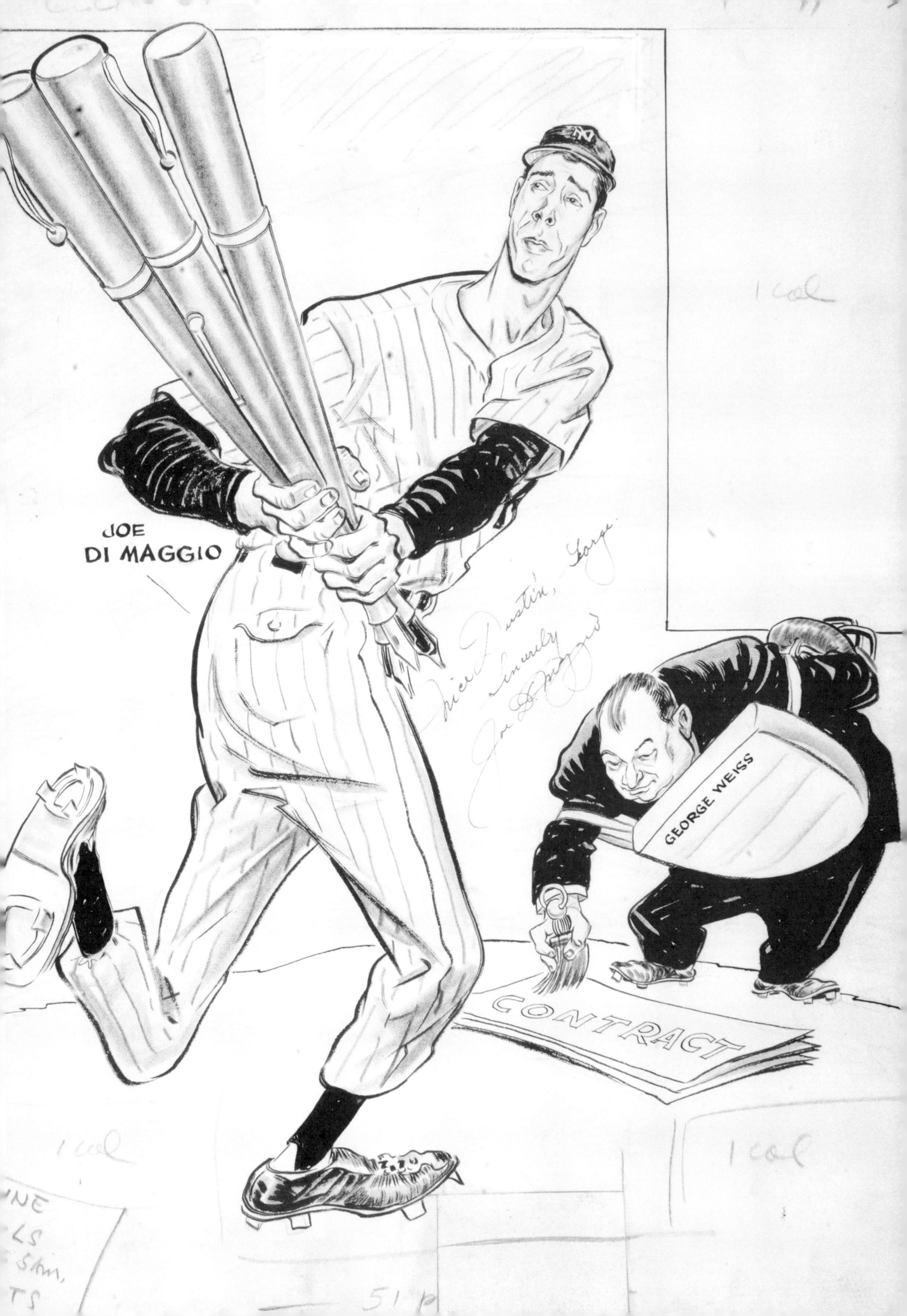
JOE
DI MAGGIO
GEORGE WEISS
CONTRACT

With nothing at stake, Red Sox manager Joe Cronin offered to let Williams sit out the doubleheader to protect his .400 average. The slugger was having none of that. If he was going to hit .400, it would be with a bat in his hands, not hiding in the dugout.

Williams singled in his first at-bat and homered in his next swing. He went 4-for-5 in the opener and 2-for-3 in the second game. The six hits in eight at-bats raised his batting average for the season to .406.

He explained his approach, saying, "If I couldn't hit .400 all the way, I didn't deserve it."

Infielder Pete Suder of the Philadelphia Athletics was in his first Major League season in 1941 and on the other side of the field on that last day. He remembered his reaction to the heroics of DiMaggio and Williams. "Here I am a rookie and I see one guy hit in 56 straight games and another guy hit .406," he said. "I'm hitting .245 and I think I'm in the wrong league."

The World Series that year matched the Brooklyn Dodgers and New York Yankees, the first in a series of showdowns between these intracity rivals that Willard Mullin called "The Subway Series." The nickname stuck and is still used today when the Yankees and the Mets (modern-day descendants of the long-gone Giants and Dodgers) play each other.

The Dodgers, playing in the World Series for the first time since 1920, were poised to tie the Series at two games apiece. Leading 4-3 with two out in the ninth inning of Game 5, reliever Hugh Casey struck out Tommy Henrich with a sharp breaking curve ball that some suspected was a spitball. Henrich swung and missed for what should have been the final out of the game. But the ball eluded catcher Mickey Owen and Henrich reached first on the passed ball. The Yankees then rallied for four runs to win Game 5 and then finished off the Dodgers the next day to capture the championship.

Two months after the season ended, Japan bombed the United States fleet at Pearl Harbor, Hawaii, and America was plunged into World War II.

Two days after the attack on Pearl Harbor, Bob Feller enlisted in the Navy and Hank Greenberg, who had served earlier, re-enlisted in the Army. Two of the game's biggest stars had volunteered immediately, and they soon would be followed by a parade of players. Some 500 Major Leaguers, including DiMaggio and Williams, marched off to war. Yogi Berra was part of the D-Day invasion of Normandy. Warren Spahn fought in the Battle of the Bulge. Major League rosters were drained, leaving baseball in a precarious state.

Each December, Mullin would draw a Christmas greeting card composed entirely of names of people in sports. It was an arduous effort that took him several days to complete. Perhaps none of them was as significant as the one he drew following the attack on Pearl Harbor.

With the country on a war footing, commissioner Kenesaw Mountain Landis wrote to President Franklin Delano Roosevelt and asked how baseball could best serve the war effort. The president's advice, contained in the famous "green light" letter of January 15, 1942, was to carry on.

"I honestly feel it would be best for the country to keep baseball going," the president said. "There will be fewer people unemployed and everybody will work longer hours and harder than ever before. And that means they ought to have a chance for recreation and for taking their minds off their work even more than before."

And so, baseball pressed on. Teams reached out to those who might otherwise not have had the opportunity to play in the big leagues. One day in 1944, Cincinnati used 15-year-old Joe Nuxhall to pitch. He allowed two hits and walked five batters in two-thirds of an inning, leaving with a 67.50 earned run average. Eight years later, he returned to begin a more normal and more productive Major League career.

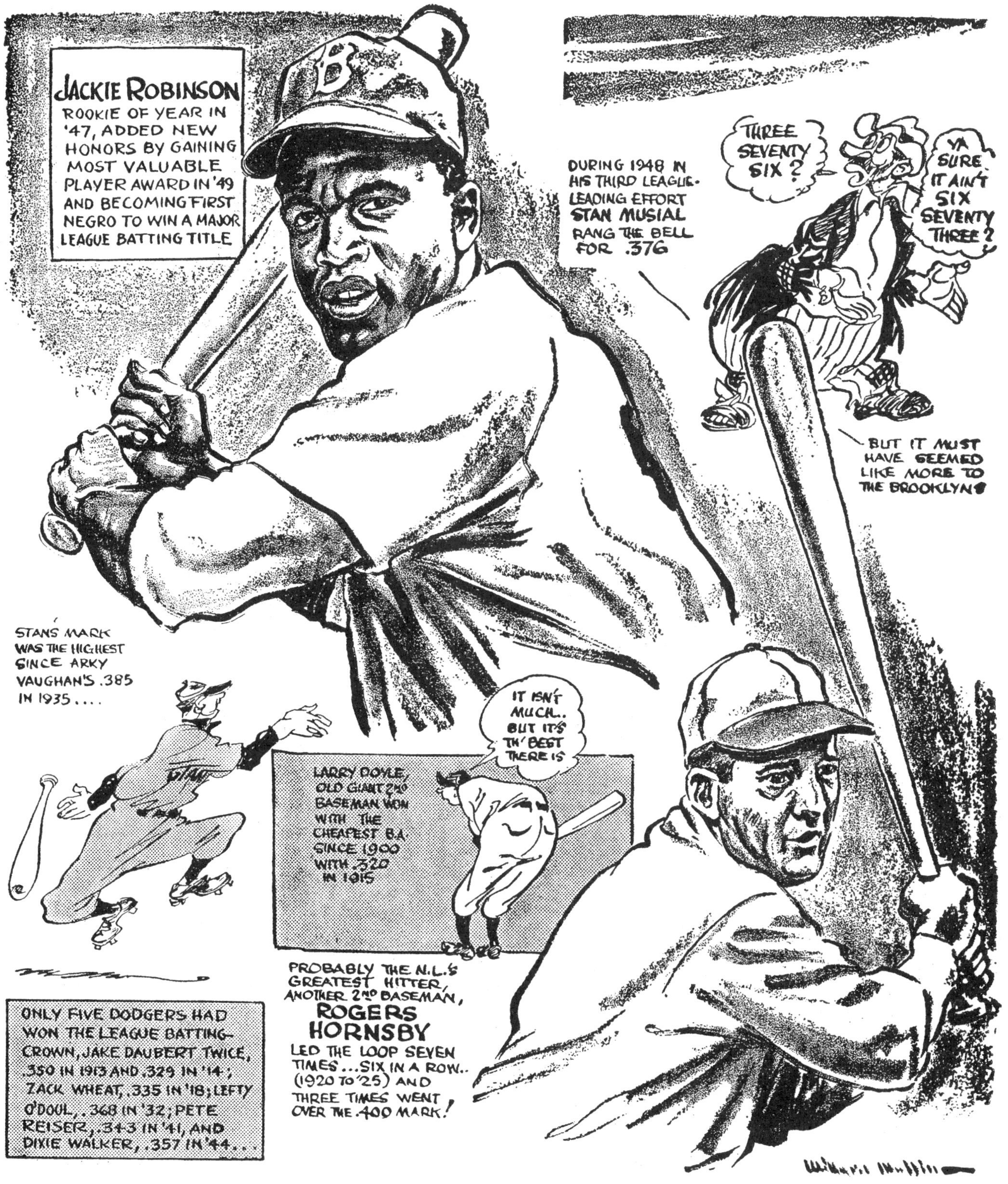

JACKIE ROBINSON
ROOKIE OF YEAR IN '47, ADDED NEW HONORS BY GAINING MOST VALUABLE PLAYER AWARD IN '49 AND BECOMING FIRST NEGRO TO WIN A MAJOR LEAGUE BATTING TITLE
DURING 1948 IN HIS THIRD LEAGUE-LEADING EFFORT STAN MUSIAL RANG THE BELL FOR .376
THREE SEVENTY SIX ?
YA SURE IT AIN'T SIX SEVENTY THREE ?
BUT IT MUST HAVE SEEMED LIKE MORE TO THE BROOKLYNS
STANS MARK WAS THE HIGHEST SINCE ARKY VAUGHAN'S .385 IN 1935....
IT ISN'T MUCH.. BUT IT'S TH' BEST THERE IS
LARRY DOYLE, OLD GIANT 2ND BASEMAN WON WITH THE CHEAPEST B.A. SINCE 1900 WITH .320 IN 1915
PROBABLY THE N.L.'S GREATEST HITTER, ANOTHER 2ND BASEMAN, ROGERS HORNSBY LED THE LOOP SEVEN TIMES...SIX IN A ROW.. (1920 TO '25) AND THREE TIMES WENT OVER THE .400 MARK!
ONLY FIVE DODGERS HAD WON THE LEAGUE BATTING-CROWN, JAKE DAUBERT TWICE, .350 IN 1913 AND .329 IN '14; ZACK WHEAT, .335 IN '18; LEFTY O'DOUL, .368 IN '32; PETE REISER, .343 IN '41, AND DIXIE WALKER, .357 IN '44...

ABOVE: Jackie Robinson had his greatest season in 1949, two years after his historic debut. Robinson led the league in hitting and stolen bases, drove in 124 runs, and, in a close vote, won the National League MVP over Stan Musial.

At the other end of the age spectrum, Babe Herman, 42, showed up in Brooklyn's outfield; Pepper Martin, 40, was resurrected by the St. Louis Cardinals; and the Waner Brothers, Lloyd and Paul, well into their 40s, made a pit stop on their way to the Hall of Fame. Slugger Jimmie Foxx, 38, another Hall of Famer, wound up pitching for the Philadelphia Phillies. He won his only decision and had a 1.59 ERA in nine games.

Willard Mullin did a drawing of the Waners, saluting the batting skills of Little Poison (Lloyd) and Big Poison (Paul) and noting that they'd learned to hit in an unusual way — swatting corncobs with broomsticks in their native Harrah, Oklahoma.

Perhaps the most extreme example of the manpower situation was when the Browns signed outfielder Pete Gray of the Southern Association, who had batted .333 at Memphis. Gray played 77 games, batting an unimpressive .218. What was impressive was that he did it with one arm. He had lost his right arm in a childhood farming accident.

Mullin noted baseball's shortage of able-bodied players with a striking portrait of Pepper Martin, who had been out of the game four years. He decorated the image with examples of the head-first antics of the man they called "The Wild Horse of the Osage." Mullin observed in the cartoon, "To us, for one, it will be a joy to watch old Pepper again … at least for as long as he holds together." And the cartoonist poked fun at the Cincinnati Reds' scheme of importing a specialist to work on the players' rhythm and movement.

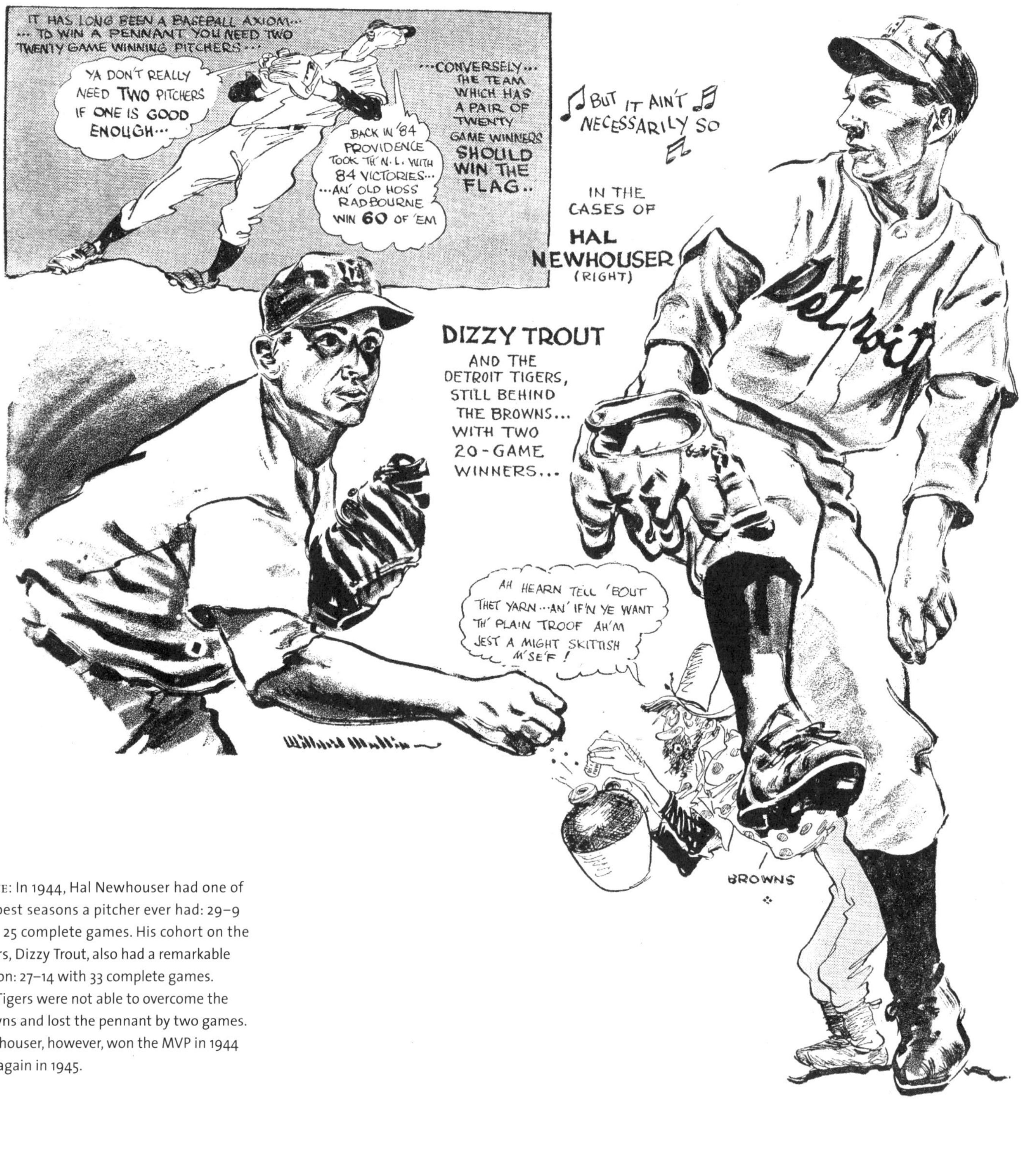
IT HAS LONG BEEN A BASEBALL AXIOM… … TO WIN A PENNANT YOU NEED TWO TWENTY GAME WINNING PITCHERS…
YA DON'T REALLY NEED TWO PITCHERS IF ONE IS GOOD ENOUGH…
…CONVERSELY… THE TEAM WHICH HAS A PAIR OF TWENTY GAME WINNERS SHOULD WIN THE FLAG..
BACK IN '84 PROVIDENCE TOOK TH' N. L. WITH 84 VICTORIES… …AN' OLD HOSS RADBOURNE WIN 60 OF 'EM
BUT IT AIN'T NECESSARILY SO
IN THE CASES OF HAL NEWHOUSER (RIGHT)
DIZZY TROUT AND THE DETROIT TIGERS, STILL BEHIND THE BROWNS… WITH TWO 20-GAME WINNERS…
Detroit
AH HEARN TELL 'BOUT THET YARN…AN' IF'N YE WANT TH' PLAIN TROOF AH'M JEST A MIGHT SKITTISH M'SE'F!
BROWNS
Willard Mullin

ABOVE: In 1944, Hal Newhouser had one of the best seasons a pitcher ever had: 29–9 with 25 complete games. His cohort on the Tigers, Dizzy Trout, also had a remarkable season: 27–14 with 33 complete games. The Tigers were not able to overcome the Browns and lost the pennant by two games. Newhouser, however, won the MVP in 1944 and again in 1945.

Then there was Leo Durocher, manager of the Dodgers, suggesting in 1944 that he might step in to play second base for Brooklyn. Mullin noted that if the manager tried that he'd put himself on the spot — "a spot as big as a dime" — and drew Durocher standing on the coin. He supplied his pal with a slingshot "for the long throw to the plate."

When the war ended and Major League players returned to baseball, some found their skills diminished. Hank Greenberg was dealt by Detroit to Pittsburgh, much the way other sluggers had moved on before him. Mullin drew him climbing a mountain labeled "Over The Hill" to the "National League Old Folks Home," a trip Babe Ruth and Jimmie Foxx had made before.

Durocher was known as Leo the Lip for good reason. He would sound off at the drop of a baseball. There was, for example, the matter of the Dodgers' longtime rivals, the New York Giants. The Giants were managed by a low-key Mel Ott, the complete opposite of the fiery Durocher. Why couldn't he be easygoing like Ott? Durocher was asked. The Dodgers' manager motioned at the Giants across the field. "Take a look at them," he said. "All nice guys. Where are they? Seventh place." That sentiment was summed up in Durocher's most famous quote: "Nice guys finish last."

The Giants never did dip that low but they also didn't contend until they fired Ott and brought in a new manager — Leo Durocher. Mullin enjoyed the irony of that and often used it in his cartoons as Durocher and the Giants constructed the "Little Miracle of Coogan's Bluff," overtaking the Dodgers to win the pennant in 1951. He also saluted Ott's batting records with the Giants as "The face of Coogan's Bluff at the Polo Grounds." And he noted the affection celebrities had for the Giants, drawing prominent fans at the Giants' home including heavyweight champion Jim Corbett, Broadway showman George M. Cohan, and restaurateur Toots Shor.

Another important managerial change occured in 1949 when the Yankees brought in Casey Stengel to run the team. Stengel was viewed as something of a baseball comedian, famous for once tipping his cap and having a bird flutter out from under it. Perfect, thought Mullin, who drew Casey flying out of general manager George Weiss's hat. When the Yankees went through an off-season with no roster changes, Mullin had Stengel waltzing with a strawberry blonde labeled "same old Yankee team" and Weiss alongside owners Del Webb and Dan Topping admiring the couple.

When baseball loosened its restriction on night games in 1944, Mullin anticipated what would occur. His cartoon depicted an alarmed, oversized player labeled "Day Ball" strapped into an electric chair, while the bosses of baseball reassured him, saying, "Now sit back and relax. We're just turning up the lights a little."

When there was talk of adding a third major league, Mullin pointed out that "getting franchises, backers, and ballparks is only the start," and drew Aladdin rubbing a magic lamp to conjure up 200 players of major league caliber.

Mullin also noted the debate on juiced-up baseballs and hopped-up hitters. What would he have thought of baseball's steroid era?

In 1944, the woebegone St. Louis Browns won the American League pennant and went to their only World Series. It was a wonder indeed, Mullin thought, considering the competition, which included the Detroit Tigers and a pair of 20-game winners in Hal Newhouser and Dizzy Trout. One of his cartoons noted that unusual feat.

Among the thousands of Americans who went off to war was Jack Roosevelt Robinson, the four-sport star from UCLA. Robinson had excelled in baseball, basketball, football, and track, but left school four months short of graduation to work for the National Youth Administration. He played in the College All-Star Game in Chicago and some semi-pro football in Los Angeles and Hawaii before being drafted in April 1942.

After some difficulty because of institutional racism, Robinson was admitted to Officer Candidate School. He was commissioned as a second lieutenant and assigned to Fort Riley, Kansas, and then Fort Hood, Texas. It was there, in July 1944, that he got into an argument with a bus driver when he refused to sit in the back of a camp bus.

This was 11 years before Rosa Parks sparked a civil rights revolution in America by doing the same thing in Montgomery, Alabama. All Jackie Robinson got for his trouble was a court martial. He was found not guilty on all counts and honorably discharged in November 1944.

Meanwhile, back in Brooklyn, Willard Mullin's beloved Bums were under new stewardship. Branch Rickey, who had molded the St. Louis Cardinals into a championship team, had replaced Larry MacPhail as boss of the Dodgers in 1942. One of Rickey's theories was to place players and teams in small cities all over America and use that minor league farm system as a feeder network for major league teams.

There was, however, the issue of housing scores of aspiring players in spring training. Mullin drew Rickey in conversation with the nursery rhyme figure Old Mother Hubbard, who lived in a shoe and had so many children she didn't know what to do. "Let me get this straight," the cartoon Rickey says, quoting from the nursery rhyme. "You give them their supper without any bread then spank them all soundly and send them to bed."

Mullin loved nursery rhyme imagery. When the Cardinals had a loaded roster headed by Hall of Famers Stan Musial and Enos Slaughter, Mullin called on the shoe image again, drawing Cards owner Sam Breadon as the old woman who had so many children (the many St. Louis stars) she didn't know what to do.

In the summer of 1949, with the Dodgers chasing the Cardinals, Mullin drew "St. Louis Daze," with the Brooklyn Bum dreaming of Musial and the other St. Louis stars. In the final week of the season, with the Dodgers one game behind and four games to play, Mullin drew the Bum barely hanging on to pennant hopes. They wound up winning, another first place finish for Rickey's team.

Two years earlier, the Dodgers had reached the World Series against the Yankees, a series perhaps best remembered for a remarkable catch by reserve outfielder Al Gionfriddo against DiMaggio. Mullin drew the catch along with the admonition from the iconic Bum that if Gionfriddo didn't make those kinds of plays he'd be working in the minors "real quick." It turned out to be the outfielder's last major league game.

Rickey was a unique character with bushy eyebrows who frequently puffed on cigars. He was once described by *Time* magazine as a cross between circus promoter Phineas T. Barnum and preacher Billy Sunday. He was all at once gruff and yet captivating, a man well ahead of others in planning and implementing change in baseball.

It was Rickey who designed baseball's minor league network. It was Rickey who introduced batting helmets, logical if minimal protection for hitters. And it was Rickey who changed baseball forever when he signed Jackie Robinson for the Brooklyn Dodgers.

Robinson, remember, was a black man and modern baseball did not tolerate persons of color. The game was a restricted, closed society, reserved for whites only, a policy endorsed and embraced by commissioner Kenesaw Mountain Landis.

When Landis died in November 1944, he was succeeded by former Kentucky governor Albert "Happy" Chandler, whose main platform was to repeatedly announce "Ah Loves Baseball." Mullin had fun with that, contrasting the gregarious Chandler with the stern Landis. When Jackie Robinson was discharged from the Army in the same month that Landis died, Branch Rickey began devising a plan to tear down baseball's racial barriers.

Rickey was a devout Methodist whose strongest expletive was "Judas Priest." He had been baseball coach at the University of Michigan while studying for his law degree in 1904, when he'd ushered his team to South Bend, Indiana, for a game against Notre Dame. When Rickey's team attempted to check into its hotel, the room clerk refused them. The problem, he said, was Rickey's catcher, Charles Thomas, who happened to be black. The hotel would not accommodate a black man.

Rickey was outraged at the rejection and negotiated a settlement with the clerk. Thomas would not need a room. He would stay in Rickey's room. Rickey secured a room key, gave it to Thomas, and sent the catcher to his room while he finished checking in the rest of his team.

When Rickey went to the room, he found the catcher seated on a chair, sobbing as he pulled at his hands. "It's my skin, Mr. Rickey. It's my skin. If I could just tear it off, I'd be like everyone else. It's my skin, Mr. Rickey. It's my skin."

The episode left a permanent scar on Rickey. Forty years later, he was determined to make things right. "I don't mean to be a crusader," he said. "My only purpose is to be fair to all people … I couldn't face my God much longer knowing His black creatures are held separate and distinct from His white creatures in the game that has given me all that I own."

And so, baseball's Great Experiment began. Rickey needed to rebuild the Brooklyn Dodgers and he knew there was a reservoir of untapped talent playing in baseball's Negro Leagues. He secretly dispatched scouts to look at the available players. There was plenty of talent there from Josh Gibson and Satchel Paige to Cool Papa Bell and Buck Leonard. And, oh yes, there was this shortstop with the Kansas City Monarchs, a fellow named Jackie Robinson.

Rickey sent his most trusted aide, Clyde Sukeforth, to check up on Robinson. Sukeforth, an old catcher turned scout, was instructed to evaluate Robinson's arm and, if he liked what he saw, to bring the player to Brooklyn to meet Rickey. Robinson was a bit suspicious, especially the part about his arm since he had a sore shoulder at the time. No problem. Sukeforth ushered Robinson to Brooklyn anyway. Now one of baseball's most important meetings began.

There was tension in the air as Rickey laid out his plan. He wanted to sign Robinson to play for the Dodgers, to break baseball's color line, to revolutionize the game. It would be hard. Robinson would have to silently endure every curse, every slur. Rickey rained down every vile word he could think of on Robinson. It was a test to see if this 26-year-old player could take the rough treatment.

Finally, Robinson snapped. "Mr. Rickey," he said, "do you want someone who's afraid to fight back?"

Rickey's brow furrowed. "No," the Dodgers' boss replied, "I want someone with the guts not to fight back."

Robinson promised to ignore the abuse he would surely face, to turn the other cheek. "I've got two cheeks, Mr. Rickey," he said.

After two hours, Rickey was convinced that Robinson could handle the situation. On October 23, 1945, the Brooklyn Dodgers announced the signing of Jackie Robinson, who would begin his career playing for the team's farm club in Montreal. Baseball was about to be changed forever.

The Montreal Royals opened their season in Jersey City, and in his second at-bat, Robinson hit a home run. He would bat .349 that season with 40 stolen bases. He dominated International League baseball and was ready for a bigger challenge. It wasn't entirely clear, however, that the Brooklyn Dodgers' players were ready for him.

During spring training, there was talk of a boycott led by a group of southerners that included Dixie Walker and Hugh Casey. When manager Leo Durocher learned what was going on, he called a team meeting at midnight and chewed out the players with a stream of invectives. The revolt was crushed before it started and on April 10, 1947, the Dodgers casually issued a two-sentence news release in the middle of an exhibition game.

"The Brooklyn Dodgers today purchased the contract of Jackie Roosevelt Robinson from the Montreal Royals. He will report immediately."

There was no mention of his race.

Robinson was in the Dodgers' Opening Day lineup against the Boston Braves but Durocher was not in the dugout. Chandler displayed some muscle when he suspended the Dodgers' manager for the season because of Durocher's affection for gambling and association with some unsavory characters. Rickey replaced him with Burt Shotton, a less combustible character.

Robinson, forced to face that first season without Durocher at his back, started by going 0-for-3 against Braves pitcher Johnny Sain. His first hit was a bunt single two days later. In the Dodgers' next series against the New York Giants, he hit his first home run. Then he slipped into a 0-for-20 slump and when the Dodgers faced Philadelphia, his oath of silence was put to its toughest test.

The manager of the Phillies was Ben Chapman, a Southerner who showered Robinson with a fusillade of the vilest racial abuse that the player ever heard. Robinson thought about discarding his pledge to Rickey and going after his tormenters. But he got through it. The abuse continued for two more days before a teammate stepped in. Eddie Stanky, another Southerner, confronted the Phillies dugout and shouted, "Listen you yellow-bellied SOBs, why don't you yell at somebody who can answer back?"

Rickey was thrilled.

"Chapman did more than anybody to unite the Dodgers," he said. "When he poured out that string of unconscionable abuse he solidified and unified 30 men, not one of whom was willing to sit by and see someone kick around a man who had his hands tied behind his back."

When Chapman's abuse became known, it seemed the episode might cost the manager his job. To save face, he sent word through a friend, asking Robinson to pose for a fence-mending picture. On the Dodgers' next trip to Philadelphia, with Rickey's blessing, the rookie and his chief tormenter met behind the batting cage. They posed together. They did not shake hands.

Robinson said later, "I have to admit that having my picture taken with that man was one of the most difficult things I had to make myself do."

The abuse continued. Robinson was forced to leave the team in some cities because hotels would not accept a black guest. It was a reminder to Rickey that not much had changed from the Charles Thomas experience in South Bend, so many years before.

There was talk of a player walkout from St. Louis, where the World Series Champion Cardinals were angry about playing a team with a black man. That was when National League President Ford Frick stepped in.

"If you do this you will be suspended from the league," Frick told the Cardinals. "You will be outcasts. I don't care if half the league strikes. Those who do it will encounter quick retribution. All will be suspended and I don't care if it wrecks the National League for five years. This is the United States of America and one citizen has as much right to play as another."

Slowly, Robinson's Dodgers teammates expressed their support. Shortstop Pee Wee Reese, another Southerner, pointedly stood with his arm over Robinson's shoulder during a pitching change, an important display of solidarity. When Robinson received death threats, outfielder Gene Hermanski suggested all the Dodgers wear Robinson's uniform, No. 42, to confuse anybody targeting him.

Seven weeks into Robinson's rookie season, Cleveland brought in outfielder Larry Doby, the first black player in the American League. Within a year, the Indians added legendary Negro League pitcher Satchel Paige. Negro League stars Roy Campanella and Don Newcombe joined Robinson in Brooklyn. The Giants signed Monte Irvin and Henry Thompson, who came up first with the St. Louis Browns. Sam Jethroe gave the Boston Braves a dimension of speed they had lacked before.

Integration changed the face of Major League Baseball. But there was a flip side to it. The migration of the best young black players to the big leagues sapped the talent from the Negro Leagues, which had functioned for years as a home for players of color. Now whole teams — the Homestead Grays, Baltimore Elite Giants, Kansas City Monarchs, and Newark Eagles among them — were driven out of business.

Rickey's Great Experiment had worked, but not without a price. ❖

OPPOSITE: The Babe was a personal friend of Mullin's, so when Ruth passed away in August of 1948 from cancer, it seemed only appropriate that Mullin would honor his old friend with a portrait that appeared in the *World-Telegram* the next day.

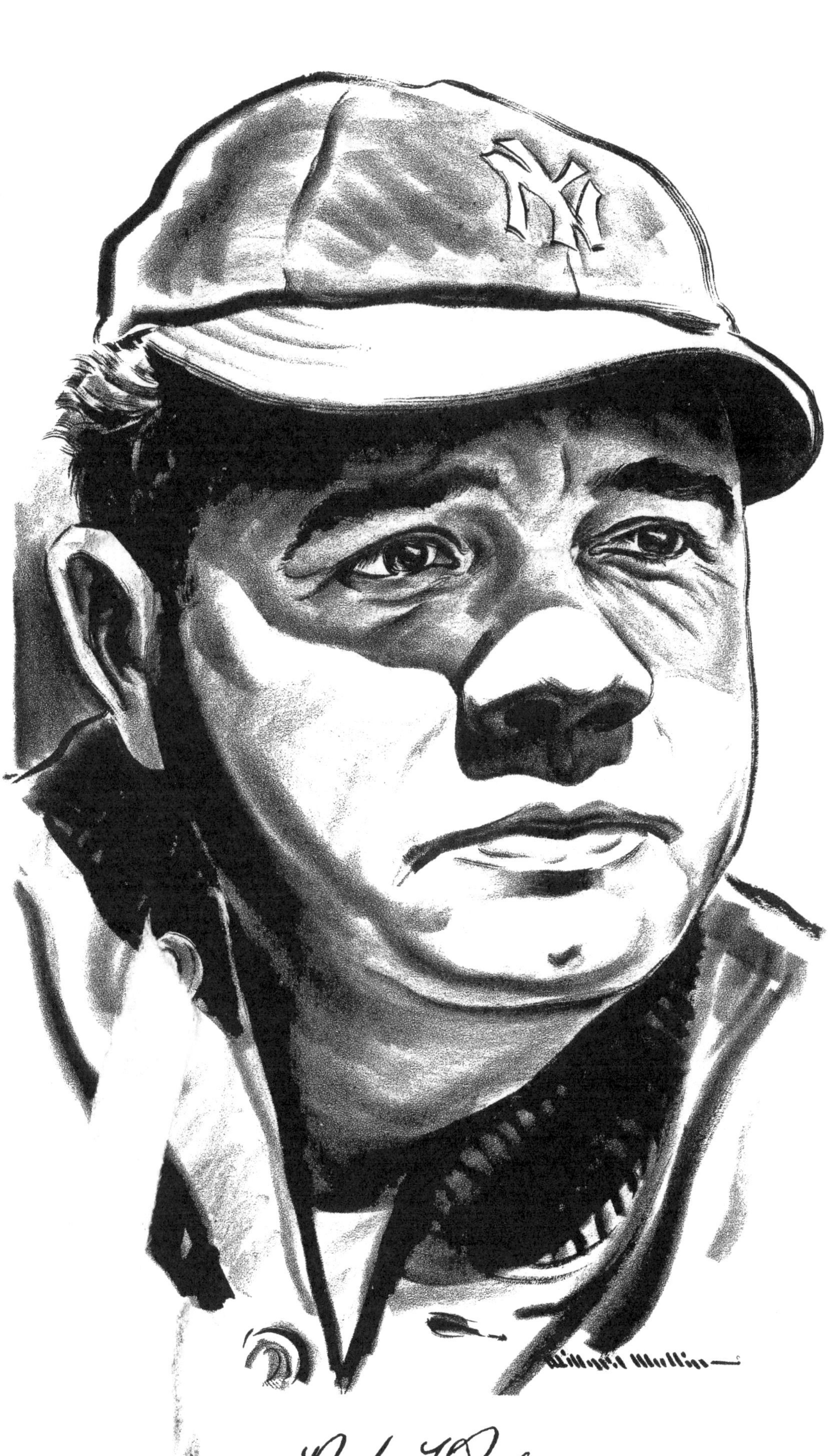

Babe Ruth

BASEBALL'S IMMORTAL

February 6, 1895—August 16, 1948

Compliments of the New York World-Telegram

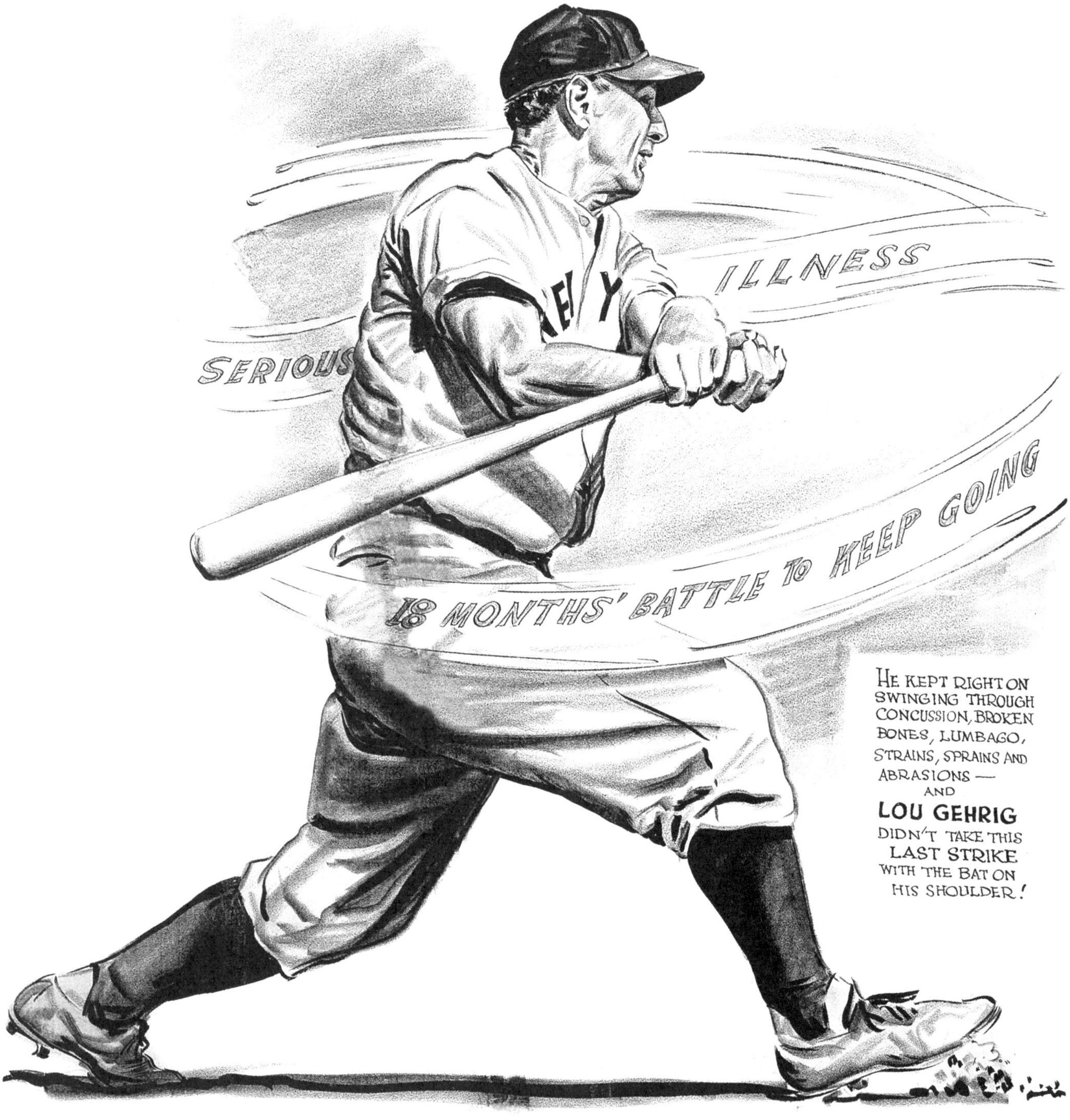
SERIOUS ILLNESS
18 MONTHS' BATTLE TO KEEP GOING
HE KEPT RIGHT ON SWINGING THROUGH CONCUSSION, BROKEN BONES, LUMBAGO, STRAINS, SPRAINS AND ABRASIONS — AND LOU GEHRIG DIDN'T TAKE THIS LAST STRIKE WITH THE BAT ON HIS SHOULDER!

In June 1941, Lou Gehrig, the "Iron Horse," lost his battle with ALS. Mullin commemorated Gehrig's fighting spirit with this drawing entitled "Iron Heart."

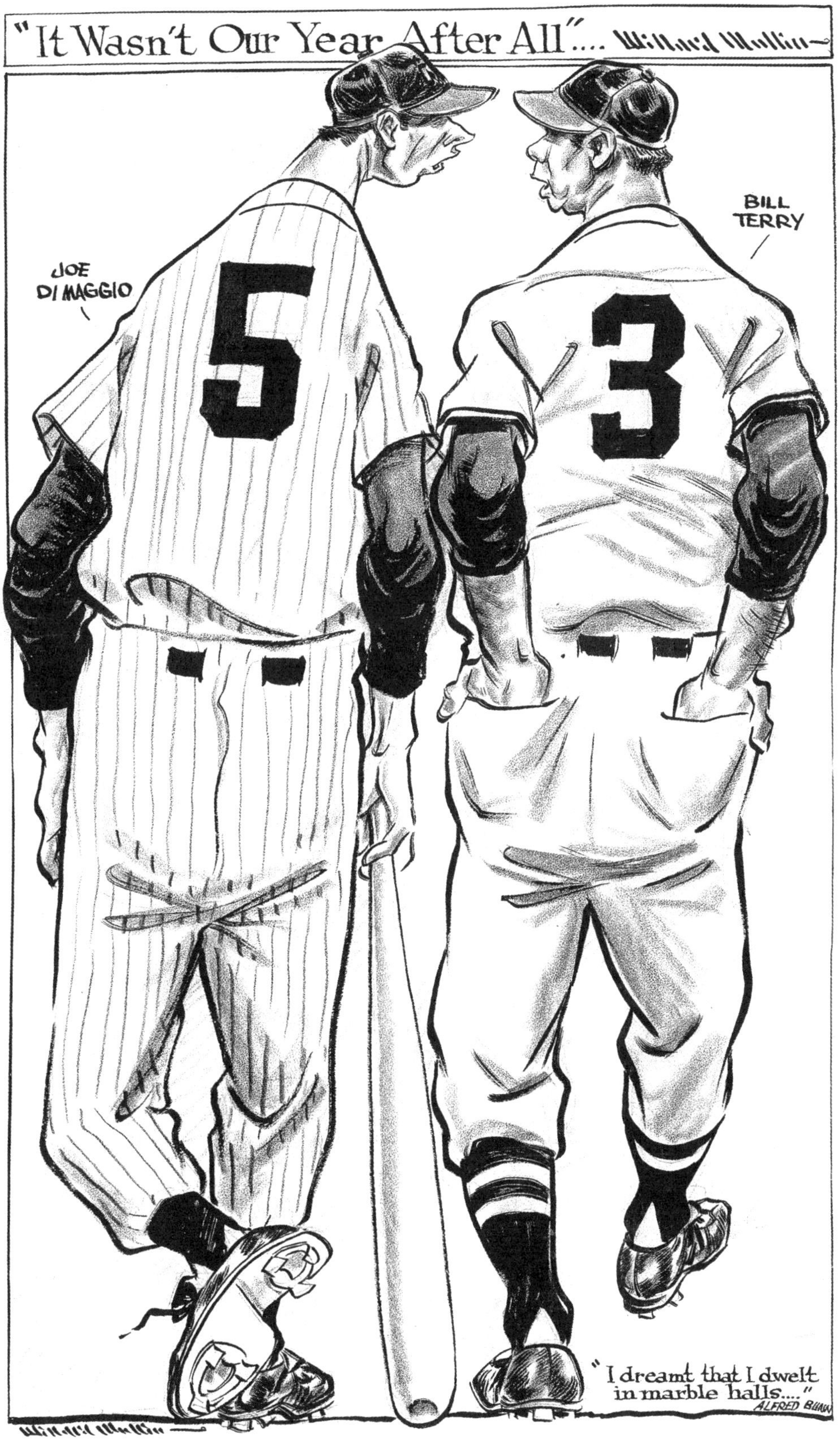
"It Wasn't Our Year After All"....
JOE DI MAGGIO
BILL TERRY
"I dreamt that I dwelt in marble halls...."
ALFRED BUNN

In 1940, the Yankees sat out the World Series for the first time since 1935. The New York Giants had won National League pennants in 1933, 1936, and 1937, but were also out that year. Joe DiMaggio, the Yankees' star center fielder, and Bill Terry, the Giants' manager, commiserate in this Mullin drawing.

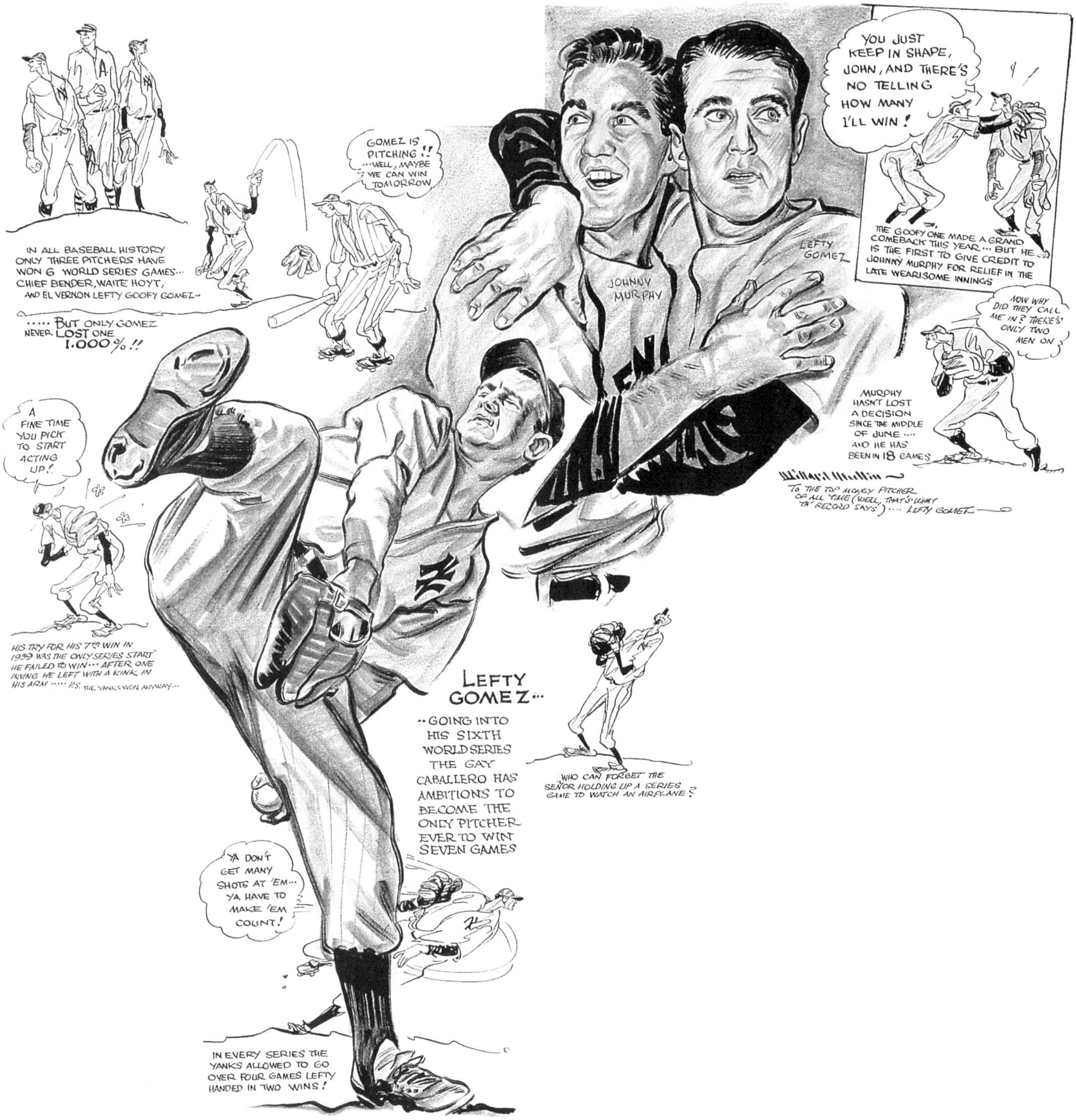
IN ALL BASEBALL HISTORY ONLY THREE PITCHERS HAVE WON 6 WORLD SERIES GAMES... CHIEF BENDER, WAITE HOYT, AND EL VERNON LEFTY GOOFY GOMEZ..
GOMEZ IS PITCHING !! ...WELL, MAYBE WE CAN WIN TOMORROW
..... BUT ONLY GOMEZ NEVER LOST ONE 1.000 % !!
JOHNNY MURPHY
LEFTY GOMEZ
YOU JUST KEEP IN SHAPE, JOHN, AND THERE'S NO TELLING HOW MANY I'LL WIN !
THE GOOFY ONE MADE A GRAND COMEBACK THIS YEAR... BUT HE IS THE FIRST TO GIVE CREDIT TO JOHNNY MURPHY FOR RELIEF IN THE LATE WEARISOME INNINGS
NOW WHY DID THEY CALL ME IN ? THERE'S ONLY TWO MEN ON
MURPHY HASN'T LOST A DECISION SINCE THE MIDDLE OF JUNE.... AND HE HAS BEEN IN 18 GAMES
A FINE TIME YOU PICK TO START ACTING UP !
TO THE TOP MONEY PITCHER OF ALL TIME (WELL, THAT'S WHAT TH' RECORD SAYS).... LEFTY GOMEZ
HIS TRY FOR HIS 7TH WIN IN 1939 WAS THE ONLY SERIES START HE FAILED TO WIN... AFTER ONE INNING HE LEFT WITH A KINK IN HIS ARM ..... P.S. THE YANKS WON ANYWAY...
LEFTY GOMEZ...
..GOING INTO HIS SIXTH WORLD SERIES THE GAY CABALLERO HAS AMBITIONS TO BECOME THE ONLY PITCHER EVER TO WIN SEVEN GAMES
WHO CAN FORGET THE SEÑOR HOLDING UP A SERIES GAME TO WATCH AN AIRPLANE ?
YA DON'T GET MANY SHOTS AT 'EM... YA HAVE TO MAKE 'EM COUNT !
IN EVERY SERIES THE YANKS ALLOWED TO GO OVER FOUR GAMES LEFTY HANDED IN TWO WINS !

Lefty Gomez had a comeback season in 1941, going 15–5, due in part to Johnny Murphy, the first great relief pitcher, who notched 15 saves with a 1.98 ERA.

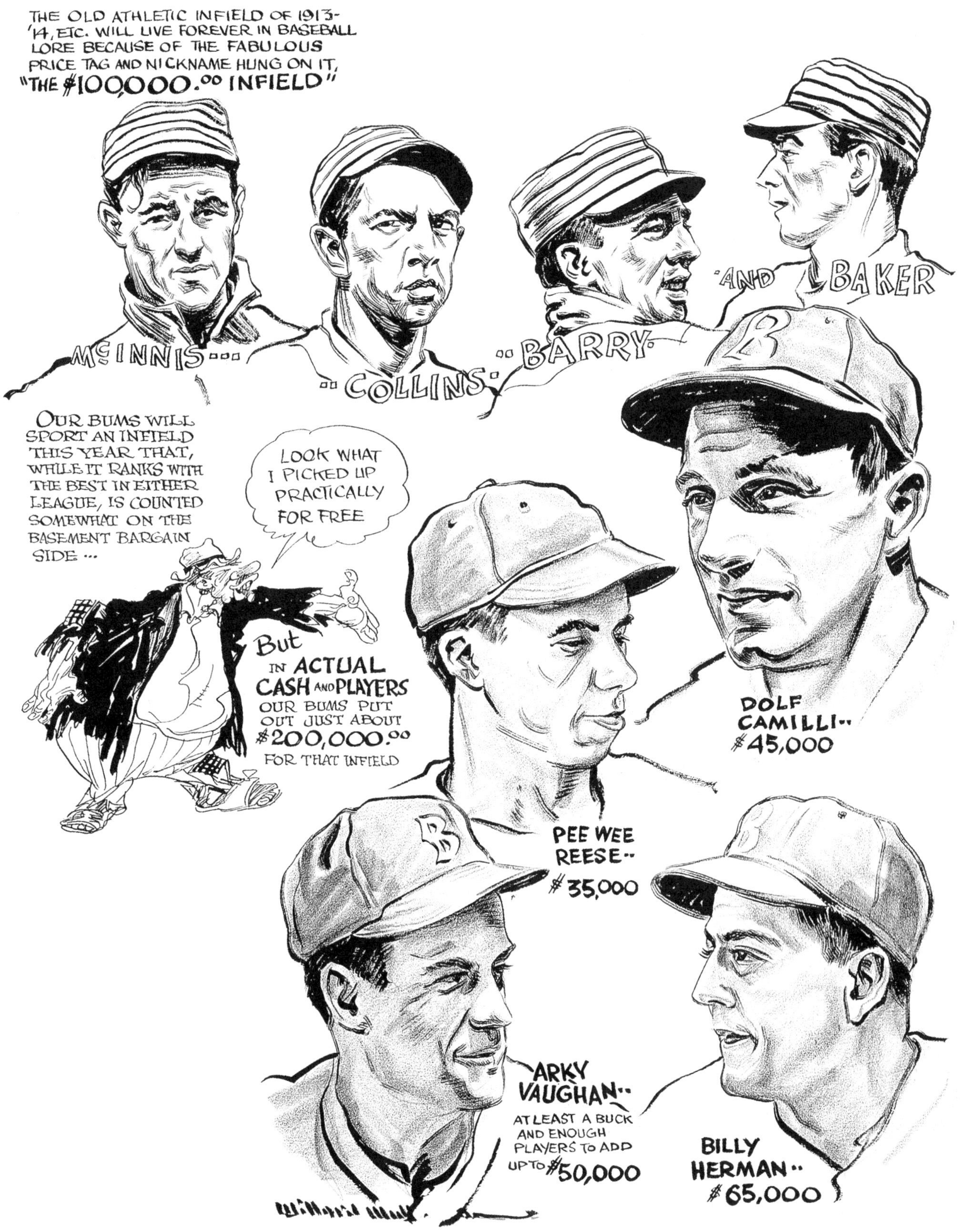
THE OLD ATHLETIC INFIELD OF 1913-'14, ETC. WILL LIVE FOREVER IN BASEBALL LORE BECAUSE OF THE FABULOUS PRICE TAG AND NICKNAME HUNG ON IT, "THE $100,000.00 INFIELD"
McINNIS...
..COLLINS..
..BARRY..
AND BAKER
OUR BUMS WILL SPORT AN INFIELD THIS YEAR THAT, WHILE IT RANKS WITH THE BEST IN EITHER LEAGUE, IS COUNTED SOMEWHAT ON THE BASEMENT BARGAIN SIDE...
LOOK WHAT I PICKED UP PRACTICALLY FOR FREE
But IN ACTUAL CASH AND PLAYERS OUR BUMS PUT OUT JUST ABOUT $200,000.00 FOR THAT INFIELD
DOLF CAMILLI.. $45,000
PEE WEE REESE.. $35,000
ARKY VAUGHAN.. AT LEAST A BUCK AND ENOUGH PLAYERS TO ADD UP TO $50,000
BILLY HERMAN.. $65,000

In 1942, the Dodgers had an infield composed of three future Hall of Famers: Arky Vaughan, Billy Herman, and Pee Wee Reese. The fourth infielder, Dolph Camilli, had led the National League in home runs and RBIs in 1941 and had been named the League's MVP. This infield was together only one season, as Reese went off to war in 1943.

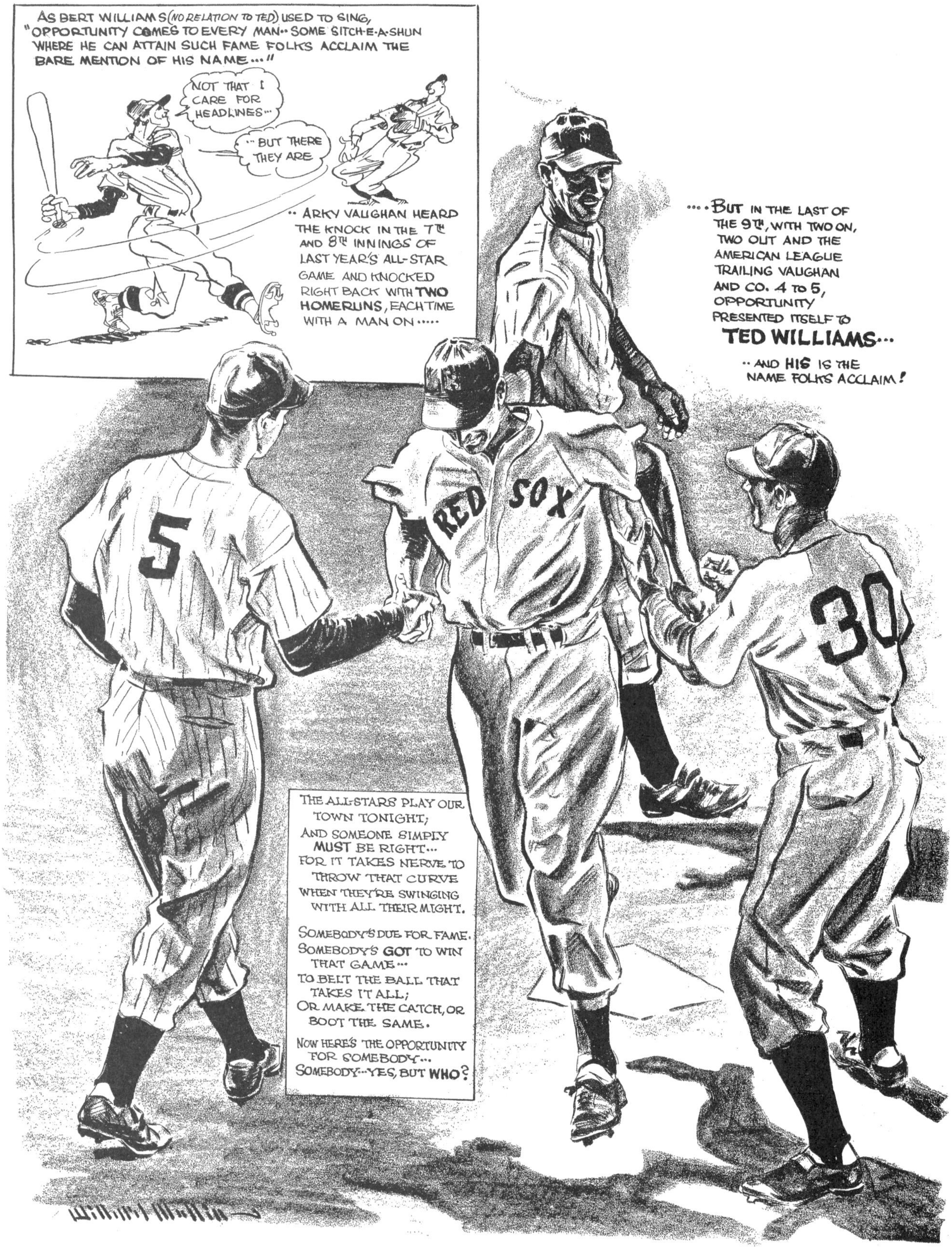
AS BERT WILLIAMS (NO RELATION TO TED) USED TO SING, "OPPORTUNITY COMES TO EVERY MAN.. SOME SITCH-E-A-SHUN WHERE HE CAN ATTAIN SUCH FAME FOLKS ACCLAIM THE BARE MENTION OF HIS NAME..."
NOT THAT I CARE FOR HEADLINES...
...BUT THERE THEY ARE
..ARKY VAUGHAN HEARD THE KNOCK IN THE 7TH AND 8TH INNINGS OF LAST YEAR'S ALL-STAR GAME AND KNOCKED RIGHT BACK WITH TWO HOMERUNS, EACH TIME WITH A MAN ON.....
....BUT IN THE LAST OF THE 9TH, WITH TWO ON, TWO OUT AND THE AMERICAN LEAGUE TRAILING VAUGHAN AND CO. 4 TO 5, OPPORTUNITY PRESENTED ITSELF TO
TED WILLIAMS...
..AND HIS IS THE NAME FOLKS ACCLAIM!
5
RED SOX
30
THE ALL-STARS PLAY OUR TOWN TONIGHT;
AND SOMEONE SIMPLY MUST BE RIGHT...
FOR IT TAKES NERVE TO THROW THAT CURVE
WHEN THEY'RE SWINGING WITH ALL THEIR MIGHT.
SOMEBODY'S DUE FOR FAME.
SOMEBODY'S GOT TO WIN THAT GAME...
TO BELT THE BALL THAT TAKES IT ALL;
OR MAKE THE CATCH, OR BOOT THE SAME.
NOW HERE'S THE OPPORTUNITY FOR SOMEBODY...
SOMEBODY...YES, BUT WHO?

In the 1941 All-Star Game, Ted Williams had hit a home run that won it for the American League in the bottom of the ninth. This drawing was done right before the 1942 All-Star Game, with Mullin wondering who would be that year's star.

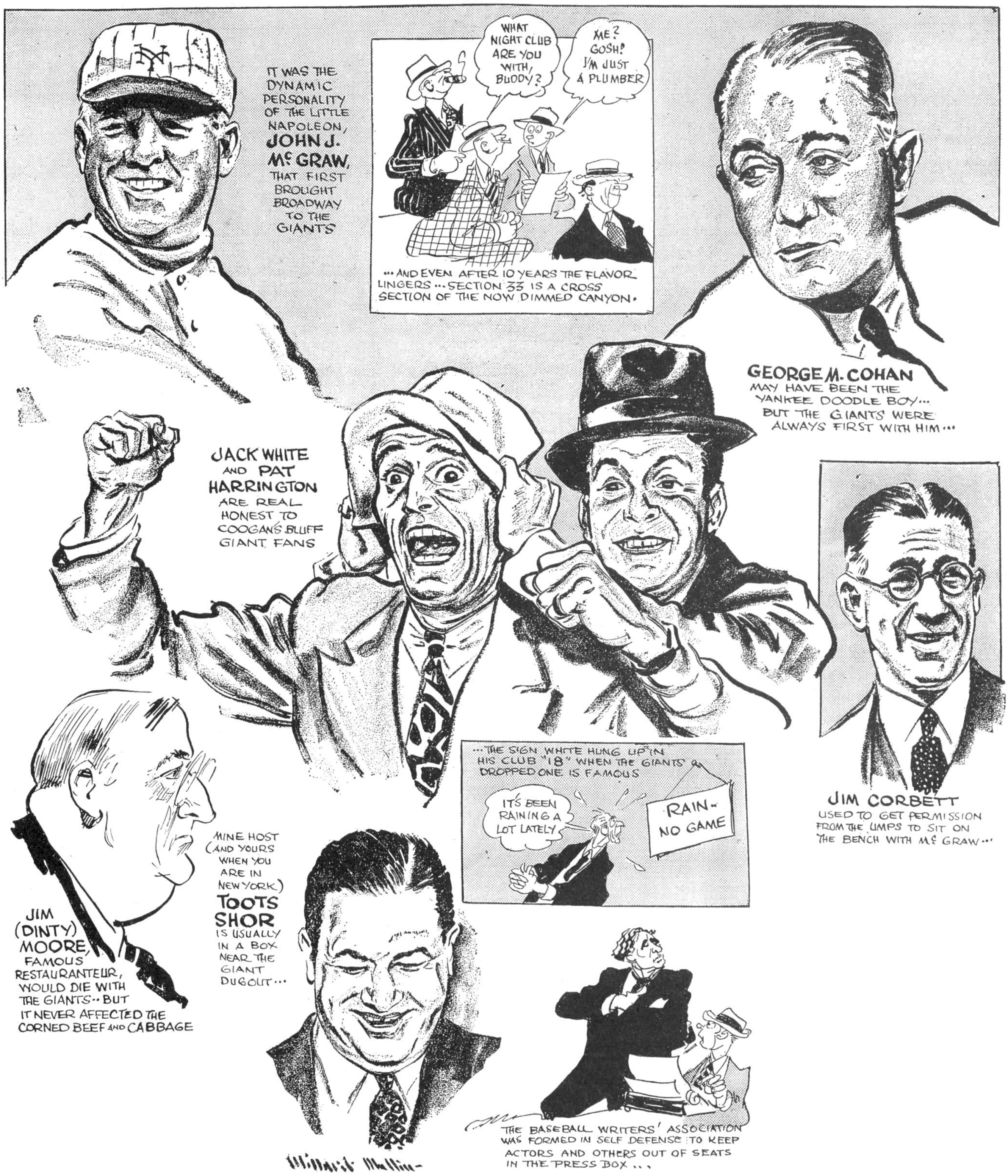
IT WAS THE DYNAMIC PERSONALITY OF THE LITTLE NAPOLEON, JOHN J. McGRAW, THAT FIRST BROUGHT BROADWAY TO THE GIANTS
WHAT NIGHT CLUB ARE YOU WITH, BUDDY?
ME? GOSH! I'M JUST A PLUMBER
...AND EVEN AFTER 10 YEARS THE FLAVOR LINGERS... SECTION 33 IS A CROSS SECTION OF THE NOW DIMMED CANYON.
GEORGE M. COHAN MAY HAVE BEEN THE YANKEE DOODLE BOY... BUT THE GIANTS WERE ALWAYS FIRST WITH HIM...
JACK WHITE AND PAT HARRINGTON ARE REAL HONEST TO COOGAN'S BLUFF GIANT FANS
JIM CORBETT USED TO GET PERMISSION FROM THE UMPS TO SIT ON THE BENCH WITH McGRAW...
...THE SIGN WHITE HUNG UP IN HIS CLUB "18" WHEN THE GIANTS' DROPPED ONE IS FAMOUS
IT'S BEEN RAINING A LOT LATELY
RAIN - NO GAME
JIM (DINTY) MOORE, FAMOUS RESTAURANTEUR, WOULD DIE WITH THE GIANTS.. BUT IT NEVER AFFECTED THE CORNED BEEF AND CABBAGE
MINE HOST (AND YOURS WHEN YOU ARE IN NEW YORK) TOOTS SHOR IS USUALLY IN A BOX NEAR THE GIANT DUGOUT...
THE BASEBALL WRITERS' ASSOCIATION WAS FORMED IN SELF DEFENSE TO KEEP ACTORS AND OTHERS OUT OF SEATS IN THE PRESS BOX...
Willard Mullin

Even though Mullin is most associated with the Dodgers, his favorite team was the New York Giants. In July 1942, he drew this piece about some of the famous fans seen at the Giants' home, the Polo Grounds.

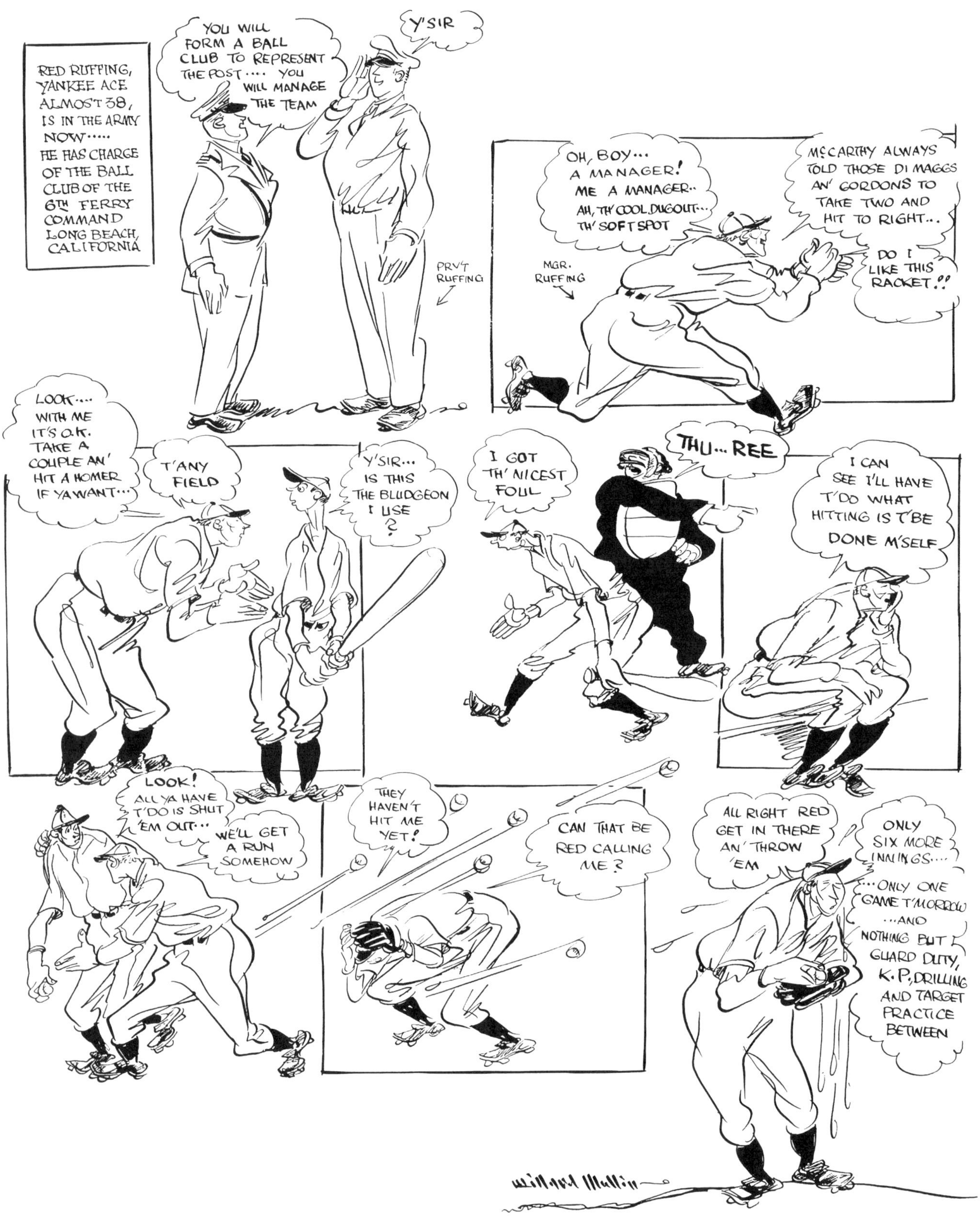
RED RUFFING, YANKEE ACE ALMOST 38, IS IN THE ARMY NOW..... HE HAS CHARGE OF THE BALL CLUB OF THE 6TH FERRY COMMAND LONG BEACH, CALIFORNIA
YOU WILL FORM A BALL CLUB TO REPRESENT THE POST.... YOU WILL MANAGE THE TEAM
Y'SIR
PRV'T RUFFING
OH, BOY... A MANAGER! ME A MANAGER.. AH, TH' COOL DUGOUT... TH' SOFT SPOT
MCCARTHY ALWAYS TOLD THOSE DI MAGGS AN' GORDONS TO TAKE TWO AND HIT TO RIGHT..
DO I LIKE THIS RACKET!!
MGR. RUFFING
LOOK... WITH ME IT'S O.K. TAKE A COUPLE AN' HIT A HOMER IF YA WANT...
T'ANY FIELD
Y'SIR... IS THIS THE BLUDGEON I USE ?
I GOT TH' NICEST FOUL
THU... REE
I CAN SEE I'LL HAVE T'DO WHAT HITTING IS T'BE DONE M'SELF
LOOK! ALL YA HAVE T'DO IS SHUT 'EM OUT..
WE'LL GET A RUN SOMEHOW
THEY HAVEN'T HIT ME YET!
CAN THAT BE RED CALLING ME?
ALL RIGHT RED GET IN THERE AN' THROW 'EM
ONLY SIX MORE INNINGS....
...ONLY ONE GAME T'MORROW ...AND NOTHING BUT GUARD DUTY, K.P., DRILLING AND TARGET PRACTICE BETWEEN
Willard Mullin

When World War II began, many major leaguers joined the military. Not all saw combat; a significant number were stationed stateside and played baseball on the service teams. Joe DiMaggio was one, as was another Yankees great, Red Ruffing, shown in this cartoon by Mullin from the mid-1940s.

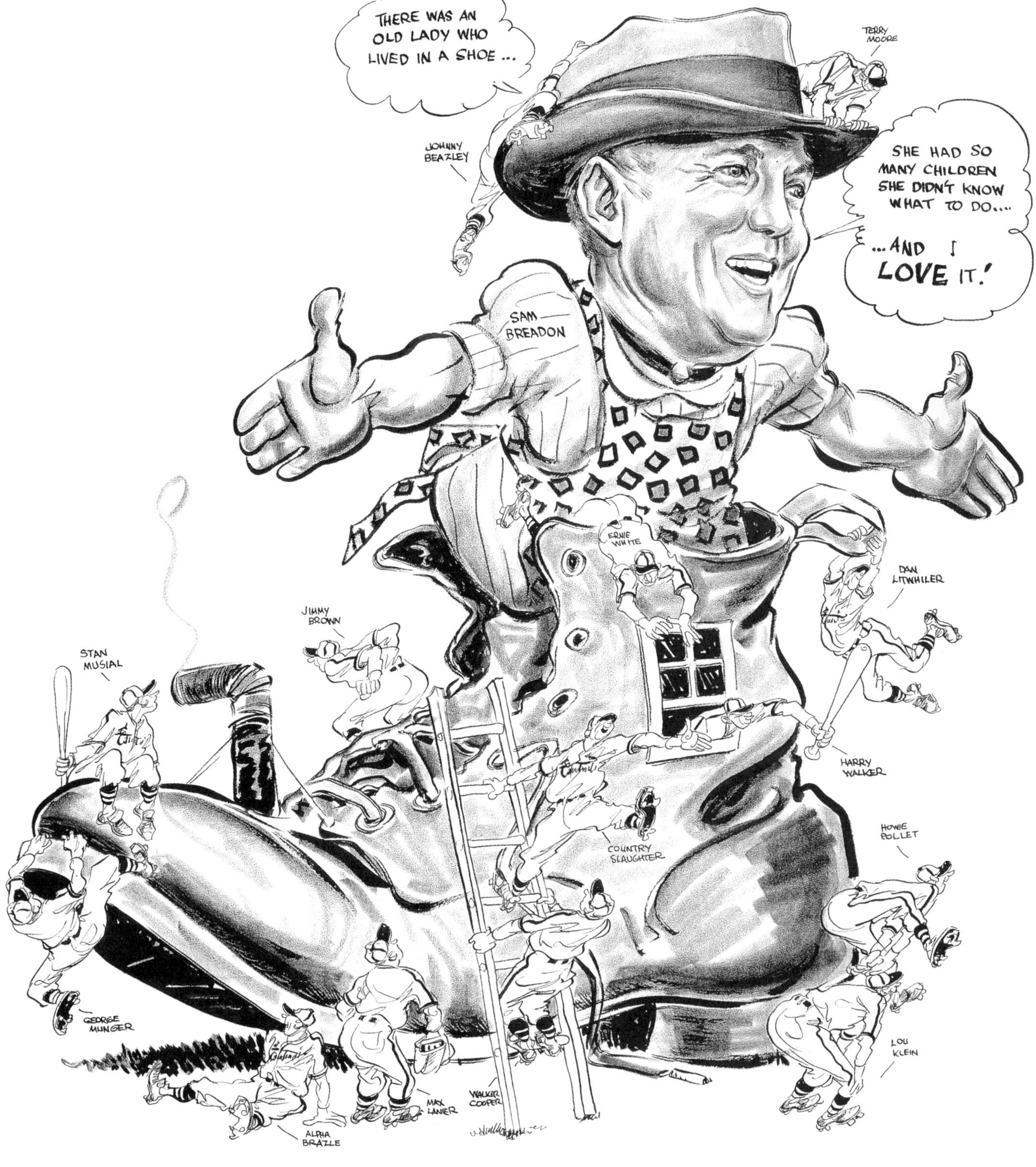
THERE WAS AN OLD LADY WHO LIVED IN A SHOE ...
SHE HAD SO MANY CHILDREN SHE DIDN'T KNOW WHAT TO DO....
...AND LOVE IT!
TERRY MOORE
JOHNNY BEAZLEY
SAM BREADON
ERNIE WHITE
DAN LITWHILER
JIMMY BROWN
STAN MUSIAL
HARRY WALKER
COUNTRY SLAUGHTER
HOWIE POLLET
GEORGE MUNGER
LOU KLEIN
WALKER COOPER
MAX LANIER
ALPHA BRAZLE

While working for the Cardinals in the 1920s and 1930s as the first general manager in baseball, Branch Rickey created the framework for the modern minor league farm system. By the early 1940s, the Cardinals had become a perennial powerhouse due to all the quality players they developed in their minor league farm system. This cartoon from the mid-1940s celebrates Cardinal owner Sam Breadon's embarrassment of riches.

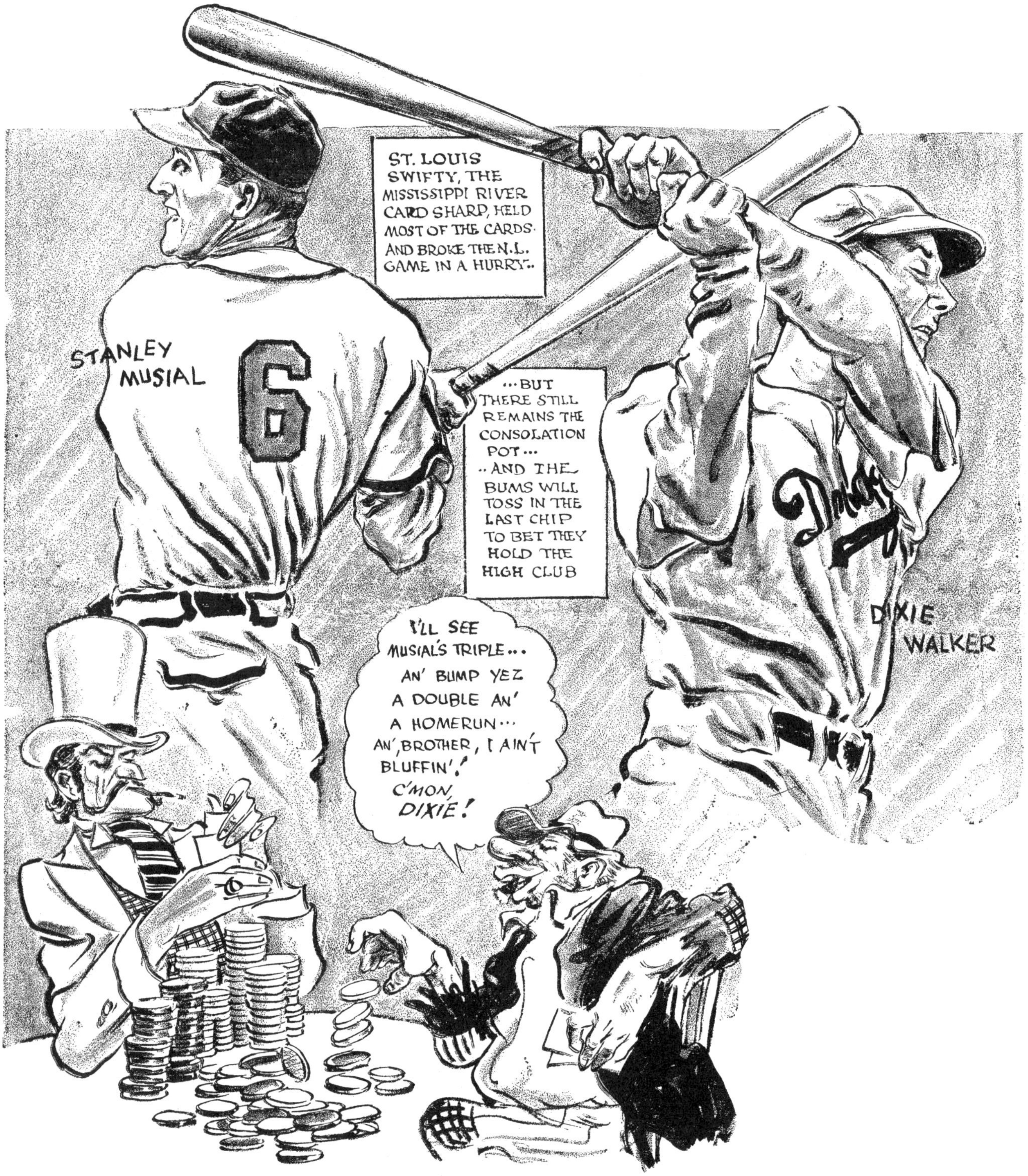
ST. LOUIS SWIFTY, THE MISSISSIPPI RIVER CARD SHARP, HELD MOST OF THE CARDS. AND BROKE THE N.L. GAME IN A HURRY..
STANLEY MUSIAL
6
...BUT THERE STILL REMAINS THE CONSOLATION POT... ..AND THE BUMS WILL TOSS IN THE LAST CHIP TO BET THEY HOLD THE HIGH CLUB
DIXIE WALKER
I'LL SEE MUSIAL'S TRIPLE... AN' BUMP YEZ A DOUBLE AN' A HOMERUN... AN', BROTHER, I AIN'T BLUFFIN'! C'MON, DIXIE!

This drawing was done early in the 1944 season. As it played out, Dixie Walker ended up winning the batting title with a .357 average, but Stan Musial's team won the pennant and the World Series. Walker's Dodgers lost 91 games and finished seventh in an eight-team league.

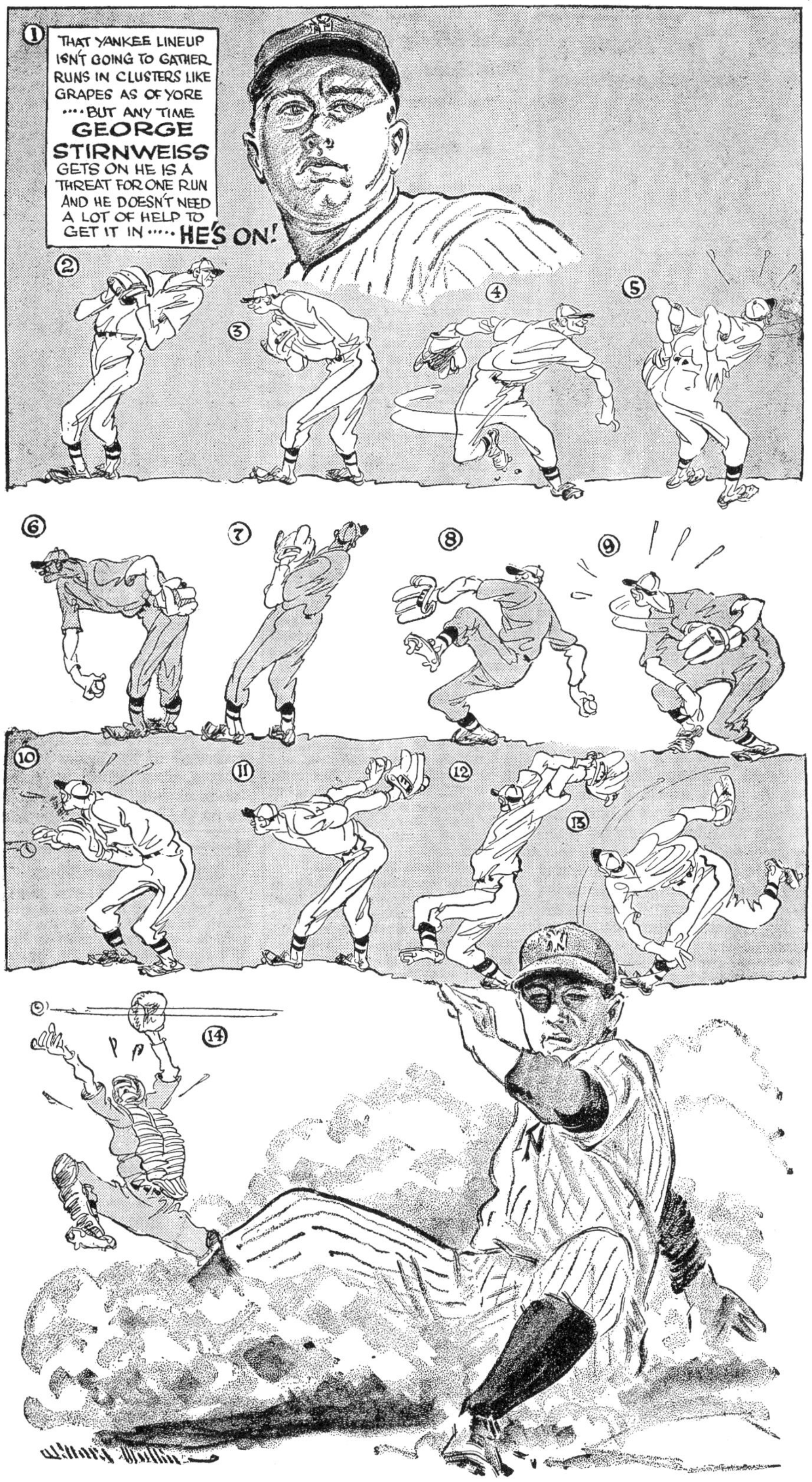
THAT YANKEE LINEUP ISN'T GOING TO GATHER RUNS IN CLUSTERS LIKE GRAPES AS OF YORE ....BUT ANY TIME GEORGE STIRNWEISS GETS ON HE IS A THREAT FOR ONE RUN AND HE DOESN'T NEED A LOT OF HELP TO GET IT IN.....HE'S ON!

By 1944, many of the Yankees' stars were in the military, including Joe DiMaggio and Phil Rizzuto, but George Stirnweiss had a stellar year for the Yankees, hitting .319 and leading the league in runs, hits, triples, and stolen bases.

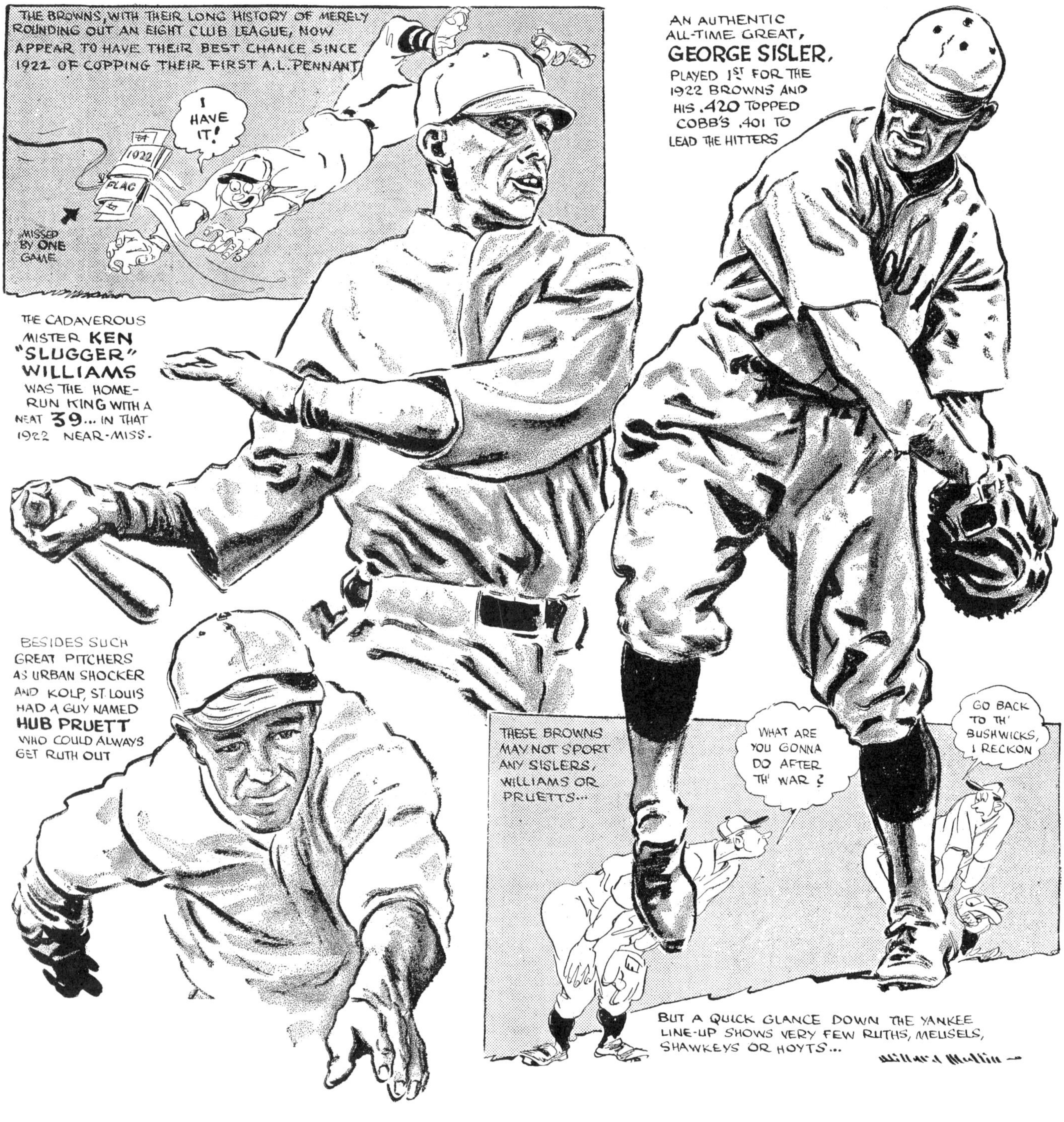
THE BROWNS, WITH THEIR LONG HISTORY OF MERELY ROUNDING OUT AN EIGHT CLUB LEAGUE, NOW APPEAR TO HAVE THEIR BEST CHANCE SINCE 1922 OF COPPING THEIR FIRST A.L. PENNANT
I HAVE IT!
1922
FLAG
MISSED BY ONE GAME
AN AUTHENTIC ALL-TIME GREAT, GEORGE SISLER, PLAYED 1ST FOR THE 1922 BROWNS AND HIS .420 TOPPED COBB'S .401 TO LEAD THE HITTERS
THE CADAVEROUS MISTER KEN "SLUGGER" WILLIAMS WAS THE HOME-RUN KING WITH A NEAT 39... IN THAT 1922 NEAR-MISS.
BESIDES SUCH GREAT PITCHERS AS URBAN SHOCKER AND KOLP, ST. LOUIS HAD A GUY NAMED HUB PRUETT WHO COULD ALWAYS GET RUTH OUT
THESE BROWNS MAY NOT SPORT ANY SISLERS, WILLIAMS OR PRUETTS...
WHAT ARE YOU GONNA DO AFTER TH' WAR?
GO BACK TO TH' BUSHWICKS, I RECKON
BUT A QUICK GLANCE DOWN THE YANKEE LINE-UP SHOWS VERY FEW RUTHS, MEUSELS, SHAWKEYS OR HOYTS...

In 1944, with the major leagues depleted by the number of players serving in the military, the St. Louis Browns won their one and only pennant, eventually losing the World Series to their crosstown rivals, the St. Louis Cardinals.

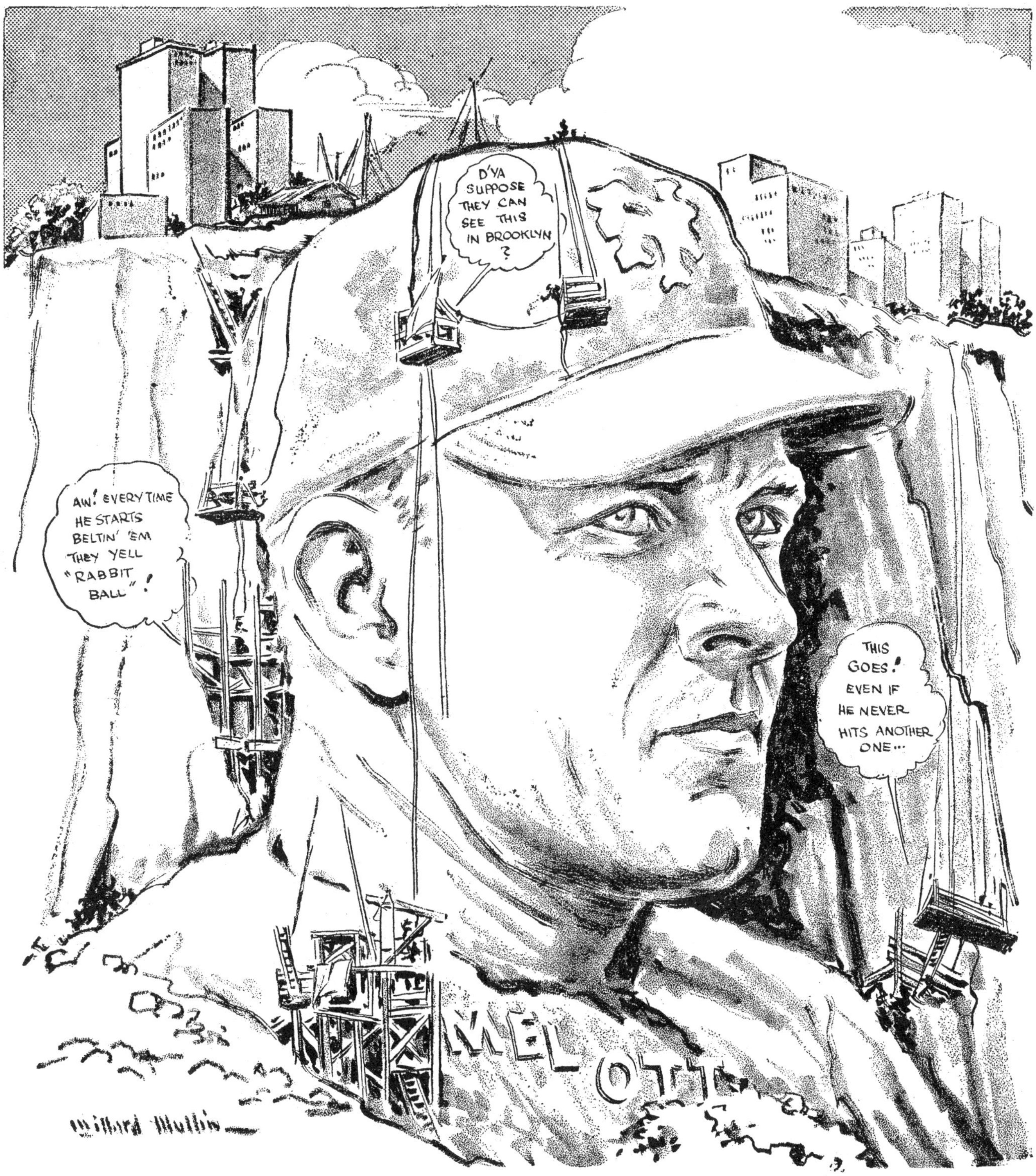
D'YA SUPPOSE THEY CAN SEE THIS IN BROOKLYN ?
AW! EVERYTIME HE STARTS BELTIN' 'EM THEY YELL "RABBIT BALL"!
THIS GOES! EVEN IF HE NEVER HITS ANOTHER ONE...
MEL OTT
Willard Mullin

Mel Ott made his debut for the New York Giants in 1926 at age 17 and played for them for the next 22 years. When he retired, he was the National League career home run leader, with 511, and had a career .304 batting average with 1,860 RBIs.

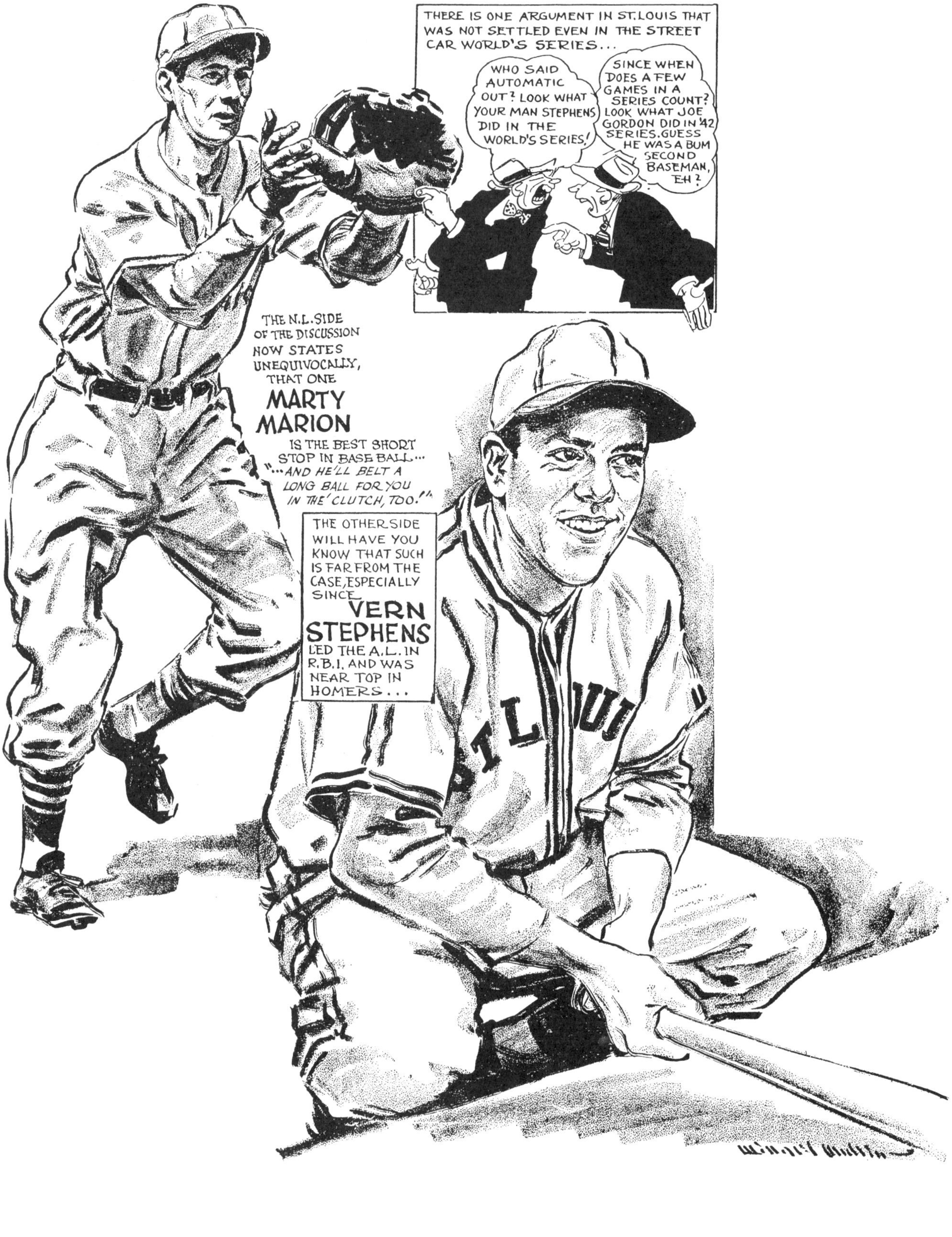
THERE IS ONE ARGUMENT IN ST. LOUIS THAT WAS NOT SETTLED EVEN IN THE STREET CAR WORLD'S SERIES...
WHO SAID AUTOMATIC OUT? LOOK WHAT YOUR MAN STEPHENS DID IN THE WORLD'S SERIES!
SINCE WHEN DOES A FEW GAMES IN A SERIES COUNT? LOOK WHAT JOE GORDON DID IN '42 SERIES. GUESS HE WAS A BUM SECOND BASEMAN, EH?
THE N.L. SIDE OF THE DISCUSSION NOW STATES UNEQUIVOCALLY, THAT ONE MARTY MARION IS THE BEST SHORT STOP IN BASE BALL... "...AND HE'LL BELT A LONG BALL FOR YOU IN THE' CLUTCH, TOO!"
THE OTHER SIDE WILL HAVE YOU KNOW THAT SUCH IS FAR FROM THE CASE, ESPECIALLY SINCE VERN STEPHENS LED THE A.L. IN R.B.I. AND WAS NEAR TOP IN HOMERS...
ST LOUI

In 1944, the city of St. Louis was home to arguably the two best shortstops in baseball: Marty Marion of the Cardinals and Vern Stephens of the Browns. Stephens led the AL in RBIs and in home runs in 1945. Marion won the NL MVP, despite a .267 batting average. Marion's Cardinals and Stephens's Browns met for the only time in the 1944 World Series. The Cards won in six games.

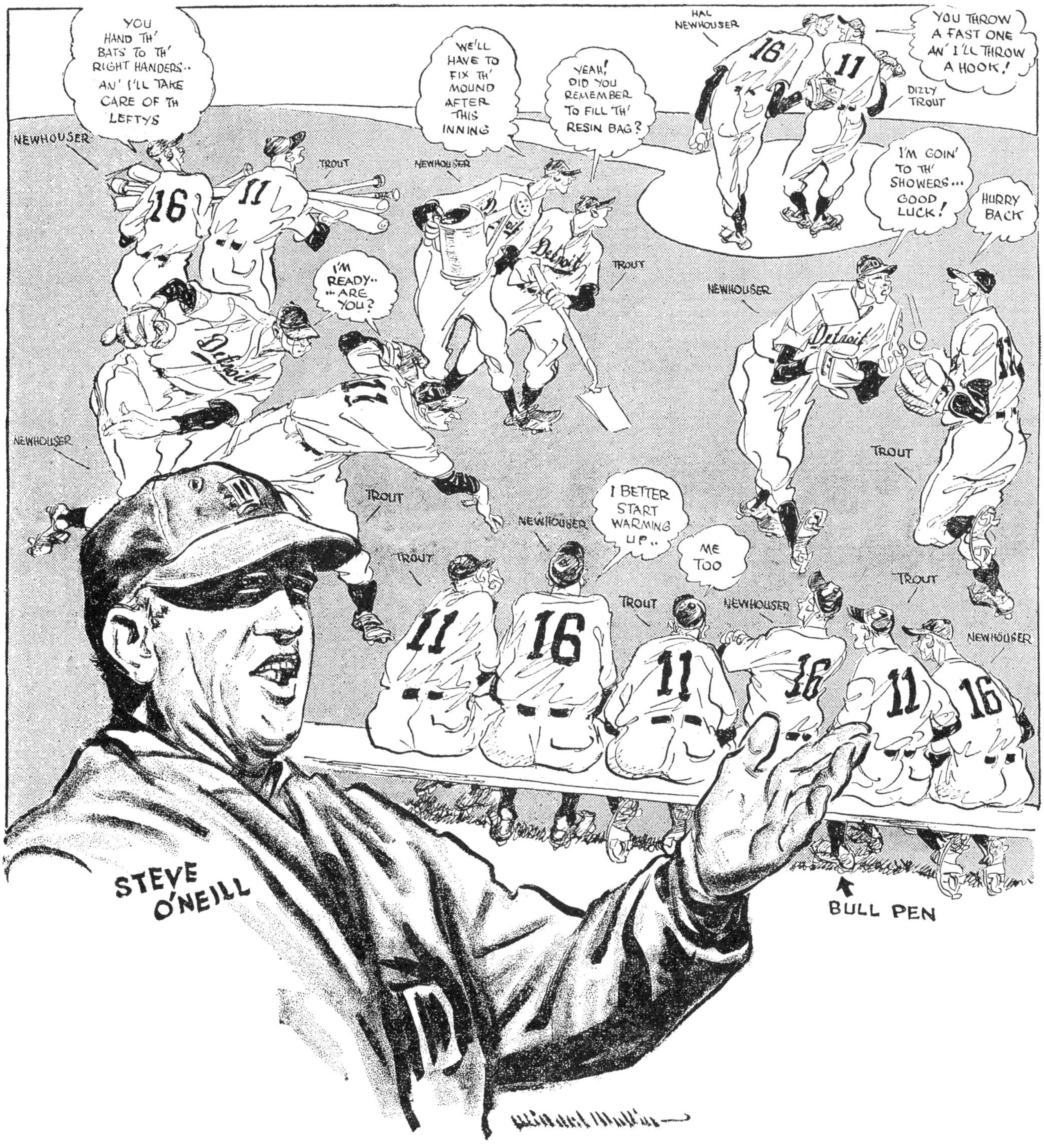
YOU HAND TH' BATS TO TH' RIGHT HANDERS.. AN' I'LL TAKE CARE OF TH LEFTYS
NEWHOUSER
TROUT
WE'LL HAVE TO FIX TH' MOUND AFTER THIS INNING
NEWHOUSER
YEAH! DID YOU REMEMBER TO FILL TH' RESIN BAG?
TROUT
HAL NEWHOUSER
YOU THROW A FAST ONE AN' I'LL THROW A HOOK!
DIZZY TROUT
I'M READY.. ..ARE YOU?
I'M GOIN' TO TH' SHOWERS... GOOD LUCK!
HURRY BACK
NEWHOUSER
NEWHOUSER
TROUT
TROUT
I BETTER START WARMING UP..
NEWHOUSER
TROUT
ME TOO
TROUT
NEWHOUSER
TROUT
NEWHOUSER
STEVE O'NEILL
BULL PEN

Starting in the mid-1940s, while most of the stars were off fighting in World War II, the Tigers became a dominant team because of two pitchers: Hal Newhouser and Dizzy Trout.

This culminated in the Tigers winning the 1945 World Series against the Chicago Cubs. The Cubs, famously, have not made it to the World Series since.

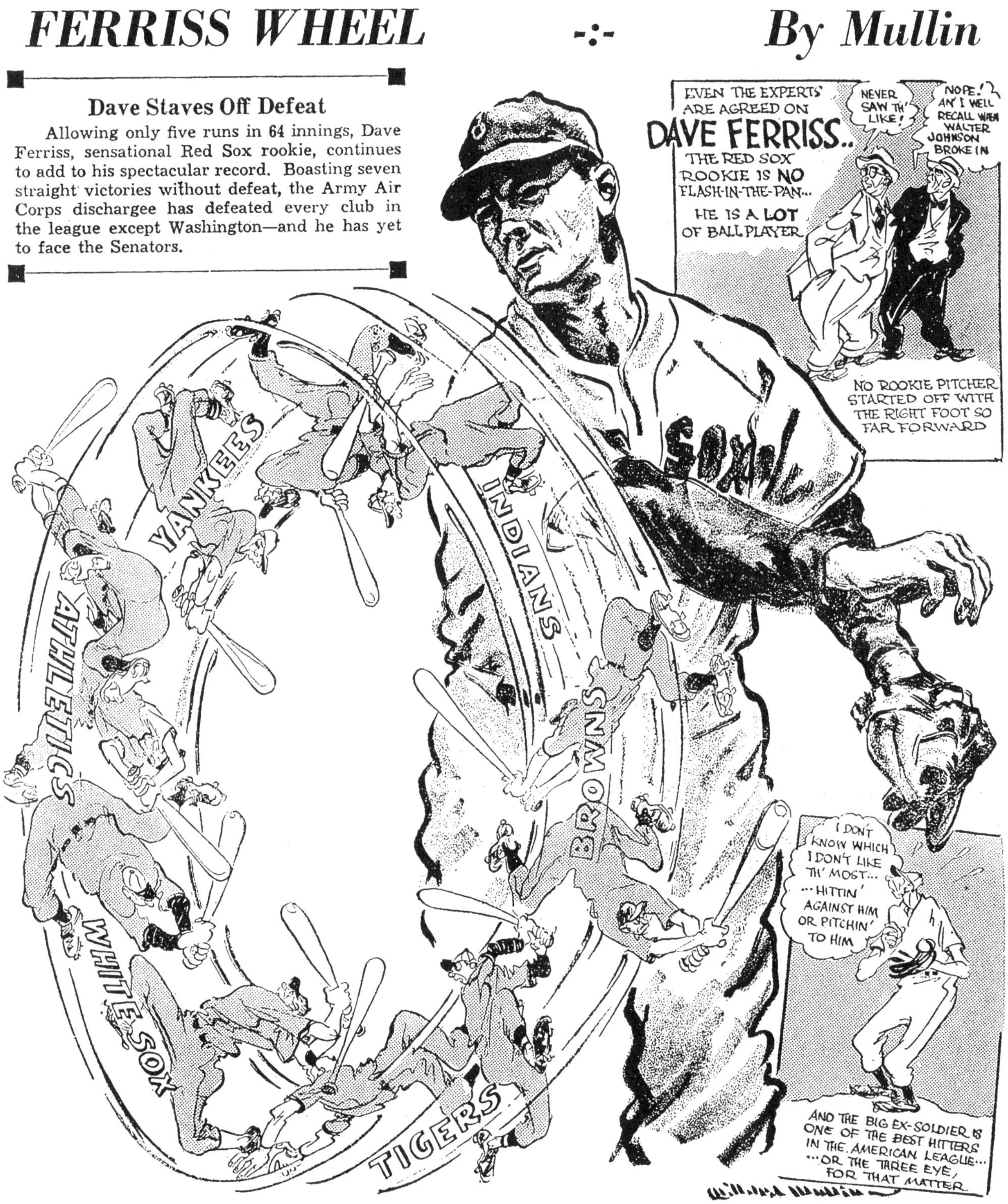
FERRISS WHEEL -:- By Mullin
Dave Staves Off Defeat
Allowing only five runs in 64 innings, Dave Ferriss, sensational Red Sox rookie, continues to add to his spectacular record. Boasting seven straight victories without defeat, the Army Air Corps dischargee has defeated every club in the league except Washington—and he has yet to face the Senators.
EVEN THE EXPERTS' ARE AGREED ON DAVE FERRISS.. THE RED SOX ROOKIE IS NO FLASH-IN-THE-PAN... HE IS A LOT OF BALL PLAYER
NEVER SAW TH' LIKE!
NOPE! AN' I WELL RECALL WHEN WALTER JOHNSON BROKE IN
NO ROOKIE PITCHER STARTED OFF WITH THE RIGHT FOOT SO FAR FORWARD
YANKEES
INDIANS
ATHLETICS
BROWNS
WHITE SOX
TIGERS
I DON'T KNOW WHICH I DON'T LIKE TH' MOST... ...HITTIN' AGAINST HIM OR PITCHIN' TO HIM
AND THE BIG EX-SOLDIER IS ONE OF THE BEST HITTERS IN THE AMERICAN LEAGUE... ...OR THE THREE EYE, FOR THAT MATTER

Dave Ferris came to the majors with a splash in 1945, going 21–10. He followed that by going 25–6 and winning a World Series game for the Red Sox in 1946. Unfortunately, Ferris later had arm trouble and was out of baseball by 1950.

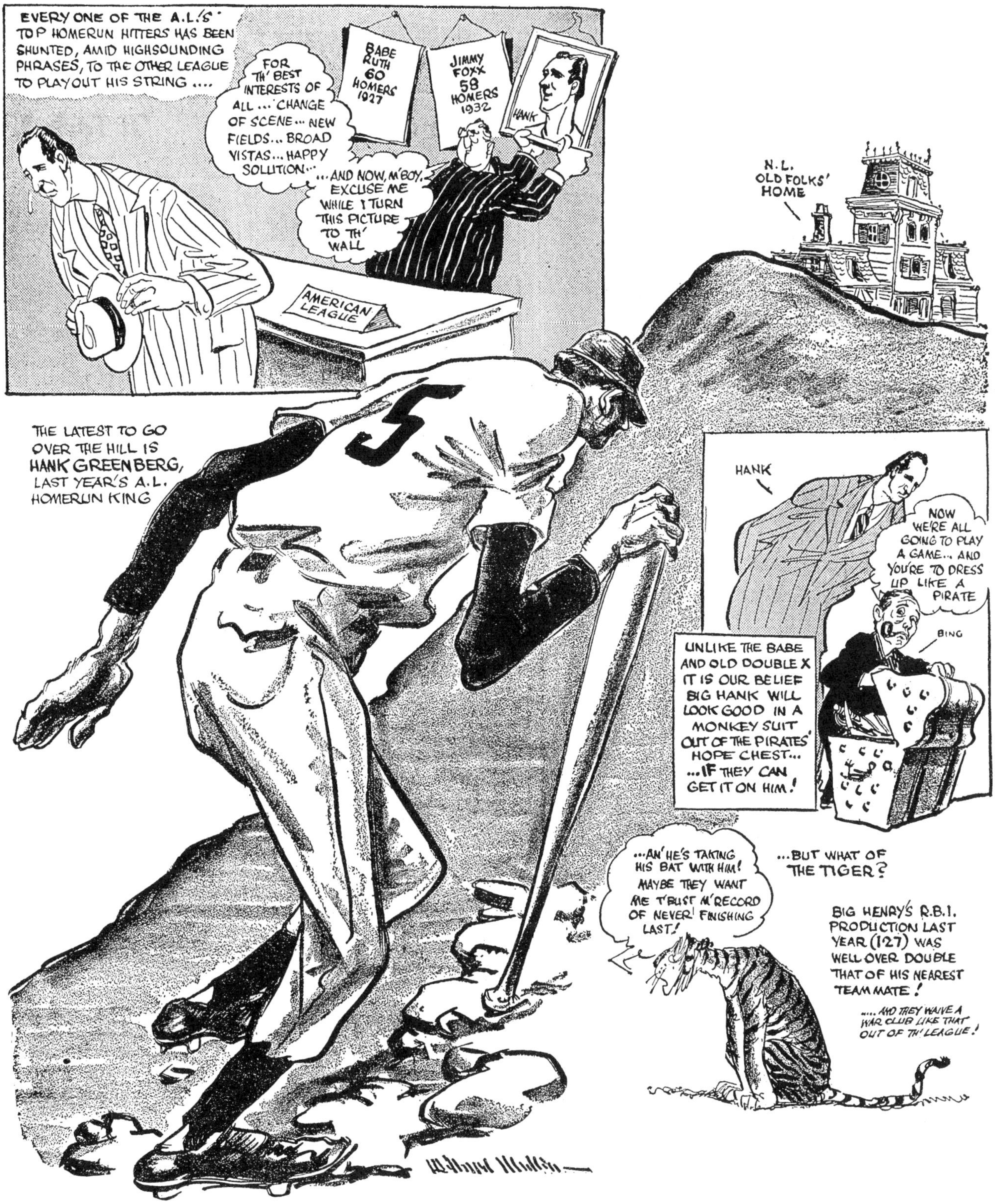
EVERY ONE OF THE A.L.'S TOP HOMERUN HITTERS HAS BEEN SHUNTED, AMID HIGHSOUNDING PHRASES, TO THE OTHER LEAGUE TO PLAY OUT HIS STRING ....
FOR TH' BEST INTERESTS OF ALL ... CHANGE OF SCENE... NEW FIELDS... BROAD VISTAS... HAPPY SOLUTION...
BABE RUTH 60 HOMERS 1927
JIMMY FOXX 58 HOMERS 1932
HANK
...AND NOW, M'BOY, EXCUSE ME WHILE I TURN THIS PICTURE TO TH' WALL
AMERICAN LEAGUE
N.L. OLD FOLKS' HOME
THE LATEST TO GO OVER THE HILL IS HANK GREENBERG, LAST YEAR'S A.L. HOMERUN KING
HANK
NOW WE'RE ALL GOING TO PLAY A GAME... AND YOU'RE TO DRESS UP LIKE A PIRATE
BING
UNLIKE THE BABE AND OLD DOUBLE X IT IS OUR BELIEF BIG HANK WILL LOOK GOOD IN A MONKEY SUIT OUT OF THE PIRATES' HOPE CHEST... ...IF THEY CAN GET IT ON HIM!
...AN' HE'S TAKING HIS BAT WITH HIM! MAYBE THEY WANT ME T'BUST M'RECORD OF NEVER FINISHING LAST!
...BUT WHAT OF THE TIGER?
BIG HENRY'S R.B.I. PRODUCTION LAST YEAR (127) WAS WELL OVER DOUBLE THAT OF HIS NEAREST TEAM MATE!
.... AND THEY WAIVE A WAR CLUB LIKE THAT OUT OF TH' LEAGUE!

Hank Greenberg missed more than four seasons due to his military service in World War II. In 1946, his first full season back with the Tigers, Greenberg led the American League in home runs (44) and RBIs (127).

But the Tigers apparently felt that, at 35 years old, Greenberg was over the hill and traded him to Bing Crosby's Pittsburgh Pirates. Greenberg played one more season and then retired for good.

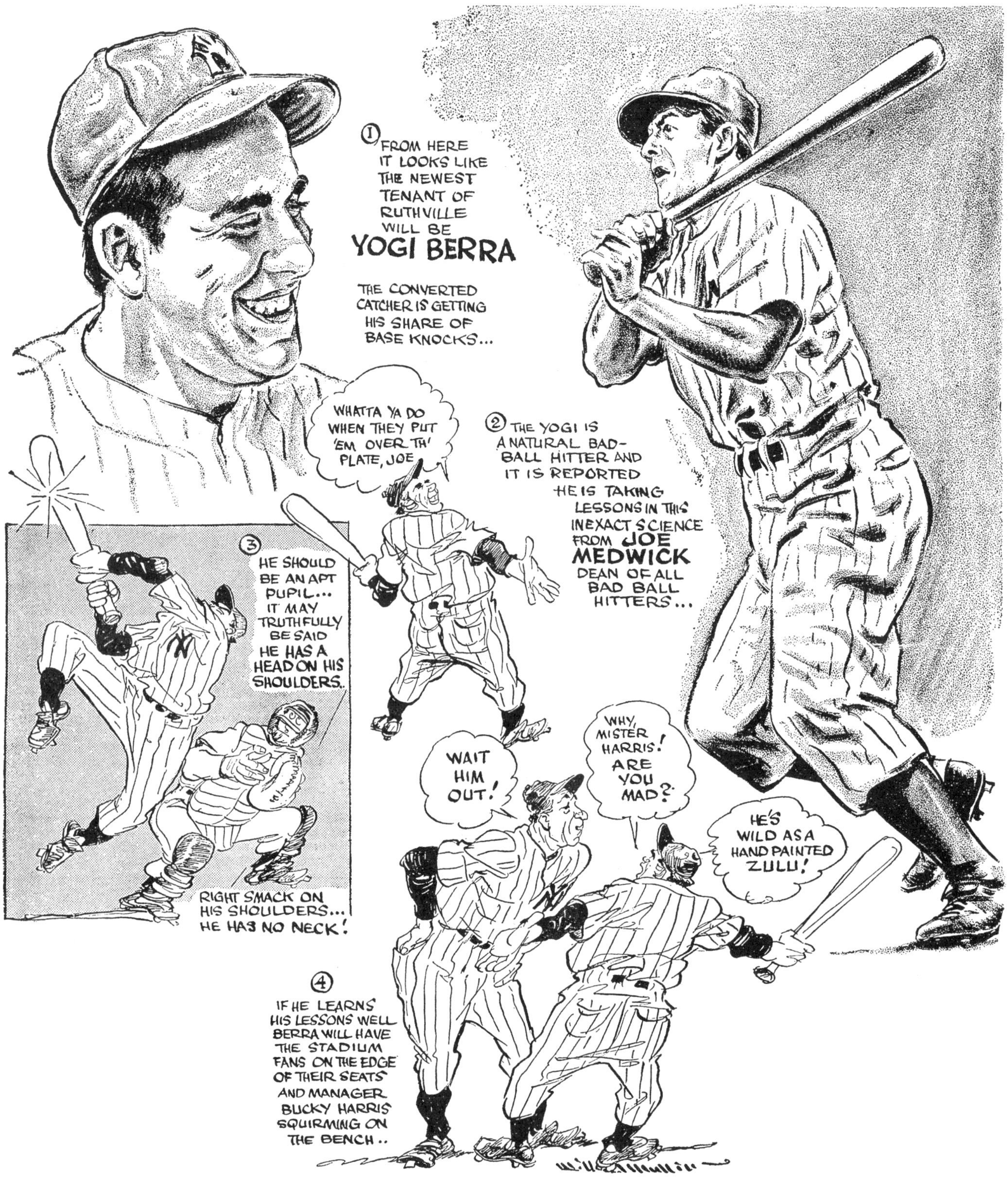
① FROM HERE IT LOOKS LIKE THE NEWEST TENANT OF RUTHVILLE WILL BE
YOGI BERRA
THE CONVERTED CATCHER IS GETTING HIS SHARE OF BASE KNOCKS...
WHATTA YA DO WHEN THEY PUT 'EM OVER TH' PLATE, JOE
② THE YOGI IS A NATURAL BAD-BALL HITTER AND IT IS REPORTED HE IS TAKING LESSONS IN THIS INEXACT SCIENCE FROM JOE MEDWICK DEAN OF ALL BAD BALL HITTERS...
③ HE SHOULD BE AN APT PUPIL... IT MAY TRUTHFULLY BE SAID HE HAS A HEAD ON HIS SHOULDERS.
RIGHT SMACK ON HIS SHOULDERS... HE HAS NO NECK!
WAIT HIM OUT!
WHY, MISTER HARRIS! ARE YOU MAD?
HE'S WILD AS A HAND PAINTED ZULU!
④ IF HE LEARNS HIS LESSONS WELL BERRA WILL HAVE THE STADIUM FANS ON THE EDGE OF THEIR SEATS AND MANAGER BUCKY HARRIS SQUIRMING ON THE BENCH..

When Yogi Berra joined the Yankees in 1947, few thought he would last as a ballplayer, much less make the Hall of Fame, but Mullin had an uncanny knack for spotting talent and anointed him for stardom in this drawing from April 1947.

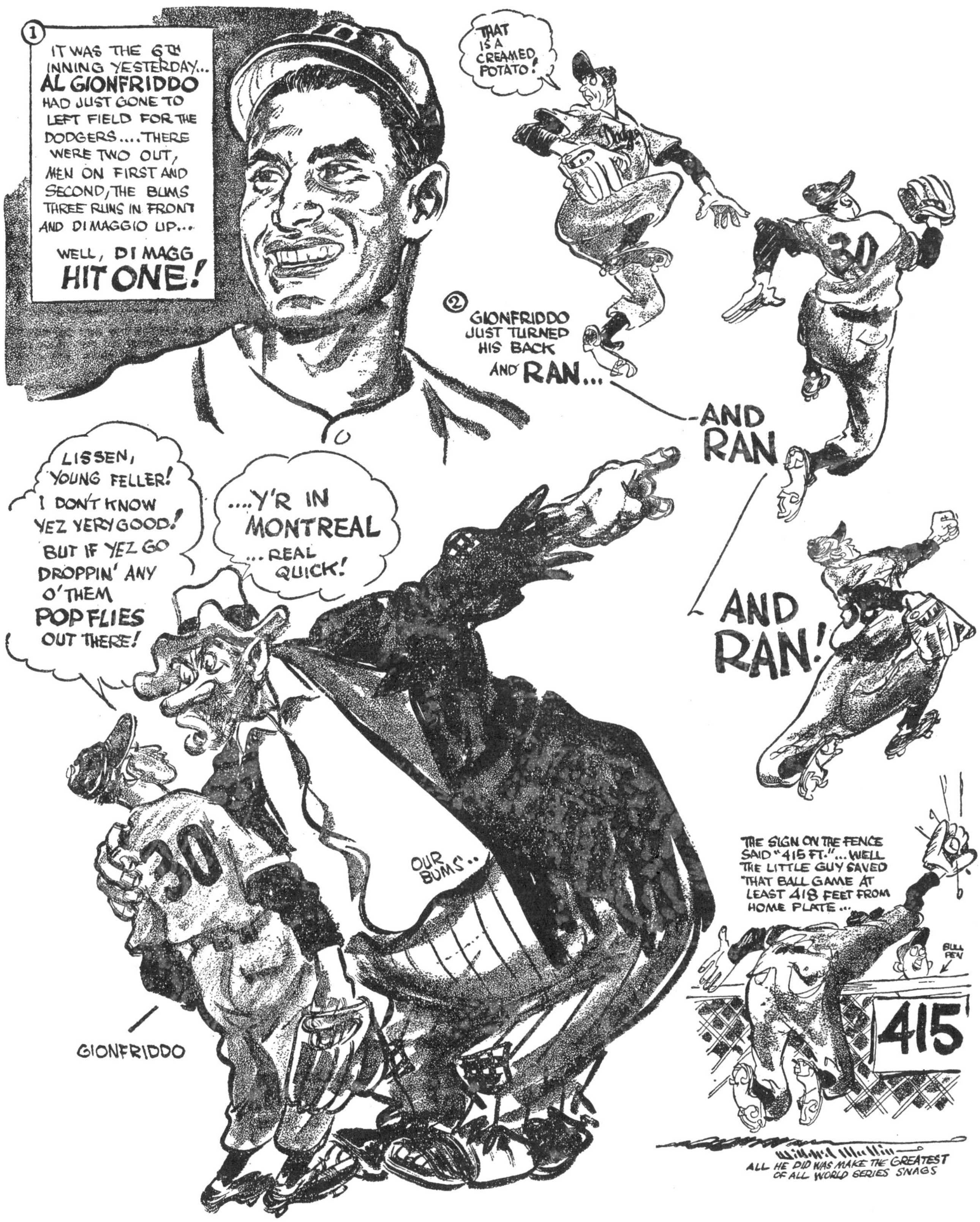
1
IT WAS THE 6TH INNING YESTERDAY... AL GIONFRIDDO HAD JUST GONE TO LEFT FIELD FOR THE DODGERS.... THERE WERE TWO OUT, MEN ON FIRST AND SECOND, THE BUMS THREE RUNS IN FRONT AND DI MAGGIO UP...
WELL, DI MAGG HIT ONE!
THAT IS A CREAMED POTATO!
2
GIONFRIDDO JUST TURNED HIS BACK AND RAN...
-AND RAN
AND RAN!
LISSEN, YOUNG FELLER! I DON'T KNOW YEZ VERY GOOD! BUT IF YEZ GO DROPPIN' ANY O'THEM POP FLIES OUT THERE!
...Y'R IN MONTREAL ...REAL QUICK!
OUR BUMS..
30
GIONFRIDDO
THE SIGN ON THE FENCE SAID "415 FT."... WELL THE LITTLE GUY SAVED THAT BALL GAME AT LEAST 418 FEET FROM HOME PLATE...
BULL PEN
415
ALL HE DID WAS MAKE THE GREATEST OF ALL WORLD SERIES SNAGS

In the 1947 World Series, Al Gionfriddo made the catch of a lifetime, robbing Yankees great Joe DiMaggio of a game-tying home run. The Dodgers hung on to win game 6, 8–6, but the Yankees won game 7 — and the Series — the next day.

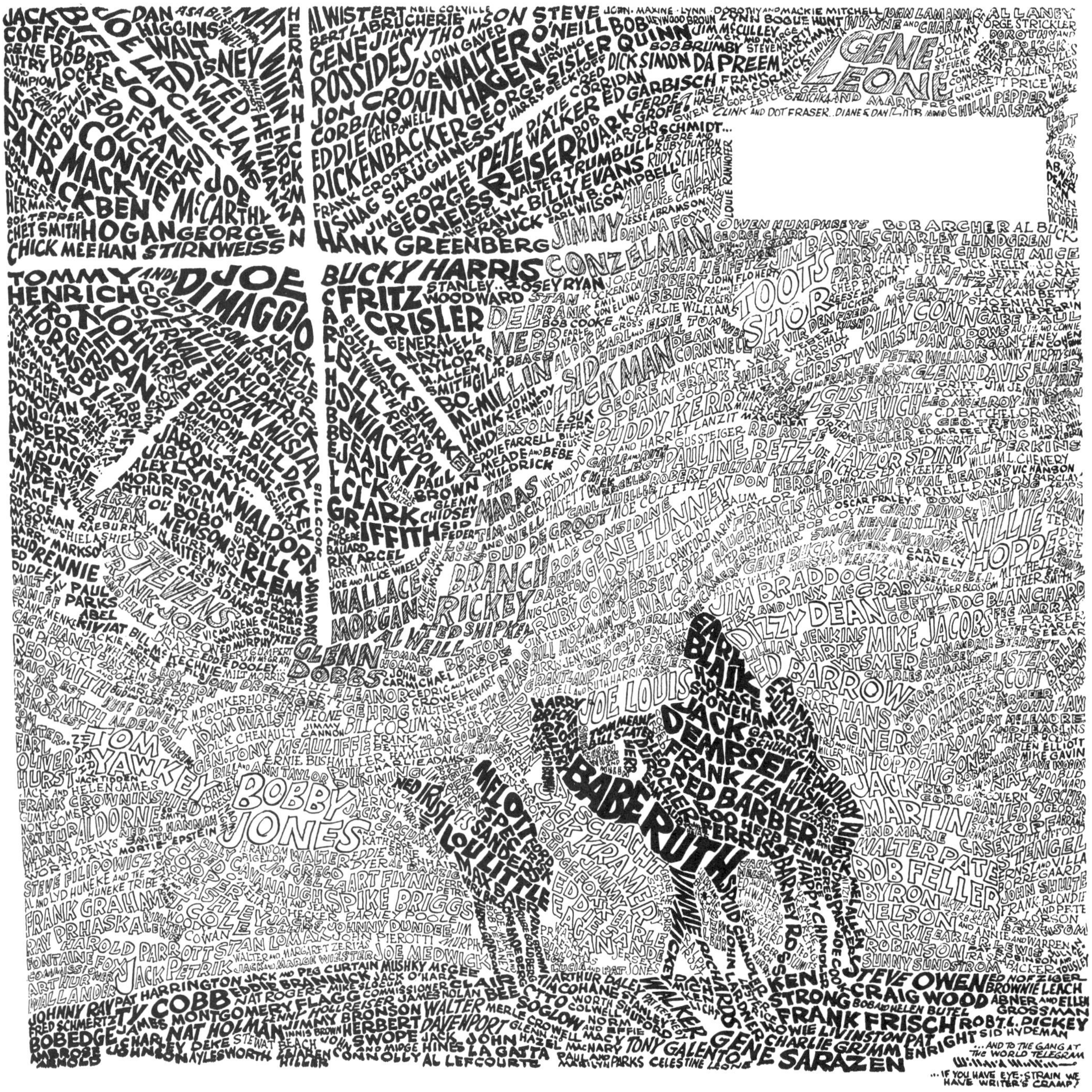
JOE DIMAGGIO
GENE LEONE
BUCKY HARRIS
FRITZ CRISLER
HANK GREENBERG
CONZELMAN
TOOTS SHOR
SID LUCKMAN
BILLY CONN
JOE LOUIS
JACK DEMPSEY
BABE RUTH
RED BARBER
BOBBY JONES
DIZZY DEAN
JIM BRADDOCK
MIKE JACOBS
BOB FELLER
GENE SARAZEN
FRANK FRISCH
CRAIG WOOD
STEVE OWEN
TY COBB
NAT HOLMAN
GLENN DOBBS
WILLIE HOPPE
HAGEN
DISNEY
CONNIE MACK
...AND TO THE GANG AT THE WORLD TELEGRAM
...IF YOU HAVE EYE-STRAIN WE HAVE WRITER'S CRAMP!

Beginning in the 1940s, Mullin composed Christmas cards using all of the great names in sports. These drawings, all hand-lettered by Mullin, would take up to four days to complete.

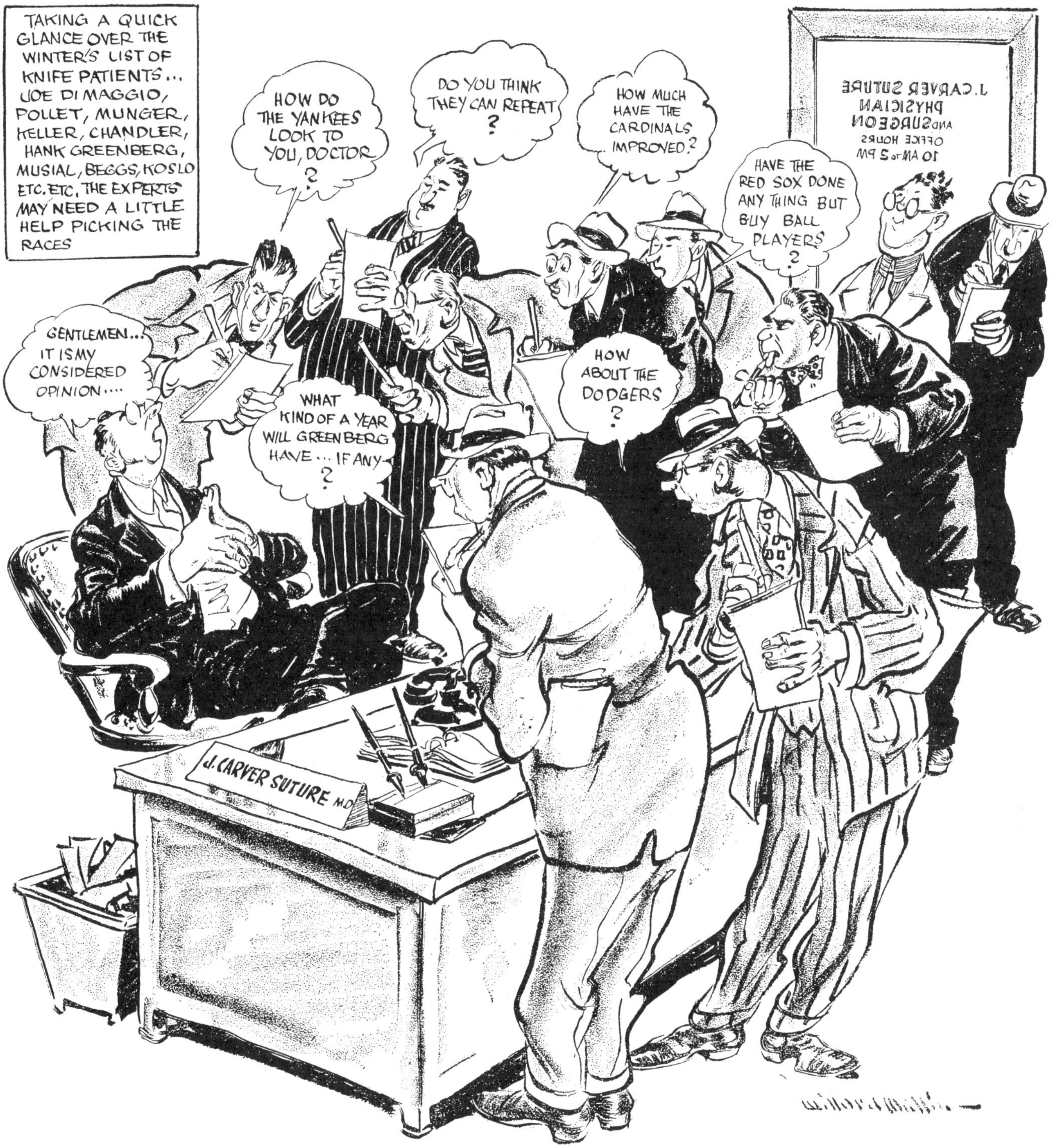
TAKING A QUICK GLANCE OVER THE WINTER'S LIST OF KNIFE PATIENTS... JOE DI MAGGIO, POLLET, MUNGER, KELLER, CHANDLER, HANK GREENBERG, MUSIAL, BEGGS, KOSLO ETC. ETC. THE EXPERTS MAY NEED A LITTLE HELP PICKING THE RACES
J. CARVER SUTURE PHYSICIAN AND SURGEON OFFICE HOURS 10 AM to 2 PM
HOW MUCH HAVE THE CARDINALS IMPROVED?
DO YOU THINK THEY CAN REPEAT?
HOW DO THE YANKEES LOOK TO YOU, DOCTOR?
HAVE THE RED SOX DONE ANY THING BUT BUY BALL PLAYERS?
HOW ABOUT THE DODGERS?
WHAT KIND OF A YEAR WILL GREENBERG HAVE... IF ANY?
GENTLEMEN... IT IS MY CONSIDERED OPINION....
J. CARVER SUTURE M.D.

In the 1947–1948 off-season, a number of star players had surgery for one ailment or another. Joe DiMaggio was probably the most famous, followed by Hank Greenberg. Greenberg had surgery on his elbow in December 1947, but he still decided to retire before the start of the 1948 season.

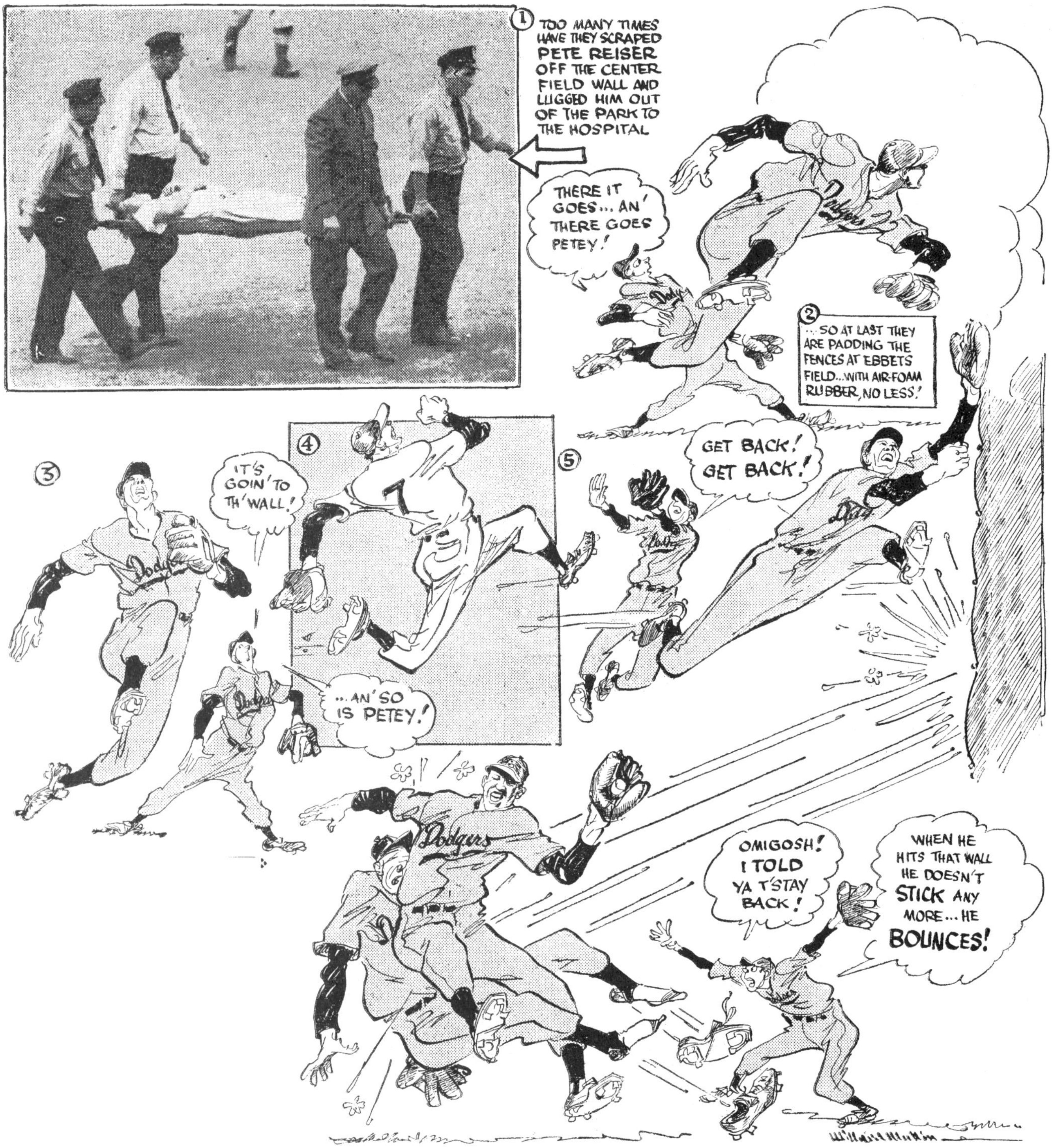
① TOO MANY TIMES HAVE THEY SCRAPED PETE REISER OFF THE CENTER FIELD WALL AND LUGGED HIM OUT OF THE PARK TO THE HOSPITAL
THERE IT GOES... AN' THERE GOES PETEY!
② ...SO AT LAST THEY ARE PADDING THE FENCES AT EBBETS FIELD...WITH AIR-FOAM RUBBER, NO LESS!
③
IT'S GOIN' TO TH' WALL!
...AN' SO IS PETEY!
④
⑤
GET BACK! GET BACK!
OMIGOSH! I TOLD YA T'STAY BACK!
WHEN HE HITS THAT WALL HE DOESN'T STICK ANY MORE... HE BOUNCES!

As a 22-year-old rookie in 1941, Peter Reiser led the National League in hitting. The following year, he was hitting .383 in August when he ran full speed into the outfield wall. This began a series of injuries that ultimately curtailed his career and robbed him of his greatness. Reiser was taken off the field on a stretcher a record 11 times. When Mullin drew this cartoon in 1948, Reiser was at the end of his career with the Dodgers. He only played parts of four more seasons before retiring completely.

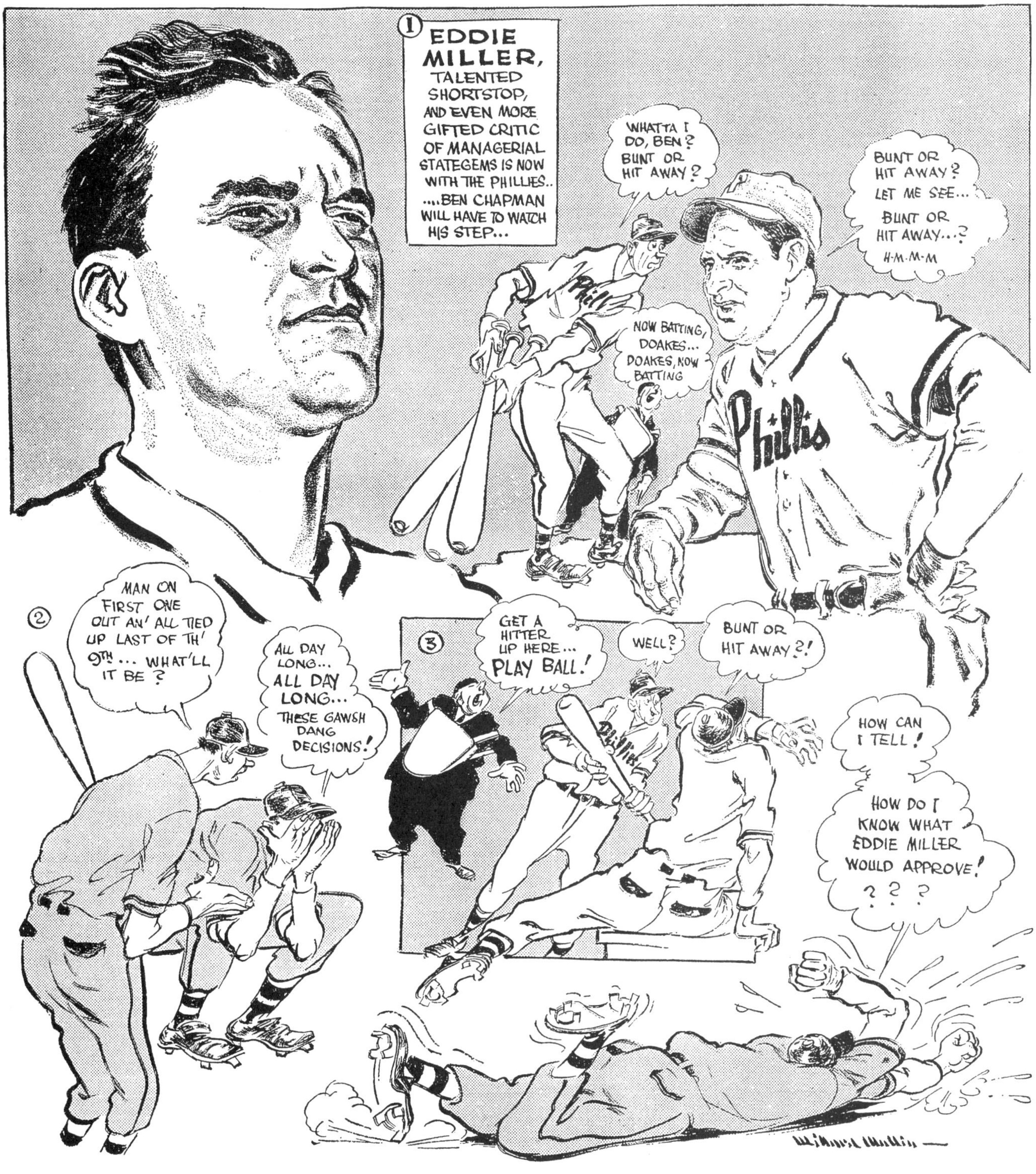

1
EDDIE MILLER, TALENTED SHORTSTOP, AND EVEN MORE GIFTED CRITIC OF MANAGERIAL STATEGEMS IS NOW WITH THE PHILLIES.. ....BEN CHAPMAN WILL HAVE TO WATCH HIS STEP...
WHATTA I DO, BEN? BUNT OR HIT AWAY?
BUNT OR HIT AWAY? LET ME SEE... BUNT OR HIT AWAY...? H-M-M-M
NOW BATTING, DOAKES... DOAKES, NOW BATTING
Phillies
2
MAN ON FIRST ONE OUT AN' ALL TIED UP LAST OF TH' 9TH... WHAT'LL IT BE?
ALL DAY LONG... ALL DAY LONG... THESE GAWSH DANG DECISIONS!
3
GET A HITTER UP HERE... PLAY BALL!
WELL?
BUNT OR HIT AWAY?!
HOW CAN I TELL!
HOW DO I KNOW WHAT EDDIE MILLER WOULD APPROVE! ? ? ?

Ben Chapman joined the New York Yankees in 1930 and played for a number of teams through 1947. In 1945, he was named manager of the last-place Phillies. In 1947, Chapman, one of the most notorious bigots ever to play baseball, opposed the Dodgers' bringing Jackie Robinson into the major leagues. His vitriol was so intense that it actually increased public sympathy for Robinson. Chapman was fired as manager a couple of months after this drawing appeared in February of 1948.

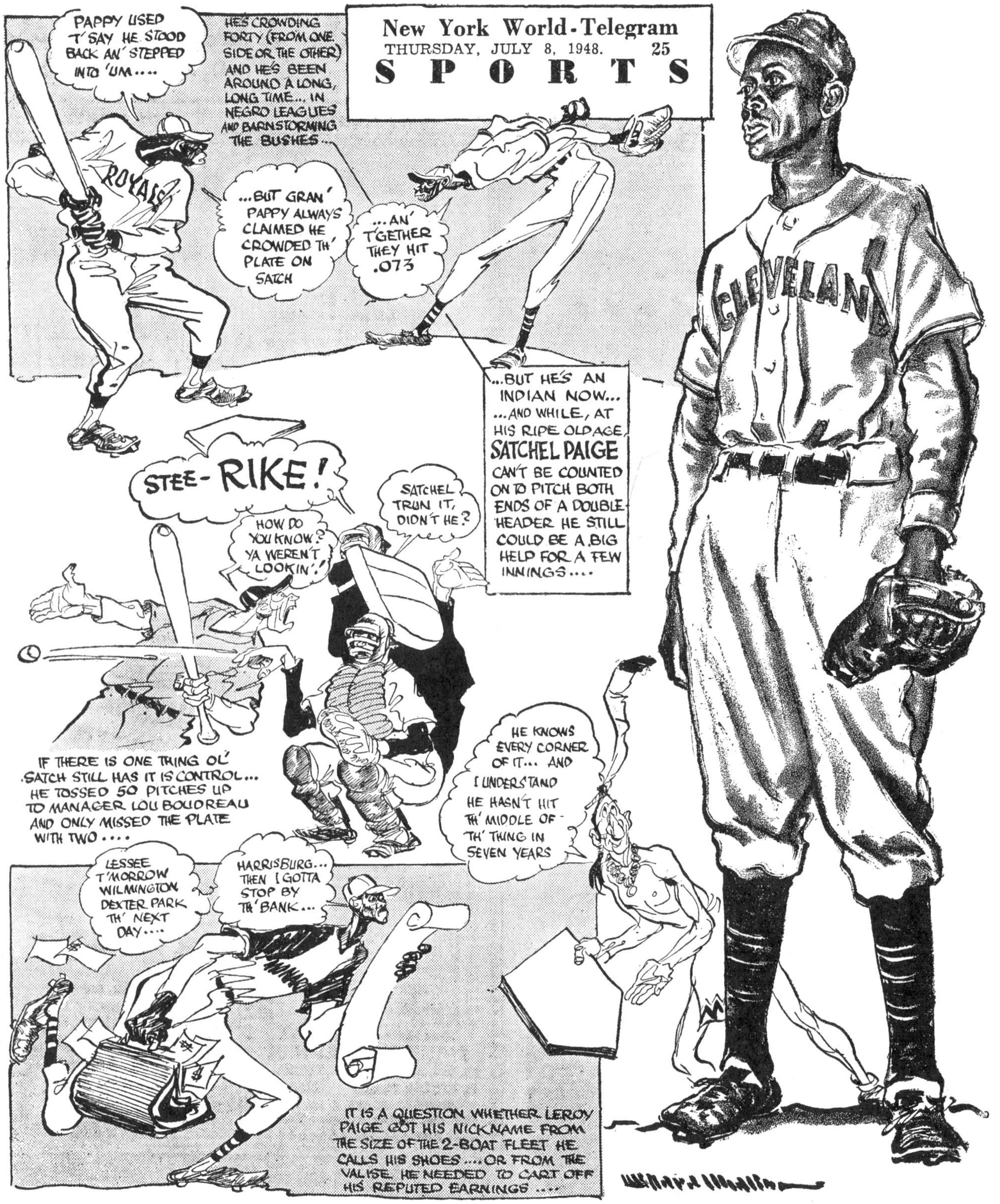
New York World-Telegram
THURSDAY, JULY 8, 1948. 25
SPORTS
PAPPY USED T' SAY HE STOOD BACK AN' STEPPED INTO 'UM....
HE'S CROWDING FORTY (FROM ONE SIDE OR THE OTHER) AND HE'S BEEN AROUND A LONG, LONG TIME... IN NEGRO LEAGUES AND BARNSTORMING THE BUSHES...
ROYALS
...BUT GRAN' PAPPY ALWAYS CLAIMED HE CROWDED TH' PLATE ON SATCH
...AN' T'GETHER THEY HIT .073
...BUT HE'S AN INDIAN NOW... ...AND WHILE, AT HIS RIPE OLD AGE, SATCHEL PAIGE CAN'T BE COUNTED ON TO PITCH BOTH ENDS OF A DOUBLE-HEADER HE STILL COULD BE A BIG HELP FOR A FEW INNINGS....
CLEVELAND
STEE-RIKE!
SATCHEL TRUN IT, DIDN'T HE?
HOW DO YOU KNOW? YA WEREN'T LOOKIN'!
IF THERE IS ONE THING OL' SATCH STILL HAS IT IS CONTROL... HE TOSSED 50 PITCHES UP TO MANAGER LOU BOUDREAU AND ONLY MISSED THE PLATE WITH TWO....
HE KNOWS EVERY CORNER OF IT... AND I UNDERSTAND HE HASN'T HIT TH' MIDDLE OF TH' THING IN SEVEN YEARS
LESSEE T'MORROW WILMINGTON DEXTER PARK TH' NEXT DAY....
HARRISBURG... THEN I GOTTA STOP BY TH' BANK...
IT IS A QUESTION WHETHER LEROY PAIGE GOT HIS NICKNAME FROM THE SIZE OF THE 2-BOAT FLEET HE CALLS HIS SHOES....OR FROM THE VALISE HE NEEDED TO CART OFF HIS REPUTED EARNINGS....

The legendary Satchel Paige played in the Negro Leagues for over 20 years before he was called up to the Cleveland Indians in July 1948 as a 42-year-old rookie. Paige played for the Indians and the Browns through 1953. In 1948, Paige became the first African American to pitch in the World Series.

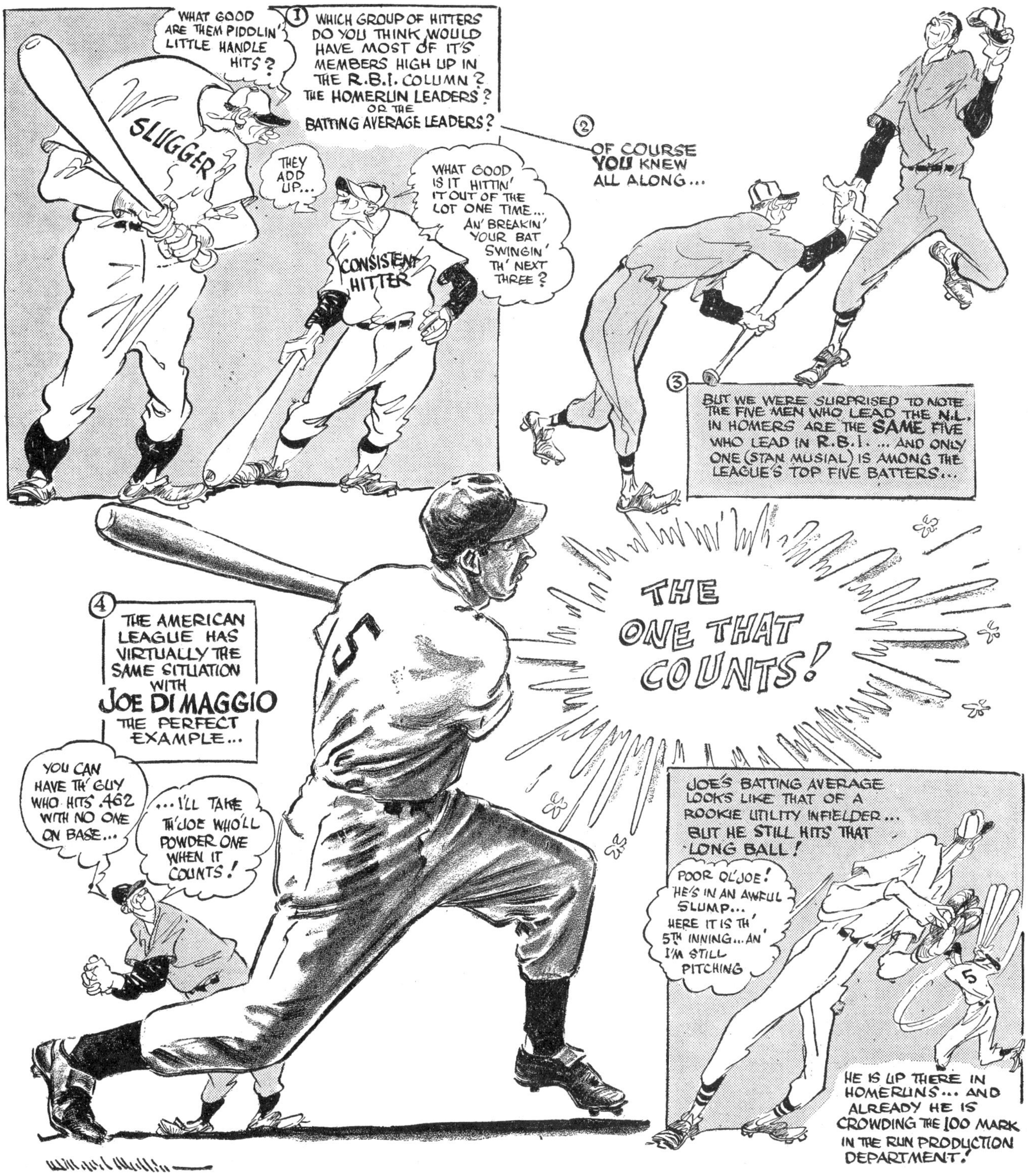

1 WHICH GROUP OF HITTERS DO YOU THINK WOULD HAVE MOST OF IT'S MEMBERS HIGH UP IN THE R.B.I. COLUMN? THE HOMERUN LEADERS? OR THE BATTING AVERAGE LEADERS?
WHAT GOOD ARE THEM PIDDLIN' LITTLE HANDLE HITS?
SLUGGER
THEY ADD UP...
WHAT GOOD IS IT HITTIN' IT OUT OF THE LOT ONE TIME... AN' BREAKIN' YOUR BAT SWINGIN' TH' NEXT THREE?
CONSISTENT HITTER
2 OF COURSE YOU KNEW ALL ALONG...
3 BUT WE WERE SURPRISED TO NOTE THE FIVE MEN WHO LEAD THE N.L. IN HOMERS ARE THE SAME FIVE WHO LEAD IN R.B.I. ... AND ONLY ONE (STAN MUSIAL) IS AMONG THE LEAGUE'S TOP FIVE BATTERS...
THE ONE THAT COUNTS!
4 THE AMERICAN LEAGUE HAS VIRTUALLY THE SAME SITUATION WITH JOE DI MAGGIO THE PERFECT EXAMPLE...
5
YOU CAN HAVE TH' GUY WHO HITS .462 WITH NO ONE ON BASE...
...I'LL TAKE TH' JOE WHO'LL POWDER ONE WHEN IT COUNTS!
JOE'S BATTING AVERAGE LOOKS LIKE THAT OF A ROOKIE UTILITY INFIELDER... BUT HE STILL HITS THAT LONG BALL!
POOR OL' JOE! HE'S IN AN AWFUL SLUMP... HERE IT IS TH' 5TH INNING... AN' I'M STILL PITCHING
HE IS UP THERE IN HOMERUNS... AND ALREADY HE IS CROWDING THE 100 MARK IN THE RUN PRODUCTION DEPARTMENT!

For much of 1948, Joe DiMaggio's batting average hovered under .300. Still, he was an extremely effective power hitter. While a late surge put his batting average above .300, he also led the American League in home runs (39) and RBIs (155).

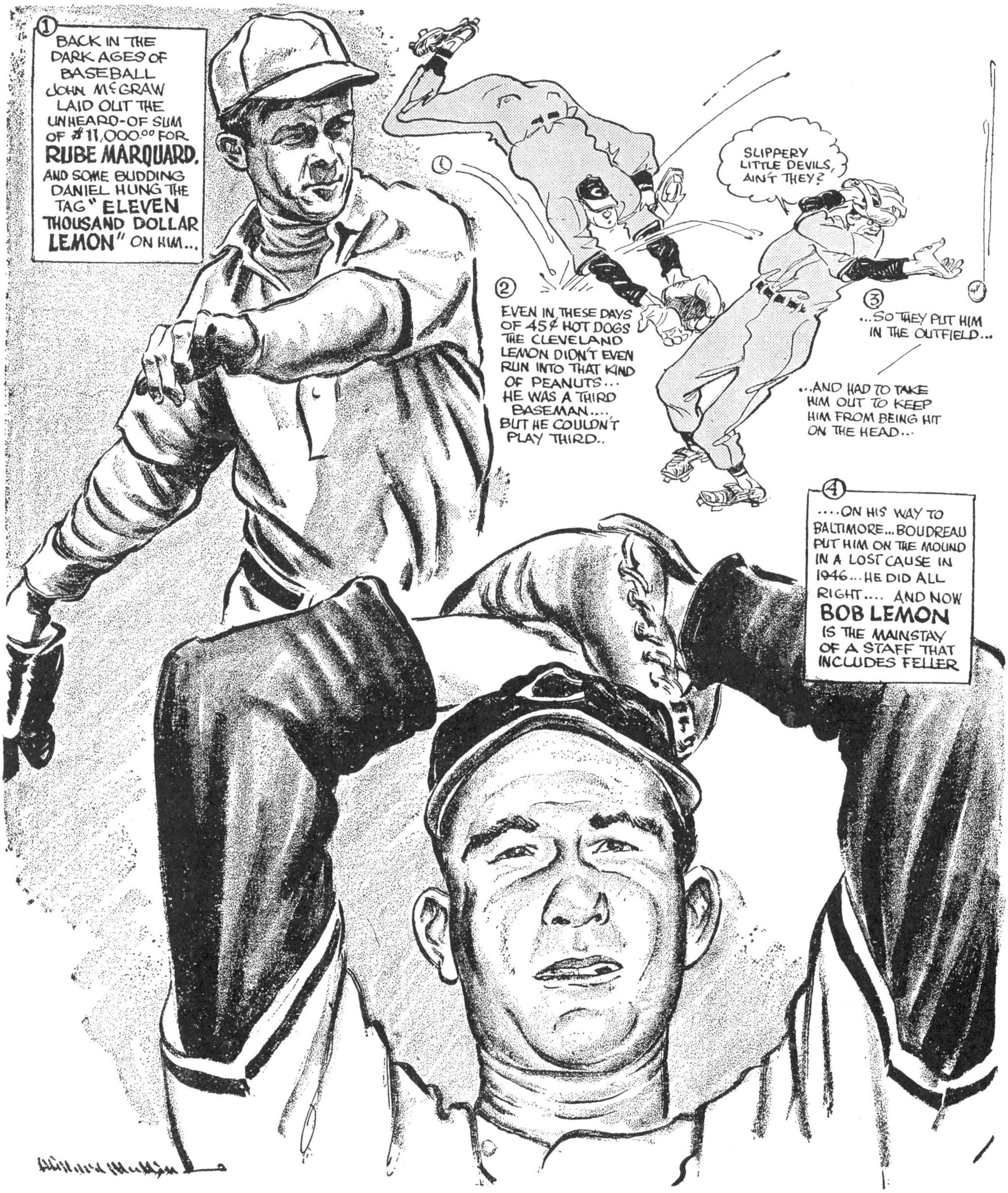

1
BACK IN THE DARK AGES OF BASEBALL JOHN McGRAW LAID OUT THE UNHEARD-OF SUM OF $11,000.00 FOR RUBE MARQUARD. AND SOME BUDDING DANIEL HUNG THE TAG "ELEVEN THOUSAND DOLLAR LEMON" ON HIM...
2
EVEN IN THESE DAYS OF 45¢ HOT DOGS THE CLEVELAND LEMON DIDN'T EVEN RUN INTO THAT KIND OF PEANUTS... HE WAS A THIRD BASEMAN.... BUT HE COULDN'T PLAY THIRD..
SLIPPERY LITTLE DEVILS, AIN'T THEY?
3
...SO THEY PUT HIM IN THE OUTFIELD...
...AND HAD TO TAKE HIM OUT TO KEEP HIM FROM BEING HIT ON THE HEAD...
4
....ON HIS WAY TO BALTIMORE...BOUDREAU PUT HIM ON THE MOUND IN A LOST CAUSE IN 1946... HE DID ALL RIGHT.... AND NOW BOB LEMON IS THE MAINSTAY OF A STAFF THAT INCLUDES FELLER

Bob Lemon was signed by the Cleveland Indians out of Woodrow Wilson High School in Long Beach, California, as a third baseman, but he proved to be such a miserable fielder that he was converted to a pitcher by manager Lou Boudreau in 1946. Lemon went on to seven seasons of 20 or more pitching wins and was elected to the Hall of Fame in 1976.

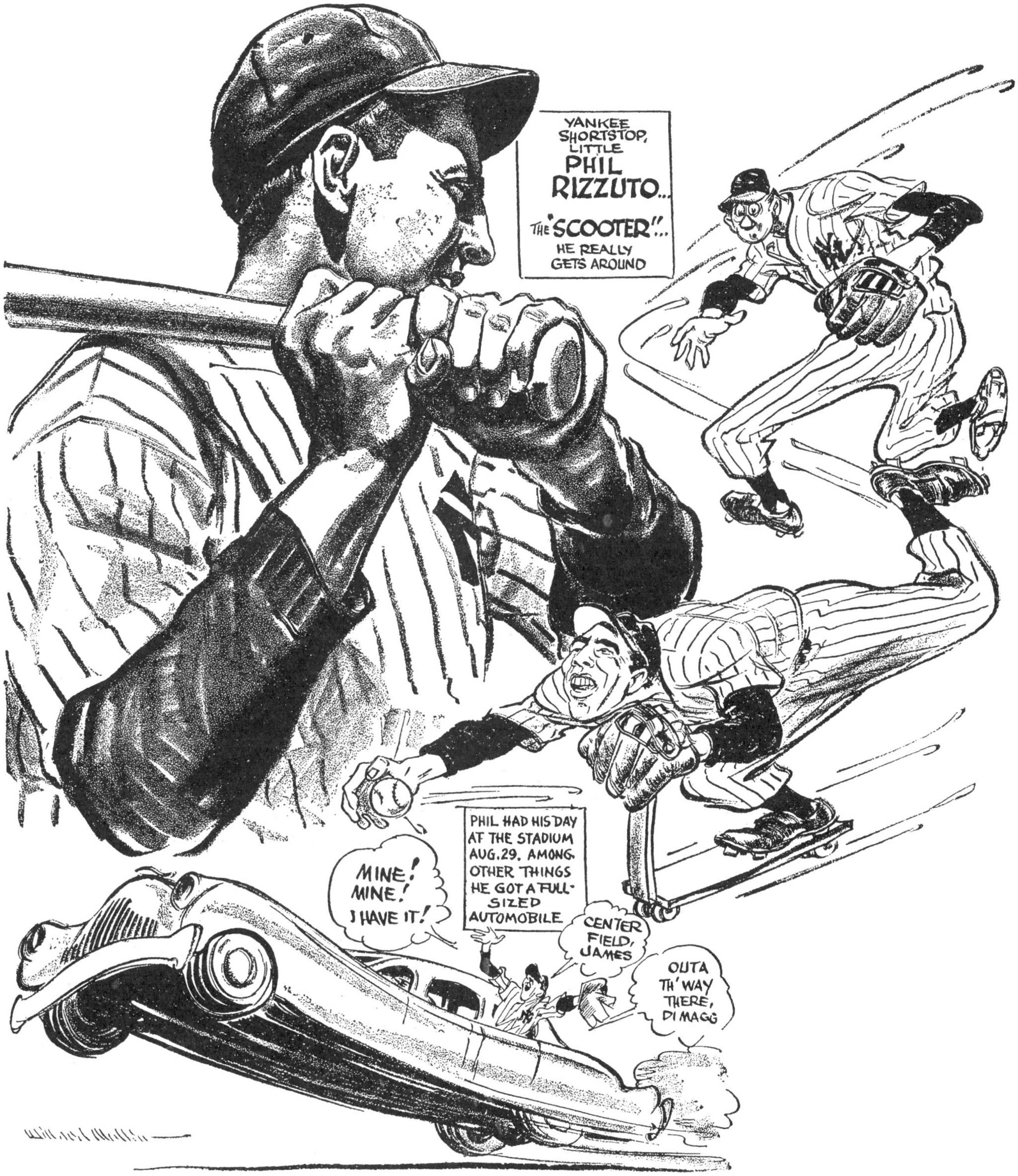
YANKEE SHORTSTOP, LITTLE PHIL RIZZUTO...
THE "SCOOTER"... HE REALLY GETS AROUND
PHIL HAD HIS DAY AT THE STADIUM AUG. 29. AMONG OTHER THINGS HE GOT A FULL-SIZED AUTOMOBILE
MINE! MINE! I HAVE IT!
CENTER FIELD, JAMES
OUTA TH' WAY THERE, DI MAGG

Phil Rizzuto joined the Yankees in 1941. By 1948, when this drawing was done, he was the premier defensive shortstop in baseball. He would further burnish his Hall of Fame credentials by hitting .324 in 1950 and winning the AL MVP.

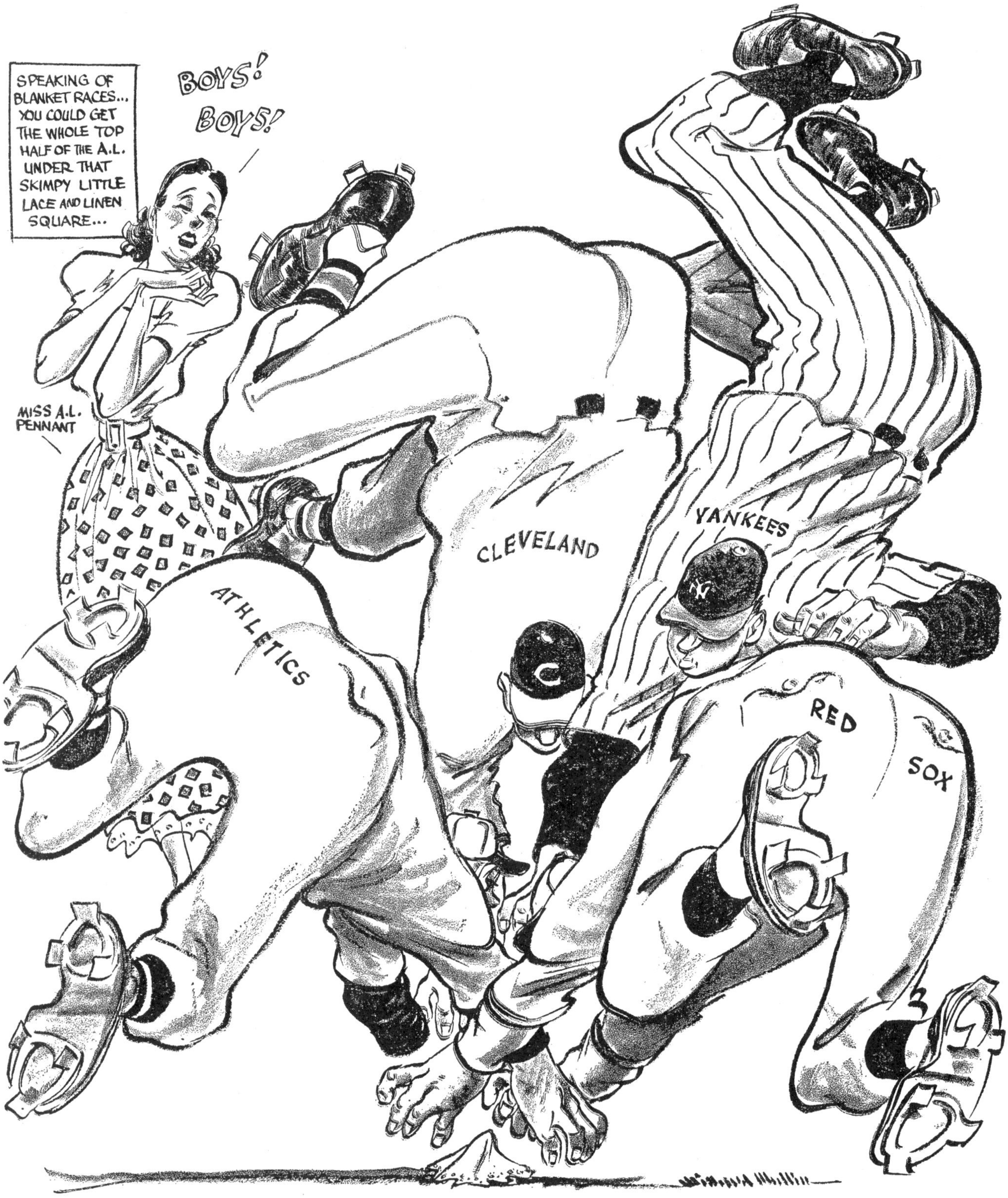
SPEAKING OF BLANKET RACES... YOU COULD GET THE WHOLE TOP HALF OF THE A.L. UNDER THAT SKIMPY LITTLE LACE AND LINEN SQUARE...
BOYS! BOYS!
MISS A.L. PENNANT
CLEVELAND
YANKEES
ATHLETICS
RED SOX

The 1948 American League pennant race was especially contentious, with the Cleveland Indians beating the Red Sox in a one-game playoff after the two teams finished the regular season tied. The Yankees were not far behind, finishing two-and-a-half games back of the Indians and one-and-a-half back of the Red Sox.

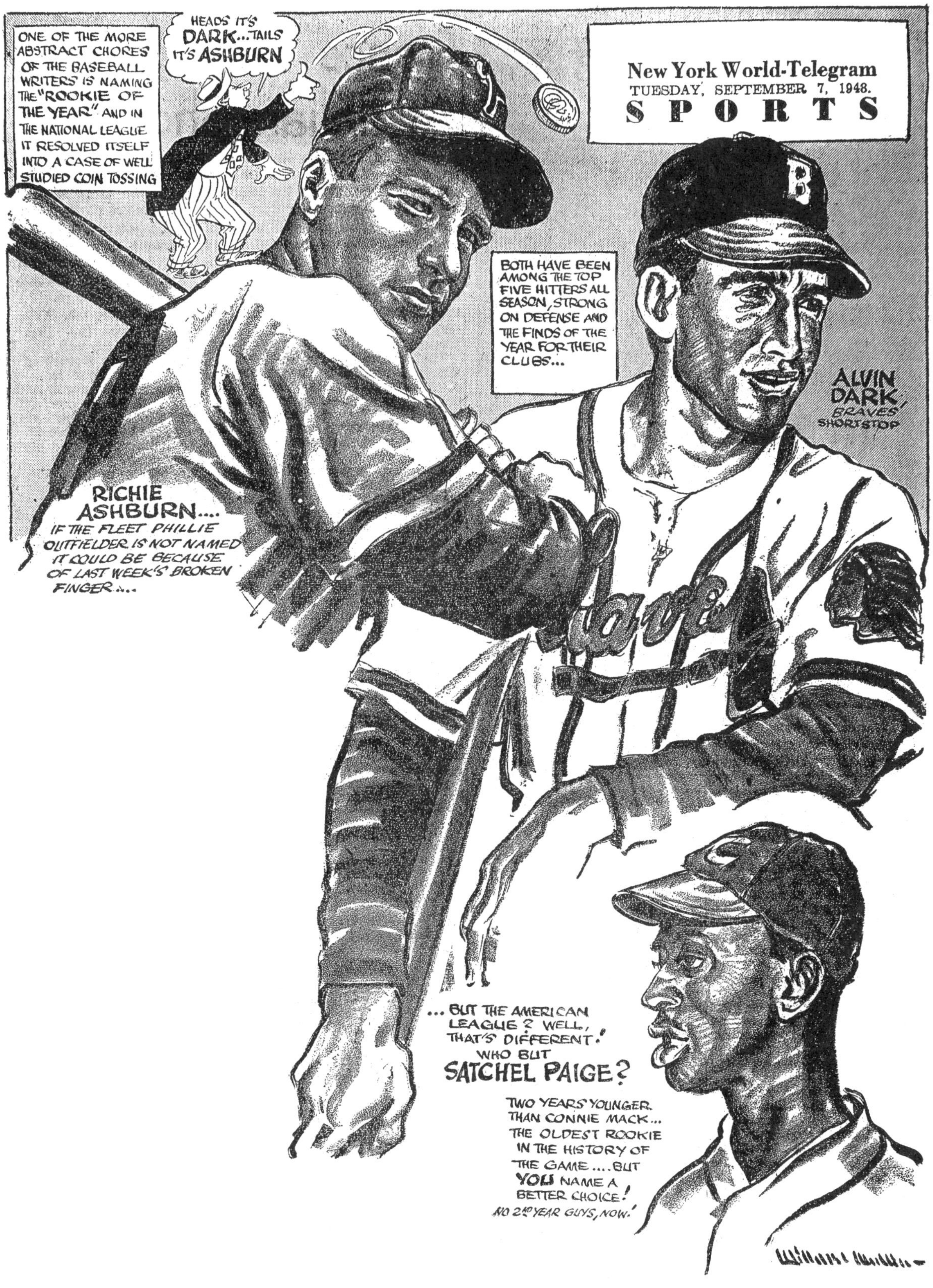
ONE OF THE MORE ABSTRACT CHORES OF THE BASEBALL WRITERS' IS NAMING THE "ROOKIE OF THE YEAR" AND IN THE NATIONAL LEAGUE IT RESOLVED ITSELF INTO A CASE OF WELL STUDIED COIN TOSSING
HEADS IT'S DARK...TAILS IT'S ASHBURN
New York World-Telegram
TUESDAY, SEPTEMBER 7, 1948.
SPORTS
BOTH HAVE BEEN AMONG THE TOP FIVE HITTERS ALL SEASON, STRONG ON DEFENSE AND THE FINDS OF THE YEAR FOR THEIR CLUBS...
ALVIN DARK, BRAVES' SHORTSTOP
RICHIE ASHBURN....
IF THE FLEET PHILLIE OUTFIELDER IS NOT NAMED IT COULD BE BECAUSE OF LAST WEEK'S BROKEN FINGER...
...BUT THE AMERICAN LEAGUE? WELL, THAT'S DIFFERENT! WHO BUT
SATCHEL PAIGE?
TWO YEARS YOUNGER THAN CONNIE MACK... THE OLDEST ROOKIE IN THE HISTORY OF THE GAME....BUT YOU NAME A BETTER CHOICE!
NO 2ND YEAR GUYS, NOW!

1948 was only the second year that the Baseball Writers' Association chose a "Rookie of the Year." In 1947, the winner was Jackie Robinson. In 1948, the choice came down to one of three: Alvin Dark and future Hall of Famers Richie Ashburn and Satchel Paige. Dark won the honor, but Paige and Ashburn certainly had more impressive careers.

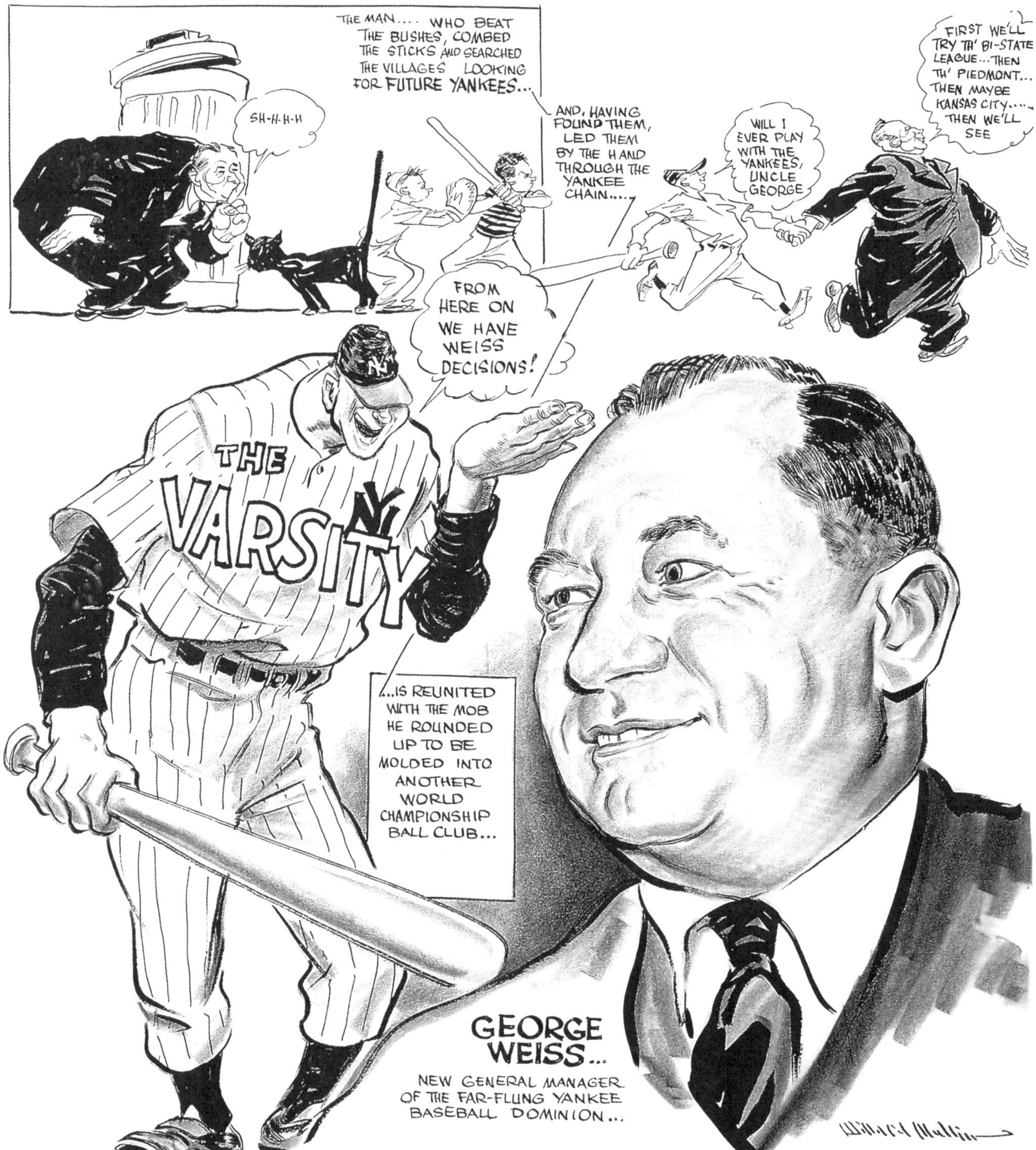
THE MAN.... WHO BEAT THE BUSHES, COMBED THE STICKS AND SEARCHED THE VILLAGES LOOKING FOR FUTURE YANKEES...
SH-H-H-H
AND, HAVING FOUND THEM, LED THEM BY THE HAND THROUGH THE YANKEE CHAIN....
WILL I EVER PLAY WITH THE YANKEES, UNCLE GEORGE
FIRST WE'LL TRY TH' BI-STATE LEAGUE...THEN TH' PIEDMONT...THEN MAYBE KANSAS CITY..... THEN WE'LL SEE
FROM HERE ON WE HAVE WEISS DECISIONS!
THE VARSITY
NY
...IS REUNITED WITH THE MOB HE ROUNDED UP TO BE MOLDED INTO ANOTHER WORLD CHAMPIONSHIP BALL CLUB...
GEORGE WEISS...
NEW GENERAL MANAGER OF THE FAR-FLUNG YANKEE BASEBALL DOMINION...

In 1932, the Yankees' George Weiss started building one of the best farm systems in baseball. By 1947, when Weiss was appointed General Manager (GM), that farm system had produced Joe DiMaggio, Phil Rizzuto, and Yogi Berra. During Weiss's tenure as GM, the Yankees won 10 pennants and seven World Series between 1947 and 1960.

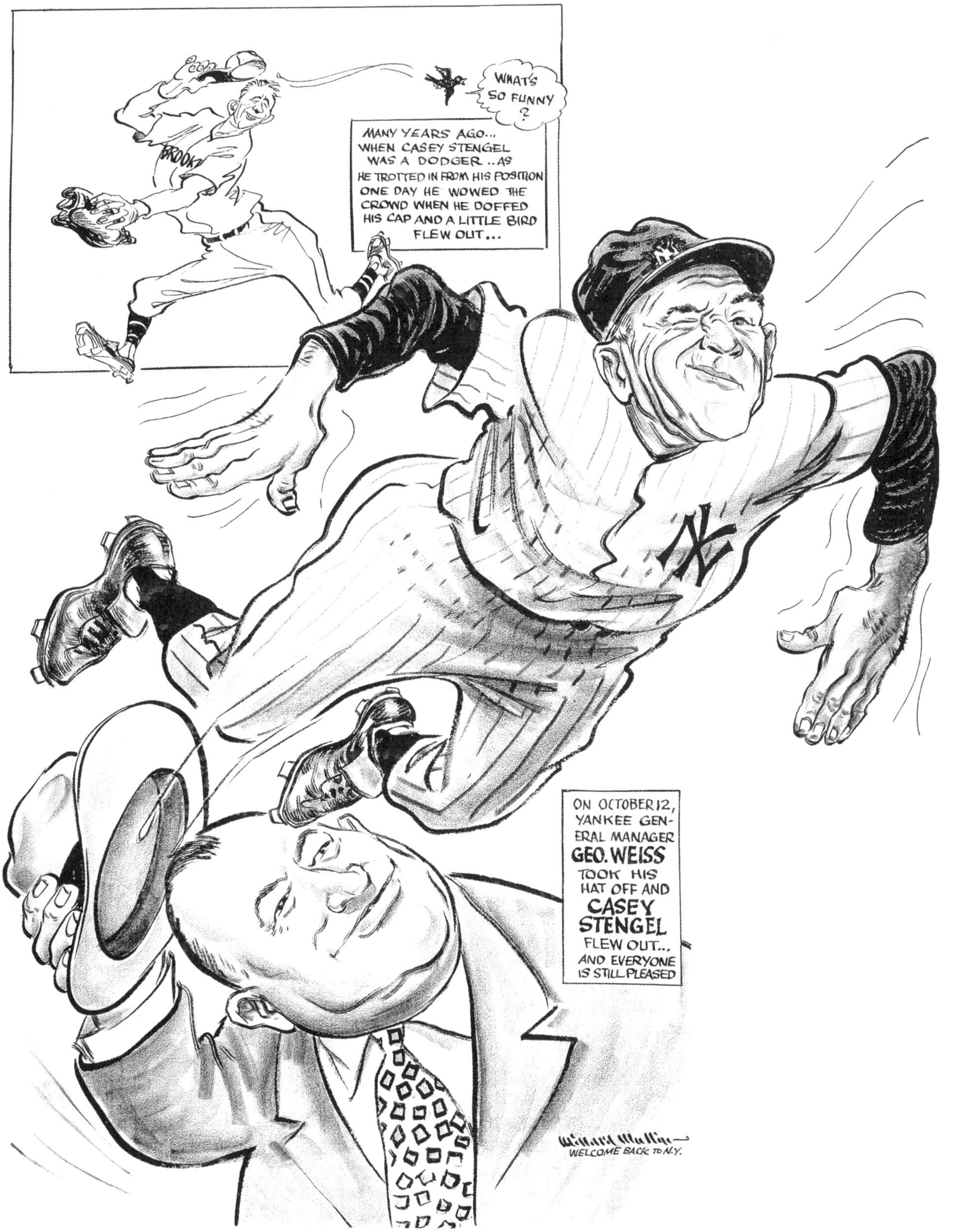
WHAT'S SO FUNNY ?
MANY YEARS AGO... WHEN CASEY STENGEL WAS A DODGER.. AS HE TROTTED IN FROM HIS POSITION ONE DAY HE WOWED THE CROWD WHEN HE DOFFED HIS CAP AND A LITTLE BIRD FLEW OUT...
ON OCTOBER 12, YANKEE GENERAL MANAGER GEO. WEISS TOOK HIS HAT OFF AND CASEY STENGEL FLEW OUT... AND EVERYONE IS STILL PLEASED
WELCOME BACK TO N.Y.

Casey Stengel was a surprise pick to manage the American League Yankees in 1949, after unsuccessful stints with Brooklyn and Boston in the National League. Mullin parodied an incident from Stengel's playing career in this cartoon from late 1948.

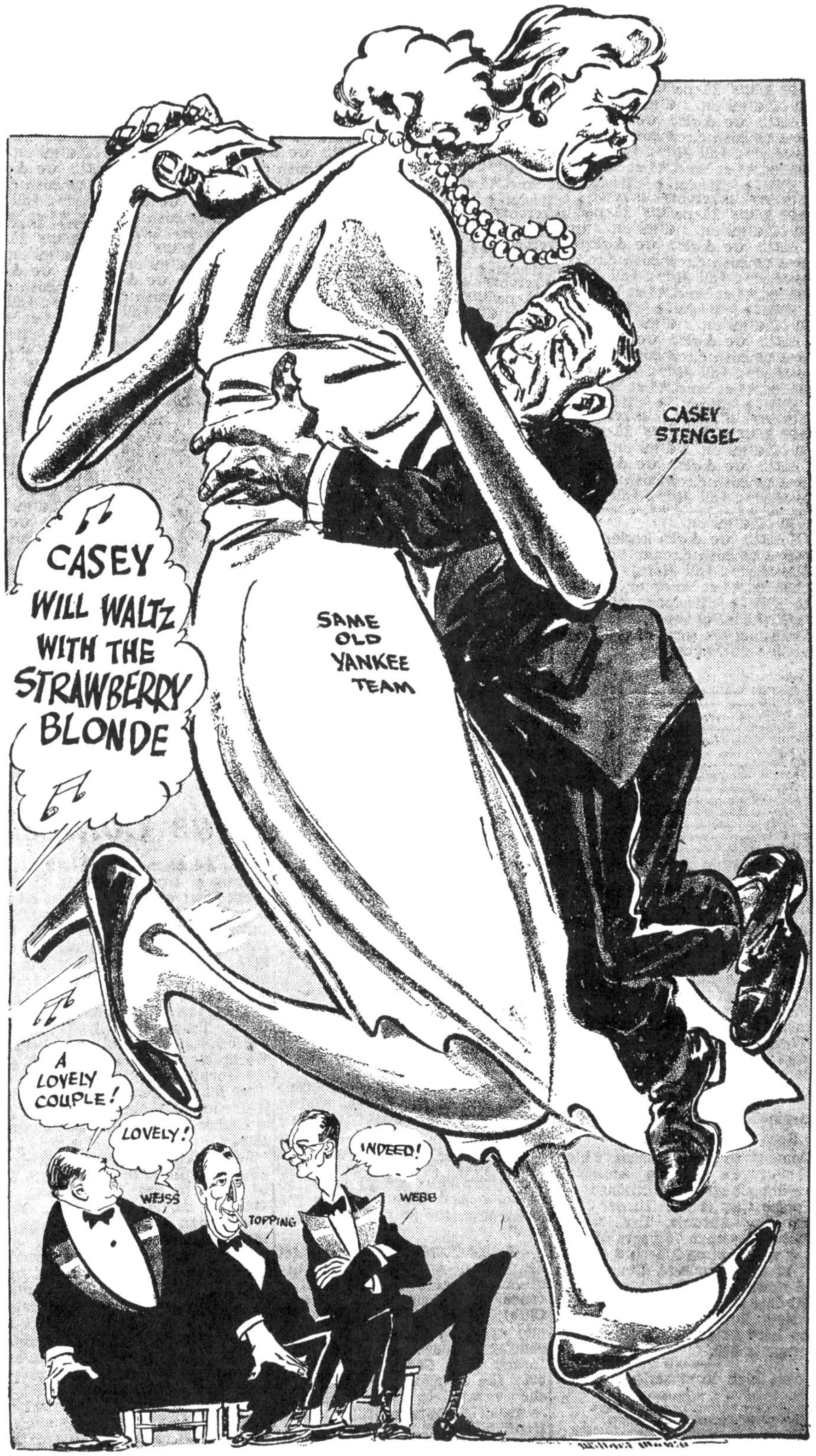
CASEY STENGEL
CASEY WILL WALTZ WITH THE STRAWBERRY BLONDE
SAME OLD YANKEE TEAM
A LOVELY COUPLE!
LOVELY!
INDEED!
WEISS
TOPPING
WEBB

When Casey Stengel took over as manager of the Yankees in 1949, they were a veteran team with their two biggest stars, Joe DiMaggio and Tommy Henrich, well into their 30s. It would be a couple of more years before the changing of the guard, when Whitey Ford joined the team in 1950 and Mickey Mantle arrived in 1951.

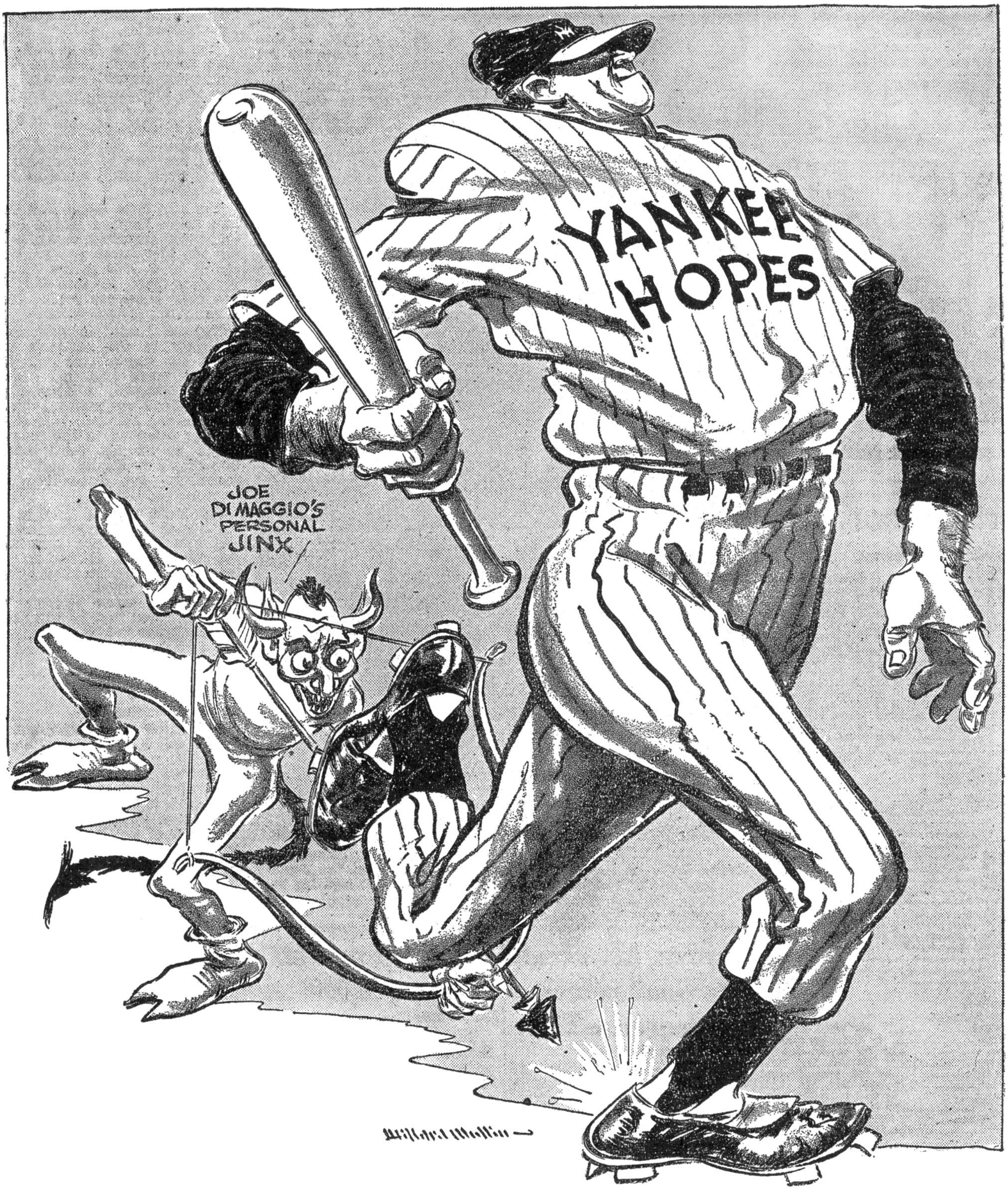
YANKEE HOPES
JOE DI MAGGIO'S PERSONAL JINX
Willard Mullin

Joe DiMaggio played most of 1948 with pain in his heel due to bone spurs. He began the 1949 season still in pain. But one day in mid-June he woke up and the pain was gone. DiMaggio then went on a tear with the Yankees, beating the Red Sox in the final game of the season to win the AL pennant.

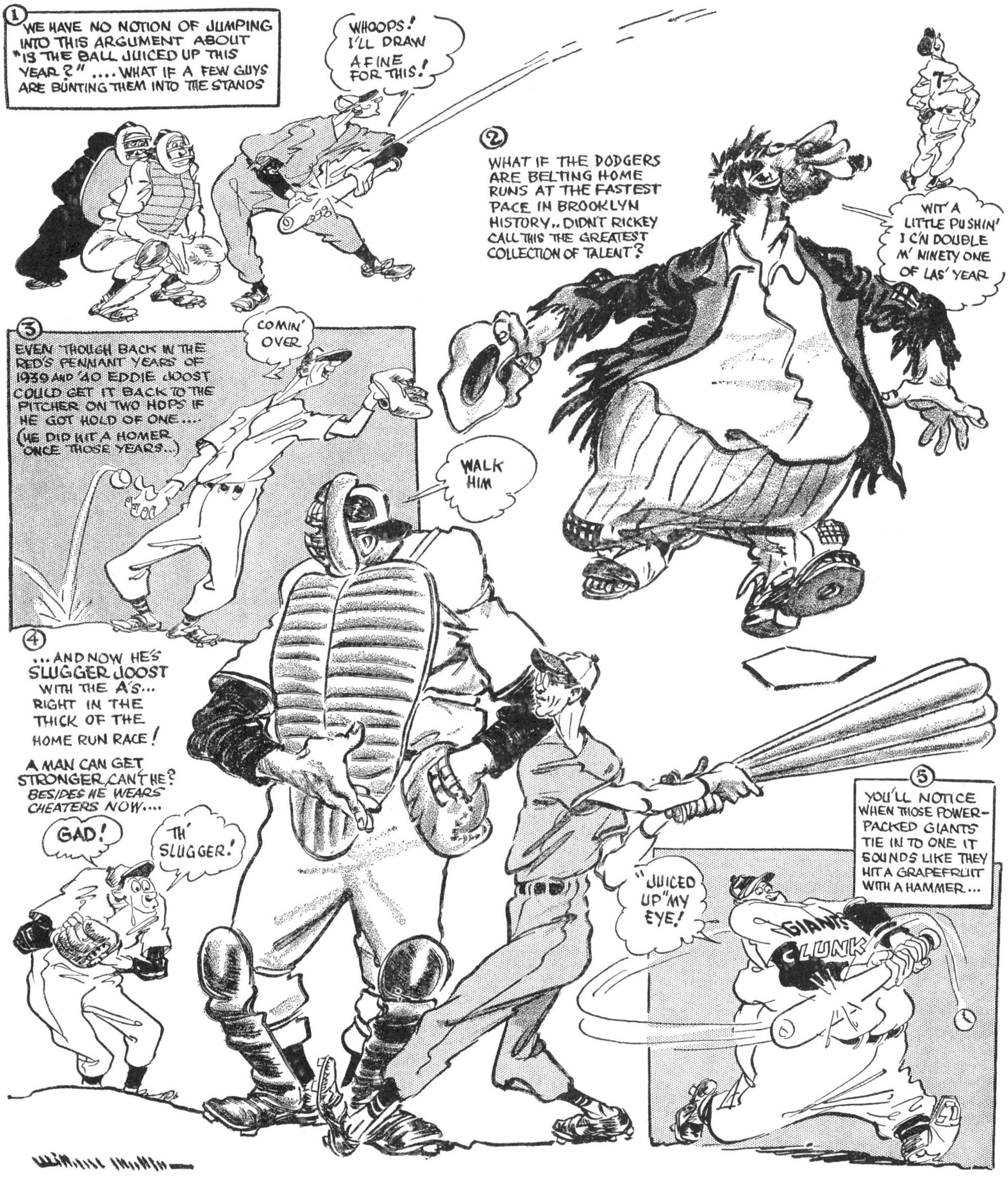
1
WE HAVE NO NOTION OF JUMPING INTO THIS ARGUMENT ABOUT "IS THE BALL JUICED UP THIS YEAR?" .... WHAT IF A FEW GUYS ARE BUNTING THEM INTO THE STANDS
WHOOPS! I'LL DRAW A FINE FOR THIS!
2
WHAT IF THE DODGERS ARE BELTING HOME RUNS AT THE FASTEST PACE IN BROOKLYN HISTORY.. DIDN'T RICKEY CALL THIS THE GREATEST COLLECTION OF TALENT?
WIT' A LITTLE PUSHIN' I C'N DOUBLE M' NINETY ONE OF LAS' YEAR
3
EVEN THOUGH BACK IN THE RED'S PENNANT YEARS OF 1939 AND '40 EDDIE JOOST COULD GET IT BACK TO THE PITCHER ON TWO HOPS IF HE GOT HOLD OF ONE....
(HE DID HIT A HOMER ONCE THOSE YEARS...)
COMIN' OVER
WALK HIM
4
...AND NOW HE'S SLUGGER JOOST WITH THE A'S... RIGHT IN THE THICK OF THE HOME RUN RACE!
A MAN CAN GET STRONGER, CAN'T HE? BESIDES HE WEARS CHEATERS NOW....
GAD!
TH' SLUGGER!
"JUICED UP" MY EYE!
5
YOU'LL NOTICE WHEN THOSE POWER-PACKED GIANTS TIE IN TO ONE IT SOUNDS LIKE THEY HIT A GRAPEFRUIT WITH A HAMMER...
GIANTS
CLUNK

There have always been allegations that the baseball has been made livelier — "juiced." 1949 was one of those years, with Mullin definitely staking the middle ground.

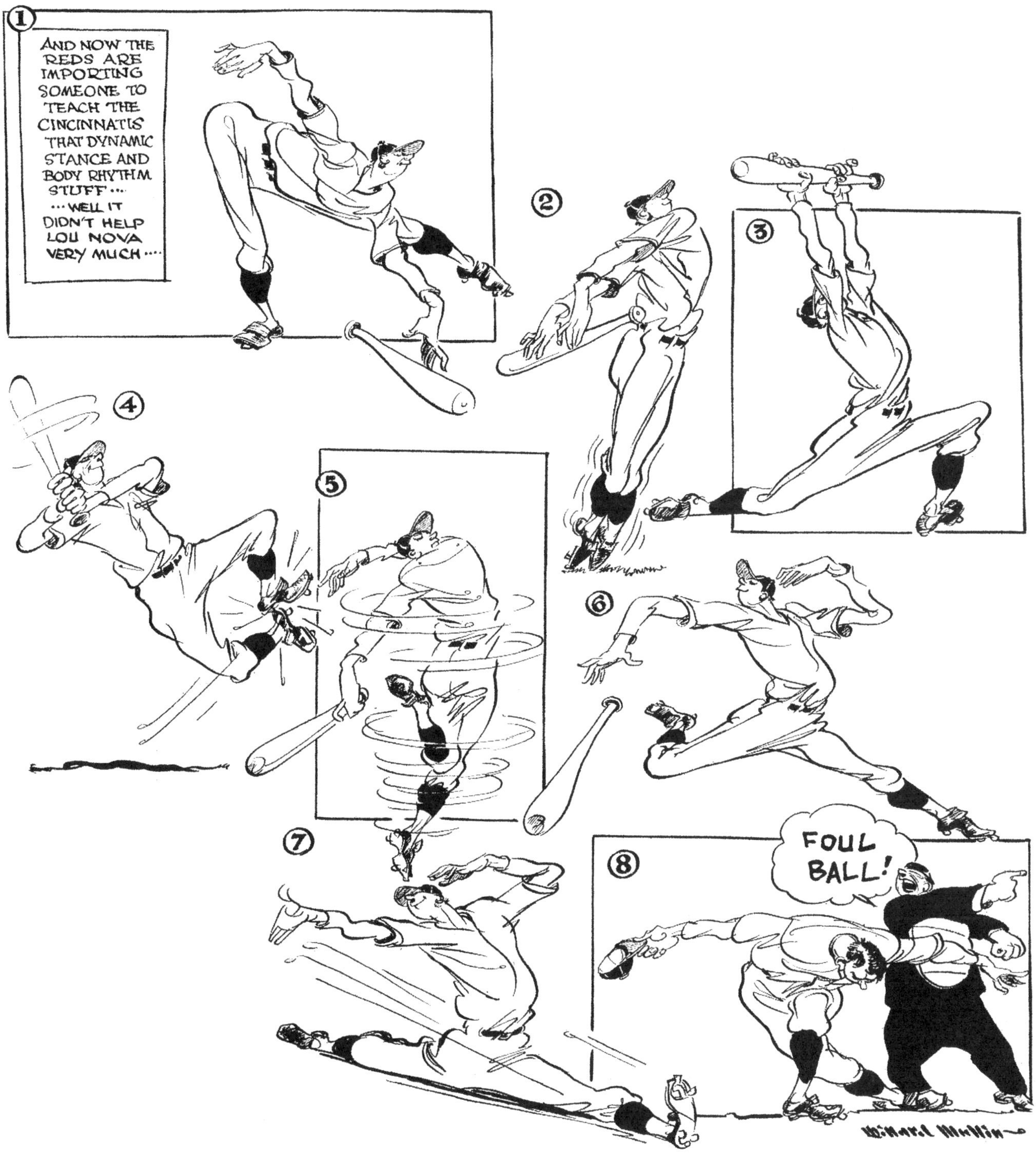
AND NOW THE REDS ARE IMPORTING SOMEONE TO TEACH THE CINCINNATIS THAT DYNAMIC STANCE AND BODY RHYTHM STUFF... ...WELL IT DIDN'T HELP LOU NOVA VERY MUCH....
FOUL BALL!
Willard Mullin

Mullin's ability to animate the body was legendary, and this drawing from the late 1940s illustrates the master at his best.

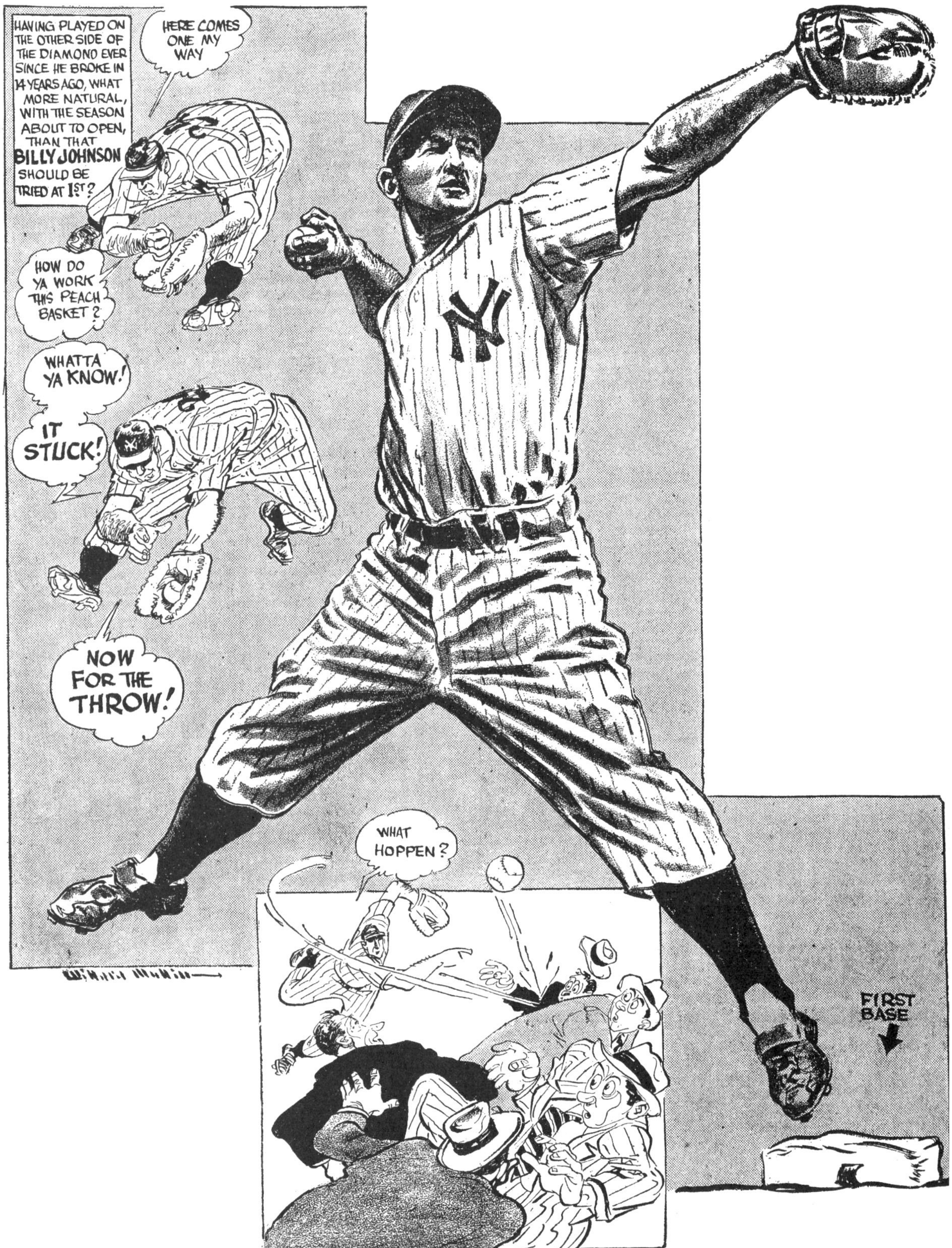
HAVING PLAYED ON THE OTHER SIDE OF THE DIAMOND EVER SINCE HE BROKE IN 14 YEARS AGO, WHAT MORE NATURAL, WITH THE SEASON ABOUT TO OPEN, THAN THAT BILLY JOHNSON SHOULD BE TRIED AT 1ST?
HERE COMES ONE MY WAY
HOW DO YA WORK THIS PEACH BASKET?
WHATTA YA KNOW!
IT STUCK!
NOW FOR THE THROW!
WHAT HOPPEN?
FIRST BASE

Billy Johnson was a utility infielder who mostly played third base during his 10-year major league career, but in the spring of 1949, new Yankees manager Casey Stengel apparently tried him out at first base.

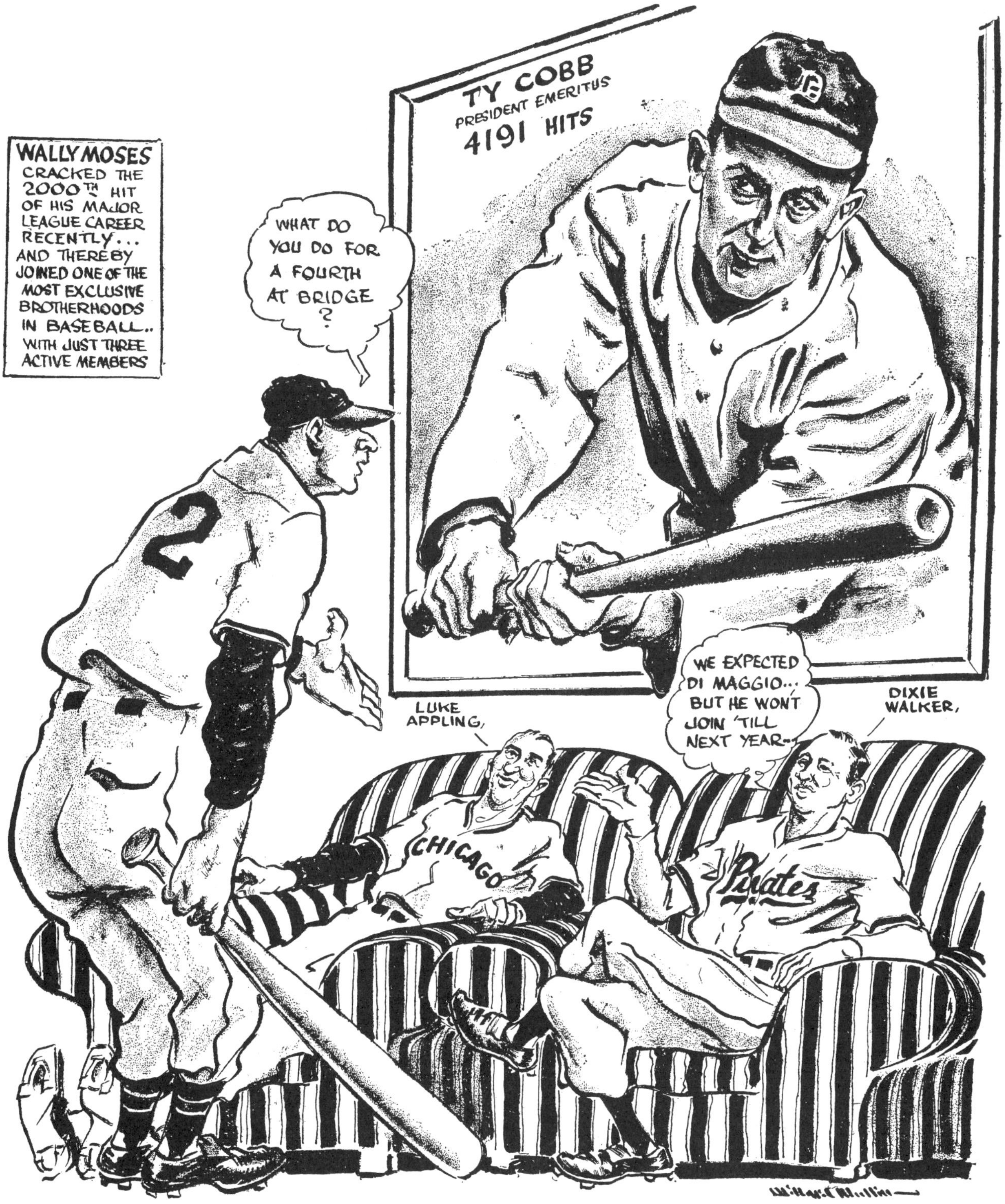
WALLY MOSES CRACKED THE 2000TH HIT OF HIS MAJOR LEAGUE CAREER RECENTLY... AND THEREBY JOINED ONE OF THE MOST EXCLUSIVE BROTHERHOODS IN BASEBALL.. WITH JUST THREE ACTIVE MEMBERS
TY COBB
PRESIDENT EMERITUS
4191 HITS
WHAT DO YOU DO FOR A FOURTH AT BRIDGE ?
WE EXPECTED DI MAGGIO... BUT HE WON'T JOIN 'TILL NEXT YEAR-
LUKE APPLING,
DIXIE WALKER,
CHICAGO
Pirates
2

In 1949, at the age of 38, Wally Moses got his 2,000th career hit. At that time, a player hadn't amassed 3,000 since Paul Waner had done it in 1942, and there would not be another member to join the 3,000-hit club until Stan Musial in 1958.

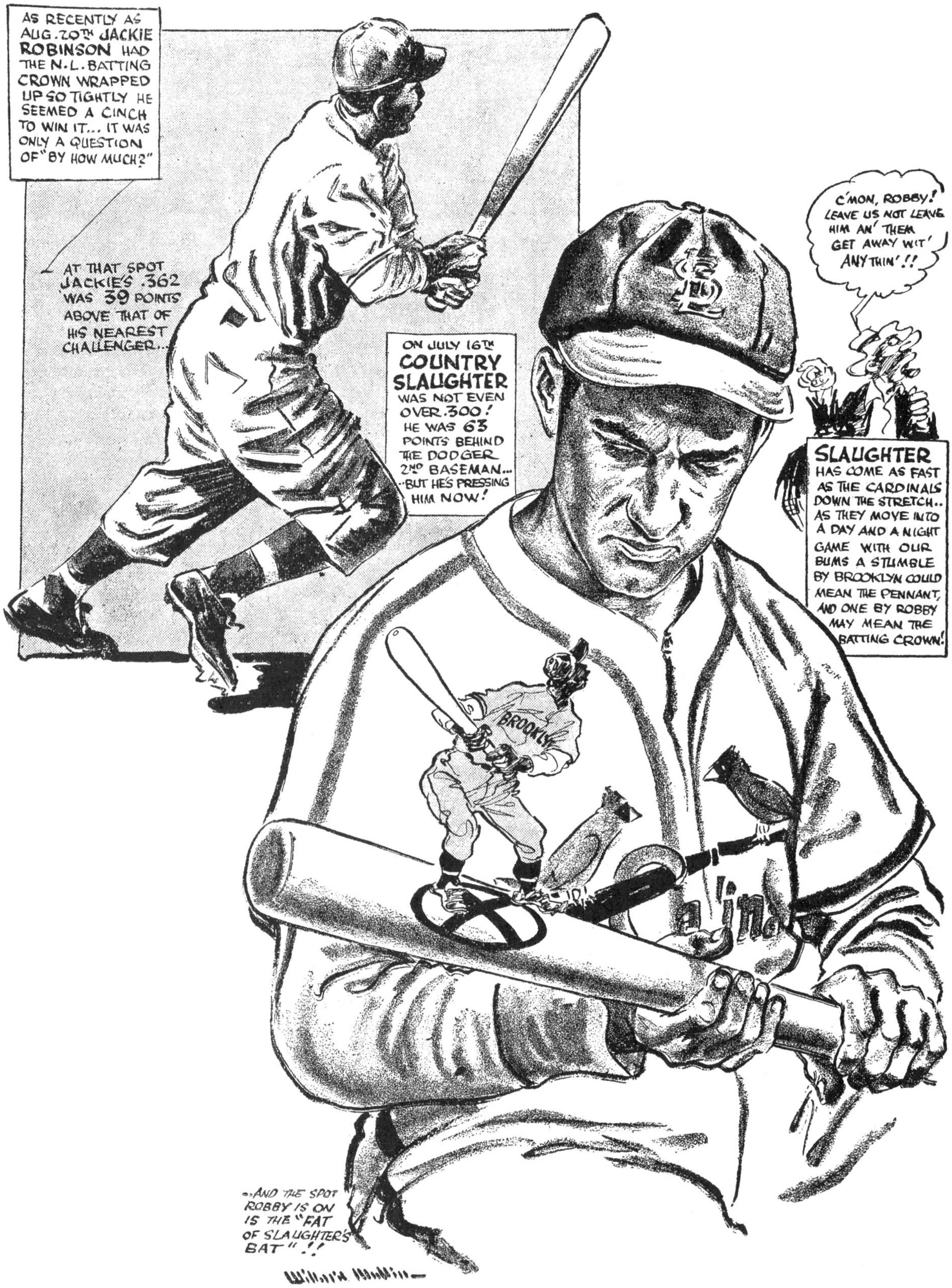

AS RECENTLY AS AUG. 20TH JACKIE ROBINSON HAD THE N.L. BATTING CROWN WRAPPED UP SO TIGHTLY HE SEEMED A CINCH TO WIN IT... IT WAS ONLY A QUESTION OF "BY HOW MUCH?"
AT THAT SPOT JACKIE'S .362 WAS 39 POINTS ABOVE THAT OF HIS NEAREST CHALLENGER...
ON JULY 16TH COUNTRY SLAUGHTER WAS NOT EVEN OVER .300! HE WAS 63 POINTS BEHIND THE DODGER 2ND BASEMAN... BUT HE'S PRESSING HIM NOW!
C'MON, ROBBY! LEAVE US NOT LEAVE HIM AN' THEM GET AWAY WIT' ANYTHIN'!!
SLAUGHTER HAS COME AS FAST AS THE CARDINALS DOWN THE STRETCH.. AS THEY MOVE INTO A DAY AND A NIGHT GAME WITH OUR BUMS A STUMBLE BY BROOKLYN COULD MEAN THE PENNANT, AND ONE BY ROBBY MAY MEAN THE BATTING CROWN!
BROOKLYN
..AND THE SPOT ROBBY IS ON IS THE "FAT OF SLAUGHTER'S BAT"!!

In 1949, Jackie Robinson won the National League batting crown but had to hold off a late charge by the Cardinals' Enos Slaughter.

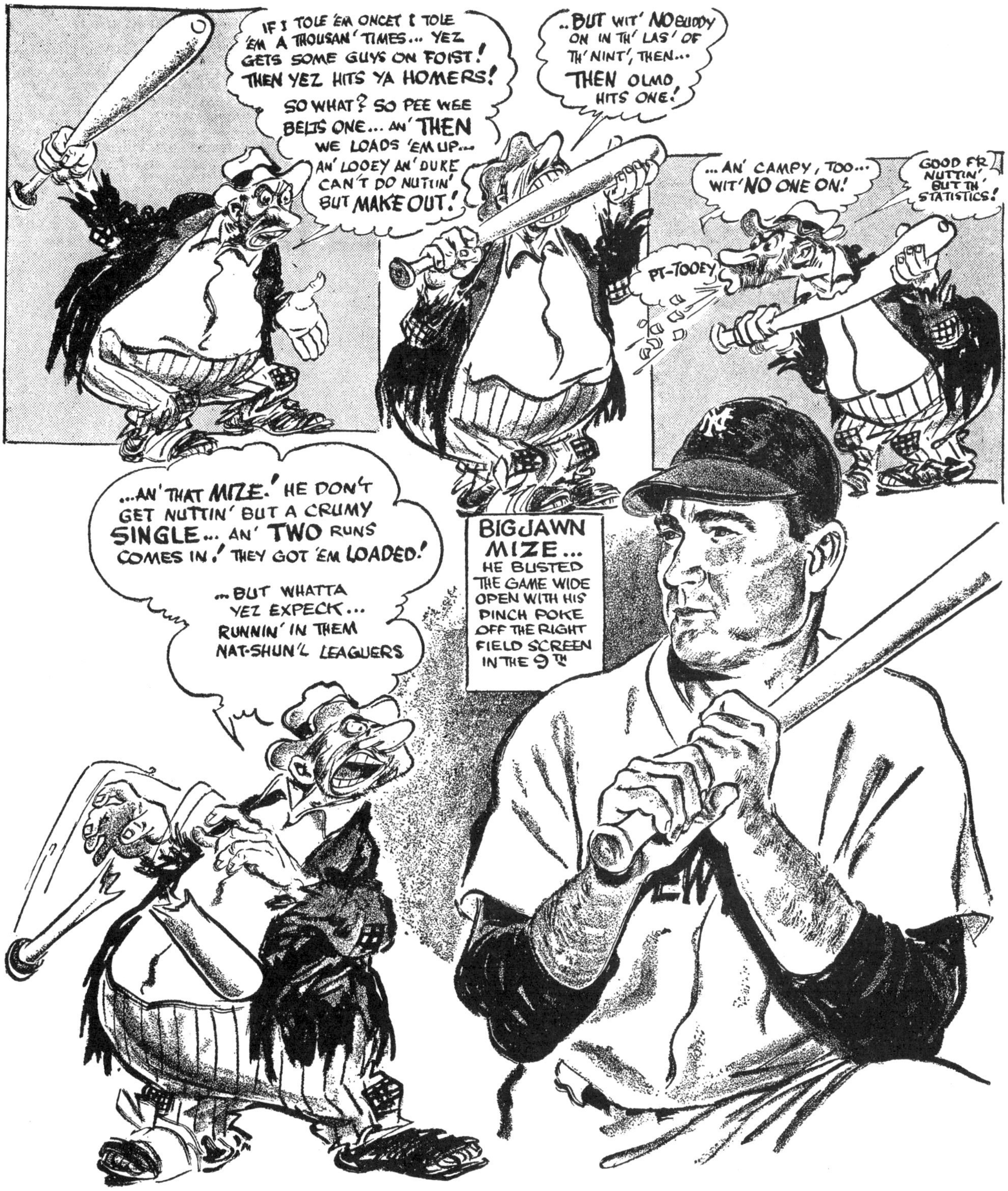
IF I TOLE 'EM ONCET I TOLE 'EM A THOUSAN' TIMES... YEZ GETS SOME GUYS ON FOIST! THEN YEZ HITS YA HOMERS!
SO WHAT? SO PEE WEE BELTS ONE... AN' THEN WE LOADS 'EM UP... AN' LOOEY AN' DUKE CAN'T DO NUTTIN' BUT MAKE OUT!
..BUT WIT' NOBUDDY ON IN TH' LAS' OF TH' NINT', THEN... THEN OLMO HITS ONE!
... AN' CAMPY, TOO... WIT' NO ONE ON!
GOOD FR NUTTIN' BUT TH STATISTICS!
PT-TOOEY
...AN' THAT MIZE! HE DON'T GET NUTTIN' BUT A CRUMY SINGLE... AN' TWO RUNS COMES IN! THEY GOT 'EM LOADED!
...BUT WHATTA YEZ EXPECK... RUNNIN' IN THEM NAT-SHUN'L LEAGUERS
BIG JAWN MIZE... HE BUSTED THE GAME WIDE OPEN WITH HIS PINCH POKE OFF THE RIGHT FIELD SCREEN IN THE 9TH

Late in the 1949 season, Johnny Mize was traded to the Yankees. In game 4 of the World Series, he pinch-hit a single that drove in two runs and won the game for them.

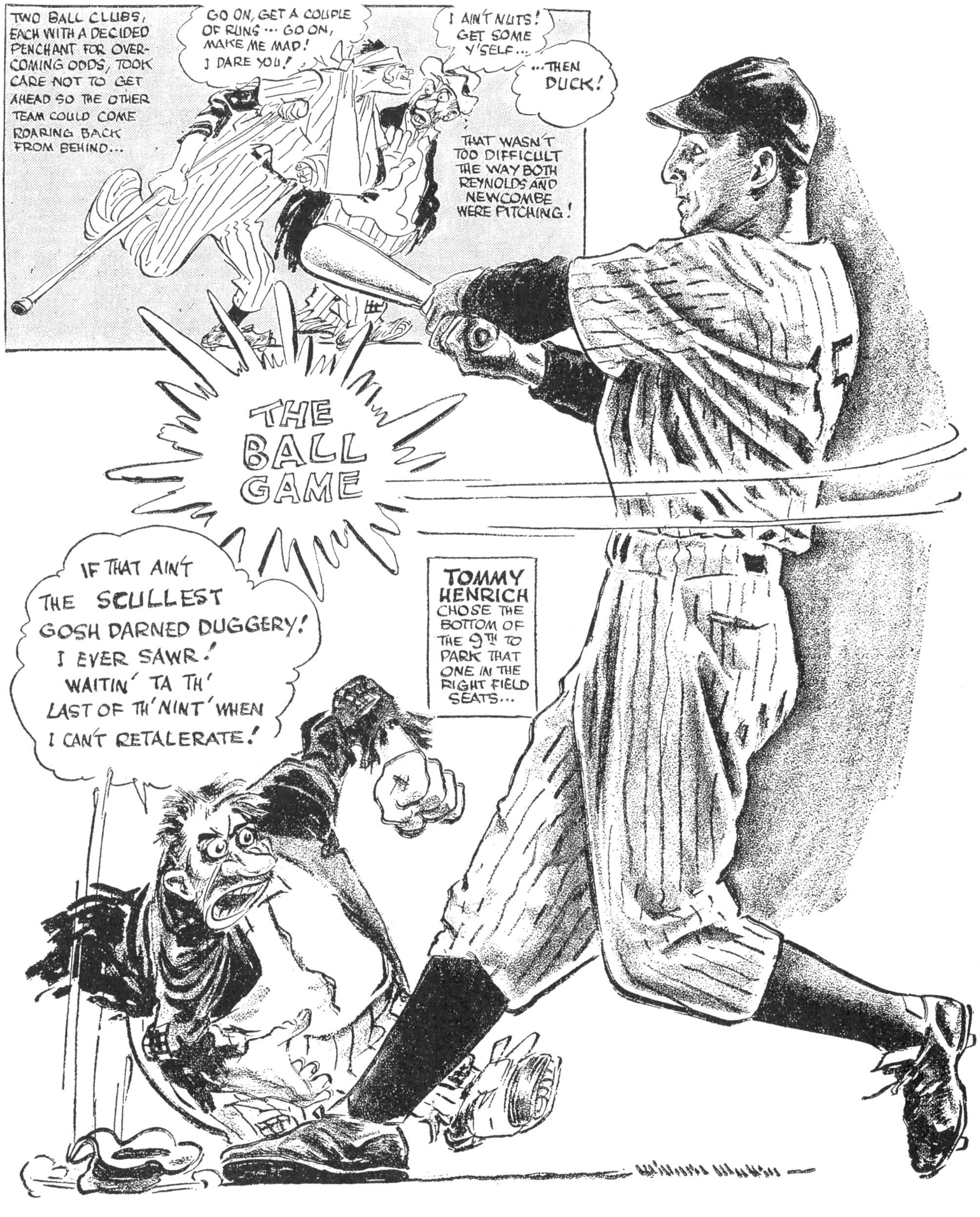
TWO BALL CLUBS, EACH WITH A DECIDED PENCHANT FOR OVER-COMING ODDS, TOOK CARE NOT TO GET AHEAD SO THE OTHER TEAM COULD COME ROARING BACK FROM BEHIND...
GO ON, GET A COUPLE OF RUNS ··· GO ON, MAKE ME MAD! I DARE YOU!
I AIN'T NUTS! GET SOME Y'SELF...
...THEN DUCK!
THAT WASN'T TOO DIFFICULT THE WAY BOTH REYNOLDS AND NEWCOMBE WERE PITCHING!
THE BALL GAME
IF THAT AIN'T THE SCULLEST GOSH DARNED DUGGERY! I EVER SAWR! WAITIN' TA TH' LAST OF TH' NINT' WHEN I CAN'T RETALERATE!
TOMMY HENRICH CHOSE THE BOTTOM OF THE 9TH TO PARK THAT ONE IN THE RIGHT FIELD SEATS...

In the first game of the 1949 series against the Dodgers, the Yankees' Tommy Henrich became the first player ever to win a World Series game with a walk-off homer in the ninth.

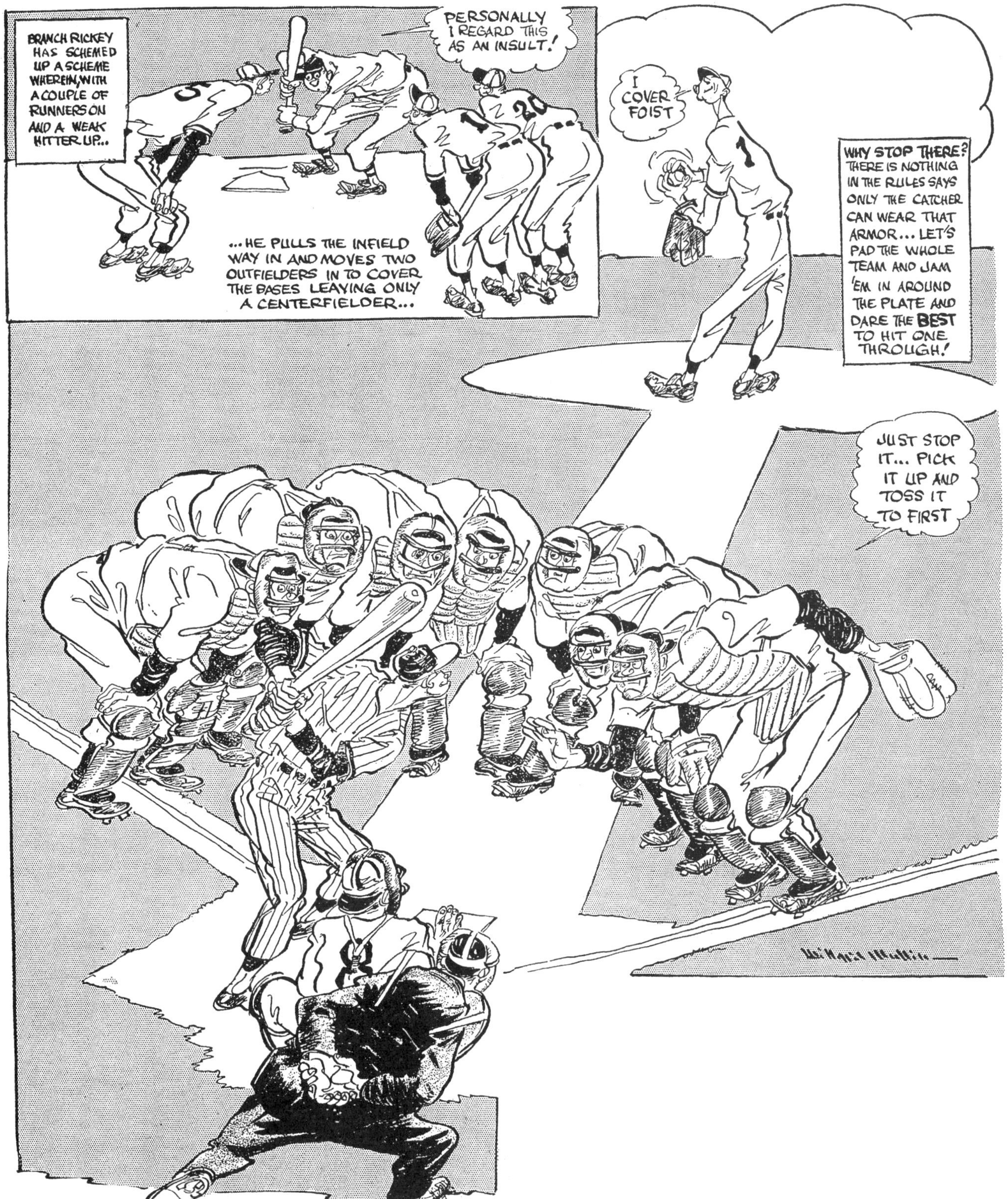
BRANCH RICKEY HAS SCHEMED UP A SCHEME WHEREIN, WITH A COUPLE OF RUNNERS ON AND A WEAK HITTER UP...
PERSONALLY I REGARD THIS AS AN INSULT!
...HE PULLS THE INFIELD WAY IN AND MOVES TWO OUTFIELDERS IN TO COVER THE BASES LEAVING ONLY A CENTERFIELDER...
I COVER FOIST
WHY STOP THERE? THERE IS NOTHING IN THE RULES SAYS ONLY THE CATCHER CAN WEAR THAT ARMOR... LET'S PAD THE WHOLE TEAM AND JAM 'EM IN AROUND THE PLATE AND DARE THE BEST TO HIT ONE THROUGH!
JUST STOP IT... PICK IT UP AND TOSS IT TO FIRST

Mullin's drawing comments on a strategy Branch Rickey advocated when he was General Manager of the Dodgers.

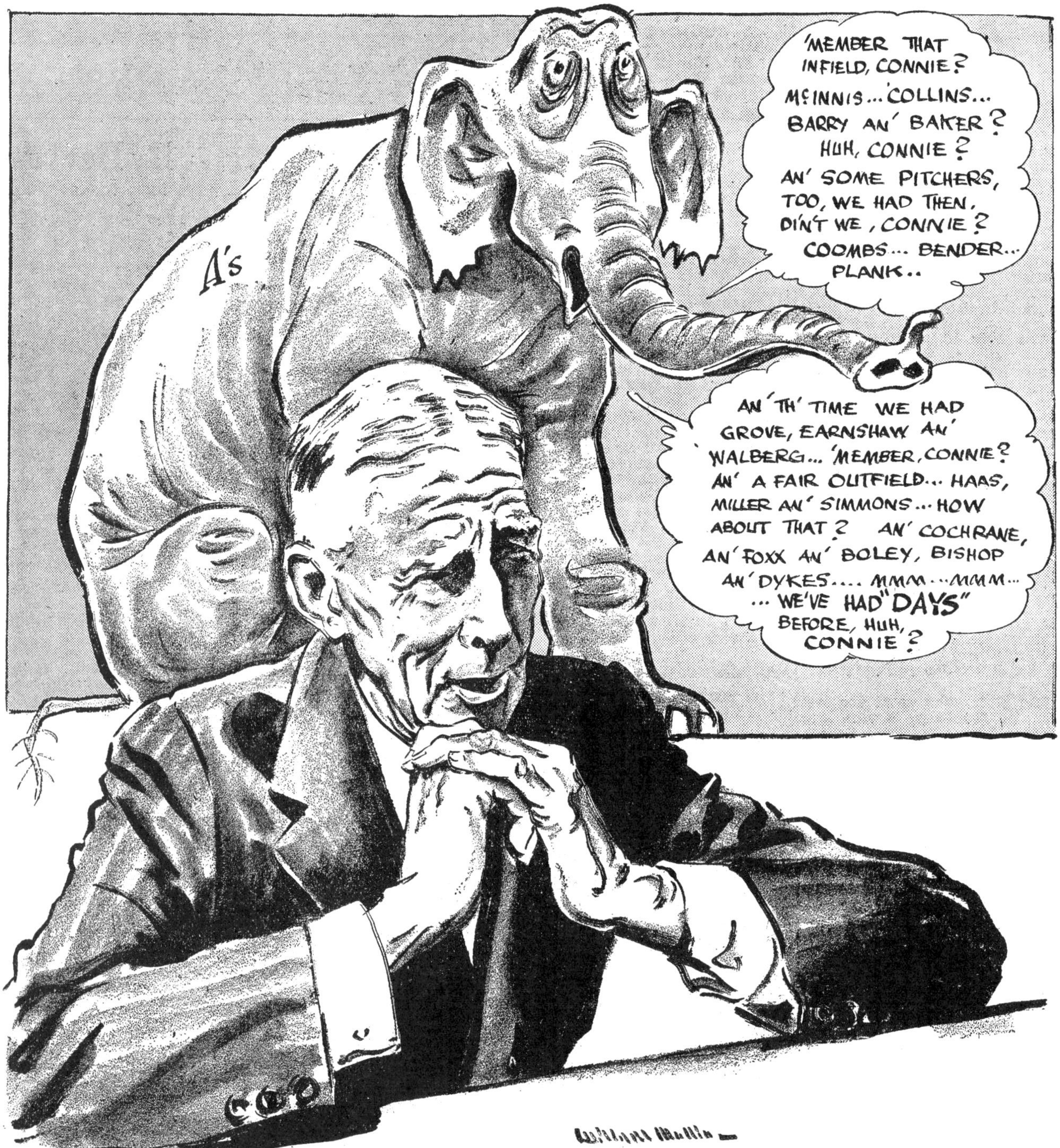
A's
'MEMBER THAT INFIELD, CONNIE? McINNIS... COLLINS... BARRY AN' BAKER? HUH, CONNIE? AN' SOME PITCHERS, TOO, WE HAD THEN, DIN'T WE, CONNIE? COOMBS... BENDER... PLANK..
AN' TH' TIME WE HAD GROVE, EARNSHAW AN' WALBERG... 'MEMBER, CONNIE? AN' A FAIR OUTFIELD... HAAS, MILLER AN' SIMMONS... HOW ABOUT THAT? AN' COCHRANE, AN' FOXX AN' BOLEY, BISHOP AN' DYKES.... MMM...MMM... ...WE'VE HAD "DAYS" BEFORE, HUH, CONNIE?

Connie Mack managed the Philadelphia Athletics for 50 years, from 1901 to 1950. During that time, the Athletics won nine AL pennants and five World Series titles. However, the last of those titles was in 1930. By 1949, when this was drawn, the Athletics had also finished last a record 17 times. Mack would end his managerial career the next season at the age of 88.

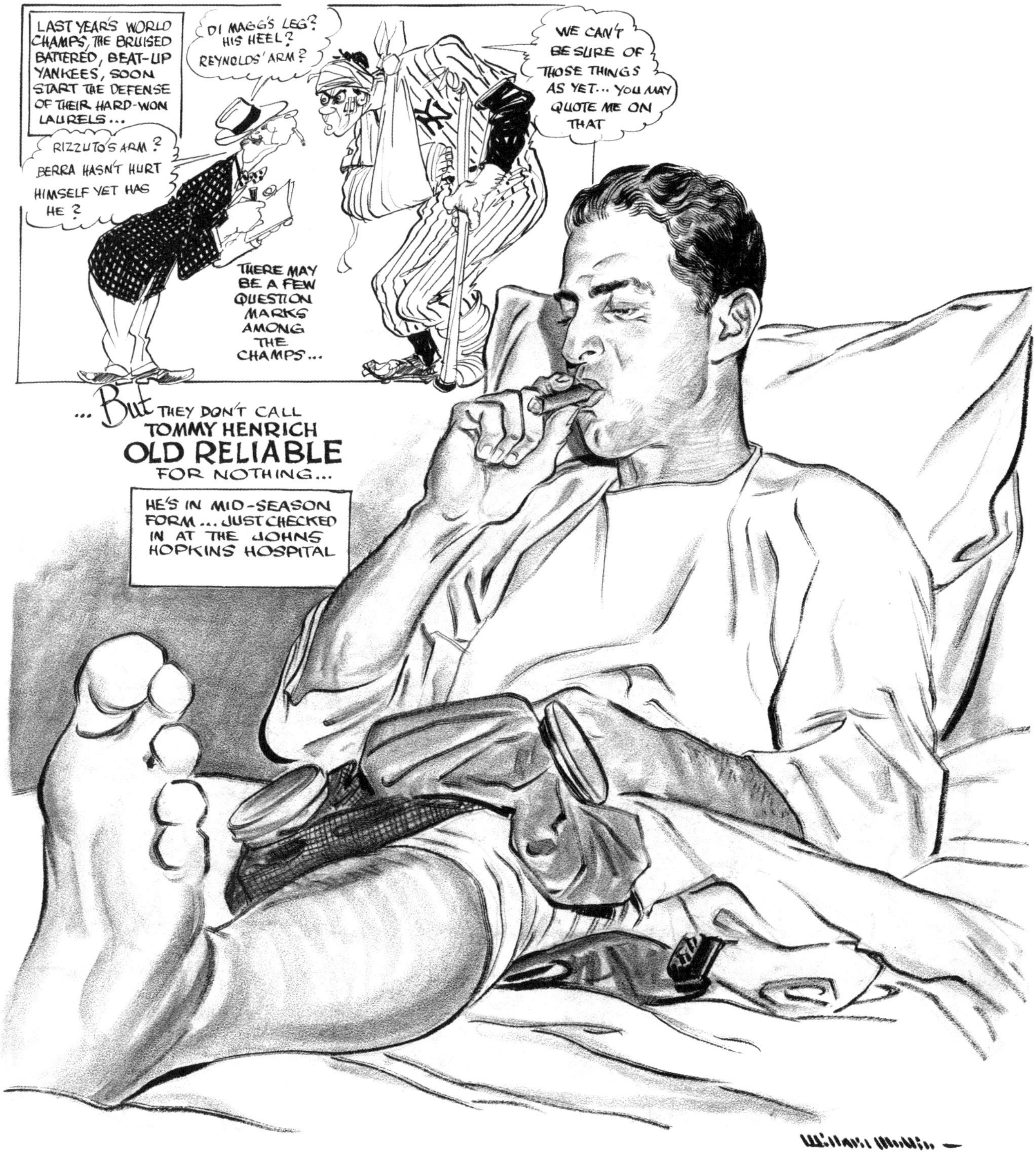
LAST YEAR'S WORLD CHAMPS, THE BRUISED BATTERED, BEAT-UP YANKEES, SOON START THE DEFENSE OF THEIR HARD-WON LAURELS...
DI MAGG'S LEG? HIS HEEL? REYNOLDS' ARM?
WE CAN'T BE SURE OF THOSE THINGS AS YET... YOU MAY QUOTE ME ON THAT
RIZZUTO'S ARM? BERRA HASN'T HURT HIMSELF YET HAS HE?
THERE MAY BE A FEW QUESTION MARKS AMONG THE CHAMPS...
... But THEY DON'T CALL TOMMY HENRICH OLD RELIABLE FOR NOTHING...
HE'S IN MID-SEASON FORM... JUST CHECKED IN AT THE JOHNS HOPKINS HOSPITAL

After the 1949 World Series, several of the Yankees' veteran stars underwent off-season surgery. Tommy Henrich, who had won game 1 of the World Series with a home run in the bottom of the ninth, was one of them.

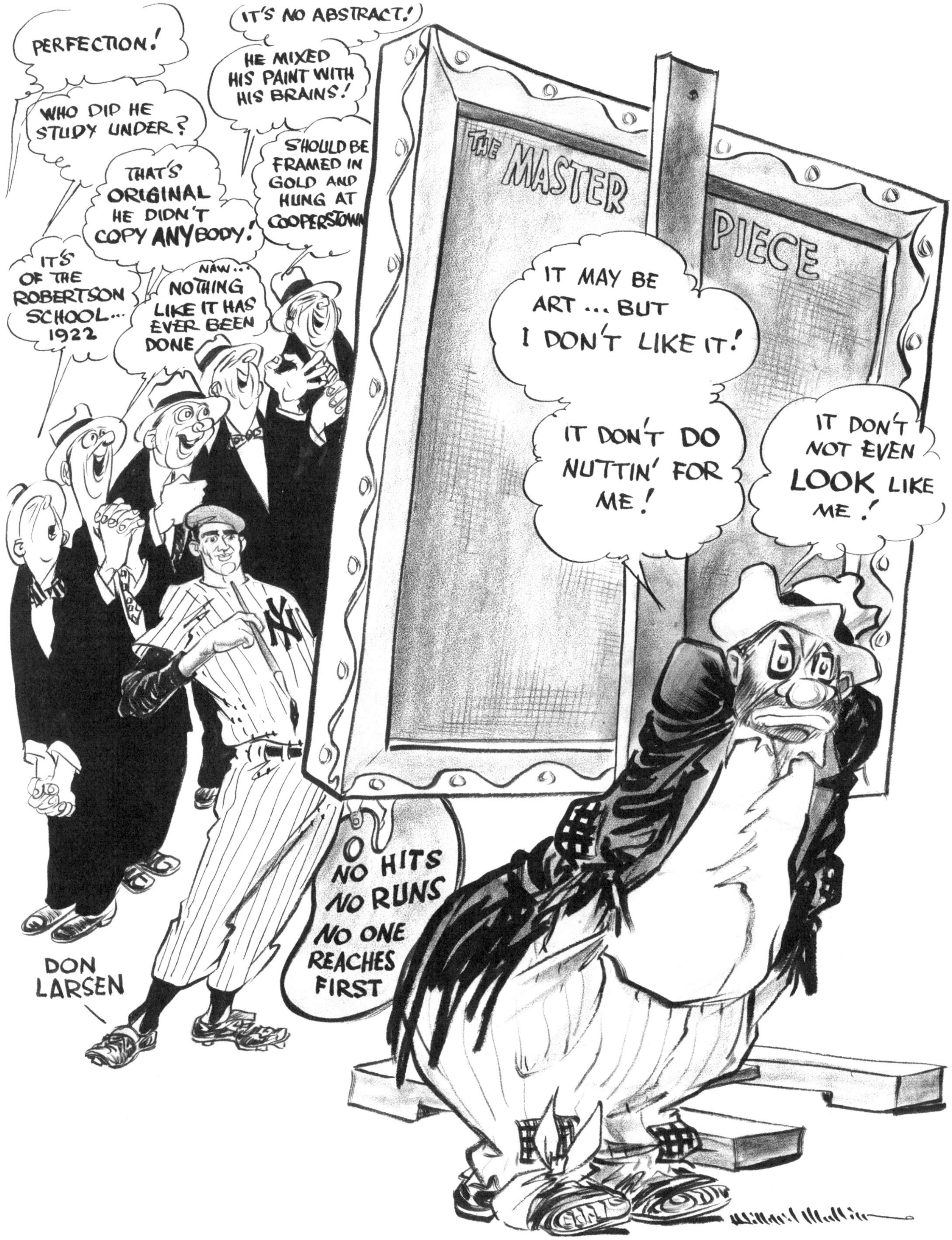

PERFECTION!
IT'S NO ABSTRACT!
HE MIXED HIS PAINT WITH HIS BRAINS!
WHO DID HE STUDY UNDER?
THAT'S ORIGINAL HE DIDN'T COPY ANYBODY!
SHOULD BE FRAMED IN GOLD AND HUNG AT COOPERSTOWN
IT'S OF THE ROBERTSON SCHOOL... 1922
NAW... NOTHING LIKE IT HAS EVER BEEN DONE
THE MASTER PIECE
IT MAY BE ART ... BUT I DON'T LIKE IT!
IT DON'T DO NUTTIN' FOR ME!
IT DON'T NOT EVEN LOOK LIKE ME!
0 NO HITS NO RUNS NO ONE REACHES FIRST
DON LARSEN

The 1950s

· · ·

For the first half of the 20th century,

baseball was the most dependable of sports, sold on stability, 16 teams anchored to longtime homes with no divisions, no artificial surfaces, no designated hitters, and no free agency.

And most of all, no players of color.

In the 1950s, that all changed. African-American and Latin players were introduced to the majors, and teams began moving from city to city, jumping like so many chess pieces from square to square, always looking for a better situation. First, the Boston Braves packed up for Milwaukee, which proved to be nothing more than a stopover before their ultimate destination in Atlanta. Emboldened by that move, the Philadelphia Athletics left for Kansas City, headed eventually to Oakland. The St. Louis Browns shed not only their city but their nickname as well, becoming the Baltimore Orioles. None of that, however, was as dramatic as the move west of the Giants and Dodgers, stripping New York of any National League representation.

And there, recording it all six times a week with bold strokes of his pen and ink was baseball's foremost cartoonist, Willard Mullin.

Baseball tipped its toe into integration ever so tentatively when the Brooklyn Dodgers signed Jackie Robinson in 1946 and promoted him to the majors the next year. Robinson had a brilliant first season, winning Rookie of the Year honors, and then capturing the Most Valuable Player award two years later. His performance shattered racial barriers. When the 1950s began, four of the 16 teams had African-American players. By decade's end, there was at least one black player on every major league roster, some added enthusiastically with talent that would take them to the Hall of Fame, others inserted grudgingly, almost as tokens quickly to be forgotten.

Some teams flourished with the change. Stars like Hank Aaron, Ernie Banks, and Frank Robinson altered the landscape of the sport significantly and were impact players as soon as they reached the majors. Their careers began in the 1950s with small hints of what they would ultimately accomplish. Aaron went on to shatter Babe Ruth's record of 714 home runs, finishing with 755. Banks won consecutive Most Valuable Player Awards on an also-ran team and accumulated 512 home runs, and Robinson finished with 586 homers and would become baseball's first black manager. They were at the forefront of baseball's class of emerging new stars, and fans flocked to see them all. Attendance records were shattered as baseball explored new markets.

Nowhere was the change felt more dramatically than in New York, where the Giants and Dodgers quickly discarded the racial divide and reaped great dividends. Before the decade was over, they also joined the search for new homes. And through it all, Mullin traced the tale with classic cartoons, sometimes comical, sometimes serious, always on target.

The introduction of black players who altered the baseball landscape was most dramatic in New York, right in sight of Mullin's easel. After Jackie Robinson joined the Dodgers, Branch Rickey quickly added power pitcher Don Newcombe, who swept the National League Most Valuable Player and Cy Young Awards in 1956, and catcher Roy Campanella, who won three MVP Awards. The Giants introduced Monte Irvin

OPPOSITE: In 1956, Don Larsen pitched the only perfect game in World Series history against the defending World Champion Brooklyn Dodgers. The Yankees would go on to win that series in seven games, reclaiming the Championship from Brooklyn. The Bum, as can be seen in this Mullin drawing, was unappreciative of Larsen's "masterpiece."

shortly after Robinson came to Brooklyn and then added 20-year-old center fielder Willie Mays, the MVP in 1954, who would become one of the game's most dynamic players. Mullin once drew Mays carrying the Giants on his back, which was not an overstatement.

Together, those players, each a future Hall of Famer, turned the National League into their personal playground, one or the other leading their teams to pennants almost every year from 1949 through 1956. That produced great fodder for Mullin's daily cartoons to chronicle one of baseball's greatest eras.

The decade started with a three-month newspaper strike in New York. Mullin moved his easel to the NEA syndicate offices and continued to draw. Harry Grayson, a senior writer, sat next to Mullin and christened the National League champion Philadelphia Phillies the Whiz Kids because they were so young. Mullin's interpretation of that was the caricature of a juvenile delinquent, baseball cap at an angle, a Dead End kid wearing a polo shirt and dungarees with a slingshot positioned casually in his back pocket, just in case he ran into some bully.

And in The Baseball World of Willard Mullin, there were plenty of bullies running around. With his whimsical view of the world and fertile mind, the nicknames of baseball teams translated easily into cartoons. Instead of the logical redbird for the St. Louis Cardinals, columnist Joe Williams suggested and Mullin adopted a riverboat gambler, looking appropriately sly, shuffling cards and rolling dice. The St. Louis Swifty wore a top hat, handlebar mustache, ascot, checkered vest, and sinister look as he confronted other teams, who would invariably be woefully overmatched dealing with this slick character. The Swifties made off with the 1946 World Series when Enos Slaughter circled the bases on a two-out, eighth-inning hit by Harry Walker, as Johnny Pesky held the relay throw an instant too long.

Pittsburgh's Pirates were a swashbuckling mob of cutthroats complete with eye patches and equipped with ominous looking pistols and cutlasses. The Milwaukee Braves were a tribe of Native Americans, intent on mayhem before the era of political correctness rendered those images inappropriate. The Chicago Cubs were baby bears, on the prowl for prey. Boston's Red Sox and Chicago's White Sox were easy pickings, appropriately colored hosiery adorned with holes. And the Athletics, who represented Philadelphia before moving on to Kansas City and then Oakland, were represented by a white elephant. The logo was embraced by A's boss Connie Mack after some trash talk by Giants manager John McGraw before an early World Series. If the white elephant was good enough for Mr. Mack, it was fine with Mr. Mullin, who had plenty of fun with the pachyderm. In one cartoon, he saluted Mack's longevity, noting that the Athletics patriarch broke into baseball when Chester A. Arthur was president and America had just 38 states.

Mullin had a picnic with this inkwell full of characters, but he never had more fun than he did with his iconic Brooklyn Bum. One time, he had the Bum blowing cigar smoke into the face of the Whiz Kid Phillies, just another bully flexing some muscle. Mullin had invented the Bum two decades earlier as a kind of clown, but by the 1950s, he had evolved into a proud but down-on-his-luck hobo, poor but independent, often looking bewildered, unshaven, with the stump of a cigar stuck in his mouth. Mullin positioned a worn hat on the Bum's head and gave him a tattered coat and baggy pants. The only parts

ABOVE: Mullin's Bum became so popular that in the 1950s a toy manufacturer produced a Brooklyn Bum squeak toy.

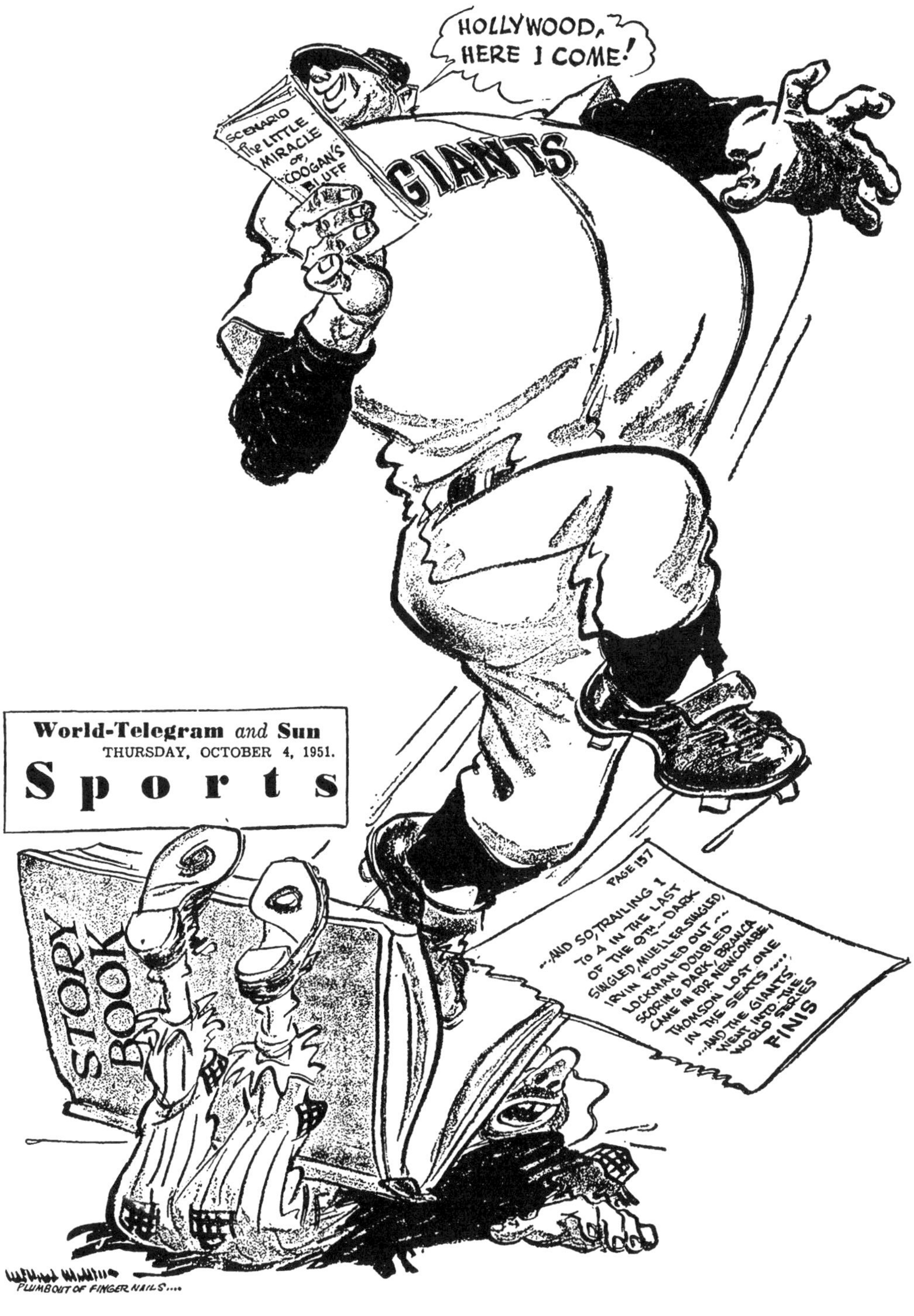
HOLLYWOOD, HERE I COME!
SCENARIO The LITTLE MIRACLE OF COOGAN'S BLUFF
GIANTS
World-Telegram and Sun
THURSDAY, OCTOBER 4, 1951.
Sports
STORY BOOK
PAGE 157
...AND SO, TRAILING 1 TO 4 IN THE LAST OF THE 9TH... DARK SINGLED, MUELLER SINGLED, IRVIN FOULED OUT... LOCKMAN DOUBLED SCORING DARK, BRANCA CAME IN FOR NEWCOMBE, THOMSON LOST ONE IN THE SEATS.... ...AND THE GIANTS WENT INTO THE WORLD SERIES
FINIS
PLUMB OUT OF FINGER NAILS....

that matched were the plaid patches that adorned each of the elbows and knees. The Bum was always cobbler challenged, one shoe held together by a neatly tied bandana, the other with a hole in the sole. The constant for Mullin's Bum was his rivalry with the crosstown Giants. Their clashes were the subject of many Mullin classics.

In his autobiography, Mullin said the Bum had been a work in progress. "He didn't just pop up," the cartoonist said. "He arrived after much fiddling and fussing." It was, however, a worthwhile effort.

Mullin was a bit kinder to New York's other teams. The tattered, unkempt Bum was in stark contrast to the haughty image that Mullin created for the Yankees — an aristocratic character strutting around with an oversized bat at the ready, chest thrust out, proud of the dynasty that ruled baseball at the time with nine World Series

ABOVE: This drawing from October 4, 1951 celebrates Bobby Thomson's pennant-winning home run, the culmination of the "Miracle of Coogan's Bluff."

appearances in 10 years, seven of them against the Giants or Dodgers. In a Mullin self portrait, he drew the proud Yankees looking over his shoulder, reminding the cartoonist of which team ruled baseball, as he worked with other teams preparing for 1956.

Because of their perennial success, Mullin had less fun with the fancy Yankees. Their annual invincibility — five straight pennants and nine in ten years — left the Giants and Dodgers in perpetual pursuit. "I've tried for 15 years to come up with a good character for the Yankees," Mullin wrote in his autobiography.

But when the team assembled an astounding list of 149 injuries in 1949, the cartoonist noted the trend with a drawing of a bloodied and bandaged Bronx Bomber, crutch in one hand, arm in a sling and head bandaged, daring anybody to knock him off the side of a mountain. Another time, he drew manager Casey Stengel leading his bedraggled troops in a baseball version of the famous Revolutionary War painting. When the Yankees beat Brooklyn in the World Series for the third time in the decade, Mullin turned lyrical with parody of Walt Whitman's "Oh Captain, My Captain." The Bum is prone again as the good ship Yankees sails away with yet another World Series Championship.

Mullin's beloved Giants were captured in an oversized character named Willy, who had a tiny head sitting atop a bulbous body. Why Willy? Mullin never said, although it seemed to fit a team that lumbered along one base at a time, eschewing sacrifice bunts, stolen bases, and other modern baseball weapons.

The three New York teams were each blessed with a Hall of Fame center fielder — Willie Mays of the Giants, Mickey Mantle of the Yankees, and Duke Snider of the Dodgers. They were the fodder of endless street corner debates among fans of the three teams and formed the inspiration for baseball balladeer Terry Cashman's haunting baseball ballad, "Talking Baseball," a tribute to that time, which was woven around their names — "Willie, Mickey, and The Duke." And every year, their teams were in the thick of the pennant chase.

The annual chase to October had a dramatic beginning in 1950 when Mullin's Whiz Kid juvenile delinquents from Philadelphia nearly blew the National League pennant on the final day of the season in Brooklyn. The Dodgers had whittled a nine-game Phillies lead down to one with the teams meeting on the last day.

Mullin had the Bum hovering over the unsuspecting Whiz Kid, ready to pounce. With the score tied at 1-1 in the bottom of the ninth inning, Brooklyn's Cal Abrams tried to score on a hit by Duke Snider. Phillies centerfielder Richie Ashburn, not known for his arm, threw Abrams out at the plate and the game hurtled into extra innings.

When Dick Sisler homered in the 10th, the Phillies had their first pennant since 1915. It was ideal material for Mullin, who simply wheeled out his often-used baleful cry of Brooklyn, with the Bum nailing up a "Wait 'til Next Year" sign to deal with the disappointment. And when the Phillies got to the World Series, Mullin reminded them that the 12-time champion Yankees were waiting for them. It was on target. New York swept the Series in four games.

That was a tough year for the Dodgers and a tough year for Mullin because of the three-month strike that shut down *The New York World-Telegram & Sun,* Mullin's newspaper home, forcing him to move his easel to the offices of the NEA newspaper syndicate where he continued drawing for various other papers. But it wasn't quite the same as occupying his perch in the corner of his paper's sports department.

There was a wealth of material to work with because baseball in the 1950s had stars all over the place — from Ted Williams, the game's last .400 hitter, who had his career interrupted twice by service in World War II and Korea, to Stan Musial, whose coiled stance produced seven batting championships and three Most Valuable Player Awards; from Warren Spahn, who became baseball's winningest left-handed pitcher with 363 victories after returning from fighting in the Battle of the Bulge, to Robin

Roberts, who won 286 games and led the National League in complete games for five straight seasons, finishing 140 of 191 starts over that stretch.

Mullin viewed Musial as one of the toughest problems for a pitcher and demonstrated that with a classic cartoon. The Cardinals slugger is in his stance at the plate while the third baseman advises his pitcher to work him inside, the better to make him pull the ball, while the first baseman, knowing no good can come of that for him, advises pitching Stan The Man outside so that he'll hit it the other way to the wise guy third baseman's side of the field.

In 1951, baseball's carnival side surfaced briefly when showman Bill Veeck, who owned the woeful St. Louis Browns, decided to push the envelope just a bit. Veeck hired Eddie Gaedel for a pinch-hitting appearance against Detroit. The fact that Gaedel was a 3-foot-7-inch midget made a base on balls just about inevitable. Wearing uniform number 1/8, Gaedel took four balls and trotted triumphantly to first base. It was his only Major League appearance. Mullin loved that kind of tomfoolery.

Veeck once hired Rogers Hornsby to manage the woebegone Browns. Hornsby was an old school, tough-as-nails baseball lifer, unprepared for the sorry St. Louis franchise, which Mullin characterized as a hillbilly equipped with a jug of moonshine. Mullin drew Hornsby with a whip, trying to get Veeck's crew to respond. It didn't work, and the manager was soon gone, leaving the beleaguered Browns behind. The same thing happened in Cincinnati, and Mullin gave Hornsby another whip, also to no avail.

The Gaedel episode was a brief respite from one of baseball's most dramatic battles, an intra-city struggle between the Giants and Dodgers that captured the imagination of New York and the rest of the baseball world. The Giants lost 11 straight games early in the season and by mid-August had fallen 13 1/2 games behind Brooklyn in the standings. Mullin drew the Bum like a racehorse, running away with the pennant.

Then New York won 37 of its final 44 games to catch the Dodgers and force a three-game playoff. The Giants' pursuit of the Dodgers provided a summer's worth of material for Mullin, including one of his iconic Bum, body parts in pieces, labeled "Falling Apart?"

When the regular season ended with the teams tied, Mullin's cartoon had the Giants flaunting their hot finish, the Bum exhausted by a 14-inning season-saving victory in the final game, and still faced with a three-game playoff and the haughty Yankees waiting ominously for the survivor.

The issue wasn't decided until Bobby Thomson's pennant-winning three-run home run in the bottom of the ninth inning of the final game. Mullin called Thomson's homer "The Shot Heard 'Round The World," and had the triumphant Giants heading for Hollywood with this remarkable saga while the Brooklyn Bum was buried under the fairy tale.

Mullin termed the saga of the Giants' comeback "The Little Miracle of Coogan's Bluff," a salute to the Polo Grounds, the team's rickety old ballpark located atop a hill in upper Manhattan. The name stuck as part of Mullin's lasting contribution to baseball's lexicon, and he often drew manager Leo Durocher reading from a tome with that title as Mullin's oafish Giant sat listening and enthralled by the fairy tale.

When the Giants won the World Series opener against the Yankees, Mullin had them standing over the American League champions, talking about writing an epilogue to the Little Miracle. It was not to be. The Yankees prevailed in six games.

The next year, the Giants' hopes for a repeat were torpedoed in spring training when slugger Monte Irvin broke his ankle. A year later, Mullin drew them still haunted by the accident and Durocher telling them to forget about it.

The Yankees' 1951 season was marked by a pair of no-hitters by Allie Reynolds, the first a 1-0 decision over Cleveland on July 12, the second against Boston on September 28. The Red Sox no-hitter was no simple matter. With two out in the ninth inning, Reynolds got the dangerous Ted Williams to hit a pop fly behind home plate. Hall of Fame catcher Yogi Berra settled under the ball and inexplicably dropped it.

Now Williams would have another chance to spoil Reynolds's gem. Incredibly, the man considered to be baseball's best hitter, winner of six batting championships, obligingly hit another pop up behind the plate. This time, Berra squeezed it for the final out.

Williams and Mullin had a private feud that the cartoonist learned about when the slugger refused to shake hands with a *World-Telegram & Sun* writer and told him that the paper's sports pages were composed of misfits and idiots — including Mullin, "who's done some terrible things of me."

Mullin responded with a cartoon he intended as a personal joke to send to Williams, depicting the star as an art critic. But then he decided to print it in the paper. "Theodore Samuel Williams, frustrated fisherman and sometime leftfielder for the Red Sox, has, perhaps with good reason, found fault with some of our efforts," Mullin printed. "Now the great man is also an art critic. We hesitate to go to press without his OK." Then in an afterthought he added, "Maybe I had better erase the whole thing, Mister Williams, and just start over."

In another cartoon, Mullin paid homage to Williams's fly fishing prowess, drawing him with a huge haul, not of fish but of dollar bills, saluting his earning power. The image was accompanied by a poem, something Mullin liked to do now and then.

The 1951 World Series between the Yankees and the Giants — the first of five between New York teams in the 1950s — started a trend which Mullin called "The Subway Series" and marked the end of Joe DiMaggio's brilliant Yankees career. Injuries were catching up with the Yankee Clipper, something Mullin had noted a year earlier in a spring training caricature.

When DiMaggio was done, Mullin marked the occasion with a portrait of him looking down on a youngster with a hand closing the book on "Joe DiMaggio, Yankee." The commentary said it all: "That, my boy, was quite a story."

A few years later, DiMaggio married Hollywood starlet Marilyn Monroe, a union of high profile stars that never quite worked out. When Marilyn returned from a tour of Armed Forces bases, she regaled DiMaggio over the reception she had received. "Oh, Joe," she gushed, "you never heard such cheering." The man who once hit in 56 consecutive games replied dryly, "Oh, yes, I have."

DiMaggio and Williams were two of baseball's best hitters during the 1950s and almost got traded for each other one night. Boston owner Tom Yawkey and Yankees boss Dan Topping were at a World Series cocktail party and the alcohol-fueled conversation drifted into how good the righty-swinging DiMaggio would be aiming at Fenway Park's Green Monster in left field and how the close-in right field fence at Yankee Stadium would be easy pickings for Williams's sweet left-handed swing. So why not swap them in a trade born of common sense, convenience, and several scotch and sodas?

The next morning when the air had cleared, it occurred to the two owners that it might not be such a good idea for fierce rivals to exchange their best players, and the deal was called off.

Dodgers disappointment was becoming an annual exercise for Brooklyn loyalists who were growing tired of repeating the old refrain of "Wait 'til Next Year" each time their team fell short. They had never won a World Series in five tries and Mullin reminded them of their agony with the Bum terrified at looking in a book of Series history as the Dodgers prepared to try one more time. Mullin tapped into their grief when he drew the cover of the team's 1952 yearbook depicting the trademark Bum looking appropriately angry while hammering a sign that declared "This Is Next Year."

Alas, it was not.

There would be two more World Series losses to the high and mighty Yankees, in 1952 and 1953. Mullin celebrated the 50th anniversary of the World Series with a winding parade of teams leading up to the Brooklyn Bum and the regal Yankees shaking hands as they prepared to face off in the 1953 Series.

On the shores at Sportsman's Palace,
By the murky big pool waters,
Stood Ted Williams of the Red Sox
Holding in his hand a fish rod,
Bamboo, long and limber fish rod,
Casting out across the waters.
  Floated out, the line descending
On the waters made no ripple.
In the crowd on watch behind him,
Watching Williams do his fishing,
No papoose so young and naïve
Did not know where Williams fishes,
Were no fish where Williams
  fishes.
Suddenly on his big reel cranking,
Pulled from out the murky waters,
Pulled out several paltry dollars
With a smile upon his features.

WITH FURTHER APOLOGIES TO LONGFELLOW....

The Yankees won that one and then the hated Giants won the Series in a four-game sweep against Cleveland in 1954, touched off by Willie Mays's back-to-the-plate catch of a drive by Vic Wertz, an iconic World Series moment.

The sweep was a most unexpected turn of events because the Indians, depicted by the cartoonish Chief Wahoo, who moved easily from their uniform sleeves to Mullin's drawing board, won 111 games that season. That was more than the regal Yankees ever won during their dynasty years, but it didn't help the Indians against the Giants. Mullin drew the Giant strutting around with the rest of baseball's member teams clenched in his hands.

ABOVE, LEFT: In 1949 and again in 1950, Ted Williams was paid $100,000 to play baseball, a salary matched at the time only by Yankees great Joe DiMaggio.

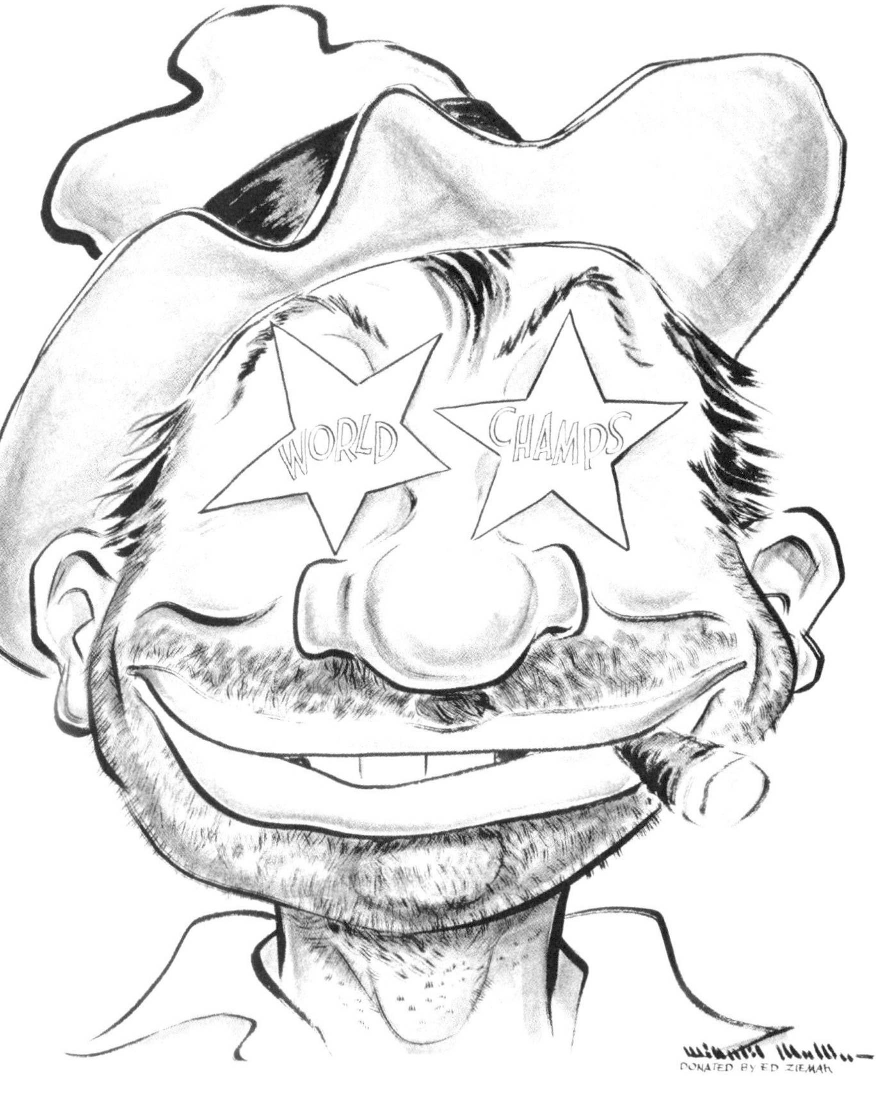
WORLD
CHAMPS

ABOVE, LEFT: Between 1941 and 1956, the Yankees and Dodgers met in the World Series seven times. The Yankees won six. In 1955, Brooklyn finally triumphed, claiming their only World Series Championship. The Bum was starry-eyed in wonder at it all.

Seeing the Yankees not finish in first place was almost unprecedented. Novelist Douglas Wallop wrote a whimsical account of a fictional season celebrating the failure. *The Year The Yankees Lost The Pennant* had a Mullin cartoon on the cover with the Yankees hanging off the end of the Devil's pitchfork. The book evolved into the Broadway hit *Damn Yankees.* And 1954 turned out to be the year the Yankees really did lose the pennant.

Seeing the hated Giants win the World Series stuck in the craw of the Brooklyn Bum. The feud between New York's two National League teams was very real, and Mullin captured it frequently, once with the Bum and the Giant facing off like a couple of boxers. Another time, Mullin drew the Bum swearing that he'd take the pennant away from the celebrating Giant. The high and mighty Yankee is in the background reminding them both that the World Series Championship was his personal property.

Then Next Year really did arrive for Brooklyn.

In 1955, the Dodgers set a record by winning their first 10 games and 22 of their first 24. It was a statement that this time, Brooklyn meant business. Mullin tracked their progress with dutiful respect. By mid-August, the Dodgers were 16 1/2 games in front, and by September 8, they had clinched the pennant, the earliest clinching in National League history.

Still, a daunting task lay ahead. They would face the hated Yankees in the World Series toting some heavy baggage — painful memories of Series losses to their rivals in 1953, 1952, 1949, 1947, and 1941. This time, though, it would be different. This time, it really was Next Year.

Powered by Johnny Podres's seventh-game shutout and a miraculous one-handed catch by left fielder Sandy Amorós, the Dodgers won their first and only World Series Championship for Brooklyn.

The accomplishment was celebrated on the front page of Mullin's paper with a string of cartoons depicting the iconic Bum with a silly grin on his face. In the place of his eyes were stars labeled "World Champions." Inside, the Bum exulted in the triumph, exclaiming, "We dood it! Woil Cham-peens! Me!" Never mind that in the picture he is in a straitjacket, being carried off by men in white coats, mental health professionals. For the Dodgers' 1956 yearbook, Mullin had his Bum grinning broadly and already planning for a repeat.

Brooklyn was overcome with joy, so much so that it hardly mattered a year later when the Yankees' Don Larsen pitched a perfect game against them for the only World Series no-hitter in history. Twenty-seven batters up and 27 batters down, accomplished with just 97 pitches. Mullin showed Larsen surrounded by critics admiring the canvas depicting the perfect game. In the foreground is the Bum, rather perturbed, proclaiming, "It may be art but I don't like it. It don't do nuttin' for me. It don't even look like me."

Later, he had Larsen and GM George Weiss on a seesaw, contemplating how much the perfect game would cost the Yankees in the pitcher's 1957 contract.

Larsen's gem was saved by Mickey Mantle's running catch in left center field. That contribution in the field was ironic in a year when Mantle did so much damage at bat, winning the Triple Crown by leading the American League with a .353 batting average, 52 home runs, and 130 runs batted in. Mullin saluted Mantle with a cartoon of the Yankees slugger and a couple of dice rolling a seven. "The Mick," after all, was a natural.

Larsen's no-hitter wasn't the best-pitched game of the decade, though. That distinction belonged to hard-luck Harvey Haddix, who threw 12 perfect innings for Pittsburgh against Milwaukee and still lost the game.

Facing the Braves on a misty May night in 1959, Haddix retired 36 consecutive batters, no hits, no walks, no errors, no base runners, nothing for a dozen innings. It was the longest stretch of perfect pitching in baseball history, but Haddix was still locked in a scoreless game as Milwaukee came to bat in the bottom of the 13th inning. An error by third baseman Don Hoak gave the Braves their first base runner and, after a sacrifice and an intentional walk, Joe Adcock tagged a home run. The greatest game ever pitched was just another loss for the Pirates and sad-eyed Harvey Haddix.

Earlier in the decade, Branch Rickey had moved from the Dodgers to the Pirates, equipped with some intriguing ideas like turning Dale Long into a left-handed catcher and positioning six players in the outfield. Mullin's cartoon questioned whether the old genius had lost his playthings, a set of marbles.

Larsen's perfect game was the exclamation point on still another Yankees Series triumph over Mullin's beloved Bums, their sixth in seven October showdowns beginning in 1941 and ending in 1956.

By then, storm clouds were gathering over New York baseball. Slowly, teams were becoming aware that the economics of the game did not require them to stay in their ancestral homes forever. In Brooklyn, Dodgers owner Walter O'Malley was keenly aware of the trend. His team was locked in a bandbox of a ballpark that barely held 32,000 fans and offered no parking.

O'Malley saw no reason to stay in that situation, not with so many other teams picking up and moving on to other cities. There was talk of a new stadium for the Dodgers and Mullin drew the Bum dreaming about it. Sadly, when it was built, the Dodgers had left town and taken the Giants with them.

O'Malley's wanderlust led him first to Jersey City, where the Dodgers played eight "home" games in 1956, a sort of a shot across the bow of New York politicians, a signal that the Dodgers were seeking greener pastures.

....BUT NOT FORGOTTEN

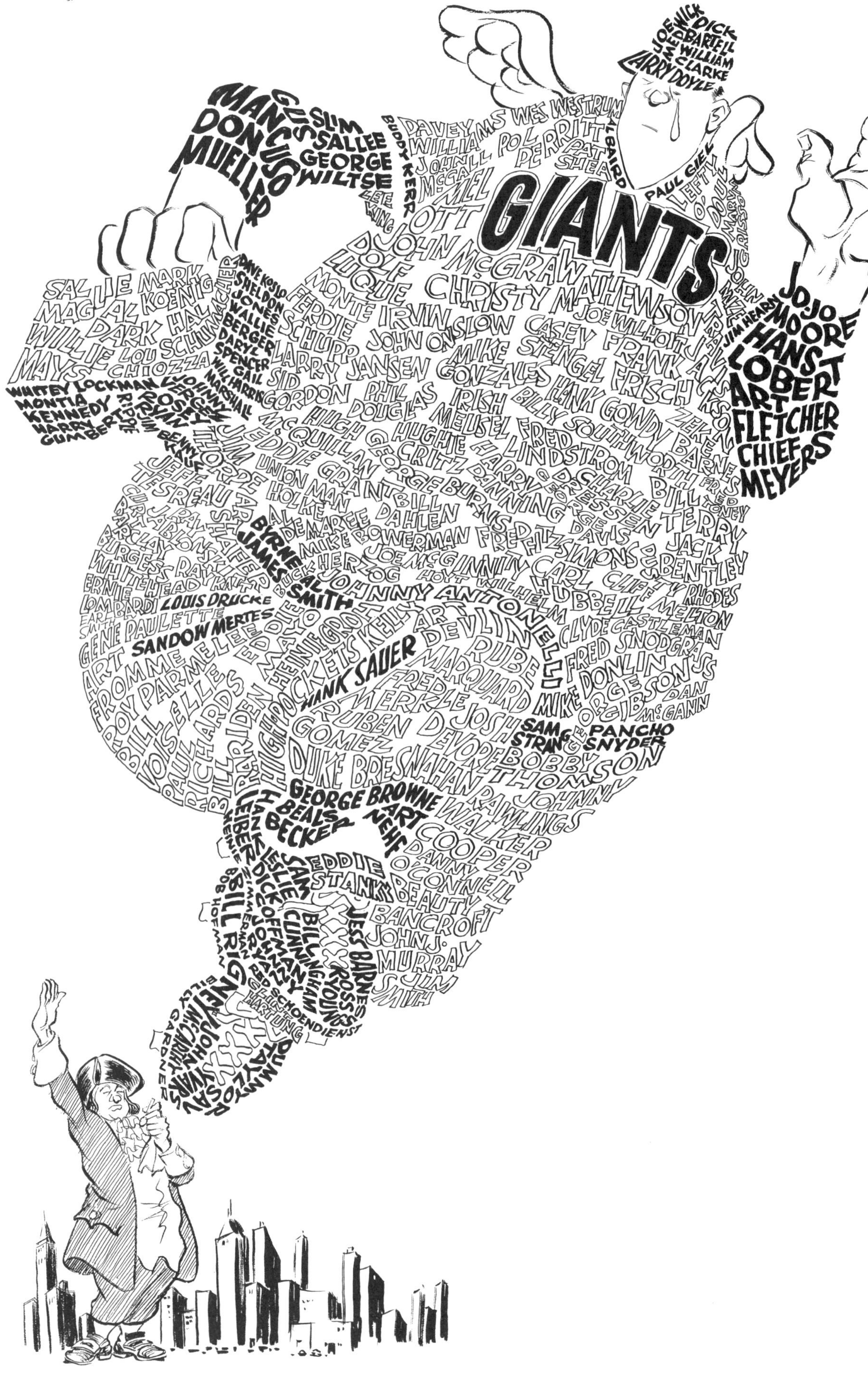
GIANTS
JOE WICK
DICK BARTELL
WILLIAM CLARKE
LARRY DOYLE
MANCUSO
GUS
DON
MUELLER
SLIM SALLEE
GEORGE WILTSE
BUDDY KERR
PAUL GIEL
JOJO MOORE
HANS LOBERT
ART FLETCHER
CHIEF MEYERS
JOHN McGRAW
CHRISTY MATHEWSON
WHITEY LOCKMAN
MONTIA KENNEDY
HARRY GUMBERT
LOUIS DRUCKE
SANDOW MERTES
HANK SAUER
JOHNNY ANTONELLI
SAM STRANG
PANCHO SNYDER
BOBBY THOMSON
GEORGE BROWNE
BEALS BECKER
ART NEHF
EDDIE STANKY
BILL RIGNEY

If New York didn't notice, Los Angeles certainly did. The city put on a full court press, dazzling O'Malley with an offer he couldn't refuse — acres of valuable downtown real estate called Chavez Ravine where Dodger Stadium would be constructed. Mullin used the novel *Of Mice and Men* for this turn of events, with a slick O'Malley dazzling the dreamy-eyed Bum with tales of the riches awaiting them both in California. Mullin could relate to that because he'd spent many of his formative years in that state.

Because of scheduling issues, O'Malley knew he couldn't go to California alone and cajoled the Giants to join him in the cross-country journey. Team owner Horace Stoneham, tired of playing in the mostly empty, dilapidated Polo Grounds, was a willing travel companion and Mullin used the same *Of Mice and Men* theme, with the owner sweet-talking his bulbous Giant about the move.

The team's board of directors approved the move to San Francisco after club officials scouted Candlestick Point, where a ballpark would be built hard by the waters of San Francisco Bay. When the Giants arrived, they found the ballpark constructed in a wind tunnel, a setting totally unfit for baseball. How could that happen? Well, the city fathers had been careful to take team officials to Candlestick in mid-day, well before the winds settled in.

In a decade of change, the biggest shock of all came when the two New York teams left town. The move of the Dodgers and Giants rocked the nation's largest city. When the Dodgers' migration plans became public, Mullin thought about its impact. "My loss will be personal," he said. "The Brooklyn Bum is indigenous to one place, and transplanted to Los Angeles he wouldn't be the same lovable guy."

When the teams moved, Mullin responded to it with a typical sense of cartoon humor. He dressed up his signature Bum in a pair of sunglasses, the better to deal with all that California sunshine, planted a beret on his head for his Hollywood incarnation, and a hobo's knapsack slung casually over his shoulder to hold all his worldly belongings. Instead of the stump of a cigar, Mullin gave the Bum a classy cigarette holder. Then, as if he really couldn't believe what had happened, Mullin crafted a cartoon of the original Bum looking at a mirror image of himself, all decked out in his Hollywood finery. The caption, in classic Brooklynese, read, "Usen't youse t' live in Brooklyn?"

Mullin was a bit more wounded by the loss of his beloved Giants. His farewell cartoon for his favorite team was composed of a mélange of names of the team's players throughout its storied history to form the big guy from head to toe. The image, much like Mullin's annual Christmas card, was made all the more emotional by the inclusion of a tear dropping from the Giant's eye as he headed west.

While new parks were being built, the Giants and Dodgers spent their early years out West in strange settings. The Giants played in Seals Stadium, a minor league ballpark that seated fewer than 23,000 fans. The Dodgers settled in the Los Angeles Coliseum, home of the 1932 Olympics, well suited to football and track, but not baseball. Nevertheless, turnstiles spun furiously in both ballparks. The Dodgers drew 1,845,556 fans in their first year and the Giants attracted 1,272,625. Prosperity had come to O'Malley and Stoneham.

With the Dodgers and Yankees packing for California, the Yankees tried to heal New York's wound by winning two more American League pennants in 1957 and 1958. They met the Milwaukee Braves in both World Series, losing in 1957 when Lew Burdette won three games for the Braves and then winning in 1958 by capturing the last three games of the Series.

Two years after their move, the Dodgers were World Champions in 1959 and Mullin marked the occasion with a picture of the original Bum, grinning broadly, Brooklyn left behind for good, a through-and-through Californian now.

That was Mullin's way — always looking for the lighter side of sports. He flourished in the 1950s in a city that dominated baseball with three teams — the haughty

OPPOSITE: The Giants were in New York from 1883 through 1957. When the Giants left for San Francisco, Mullin drew this portrait of Willy the Giant using the names of Giants greats.

Yankees in the midst of baseball's greatest dynasty, the oafish Giants, and the lovable Dodgers. That made New York the cornerstone for baseball, an ideal condition for Mullin, who always had plenty of subject matter from which to choose.

Each year, Mullin would celebrate the holiday season with a card depicting a Christmas scene composed of the names from all over the world of sports. It took several days to create, and in his autobiography, he wrote, "It never fails to astound me to find the number of people who will plow through this eye-strainer. I'll get letters like 'Hey, you got Joe Zilch in twice,' or 'I've been through your Christmas card twice and you've left out Ted Williams.'"

At the bottom of the card, Mullin added a disclaimer. "If you have eye strain," it said, "we have writer's cramp."

Mullin sometimes seemed obsessed with the contract woes the Yankees' success created for the team's penurious general manager, George Weiss. But he admired Weiss's acumen and saluted the GM by positioning him inside the Yankees' perpetual motion machine, keeping the team on a first place roll. In one memorable cartoon, he drew Weiss as George Washington with manager Casey Stengel as Betsy Ross, weaving a flag and reminding his boss of the extra stars for all those championships. Another time, Mullin had Weiss at a cashier's window at the racetrack, reluctantly doling out payoffs to his cast of stars. And when Lee MacPhail was set to succeed Weiss as GM, Mullin had Weiss instructing the new man on how to deal with Mickey Mantle. He drew a bullseye and advised the new GM to aim for the middle, $50,000, instead of the more expensive outer rings. Mantle and Weiss were frequent adversaries, and one time Mullin had them dueling, the GM armed with a pen, the slugger with a bat.

Mullin often used Weiss and Stengel together. One year, he celebrated Valentine's Day by drawing them as a pair of Cupids, hoping a cast of Yankees rookies could steal their hearts away. Another time, he drew Weiss as a young fan, pursuing the Yankees' cast of stars for autographs — on contracts, he hoped.

When the Yankees finished third in 1959, Mullin had Weiss almost chortling over the less expensive cost of his payroll in 1960. After all, third place finishers can't expect to make as much as teams that finish first. And the GM saw to it that they didn't.

During that time, the legendary Toots Shor ran a restaurant in midtown Manhattan that became the No. 1 sports hangout. The bar at Shor's was the gathering place for stars and starlets, sports figures, and Broadway types. And Mullin was a keen observer of the scene. One of his more memorable cartoons, a rush job drawn over three days for *Collier's* magazine, was a view of the crowded scene at Shor's bar where the proprietor referred to most of the customers affectionately as crumb bums. Mullin's drawing made it easy to pick out the celebrities — Bing Crosby over here and Bob Hope over there, Joe DiMaggio at one end of the crowd and Shor holding court at the other.

The Shor drawing was almost as if Mullin were holding up a magnifying glass to the decade of the 1950s, a time when sports in New York meant the Yankees, Dodgers, and Giants — perennial rulers of the baseball world. But just as the introduction of black players signaled baseball's major change at the start of the 1950s, Mullin recognized that more change would follow in the 1960s. Expansion would alter the face of the game again with the Mets returning National League baseball to New York, the Astros added in Houston, the Angels challenging his old Dodger friends in Los Angeles, and a new Senators franchise in Washington, replacing the original version, which was transplanted to Minnesota and renamed the Twins.

Mullin welcomed all the new participants, additional occupants of his whimsical world of baseball, each with his own personality, each chronicled in unforgettable fashion by the man at the easel in the corner of the newsroom. ❖

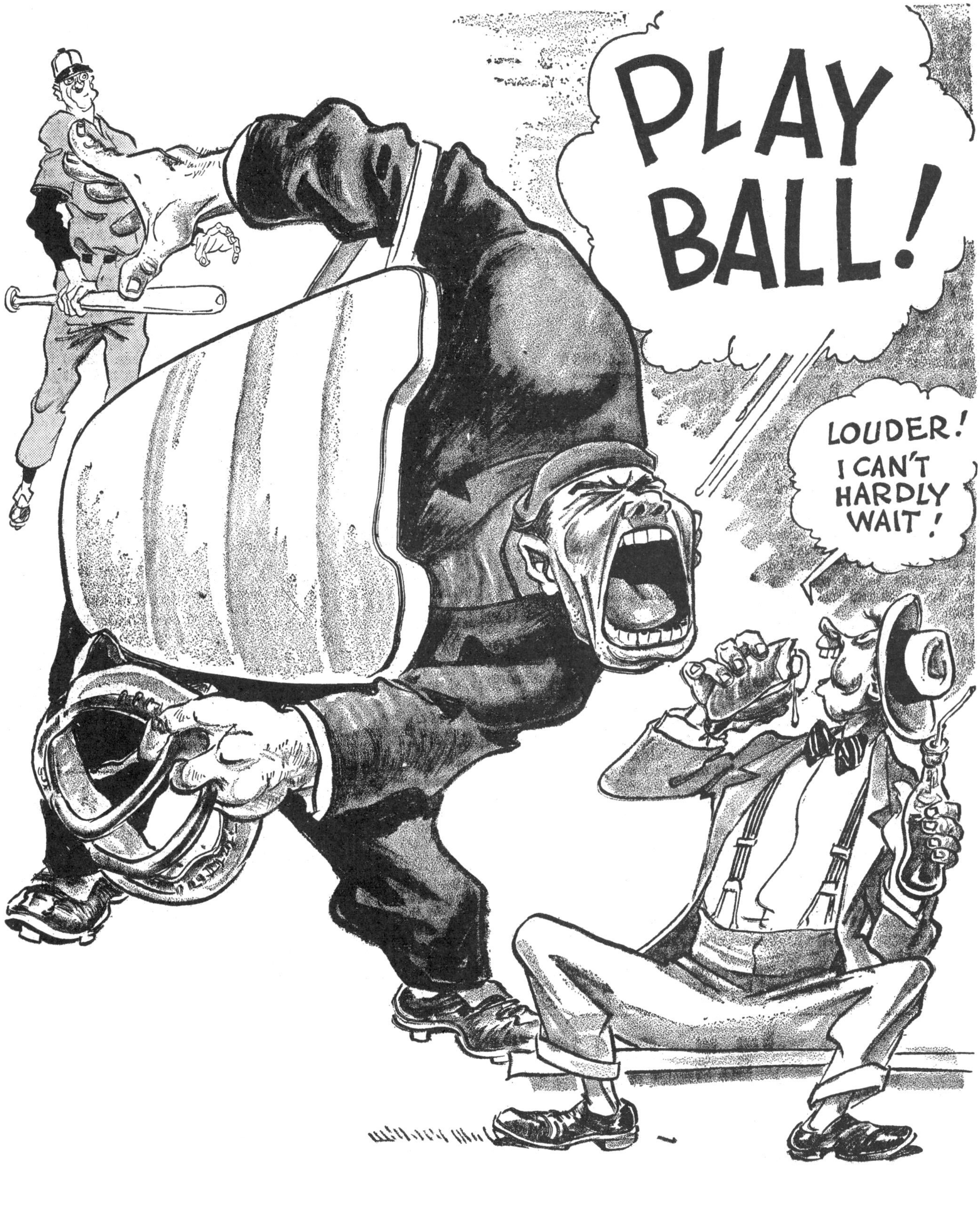
PLAY BALL!
LOUDER! I CAN'T HARDLY WAIT!

Mullin celebrated the opening of baseball season with this cartoon in April 1950.

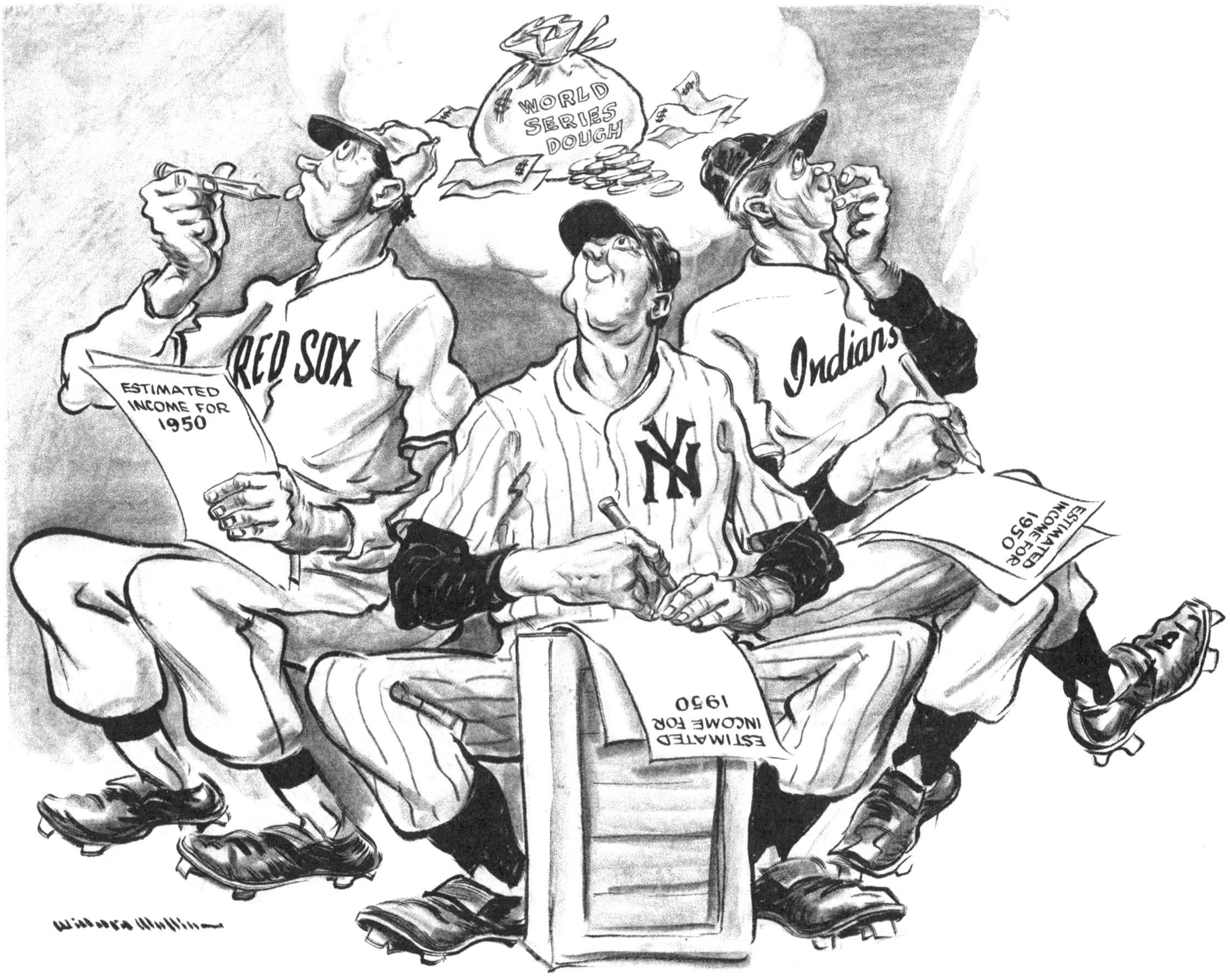
WORLD SERIES DOUGH
RED SOX
ESTIMATED INCOME FOR 1950
Indians
ESTIMATED INCOME FOR 1950
ESTIMATED INCOME FOR 1950

In 1948, the Cleveland Indians won the World Series. In 1949, the Yankees won the World Series and Boston lost a one-game playoff to the Yankees for the pennant. All three had World Series aspirations going into the 1950 season.

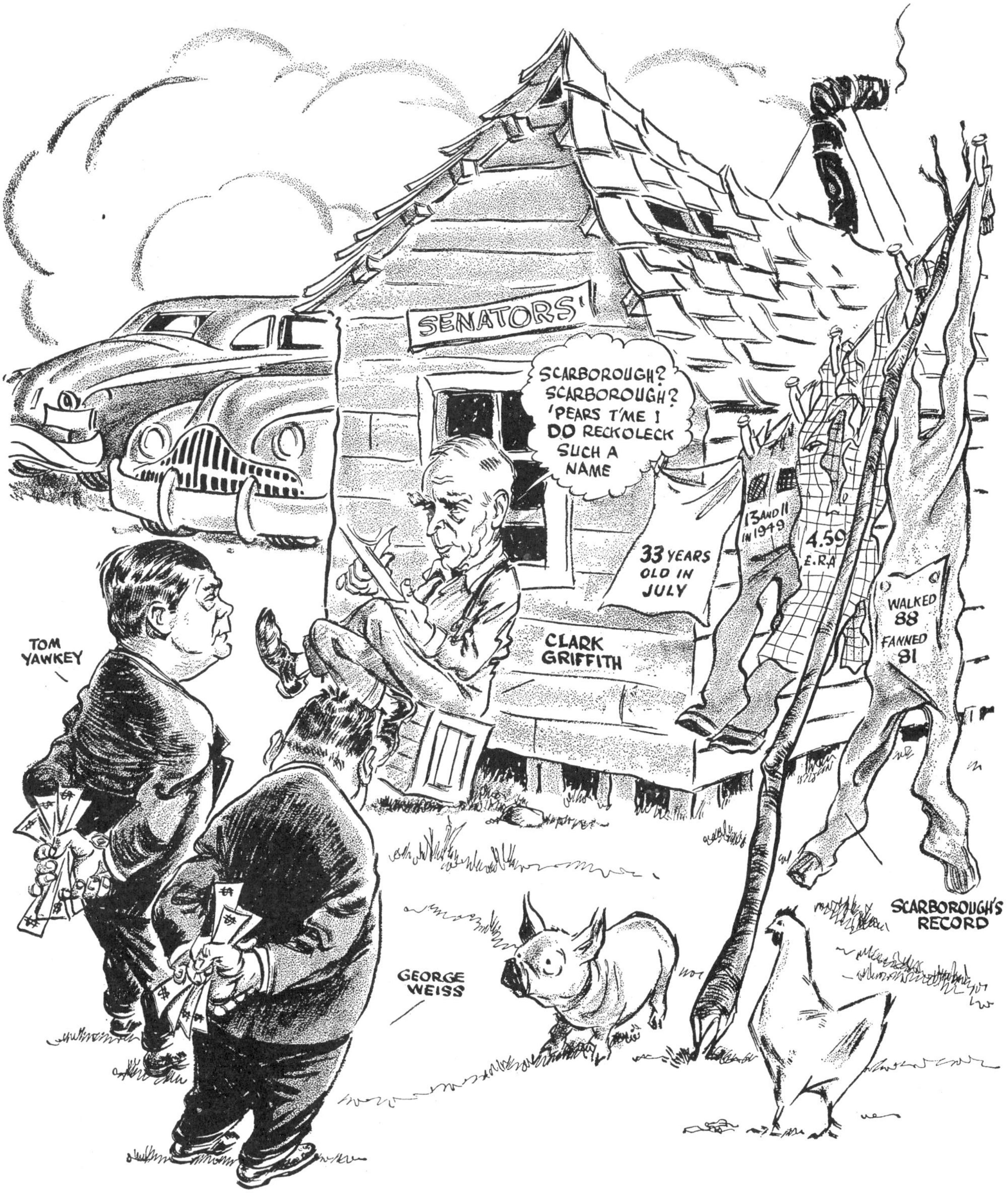
SENATORS'
SCARBOROUGH? SCARBOROUGH? 'PEARS T'ME I DO RECKOLECK SUCH A NAME
13 AND 11 IN 1949
4.59 E.R.A
33 YEARS OLD IN JULY
WALKED 88
FANNED 81
CLARK GRIFFITH
TOM YAWKEY
GEORGE WEISS
SCARBOROUGH'S RECORD

In 1950, the Yankees and the Red Sox were looking for pitching help. Both focused on Ray Scarborough, a mediocre pitcher for the Washington Senators. Scarborough ended up splitting the season between Washington and Chicago, but he did pitch for Boston in 1951 and 1952 — and for the Yankees in 1952 and 1953.

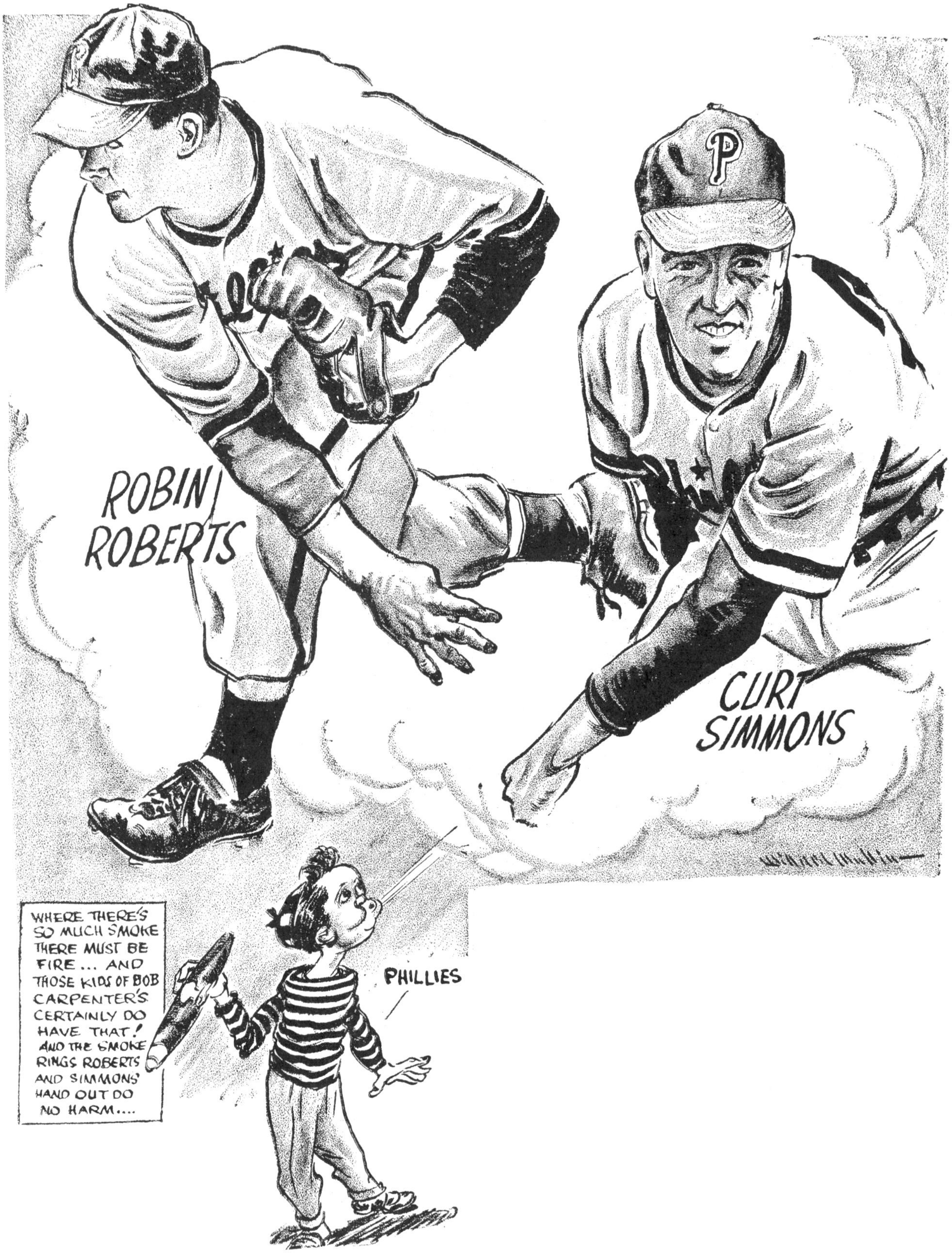
ROBIN ROBERTS
CURT SIMMONS
WHERE THERE'S SO MUCH SMOKE THERE MUST BE FIRE... AND THOSE KIDS OF BOB CARPENTER'S CERTAINLY DO HAVE THAT! AND THE SMOKE RINGS ROBERTS AND SIMMONS' HAND OUT DO NO HARM....
PHILLIES

In 1950, Robin Roberts won 20 games and Curt Simmons won 17. They led the Philadelphia Phillies "Whiz Kids" to the National League pennant.

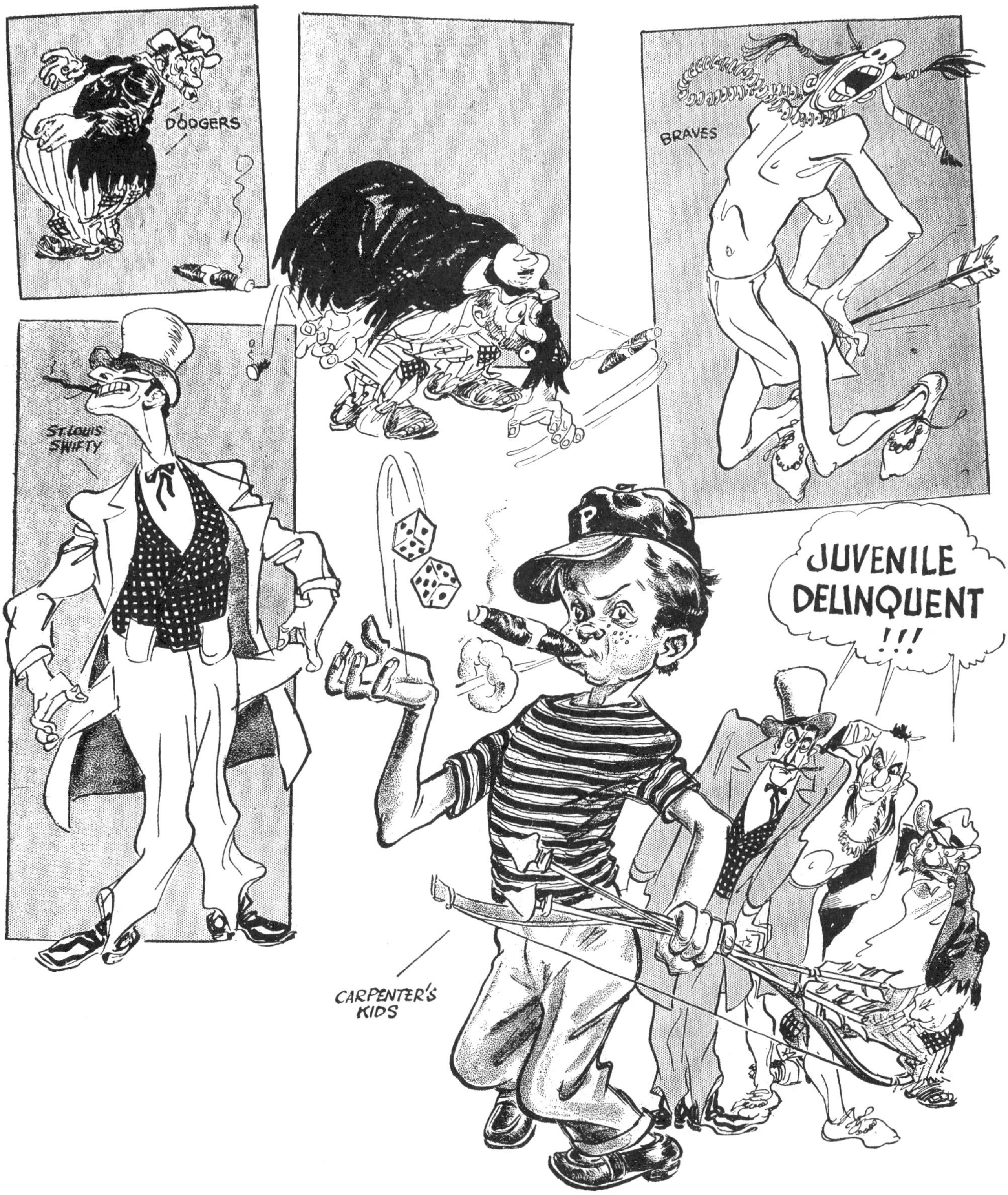
DODGERS
BRAVES
ST. LOUIS SWIFTY
JUVENILE DELINQUENT !!!
CARPENTER'S KIDS

In 1950, the starting lineup of the Philadelphia Phillies pennant-winning "Whiz Kids," averaged just 26 years old.

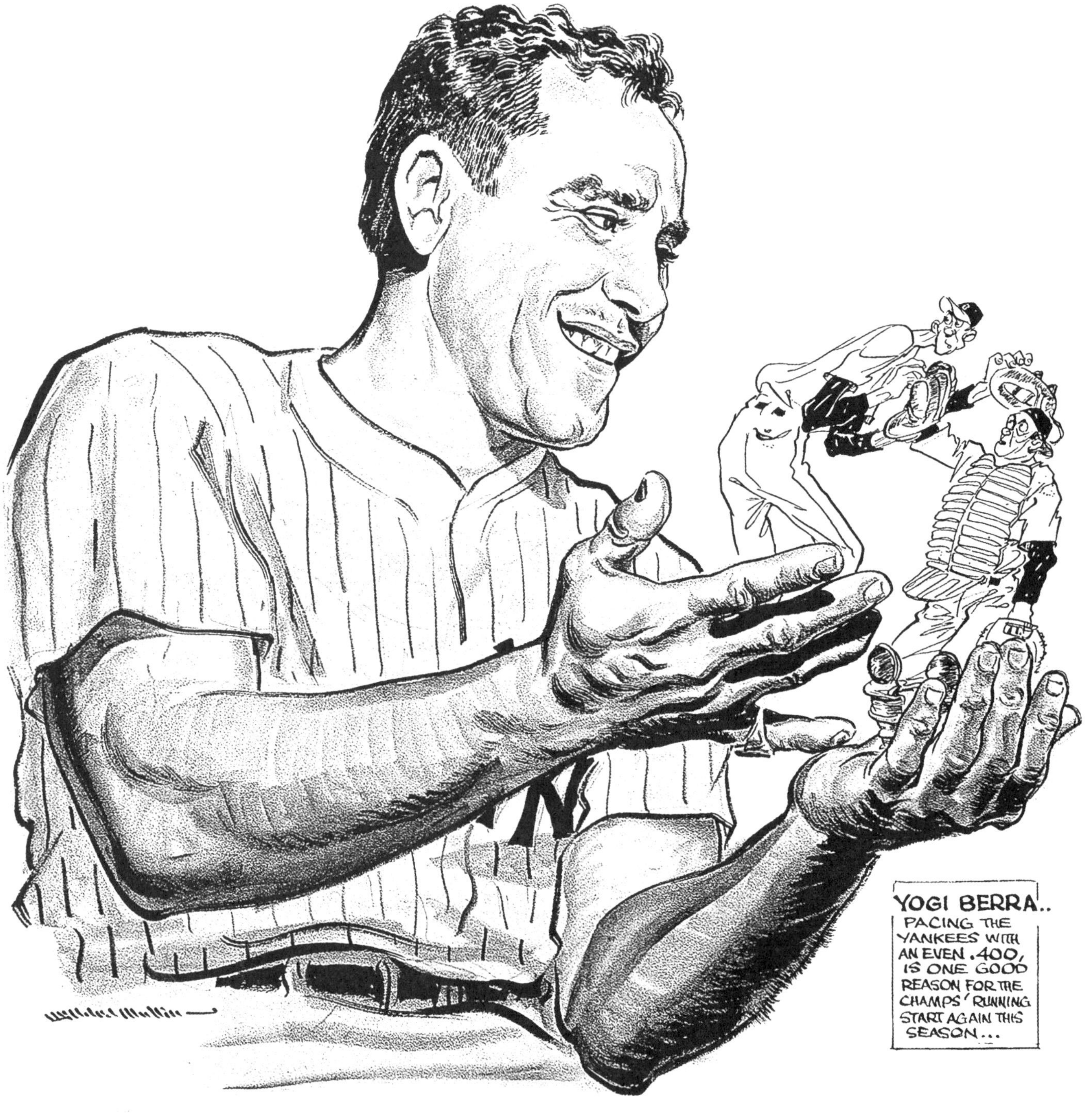
YOGI BERRA..
PACING THE YANKEES WITH AN EVEN .400, IS ONE GOOD REASON FOR THE CHAMPS' RUNNING START AGAIN THIS SEASON...

Yogi Berra won the AL MVP three times: 1951,1954, and 1955. Mullin spotted Yogi's talent early on, and this drawing from 1950 recognizes what an important part of the Yankees' success Yogi had become.

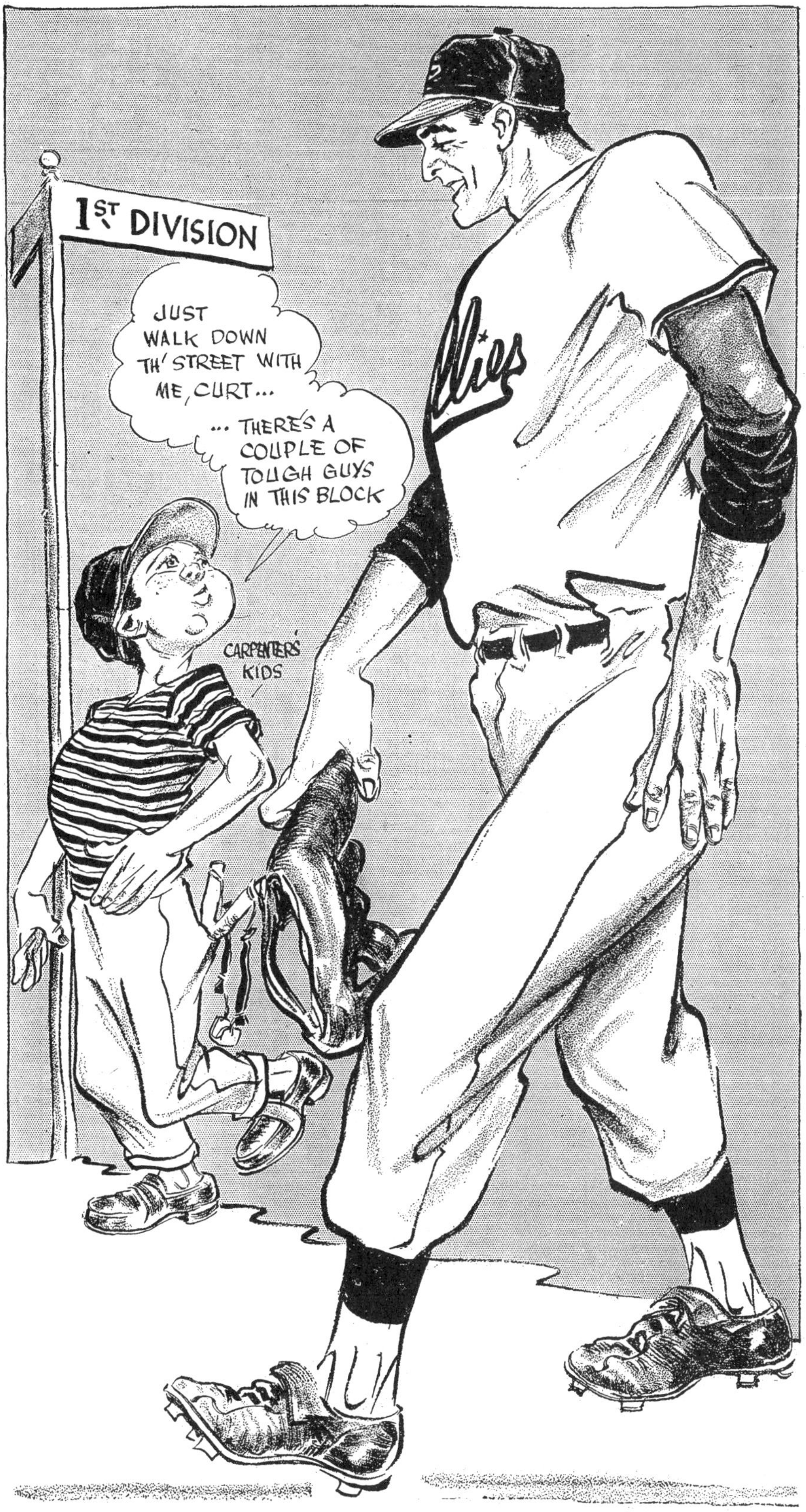
1ST DIVISION
JUST WALK DOWN TH' STREET WITH ME, CURT...
... THERE'S A COUPLE OF TOUGH GUYS IN THIS BLOCK
CARPENTERS' KIDS

In 1947, Curt Simmons was signed by the Phillies and received a $65,000 signing bonus, one of the highest ever paid to that time. Simmons was a solid, if not spectacular, pitcher for the Phillies for the next 13 years, compiling a 17–8 record in 1950 to help the Phillies win the National League pennant.

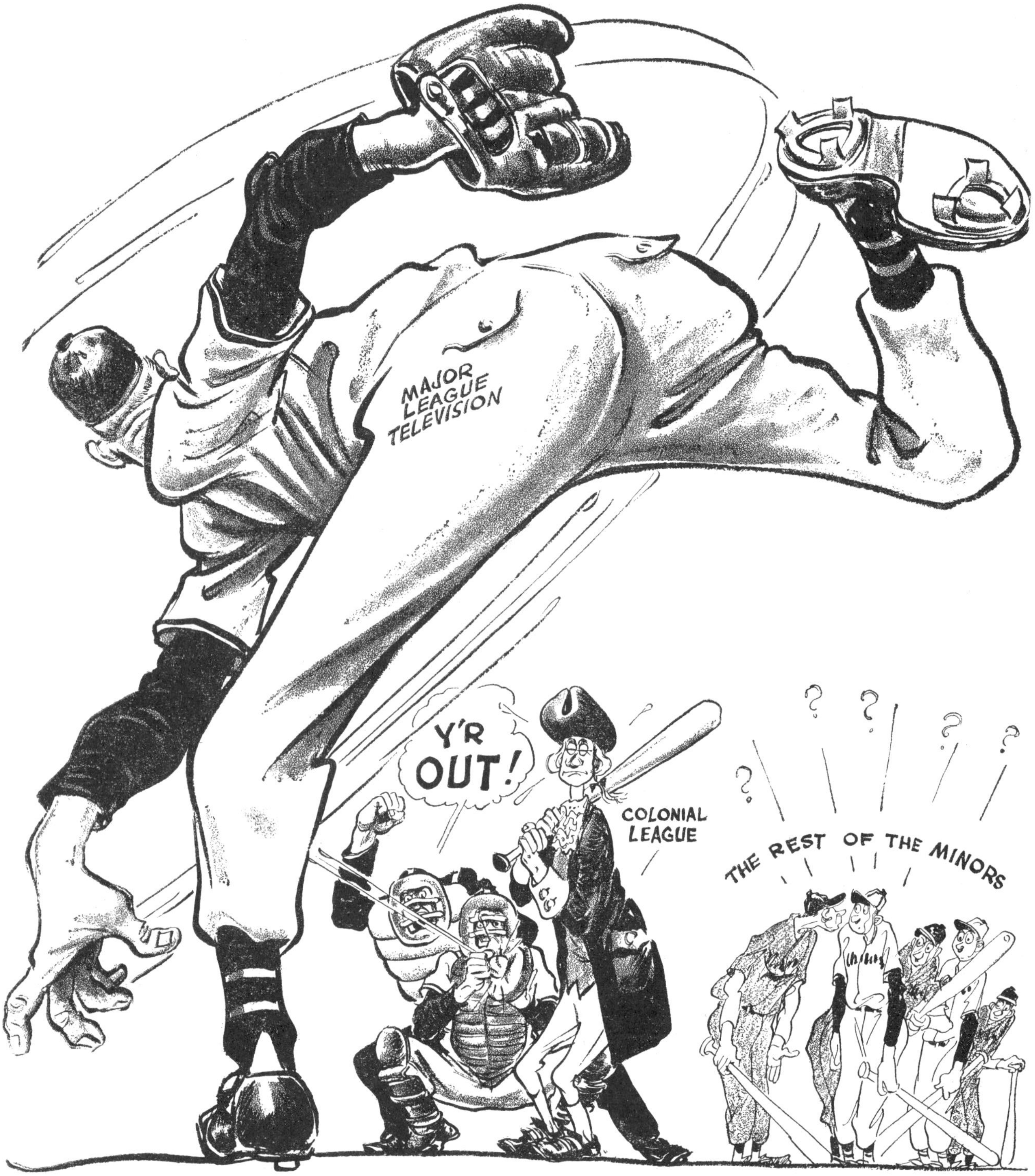
MAJOR LEAGUE TELEVISION
Y'R OUT!
COLONIAL LEAGUE
THE REST OF THE MINORS

During the post-World War II baseball boom, a number of unaffiliated minor leagues sprang up. However, with the expansion of televised major league games, these leagues began to fold. The Colonial League was one of the early casualties, shutting down July 14, 1950. Many more minor leagues would shut down over the next 10 years, something Mullin anticipated in this cartoon from mid-1950.

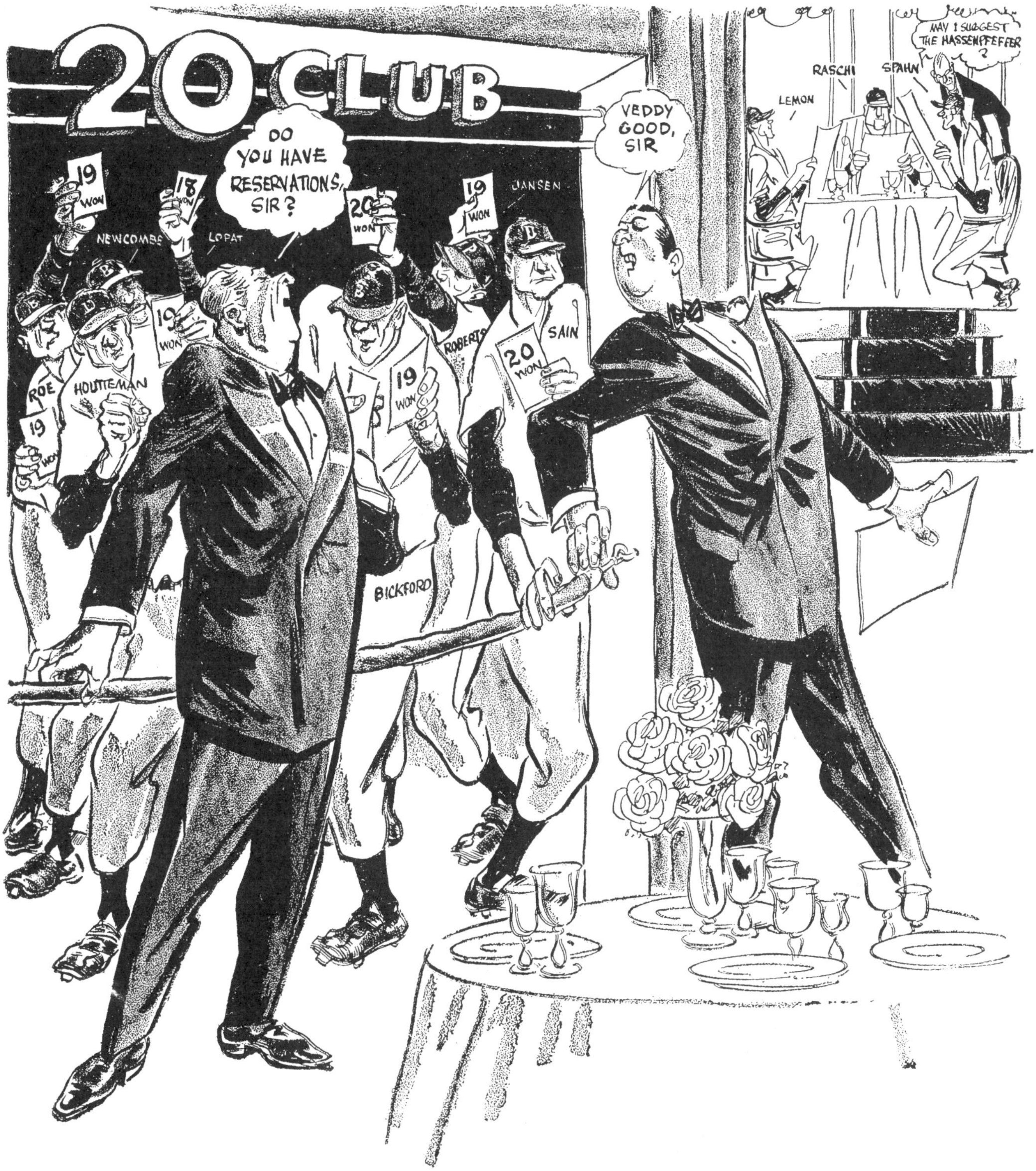
20 CLUB
DO YOU HAVE RESERVATIONS, SIR?
VEDDY GOOD, SIR
MAY I SUGGEST THE HASSENPFEFFER ?
LEMON
RASCHI
SPAHN
19 WON
18 WON
20 WON
19 WON
JANSEN
NEWCOMBE
LOPAT
19 WON
ROE
HOUTTEMAN
19 WON
ROBERTS
19 WON
20 WON
SAIN
BICKFORD

In 1950, only five pitchers in all of baseball won 20 games: Bob Lemon and Vic Raschi in the AL, and Warren Spahn, Johnny Sain, and Robin Roberts in the NL.

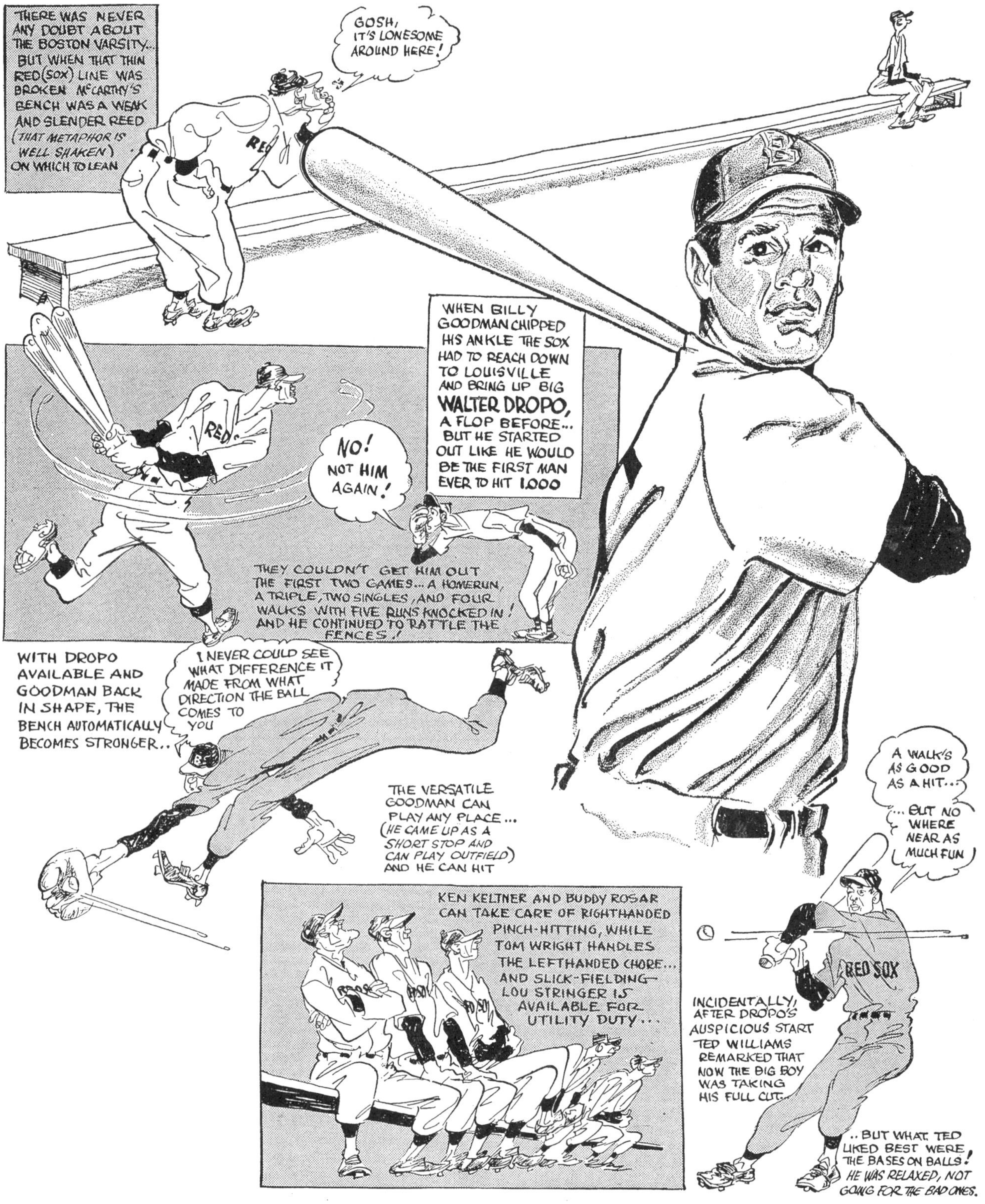
THERE WAS NEVER ANY DOUBT ABOUT THE BOSTON VARSITY.. BUT WHEN THAT THIN RED(SOX) LINE WAS BROKEN McCARTHY'S BENCH WAS A WEAK AND SLENDER REED (THAT METAPHOR IS WELL SHAKEN) ON WHICH TO LEAN
GOSH, IT'S LONESOME AROUND HERE!
WHEN BILLY GOODMAN CHIPPED HIS ANKLE THE SOX HAD TO REACH DOWN TO LOUISVILLE AND BRING UP BIG WALTER DROPO, A FLOP BEFORE... BUT HE STARTED OUT LIKE HE WOULD BE THE FIRST MAN EVER TO HIT 1.000
NO! NOT HIM AGAIN!
THEY COULDN'T GET HIM OUT THE FIRST TWO GAMES... A HOMERUN, A TRIPLE, TWO SINGLES, AND FOUR WALKS WITH FIVE RUNS KNOCKED IN! AND HE CONTINUED TO RATTLE THE FENCES!
WITH DROPO AVAILABLE AND GOODMAN BACK IN SHAPE, THE BENCH AUTOMATICALLY BECOMES STRONGER..
I NEVER COULD SEE WHAT DIFFERENCE IT MADE FROM WHAT DIRECTION THE BALL COMES TO YOU
THE VERSATILE GOODMAN CAN PLAY ANY PLACE... (HE CAME UP AS A SHORT STOP AND CAN PLAY OUTFIELD) AND HE CAN HIT
A WALK'S AS GOOD AS A HIT..
... BUT NO WHERE NEAR AS MUCH FUN!
KEN KELTNER AND BUDDY ROSAR CAN TAKE CARE OF RIGHTHANDED PINCH-HITTING, WHILE TOM WRIGHT HANDLES THE LEFTHANDED CHORE... AND SLICK-FIELDING— LOU STRINGER IS AVAILABLE FOR UTILITY DUTY...
INCIDENTALLY, AFTER DROPO'S AUSPICIOUS START TED WILLIAMS REMARKED THAT NOW THE BIG BOY WAS TAKING HIS FULL CUT.
.. BUT WHAT TED LIKED BEST WERE THE BASES ON BALLS! HE WAS RELAXED, NOT GOING FOR THE BAD ONES.

In 1950, Walt Dropo, after a great college career at the University of Connecticut, came up to the Red Sox and led the league in RBIs with 144, while hitting 34 home runs with a .322 average. This garnered Dropo the 1950 Rookie of the Year award.

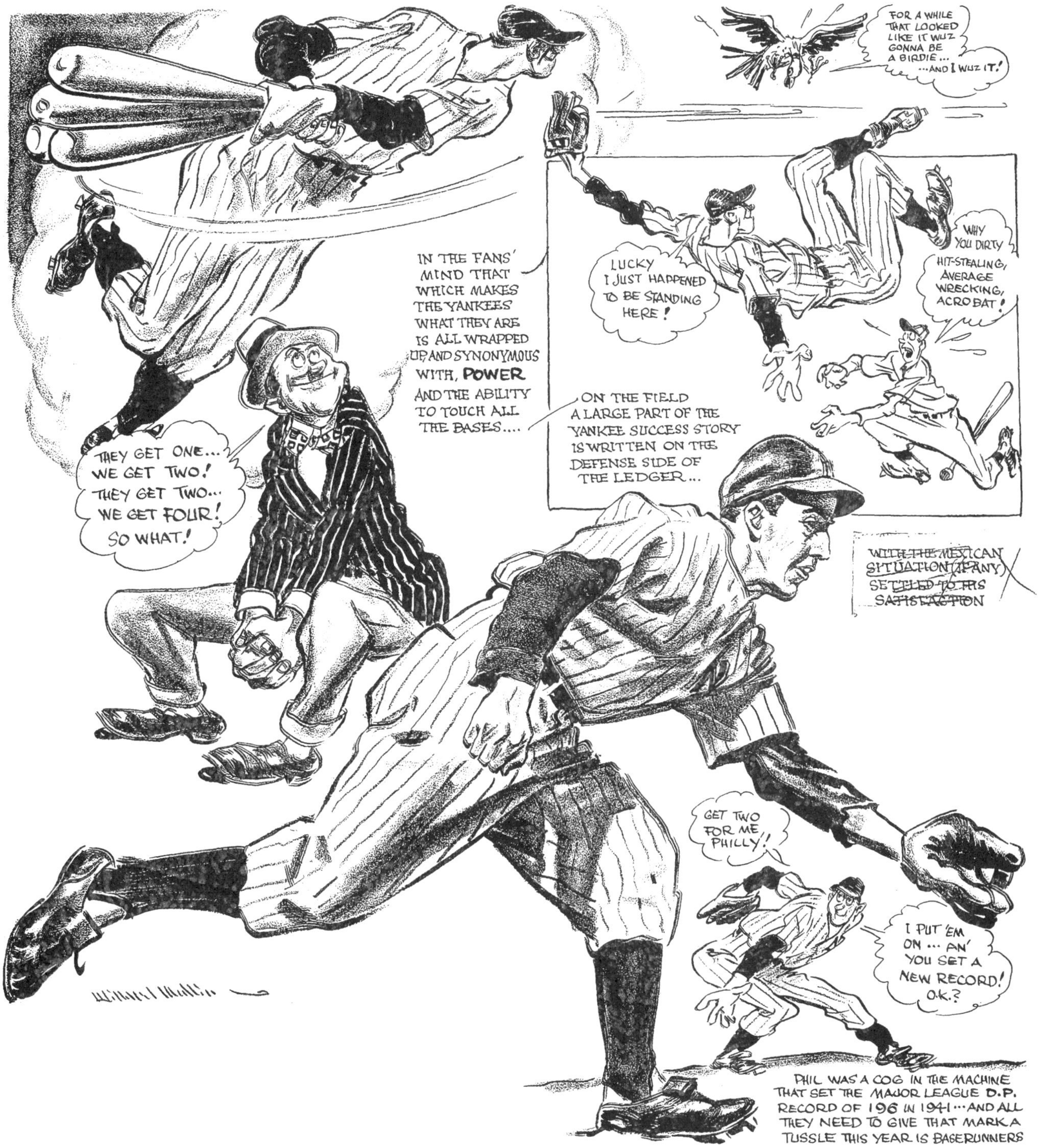
IN THE FANS' MIND THAT WHICH MAKES THE YANKEES WHAT THEY ARE IS ALL WRAPPED UP AND SYNONYMOUS WITH, POWER AND THE ABILITY TO TOUCH ALL THE BASES....
THEY GET ONE... WE GET TWO! THEY GET TWO... WE GET FOUR! SO WHAT!
FOR A WHILE THAT LOOKED LIKE IT WUZ GONNA BE A BIRDIE... ...AND I WUZ IT!
LUCKY I JUST HAPPENED TO BE STANDING HERE!
WHY YOU DIRTY HIT-STEALING, AVERAGE WRECKING, ACROBAT!
ON THE FIELD A LARGE PART OF THE YANKEE SUCCESS STORY IS WRITTEN ON THE DEFENSE SIDE OF THE LEDGER...
WITH THE MEXICAN SITUATION (IF ANY) SETTLED TO HIS SATISFACTION
GET TWO FOR ME PHILLY!
I PUT 'EM ON ... AN' YOU SET A NEW RECORD! O.K.?
PHIL WAS A COG IN THE MACHINE THAT SET THE MAJOR LEAGUE D.P. RECORD OF 196 IN 1941... AND ALL THEY NEED TO GIVE THAT MARK A TUSSLE THIS YEAR IS BASERUNNERS

Beginning with the Babe, the Yankees were known for their power hitters. However, it was their shortstop Phil Rizzuto who won the 1950 MVP with a .324 average, 92 walks, and 125 runs scored.

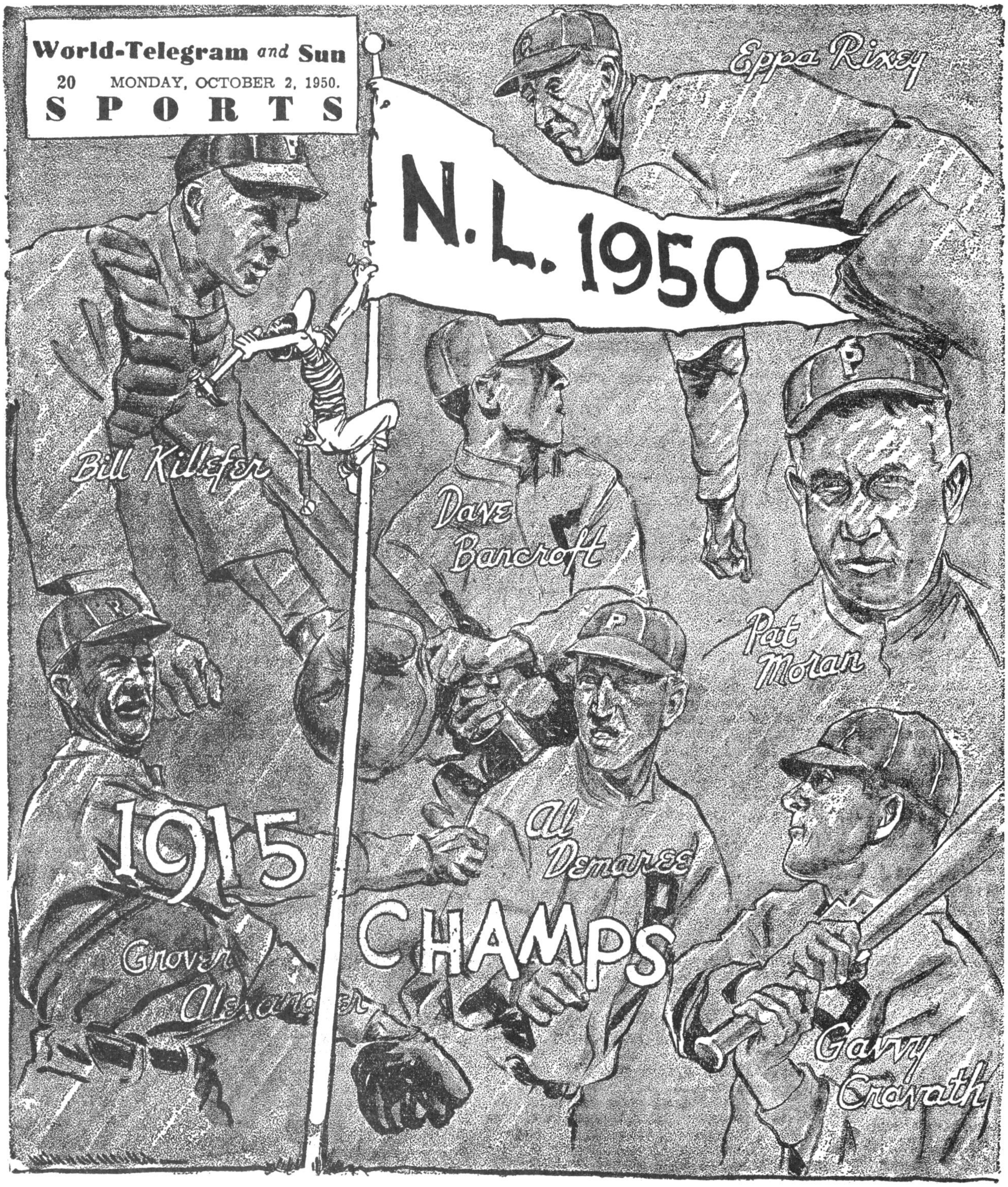
World-Telegram and Sun
20 MONDAY, OCTOBER 2, 1950.
SPORTS
N.L. 1950
Eppa Rixey
Bill Killefer
Dave Bancroft
Pat Moran
1915
Al Demaree
CHAMPS
Grover Alexander
Gavvy Cravath

In 1950, the "Whiz Kids" won Philadelphia's first pennant since 1915. However, it took a home run by Dick Sisler in the 10th inning on the last day of the season to defeat the Dodgers and clinch the pennant for the Phillies.

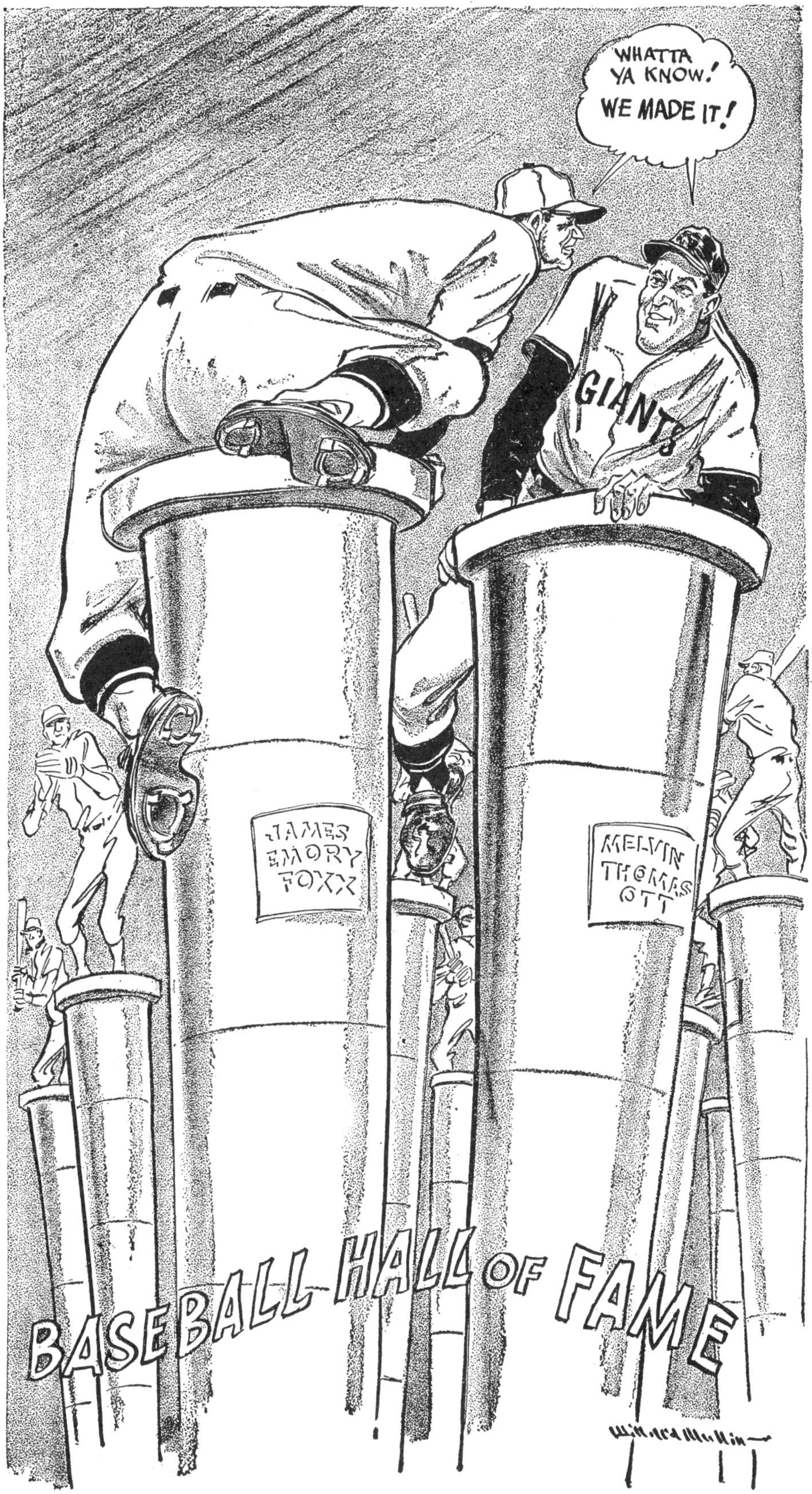
WHATTA YA KNOW! WE MADE IT!
GIANTS
JAMES EMORY FOXX
MELVIN THOMAS OTT
BASEBALL HALL OF FAME

In 1951, Jimmie Foxx and Mel Ott, both legendary home-run hitters from the 1920s and 1930s, were inducted into the Hall Of Fame.

Clark Griffith was a major league manager who owned the
Washington Senators from 1920 until his death in 1955.

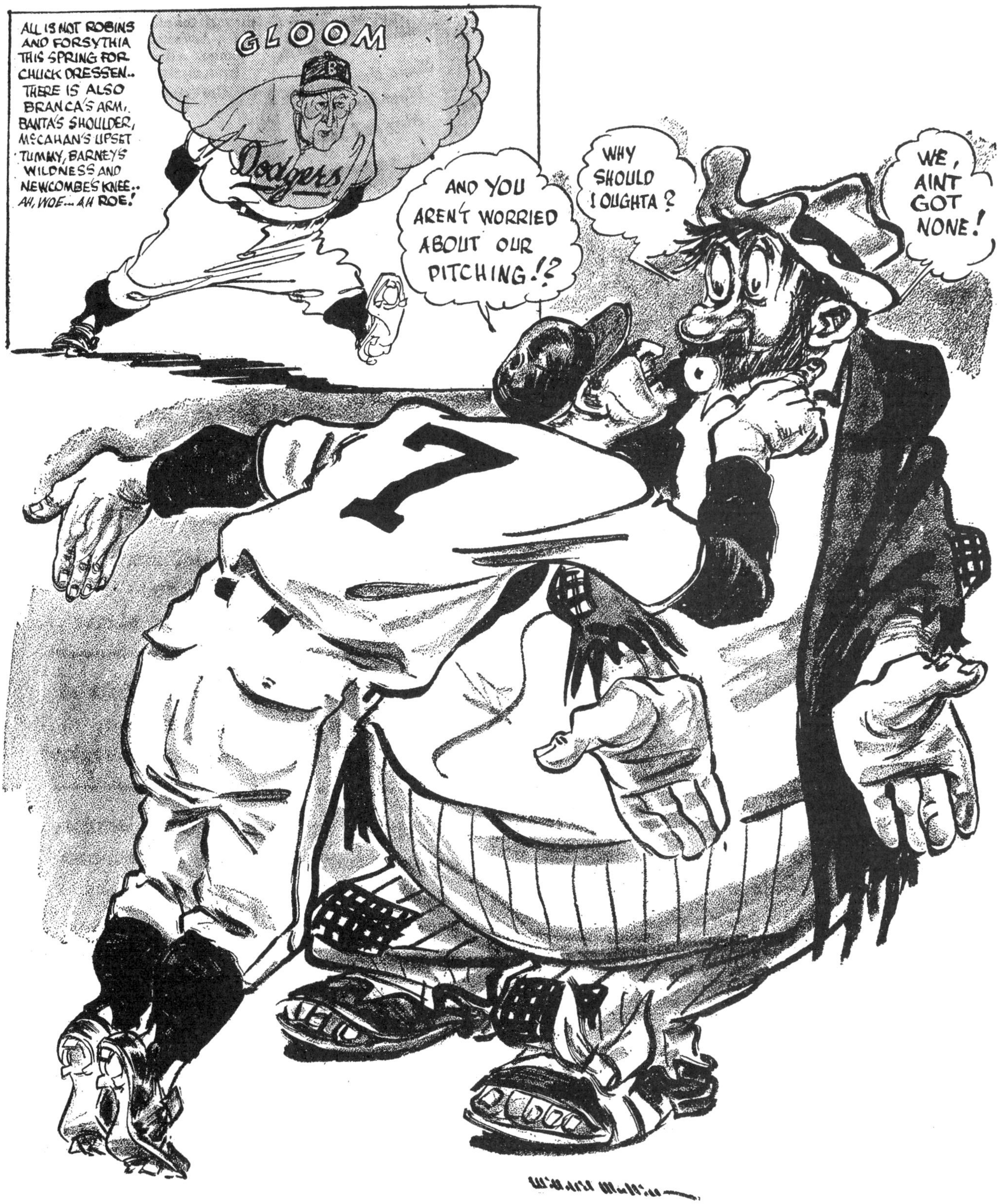
ALL IS NOT ROBINS AND FORSYTHIA THIS SPRING FOR CHUCK DRESSEN.. THERE IS ALSO BRANCA'S ARM, BANTA'S SHOULDER, McCAHAN'S UPSET TUMMY, BARNEY'S WILDNESS AND NEWCOMBE'S KNEE.. AH, WOE... AH ROE!
GLOOM
Dodgers
AND YOU AREN'T WORRIED ABOUT OUR PITCHING!?
WHY SHOULD I OUGHTA ?
WE, AINT GOT NONE!
7

Going into the 1951 season with Jackie Robinson, Roy Campanella, and Duke Snider, the Dodgers had plenty of hitting, but apparently no pitching.

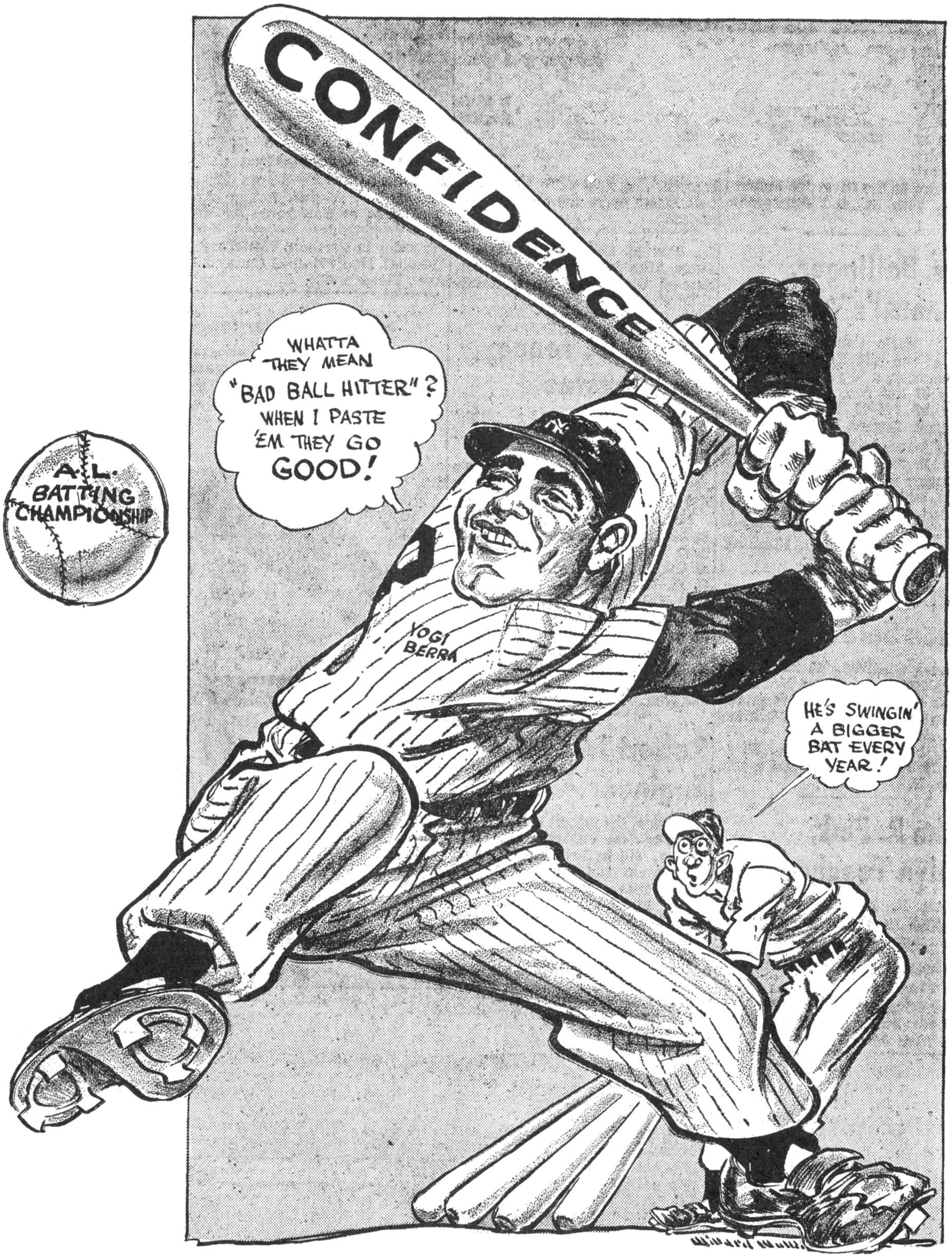
CONFIDENCE
WHATTA THEY MEAN "BAD BALL HITTER"? WHEN I PASTE 'EM THEY GO GOOD!
A.L. BATTING CHAMPIONSHIP
YOGI BERRA
HE'S SWINGIN' A BIGGER BAT EVERY YEAR!

Yogi Berra was a notorious "bad ball" hitter, and while he didn't win the American League batting championship as Mullin had predicted, he did win the first of three MVPs in 1951.

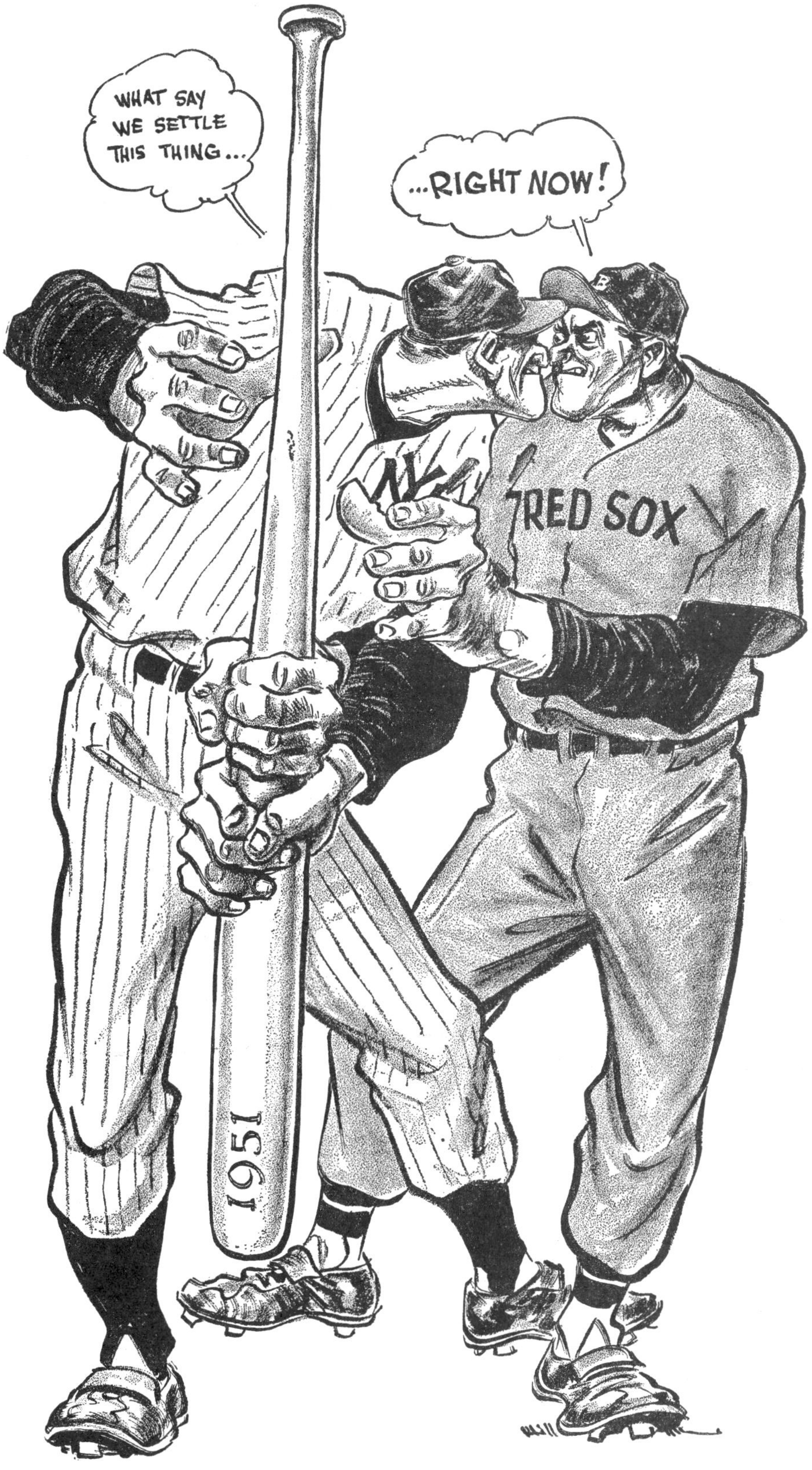
WHAT SAY WE SETTLE THIS THING...
...RIGHT NOW!
NY
RED SOX
1951

The struggle between the Yankees and the Red Sox has been one of the defining rivalries in sports. This drawing from 1951 documents just one chapter in that rivalry. The Yankees won again that year.

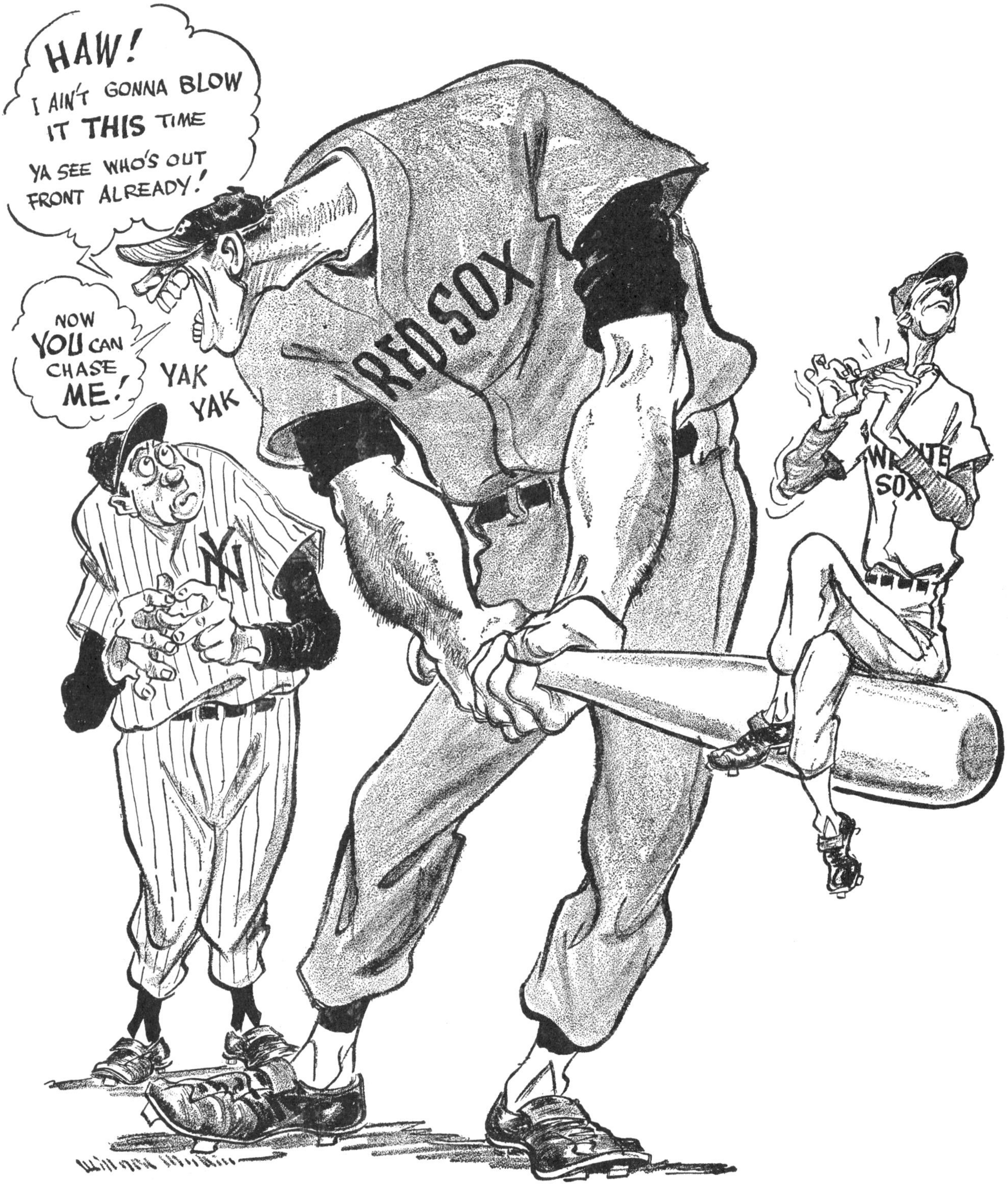
HAW!
I AIN'T GONNA BLOW IT THIS TIME
YA SEE WHO'S OUT FRONT ALREADY!
NOW YOU CAN CHASE ME!
YAK YAK
RED SOX
SOX

This cartoon from July 1951 shows the Red Sox, confident that they are not going to blow yet another pennant to the Yankees. Unfortunately, their confidence was again misplaced. Not only did they lose the pennant, but they finished in third place, 11 games behind the Yankees.

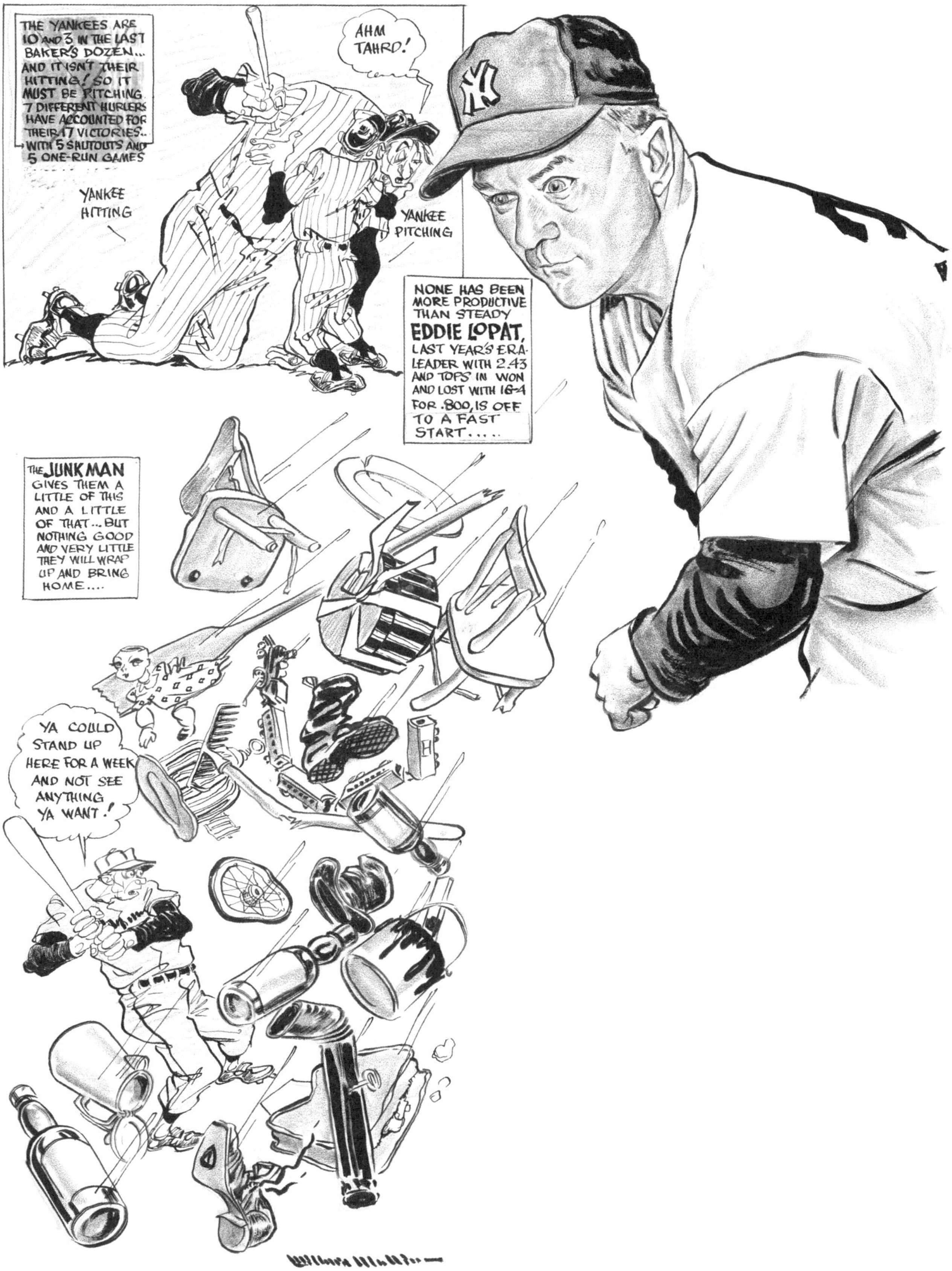
THE YANKEES ARE 10 AND 3 IN THE LAST BAKER'S DOZEN... AND IT ISN'T THEIR HITTING! SO IT MUST BE PITCHING. 7 DIFFERENT HURLERS HAVE ACCOUNTED FOR THEIR 17 VICTORIES.. WITH 5 SHUTOUTS AND 5 ONE-RUN GAMES
AHM TAHRD!
YANKEE HITTING
YANKEE PITCHING
NONE HAS BEEN MORE PRODUCTIVE THAN STEADY EDDIE LOPAT, LAST YEAR'S ERA LEADER WITH 2.43 AND TOPS IN WON AND LOST WITH 16-4 FOR .800, IS OFF TO A FAST START....
THE JUNKMAN GIVES THEM A LITTLE OF THIS AND A LITTLE OF THAT... BUT NOTHING GOOD AND VERY LITTLE THEY WILL WRAP UP AND BRING HOME....
YA COULD STAND UP HERE FOR A WEEK AND NOT SEE ANYTHING YA WANT!

When the Yankees won five straight World Series Championships (1949–1953), the anchor of their team was their pitching staff, composed of Allie Reynolds, Vic Raschi, and Ed Lopat. Lopat was the quintessential "junkball" pitcher, as Mullin humorously illustrated in this drawing.

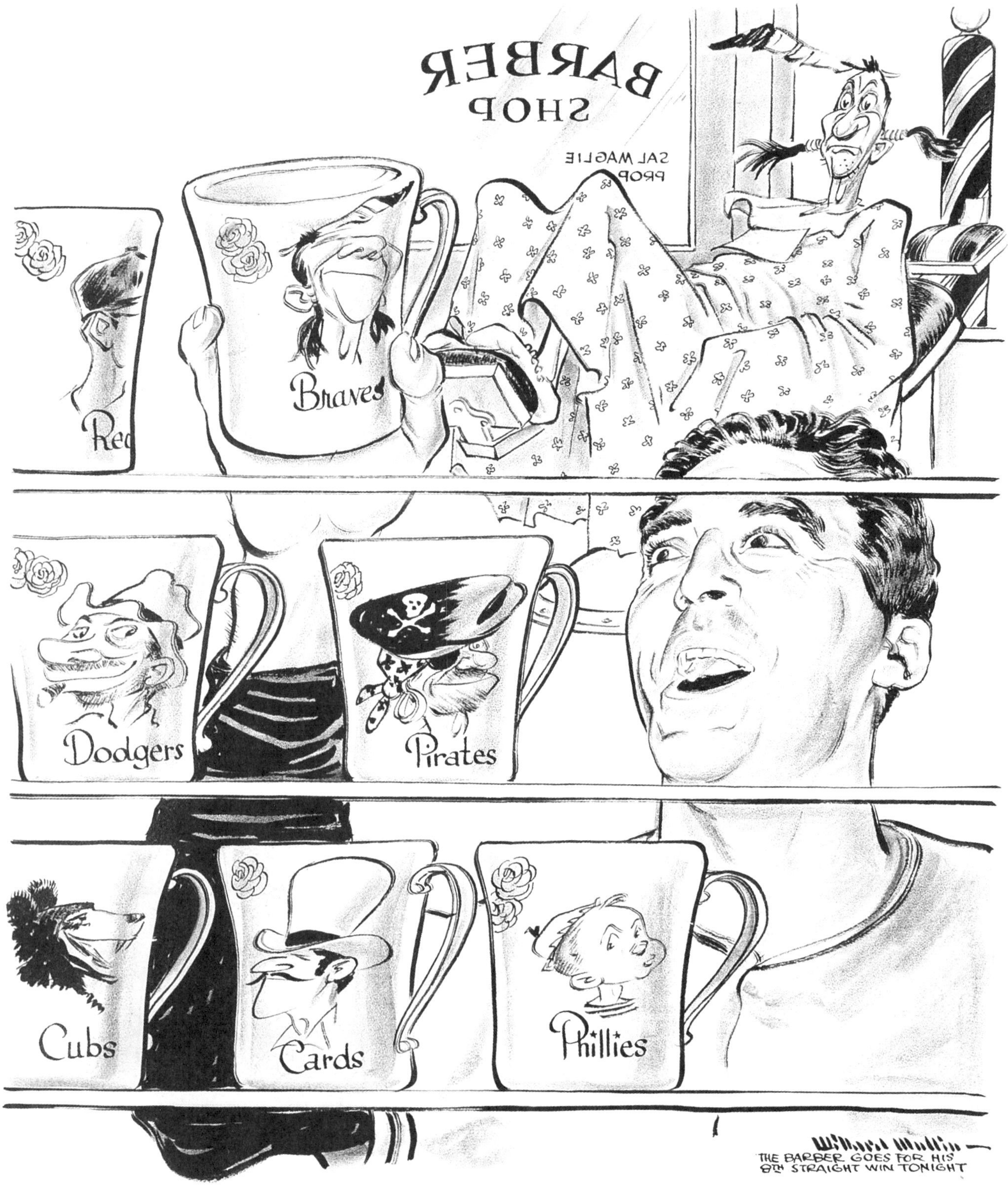
BARBER SHOP
SAL MAGLIE PROP
Braves
Dodgers
Pirates
Cubs
Cards
Phillies
THE BARBER GOES FOR HIS 8TH STRAIGHT WIN TONIGHT

Sal Maglie didn't make it to the majors until he was 28 and he didn't make it to stay until he was 33, but he won 81 games for the New York Giants between 1950 and 1954. He led the league in winning percentage in 1950 and wins (with 23) in 1951. His nickname, "The Barber," came from the "close shaves" he liked to give opposing batters with his fastball.

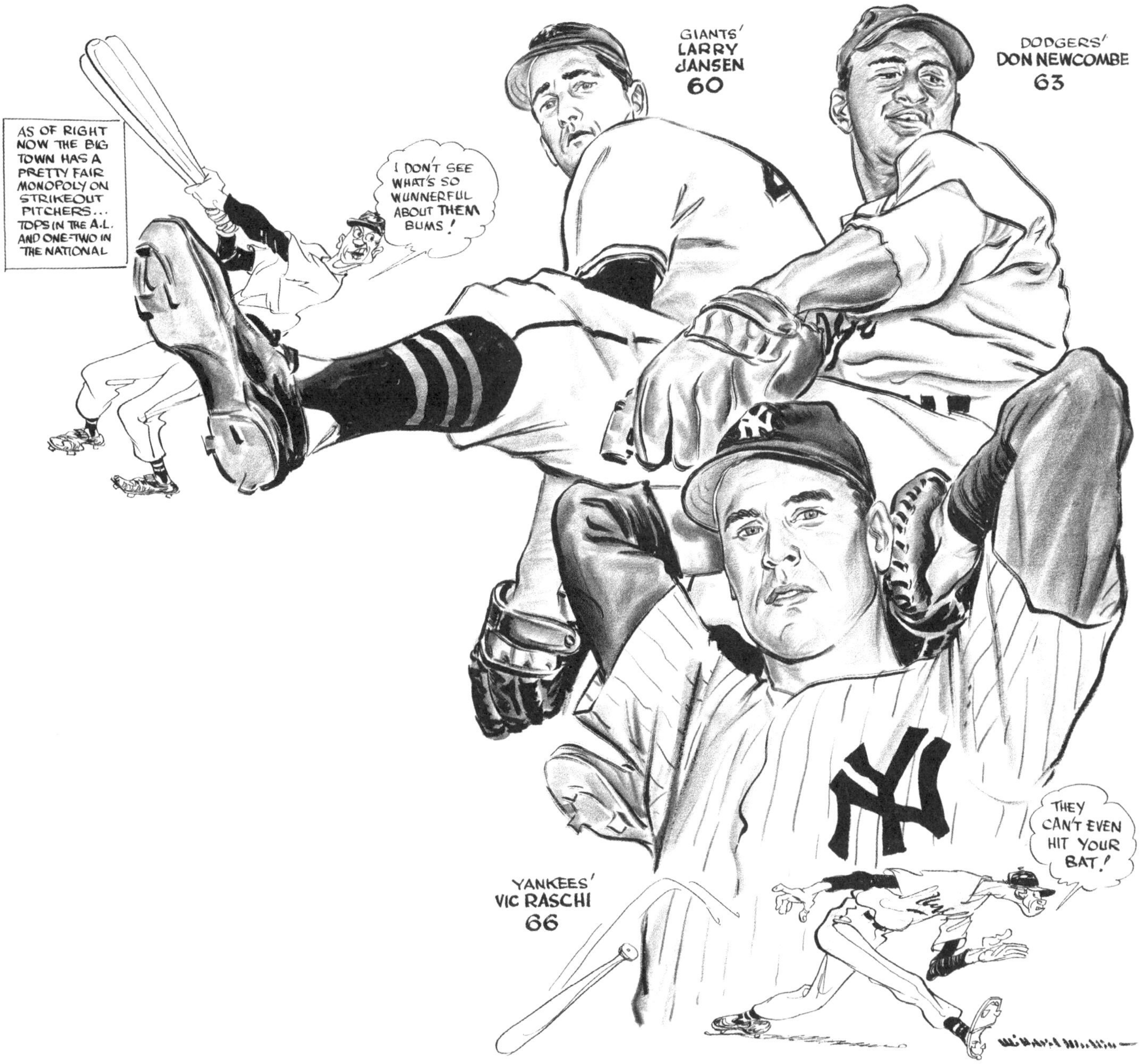
AS OF RIGHT NOW THE BIG TOWN HAS A PRETTY FAIR MONOPOLY ON STRIKEOUT PITCHERS... TOPS IN THE A.L. AND ONE-TWO IN THE NATIONAL
I DON'T SEE WHAT'S SO WUNNERFUL ABOUT THEM BUMS!
GIANTS' LARRY JANSEN 60
DODGERS' DON NEWCOMBE 63
YANKEES' VIC RASCHI 66
THEY CAN'T EVEN HIT YOUR BAT!

In 1951, the three New York teams had three of the top strike-out pitchers in baseball.

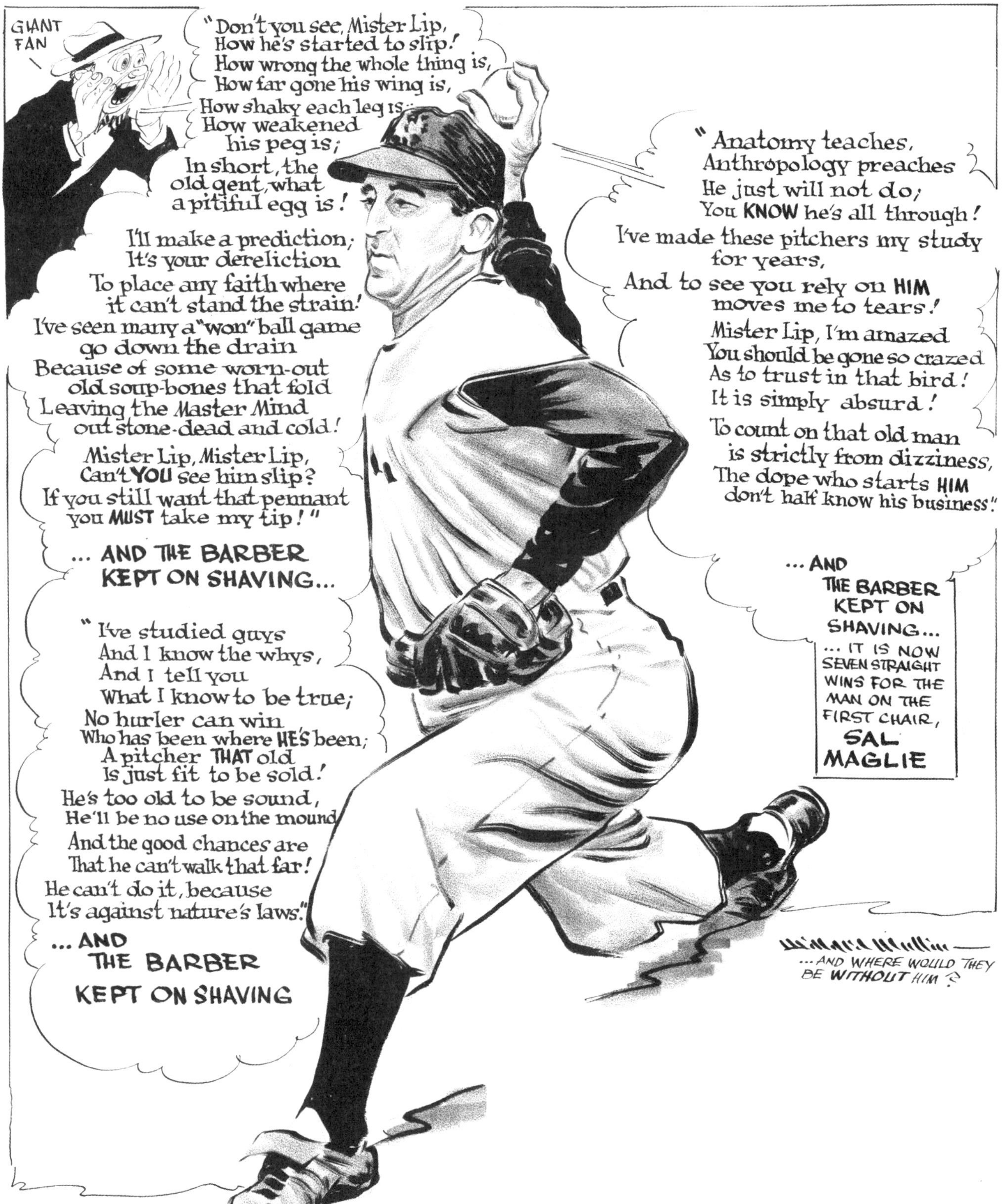
GIANT FAN
"Don't you see, Mister Lip,
How he's started to slip!
How wrong the whole thing is,
How far gone his wing is,
How shaky each leg is;
How weakened his peg is;
In short, the old gent, what a pitiful egg is!
I'll make a prediction;
It's your dereliction
To place any faith where it can't stand the strain!
I've seen many a "won" ball game go down the drain
Because of some worn-out old soup-bones that fold
Leaving the Master Mind out stone-dead and cold!
Mister Lip, Mister Lip,
Can't YOU see him slip?
If you still want that pennant you MUST take my tip!"
... AND THE BARBER KEPT ON SHAVING...
"Anatomy teaches,
Anthropology preaches
He just will not do;
You KNOW he's all through!
I've made these pitchers my study for years,
And to see you rely on HIM moves me to tears!
Mister Lip, I'm amazed
You should be gone so crazed
As to trust in that bird!
It is simply absurd!
To count on that old man is strictly from dizziness,
The dope who starts HIM don't half know his business."
... AND THE BARBER KEPT ON SHAVING...
"I've studied guys
And I know the whys,
And I tell you
What I know to be true;
No hurler can win
Who has been where HE'S been;
A pitcher THAT old
Is just fit to be sold!
He's too old to be sound,
He'll be no use on the mound
And the good chances are
That he can't walk that far!
He can't do it, because
It's against nature's laws."
... AND THE BARBER KEPT ON SHAVING
... IT IS NOW SEVEN STRAIGHT WINS FOR THE MAN ON THE FIRST CHAIR, SAL MAGLIE
... AND WHERE WOULD THEY BE WITHOUT HIM?

In 1951, Sal Maglie was a big reason the Giants won the pennant, leading the league in wins with 23.

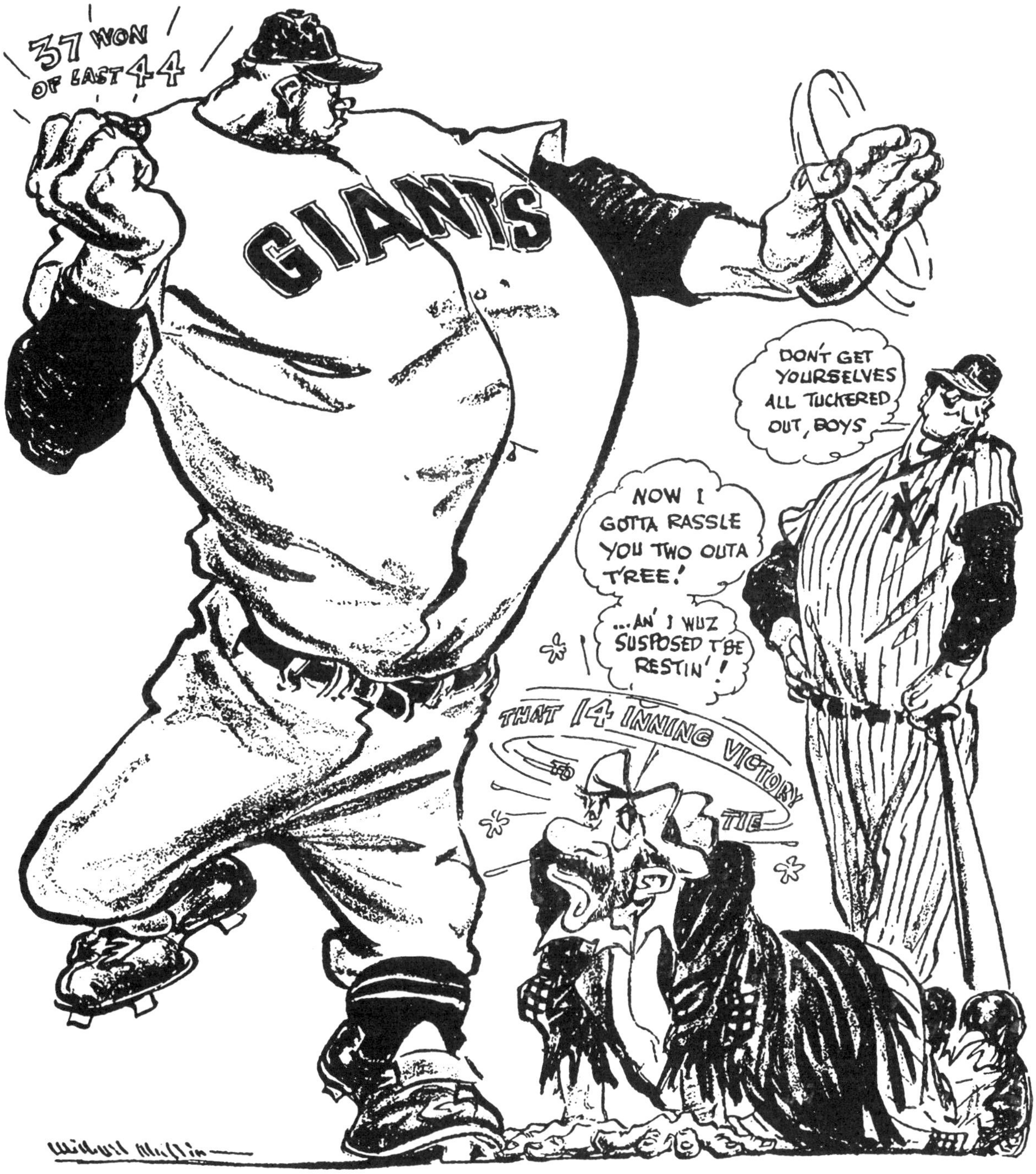
37 WON OF LAST 44
GIANTS
DON'T GET YOURSELVES ALL TUCKERED OUT, BOYS
NOW I GOTTA RASSLE YOU TWO OUTA T'REE!
...AN' I WUZ SUSPOSED T'BE RESTIN'!
THAT 14 INNING VICTORY
TIE

In 1951, the Giants won 37 of their last 44 games to tie the Dodgers at the end of the season. A three-game playoff ensued, which the Giants ultimately won on Bobby Thomson's "Shot Heard 'Round the World" home run.

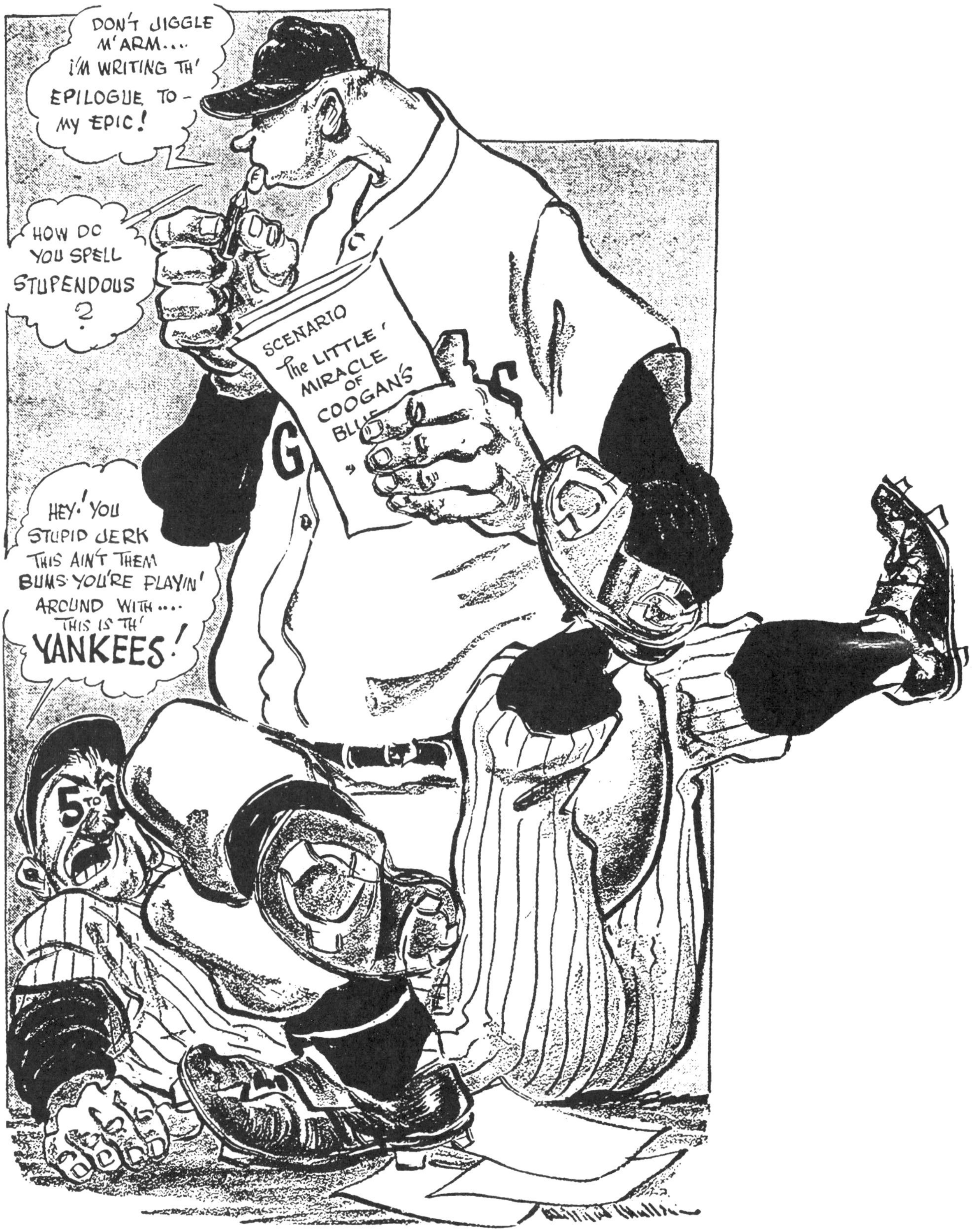
DON'T JIGGLE M'ARM.... I'M WRITING TH' EPILOGUE TO - MY EPIC!
HOW DO YOU SPELL STUPENDOUS ?
SCENARIO
The LITTLE MIRACLE OF COOGAN'S
HEY! YOU STUPID JERK THIS AIN'T THEM BUMS YOU'RE PLAYIN' AROUND WITH.... THIS IS TH' YANKEES!
5 TO 1

The Giants followed their victory over the Dodgers by taking the first game of the World Series from the Yankees. The magic would run out, however, as the Yankees took four of the next five to win their third World Series Championship in a row.

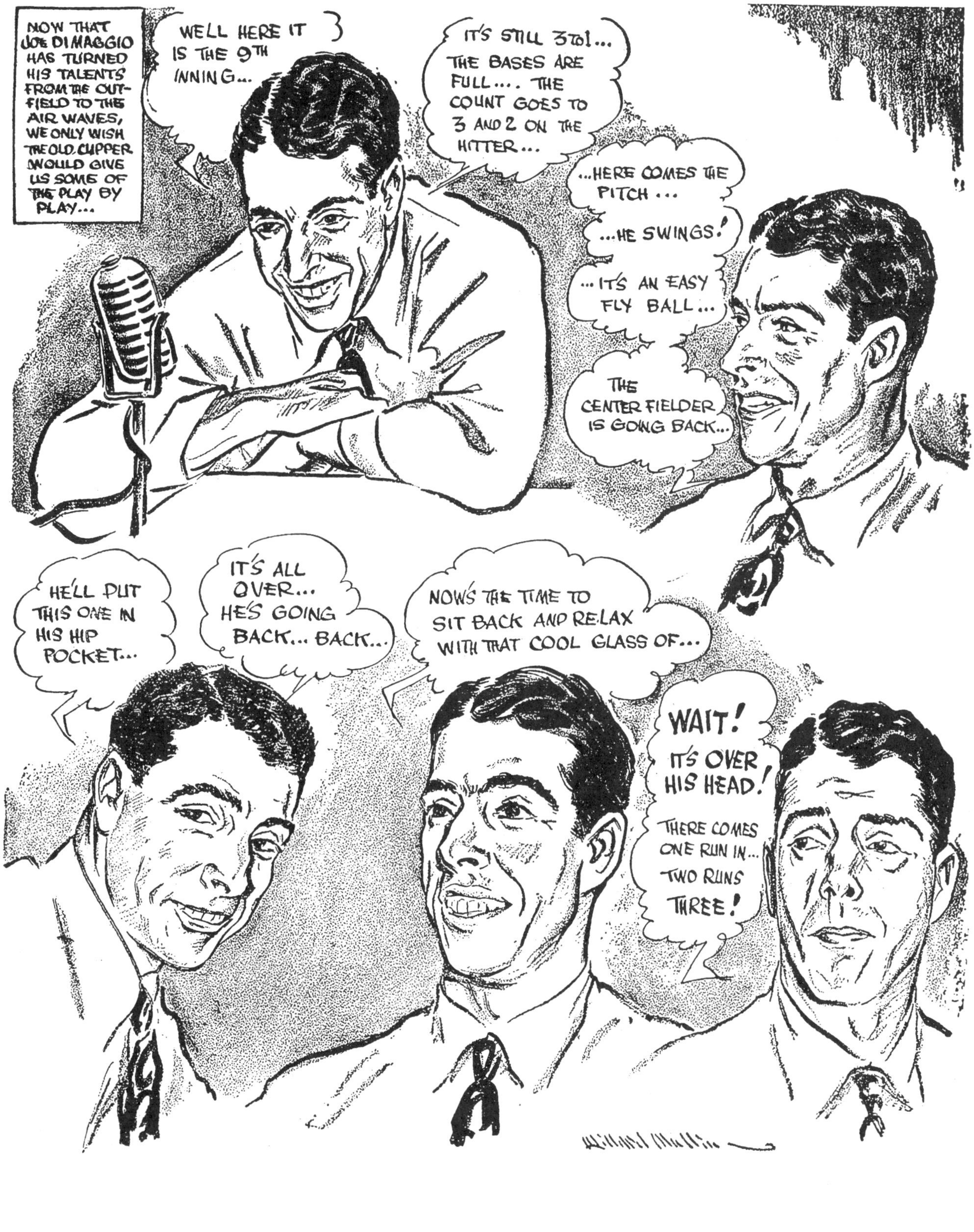
NOW THAT JOE DI MAGGIO HAS TURNED HIS TALENTS FROM THE OUT-FIELD TO THE AIR WAVES, WE ONLY WISH THE OLD CLIPPER WOULD GIVE US SOME OF THE PLAY BY PLAY...
WELL HERE IT IS THE 9TH INNING...
IT'S STILL 3 TO 1... THE BASES ARE FULL.... THE COUNT GOES TO 3 AND 2 ON THE HITTER...
...HERE COMES THE PITCH...
...HE SWINGS!
...IT'S AN EASY FLY BALL...
THE CENTER FIELDER IS GOING BACK...
HE'LL PUT THIS ONE IN HIS HIP POCKET...
IT'S ALL OVER... HE'S GOING BACK... BACK...
NOW'S THE TIME TO SIT BACK AND RE-LAX WITH THAT COOL GLASS OF...
WAIT! IT'S OVER HIS HEAD!
THERE COMES ONE RUN IN... TWO RUNS THREE!

After he retired, Joe DiMaggio worked briefly as an announcer, but he had difficulty explaining the actions of players who did not exhibit the same level of skill that he had displayed in his prime.

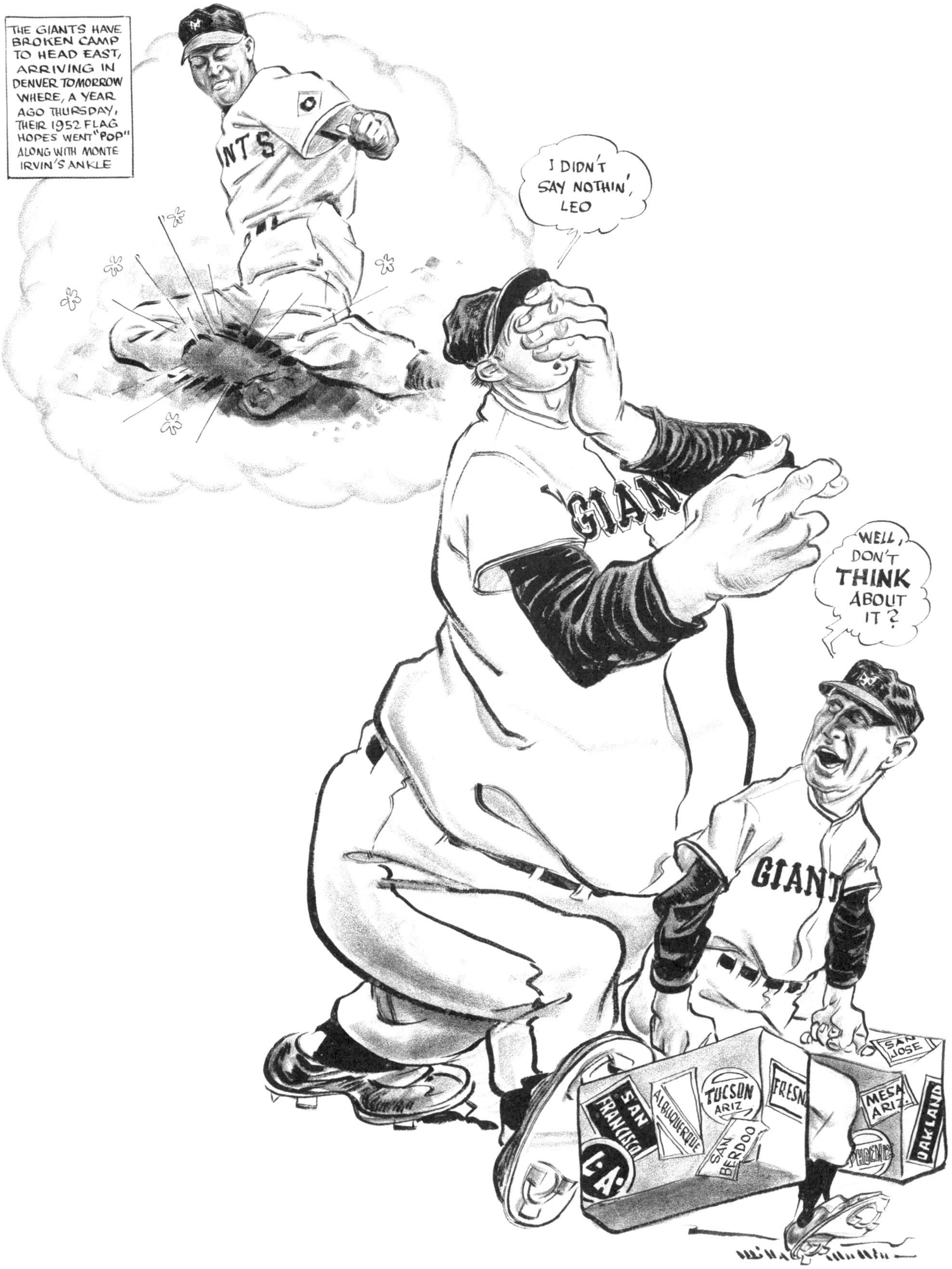
THE GIANTS HAVE BROKEN CAMP TO HEAD EAST, ARRIVING IN DENVER TOMORROW WHERE, A YEAR AGO THURSDAY, THEIR 1952 FLAG HOPES WENT "POP" ALONG WITH MONTE IRVIN'S ANKLE
I DIDN'T SAY NOTHIN', LEO
WELL, DON'T THINK ABOUT IT?
GIANTS
GIANTS
SAN FRANCISCO
ALBUQUERQUE
TUCSON ARIZ
FRESNO
SAN JOSE
MESA ARIZ
OAKLAND
SAN BERDOO
PHOENIX
L.A.

In April 1952, the Giants' hopes of defending their NL title were shortcircuited when All-Star Monte Irvin broke his ankle in Denver. A year later, the 1953 Giants were headed back to the Mile High City, hoping to avoid the same fate.

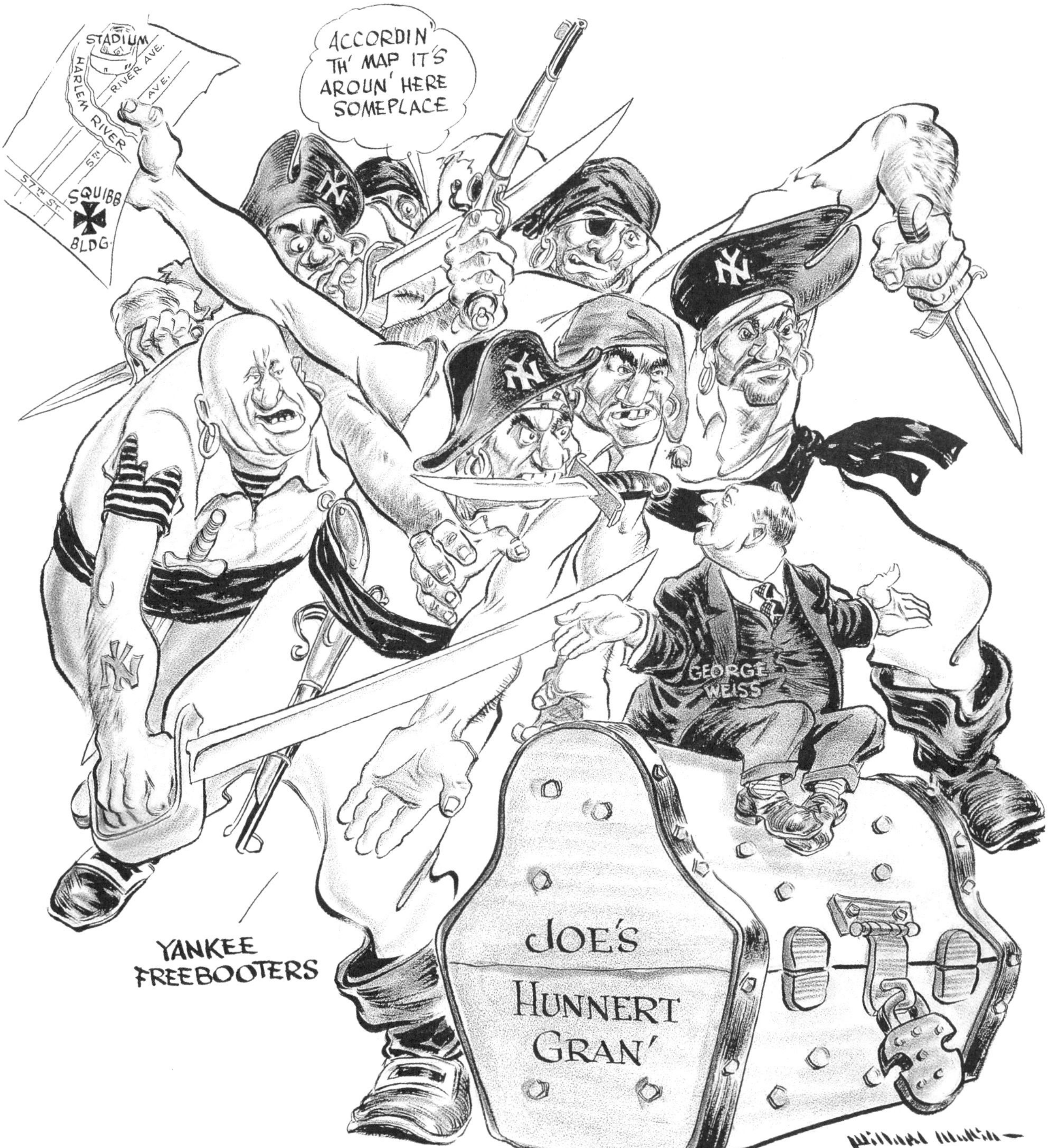
STADIUM
RIVER AVE.
HARLEM RIVER
AVE.
5TH
57TH ST.
SQUIBB BLDG.
ACCORDIN' TH' MAP IT'S AROUN' HERE SOMEPLACE
GEORGE WEISS
YANKEE FREEBOOTERS
JOE'S HUNNERT GRAN'

Joe DiMaggio retired after the 1951 season, freeing up $100,000 in salary for the next season. Mullin anticipated that a number of players would be attempting to increase their salary with some of this newly “found” money.

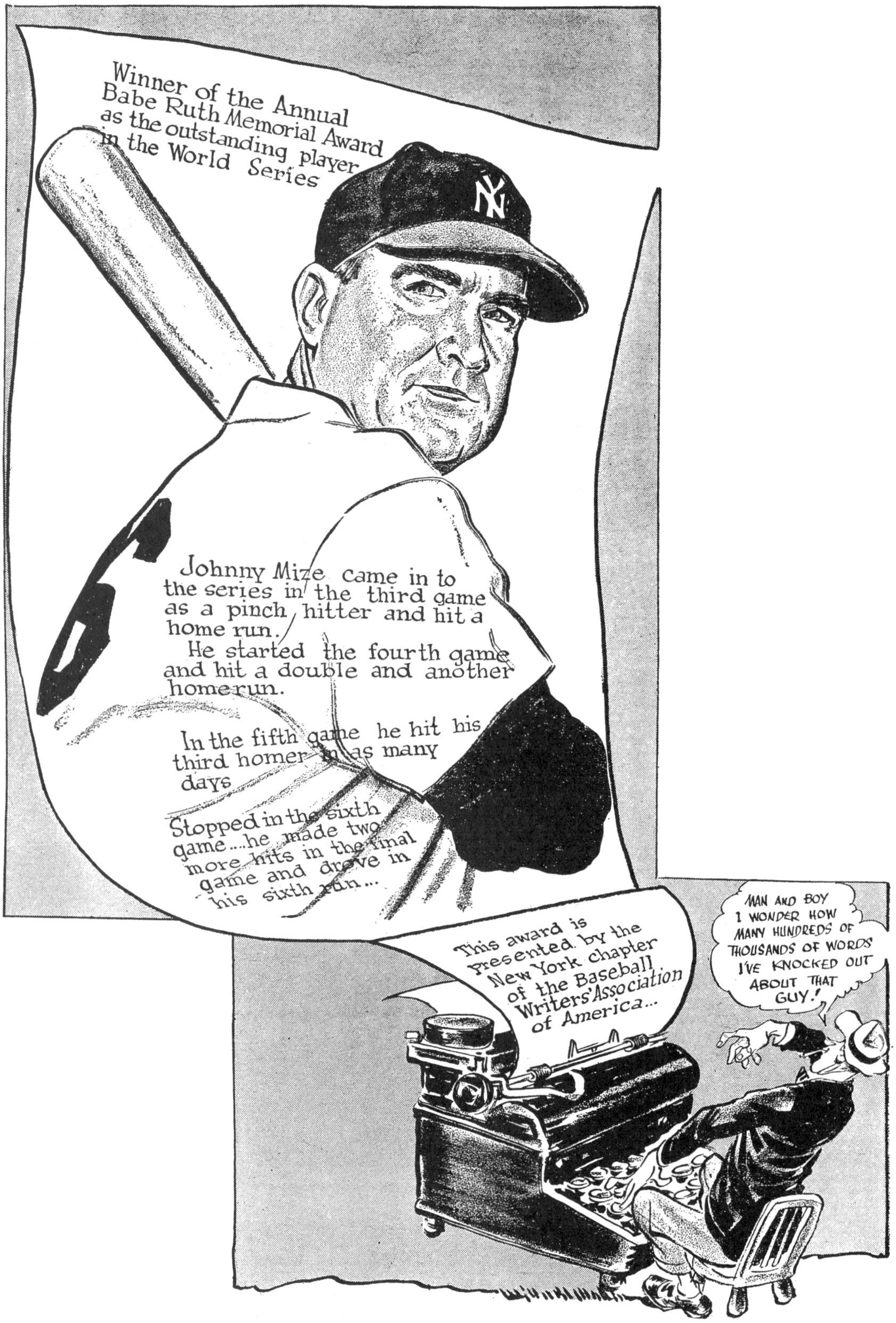
Winner of the Annual Babe Ruth Memorial Award as the outstanding player in the World Series
Johnny Mize came in to the series in the third game as a pinch hitter and hit a home run.
He started the fourth game and hit a double and another homerun.
In the fifth game he hit his third homer in as many days
Stopped in the sixth game....he made two more hits in the final game and drove in his sixth run...
This award is presented by the New York chapter of the Baseball Writers' Association of America...
MAN AND BOY I WONDER HOW MANY HUNDREDS OF THOUSANDS OF WORDS I'VE KNOCKED OUT ABOUT THAT GUY!

In the 1952 World Series, Johnny Mize hit three home runs to beat the Dodgers and help the Yankees win their fourth straight World Series.

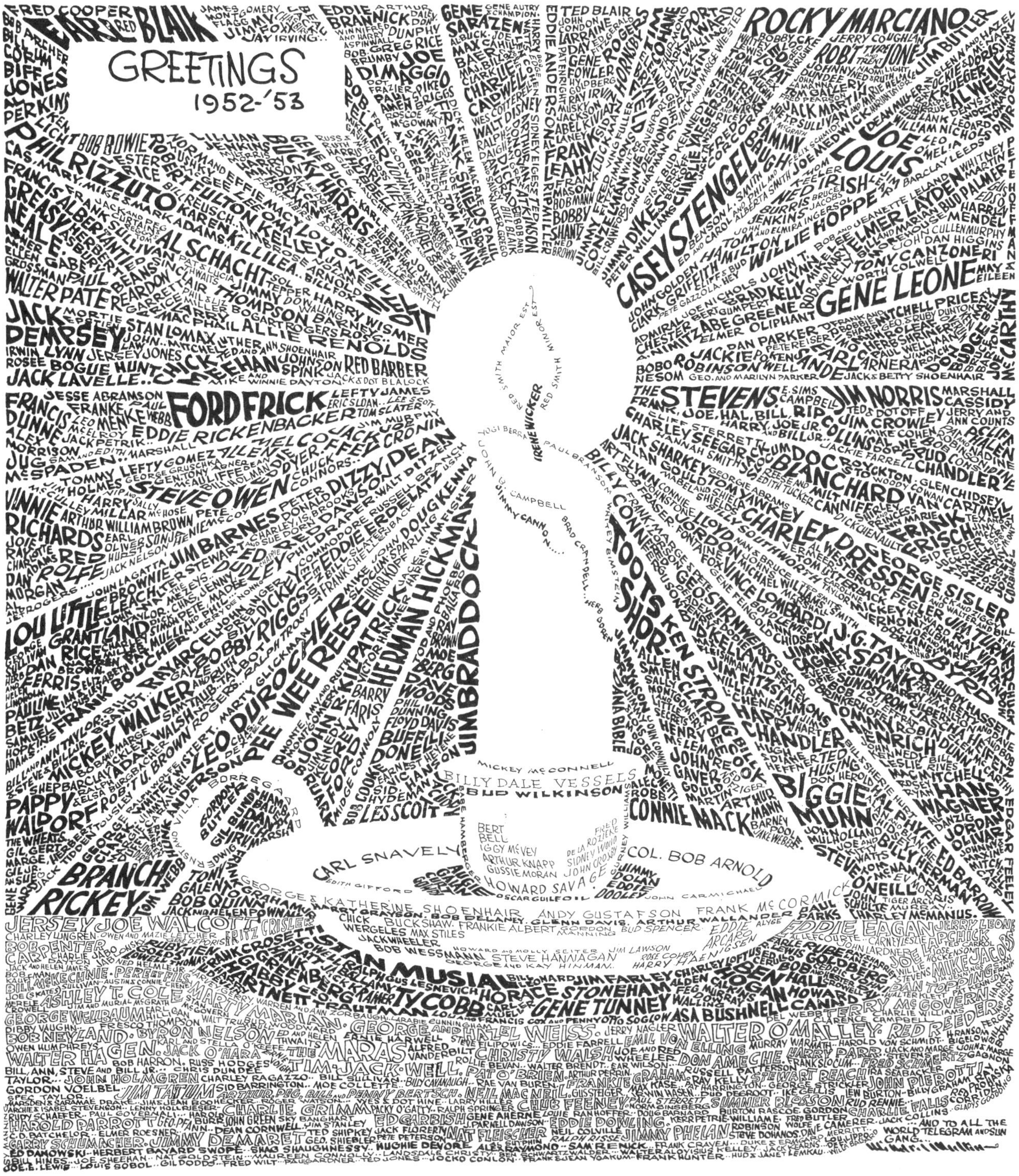
GREETINGS
1952-'53

Because of his work, Mullin knew almost everyone in the world of sports. He came up with a solution to his endless Christmas card list by creating a holiday image composed of the names of all of his friends and acquaintances. If you look closely at this one from 1952, you will see not only sports notables, but famous people from all walks of life, including actor Jimmy Cagney, Admiral Chester Nimitz, broadcaster Lowell Thomas, restauranteur Toots Shor, cartoonist Milton Caniff, and comedian Joe E. Lewis. These drawings were all hand-lettered and took Mullin up to four days to complete.

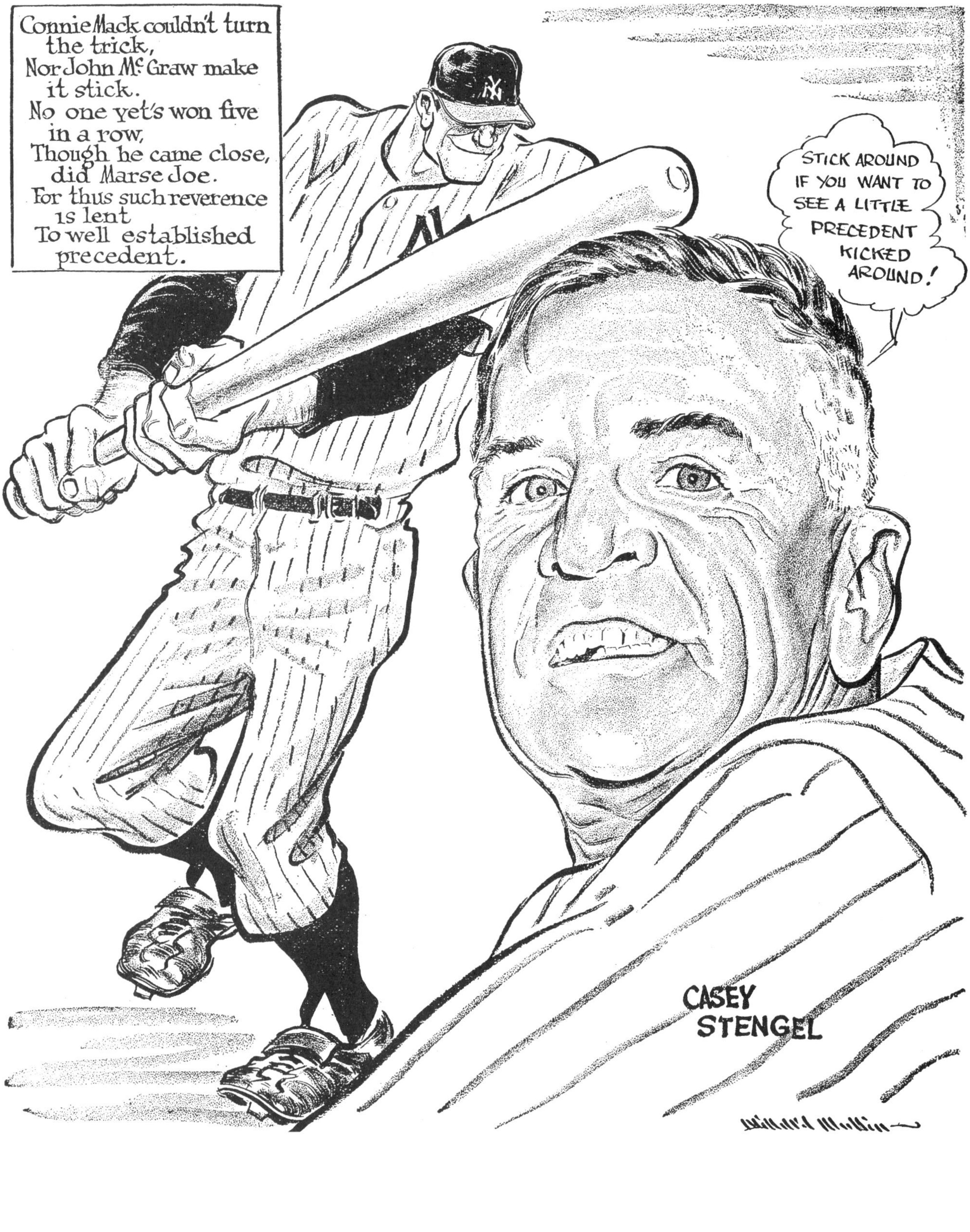
Connie Mack couldn't turn the trick,
Nor John McGraw make it stick.
No one yet's won five in a row,
Though he came close, did Marse Joe.
For thus such reverence is lent
To well established precedent.
STICK AROUND IF YOU WANT TO SEE A LITTLE PRECEDENT KICKED AROUND!
CASEY STENGEL

In 1953, Casey Stengel accomplished what no other manager has ever done before or since — he won his fifth straight World Series Championship. Mullin anticipated Stengel's accomplishment in this cartoon from April of that year.

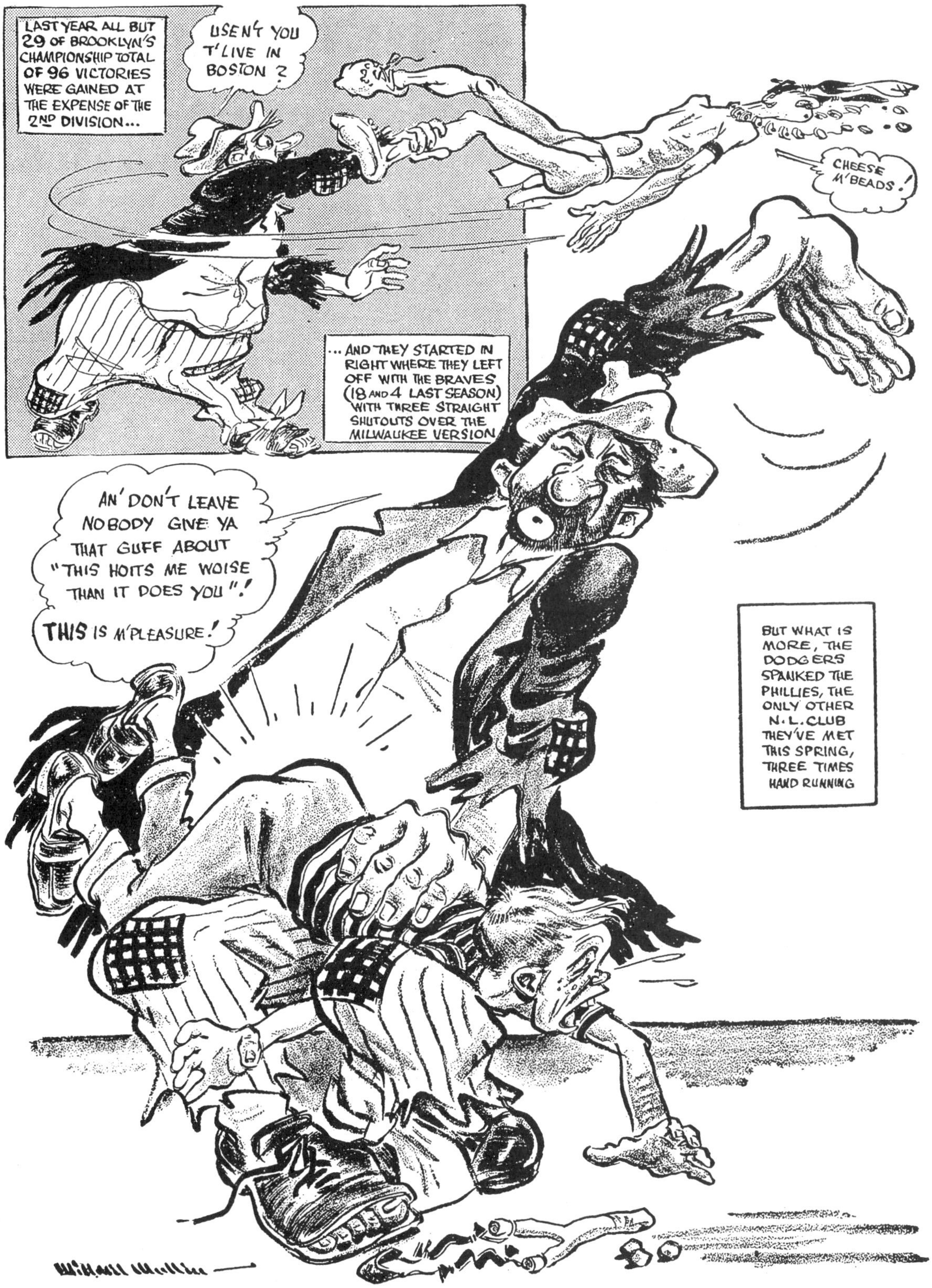
LAST YEAR ALL BUT 29 OF BROOKLYN'S CHAMPIONSHIP TOTAL OF 96 VICTORIES WERE GAINED AT THE EXPENSE OF THE 2ND DIVISION...
USEN'T YOU T'LIVE IN BOSTON ?
CHEESE M'BEADS!
...AND THEY STARTED IN RIGHT WHERE THEY LEFT OFF WITH THE BRAVES (18 AND 4 LAST SEASON) WITH THREE STRAIGHT SHUTOUTS OVER THE MILWAUKEE VERSION
AN' DON'T LEAVE NOBODY GIVE YA THAT GUFF ABOUT "THIS HOITS ME WOISE THAN IT DOES YOU"! THIS IS M'PLEASURE!
BUT WHAT IS MORE, THE DODGERS SPANKED THE PHILLIES, THE ONLY OTHER N.L. CLUB THEY'VE MET THIS SPRING, THREE TIMES HAND RUNNING

The 1953 Brooklyn Dodgers were one of the greatest baseball teams of all time. The core players of 1953 had won the National League pennant in 1949 and 1952. They would win it again that year, again in 1955, again in 1956, and they would take the World Series Championship in 1955.

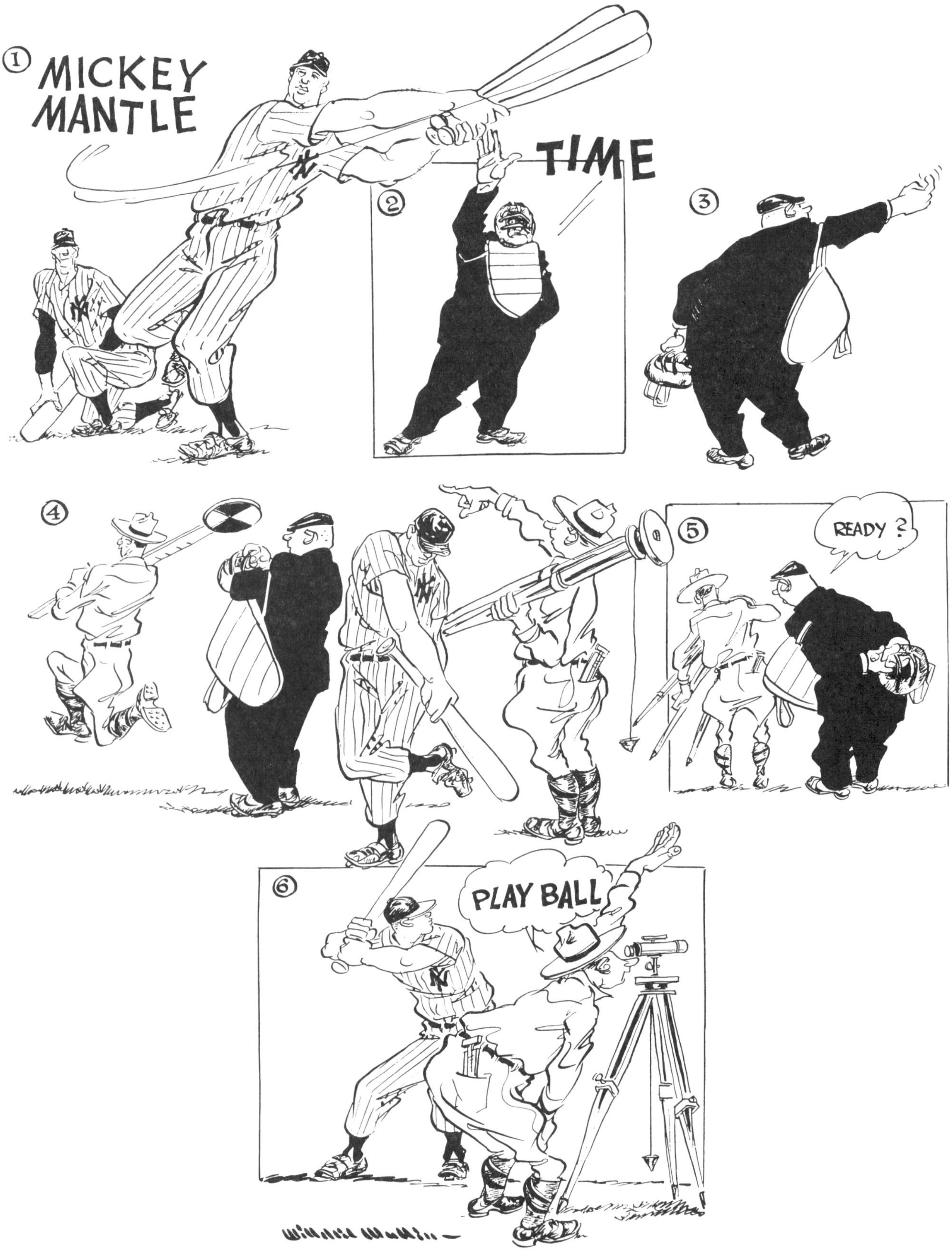
MICKEY MANTLE
TIME
READY ?
PLAY BALL

Mickey Mantle became famous for hitting what came to be referred to as “tape measure” home runs. In 1953 alone, “The Mick” hit five home runs that were measured at over 530 feet. The longest, 650 feet, ricocheted off the right-field roof at Briggs Stadium in Detroit in June. The longest slam of Mantle’s career was 734 feet in Yankee Stadium in 1963.

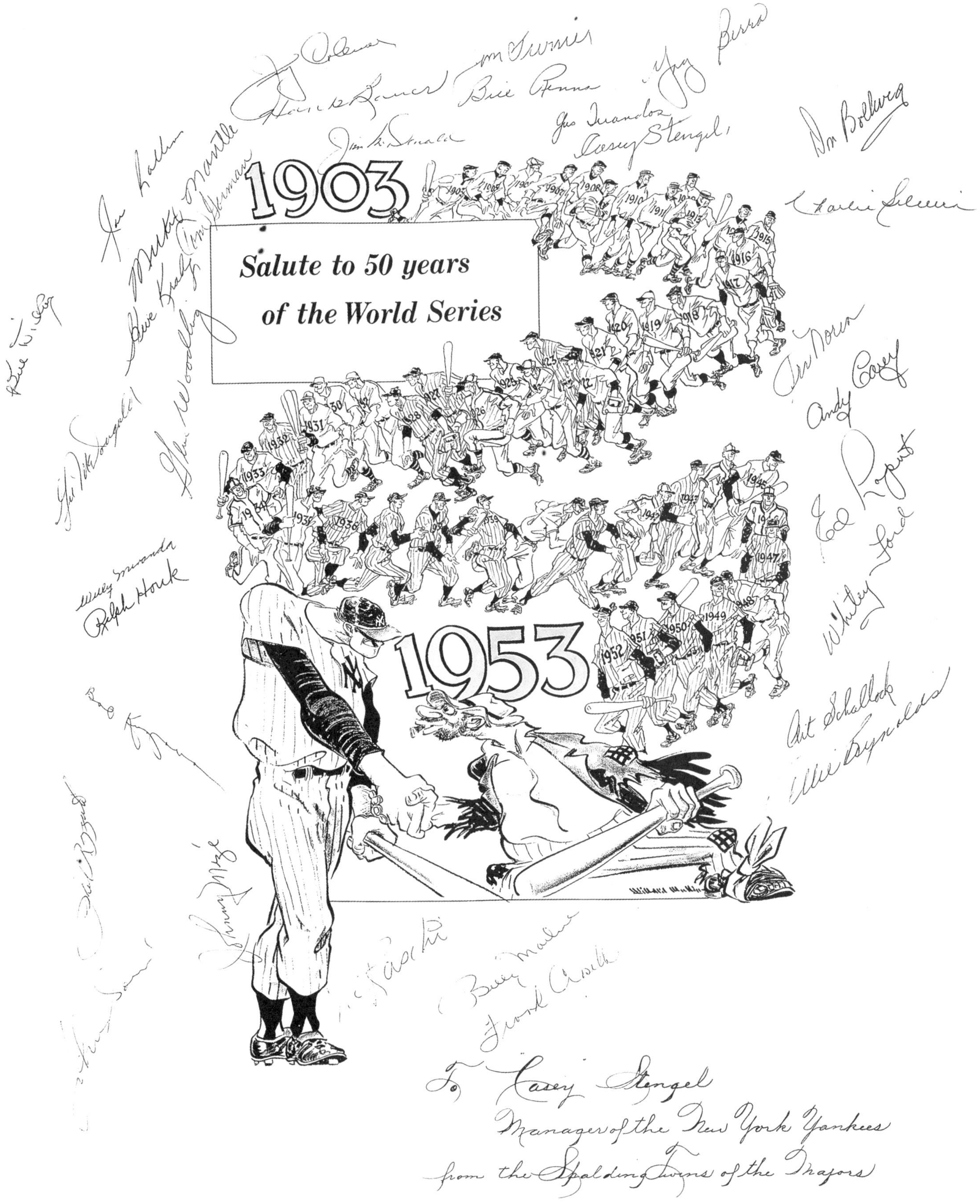
1903
Salute to 50 years
of the World Series
1953
To Casey Stengel
Manager of the New York Yankees
from the Spalding Twins of the Majors

This piece was drawn by Mullin specifically for Casey Stengel in 1953, in celebration of the 50th anniversary of the World Series.

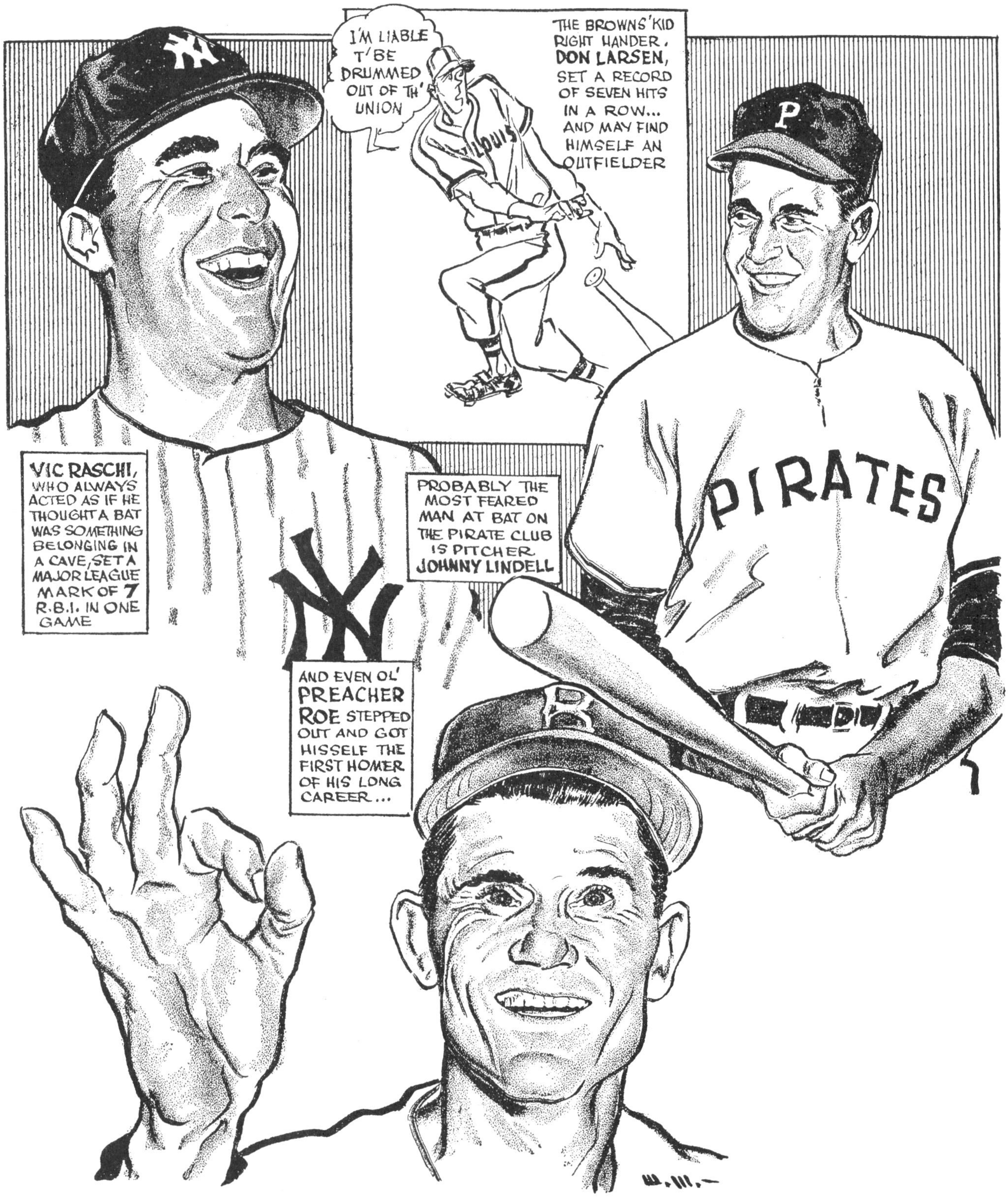
I'M LIABLE T'BE DRUMMED OUT OF TH' UNION
THE BROWNS' KID RIGHT HANDER, DON LARSEN, SET A RECORD OF SEVEN HITS IN A ROW... AND MAY FIND HIMSELF AN OUTFIELDER
VIC RASCHI, WHO ALWAYS ACTED AS IF HE THOUGHT A BAT WAS SOMETHING BELONGING IN A CAVE, SET A MAJOR LEAGUE MARK OF 7 R.B.I. IN ONE GAME
PROBABLY THE MOST FEARED MAN AT BAT ON THE PIRATE CLUB IS PITCHER JOHNNY LINDELL
PIRATES
AND EVEN OL' PREACHER ROE STEPPED OUT AND GOT HISSELF THE FIRST HOMER OF HIS LONG CAREER...

Pitchers are notoriously bad hitters, but during this 1953 stretch, several of them showed that, on occasion, they could handle a bat.

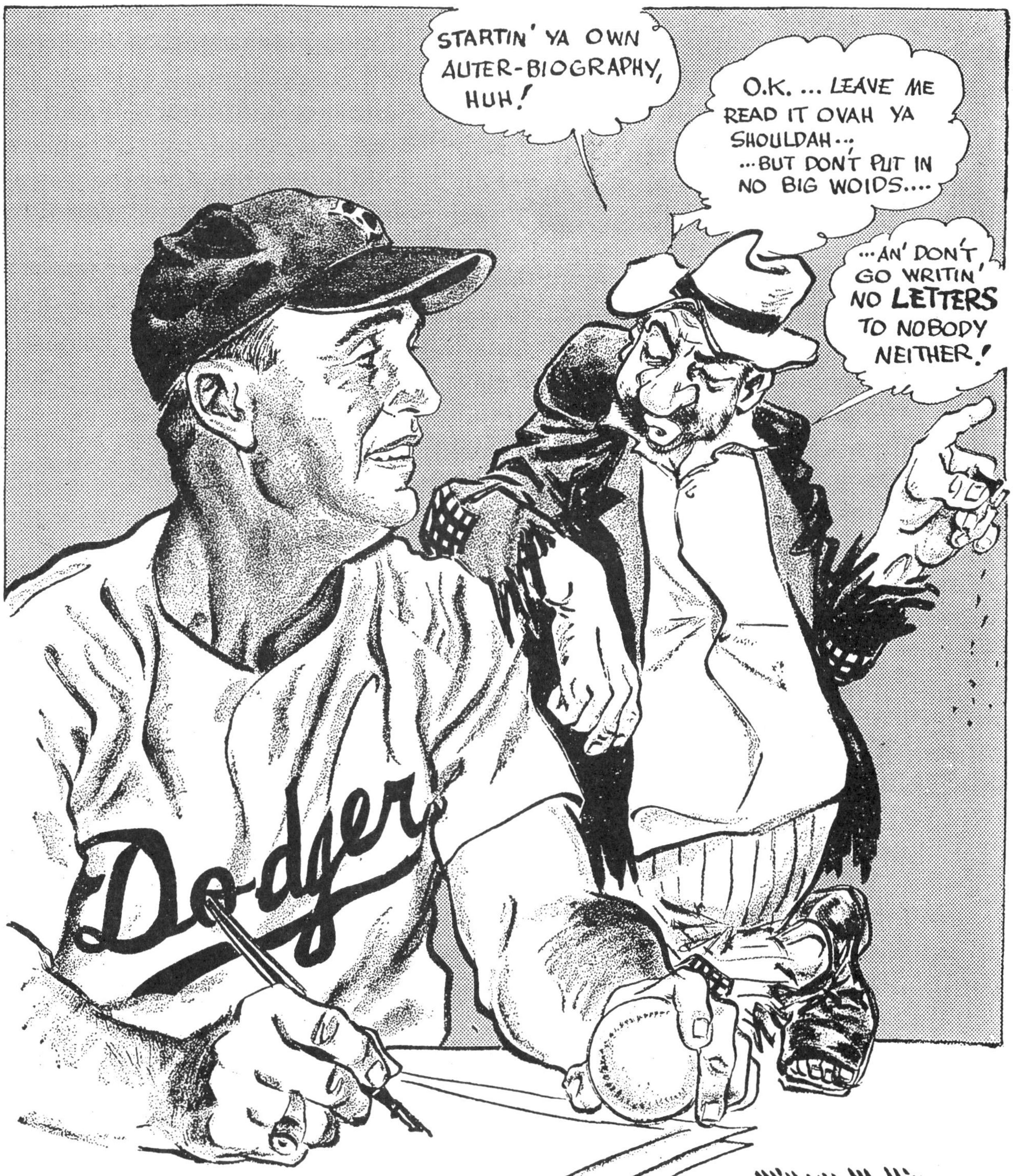
STARTIN' YA OWN AUTER-BIOGRAPHY, HUH!
O.K. ... LEAVE ME READ IT OVAH YA SHOULDAH... ...BUT DON'T PUT IN NO BIG WOIDS....
...AN' DON'T GO WRITIN' NO LETTERS TO NOBODY NEITHER!
Dodgers
Willard Mullin

In 1954, Dodgers manager Chuck Dressen demanded a better contract, which he felt he had earned after winning the 1952 and 1953 NL pennants. New majority owner Walter O'Malley felt differently and fired Dressen, hiring Walter Alston in his place. Alston would remain the Dodgers' manager for 23 years, winning seven NL pennants and four World Series.

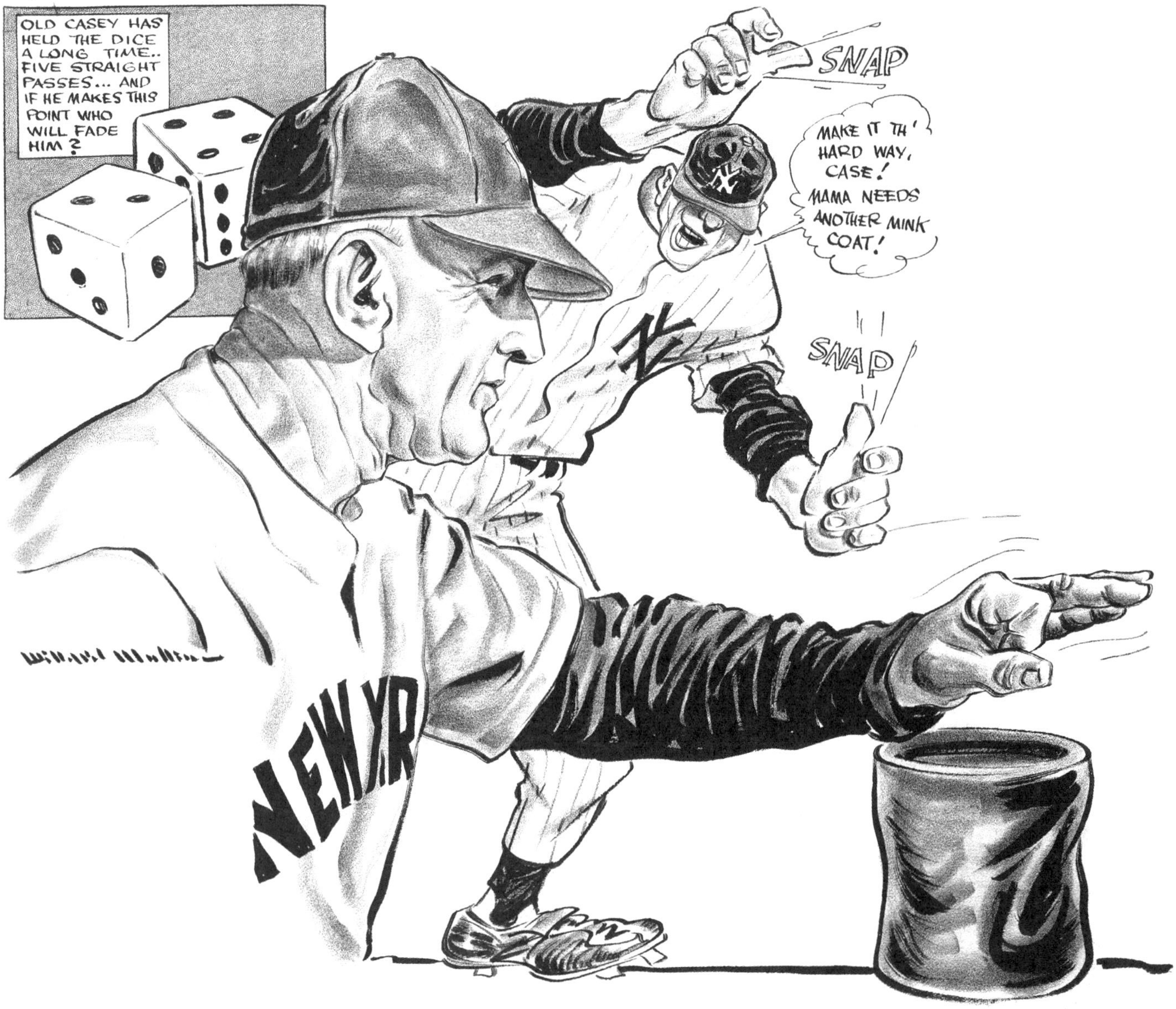
OLD CASEY HAS HELD THE DICE A LONG TIME.. FIVE STRAIGHT PASSES... AND IF HE MAKES THIS POINT WHO WILL FADE HIM?
SNAP
MAKE IT TH' HARD WAY, CASE! MAMA NEEDS ANOTHER MINK COAT!
SNAP
NEW YR

This drawing is from the spring of 1954, when the Yankees were coming off their fifth straight World Championship. Despite winning 103 games, the most ever for a Yankees team managed by Stengel, they lost the pennant to the Cleveland Indians, who won (a then-record) 111 games in a 154-game season.

.349
.339
.350
.354
.339
.334

.381
.355

FROM 1900 TO 1911
HANS WAGNER
LED THE N.L. IN
HITTING EIGHT
TIMES FOR A
LIFE TIME AVERAGE
OF .329

ROGERS
HORNSBY
TOOK OVER IN
1920 AND LED
SIX STRAIGHT
YEARS AND A
SEVENTH TIME
IN 1928 WITH
A LIFE TIME
MARK OF .358

.370
.397
.401
.384
.424
.403
.387

.357
.365
.376
.346
.355
.336

STAN MUSIAL,
WITH AN AVERAGE
OF .345 TAKES HIS
CUT AT HIS SEVENTH
NAT'L LEAGUE BATTING
CHAMPIONSHIP THIS
SEASON ....

Willard Mullin
...AND JUST WHO IS GOING TO STOP HIM?

In 1954, Stan Musial was seeking his seventh National League batting title. When Mullin drew this in June 1954, Musial was hitting .345. His average would drop to .330 by season's end, and Willie Mays would claim the crown with a .345 average. Musial would eventually win his seventh and final batting title in 1957.

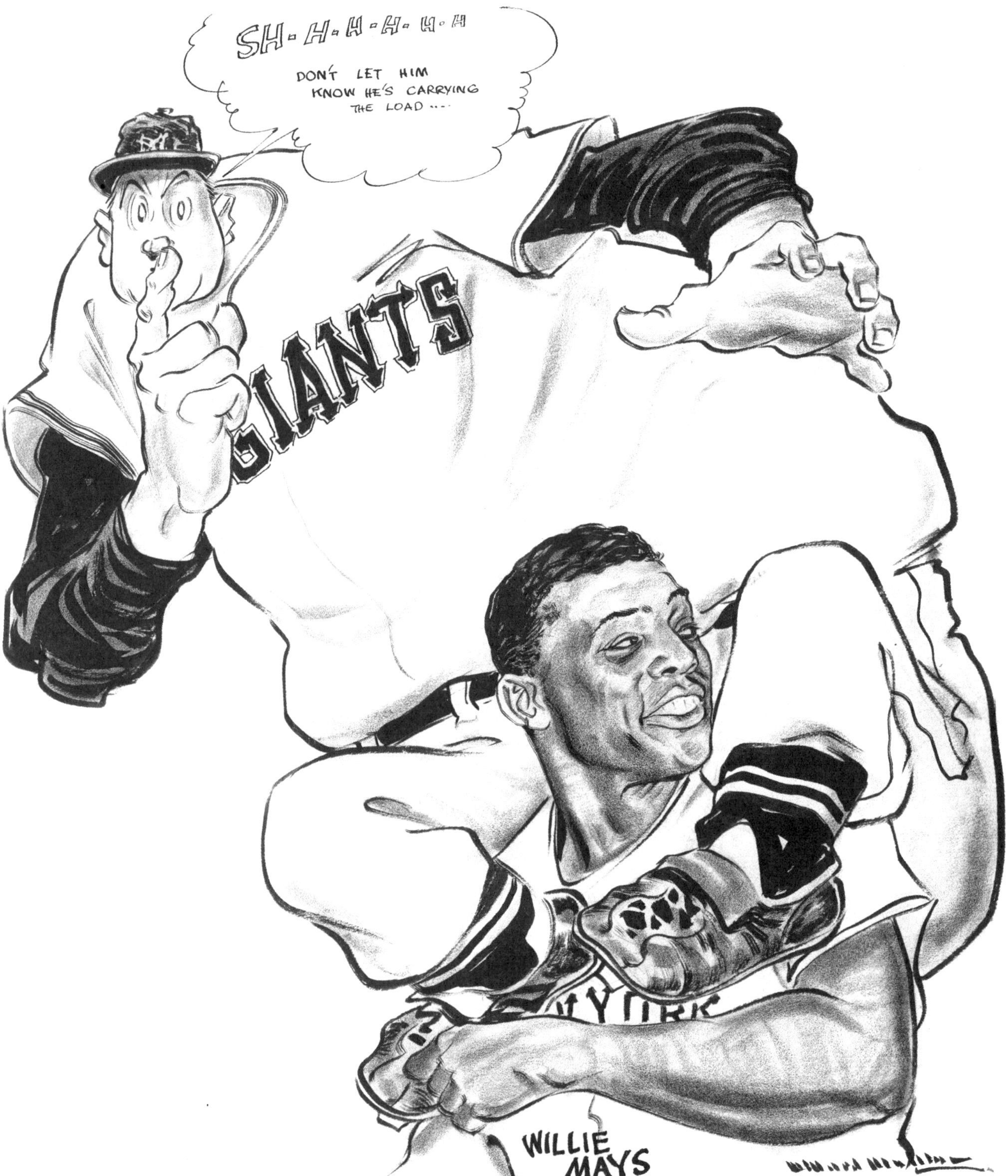
SH-H-H-H-H-H
DON'T LET HIM KNOW HE'S CARRYING THE LOAD ...
GIANTS
NEW YORK
WILLIE MAYS

Beginning in 1954, Willie Mays "carried" the Giants for almost 20 years. This drawing is from 1954, the year in which Mays won his first MVP award. That season, Mays led the league in batting averages with .345, triples with 13, home runs with 41, and RBIs with 110. In that year's World Series, which the Giants won, Mays made what is considered to be the greatest catch of all time.

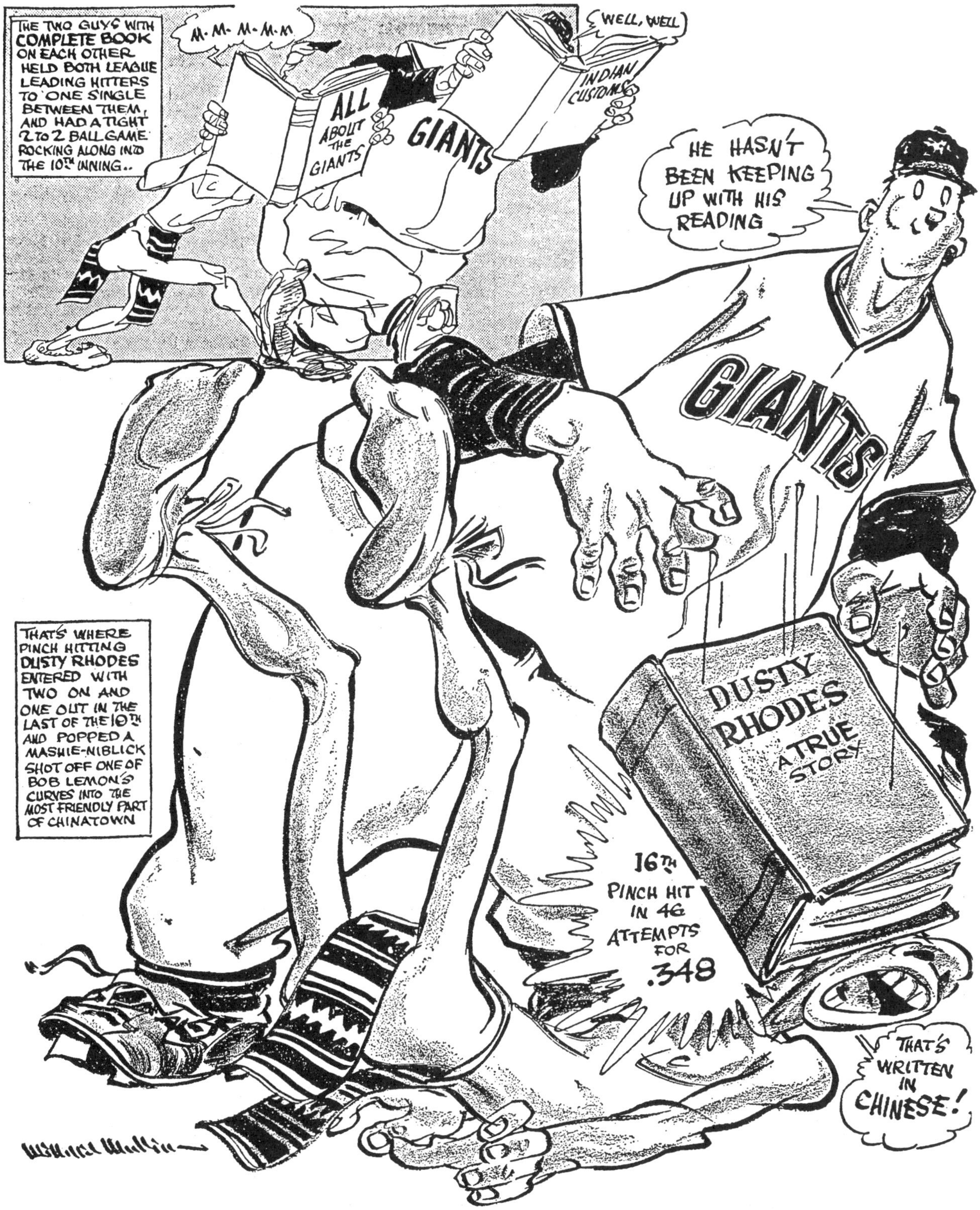
THE TWO GUYS WITH COMPLETE BOOK ON EACH OTHER HELD BOTH LEAGUE LEADING HITTERS TO ONE SINGLE BETWEEN THEM, AND HAD A TIGHT 2 TO 2 BALL GAME ROCKING ALONG INTO THE 10TH INNING..
M-M-M-M-M
WELL, WELL
ALL ABOUT THE GIANTS
INDIAN CUSTOMS
GIANTS
HE HASN'T BEEN KEEPING UP WITH HIS READING
GIANTS
THAT'S WHERE PINCH HITTING DUSTY RHODES ENTERED WITH TWO ON AND ONE OUT IN THE LAST OF THE 10TH AND POPPED A MASHIE-NIBLICK SHOT OFF ONE OF BOB LEMON'S CURVES INTO THE MOST FRIENDLY PART OF CHINATOWN
DUSTY RHODES A TRUE STORY
16TH PINCH HIT IN 46 ATTEMPTS FOR .348
THAT'S WRITTEN IN CHINESE!

The Giants won the first game of the 1954 World Series with the help of a pinch-hit home run from Dusty Rhodes. They would go on to sweep the Indians in four straight.

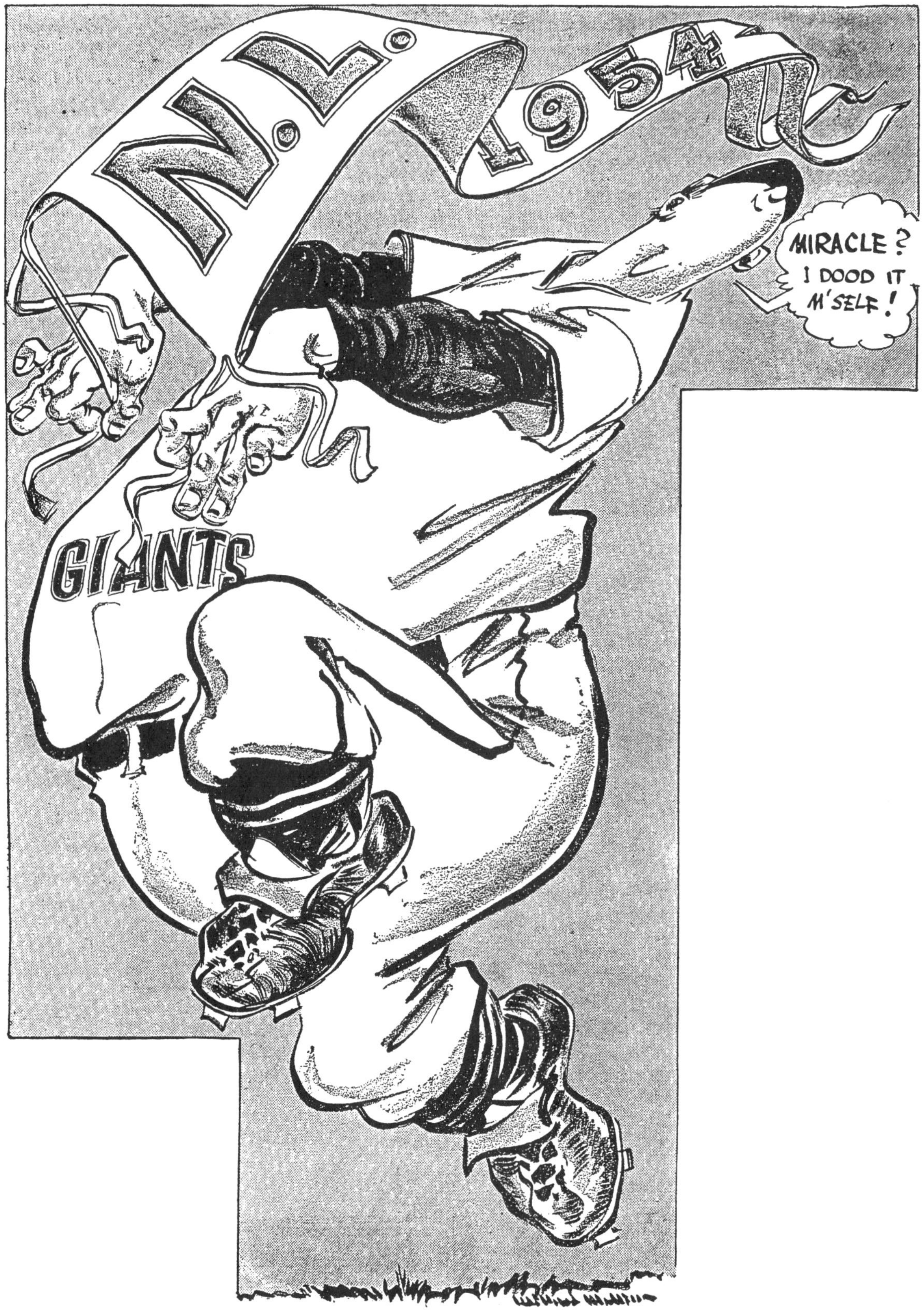
N.L.
1954
MIRACLE? I DOOD IT M'SELF!
GIANTS

In 1954 (unlike 1951), the Giants clinched the National League pennant early, without the need for another "miracle."

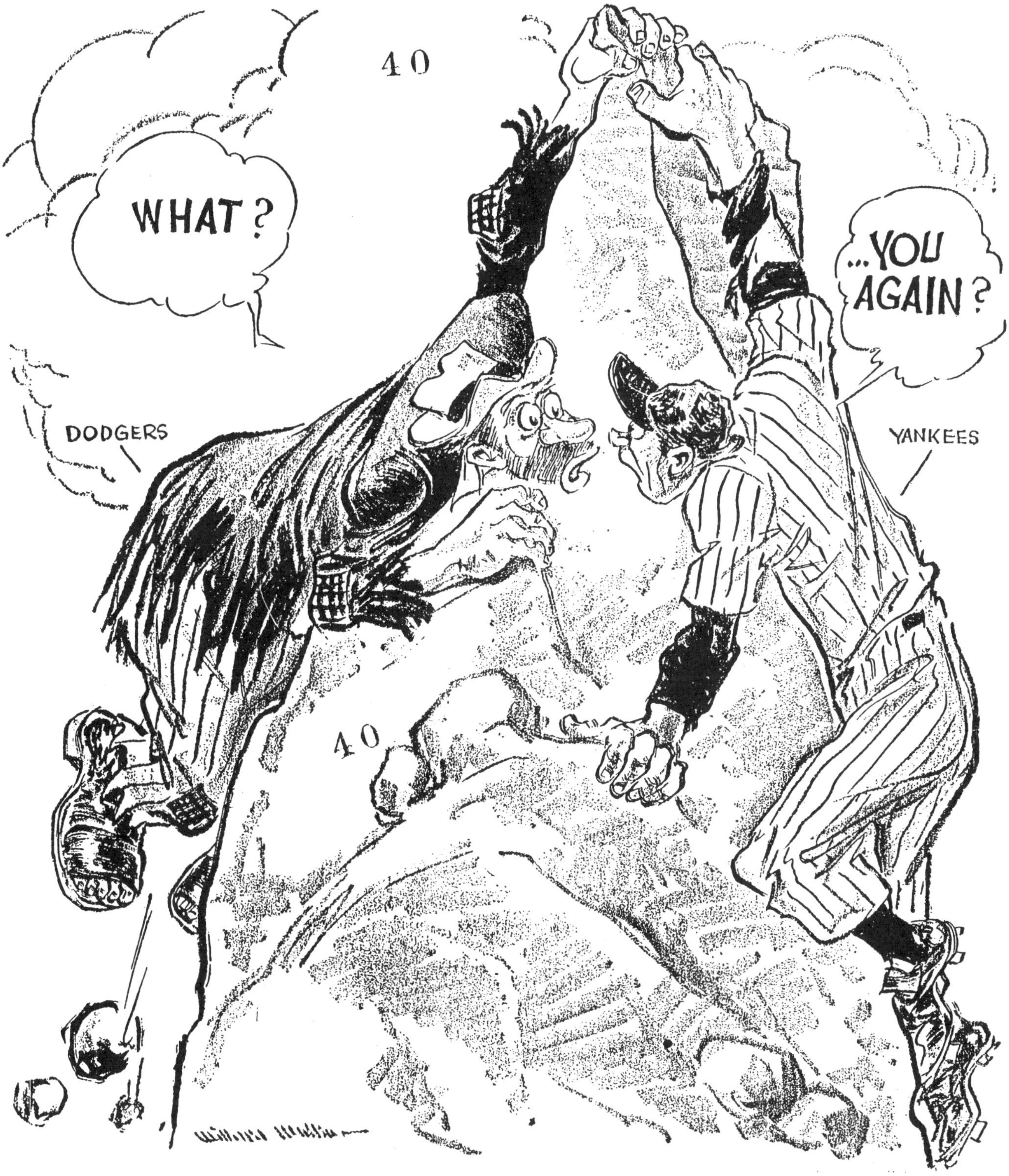
40
WHAT?
...YOU AGAIN?
DODGERS
YANKEES
40

The Yankees and the Dodgers were frequent combatants in the World Series, meeting seven times between 1941 and 1956, with the Yankees winning six of them.

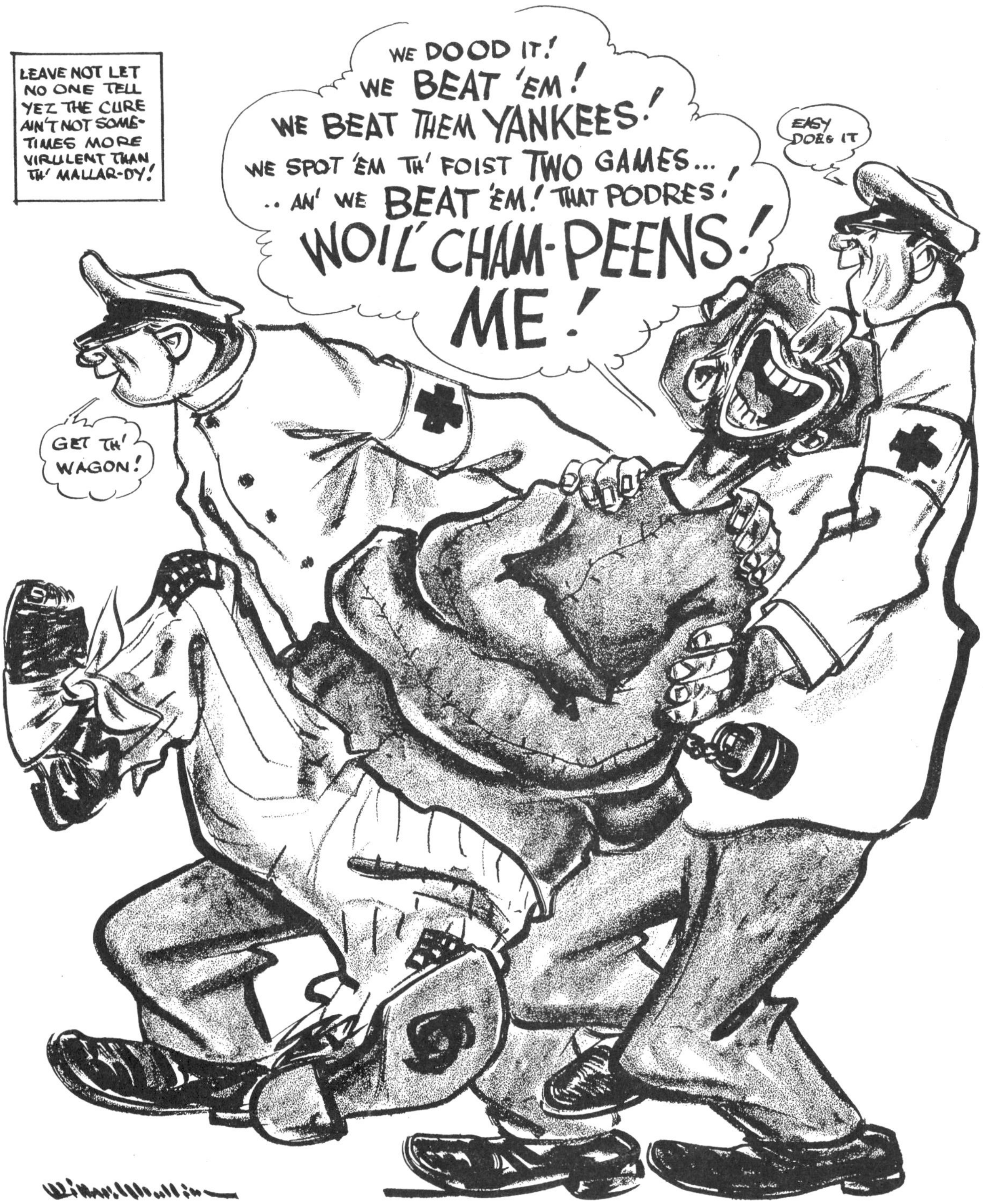
LEAVE NOT LET NO ONE TELL YEZ THE CURE AIN'T NOT SOME-TIMES MORE VIRULENT THAN TH' MALLAR-DY!
WE DOOD IT! WE BEAT 'EM! WE BEAT THEM YANKEES! WE SPOT 'EM TH' FOIST TWO GAMES... .. AN' WE BEAT 'EM! THAT PODRES! WOIL' CHAM-PEENS! ME!
EASY DOES IT
GET TH' WAGON!

In 1955, when the Dodgers finally beat the Yankees in the World Series — on their sixth try — the Bum couldn't restrain his own delirious joy. This cartoon was so popular that the *World-Telegram* received 7,000 requests for reprints.

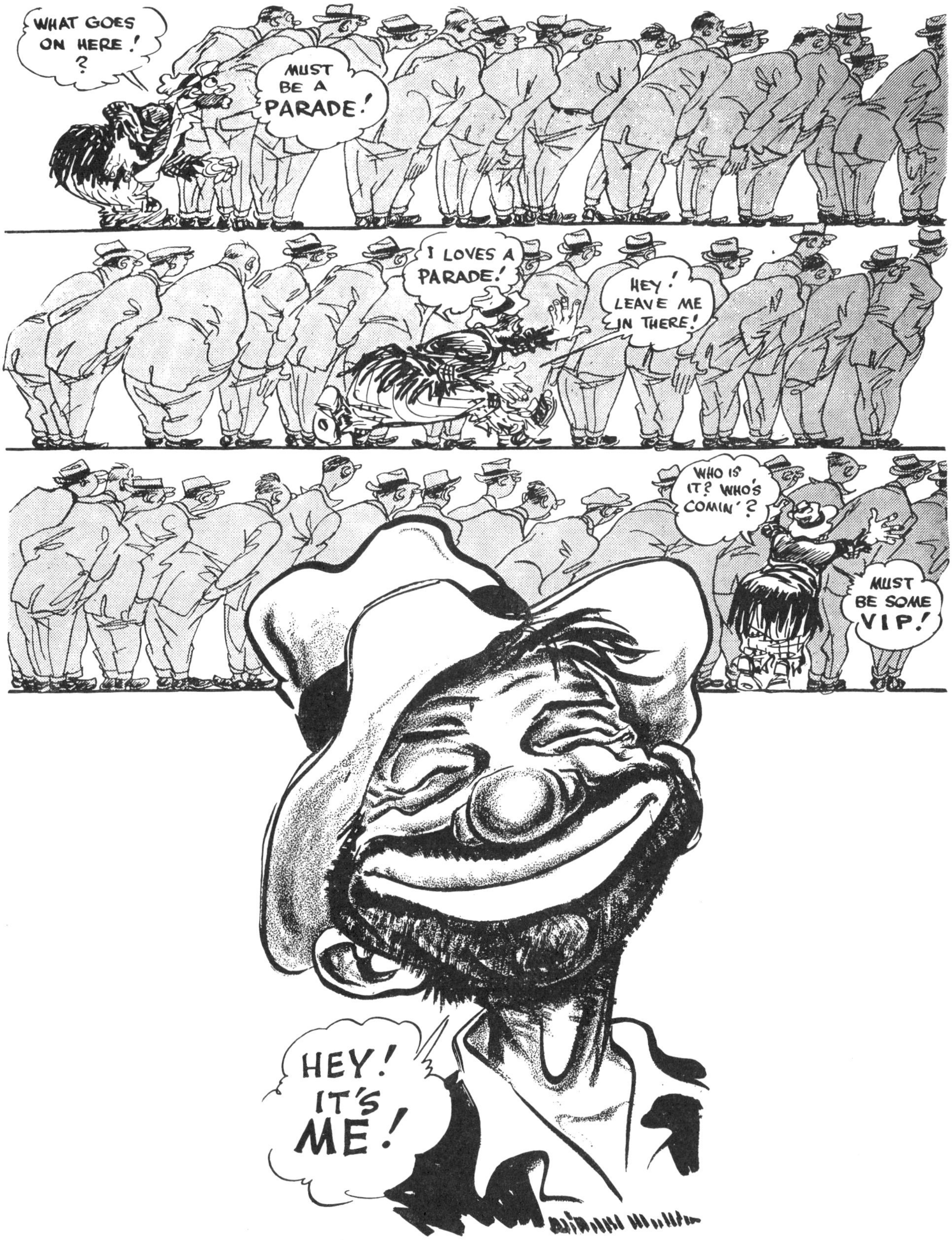
WHAT GOES ON HERE! ?
MUST BE A PARADE!
I LOVES A PARADE!
HEY! LEAVE ME IN THERE!
WHO IS IT? WHO'S COMIN'?
MUST BE SOME VIP!
HEY! IT'S ME!

The Dodgers had lost the World Series so many times that when they finally won in 1955, the Bum could hardly believe it.

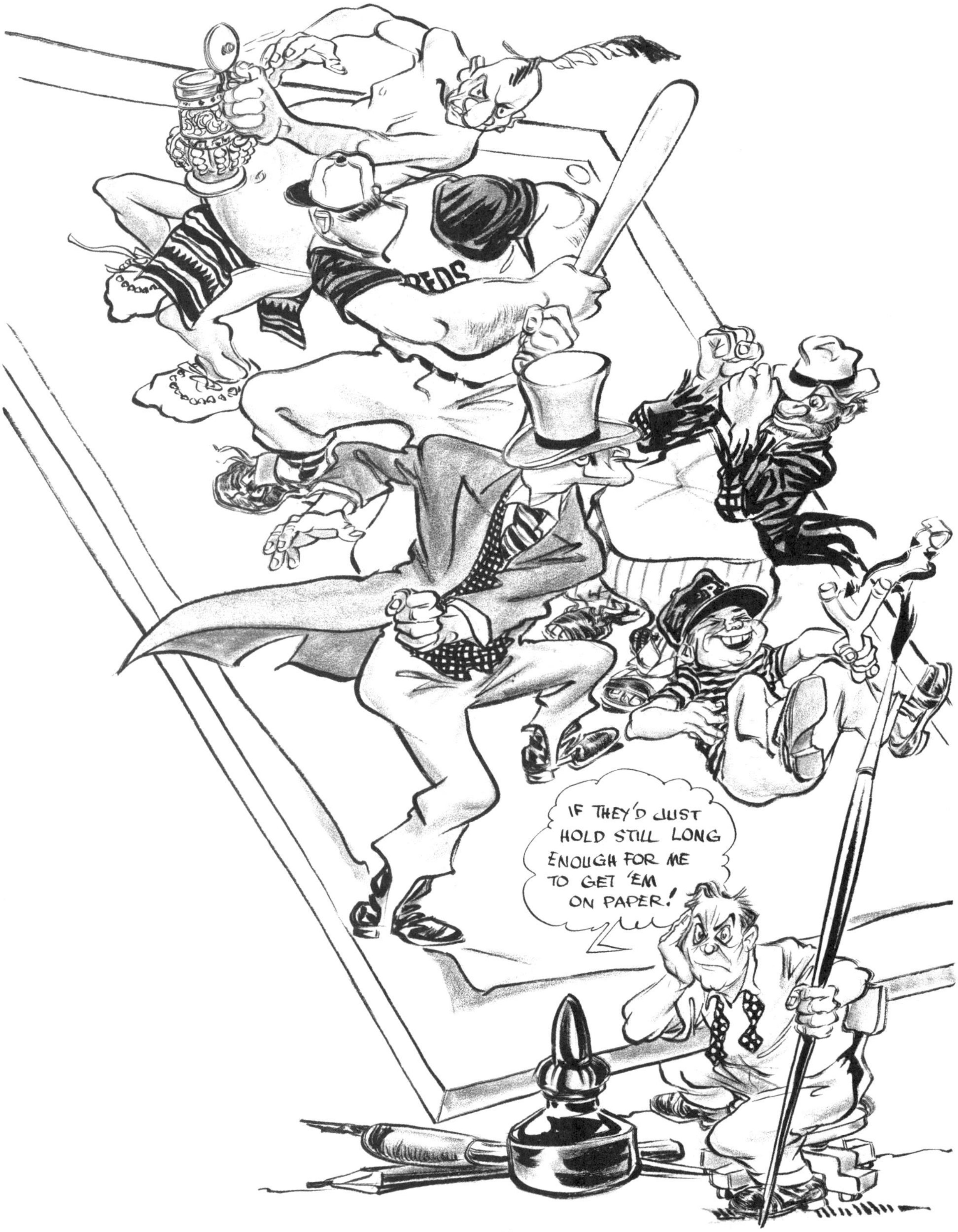
REDS
IF THEY'D JUST HOLD STILL LONG ENOUGH FOR ME TO GET 'EM ON PAPER!

This drawing from the mid-1950s shows a Mullin's-eye view of the contentious National League pennant race.

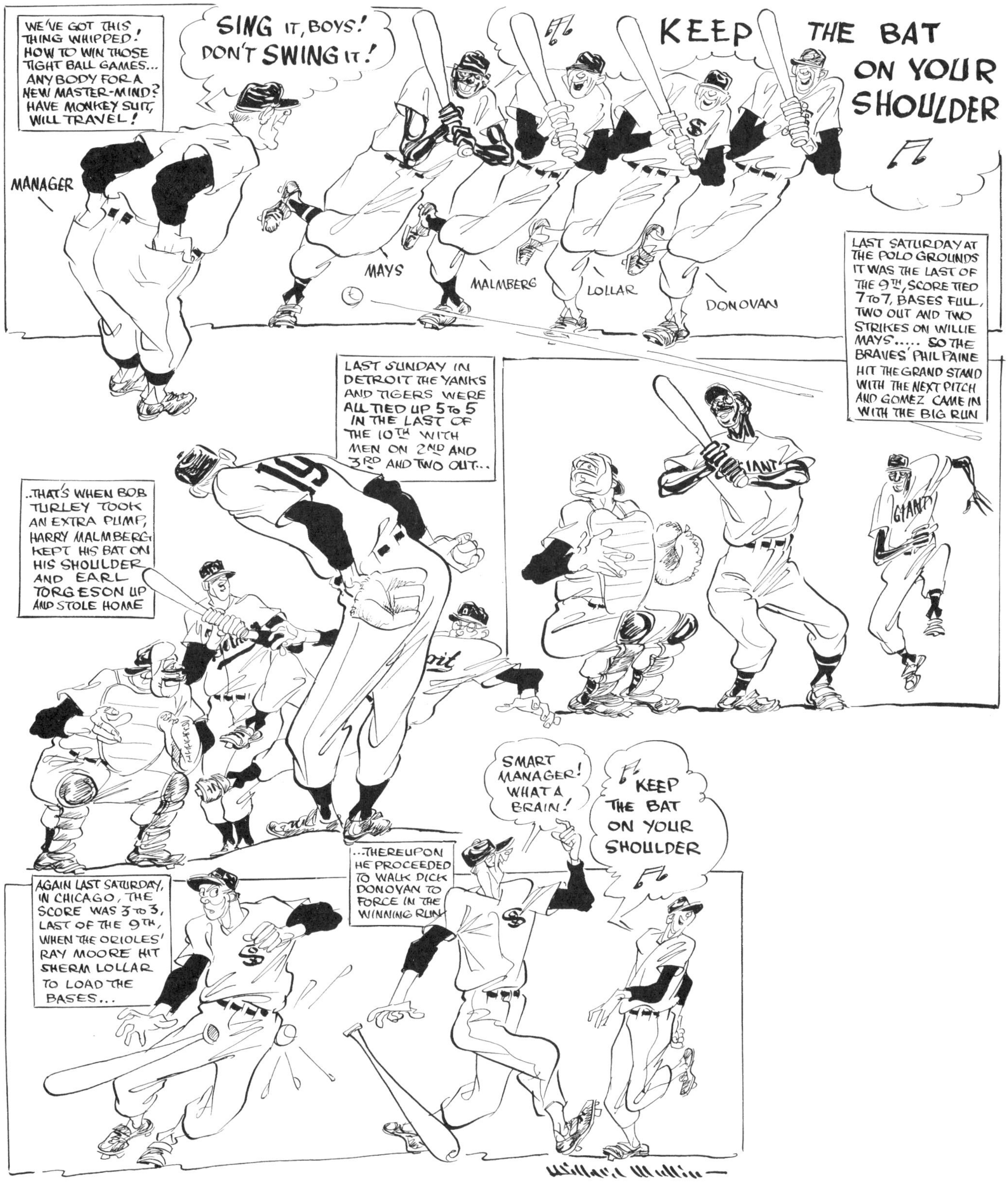
WE'VE GOT THIS THING WHIPPED! HOW TO WIN THOSE TIGHT BALL GAMES... ANYBODY FOR A NEW MASTER-MIND? HAVE MONKEY SUIT, WILL TRAVEL!
SING IT, BOYS! DON'T SWING IT!
KEEP THE BAT ON YOUR SHOULDER
MANAGER
MAYS
MALMBERG
LOLLAR
DONOVAN
LAST SATURDAY AT THE POLO GROUNDS IT WAS THE LAST OF THE 9TH, SCORE TIED 7 TO 7, BASES FULL, TWO OUT AND TWO STRIKES ON WILLIE MAYS..... SO THE BRAVES' PHIL PAINE HIT THE GRAND STAND WITH THE NEXT PITCH AND GOMEZ CAME IN WITH THE BIG RUN
LAST SUNDAY IN DETROIT THE YANKS AND TIGERS WERE ALL TIED UP 5 TO 5 IN THE LAST OF THE 10TH WITH MEN ON 2ND AND 3RD AND TWO OUT...
...THAT'S WHEN BOB TURLEY TOOK AN EXTRA PUMP, HARRY MALMBERG KEPT HIS BAT ON HIS SHOULDER AND EARL TORGESON UP AND STOLE HOME
AGAIN LAST SATURDAY, IN CHICAGO, THE SCORE WAS 3 TO 3, LAST OF THE 9TH, WHEN THE ORIOLES' RAY MOORE HIT SHERM LOLLAR TO LOAD THE BASES...
...THEREUPON HE PROCEEDED TO WALK DICK DONOVAN TO FORCE IN THE WINNING RUN
SMART MANAGER! WHAT A BRAIN!
KEEP THE BAT ON YOUR SHOULDER
Willard Mullin

Mullin reveled in the sometimes wacky occurrences in baseball and illustrated them with aplomb.

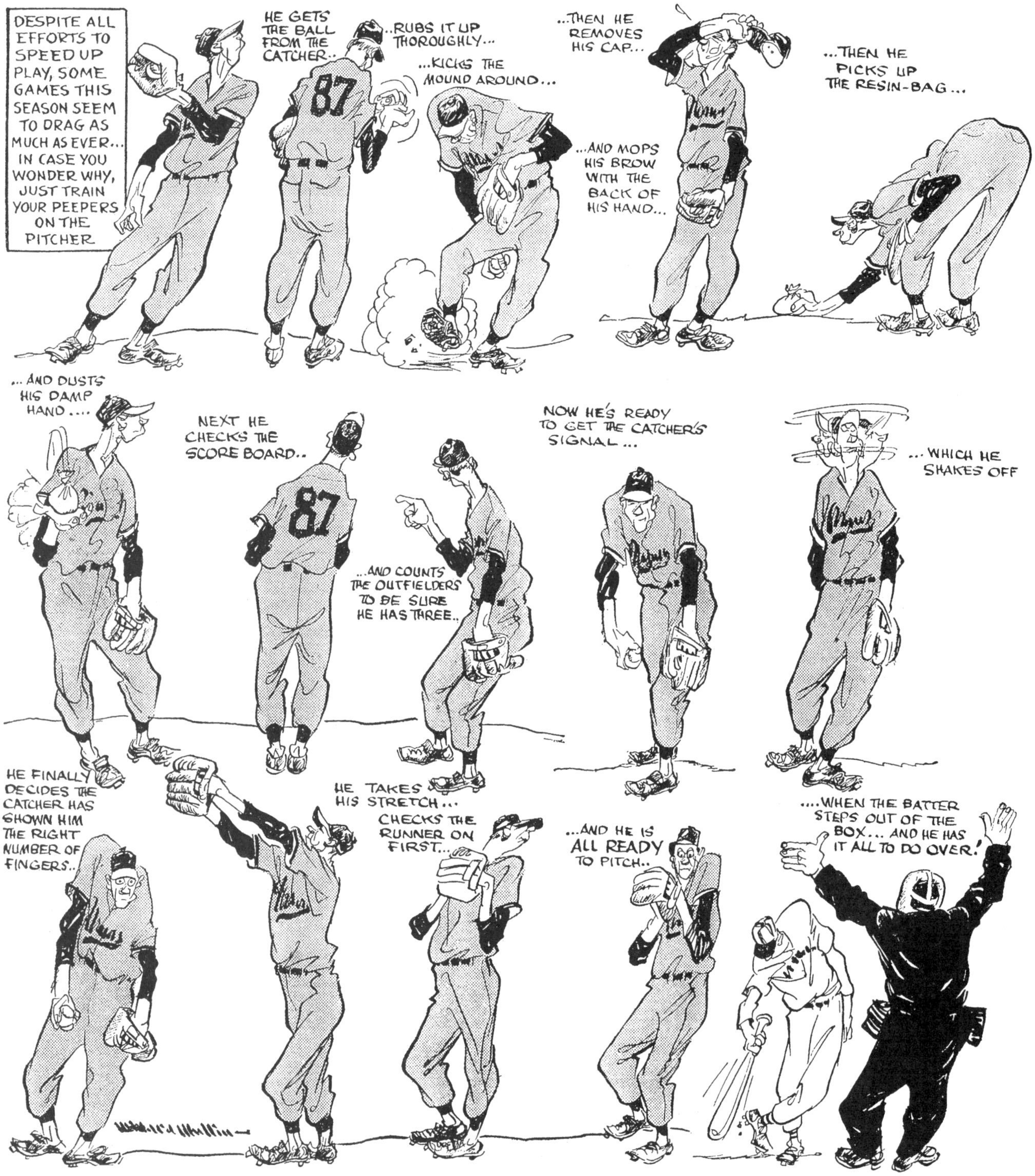
DESPITE ALL EFFORTS TO SPEED UP PLAY, SOME GAMES THIS SEASON SEEM TO DRAG AS MUCH AS EVER... IN CASE YOU WONDER WHY, JUST TRAIN YOUR PEEPERS ON THE PITCHER
HE GETS THE BALL FROM THE CATCHER..
..RUBS IT UP THOROUGHLY...
...KICKS THE MOUND AROUND...
...THEN HE REMOVES HIS CAP...
...AND MOPS HIS BROW WITH THE BACK OF HIS HAND...
...THEN HE PICKS UP THE RESIN-BAG...
...AND DUSTS HIS DAMP HAND....
NEXT HE CHECKS THE SCORE BOARD..
...AND COUNTS THE OUTFIELDERS TO BE SURE HE HAS THREE..
NOW HE'S READY TO GET THE CATCHER'S SIGNAL...
...WHICH HE SHAKES OFF
HE FINALLY DECIDES THE CATCHER HAS SHOWN HIM THE RIGHT NUMBER OF FINGERS..
HE TAKES HIS STRETCH...
CHECKS THE RUNNER ON FIRST...
...AND HE IS ALL READY TO PITCH..
....WHEN THE BATTER STEPS OUT OF THE BOX... AND HE HAS IT ALL TO DO OVER!

Mullin was fascinated and exasperated by the peculiarities of the pitcher, as can be seen in this drawing from 1956.

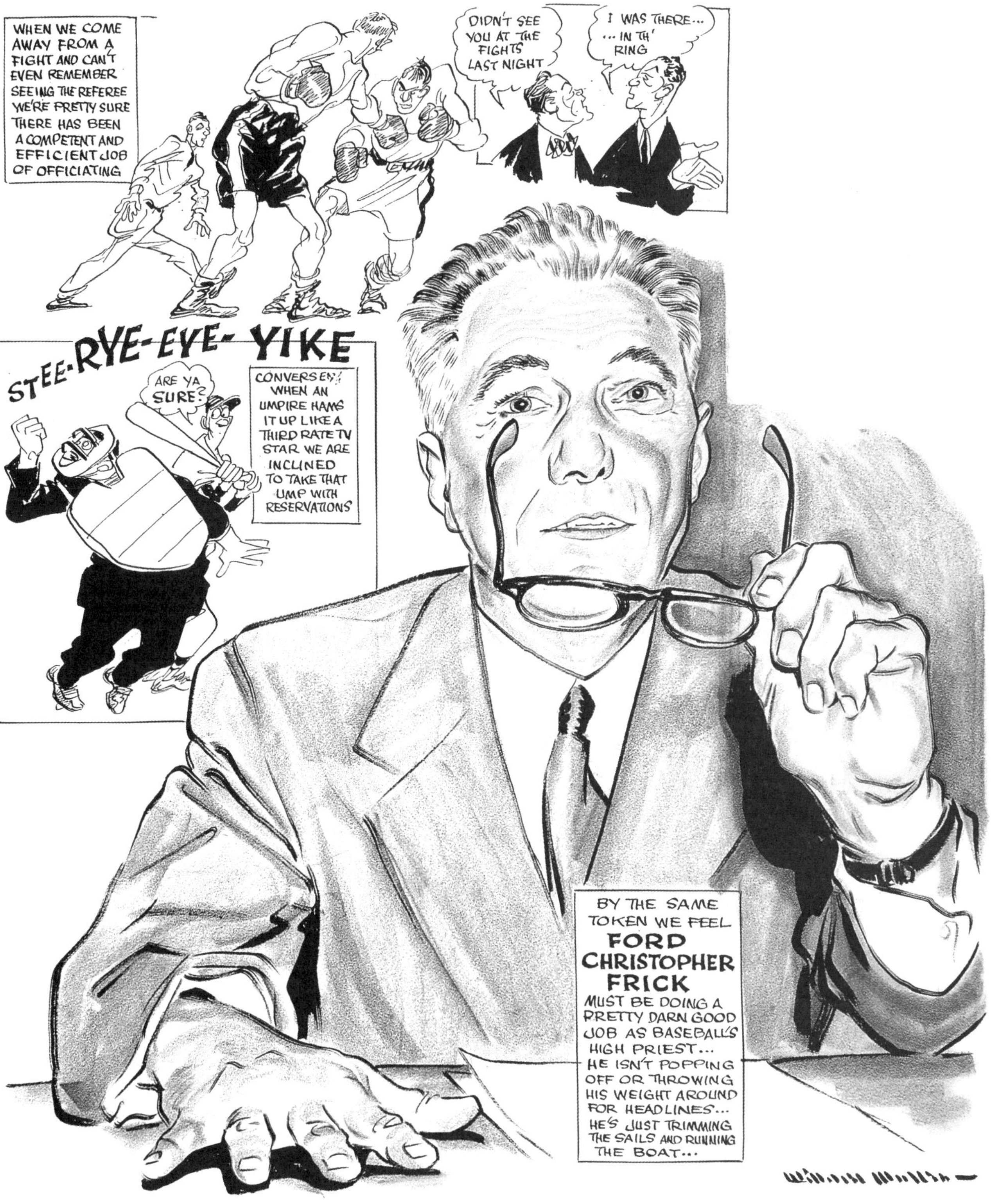
WHEN WE COME AWAY FROM A FIGHT AND CAN'T EVEN REMEMBER SEEING THE REFEREE WE'RE PRETTY SURE THERE HAS BEEN A COMPETENT AND EFFICIENT JOB OF OFFICIATING
DIDN'T SEE YOU AT THE FIGHTS LAST NIGHT
I WAS THERE... ...IN TH' RING
STEE-RYE-EYE-YIKE
ARE YA SURE?
CONVERSELY! WHEN AN UMPIRE HAMS IT UP LIKE A THIRD RATE TV STAR WE ARE INCLINED TO TAKE THAT UMP WITH RESERVATIONS
BY THE SAME TOKEN WE FEEL FORD CHRISTOPHER FRICK MUST BE DOING A PRETTY DARN GOOD JOB AS BASEBALL'S HIGH PRIEST... HE ISN'T POPPING OFF OR THROWING HIS WEIGHT AROUND FOR HEADLINES... HE'S JUST TRIMMING THE SAILS AND RUNNING THE BOAT...

Ford Frick had started out as a sportswriter but was appointed president of the National League in 1934. He was elected commissioner of all of baseball in 1951, serving until 1965.

Mullin drew this in the mid-1950s, several years before Frick's famous edict in conjunction with Roger Maris's 1961 challenge of Babe Ruth's single-season home run record.

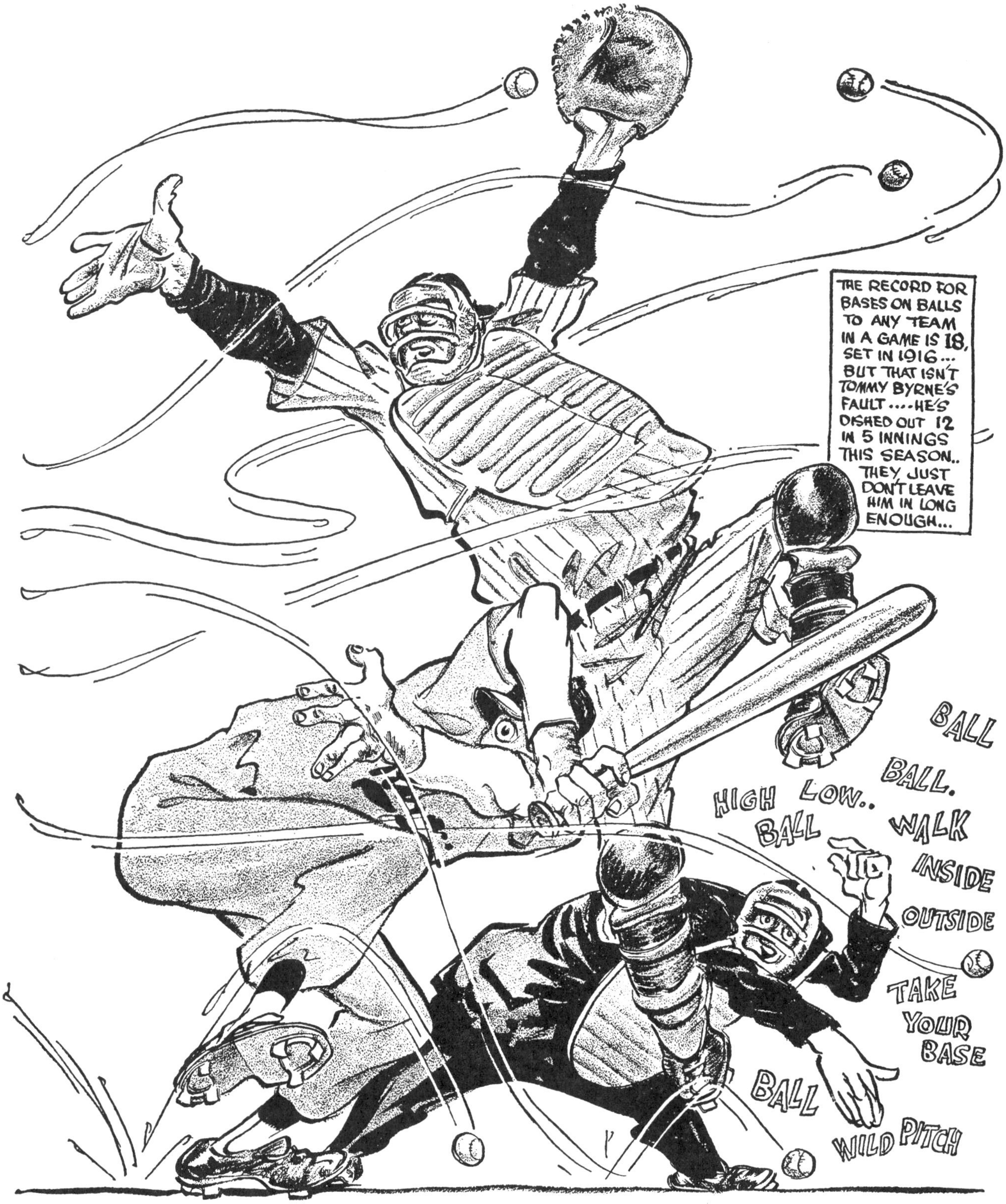
THE RECORD FOR BASES ON BALLS TO ANY TEAM IN A GAME IS 18, SET IN 1916... BUT THAT ISN'T TOMMY BYRNE'S FAULT....HE'S DISHED OUT 12 IN 5 INNINGS THIS SEASON.. THEY JUST DON'T LEAVE HIM IN LONG ENOUGH...
BALL
BALL.
HIGH
LOW..
BALL
WALK
INSIDE
OUTSIDE
TAKE YOUR BASE
BALL
WILD PITCH

Tommy Byrne played 11 seasons with the Yankees as a left-handed pitcher. His nickname was "Wild Man." He led the league in hit batsmen five times and in walks three times. In 1955, however, he did go 16–5 with a 3.15 ERA and led the league in winning percentage.

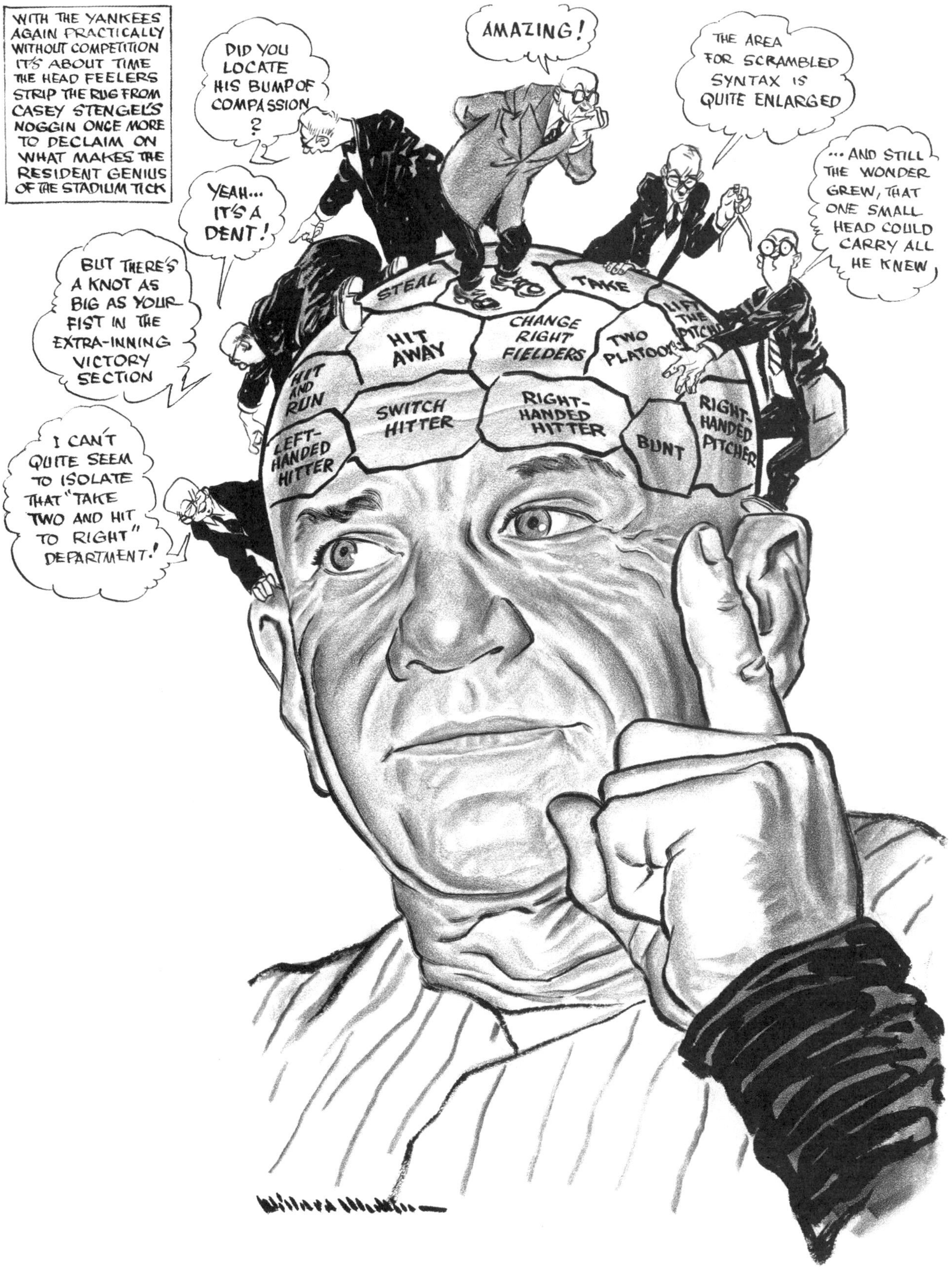
WITH THE YANKEES AGAIN PRACTICALLY WITHOUT COMPETITION IT'S ABOUT TIME THE HEAD FEELERS STRIP THE RUG FROM CASEY STENGEL'S NOGGIN ONCE MORE TO DECLAIM ON WHAT MAKES THE RESIDENT GENIUS OF THE STADIUM TICK
DID YOU LOCATE HIS BUMP OF COMPASSION ?
AMAZING!
THE AREA FOR SCRAMBLED SYNTAX IS QUITE ENLARGED
... AND STILL THE WONDER GREW, THAT ONE SMALL HEAD COULD CARRY ALL HE KNEW
YEAH... IT'S A DENT!
BUT THERE'S A KNOT AS BIG AS YOUR FIST IN THE EXTRA-INNING VICTORY SECTION
I CAN'T QUITE SEEM TO ISOLATE THAT "TAKE TWO AND HIT TO RIGHT" DEPARTMENT!
STEAL
TAKE
HIT AWAY
CHANGE RIGHT FIELDERS
TWO PLATOO
LIFT THE PITCH
HIT AND RUN
SWITCH HITTER
RIGHT-HANDED HITTER
BUNT
RIGHT-HANDED PITCHER
LEFT-HANDED HITTER

Casey Stengel was the manager of the Yankees from 1949 through 1960. In that time, they won seven World Series and 10 pennants. This drawing from the mid-1950s celebrates Stengel's genius.

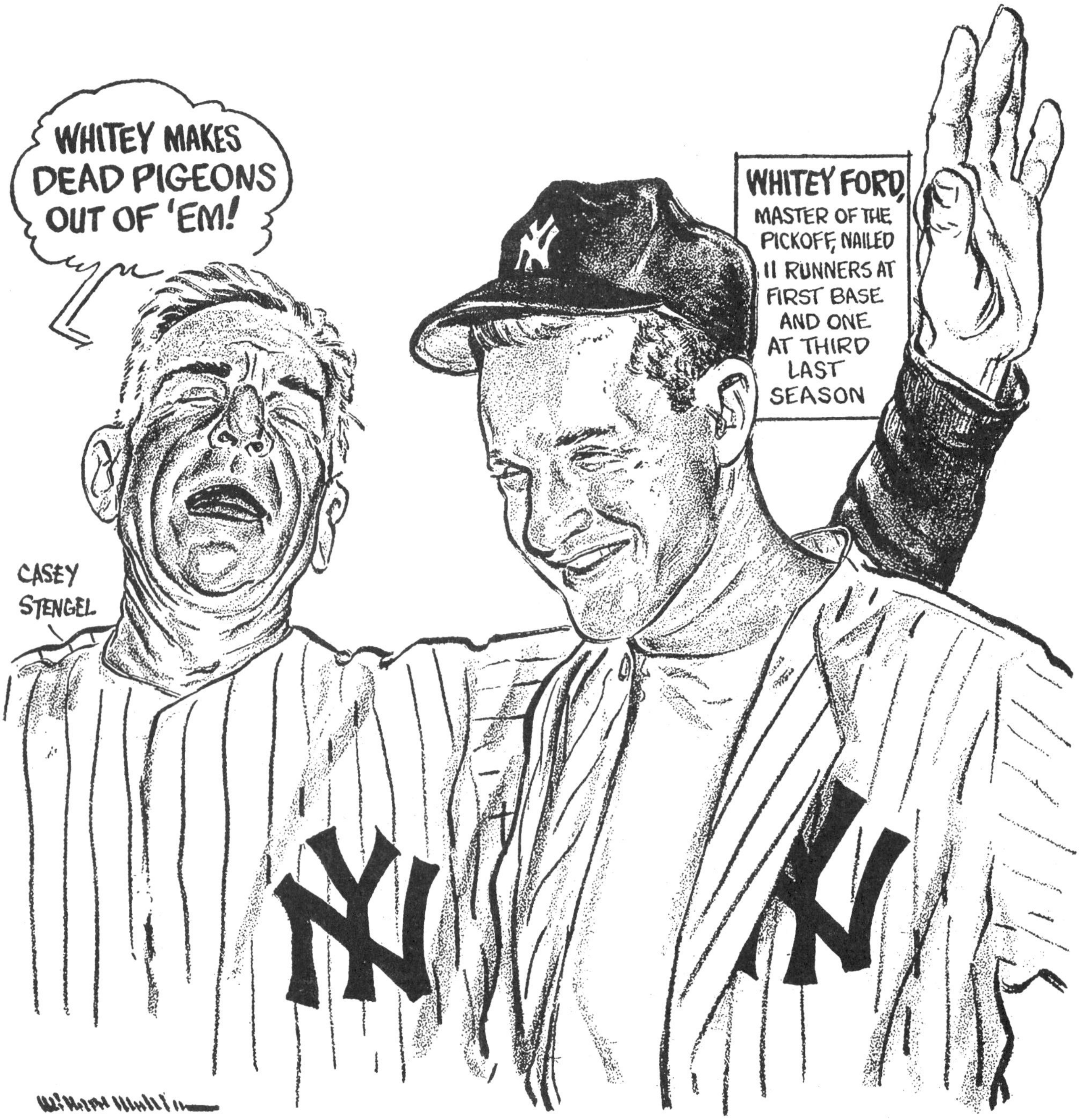
WHITEY MAKES DEAD PIGEONS OUT OF 'EM!
CASEY STENGEL
WHITEY FORD, MASTER OF THE PICKOFF, NAILED 11 RUNNERS AT FIRST BASE AND ONE AT THIRD LAST SEASON

Whitey Ford used a barnstorming tour in Japan after the 1955 season to work on his pickoff move. It proved worthwhile for him. He led all pitchers in pickoffs during the 1956 season.

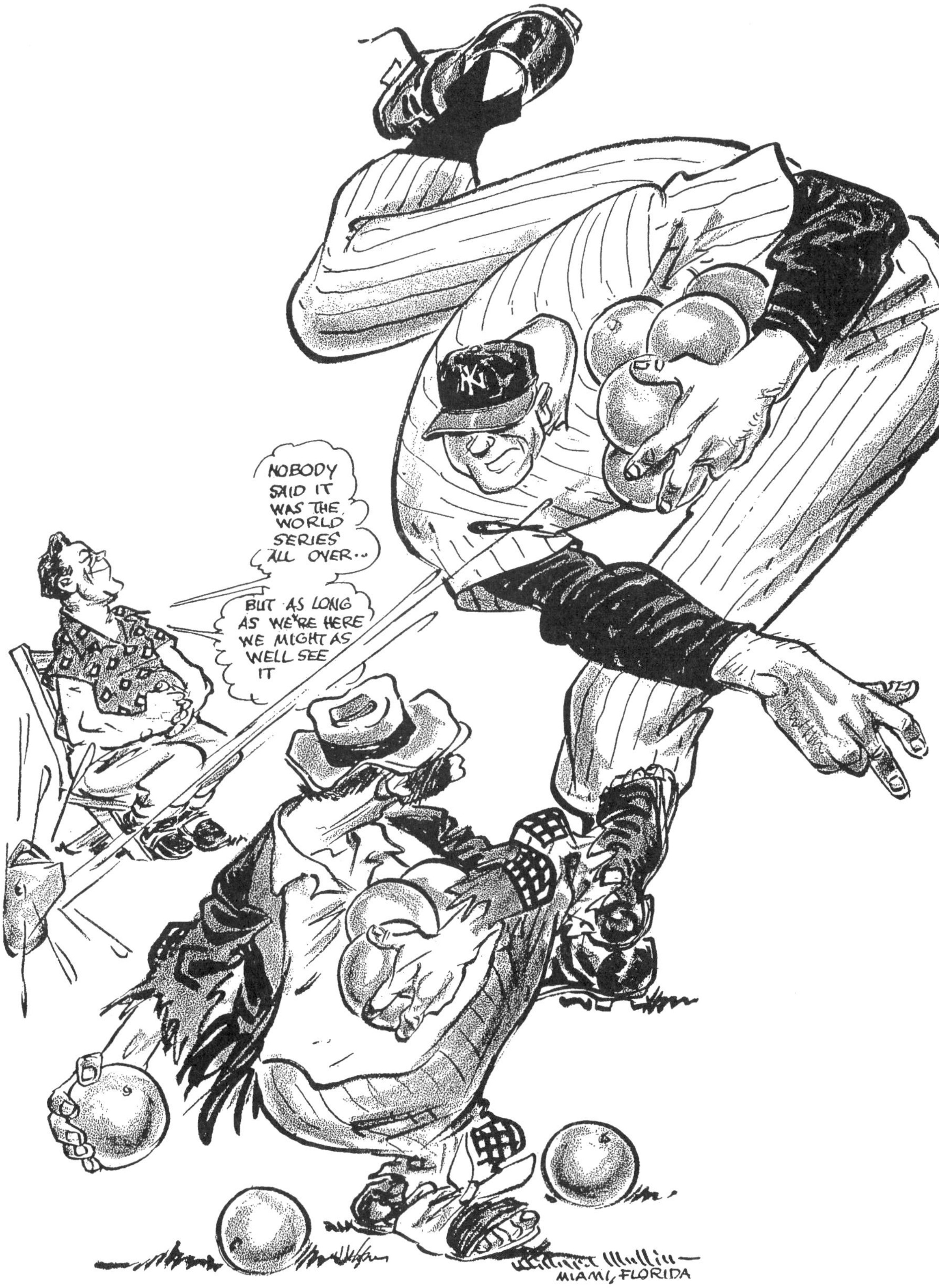
NOBODY SAID IT WAS THE WORLD SERIES ALL OVER..
BUT AS LONG AS WE'RE HERE WE MIGHT AS WELL SEE IT
MIAMI, FLORIDA

The Yankees and the Dodgers met in the World Series seven times between 1941 and 1956. They also met in spring training every year in Florida.

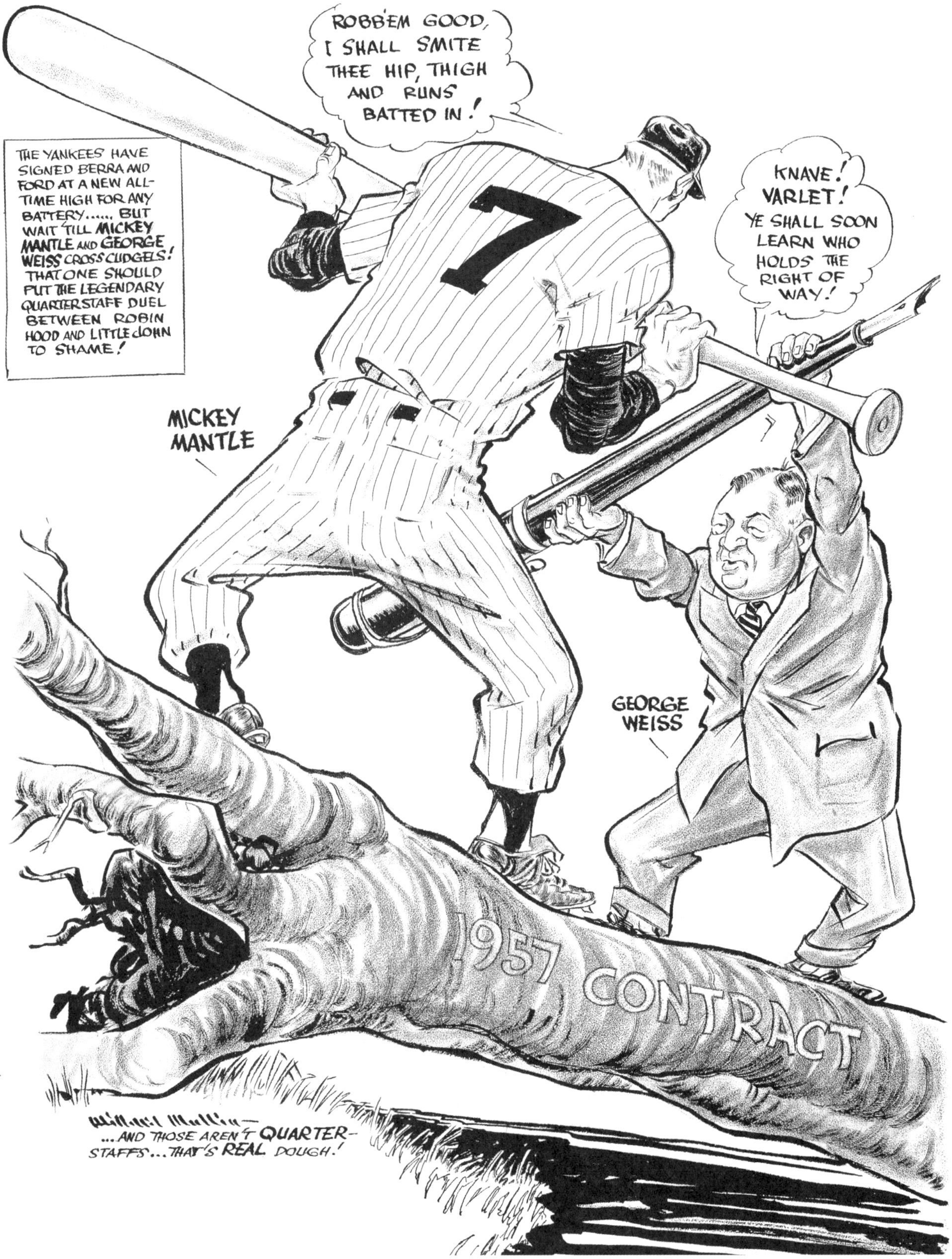
ROBB'EM GOOD, I SHALL SMITE THEE HIP, THIGH AND RUNS BATTED IN!
THE YANKEES HAVE SIGNED BERRA AND FORD AT A NEW ALL-TIME HIGH FOR ANY BATTERY..... BUT WAIT TILL MICKEY MANTLE AND GEORGE WEISS CROSS CUDGELS! THAT ONE SHOULD PUT THE LEGENDARY QUARTERSTAFF DUEL BETWEEN ROBIN HOOD AND LITTLE JOHN TO SHAME!
KNAVE! VARLET! YE SHALL SOON LEARN WHO HOLDS THE RIGHT OF WAY!
7
MICKEY MANTLE
GEORGE WEISS
1957 CONTRACT
...AND THOSE AREN'T QUARTER-STAFFS...THAT'S REAL DOUGH!

In 1956, Mickey Mantle had his greatest season, winning the Triple Crown (leading the league in batting average, home runs, and runs batted in). "The Mick," rightfully, was expecting a hefty salary increase. He did get one, but only after a battle with George Weiss, the Yankees' General Manager. Mullin anticipated that clash with this parody of the famous fight between Little John and Robin Hood.

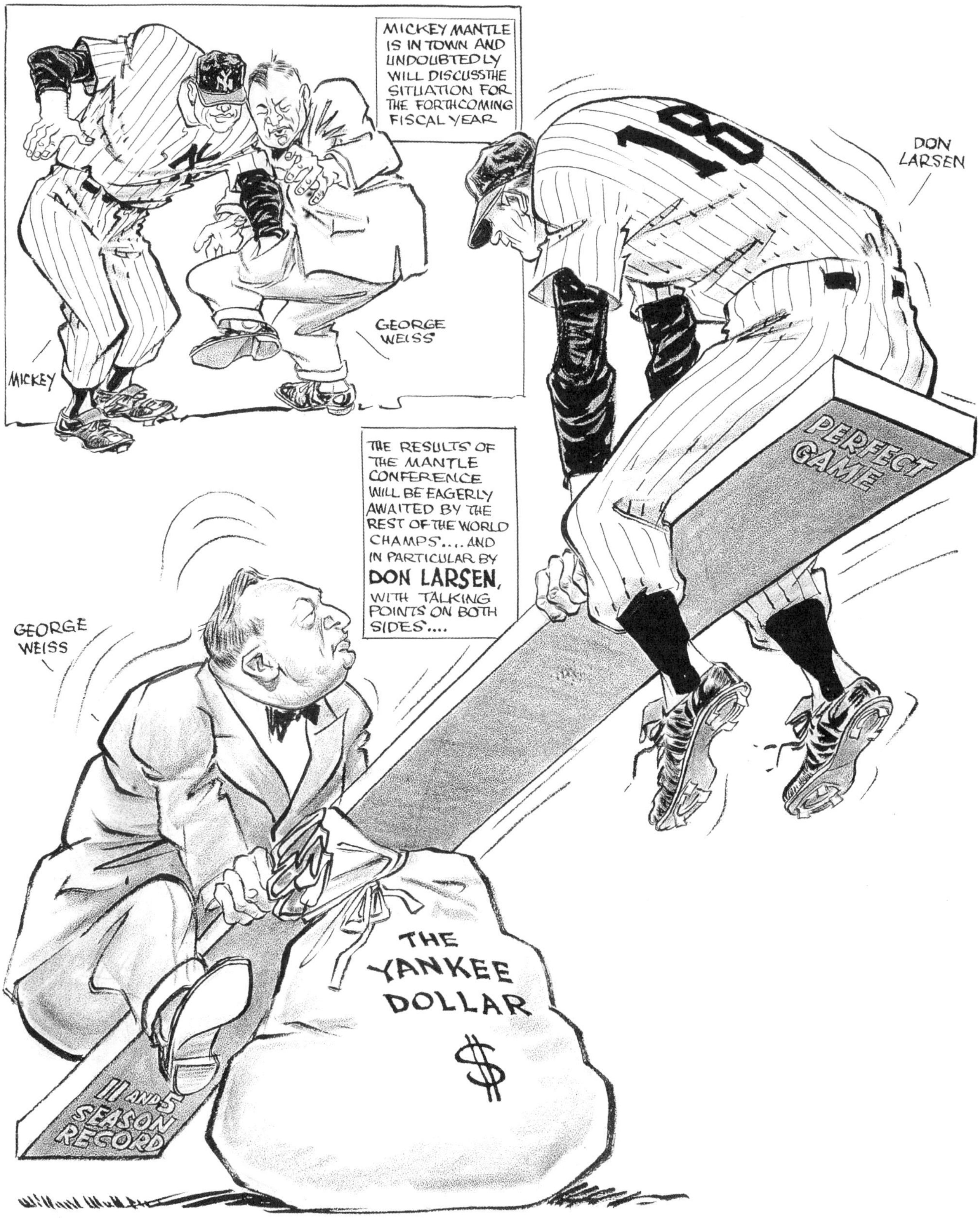
MICKEY MANTLE IS IN TOWN AND UNDOUBTEDLY WILL DISCUSS THE SITUATION FOR THE FORTHCOMING FISCAL YEAR
MICKEY
GEORGE WEISS
DON LARSEN
18
THE RESULTS OF THE MANTLE CONFERENCE WILL BE EAGERLY AWAITED BY THE REST OF THE WORLD CHAMPS'.... AND IN PARTICULAR BY **DON LARSEN**, WITH TALKING POINTS ON BOTH SIDES....
PERFECT GAME
GEORGE WEISS
THE YANKEE DOLLAR
$
11 AND 5 SEASON RECORD

In 1956, Don Larsen threw the only perfect game in World Series history. When it came time to discuss his 1957 contract, he felt that his performance warranted a raise. General Manager George Weiss was unimpressed, especially in light of Larsen's mediocre 11-5 regular season record.

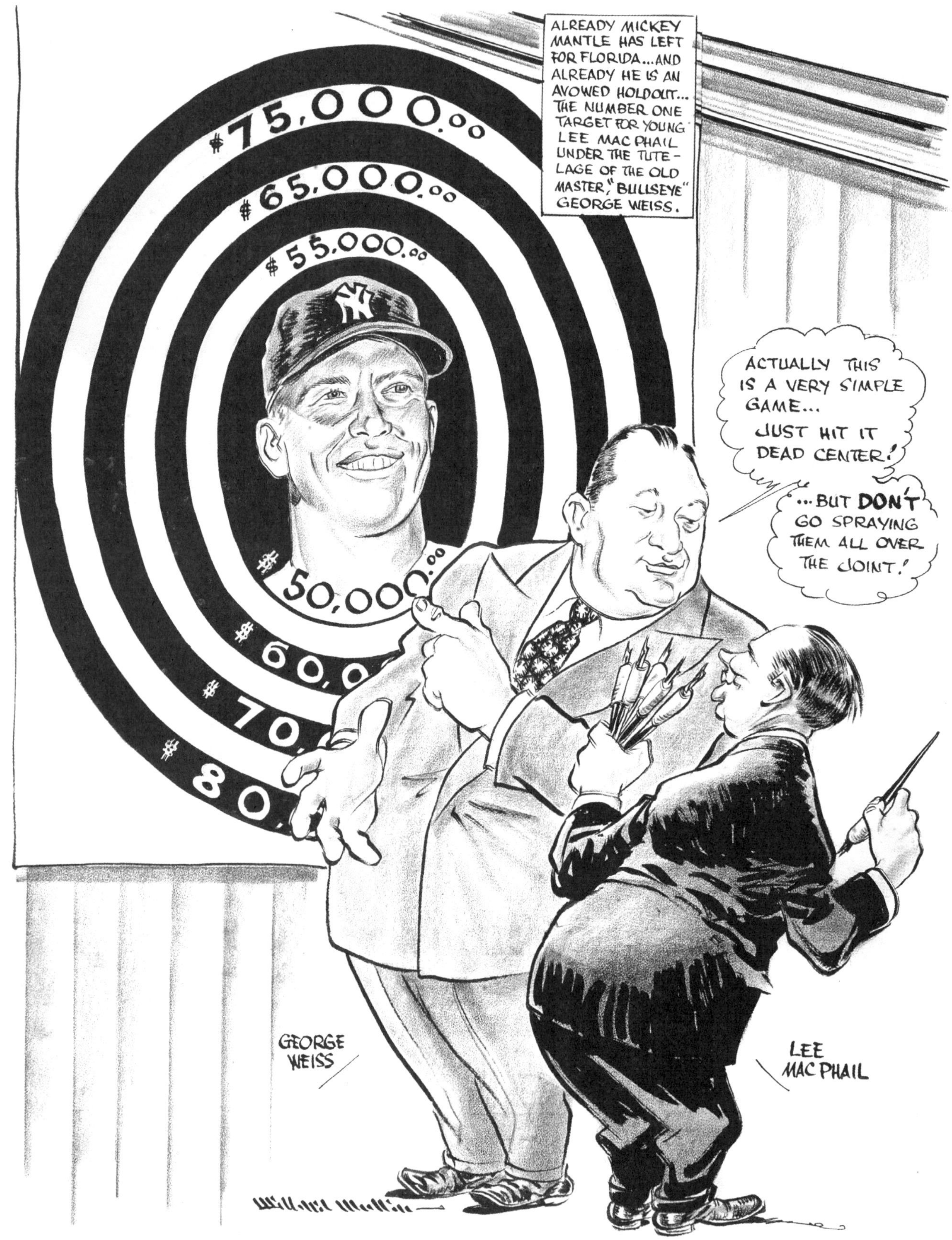
ALREADY MICKEY MANTLE HAS LEFT FOR FLORIDA...AND ALREADY HE IS AN AVOWED HOLDOUT... THE NUMBER ONE TARGET FOR YOUNG LEE MAC PHAIL UNDER THE TUTE-LAGE OF THE OLD MASTER, "BULLSEYE" GEORGE WEISS.
$75,000.00
$65,000.00
$55,000.00
$50,000.00
ACTUALLY THIS IS A VERY SIMPLE GAME... JUST HIT IT DEAD CENTER!
...BUT DON'T GO SPRAYING THEM ALL OVER THE JOINT!
GEORGE WEISS
LEE MAC PHAIL

After his Triple Crown season of 1956, Mickey Mantle had to battle the Yankees over a raise. This included a brief holdout. Mick finally settled for $58,000, an increase over the $33,000 he had earned the year before.

WHOOPEEEEE
HANK AARON
400+PROOF
TWENTY FIVE
YEARS OLD

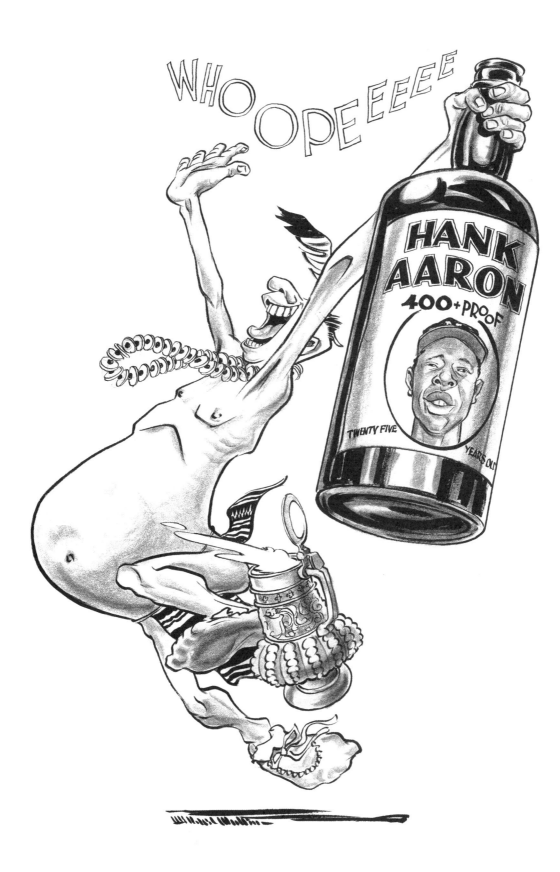

In 1957, Hank Aaron led the Milwaukee Braves to the first of two National League pennants — and won the batting title to boot!

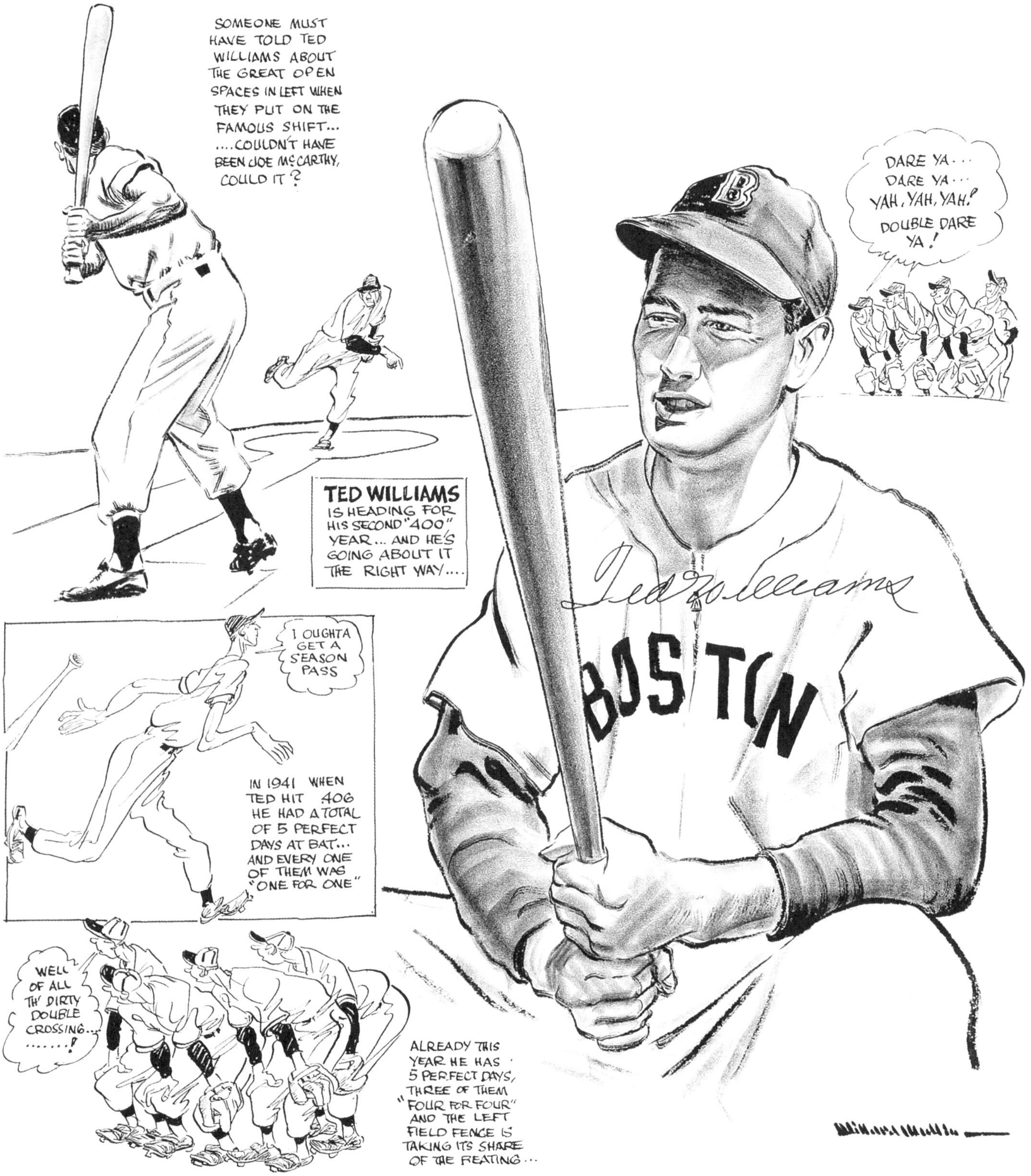
SOMEONE MUST HAVE TOLD TED WILLIAMS ABOUT THE GREAT OPEN SPACES IN LEFT WHEN THEY PUT ON THE FAMOUS SHIFT... ....COULDN'T HAVE BEEN JOE McCARTHY, COULD IT?
DARE YA... DARE YA... YAH, YAH, YAH! DOUBLE DARE YA!
TED WILLIAMS IS HEADING FOR HIS SECOND "400" YEAR... AND HE'S GOING ABOUT IT THE RIGHT WAY....
Ted Williams
BOSTON
I OUGHTA GET A SEASON PASS
IN 1941 WHEN TED HIT 406 HE HAD A TOTAL OF 5 PERFECT DAYS AT BAT... AND EVERY ONE OF THEM WAS "ONE FOR ONE"
WELL OF ALL TH' DIRTY DOUBLE CROSSING........!
ALREADY THIS YEAR HE HAS 5 PERFECT DAYS, THREE OF THEM "FOUR FOR FOUR" AND THE LEFT FIELD FENCE IS TAKING ITS SHARE OF THE BEATING...

In 1957, at the age of 38, Ted Williams won his fifth batting title, hitting .388 and beating runner-up Mickey Mantle by 23 points. For much of the season, Williams flirted with .400, something Mullin noted in this drawing from later in the 1957 season.

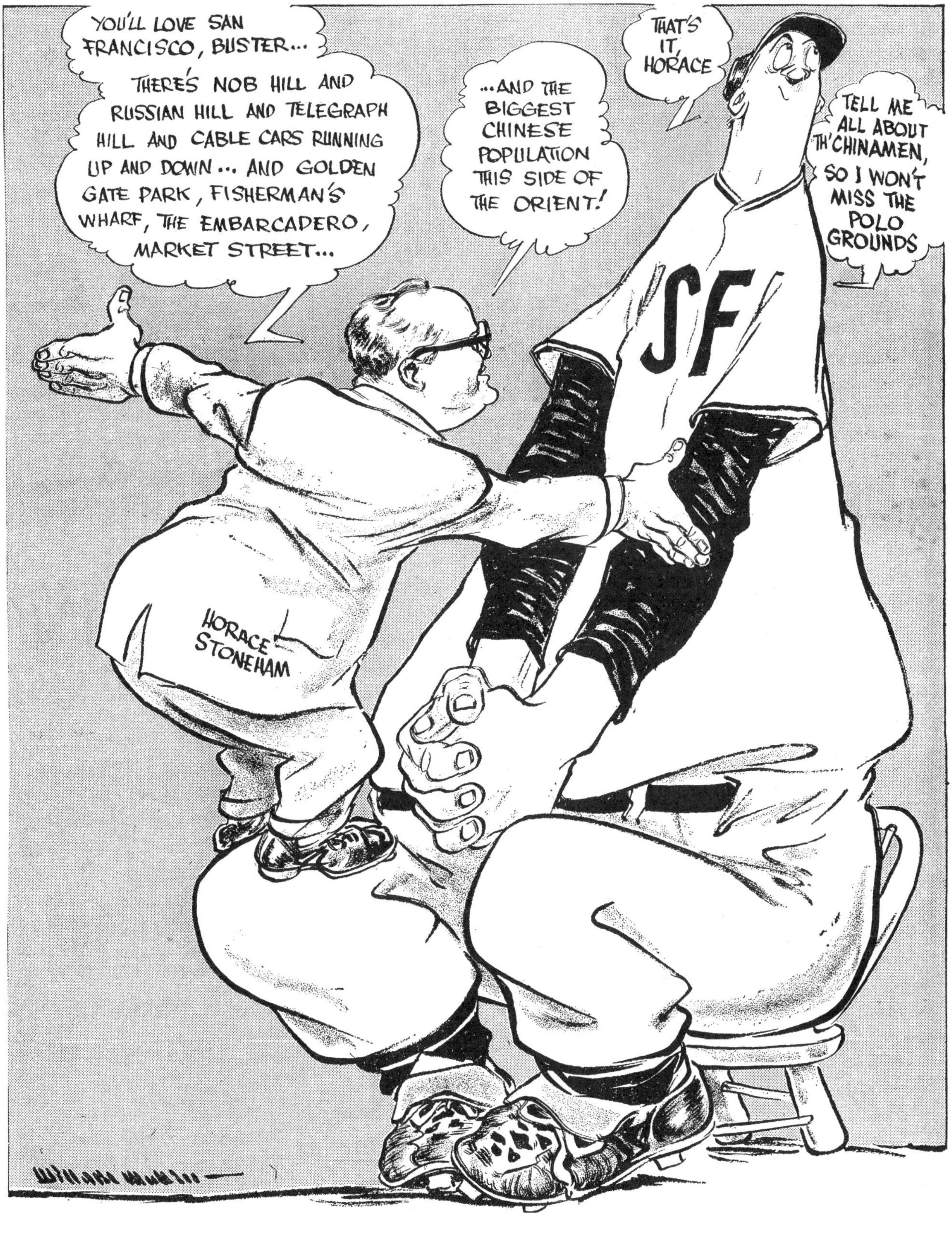
YOU'LL LOVE SAN FRANCISCO, BUSTER...
THERE'S NOB HILL AND RUSSIAN HILL AND TELEGRAPH HILL AND CABLE CARS RUNNING UP AND DOWN... AND GOLDEN GATE PARK, FISHERMAN'S WHARF, THE EMBARCADERO, MARKET STREET...
...AND THE BIGGEST CHINESE POPULATION THIS SIDE OF THE ORIENT!
THAT'S IT, HORACE
TELL ME ALL ABOUT TH'CHINAMEN, SO I WON'T MISS THE POLO GROUNDS
SF
HORACE STONEHAM

In September 1957, Horace Stoneham attempts to convince Willy the Giant that he is going to love his new home in San Francisco.

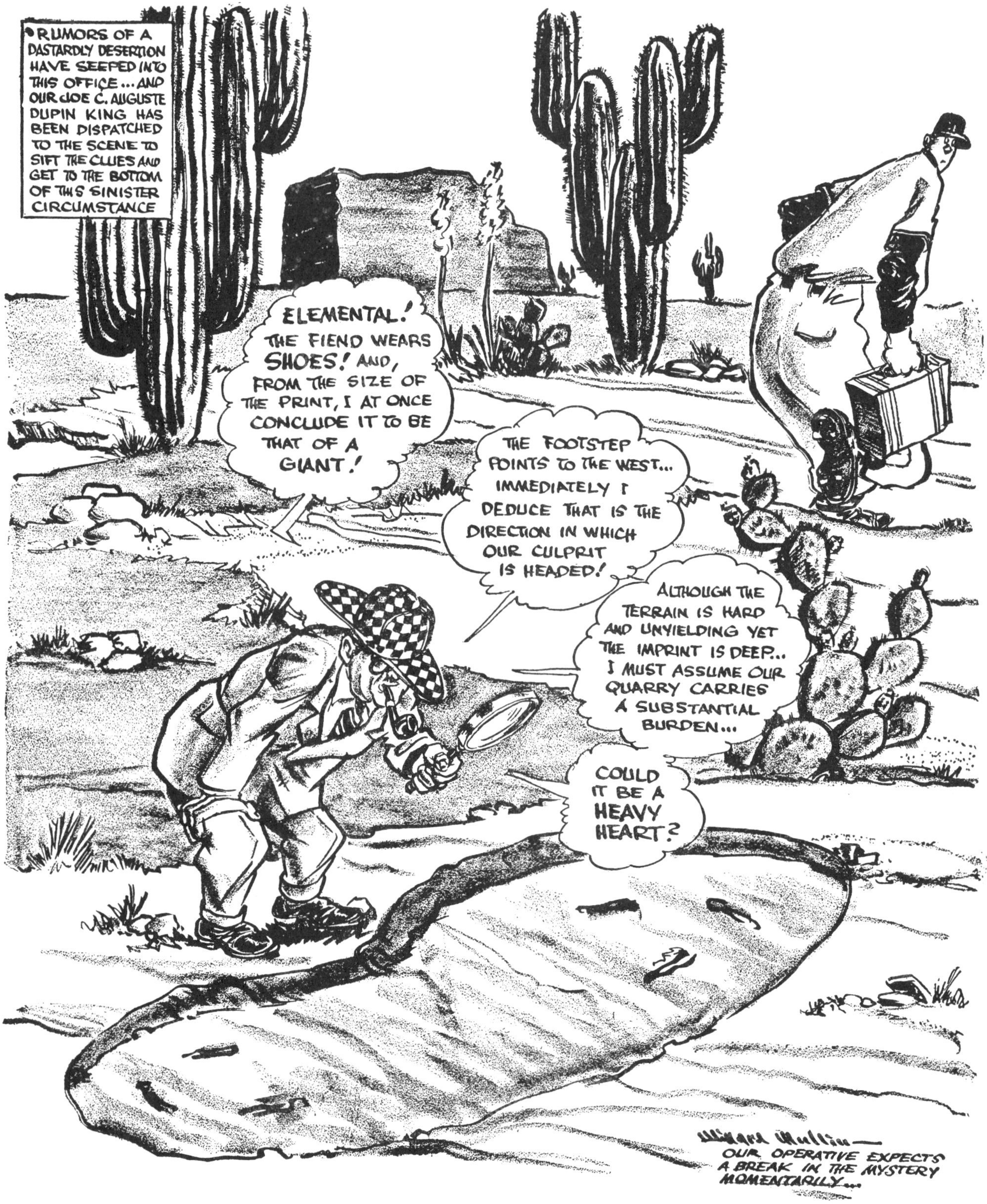

RUMORS OF A DASTARDLY DESERTION HAVE SEEPED INTO THIS OFFICE... AND OUR JOE C. AUGUSTE DUPIN KING HAS BEEN DISPATCHED TO THE SCENE TO SIFT THE CLUES AND GET TO THE BOTTOM OF THIS SINISTER CIRCUMSTANCE
ELEMENTAL! THE FIEND WEARS SHOES! AND, FROM THE SIZE OF THE PRINT, I AT ONCE CONCLUDE IT TO BE THAT OF A GIANT!
THE FOOTSTEP POINTS TO THE WEST... IMMEDIATELY I DEDUCE THAT IS THE DIRECTION IN WHICH OUR CULPRIT IS HEADED!
ALTHOUGH THE TERRAIN IS HARD AND UNYIELDING YET THE IMPRINT IS DEEP... I MUST ASSUME OUR QUARRY CARRIES A SUBSTANTIAL BURDEN...
COULD IT BE A HEAVY HEART?
OUR OPERATIVE EXPECTS A BREAK IN THE MYSTERY MOMENTARILY...

In the spring of 1958, after 74 years, the Giants left New York for California, as did the Dodgers.

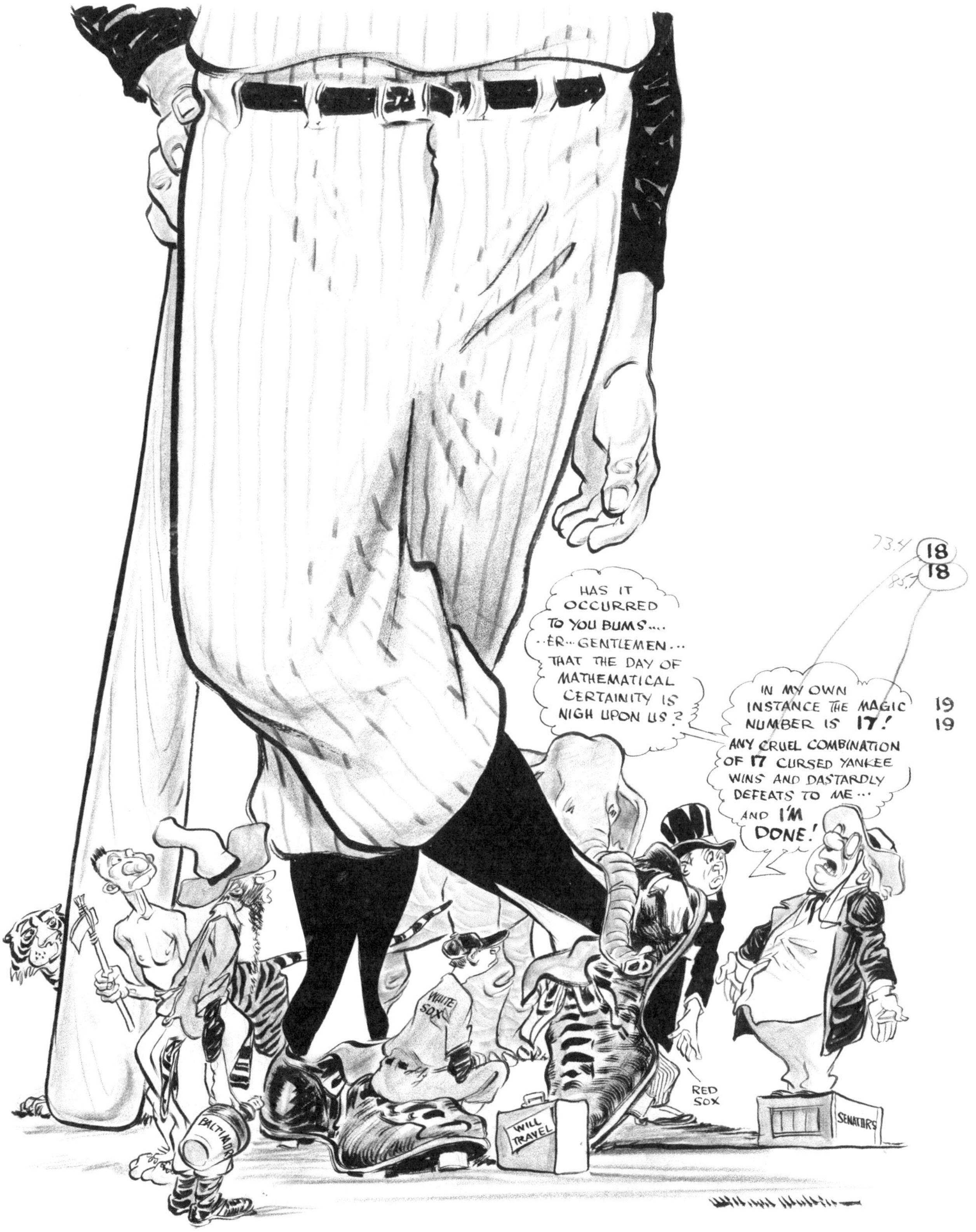
HAS IT OCCURRED TO YOU BUMS.... ..ER...GENTLEMEN... THAT THE DAY OF MATHEMATICAL CERTAINITY IS NIGH UPON US?
IN MY OWN INSTANCE THE MAGIC NUMBER IS 17! ANY CRUEL COMBINATION OF 17 CURSED YANKEE WINS AND DASTARDLY DEFEATS TO ME... AND I'M DONE!
18
18
19
19
WHITE SOX
RED SOX
WILL TRAVEL
SENATORS

While the NL pennant races of the 1950s weren't dominated by any one team, in the AL, the Yankees won eight of 10 pennants, with only the 1954 Cleveland Indians and the 1959 Chicago White Sox able to break their stranglehold. Note the additional numbers in the right margin. Mullin put them there because he had to draw his cartoon for the next day before the results of that night's games were in. The "Magic Number" and the "Cruel Combination" could have been 17, 18, or 19. The original artwork still carries the editor's marks telling the composing room which numbers to use.

BASEBALL OFFICIAL GUIDE

THE SULTAN AND THE RAJAH

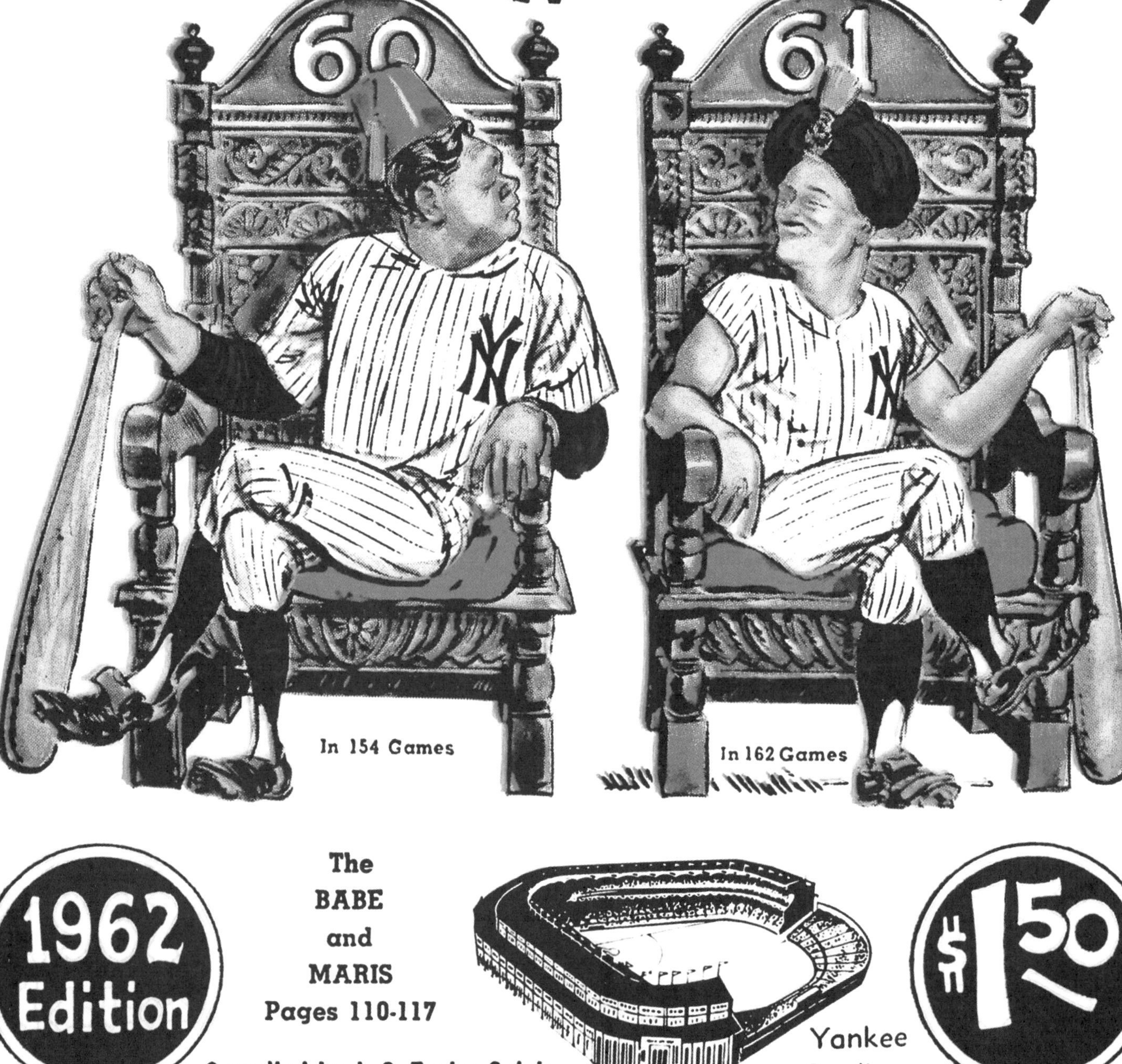

60
61
In 154 Games
In 162 Games

1962 Edition

The BABE and MARIS Pages 110-117

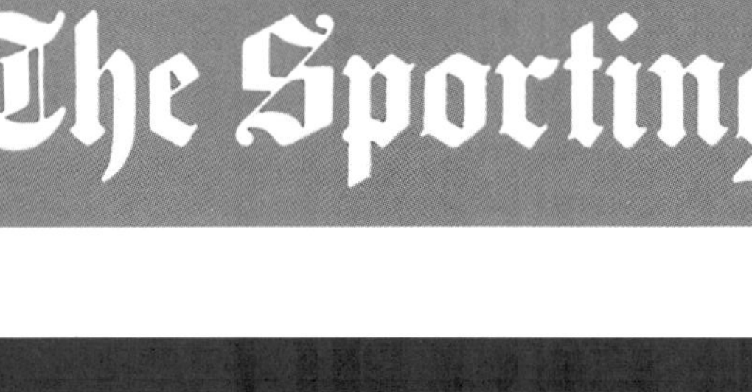

Yankee Stadium

$1.50

Compiled by J. G. Taylor Spink

PUBLISHED BY The Sporting News

The 1960s and 1970s

• • •

Ever since Babe Ruth hit 60 home runs in 1927,

the long ball has been baseball's exclamation point. One swing of the bat can change a ball game, even a season. In 1960, there were two monumental home runs at the end of the season, one in a meaningless September game, the other in the final game of the World Series.

It had been a dreary season for the Boston Red Sox, mired in seventh place, 32 games behind the New York Yankees, stuck on a treadmill to oblivion. And yet, the Sox could not be ignored, not with Ted Williams winding down a Hall of Fame career. Williams's often stormy career was interrupted twice, first for three years of service during World War II, then again for almost two more years during the Korean conflict. He had won six batting titles, including 1941 when he batted .406 and 1957 when he batted .388 at age 39. There had been six RBI titles and four home run titles and now, at age 42, he was done.

In his final Major League at-bat in Fenway Park, Williams left in style, hitting the 521st home run of his magnificent career. He put his head down and trotted around the bases as if it were no big deal. The fans, aware of the significance of the moment, were on their feet, giving him a standing ovation. But Williams never acknowledged them. There was no tip of the cap, no curtain call. It was as if he were in a hurry to put baseball behind him and get to some lake or pond with rod and reel. There were fish to be caught and no time to waste getting to them.

Throughout his career, Williams had issues with the press and sometimes fans. Once, he expressed his disdain for his critics in spectacular fashion by spitting in the direction of the fans. The Red Sox responded by fining him $5,000. The whimsical Willard Mullin commemorated the episode by drawing a Yankees player holding an umbrella and Williams emerging from a spittoon, declaring, "I challenge the world for distance, accuracy, or price."

Equipped with a long memory, Williams wasn't about to mend fences with the fans or anyone else at the end of his career. Renowned author John Updike was in Fenway that last day and noted the slugger's refusal to react to the acclamation of the fans. In an article in the *New Yorker* magazine, Updike wrote of Williams's snub, "Gods do not answer letters." It seemed to sum up this complex star perfectly.

Williams's retirement was followed by the exits of several other Hall of Famers. Mickey Mantle (536 home runs) and Yogi Berra (258 home runs) both left the Yankees. Berra became the manager in 1964, took his team to the seventh game of the World Series, and then was fired. Mantle left more gracefully four years later. Stan Musial was finished after a .331 career batting average and 475 home runs.

Warren Spahn retired with a record 363 wins for a left-hander — the first one at age 25 after he fought in World War II. When he returned to baseball after fighting in the battle for the Bridge at Remagen, Spahn mused, "Wow, if I don't do well, nobody's going to shoot me." He did very well, winning 20 or more games 13 times, throwing 63 shutouts and 382 complete games.

A couple of weeks after Williams departed, Pittsburgh found itself in the World Series for the first time since 1927. Back then, those Pirates stood around and watched

OPPOSITE: In 1961, Roger Maris broke Babe Ruth's single-season home run record, albeit in a 162-game season. As a result, Maris shared the "throne" with the Babe on the cover of the *Sporting News Official Baseball Guide* in 1962.

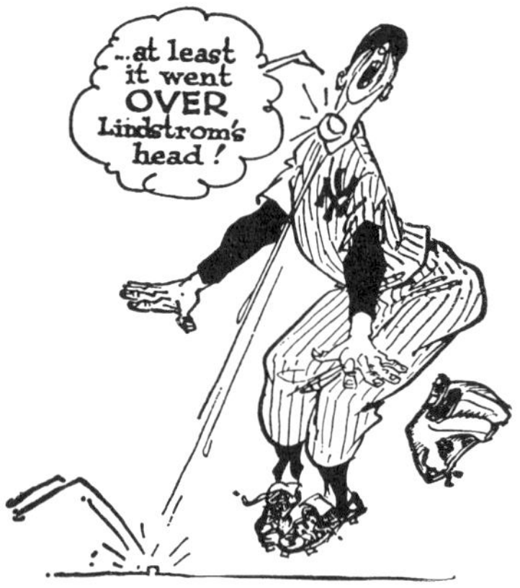
...at least it went OVER Lindstrom's head!

in awe as the New York Yankees Murderers' Row put on a long ball batting practice show and then swept the Series in four games. Now, these Pirates would be punished again by the Yankees, who scored 55 runs on 91 hits, 27 for extra bases, in seven games. The Yankees batted .338 and won games 16-3, 10-0, and 12-0. This time, though, it was the Pirates who won the World Series.

In one of the stranger battles for baseball supremacy, Pittsburgh became World Champions when Bill Mazeroski, a second baseman better known for his glove than his bat, led off the bottom of the ninth inning in Game Seven with a home run. It was the first time in history that a World Series ended with the drama of a home run.

Yogi Berra, in the twilight of his Hall of Fame career as a catcher, was in left field, looking up as Mazeroski's home run dropped over the vine-covered fence at Forbes Field that day. More significant were the two other Yankees outfielders that day — Mickey Mantle in center field and Roger Maris in right.

When the Giants and Dodgers had left for California, it was a body blow to the psyche of the nation's largest city. Willard Mullin had some fun with the departures, drawing Brooklyn's Walter O'Malley and New York's Horace Stoneham extolling the virtues of their new homes to their teams. The iconic Brooklyn Bum and Willy, the New York Giant, look a bit wary of this adventure but when their bosses said move, they moved.

There was plenty of anguish among their fans when the two teams departed, none of it, however, from baseball officials. National League President Warren Giles sneered, "Who needs New York?"

Well, maybe baseball did after all. By 1962, five years after the exodus, there was a dramatic U-turn and a triumphant return to the Big Apple when New York — along with Washington, Houston, and Los Angeles — was added to the Major Leagues through expansion.

The impetus for adding the new teams came shortly after Major League Baseball expressed no interest in providing the country's largest city with a National League team. No problem, said New York. There were other solutions available. Why not a new league?

Branch Rickey, one of the game's greatest innovators, was always up for new challenges, and he would help organize the Continental League, an alternative to the establishment, which would place teams in cities thirsting for baseball. Rickey and New York attorney William Shea drew up plans. The new league would have teams in New York, Buffalo, Atlanta, Toronto, Denver, Houston, Minneapolis-St. Paul, and Dallas-Fort Worth.

Major League Baseball was not amused, and with Rickey involved there was a fear that this threat was serious. So the establishment moved to cut off the Continentals before the rival league ever got started — the American and National Leagues would expand. In 1961, the AL would get a team for Los Angeles to rival the transplanted Dodgers, and a team for Washington to replace the one that had moved to Minnesota. The next year, the NL would get the Colt .45s (later the Astros) in Houston and the Mets (to replace the Giants and Dodgers) in New York.

All this meant stretching the schedule, adding eight extra games.

Mickey Mantle was a homebred star, who grew up in the Yankees organization. He was not always beloved because by playing center field, he was replacing one of the team's most iconic figures, Joe DiMaggio. But Mantle was a terrific hitter right from the start of his career, and when he won the Triple Crown in 1956, leading the league in batting average, home runs, and runs batted in, he certified himself as one of baseball's greatest sluggers.

Willard Mullin had celebrated the switch hitter at the start of his career as "The Natural," the cartoon highlighted by a pair of dice that came up two and five — a seven. In the drawing, Mantle has his original No. 6 uniform, which he soon traded in for No. 7, naturally.

ABOVE: A key play in the seventh game of the 1960 World Series, won by the Pittsburgh Pirates, came in the eighth inning. With one man on, Bill Virdon hit what appeared to be a double-play ball to Yankees shortstop Tony Kubek. However, the ball hit a loose pebble and ricocheted up, hitting Kubek in the throat. Kubek was forced to leave the game, and instead of two outs and no one on, there were two on and no one out.

OPPOSITE: The Yankees outscored the Pirates 55-27 overall in that World Series but the Pirates clinched the Series win with Bill Mazeroski's dramatic home run in the bottom of the ninth in the seventh game.

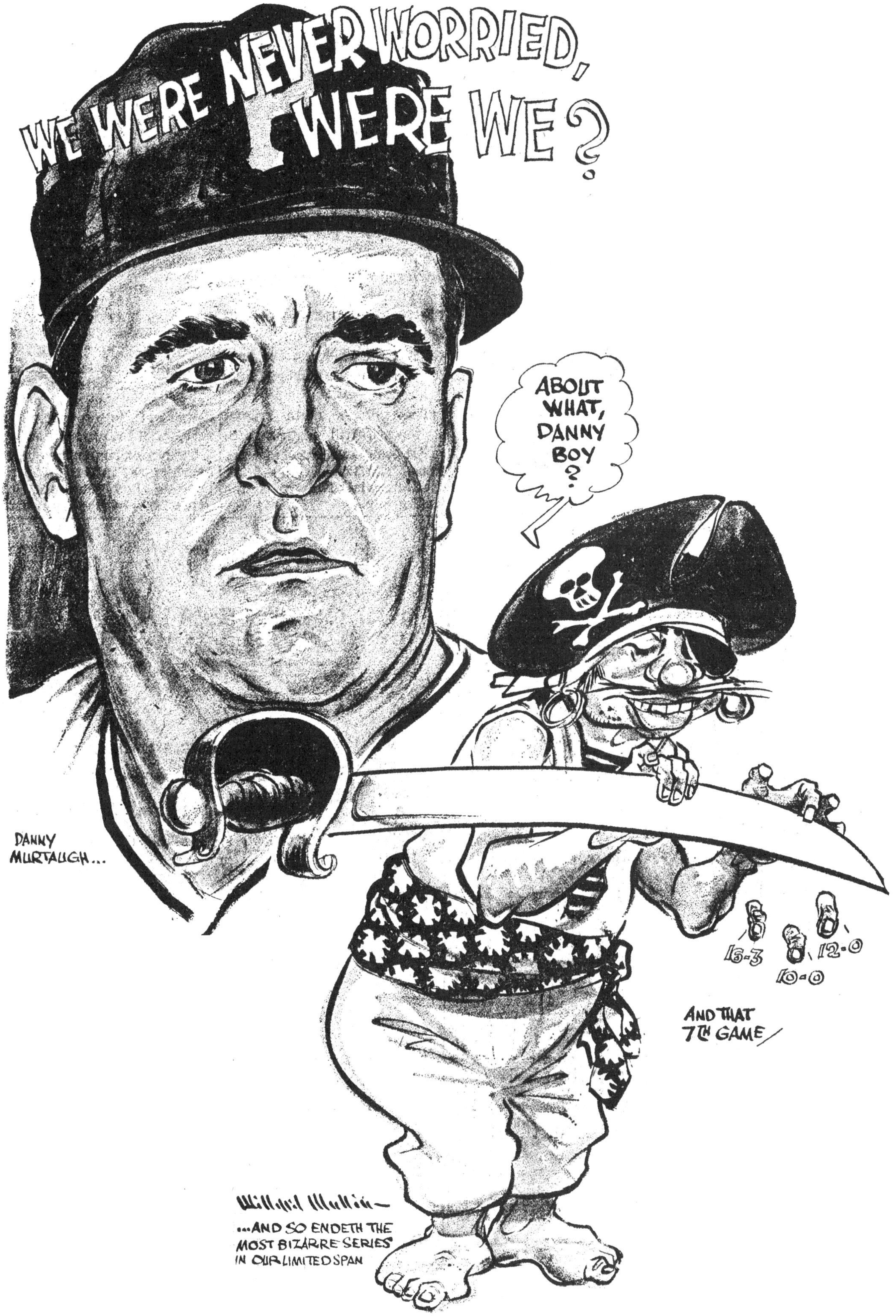
WE WERE NEVER WORRIED, WERE WE?
ABOUT WHAT, DANNY BOY?
DANNY MURTAUGH...
16-3
10-0
12-0
AND THAT 7TH GAME/
...AND SO ENDETH THE MOST BIZARRE SERIES IN OUR LIMITED SPAN

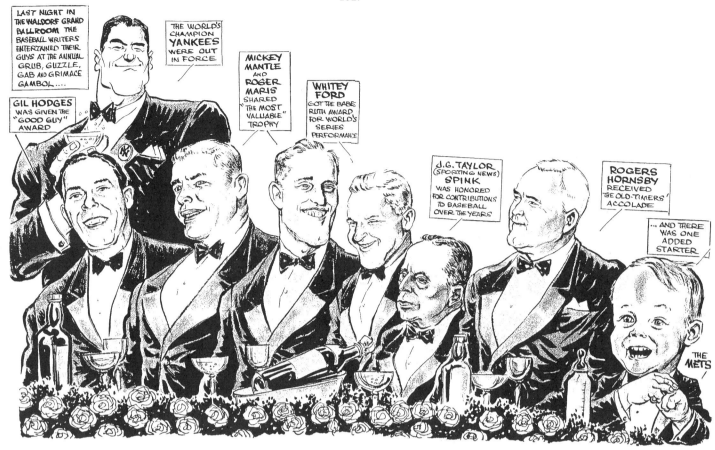

LAST NIGHT IN THE WALDORF GRAND BALLROOM THE BASEBALL WRITERS ENTERTAINED THEIR GUYS AT THE ANNUAL GRUB, GUZZLE, GAB AND GRIMACE GAMBOL....
GIL HODGES WAS GIVEN THE "GOOD GUY" AWARD
THE WORLD'S CHAMPION YANKEES WERE OUT IN FORCE
MICKEY MANTLE AND ROGER MARIS SHARED "THE MOST VALUABLE" TROPHY
WHITEY FORD GOT THE BABE RUTH AWARD FOR WORLD'S SERIES PERFORMANCE
J.G. TAYLOR (SPORTING NEWS) SPINK WAS HONORED FOR CONTRIBUTIONS TO BASEBALL OVER THE YEARS
ROGERS HORNSBY RECEIVED THE OLD-TIMERS' ACCOLADE
... AND THERE WAS ONE ADDED STARTER
THE METS

Roger Maris was the imported slugger, traded to New York from Kansas City before the 1960 season in one of those multi-player deals the Yankees arranged every so often. He was equipped with the perfect left-handed swing, built for the cozy right field stands at Yankee Stadium. His 39 home runs in his first season in New York left him one behind Mantle, the league leader.

The next season Maris and Mantle went on a long ball rampage, tagging home runs at a record pace that eventually would challenge Babe Ruth's 60-home run record set 34 years earlier.

Their run to the record was not simple. It was made more involved because of the addition of those two new American League teams that season, which resulted in extending the schedule from the traditional 154 games to 162. That was the ultimate result of the 1958 exodus of the Giants and Dodgers from New York.

When it became apparent that Ruth's record would be under a season-long attack by Mantle and Maris in 1961, commissioner Ford Frick decided to protect the Babe, declaring Ruth's record would stand unless it was broken in the same 154 games Ruth had played. The new record would be marked with an indication that it was achieved in more games. It would get an asterisk.

That solution pleased no one, but it became significant. Maris shrugged off the matter, saying simply, "A season is a season." That seemed to make sense but it hardly quelled the controversy.

Two weeks into September, Maris was three home runs ahead of Mantle, 56-53, with 18 games to play. Fans were pulling for Mantle because he was considered "a true Yankee," produced by the organization, unlike the imported Maris.

It was a role reversal for Mantle, who had become accustomed to being booed for having the audacity to replace the iconic Joe DiMaggio. Now Maris was the bad guy for challenging Babe Ruth's beloved home run record.

Their contest ended abruptly. Mantle developed a head cold and Yankees broadcaster Mel Allen recommended a doctor who was known affectionately among the

ABOVE: This drawing from the January 1962 Baseball Writers' Dinner celebrates the record-setting season of the New York Yankees and Roger Maris in 1961. It includes the first appearance of Mullin's "The Mets," representing the new New York team who would begin play in April of 1962. The model for "The Mets" was Mullin's 3-year-old grandson, Teddy Rhodes.

players as Dr. Feelgood. Mantle got an injection from the not-so-good doctor and an abscess developed on his hip. He was hospitalized and managed just one more home run the rest of the season. Maris finished the Ruth race alone, hitting No. 60 in the Yankees' 159th game and then No. 61 in the season's final game. It was the Yankees' 163rd game (because they re-played a rainout earlier in the season) and Maris's 161st game. So, he either broke Ruth's record or didn't, depending on your opinion of Ford Frick's ruling. Maris's record went into the record book as most home runs in a 162-game season. There never was an asterisk.

The new teams were suitably awful. The Angels finished in eighth place and the new Senators finished tied for last. Their ineptitude was nothing compared to what New York would experience the next year with the arrival of the Mets. The new team hired elderly Casey Stengel as manager two years after the Yankees had dismissed him because, despite 10 pennants and seven World Series Championships in 12 years, the team felt that, at age 70, the manager had fallen out of touch. "I'll never make the mistake of being 70 again," Stengel quipped.

The general manager was George Weiss, Stengel's old pal from their Yankees days. Hazel Weiss heartily endorsed her husband's return to baseball. "I married him for better or worse," she said, "but not for lunch." Suspecting Weiss might have a difficult task stocking the team, Mullin drew him pondering choices from what he called "The NL Thrift Shoppe." There were, alas, no bargains to be had.

Stengel was essential to the new team because of his ability to entertain listeners with stream-of-consciousness conversation that was dotted with fractured syntax and other violations of the English language. When he was called before Congress during antitrust hearings, Stengel left the politicians looking a bit confused as they listened to his testimony. When Mantle followed him as a witness, the slugger wisely said, "I agree with Casey."

Mullin saluted Stengel's oratory with a cartoon that celebrated the art of double-talk, a winding path through the language that was warmly known in baseball circles as Stengelese.

Stengel's act diverted attention from the field where the Mets were worse than anyone could have imagined. Eventually, the elderly manager expressed his frustration with a plaintive lament, wondering wearily, "Can't anybody here play this game?"

The answer was barely.

The Mets lost a record 120 games in their first season and provided plenty of fodder for Willard Mullin's array of pens and brushes. Mullin created the first Met, a baby fashioned after the cartoonist's grandson, Teddy. The little fellow wore a pair of spikes, a diaper, and a baseball cap on his head. The team colors were tributes to their departed predecessors, orange and blue. Orange for the Giants and blue for the Dodgers.

How bad were the Mets? Well, their first pick in the expansion draft to stock their team was journeyman catcher Hobie Landrith. Asked to explain the selection, Stengel responded brightly, "If you don't have a catcher, you get a lot of passed balls."

When the Mets traded Landrith, they acquired first baseman Marv Throneberry, a well-intentioned fellow who had more misadventures on the field than most players. There was the time Throneberry sent a long shot that allowed him to reach third base with an apparent triple. On an appeal play, he was ruled out for failing to touch second base. As Stengel came limping out of the dugout to argue the call, first base coach Cookie Lavagetto intercepted him. "Forget it, Case," the coach advised the manager. "He didn't touch first, either."

Another time, the Mets acquired catcher Harry Chiti for a player to be named later. When it came time to deliver the player they owed, the Mets chose to move Chiti back from whence he came, making him one of the few players who was ever traded for himself.

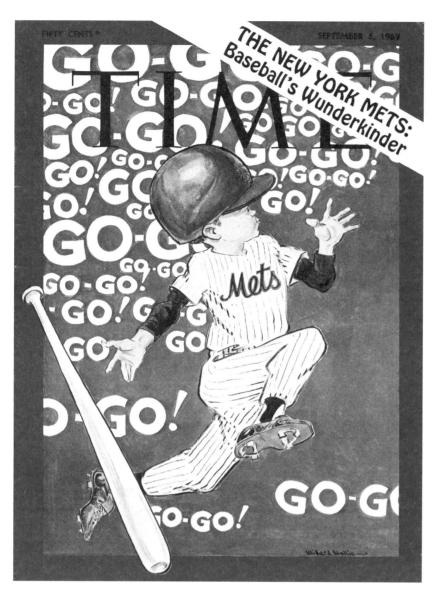

FIFTY CENTS
SEPTEMBER 5, 1969
TIME
THE NEW YORK METS:
Baseball's Wunderkinder
Mets

Then there was a memorable Memorial Day doubleheader against San Francisco in 1964. The Mets lost both games. Considering their level of achievement in those days, there was nothing special about that. What was special, however, was that the second game went 23 innings over 7 hours and 23 minutes. It was the longest game in elapsed time in Major League history. Combined with the first game, it completed the longest doubleheader in history—9 hours, 52 minutes.

Teenaged first baseman Ed Kranepool, called up from the minors by the Mets the day before, played all 32 innings. Gaylord Perry worked 10 innings of scoreless relief for the Giants and later said that was when he began fooling around with a spitball for the first time. He refined the long-banned pitch and went on to win 314 games and a ticket to the Hall of Fame.

The 23-inning game was impressive, but 10 years later, the Mets played a 25-inning affair against the St. Louis Cardinals. They lost that one, too.

The Mets were perpetual underdogs, especially in their own town where the lordly Yankees reigned supreme. In 1964, after they were eliminated, they snuck up on contenders and Mullin celebrated their surprise success. When they swept three important games from the Cardinals, he had the St. Louis Swifty snarl at the juvenile Mets, "Why don't you turn yourself in to the truant officer?"

The Mets took their triumphs wherever they could, and Mullin cooperated when the new team acquired a legitimate star in Ken Boyer, whose brother, Clete, was the longtime Yankees third baseman. Two other Boyers worked in the Yankees organization. Mullin had his diminutive Met taunting the regal Yankee, with "Nyah, nyah, we got one, too." And when the Mets had a surprising success in spring training, Mullin saluted the positive thinking of manager Wes Westrum. The success did not, however, carry over to the regular season.

While the Mets had trouble on the field, Houston had problems *with* the field. After three years of swatting mosquitoes in their open-air ballpark, the Colt .45s were renamed the Astros — in recognition of their city's role in the American space program — and moved to the Houston Astrodome, billed as the eighth wonder of the world. Equipped with a roof, the dome was air conditioned as protection against the Houston humidity. But grass needs sun to grow, and sunlight was unavailable under the roof of the Astrodome. And so was created AstroTurf — artificial grass that soon sprouted in a number of ballparks around the majors.

The 1960s began with the Mantle-Maris assault on Babe Ruth's single season home run record, touching off a decade in which a number of other marks tumbled. No one was near Ruth's lifetime total of 714 homers when the decade began. But when it ended, Hank Aaron was closing in on the mark, which he shattered in 1974.

Bob Feller posted 348 strikeouts in 1946 then watched a young left-hander, Sandy Koufax, strike out 382 in 1965. When the 1960s began, only two men in baseball

ABOVE: This is one of the last pieces Mullin did before his retirement in 1970. This *Time* magazine cover celebrates the "Go-Go Mets," who would win the World Series in just their eighth year in existence.

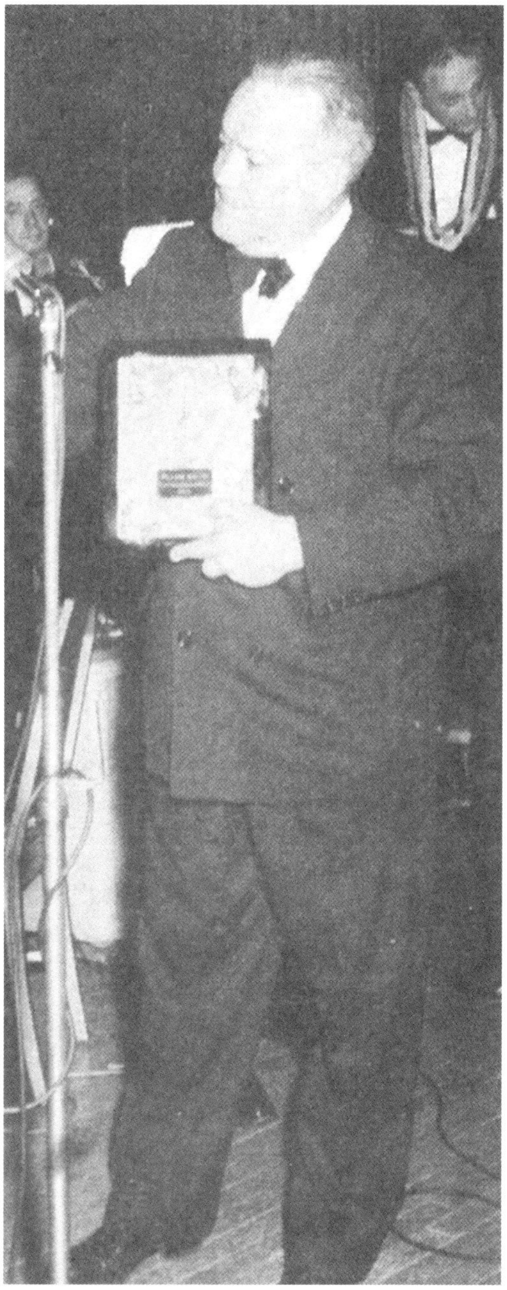

history, Feller and Cy Young, had thrown three no-hitters. Then Koufax threw four of them in four years, the last one a perfect game. He bordered on the unhittable with five straight earned run average crowns and three Cy Young Awards before an arthritic condition in his elbow ended his career prematurely at age 31.

The stolen base had fallen out of fashion. Ty Cobb's 96 steals in 1915 and 892 for his career were the standards and were never threatened. Then Maury Wills came along and stole 104 bases in 1962. Subsequent speedsters like Lou Brock and Rickey Henderson upped the ante to the point where Cobb's numbers seemed like those posted by a slowpoke.

For a long time, Feller's 18 strikeouts in a game stood as the record. Koufax matched it twice, in 1959 and then again in 1962. Then Steve Carlton struck out 19 in 1969 against a Mets team that was no longer woeful. In fact, the Miracle Mets staged one of the great reversals in baseball history, going from a perennial woebegone team of losers to, of all things, World Series Champions.

In the Mets bullpen that season was a somewhat erratic righthander named Nolan Ryan. When he harnessed his talents, he became a 300-game winner, struck out 5,714 batters, and blew past Koufax's record of four no-hitters to throw seven of his own.

Pete Rose broke in with Cincinnati in 1963 and went on to amass 4,256 hits, more hits than any player in Major League history. But Rose's career was tainted when he was banned from baseball for betting on games. It was reminiscent of the 1919 Black Sox scandal, only this time there was just one player involved and he happened to be baseball's all-time hit king.

After the excitement of the Mantle-Maris home run record chase, pitchers began to dominate baseball. Koufax led the way, and by 1968, the game had tilted dramatically away from hitters. Denny McLain won 31 games for Detroit, becoming baseball's first 30-game winner since 1934. Bob Gibson of the St. Louis Cardinals won 22 games and posted a 1.12 earned run average. In the opening game of the World Series, Gibson set a record by striking out 17 Detroit hitters. However, the Tigers recovered from a 3–1 Series deficit, sweeping the last three games and the World Championship.

There were consecutive Triple Crown winners in the American League. Frank Robinson, dismissed by Cincinnati as "an old 30," swept the home run, batting average, and RBI titles for Baltimore in 1966, and Carl Yastrzemski, the left field successor to

ABOVE, LEFT: At the time of his retirement in 1970, Mullin was recognized by his peers as the "Sports Cartoonist of the 20th Century."

Ted Williams in Boston, did it in 1967. But when Yastrzemski led the league in hitting with a .301 average in 1968, it was a red flag. Hitting was on the wane.

Alarmed by the drain on offenses, baseball took a dramatic step by lowering the pitcher's mound in 1969 to help the hitters. Four years later, the designated hitter was introduced to replace pitchers in the batting order. The National League balked at the change and never adopted it, leaving the two leagues playing with different rules, the AL with a 10-man batting order and the NL with the traditional nine.

Four more teams were added to the Major League lineup in 1969 — Kansas City and Seattle in the American League, and San Diego and Montreal in the National. The Seattle experiment lasted just one season before the team moved to Milwaukee to replace the Braves, who had fled to Atlanta. To accommodate the new teams, the two leagues split into divisions, and baseball introduced postseason playoffs, with the division champions playing each other to earn a ticket to the World Series.

The Kansas City franchise replaced the Athletics, who had moved to Oakland after a stormy stay in the Midwest under the ownership of insurance tycoon Charles O. Finley. After buying the team, he became a baseball Barnum with all manner of gimmicks that often blurred the games. Finley installed a mechanical rabbit behind home plate to deliver baseballs to the umpire. There were farm animals grazing beyond the outfield fences and a pet mule affectionately named Charlie-O, who accompanied the team to Oakland. The mule had the run of the A's home park. At a World Series press party, he nudged Hall of Famer Stan Musial on the buffet line. Musial, a genial sort, just laughed it off.

Meanwhile, in New York, labor problems had beset the newspaper industry. There were several strikes that in 1966 led to an ill-conceived merger of the *World-Telegram & Sun, Journal-American,* and *Herald Tribune.* The hybrid *New York World Journal Tribune* lasted less than a year before disappearing, leaving New York with just three daily newspapers — the *Times,* the *Daily News,* and the *Post.* It was about that time that Willard Mullin's cartoons disappeared from the daily press. But Mullin was not done drawing, and the Mets were perfect subjects as they evolved from awful to mediocre to World Champions.

Mullin drew the Mets' yearbook covers for several years in the 1960s, tracing the sometimes laborious progress of New York's National League baseball team. In 1964 he had Casey Stengel and his toddler Mets ready to pull the rug out from under the rest of the NL. In 1965, he had the young Met saluting one of the many sellouts at Shea Stadium with him saying, "You're the most." In 1966, the theme was a "Go, Go, Go Mets" banner and the youngster saying "That Means Me." The 1967 cover showed the team's progress on a set of stairs from 40 wins in 1962, to 66 in 1966. By 1968, Gil Hodges had arrived as manager and Mullin used a portrait of the onetime Brooklyn Dodger first baseman as the centerpiece of his cover.

A year later, the Mets ruled the baseball world, winning the World Series over the Baltimore Orioles. Mullin was in his glory. There was a *Time* magazine cover, a rare departure from the magazine's usual political and world focus, in which Mullin's Met is dashing across the page. The team's yearbook showed Mullin's original Met toddler all grown up, holding up a picture of the 1962 version and saying, "Remember Me?"

For the World Series record book, Mullin depicted a pint-sized David in a Mets shirt decking an oversized Goliath with the caption, "You big oaf, you stepped on my toe."

Two years later, after a career that produced some 10,000 cartoons, Mullin packed up his easel, inkwell, pens, and brushes and followed all those other Hall of Famers into retirement, hailed by his peers as the "Sports Cartoonist of the 20th Century." ❖

OPPOSITE: After his official retirement in 1970, Mullin continued to do a few jobs from time to time. These drawings were done for a 1972 Red Sox TV schedule. Even at 70 years old, Mullin's draftsmanship was second to none.

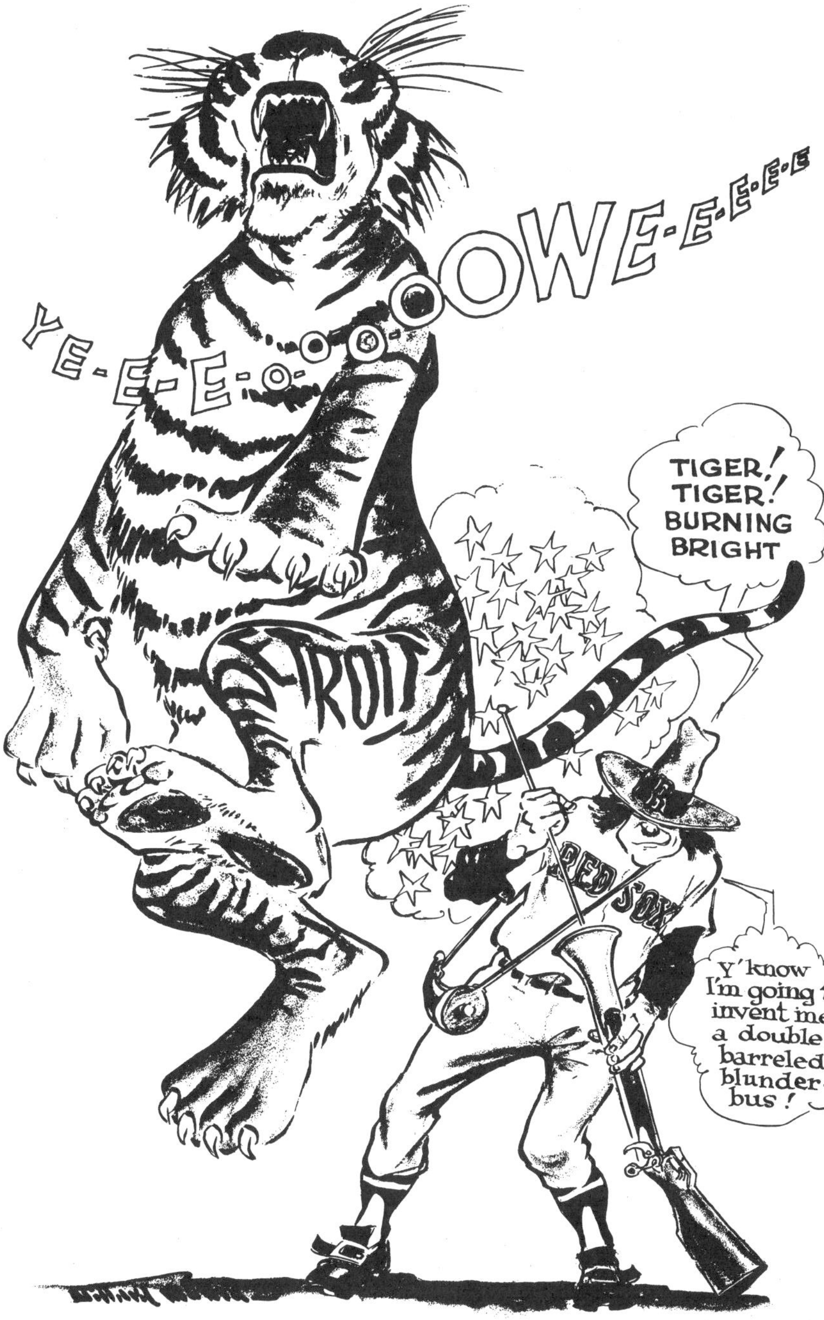
YE-E-E-O-O-O-OOWE-E-E-E-E
TIGER! TIGER! BURNING BRIGHT
DETROIT
RED SOX
Y'know I'm going to invent me a double-barreled blunderbus!

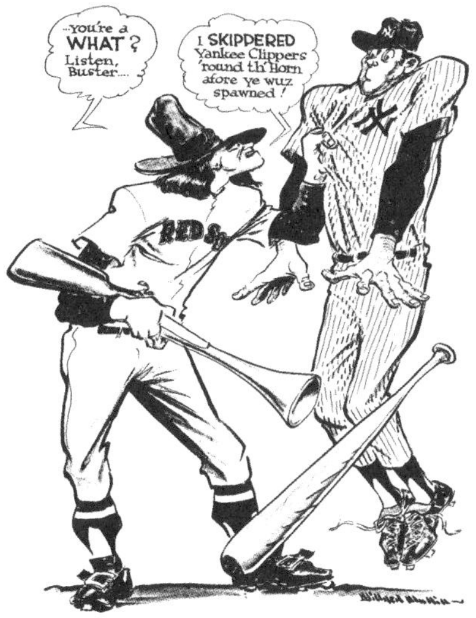
...You're a WHAT? Listen, Buster....
I SKIPPERED Yankee Clippers 'round th' Horn afore ye wuz spawned!

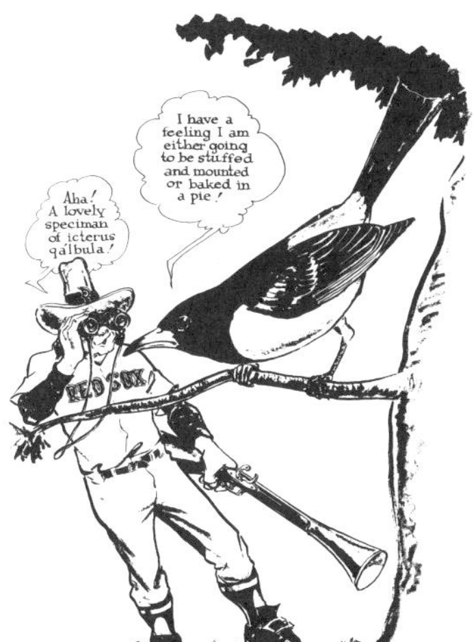
Aha! A lovely speciman of icterus qálbula!
I have a feeling I am either going to be stuffed and mounted or baked in a pie!
RED SOX

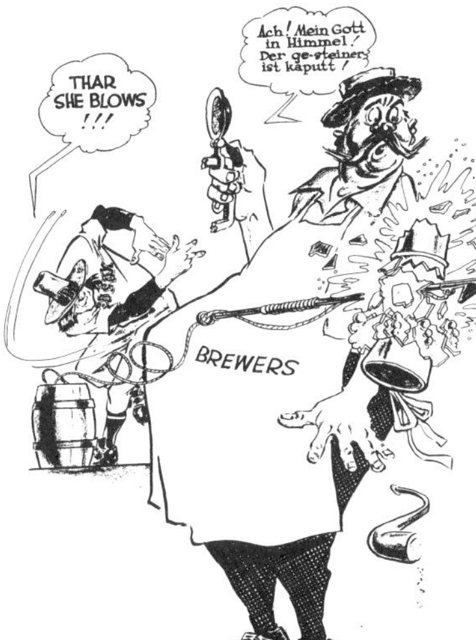
THAR SHE BLOWS !!!
Ach! Mein Gott in Himmel! Der ge-steiner ist kaputt!
BREWERS

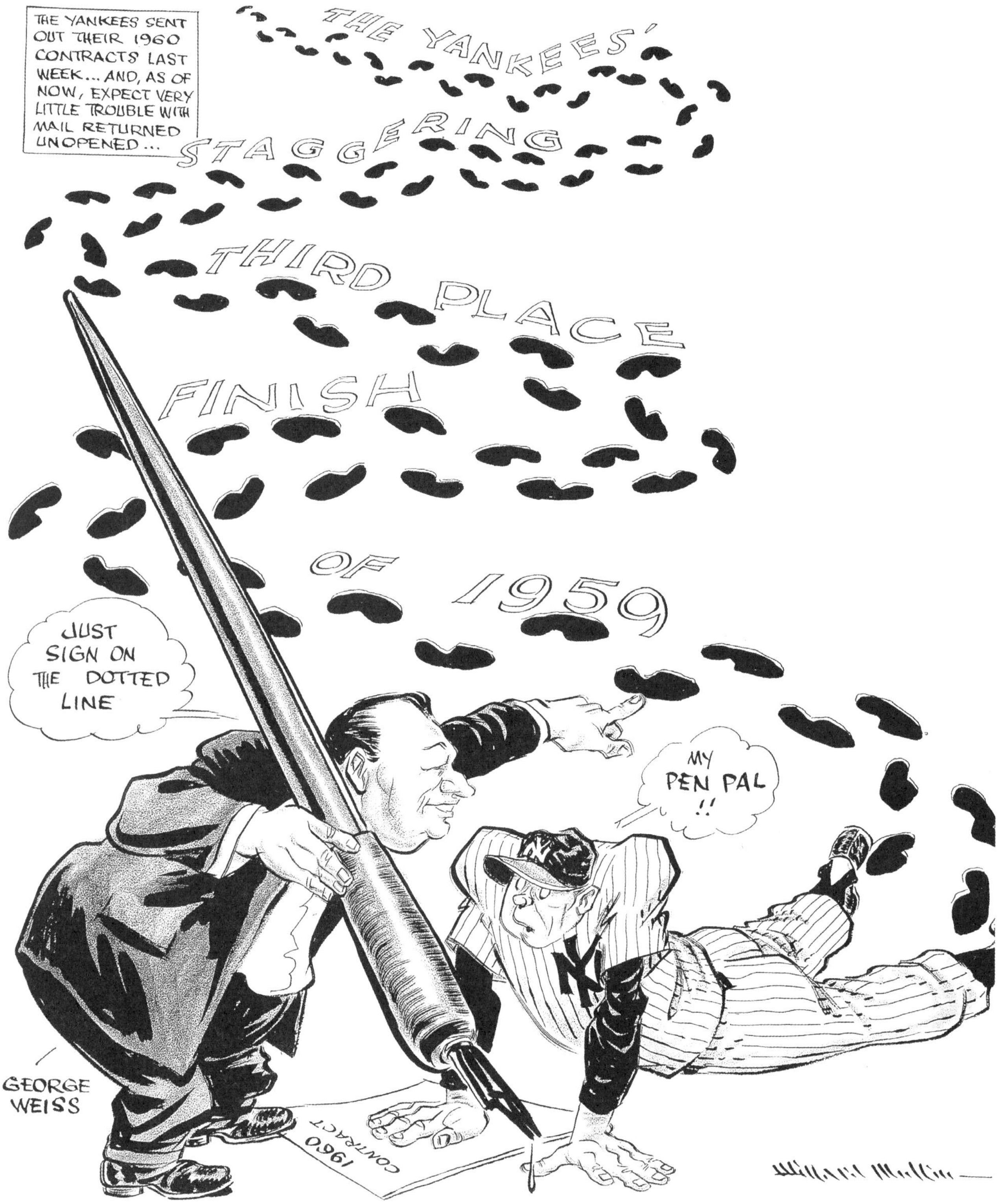
THE YANKEES SENT OUT THEIR 1960 CONTRACTS LAST WEEK... AND, AS OF NOW, EXPECT VERY LITTLE TROUBLE WITH MAIL RETURNED UNOPENED...
THE YANKEES' STAGGERING THIRD PLACE FINISH OF 1959
JUST SIGN ON THE DOTTED LINE
MY PEN PAL !!
GEORGE WEISS
1960 CONTRACT

In the 18 years from 1947 through 1964, the Yankees won 15 American League pennants. Their worst season during this run was 1959, when they went 79–75 and finished 15 games behind the pennant-winning White Sox.

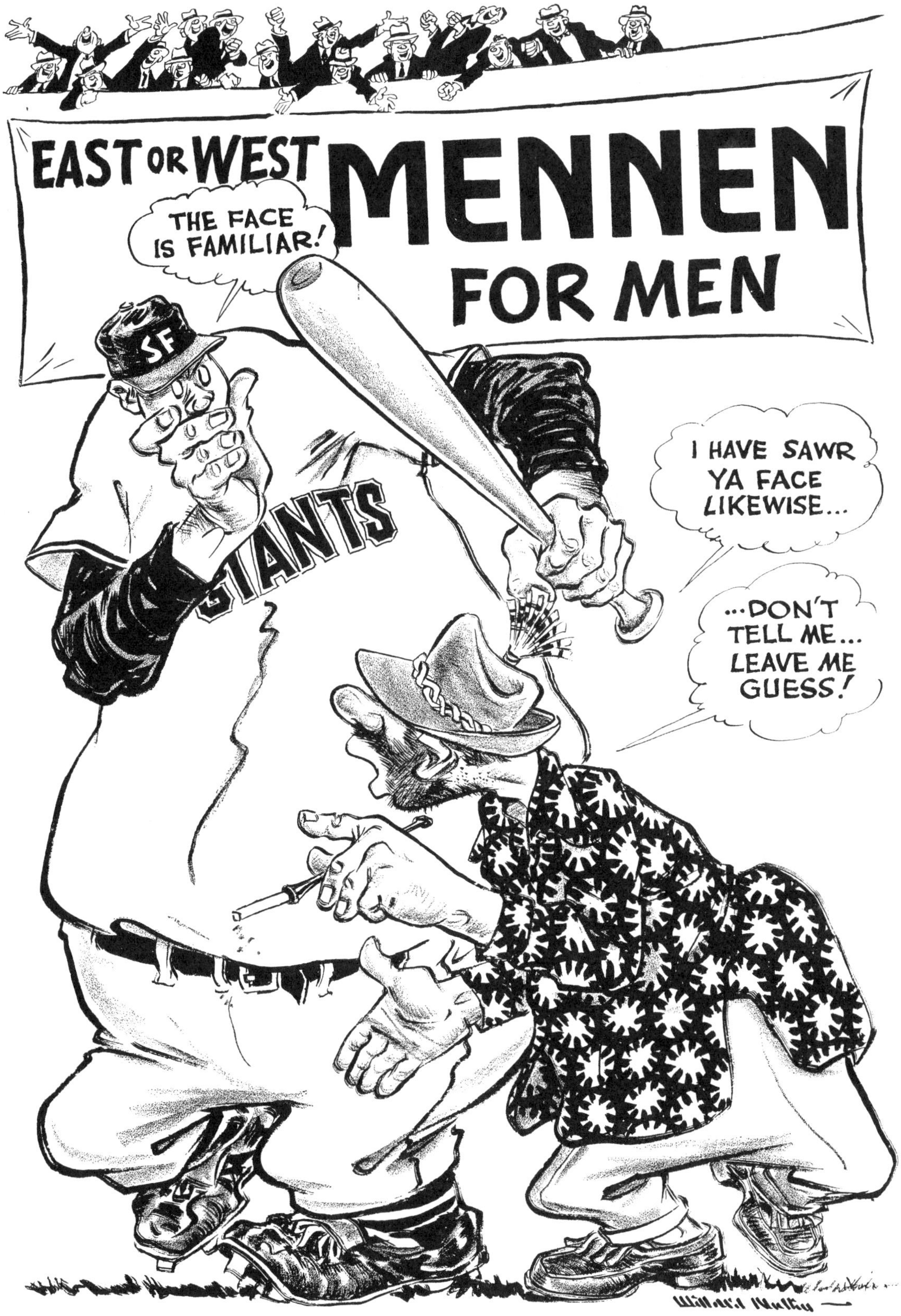
EAST OR WEST MENNEN FOR MEN
THE FACE IS FAMILIAR!
SF
GIANTS
I HAVE SAWR YA FACE LIKEWISE...
...DON'T TELL ME... LEAVE ME GUESS!
Willard Mullin

Even after the Dodgers and Giants moved West, the rivalry continued. Here, the San Francisco Giant and the Hollywood Bum get reacquainted.

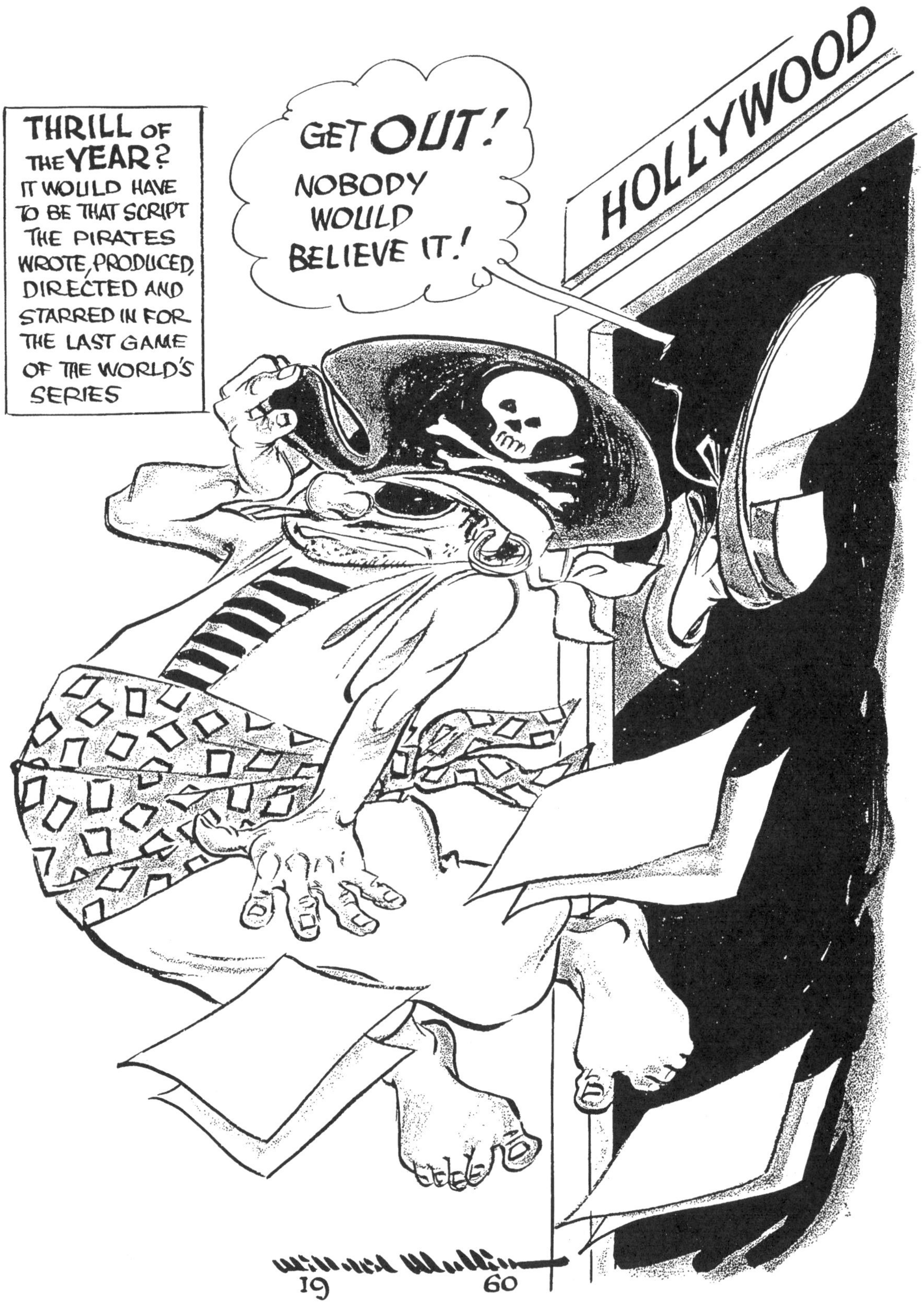
THRILL OF THE YEAR? IT WOULD HAVE TO BE THAT SCRIPT THE PIRATES WROTE, PRODUCED, DIRECTED AND STARRED IN FOR THE LAST GAME OF THE WORLD'S SERIES
GET OUT! NOBODY WOULD BELIEVE IT!
HOLLYWOOD
19 60

In 1960, the Pittsburgh Pirates, who had not been to the World Series since 1927, confounded the experts. Not only did they win the National League pennant but they also clobbered the Yankees in the World Series in the seventh game with Bill Mazeroski's improbable over–the-fence ninth-inning home run — the most dramatic homer in World Series history.

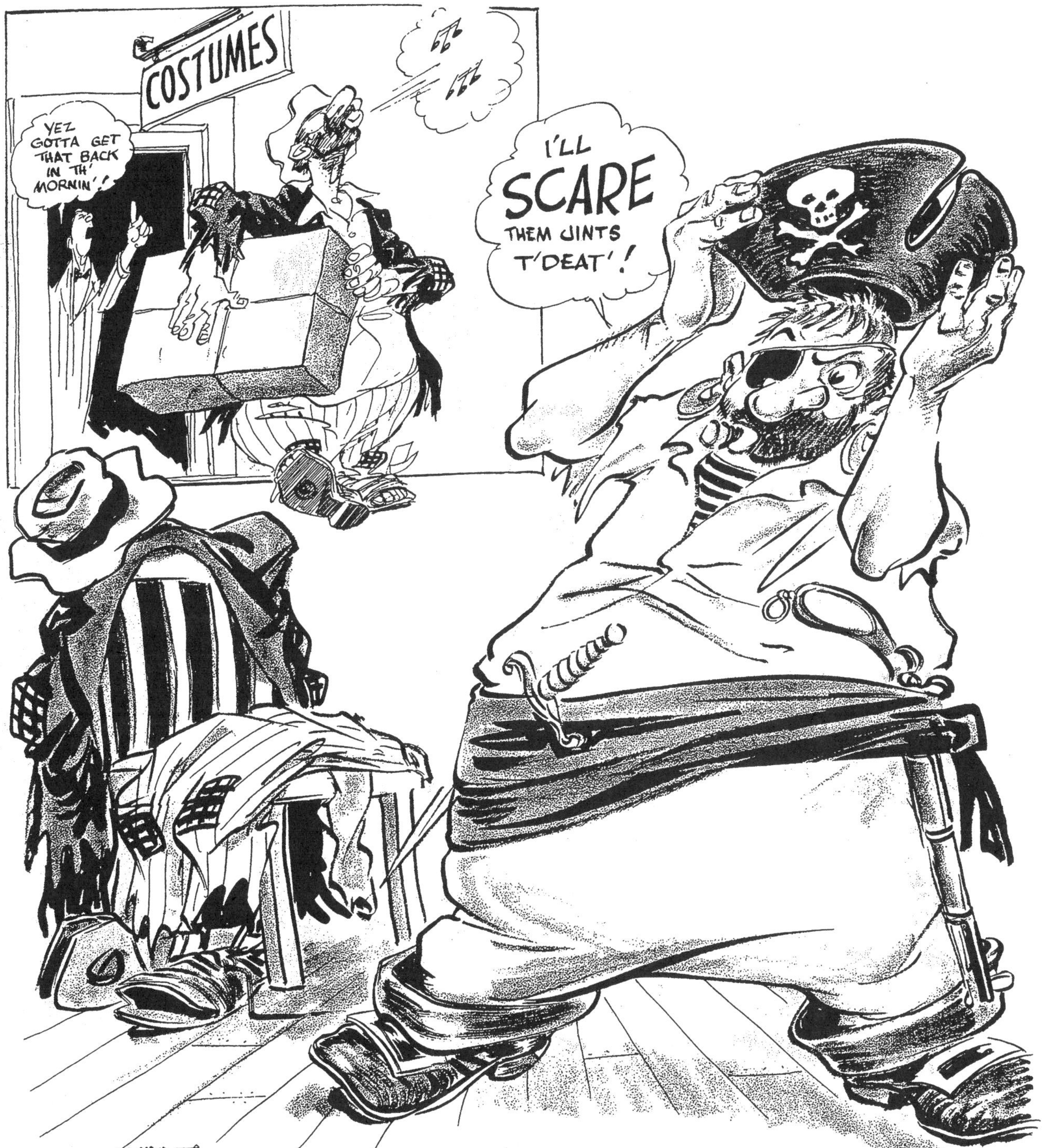
COSTUMES
YEZ GOTTA GET THAT BACK IN TH' MORNIN'!
I'LL SCARE THEM JINTS T'DEAT'!

During the regular season, in the run-up to their World Series Championship, the 1960 Pirates were particularly successful against the Giants. In this cartoon, the Bum attempts to co-opt a little of Pittsburgh's success by masquerading as a Pirate.

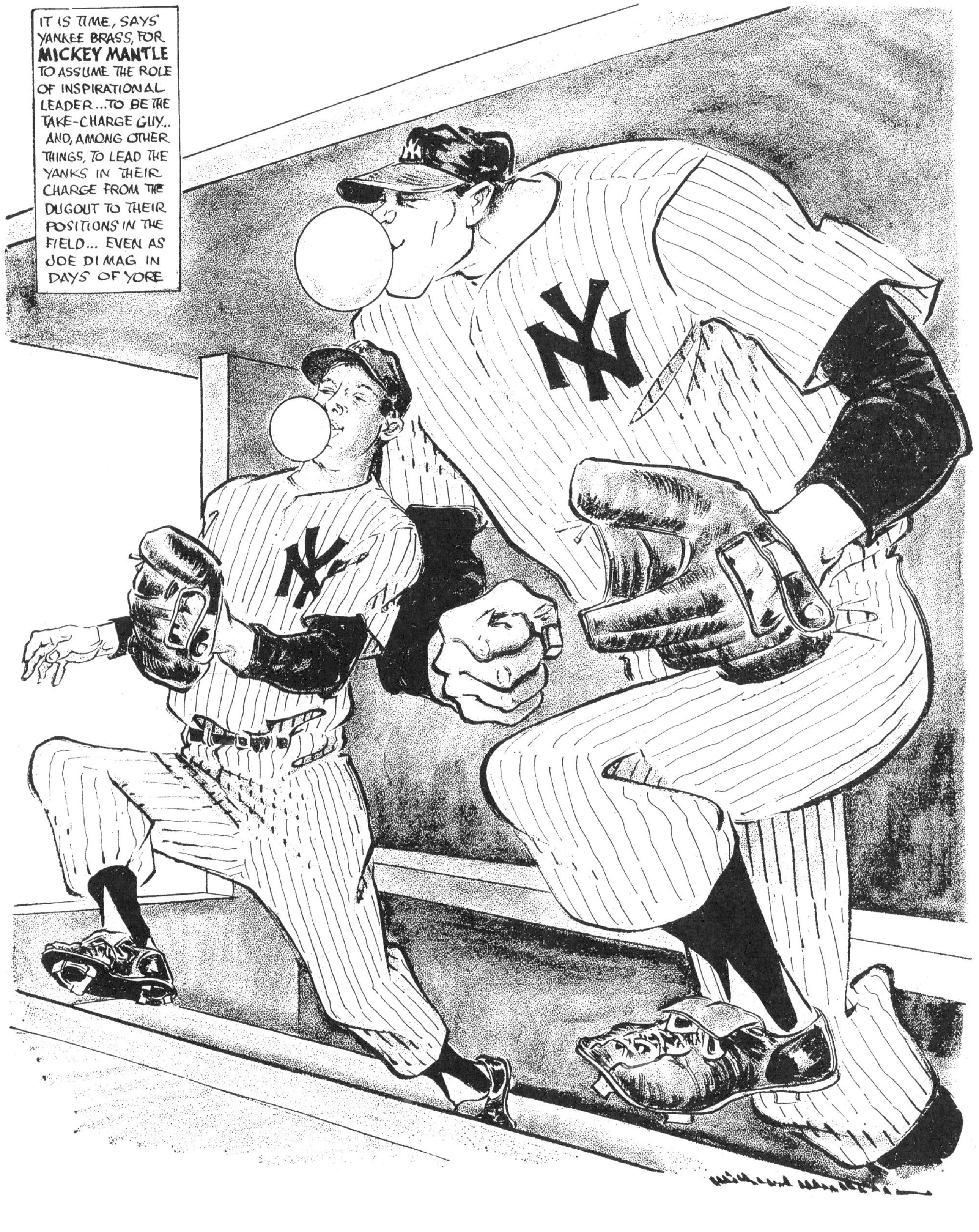
IT IS TIME, SAYS YANKEE BRASS, FOR MICKEY MANTLE TO ASSUME THE ROLE OF INSPIRATIONAL LEADER...TO BE THE TAKE-CHARGE GUY.. AND, AMONG OTHER THINGS, TO LEAD THE YANKS IN THEIR CHARGE FROM THE DUGOUT TO THEIR POSITIONS IN THE FIELD... EVEN AS JOE DI MAG IN DAYS OF YORE
NY
NY

Casey Stengel was fired as Yankees manager after the team lost the 1960 World Series. Stengel was replaced by Ralph Houk. Mickey Mantle was in his 11th season with the Yankees, and Houk looked for Mantle to assume more of a leadership role at the beginning of the 1961 campaign.

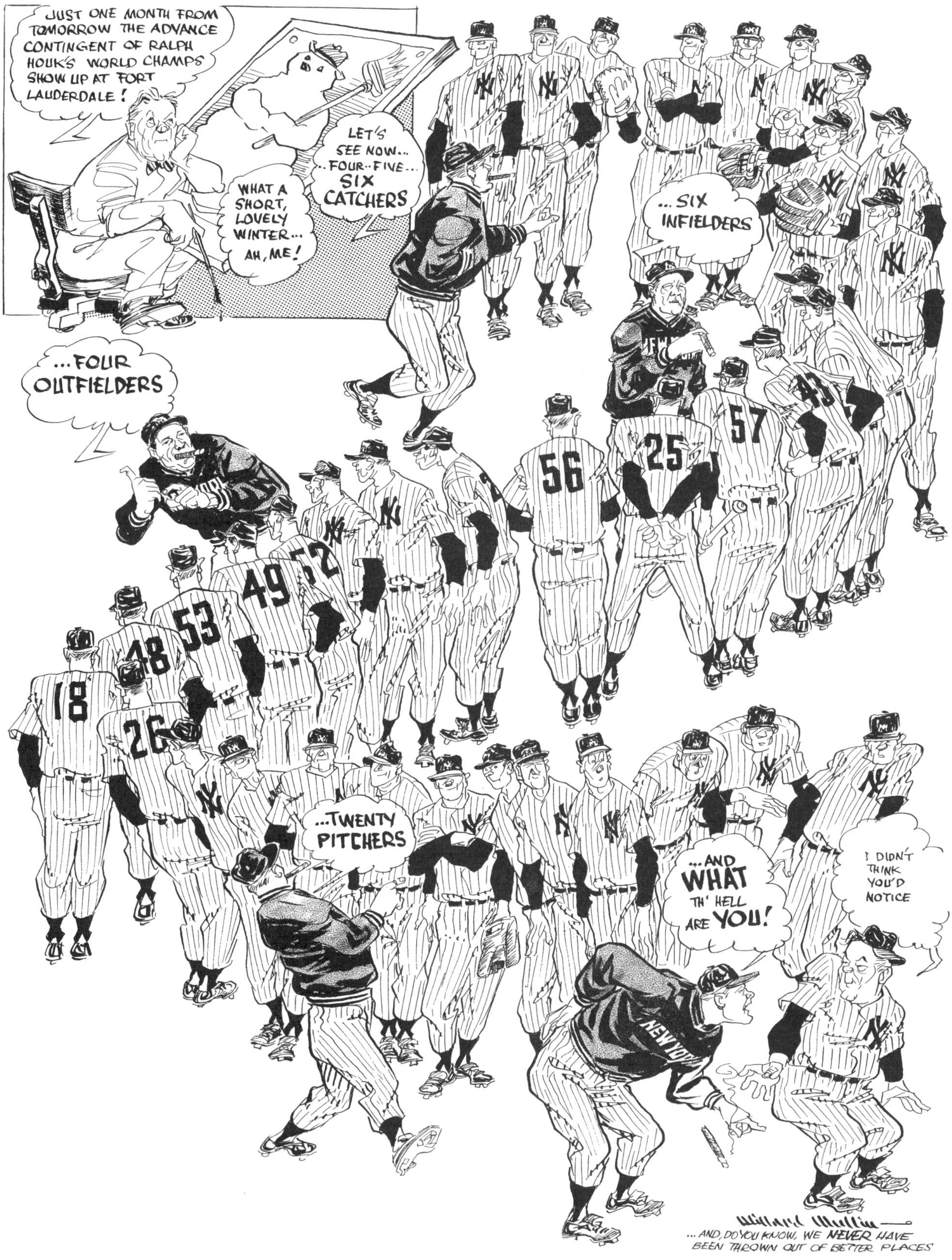
JUST ONE MONTH FROM TOMORROW THE ADVANCE CONTINGENT OF RALPH HOUK'S WORLD CHAMPS SHOW UP AT FORT LAUDERDALE!
WHAT A SHORT, LOVELY WINTER... AH, ME!
LET'S SEE NOW... ..FOUR..FIVE... SIX CATCHERS
...SIX INFIELDERS
...FOUR OUTFIELDERS
...TWENTY PITCHERS
...AND WHAT TH' HELL ARE YOU!
I DIDN'T THINK YOU'D NOTICE
Willard Mullin
...AND, DO YOU KNOW, WE NEVER HAVE BEEN THROWN OUT OF BETTER PLACES

In 1961, Ralph Houk's first year as manager of the Yankees, the team, led by Roger Maris and Mickey Mantle, won the franchise's 19th World Series title. In the spring of 1962, Houk had a plethora of pitchers vying for a spot on the roster (along with one slightly over-the-hill sports cartoonist).

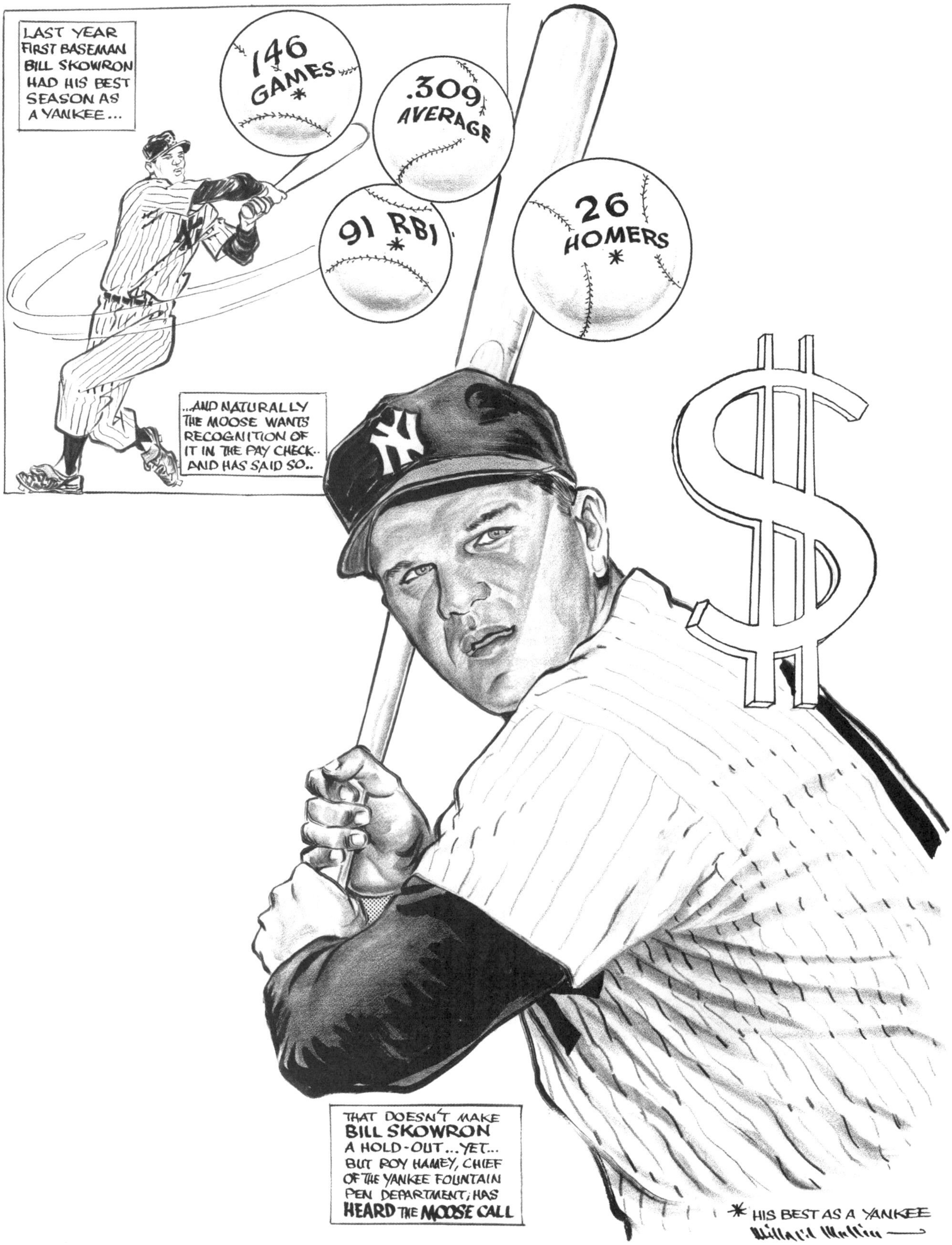
LAST YEAR FIRST BASEMAN BILL SKOWRON HAD HIS BEST SEASON AS A YANKEE...
146 GAMES *
.309 AVERAGE
91 RBI *
26 HOMERS *
...AND NATURALLY THE MOOSE WANTS RECOGNITION OF IT IN THE PAY CHECK.. AND HAS SAID SO..
THAT DOESN'T MAKE BILL SKOWRON A HOLD-OUT...YET... BUT ROY HAMEY, CHIEF OF THE YANKEE FOUNTAIN PEN DEPARTMENT, HAS HEARD THE MOOSE CALL
* HIS BEST AS A YANKEE

Moose Skowron played for the Yankees from 1954 through 1962. His best season was in 1960, when he contributed 26 home runs and 91 RBIs.

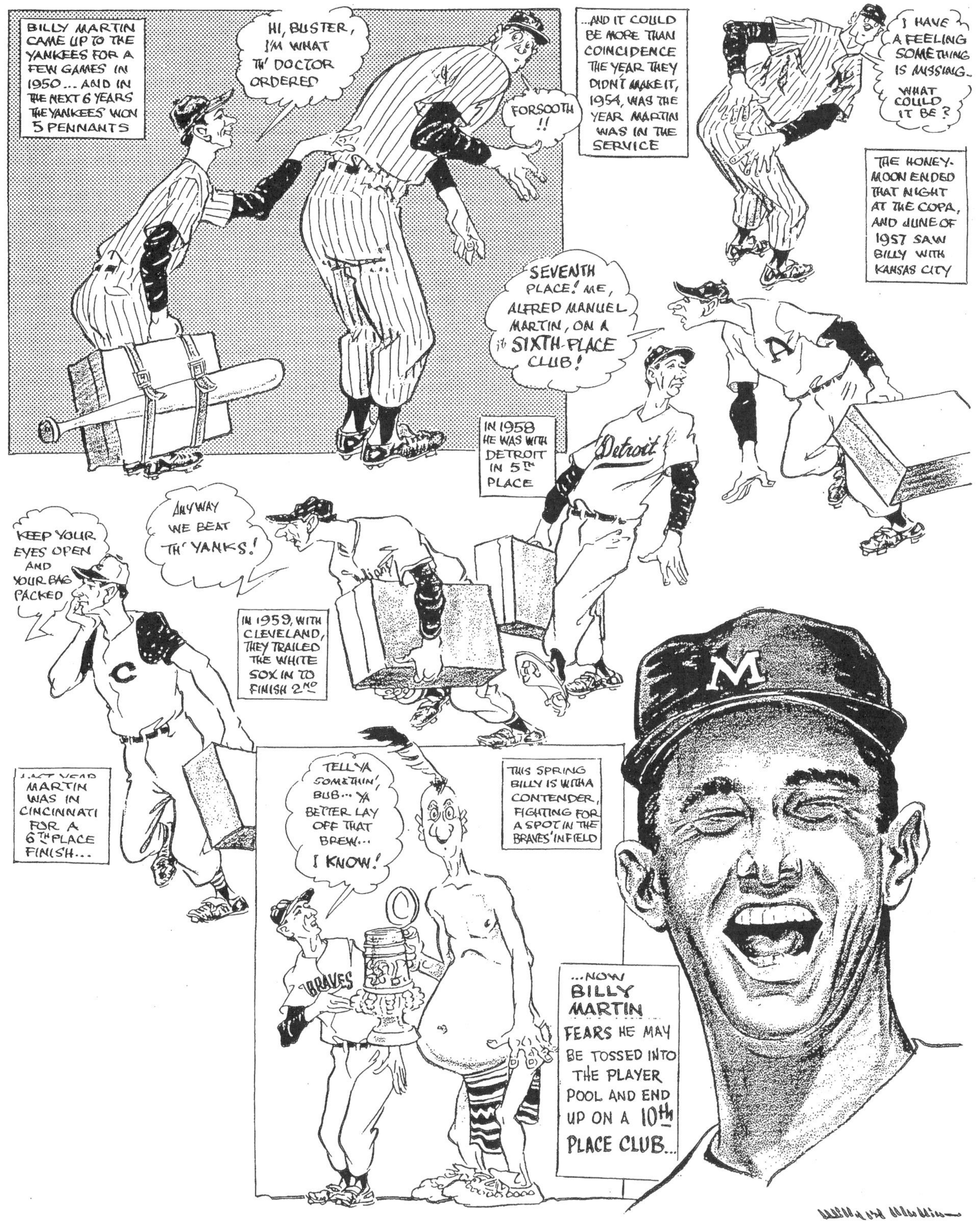
BILLY MARTIN CAME UP TO THE YANKEES FOR A FEW GAMES IN 1950... AND IN THE NEXT 6 YEARS THE YANKEES WON 5 PENNANTS
HI, BUSTER, I'M WHAT TH' DOCTOR ORDERED
FORSOOTH !!
...AND IT COULD BE MORE THAN COINCIDENCE THE YEAR THEY DIDN'T MAKE IT, 1954, WAS THE YEAR MARTIN WAS IN THE SERVICE
I HAVE A FEELING SOMETHING IS MISSING... WHAT COULD IT BE ?
THE HONEYMOON ENDED THAT NIGHT AT THE COPA, AND JUNE OF 1957 SAW BILLY WITH KANSAS CITY
SEVENTH PLACE! ME, ALFRED MANUEL MARTIN, ON A SIXTH-PLACE CLUB!
IN 1958 HE WAS WITH DETROIT IN 5TH PLACE
KEEP YOUR EYES OPEN AND YOUR BAG PACKED
ANYWAY WE BEAT TH' YANKS!
IN 1959, WITH CLEVELAND, THEY TRAILED THE WHITE SOX IN TO FINISH 2ND
MARTIN WAS IN CINCINNATI FOR A 6TH PLACE FINISH...
TELL YA SOMETHIN', BUB... YA BETTER LAY OFF THAT BREW... I KNOW!
THIS SPRING BILLY IS WITH A CONTENDER, FIGHTING FOR A SPOT IN THE BRAVES' INFIELD
...NOW BILLY MARTIN FEARS HE MAY BE TOSSED INTO THE PLAYER POOL AND END UP ON A 10TH PLACE CLUB...

Billy Martin came up to the Yankees in 1950. Over the next six years he was the starting second baseman for five pennant-winning teams. After an incident at the Copacabana in 1957 involving Martin, Mickey Mantle, Hank Bauer, and some drunken fans, Martin was unceremoniously traded to Kansas City. He was subsequently traded to the Tigers, the Indians, and the Reds. By the time of this drawing, in the spring of 1961, Martin was with his fifth team in five years, the Milwaukee Braves. Martin's playing career would end shortly thereafter, but not without one more stop: Minnesota.

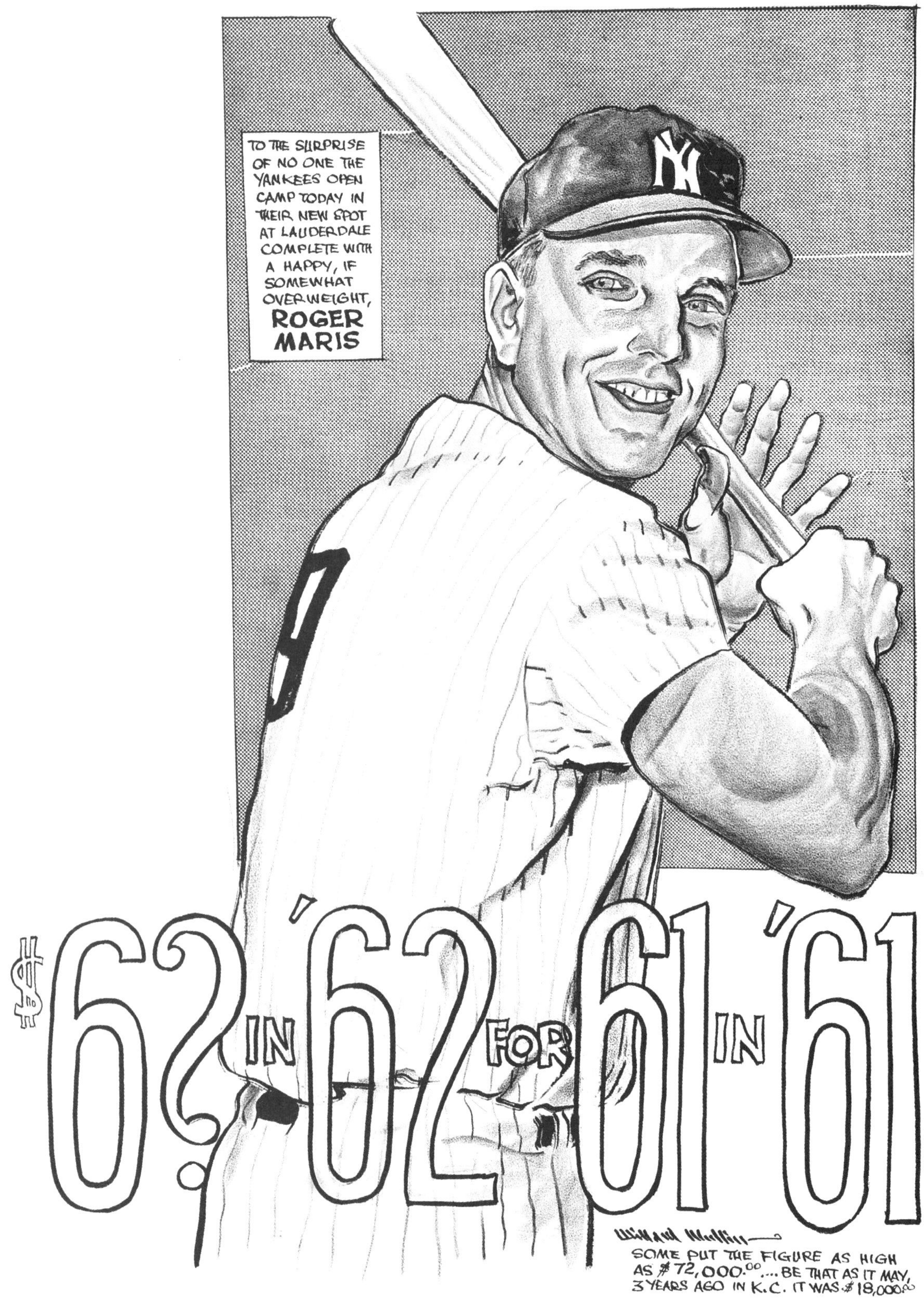
TO THE SURPRISE OF NO ONE THE YANKEES OPEN CAMP TODAY IN THEIR NEW SPOT AT LAUDERDALE COMPLETE WITH A HAPPY, IF SOMEWHAT OVERWEIGHT, ROGER MARIS
$62? IN '62 FOR 61 IN '61
SOME PUT THE FIGURE AS HIGH AS $72,000.00 .... BE THAT AS IT MAY, 3 YEARS AGO IN K.C. IT WAS $18,000.00

In 1961, Roger Maris broke the Babe's record by hitting 61 home runs in a season. He was rewarded with a significant pay increase. Mullin speculated that Maris might hit 62 in '62 and win himself another pay hike.

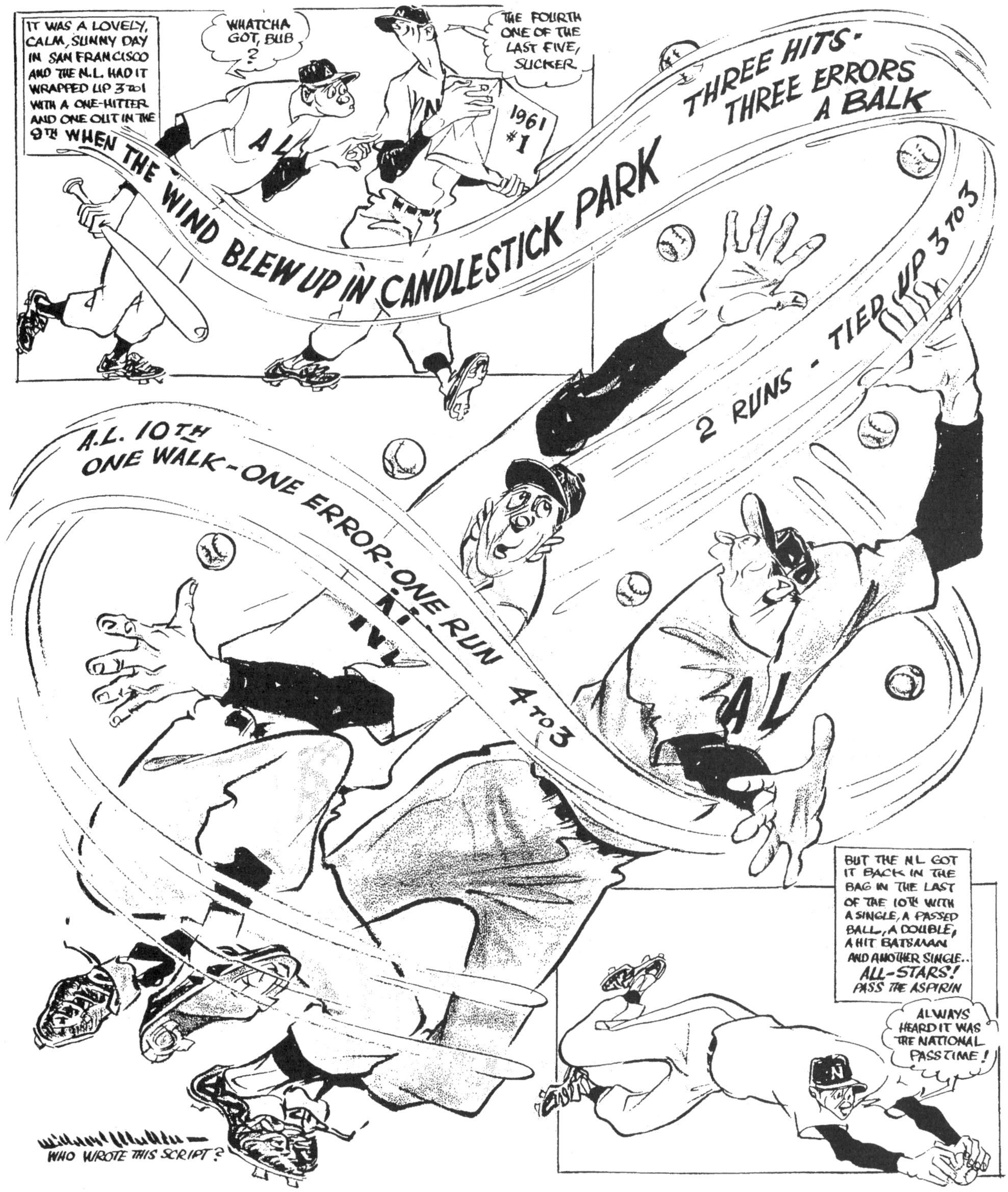
IT WAS A LOVELY, CALM, SUNNY DAY IN SAN FRANCISCO AND THE N.L. HAD IT WRAPPED UP 3 TO 1 WITH A ONE-HITTER AND ONE OUT IN THE 9TH WHEN
WHATCHA GOT, BUB ?
THE FOURTH ONE OF THE LAST FIVE, SUCKER
1961 #1
THE WIND BLEW UP IN CANDLESTICK PARK
THREE HITS - THREE ERRORS A BALK
2 RUNS - TIED UP 3 TO 3
A.L. 10TH ONE WALK - ONE ERROR - ONE RUN 4 TO 3
BUT THE N.L. GOT IT BACK IN THE BAG IN THE LAST OF THE 10TH WITH A SINGLE, A PASSED BALL, A DOUBLE, A HIT BATSMAN AND ANOTHER SINGLE.. ALL-STARS! PASS THE ASPIRIN
ALWAYS HEARD IT WAS THE NATIONAL PASSTIME!
WHO WROTE THIS SCRIPT?

From the time it opened in April 1960, Candlestick Park in San Francisco had strong winds, which often swirled down into the stadium and created havoc with the playing conditions. In the 1961 All-Star Game held at Candlestick, the National League led 3–2 in the ninth when a strong gust of wind blew Giants reliever Stu Miller off the mound, causing a balk and allowing the tying run to score. Despite this, the National League won the game in 10 innings on consecutive singles by Hank Aaron, Willie Mays, and Roberto Clemente.

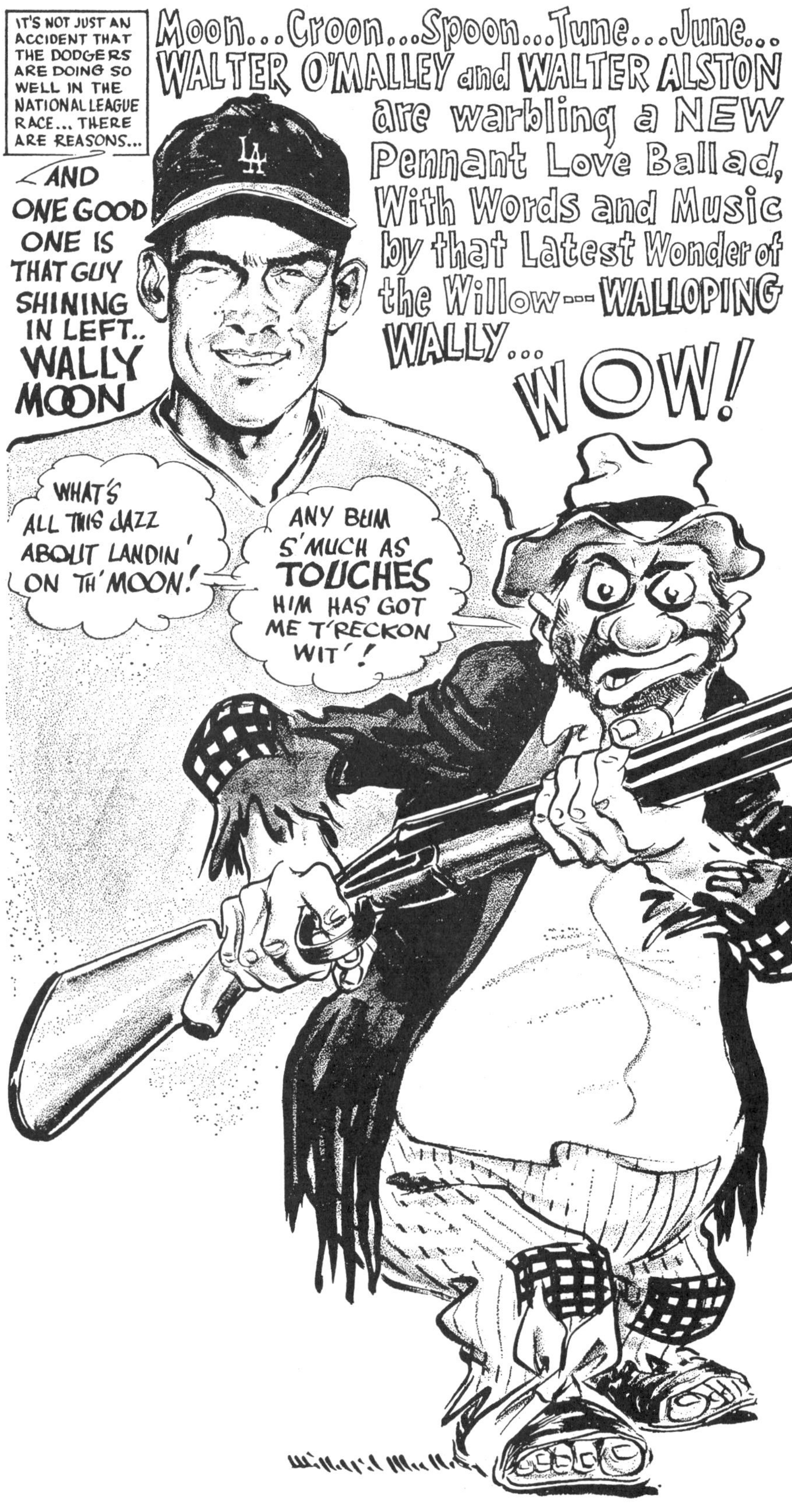
IT'S NOT JUST AN ACCIDENT THAT THE DODGERS ARE DOING SO WELL IN THE NATIONAL LEAGUE RACE... THERE ARE REASONS...
AND ONE GOOD ONE IS THAT GUY SHINING IN LEFT.. WALLY MOON
Moon...Croon...Spoon...Tune...June... WALTER O'MALLEY and WALTER ALSTON are warbling a NEW Pennant Love Ballad, With Words and Music by that Latest Wonder of the Willow--- WALLOPING WALLY... WOW!
WHAT'S ALL THIS JAZZ ABOUT LANDIN' ON TH' MOON!
ANY BUM S'MUCH AS TOUCHES HIM HAS GOT ME T'RECKON WIT'!

Wally Moon played in the majors for 12 years, the last seven with the Los Angeles Dodgers. Moon was NL Rookie of the Year in 1954, a three-time All-Star, a Gold Glove-winning outfielder, and a two-time World Series Champion.

In 1961, President John F. Kennedy announced the goal of landing a man on the moon by the end of the decade. 1961 was also one of Moon's best years. He hit .328 with 17 home runs and 88 RBIs and led the league in on-base percentage.

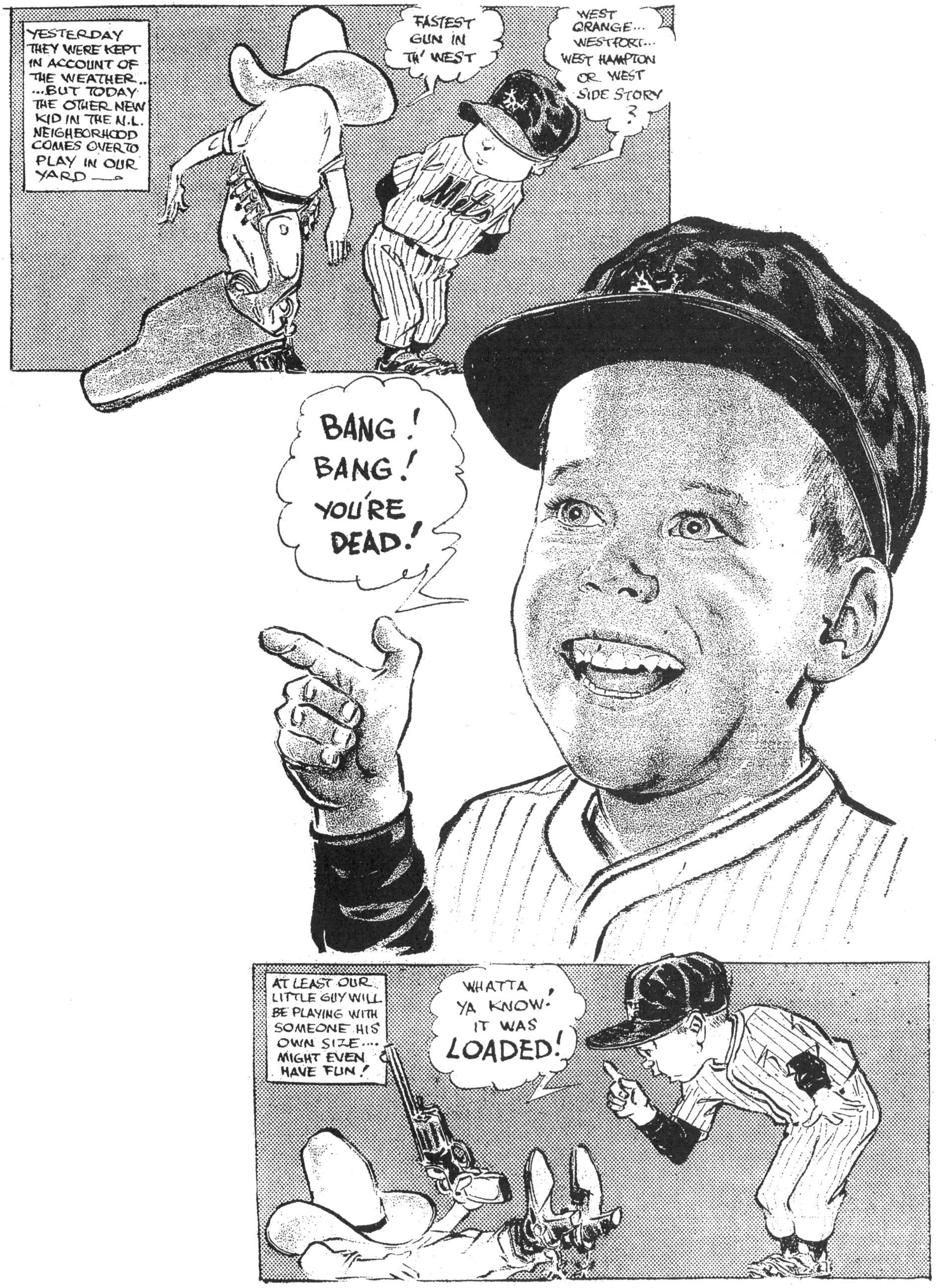
YESTERDAY THEY WERE KEPT IN ACCOUNT OF THE WEATHER.. ...BUT TODAY THE OTHER NEW KID IN THE N.L. NEIGHBORHOOD COMES OVER TO PLAY IN OUR YARD —
FASTEST GUN IN TH' WEST
WEST ORANGE... WESTPORT... WEST HAMPTON OR WEST SIDE STORY ?
BANG! BANG! YOU'RE DEAD!
AT LEAST OUR LITTLE GUY WILL BE PLAYING WITH SOMEONE HIS OWN SIZE.... MIGHT EVEN HAVE FUN!
WHATTA YA KNOW! IT WAS LOADED!

In 1962, the National League added two new franchises, the New York Mets and the Houston Colt .45s. Mullin drew this cartoon in April, during the first series between the two new teams.

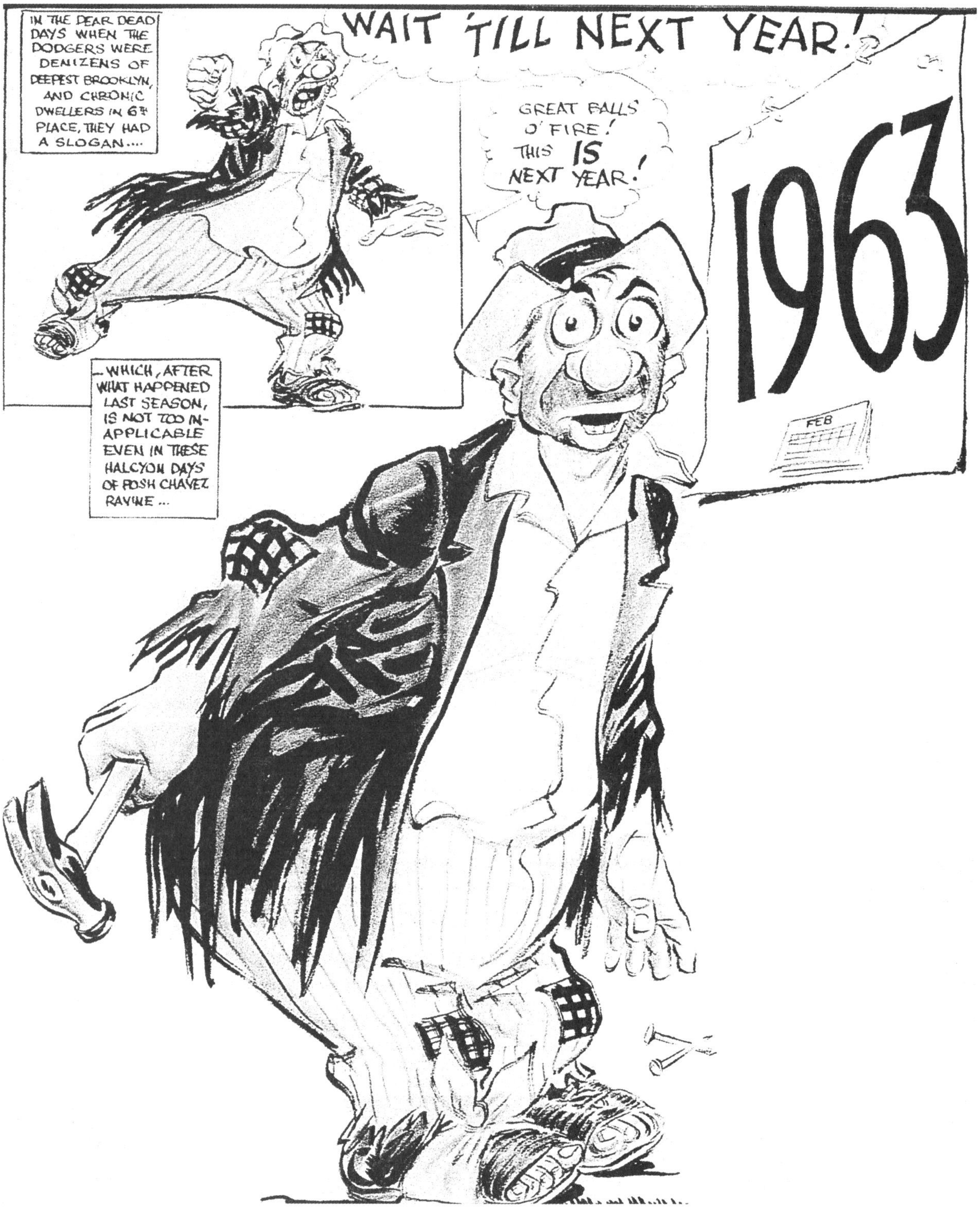
IN THE DEAR DEAD DAYS WHEN THE DODGERS WERE DENIZENS OF DEEPEST BROOKLYN, AND CHRONIC DWELLERS IN 6TH PLACE, THEY HAD A SLOGAN....
WAIT 'TILL NEXT YEAR!
...WHICH, AFTER WHAT HAPPENED LAST SEASON, IS NOT TOO IN-APPLICABLE EVEN IN THESE HALCYON DAYS OF POSH CHAVEZ RAVINE...
GREAT BALLS O' FIRE! THIS IS NEXT YEAR!
1963
FEB

Back in the glory years of the Brooklyn Dodgers in the 1950s, the eternal cry heard from the faithful was "wait 'til next year" as the "Bums" lost three out of four World Series to the Yankees (six out of seven since 1941) and, in 1951, the most dramatic playoff in history to the New York Giants. History repeated itself in 1962, with the San Francisco Giants again beating the Los Angeles Dodgers in a dramatic playoff to capture the National League pennant.

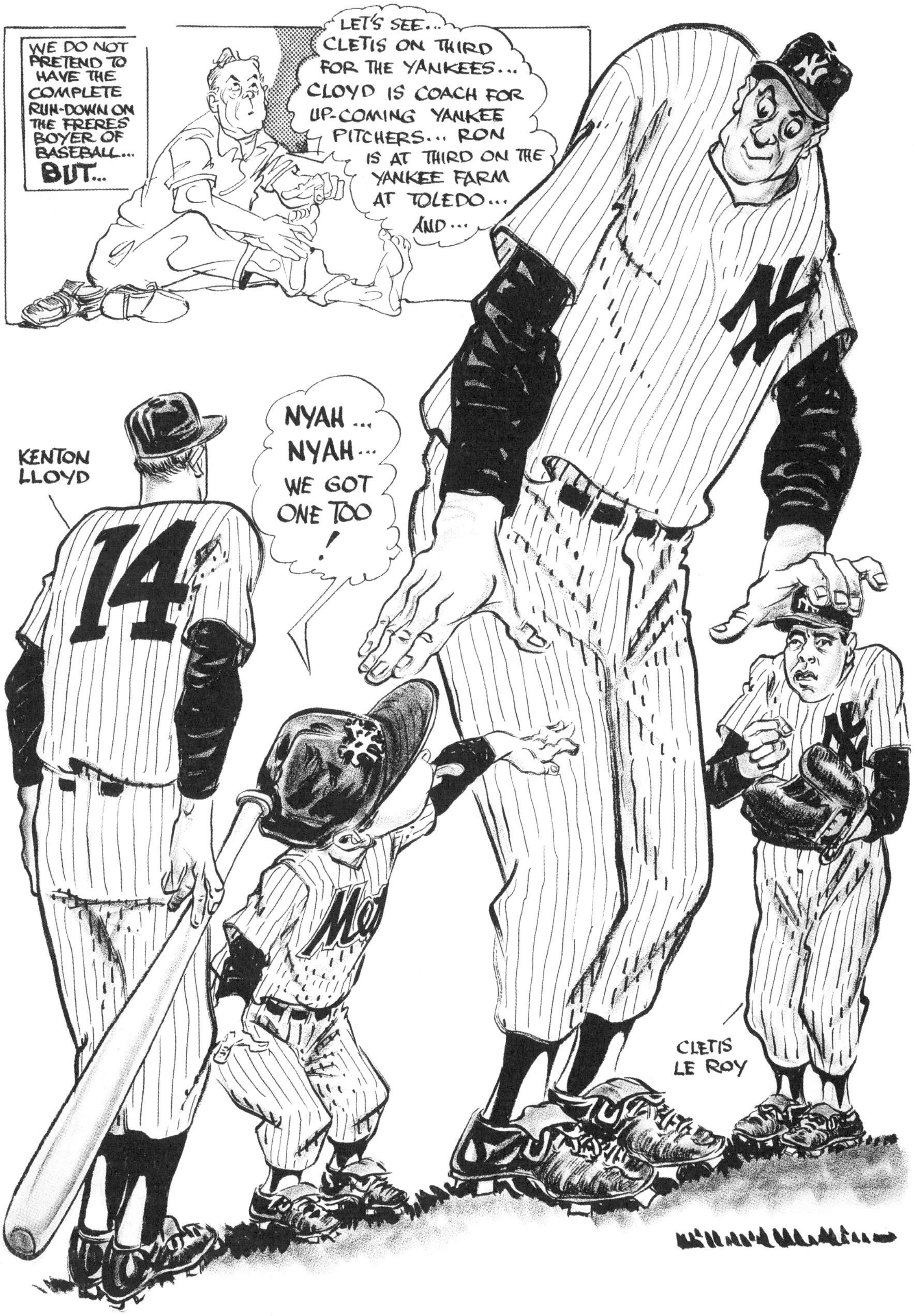
WE DO NOT PRETEND TO HAVE THE COMPLETE RUN-DOWN ON THE FRERES' BOYER OF BASEBALL... BUT...
LET'S SEE... CLETIS ON THIRD FOR THE YANKEES... CLOYD IS COACH FOR UP-COMING YANKEE PITCHERS... RON IS AT THIRD ON THE YANKEE FARM AT TOLEDO... AND...
KENTON LLOYD
NYAH... NYAH... WE GOT ONE TOO !
CLETIS LE ROY

During the 1950s and 1960s, the Boyer family had three brothers who played in the major leagues and another three who played in the minor leagues. The best was probably Ken Boyer, who won the 1964 NL MVP while playing for the Cardinals.

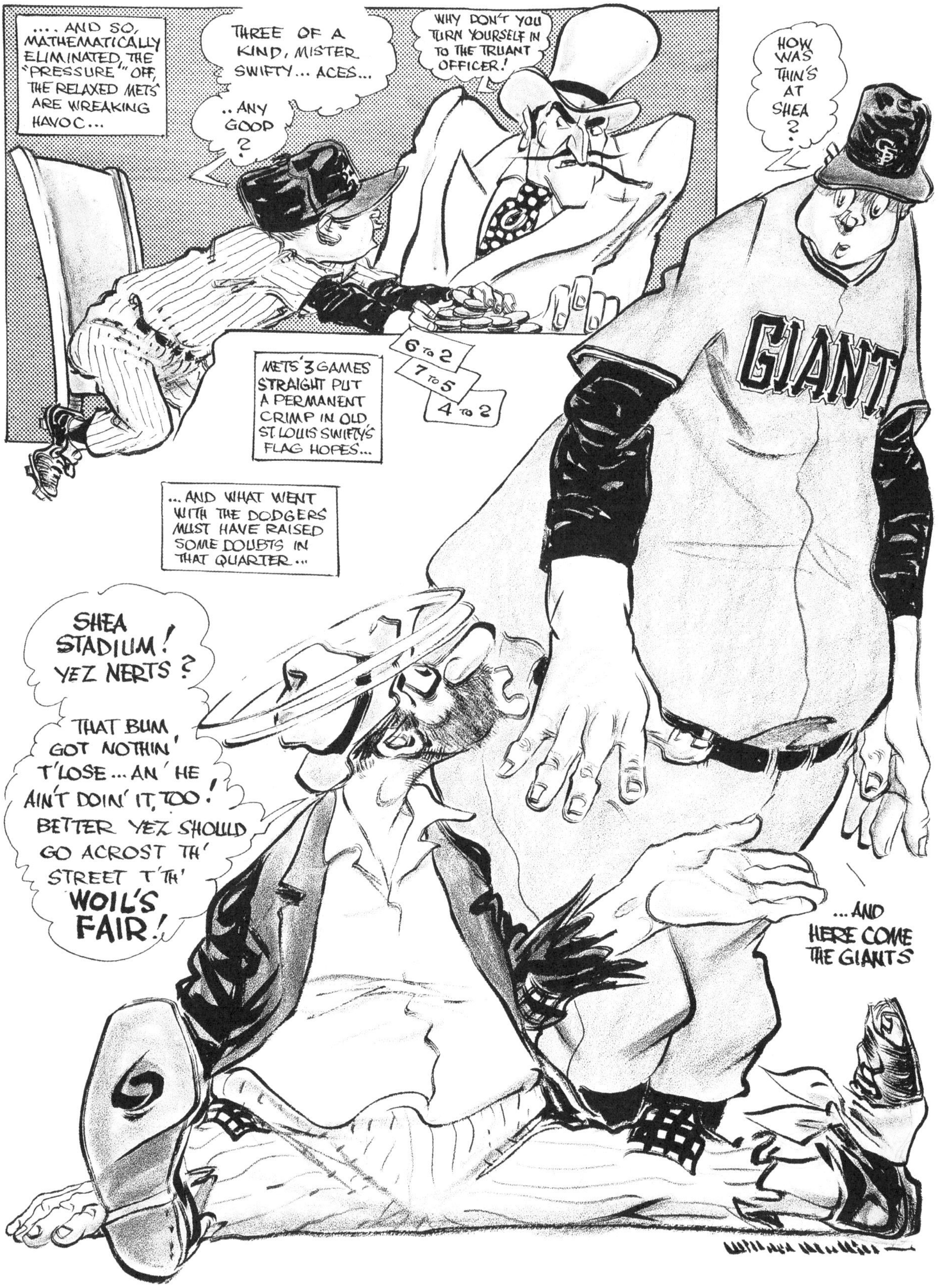
.... AND SO, MATHEMATICALLY ELIMINATED, THE "PRESSURE" OFF, THE RELAXED METS ARE WREAKING HAVOC...
THREE OF A KIND, MISTER SWIFTY... ACES...
.. ANY GOOD ?
WHY DON'T YOU TURN YOURSELF IN TO THE TRUANT OFFICER!
HOW WAS THIN'S AT SHEA ?
METS' 3 GAMES STRAIGHT PUT A PERMANENT CRIMP IN OLD ST. LOUIS SWIFTY'S FLAG HOPES...
6 TO 2
7 TO 5
4 TO 2
... AND WHAT WENT WITH THE DODGERS MUST HAVE RAISED SOME DOUBTS IN THAT QUARTER...
SHEA STADIUM! YEZ NERTS ?
THAT BUM GOT NOTHIN' T'LOSE... AN' HE AIN'T DOIN' IT, TOO! BETTER YEZ SHOULD GO ACROST TH' STREET T'TH' WOIL'S FAIR!
... AND HERE COME THE GIANTS

In 1964, the New York Mets moved into Shea Stadium and still managed to lose 109 games. But, late in the season, in their new home ballpark, they did beat several of the pennant contenders, most notably the Dodgers and the Cardinals.

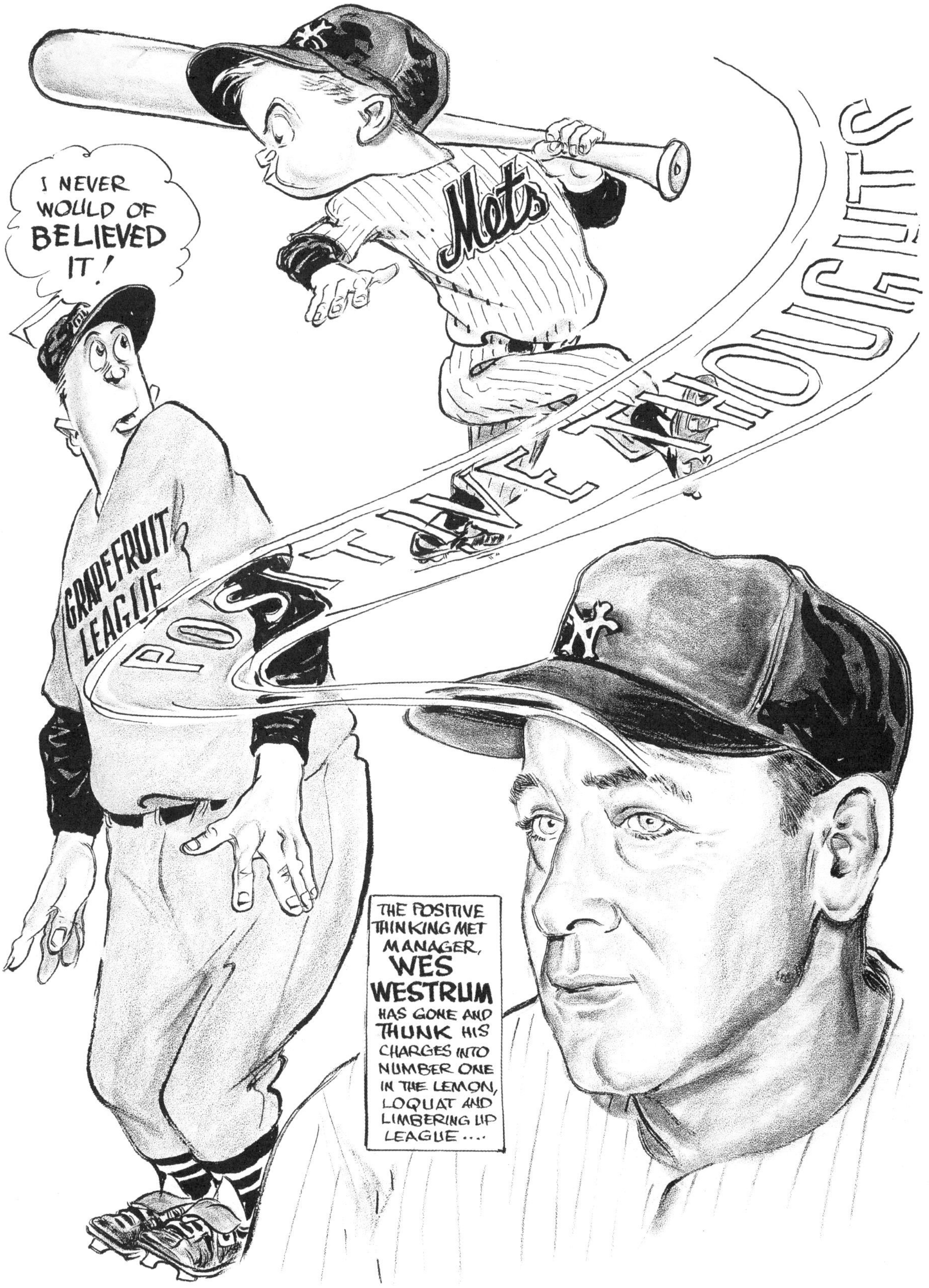
I NEVER WOULD OF BELIEVED IT!
Mets
POSITIVE THOUGHTS
GRAPEFRUIT LEAGUE
THE POSITIVE THINKING MET MANAGER, WES WESTRUM HAS GONE AND THUNK HIS CHARGES INTO NUMBER ONE IN THE LEMON, LOQUAT AND LIMBERING UP LEAGUE....

In August of 1965, Casey Stengel injured his hip and retired from baseball after 53 years. Wes Westrum was named manager, and then led the Mets to a ninth-place finish in 1966 — the first time they did not finish last since their inception in 1962.

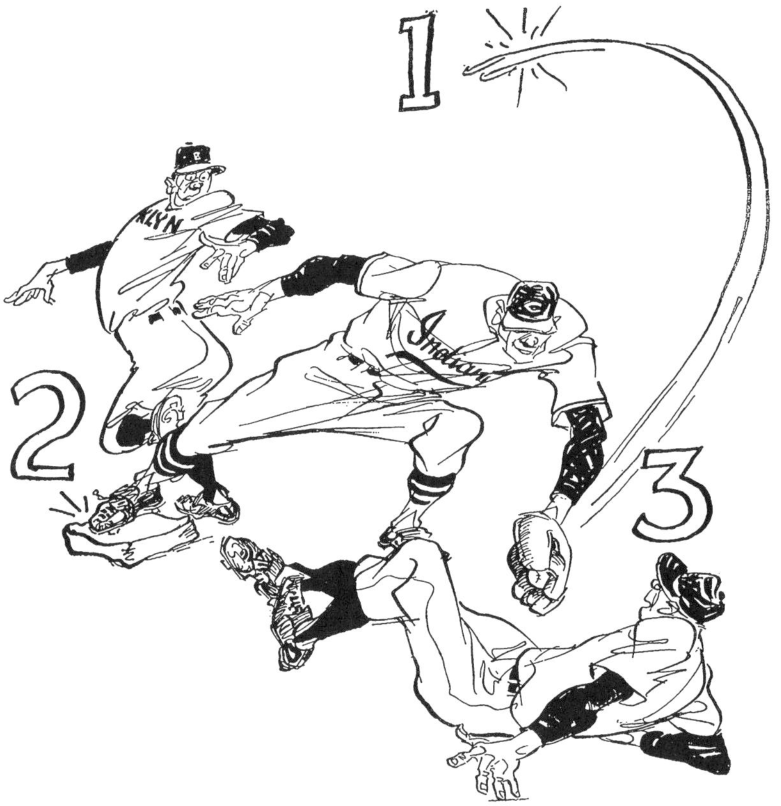
1
2
3
BKLYN
Indians

This drawing is from the 1961 *World Series Encyclopedia*. It illustrates, as only Mullin could, Bill Wambsganss's unassisted triple play for Cleveland in the 1920 World Series. It remains the only triple play, unassisted or otherwise, in World Series history.

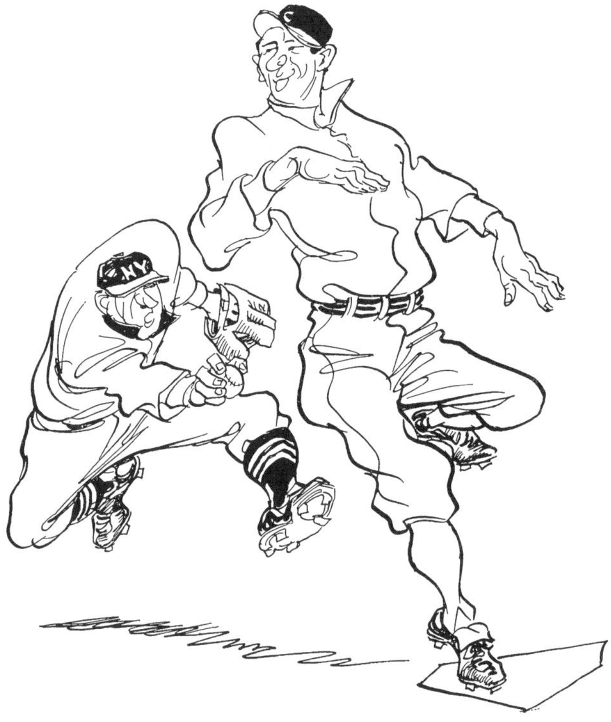

Another illustration from the *World Series Encyclopedia* shows the New York Giants' third baseman Heinie Zimmerman futilely chasing the Chicago White Sox's Eddie Collins across an uncovered home plate in a key play from the 1917 World Series. The Sox won the Series that year.

Starting in the mid-1950s, Mullin illustrated "So You Think You Know Baseball!" a feature for the *Saturday Evening Post.* It was a series of quizzes that called for interpretations of baseball's rules as applied to various scenarios that occurred during the course of a game. Mullin's images were so vividly drawn that you can almost feel the batter's pain in this illustration.

SO YOU THINK YOU KNOW BASEBALL!

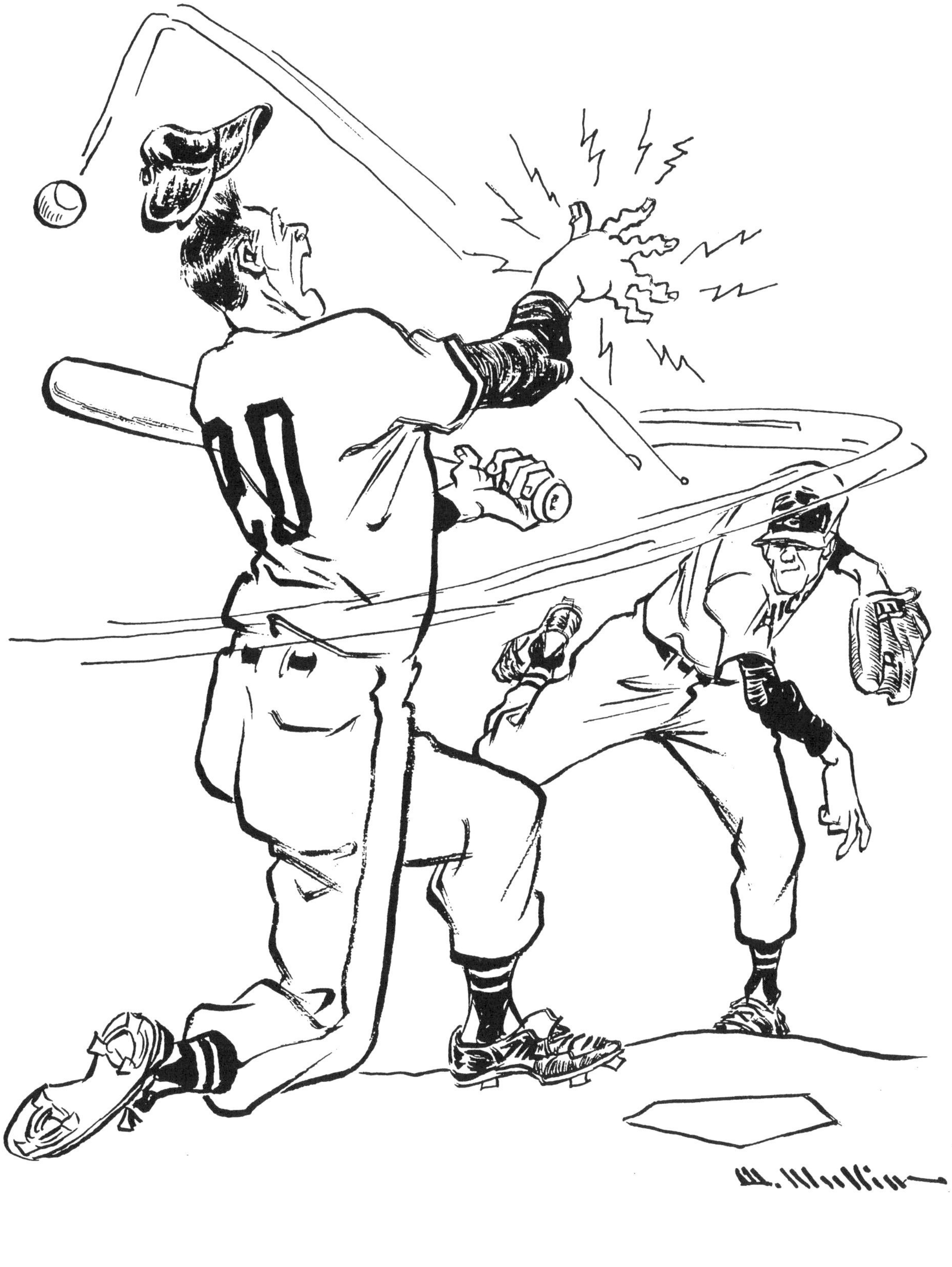

Sometimes baseball rules appear illogical. Take this simulated major-league scramble, based on a play which actually occurred elsewhere last year.

The San Francisco Giants come to bat in the last of the eighth. Willie Kirkland is walked. Willie Mays slams the ball far and deep into center field. The outfielder chasing it slips and falls heavily. The ball bounces to the center field wall and bounces about before the Braves' right fielder reaches it.

Meanwhile Kirkland crosses the plate with Mays behind him. But the Giants' first base coach waves Kirkland back to second, for the coach noted that he failed to touch that base. Kirkland obliges, carefully touching home plate and third on the way back. He reaches second safely as the ball is returned to the infield. Mays is already in the dugout.

A big question arises: Can a runner score when a player ahead of him in the batting order is still on base?

SO YOU THINK YOU KNOW BASEBALL!

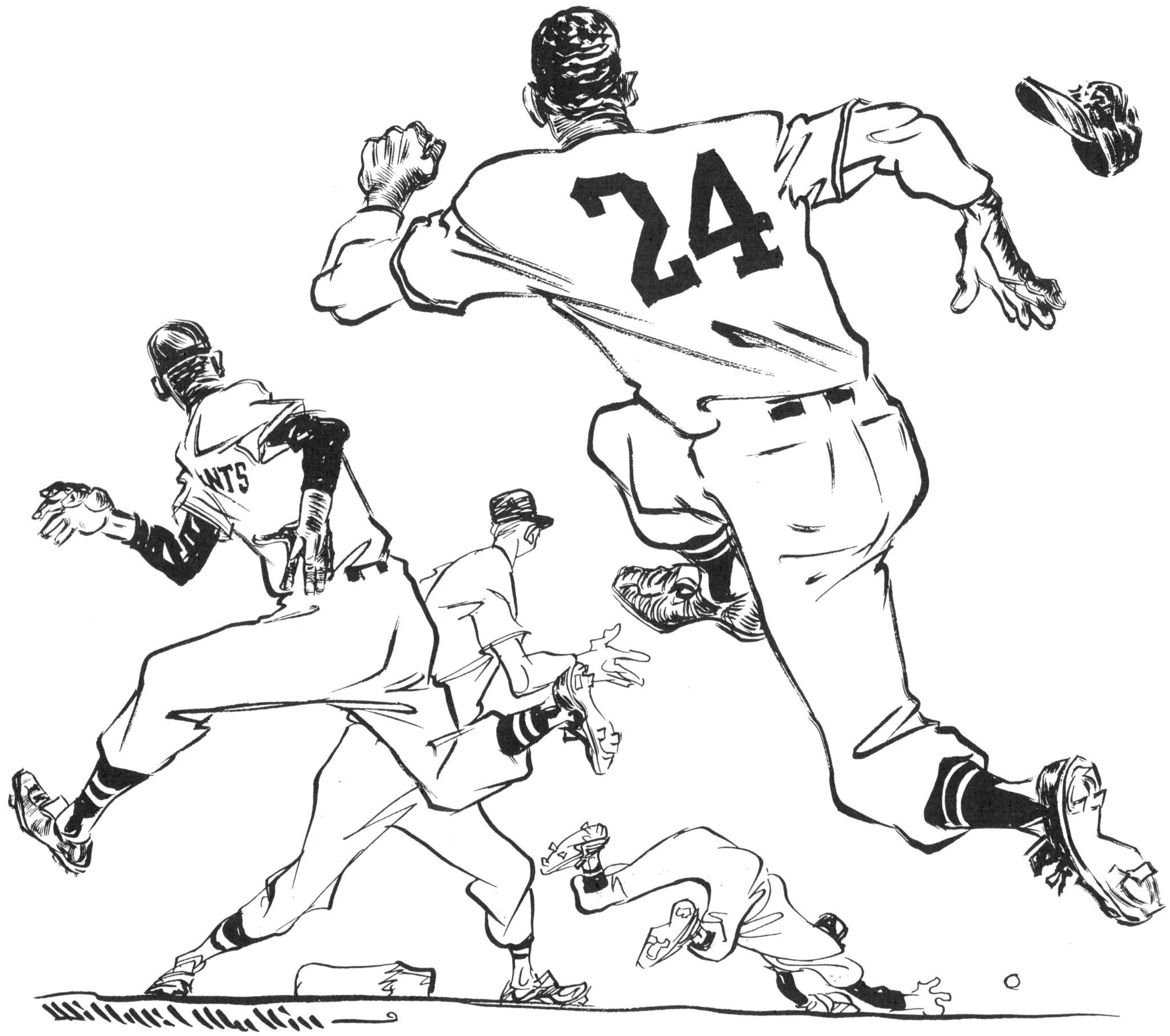
24
NTS

ANSWER: A ruling by the Official Playing Rules Interpretation Committee was necessary on this one. Under it, Mays would be out. No runs count. Section 7.12, which reads in part: "Unless two are out, the status of a following runner is not affected by a preceding runner's failure to touch a base," was held inadequate in this case. An 1897 rule, dropped from the books in 1931 for no apparent reason, would have covered the situation. It provided: "No base runner shall score a run to count in the game ahead of the base runner preceding him in the batting order, if there be such preceding base runner who had not been put out in that inning."

Oddly, if Kirkland had been thrown out while attempting to regain second base, Mays' run would have counted.

Can a team fail to win a game simply because its last batter belted a home run? Here in simulated major-league setting is an odd problem, indeed.

On an overcast afternoon in New York, after the Yankees have taken a 2–1 lead in the sixth, the Kansas City Athletics go ahead in the seventh with three runs.

With the score now 4–2, Gil McDougald leads off for the Yankees with a single to left. Mickey Mantle smashes a homer into the rightfield stand. It ties the count at 4–4. As Mickey rounds the bases, a torrential rain pours down. Time is called after he crosses the plate. With the field in a quagmire, the umpires call off the game half an hour later.

Kansas City claims a 4–4 tie. The Yankees contend that as they never completed their half of the seventh inning, the score must revert to the last full inning — giving them a 2–1 win.

If you were umpiring, how would you decide?

SO YOU THINK YOU KNOW BASEBALL!

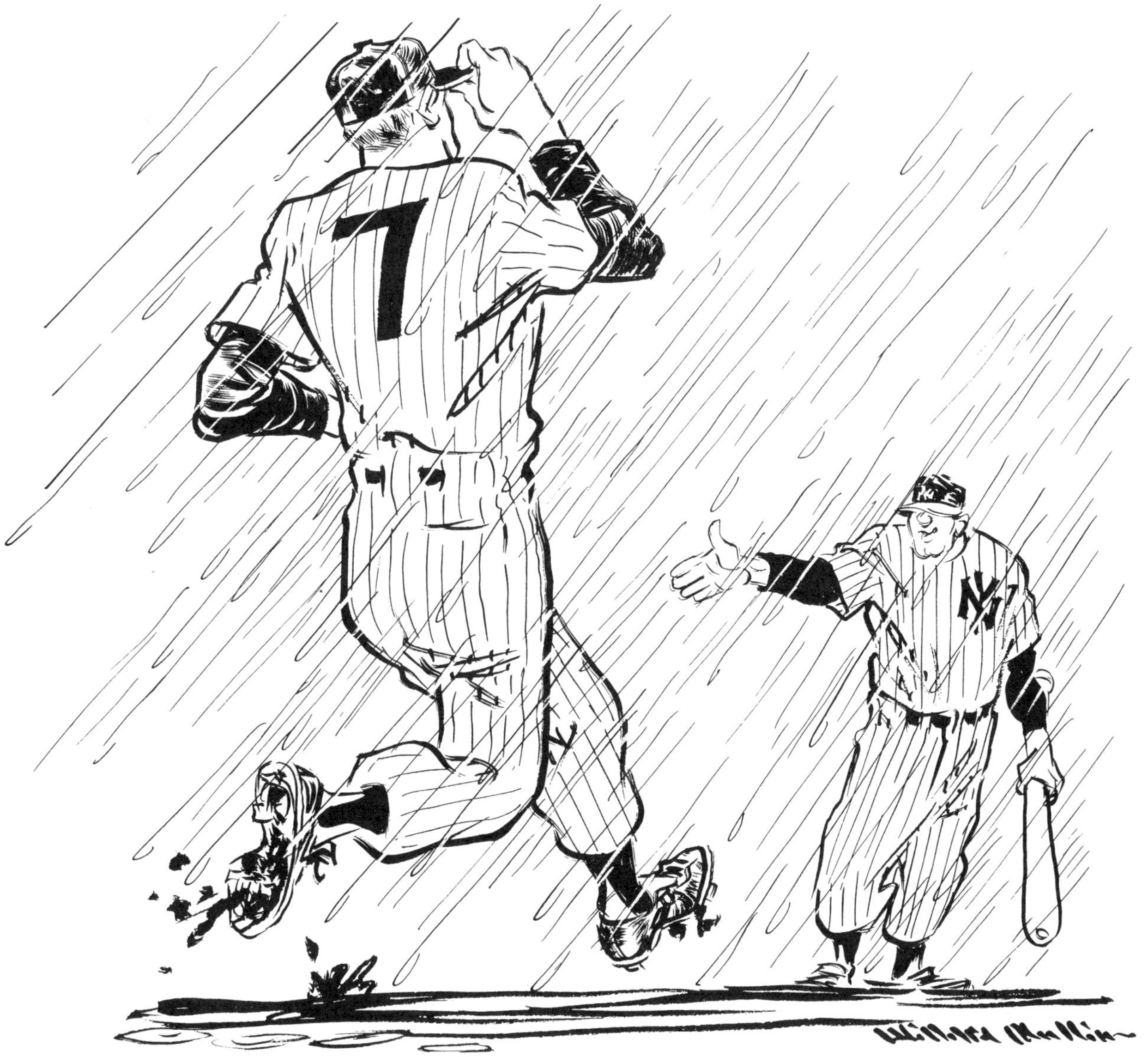

ANSWER: It is a 4–4 tie.

(Section 4.11b: "A regulation drawn game shall be declared by the umpire-in-chief if he terminates play because of weather … if, after five or more completed innings, the home team is at bat when play terminates and scores enough runs in an incompleted inning to make its total score equal to the visiting team's total score…."

Had Mantle struck out, grounded into a double play, or even stopped at third base when the rain started, the score would have reverted to the previous inning and the Yankees would have won, 2–1.

Say San Francisco leads Cincinnati, 5–3, as the Giants bat in the last of the seventh. Singles by Ed Bressoud and Jim Davenport, and a walk to Orlando Cepeda load the bases with none out. With Don Blasingame coming to bat, a squeeze is ordered.

Bressoud leaves third base as the Reds' pitcher goes into his windup, and slides across the plate just as the ball zooms into the strike zone. The ball hits Bressoud on the back. It then drops in front of the plate. The Reds' catcher picks it up and throws to third base in time for the baseman to tag Jim Davenport, coming from second.

The Reds' manager, meanwhile, charges interference by Bressoud. He claims that the pitch is the overriding part of any play, and that the Giants runner is out for interfering with the delivery. But that covers only part of the play.

If you umpiring, how would you rule?

SO YOU THINK YOU KNOW BASEBALL!

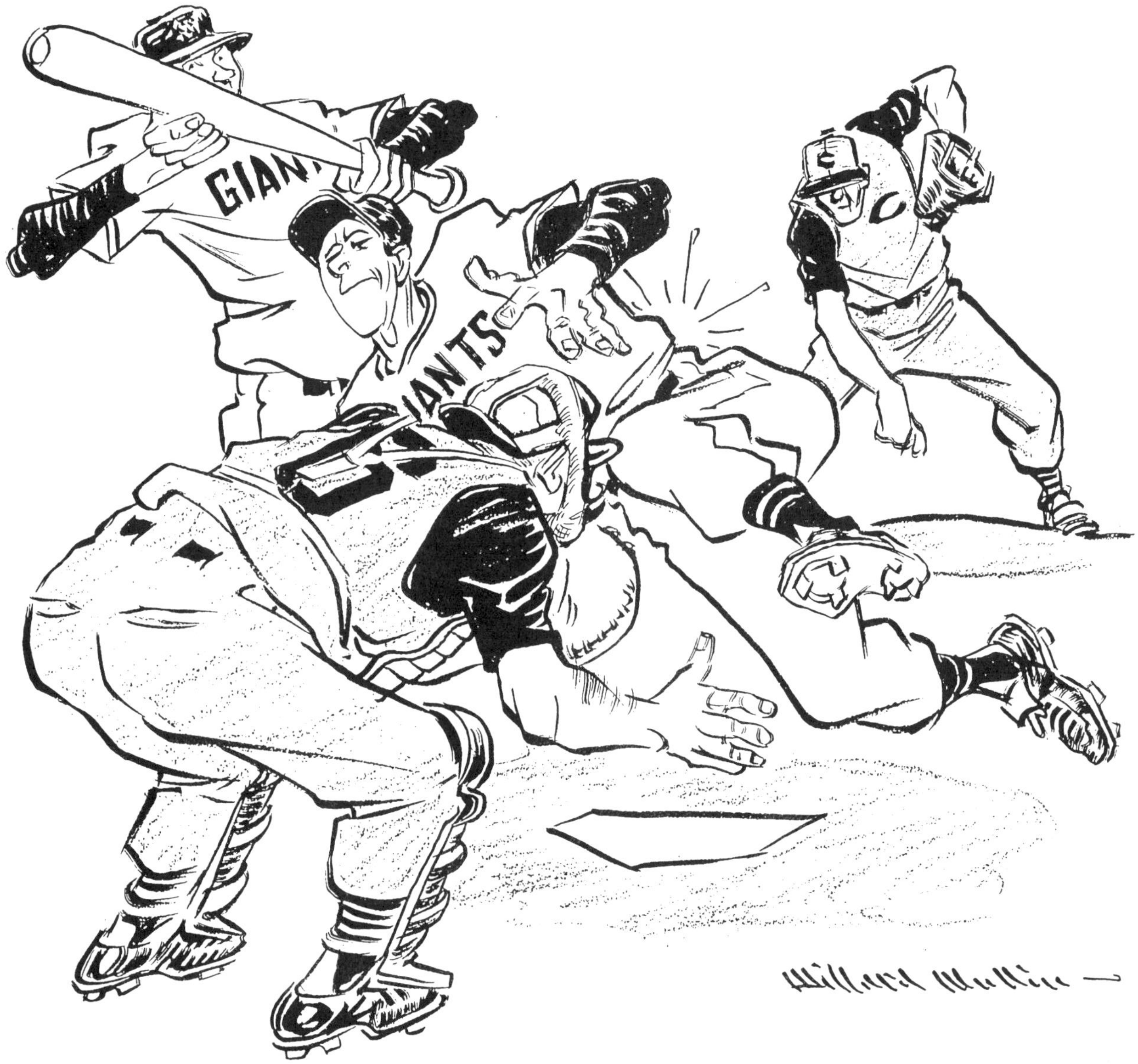
GIAN
GIANTS

ANSWER: Bressoud's run counts, and the ball is instantly dead. Place Davenport on third and Cepeda on second. (Section 5.09j: "The ball becomes dead and runners advance one base … without liability to be put out, when any legal pitch touches a runner trying to score….") Call a strike on Blasingame as Section 6.05n provides when a pitch hits a runner in the batter's strike zone.

Quick thinking is an asset to any ballplayer, but sometimes it can be overdone. Here, in a hypothetical setting, is the case of a clever catcher who anticipated a play that never happened.

Say the Senators and White Sox are tied, 2–2, and the Senators come to bat in the bottom of the seventh inning. Steve Korcheck walks. Pedro Ramos is called on to bunt. Ramos's attempted sacrifice hit turns into a little pop-up in front of the plate. Korcheck streaks for second, but the Sox catcher, sensing that he will

hurry back to first base, gets his hands on the ball and then deliberately drops it. Picking it up, he whirls and throws to second in hopes of a force play on Korcheck. But Korcheck is already hugging the base. The relay to nab Ramos at first is too late.

The umpire, however, has his own ideas about the situation, inasmuch as it is illegal for a fielder to drop a fly ball or line drive intentionally. **If you were umping, what would you do?**

SO YOU THINK YOU KNOW BASEBALL!

ANSWER: Declare Korcheck safe at second, but call Ramos out. Curiously, the intentionally dropped ball is ruled a catch although advancing runners need not tag up.

(Section 6.051: "A batter is out when a fielder intentionally

drops a fair fly ball or line drive, with first, first and second, first and third, or first, second and third base occupied before two are out. Runners need not re-touch and may advance at their own peril.")

The YEAR THE YANKEES LOST THE PENNANT

A NOVEL
BY
DOUGLASS
WALLOP

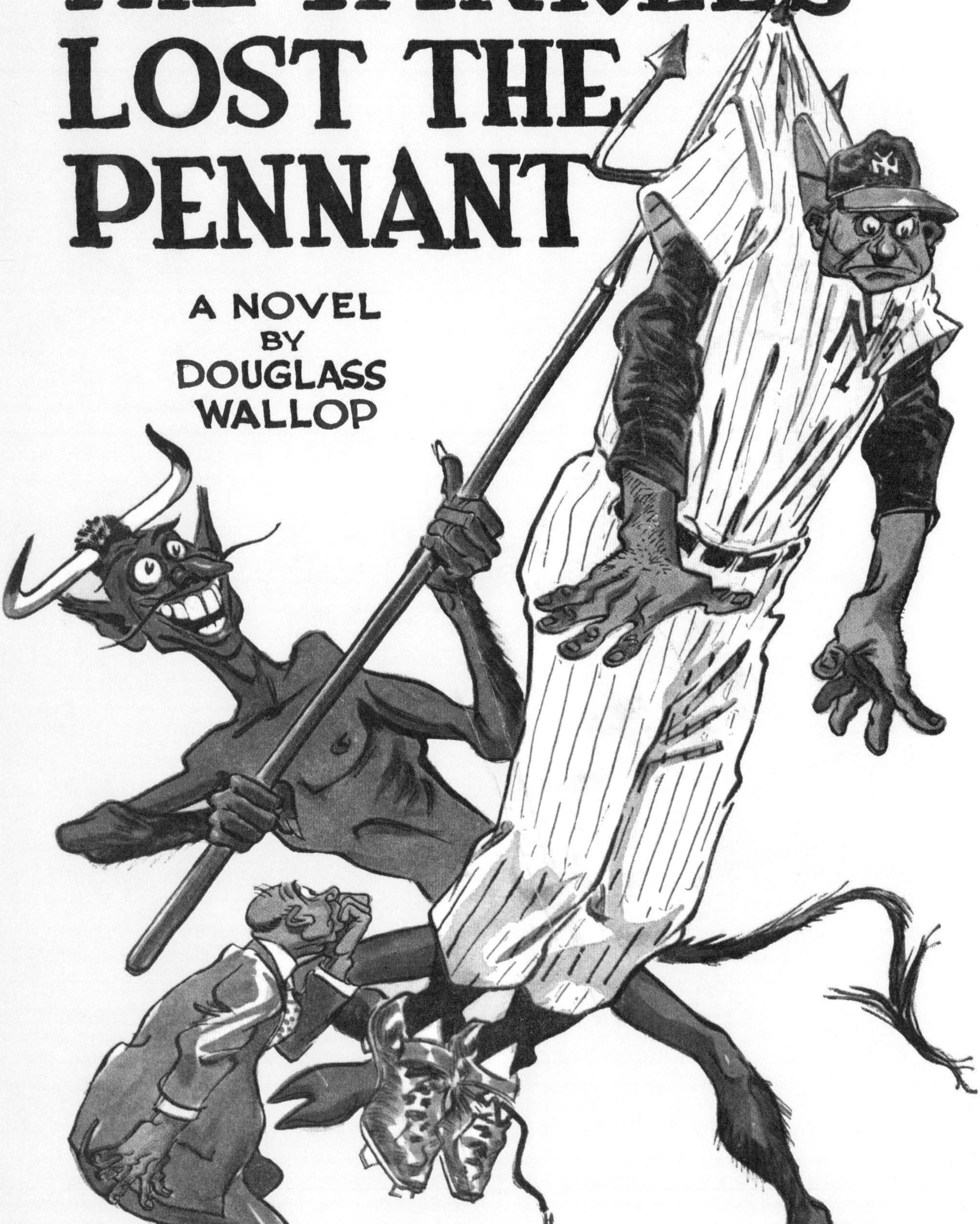

Color Work

Most of Mullin's images were in black-and-white because he was drawing for a newspaper. However, he also did outside color work for the *Sporting News,* various baseball clubs, and commercial clients. What follows is a sample of some of that work, including iconic Dodgers yearbooks and covers from the *Sporting News's* baseball specials and *Time*.

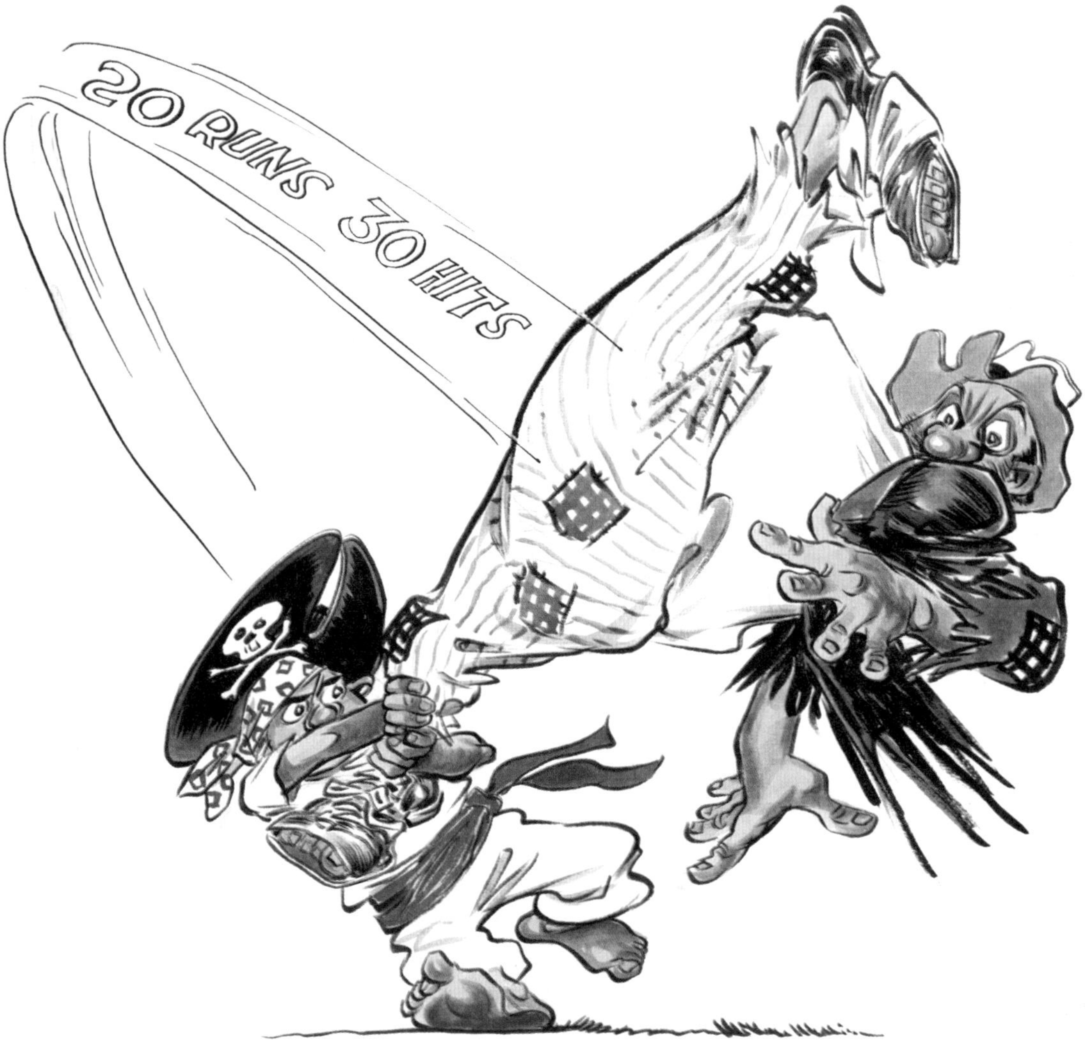
20 RUNS 30 HITS

OPPOSITE: By 1954, the New York Yankees had won five straight World Series Championships, so Douglass Wallop's novel was welcomed with open arms by fans of all of the other teams in baseball. Mullin's cover art is classic. *The Year the Yankees Lost the Pennant* would become the basis for the famous musical, *Damn Yankees.*

ABOVE: In 1960, the long-dormant Pittsburgh Pirates came to life and dramatically won the World Series against the New York Yankees. In capturing the National League pennant, they dominated their rivals. The Pirates finished 13 games ahead of the Dodgers, nine ahead of the Cardinals, and seven ahead of the second-place Milwaukee Braves.

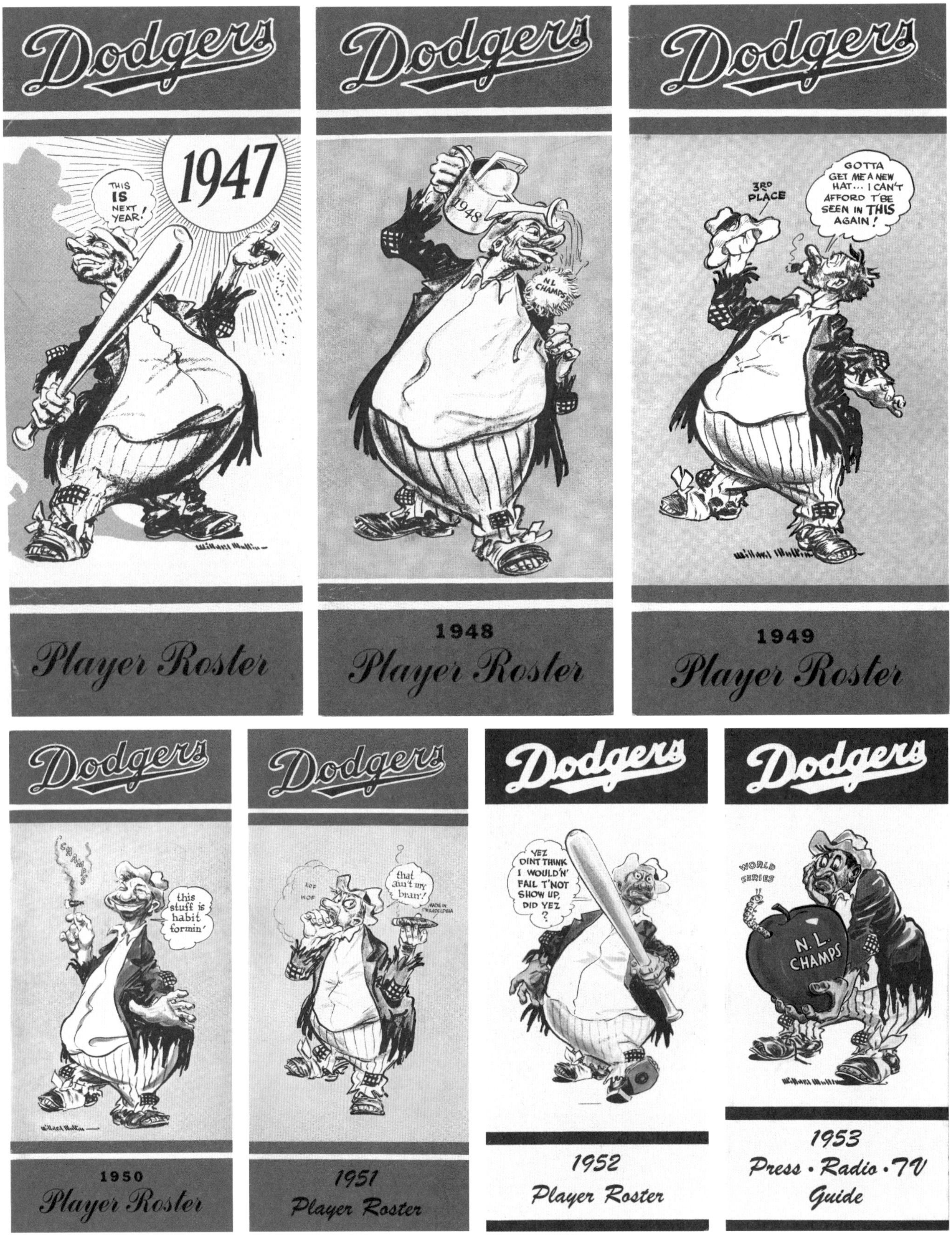
Dodgers
1947
THIS IS NEXT YEAR!
Player Roster
Dodgers
1948
N.L. CHAMPS
1948
Player Roster
Dodgers
3RD PLACE
GOTTA GET ME A NEW HAT... I CAN'T AFFORD T'BE SEEN IN THIS AGAIN!
1949
Player Roster
Dodgers
CHAMPS
this stuff is habit formin'
1950
Player Roster
Dodgers
that ain't my bran'!
1951
Player Roster
Dodgers
YEZ DINT THINK I WOULD'N' FAIL T'NOT SHOW UP, DID YEZ?
1952
Player Roster
Dodgers
WORLD SERIES
N.L. CHAMPS
1953
Press • Radio • TV
Guide

Starting in 1947, Mullin did the cover art for the Dodgers' spring training rosters. The Bum reflected not only the Dodgers' hopes for the coming season but also their recent successes or failures.

BASEBALL GUIDE
OFFICIAL MAJOR and MINOR LEAGUE AVERAGES
1944
BASEBALL RULES and REGULATIONS
50¢
HAUL-OF-FAMERS
The Sporting News
RECORD BOOK

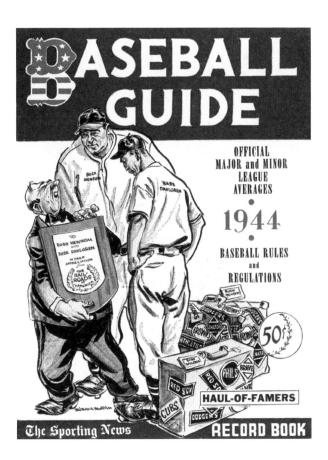

In 1944, tongue planted firmly in cheek, Mullin chose Bobo Newsom and Babe Dahlgren as "Haul-of-Famers." Over the course of his career, Dahlgren played for eight different ball clubs. In a career that spanned four decades (1929 to 1953), Newsom played for 17 teams.

Phillies
1946
Phillies
OFFICIAL
SCORE CARD
1946 - 1st NO.
10 CENTS
FEATURES-
BILL DOOLY
WILLARD MULLIN
ED DELANEY

FIRST DIVISION 1947
OFFICIAL
SCORE CARD
AND PROGRAM
1ST NO. 1947
10 CENTS
FEATURES
BILL DOOLY
WILLARD MULLIN
5TH PLACE 1946
Phillies
FOR RENT

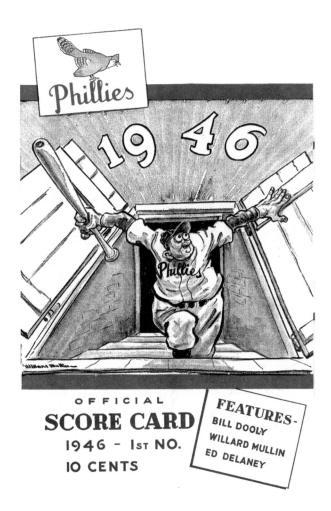

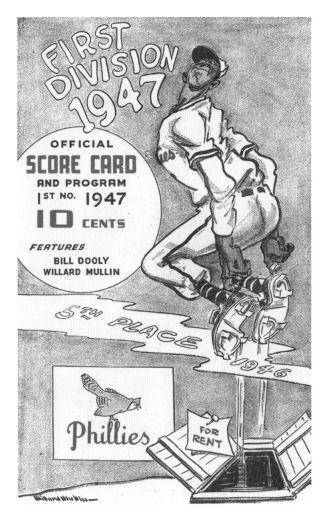

The Philadelphia Phillies were simply awful for most of the 1930s and 1940s, so when they finished fifth among eight teams in the National League in 1946, it was cause for celebration.

Dodgers
1950
1949
1947
50¢

Starting in 1951, Mullin drew the cover art for the *Dodgers Year Book* every year until they left for Los Angeles in 1958.

Dodgers
YEAR
BOOK
1954
A NEW HOME!
50¢

By 1954, the Dodgers had outgrown the by-then-antiquated Ebbets Field and were looking for a new home. Speculation was rampant as to where exactly it would be, which Mullin acknowledged on his 1954 *Year Book* cover.

DODGER
YEAR BOOK
1955
FIFTY CENTS

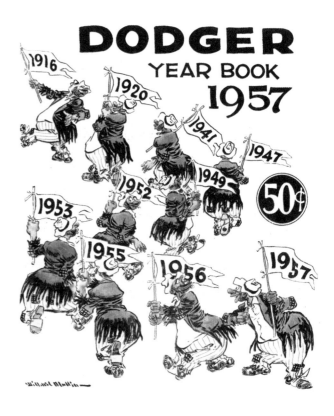

The 1955 *Dodgers Year Book* is the most sought-after of Mullin's *Dodgers Year Books.* That was the year Brooklyn won their one and only World Series Championship.

DODGER
YEAR BOOK
1957
1916
1920
1941
1947
1949
1952
1953
50¢
1955
1956
1957

The Dodgers' last year in Brooklyn. Mullin's cover celebrated all of the Dodgers' pennants over the years.

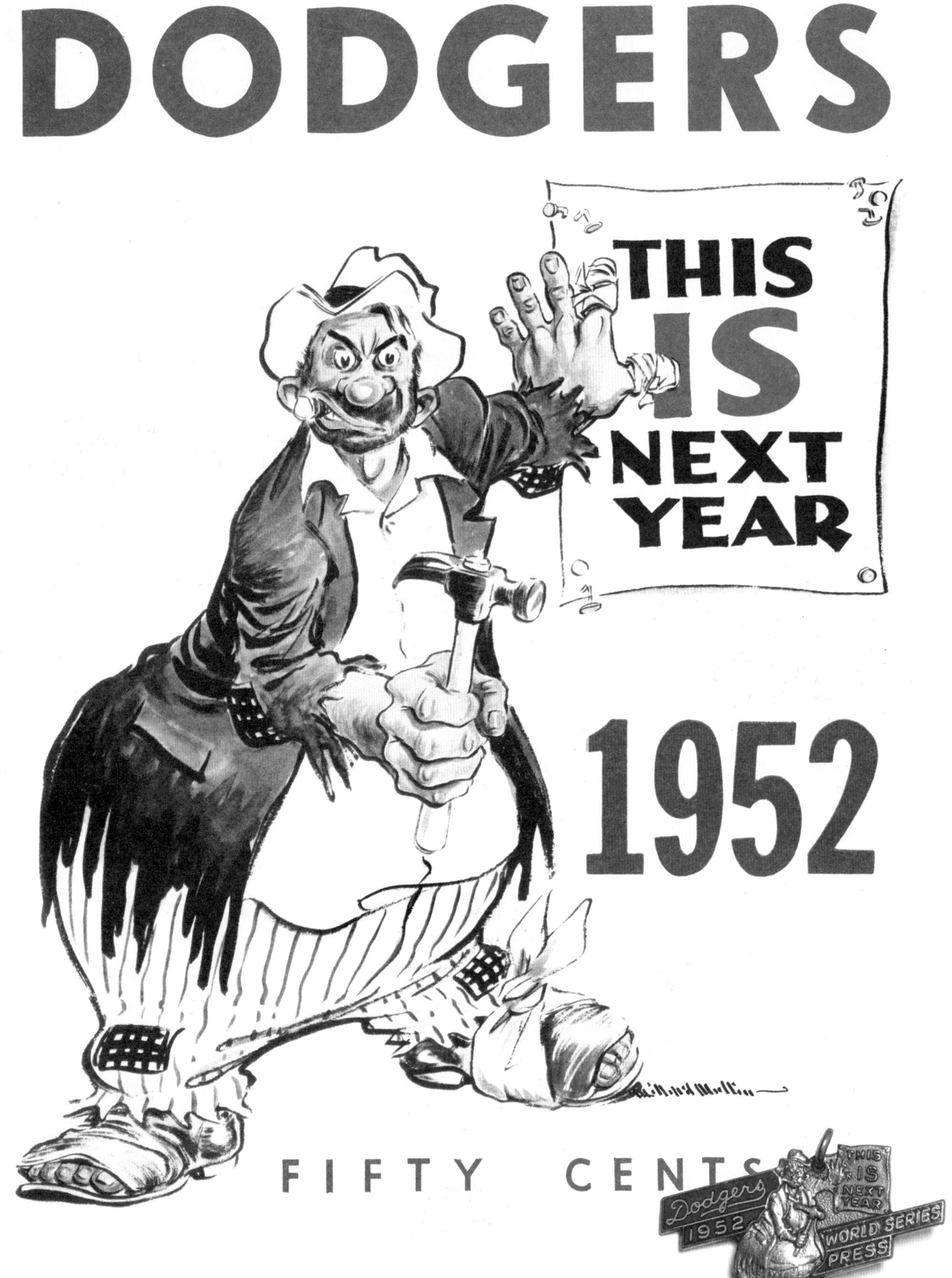
DODGERS
THIS IS NEXT YEAR
1952
FIFTY CENTS
THIS IS NEXT YEAR
Dodgers
1952
WORLD SERIES
PRESS

This 1952 cover is probably Mullin's most famous. It is an homage to Mullin's mentor, James Montgomery Flagg, creator of the famous World War I "Uncle Sam Wants You" image. The structure of this piece and the palette used by Mullin is identical to Flagg's Uncle Sam. This image was so well-received that the Dodgers used it for their World Series press pin that fall.

NEW YORK
Giants
50¢
READ IT TO ME ALL OVER AGAIN, LEO
THE LITTLE MIRACLE OF COOGAN'S BLUFF
1952

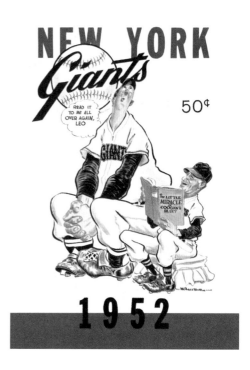

On August 11, 1951, the Giants lost to the Phillies, dropping them 13-1/2 games behind the Dodgers. Mullin dubbed what happened after that the "Miracle of Coogan's Bluff." It culminated in Bobby Thomson's "Shot Heard 'Round the World," which clinched the pennant for the Giants. Mullin's cover for the 1952 Giants Year Book shows Willy the Giant and Leo Durocher hoping for a repeat.

YEAR BOOK
SAN FRANCISCO
GIANTS
1958
THE SAGA OF CHRISTY MATHEWSON
McGINNITY to MAGLIE
HOW to MAKE FRIENDS BY EDDIE BRANNICK AS TOLD TO DALE CARNEGIE
IT'S GREAT TO BE YOUNG AND A GIANT LARRY DOYLE
THIS YEAR BY BILL RIGNEY
A TRUE STORY
The LITTLE MIRACLE of COOGAN'S BLUFF
1951
INCOMPLETE
1954
50¢

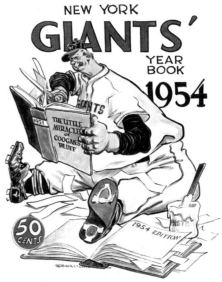

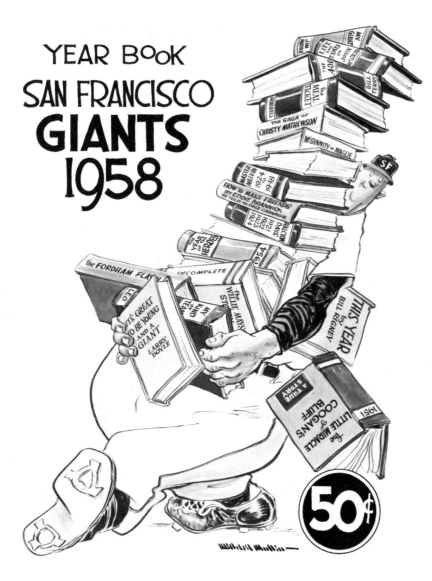

With their move to Los Angeles, Mullin's string of *Dodgers Year Books* came to an end. Not so with the Giants, however, who used Mullin's cover art for the very first *San Francisco Giants Year Book.*

NEW YORK
GIANTS'
YEAR BOOK
1954
THE LITTLE MIRACLE OF COOGAN'S BLUFF
1951
50 CENTS
1954 EDITION

The Giants began 1954 still hoping to duplicate the success of 1951's "Miracle of Coogan's Bluff," as can be seen from Mullin's 1954 cover featuring Willy the Giant eager to repeat that chapter.

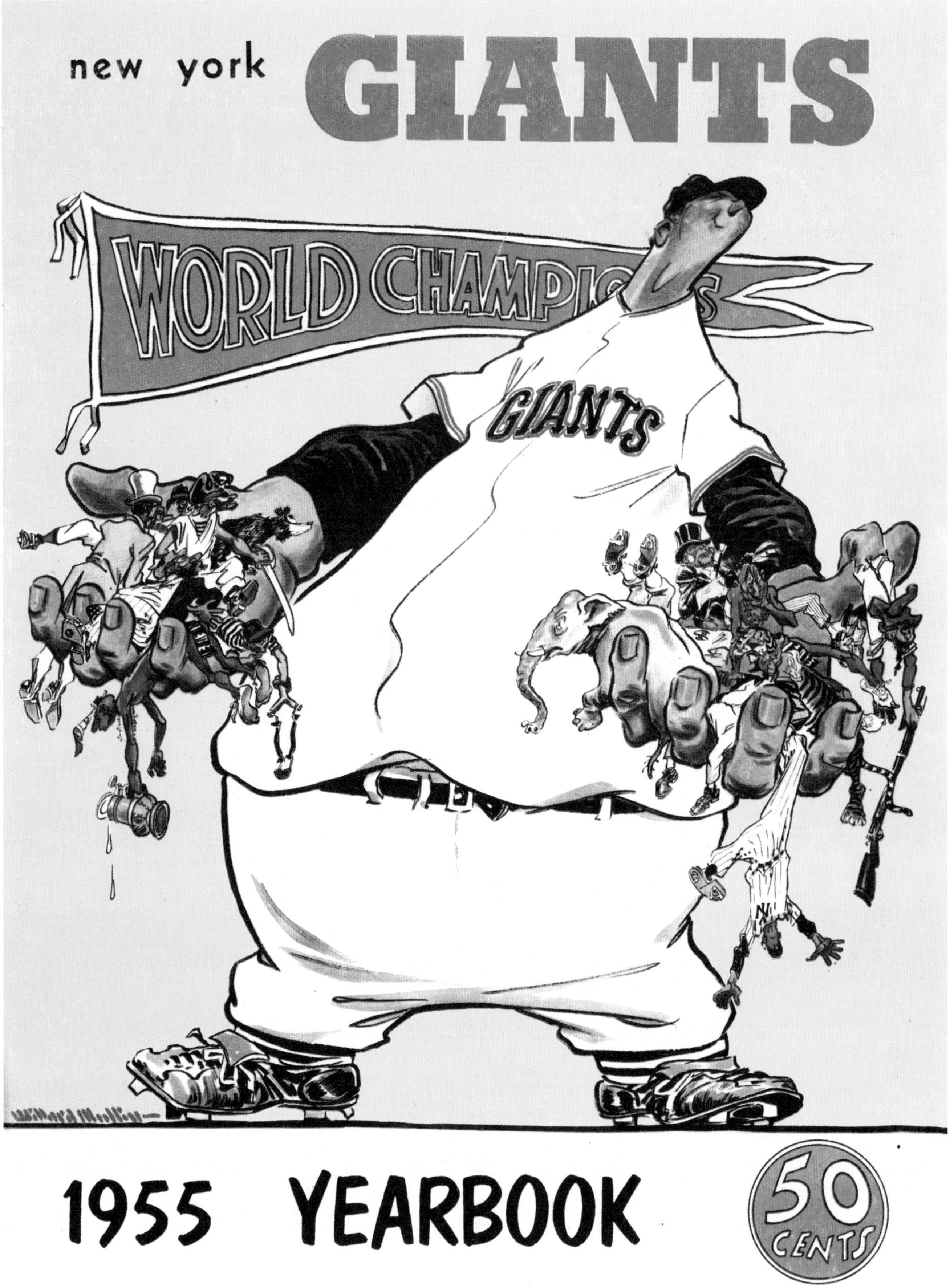
new york GIANTS
WORLD CHAMPIONS
GIANTS
1955 YEARBOOK
50 CENTS

Willy's hopes came to fruition in 1954 with the Giants not only winning the National League pennant but also sweeping the Cleveland Indians to win the World Series. The Giants' newfound status as World Series Champs is reflected in the Mullin cover for the 1955 yearbook.

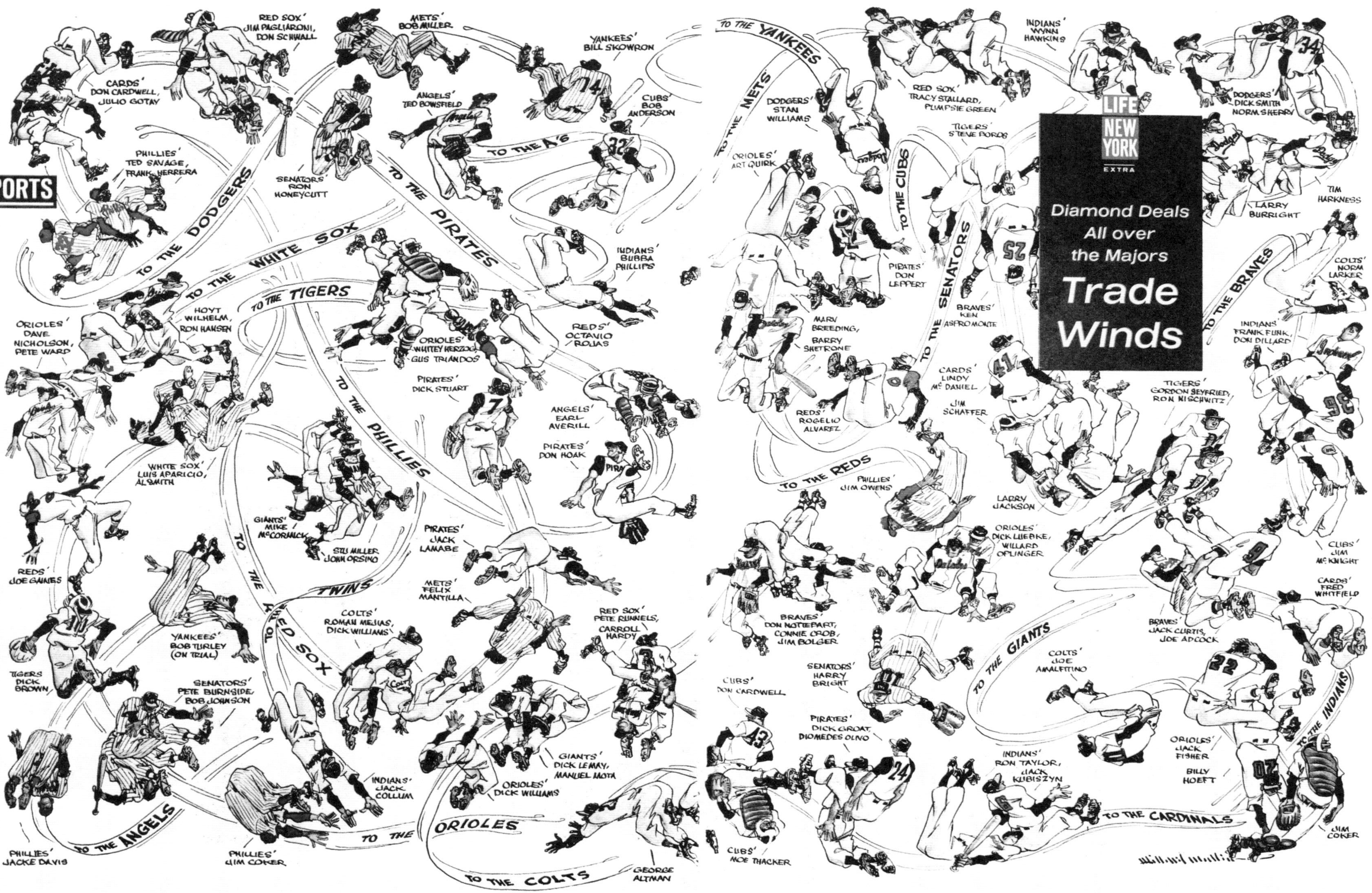
LIFE
NEW YORK
EXTRA
Diamond Deals
All over
the Majors
Trade
Winds
CARDS' DON CARDWELL, JULIO GOTAY
RED SOX' JIM PAGLIARONI, DON SCHWALL
METS' BOB MILLER
YANKEES' BILL SKOWRON
CUBS' BOB ANDERSON
ANGELS' TED BOWSFIELD
TO THE A'S
PHILLIES' TED SAVAGE, FRANK HERRERA
SENATORS' RON HONEYCUTT
TO THE DODGERS
TO THE PIRATES
INDIANS' BUBBA PHILLIPS
TO THE WHITE SOX
TO THE TIGERS
HOYT WILHELM, RON HANSEN
ORIOLES' DAVE NICHOLSON, PETE WARD
ORIOLES' WHITEY HERZOG, GUS TRIANDOS
REDS' OCTAVIO ROJAS
PIRATES' DICK STUART
ANGELS' EARL AVERILL
PIRATES' DON HOAK
TO THE PHILLIES
WHITE SOX' LUIS APARICIO, AL SMITH
GIANTS' MIKE McCORMICK
STU MILLER JOHN ORSINO
PIRATES' JACK LAMABE
REDS' JOE GAINES
TWINS
METS' FELIX MANTILLA
YANKEES' BOB TURLEY (ON TRIAL)
TO THE RED SOX
COLTS' ROMAN MEJIAS, DICK WILLIAMS
RED SOX' PETE RUNNELS, CARROLL HARDY
TIGERS DICK BROWN
SENATORS' PETE BURNSIDE, BOB JOHNSON
GIANTS' DICK LEMAY, MANUEL MOTA
INDIANS' JACK COLLUM
ORIOLES' DICK WILLIAMS
TO THE ANGELS
TO THE ORIOLES
PHILLIES' JACKE DAVIS
PHILLIES' JIM COKER
TO THE COLTS
GEORGE ALTMAN
TO THE YANKEES
TO THE METS
DODGERS' STAN WILLIAMS
INDIANS' WYNN HAWKINS
RED SOX' TRACY STALLARD, PUMPSIE GREEN
TIGERS' STEVE BOROS
DODGERS' DICK SMITH NORM SHERRY
ORIOLES' ART QUIRK
TO THE CUBS
LARRY BURRIGHT
TIM HARKNESS
PIRATES' DON LEPPERT
TO THE SENATORS
BRAVES' KEN ASPROMONTE
TO THE BRAVES
COLTS' NORM LARKER
INDIANS' FRANK FUNK, DON DILLARD
MARV BREEDING, BARRY SHETRONE
CARDS' LINDY McDANIEL
JIM SCHAFFER
REDS' ROGELIO ALVAREZ
TIGERS' GORDON SEYFRIED, RON NISCHWITZ
TO THE REDS
PHILLIES' JIM OWENS
LARRY JACKSON
ORIOLES' DICK LUEBKE, WILLARD OPLINGER
CUBS' JIM McKNIGHT
CARDS' FRED WHITFIELD
BRAVES' DON NOTTEBART, CONNIE GROB, JIM BOLGER
BRAVES' JACK CURTIS, JOE ADCOCK
TO THE GIANTS
COLTS' JOE AMALFITANO
SENATORS' HARRY BRIGHT
CUBS' DON CARDWELL
PIRATES' DICK GROAT, DIOMEDES OLIVO
ORIOLES' JACK FISHER
BILLY HOEFT
TO THE INDIANS
INDIANS' RON TAYLOR, JACK KUBISZYN
TO THE CARDINALS
CUBS' MOE THACKER
JIM COKER

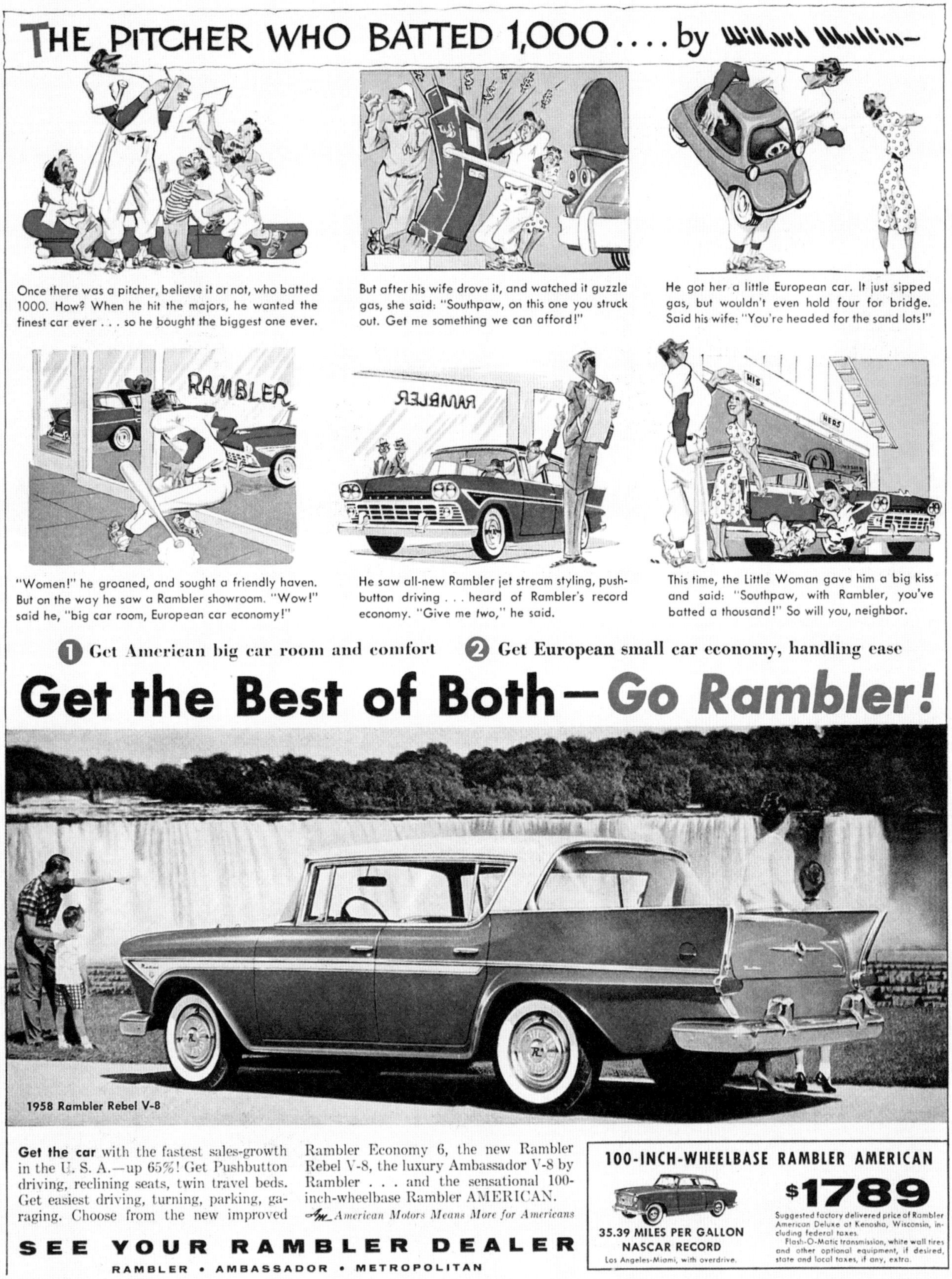
THE PITCHER WHO BATTED 1,000.... by
Once there was a pitcher, believe it or not, who batted 1000. How? When he hit the majors, he wanted the finest car ever . . . so he bought the biggest one ever.
But after his wife drove it, and watched it guzzle gas, she said: "Southpaw, on this one you struck out. Get me something we can afford!"
He got her a little European car. It just sipped gas, but wouldn't even hold four for bridge. Said his wife: "You're headed for the sand lots!"
RAMBLER
"Women!" he groaned, and sought a friendly haven. But on the way he saw a Rambler showroom. "Wow!" said he, "big car room, European car economy!"
He saw all-new Rambler jet stream styling, push-button driving . . . heard of Rambler's record economy. "Give me two," he said.
HIS
HERS
This time, the Little Woman gave him a big kiss and said: "Southpaw, with Rambler, you've batted a thousand!" So will you, neighbor.
1 Get American big car room and comfort
2 Get European small car economy, handling ease
Get the Best of Both—Go Rambler!
1958 Rambler Rebel V-8
Get the car with the fastest sales-growth in the U. S. A.—up 65%! Get Pushbutton driving, reclining seats, twin travel beds. Get easiest driving, turning, parking, garaging. Choose from the new improved Rambler Economy 6, the new Rambler Rebel V-8, the luxury Ambassador V-8 by Rambler . . . and the sensational 100-inch-wheelbase Rambler AMERICAN.
American Motors Means More for Americans
SEE YOUR RAMBLER DEALER
RAMBLER • AMBASSADOR • METROPOLITAN
100-INCH-WHEELBASE RAMBLER AMERICAN
35.39 MILES PER GALLON
NASCAR RECORD
Los Angeles-Miami, with overdrive.
$1789
Suggested factory delivered price of Rambler American Deluxe at Kenosha, Wisconsin, including federal taxes.
Flash-O-Matic transmission, white wall tires and other optional equipment, if desired, state and local taxes, if any, extra.

OPPOSITE: The American League expanded to 10 teams in 1961 and the National League to 10 in 1962. By the off-season in 1962-1963, there was a plethora of players being traded among the teams in the newly expanded leagues.

ABOVE: Mullin also did other commercial work, including this 1958 ad for American Motors.

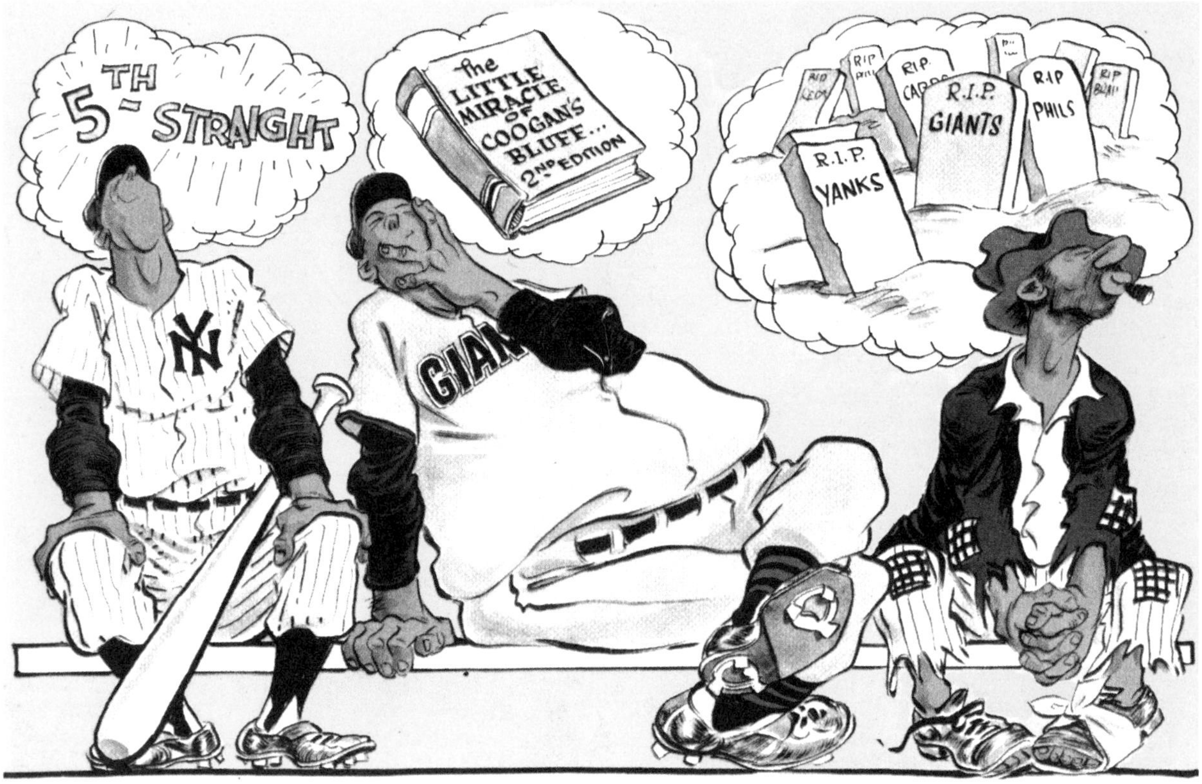
5TH - STRAIGHT
The LITTLE MIRACLE OF COOGAN'S BLUFF... 2ND EDITION
R.I.P. YANKS
R.I.P. GIANTS
RIP PHILS

Beginning in 1953, Mullin did the artwork for the Manufacturers Trust Company's pocket-sized combined New York baseball schedule, which included the Yankees, Giants, and Dodgers. He always included a two-page spread featuring the three New York ball clubs. In this first one, the Yankee is dreaming of a fifth straight World Series Championship; the Giant is still dreaming of another "Miracle of Coogan's Bluff"; and the Bum is just wishing all his rivals were dead!

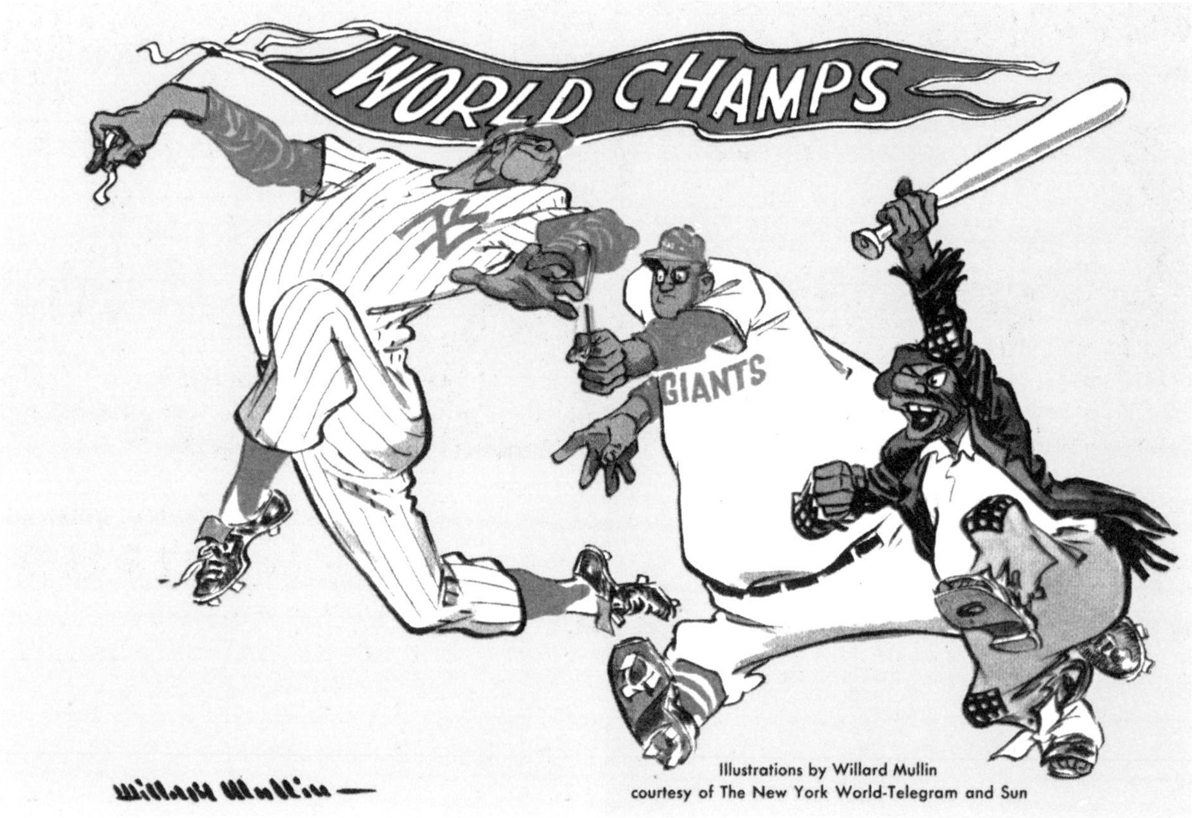
WORLD CHAMPS
GIANTS
Illustrations by Willard Mullin
courtesy of The New York World-Telegram and Sun

This spread from the 1954 schedule depicts the Yankees flaunting their fifth straight World Series Championship (in 1953) with the Dodgers and Giants in hot pursuit.

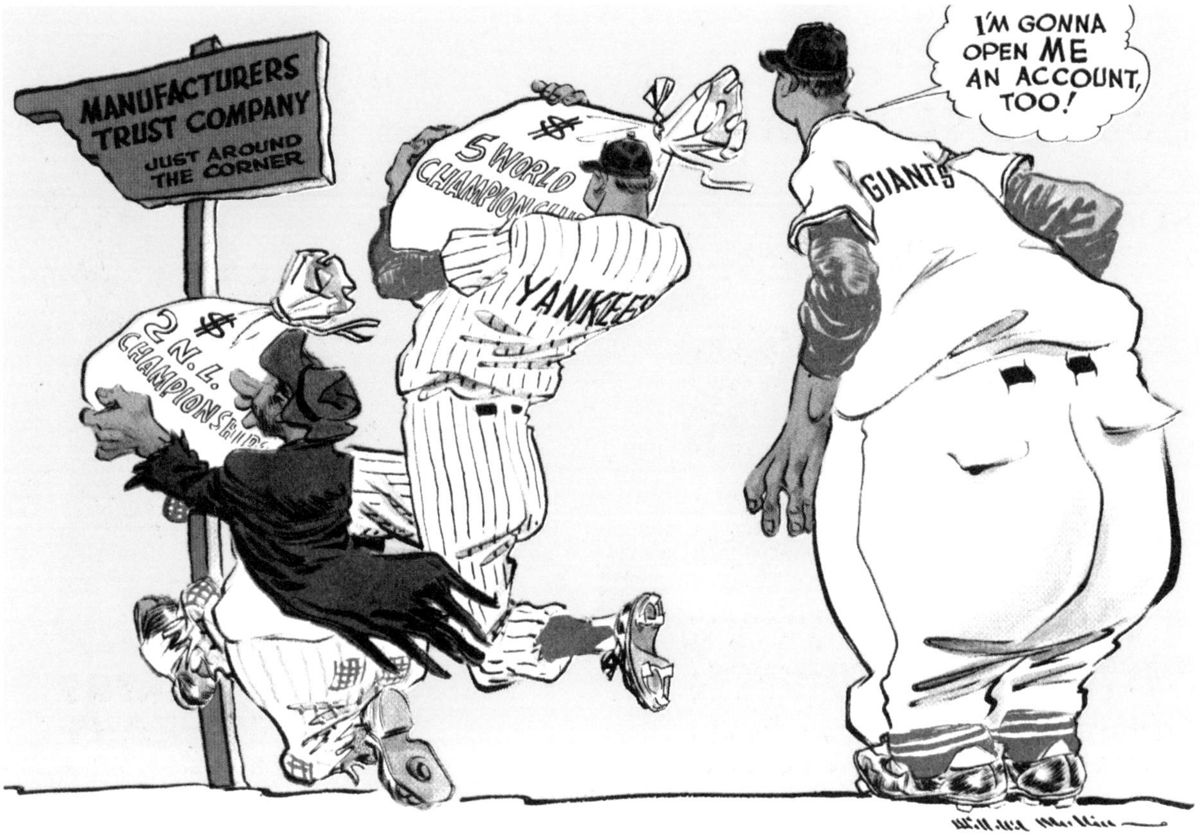
MANUFACTURERS TRUST COMPANY
JUST AROUND THE CORNER
2 N.L.
5 WORLD
YANKEES
GIANTS
I'M GONNA OPEN ME AN ACCOUNT, TOO!

At the beginning of the 1954 season, the Yankees were coming off five straight World Series Championships, and the Dodgers had claimed two straight National League pennants. The Giants would catch up by the end of 1954, sweeping the Cleveland Indians to win the World Series.

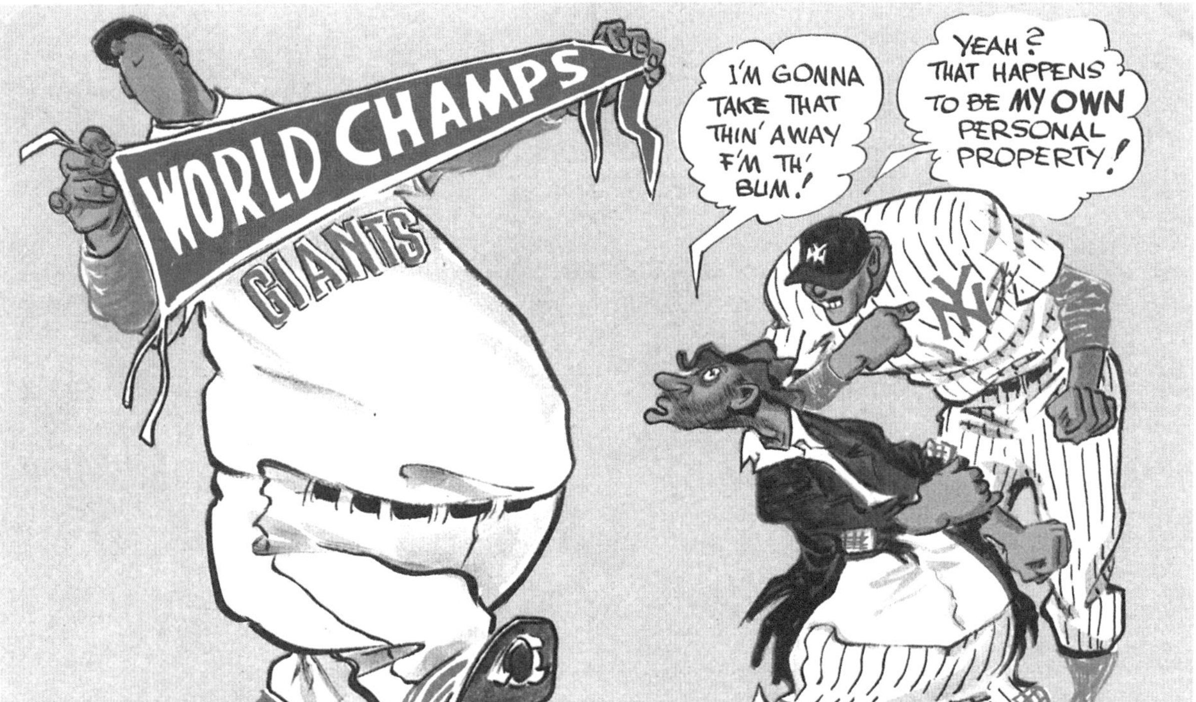
WORLD CHAMPS
GIANTS
I'M GONNA TAKE THAT THIN' AWAY F'M TH' BUM!
YEAH? THAT HAPPENS TO BE MY OWN PERSONAL PROPERTY!

Illustrations by Willard Mullin courtesy of the New York World-Telegram and Sun

This spread from the 1955 schedule celebrates the Giants' sweep of the Cleveland Indians in the 1954 World Series, ending the Yankees' run after five straight World Series Championships.

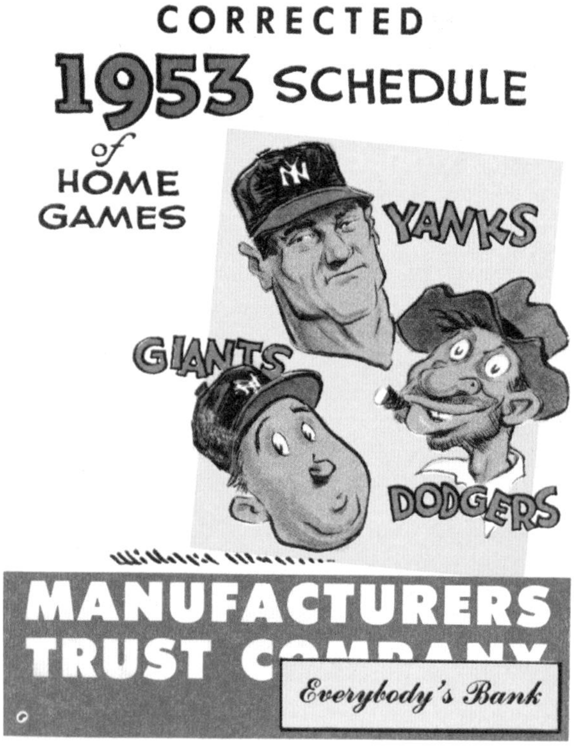
CORRECTED
1953 SCHEDULE
of
HOME
GAMES
YANKS
GIANTS
DODGERS
MANUFACTURERS
TRUST COMPANY
Everybody's Bank

The cover from the combined Yankees, Dodgers, and Giants schedule from 1953.

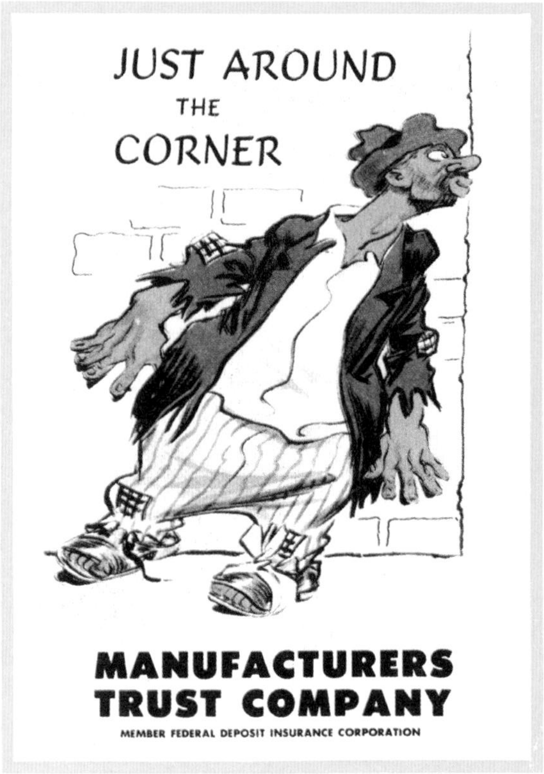
JUST AROUND
THE
CORNER
MANUFACTURERS
TRUST COMPANY
MEMBER FEDERAL DEPOSIT INSURANCE CORPORATION

A classic image of the Bum from the back cover of the 1953 combined schedule.

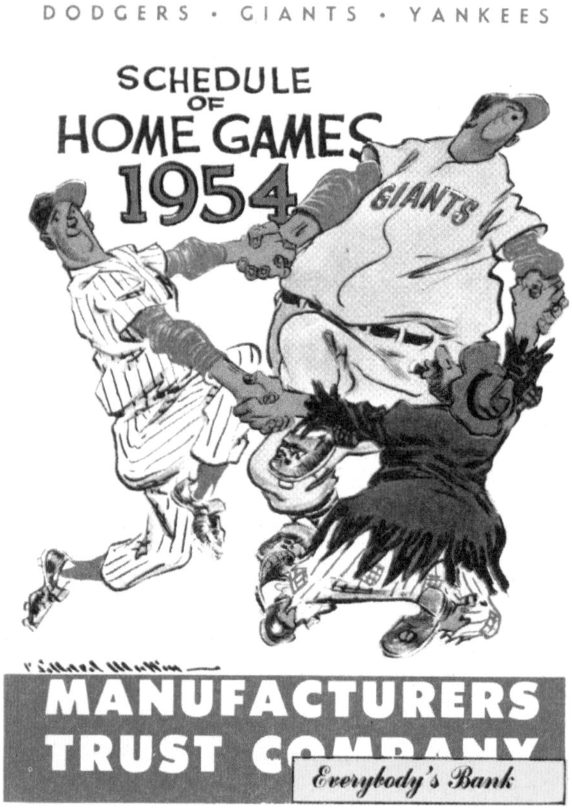
DODGERS • GIANTS • YANKEES
SCHEDULE
OF
HOME GAMES
1954
GIANTS
MANUFACTURERS
TRUST COMPANY
Everybody's Bank

The cover from the combined Yankees, Giants, and Dodgers schedule from 1954.

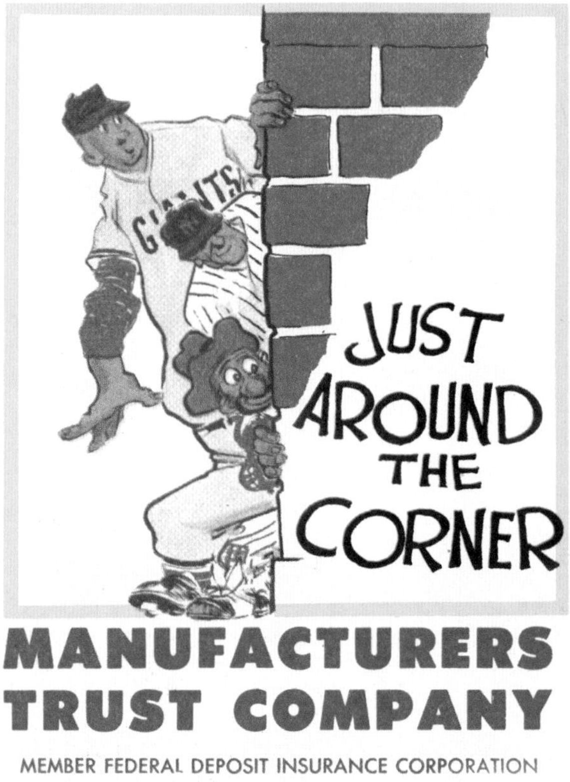
JUST
AROUND
THE
CORNER
MANUFACTURERS
TRUST COMPANY
MEMBER FEDERAL DEPOSIT INSURANCE CORPORATION

Willy the Giant, the Yankee, and The Bum from 1954.

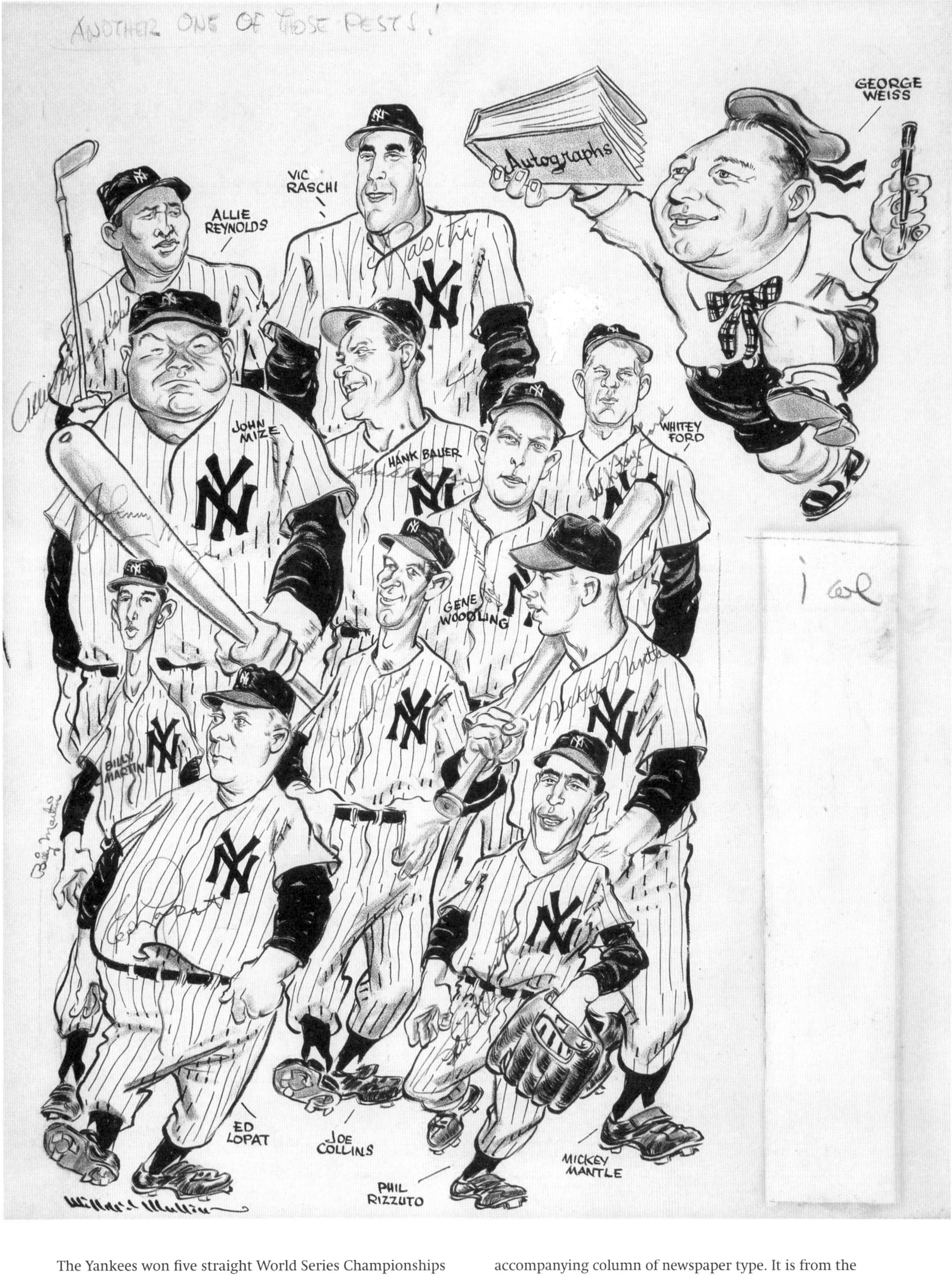
ANOTHER ONE OF THOSE PESTS!
GEORGE WEISS
Autographs
VIC RASCHI
ALLIE REYNOLDS
JOHN MIZE
HANK BAUER
WHITEY FORD
GENE WOODLING
BILLY MARTIN
ED LOPAT
JOE COLLINS
MICKEY MANTLE
PHIL RIZZUTO
Willard Mullin
1 col

The Yankees won five straight World Series Championships from 1949 to 1953. These players, along with Yogi Berra, represented the core of those Championship teams. This original Mullin drawing leaves space on the right for the accompanying column of newspaper type. It is from the personal collection of Yankees GM George Weiss and now resides at the Baseball Hall Of Fame.

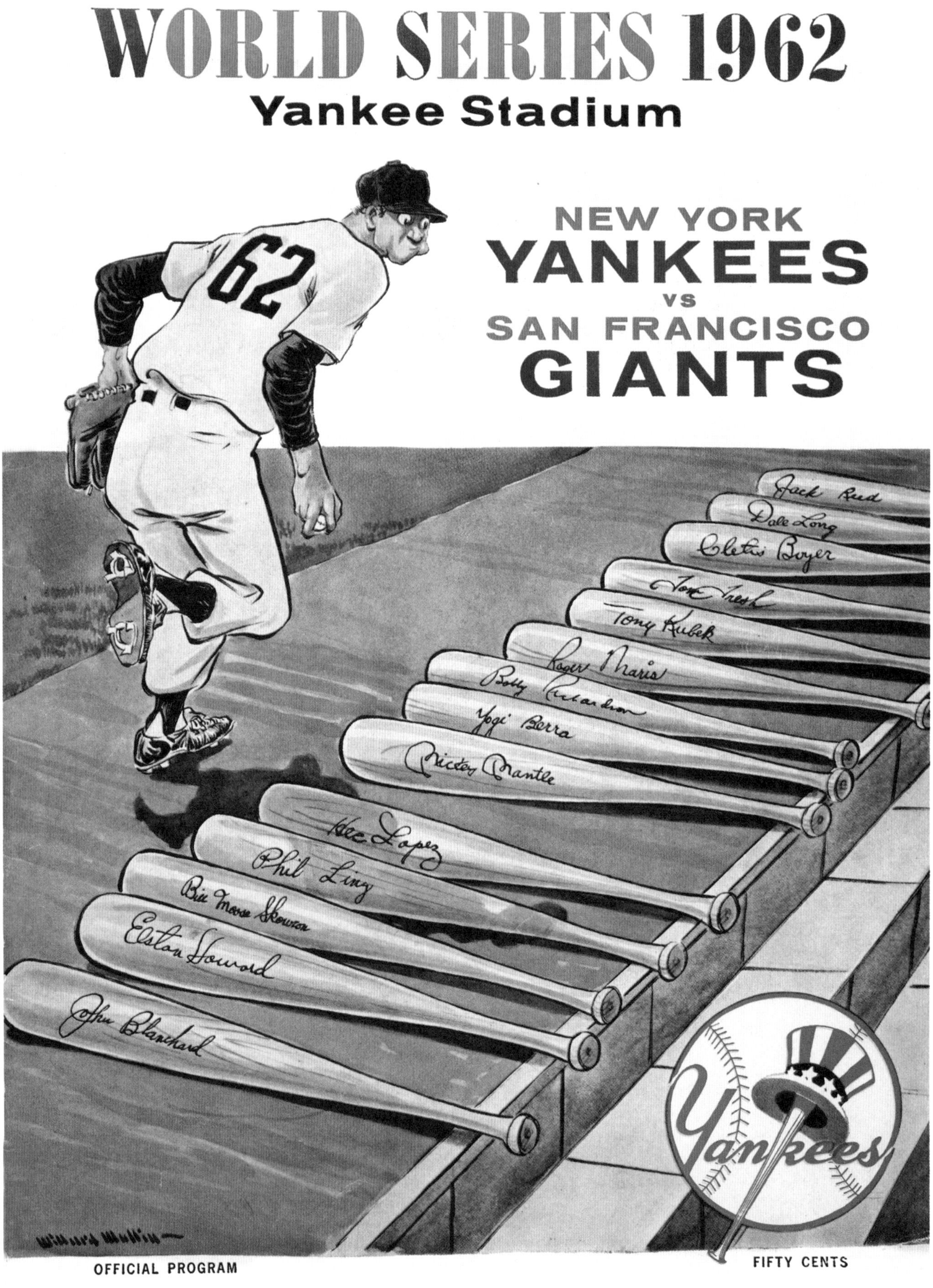
WORLD SERIES 1962
Yankee Stadium
NEW YORK
YANKEES
VS
SAN FRANCISCO
GIANTS
Yankees
OFFICIAL PROGRAM
FIFTY CENTS

The 1962 World Series was the first meeting between any of the New York teams since the Giants and Dodgers moved West after the 1957 season.

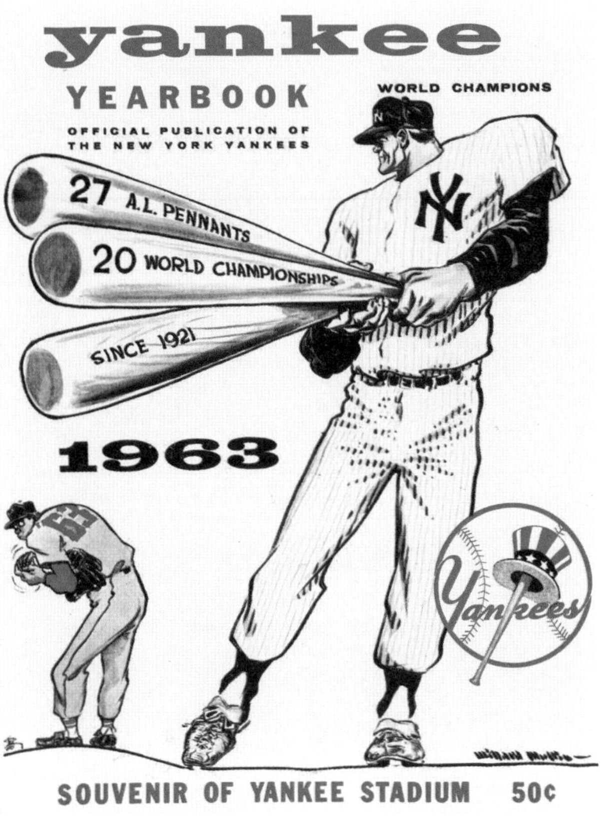
yankee
YEARBOOK
OFFICIAL PUBLICATION OF THE NEW YORK YANKEES
WORLD CHAMPIONS
27 A.L. PENNANTS
20 WORLD CHAMPIONSHIPS
SINCE 1921
1963
Yankees
SOUVENIR OF YANKEE STADIUM 50¢

By 1963, the Yankees had won 10 of the last 16 World Series and 13 of the last 16 American League pennants, cementing their claim as the greatest sports franchise in history.

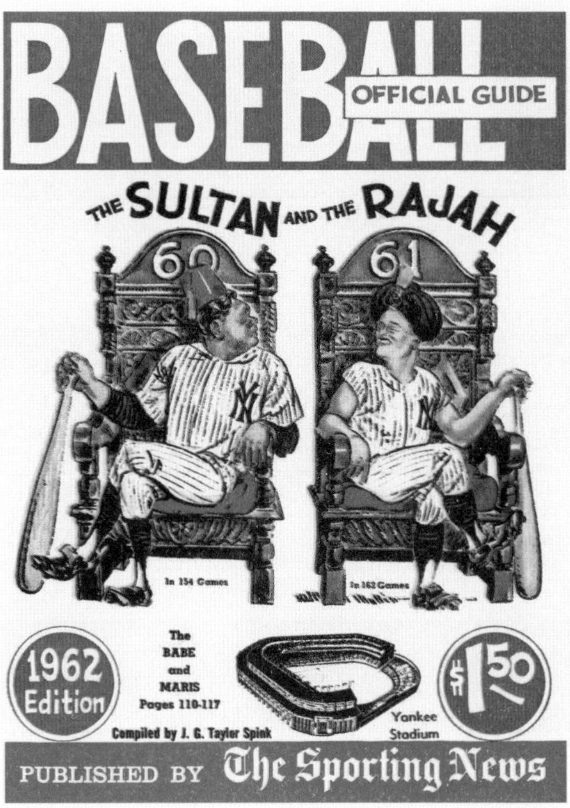
BASEBALL
OFFICIAL GUIDE
THE SULTAN AND THE RAJAH
60
61
In 154 Games
In 162 Games
The BABE and MARIS Pages 110-117
1962 Edition
$1.50
Yankee Stadium
Compiled by J. G. Taylor Spink
PUBLISHED BY The Sporting News

Cover of the 1962 edition of the *Sporting News Official Baseball Guide* featuring "The Sultan and the Rajah."

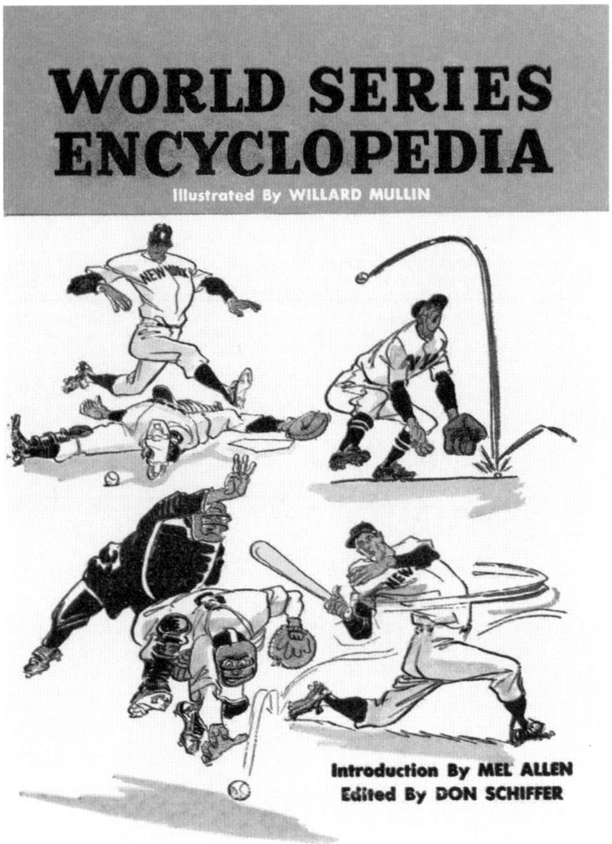
WORLD SERIES ENCYCLOPEDIA
Illustrated By WILLARD MULLIN
Introduction By MEL ALLEN
Edited By DON SCHIFFER

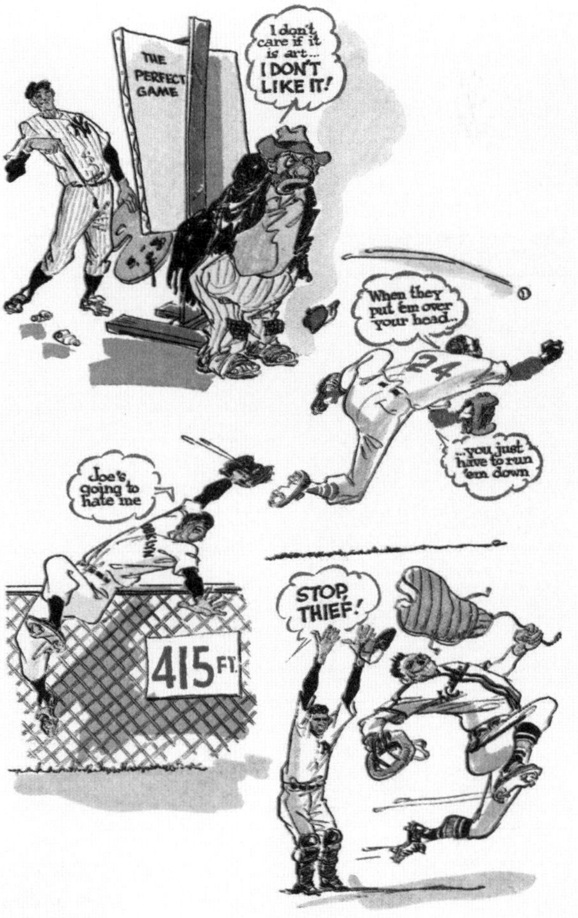
THE PERFECT GAME
I don't care if it is art... I DON'T LIKE IT!
When they put 'em over your head...
...you just have to run 'em down
Joe's going to hate me
STOP THIEF!
415 FT.

Front and back cover art for the 1961 *World Series Encyclopedia.*

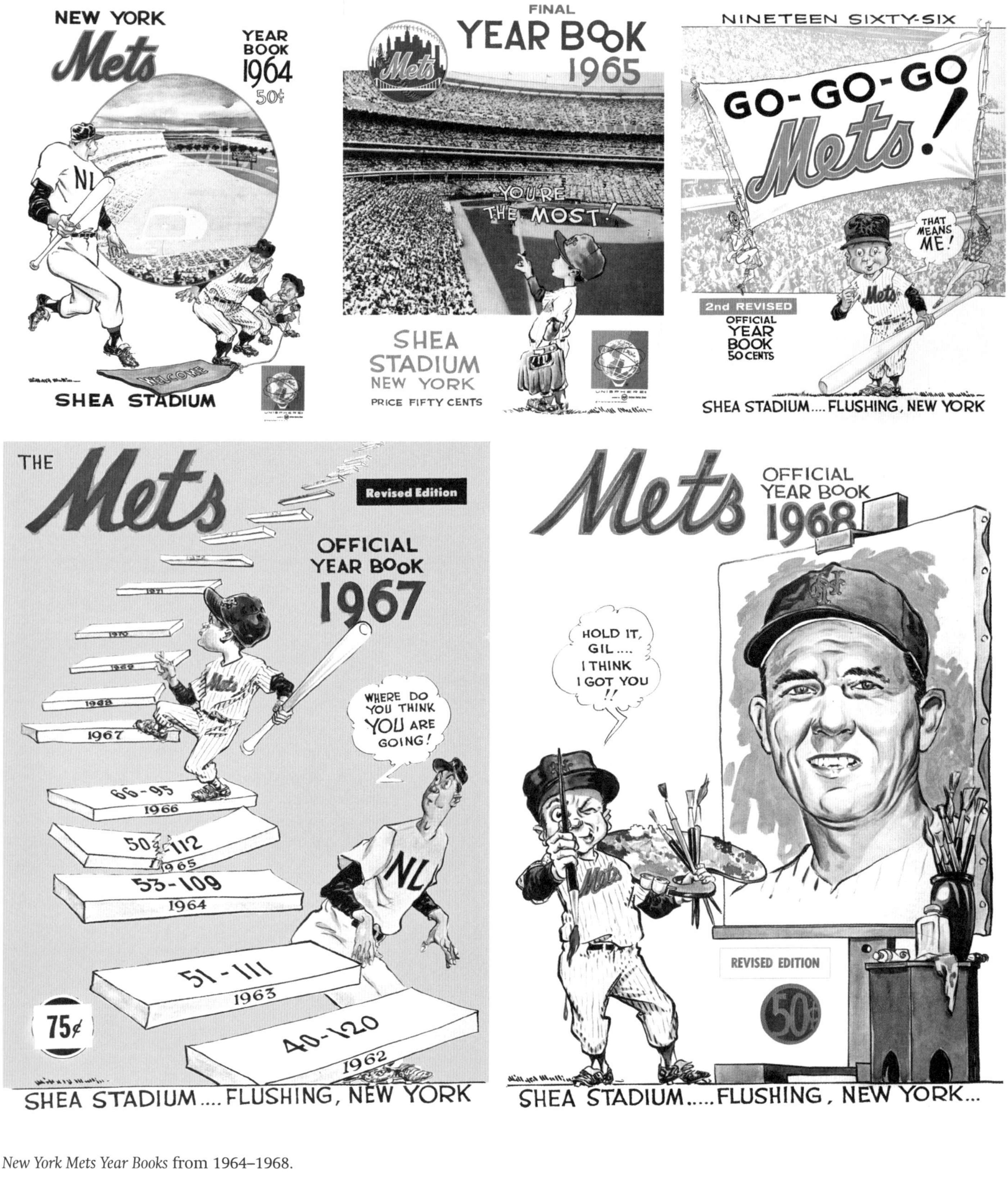
NEW YORK
Mets
YEAR BOOK 1964
50¢
NL
WELCOME
SHEA STADIUM
FINAL
YEAR BOOK
1965
Mets
YOU'RE THE MOST!
SHEA STADIUM NEW YORK
PRICE FIFTY CENTS
NINETEEN SIXTY-SIX
GO-GO-GO
Mets!
THAT MEANS ME!
Mets
2nd REVISED
OFFICIAL YEAR BOOK 50 CENTS
SHEA STADIUM.... FLUSHING, NEW YORK
THE
Mets
Revised Edition
OFFICIAL YEAR BOOK
1967
WHERE DO YOU THINK YOU ARE GOING!
1970
1969
1968
1967
Mets
66-95
1966
50-112
1965
53-109
1964
NL
51-111
1963
40-120
1962
75¢
SHEA STADIUM.... FLUSHING, NEW YORK
Mets
OFFICIAL YEAR BOOK
1968
HOLD IT, GIL.... I THINK I GOT YOU !!
Mets
REVISED EDITION
50¢
SHEA STADIUM..... FLUSHING, NEW YORK...

New York Mets Year Books from 1964–1968.

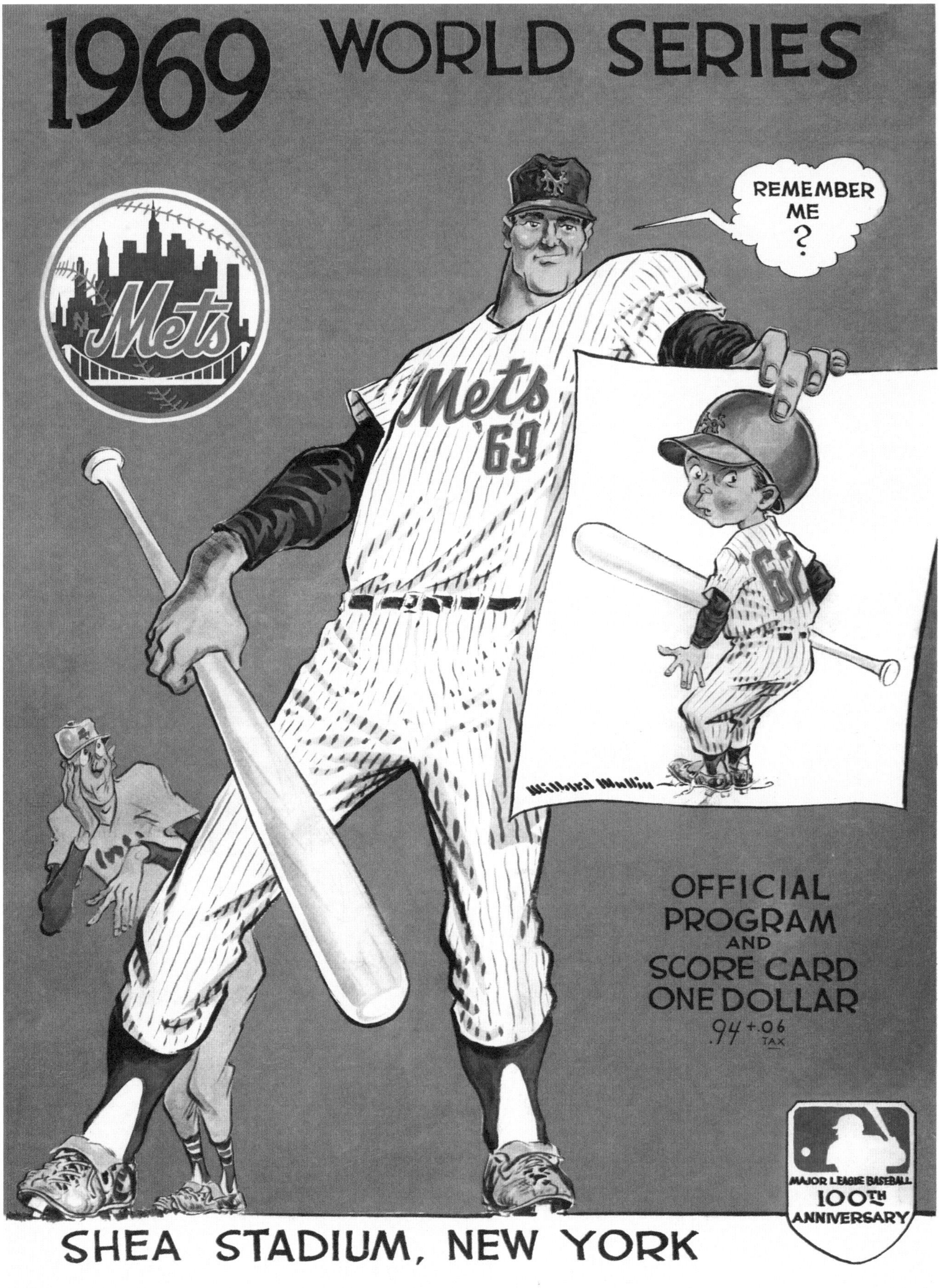
1969 WORLD SERIES
REMEMBER ME ?
Mets
Mets '69
62
Willard Mullin
OFFICIAL PROGRAM AND SCORE CARD ONE DOLLAR
.94 +.06 TAX
MAJOR LEAGUE BASEBALL 100TH ANNIVERSARY
SHEA STADIUM, NEW YORK

When the Mets were formed in 1962, Mullin depicted them as a little kid. By 1969, when they won the National League pennant and the World Series, they were clearly fully grown.

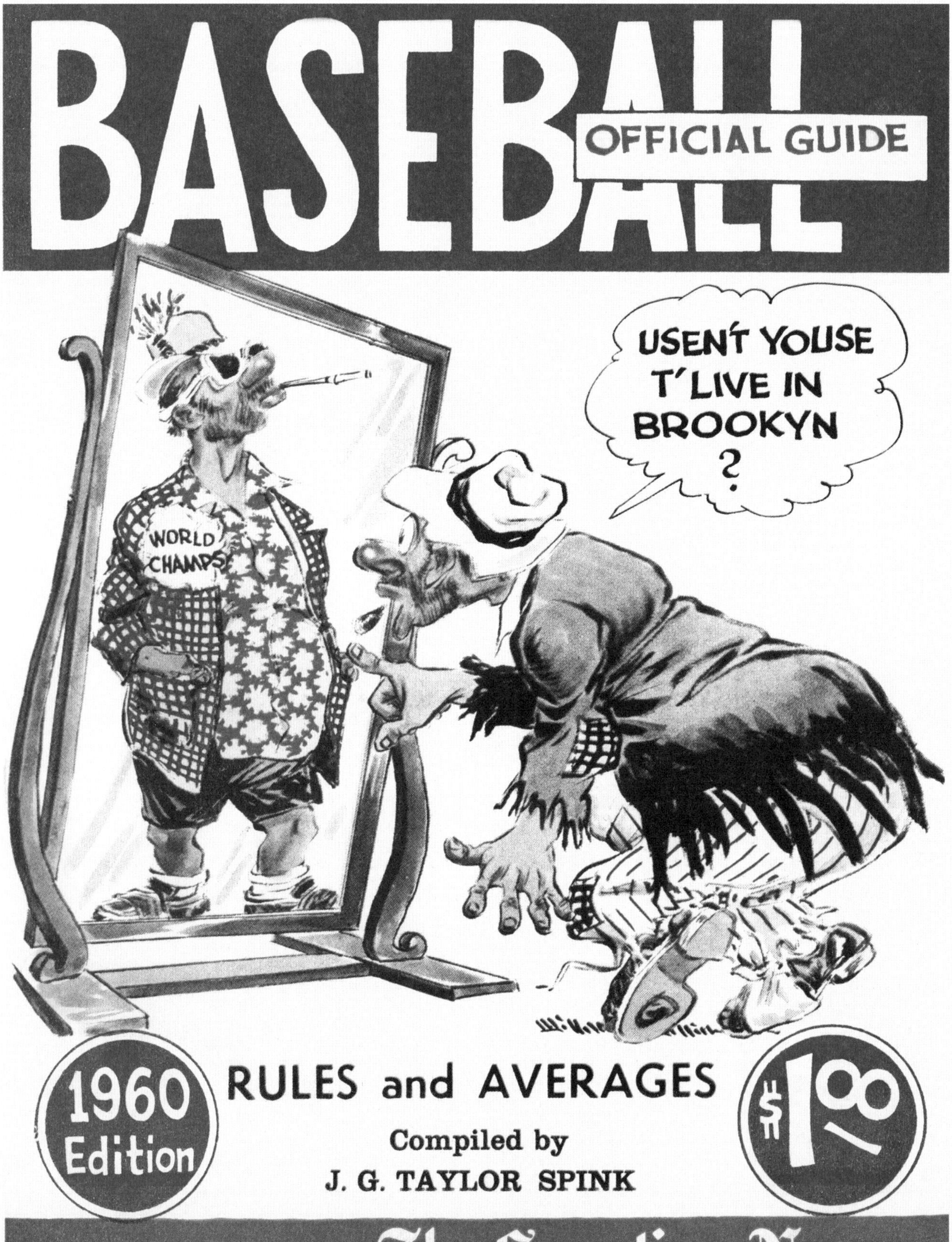
BASEBALL
OFFICIAL GUIDE
USEN'T YOUSE T'LIVE IN BROOKYN ?
WORLD CHAMPS
1960 Edition
RULES and AVERAGES
Compiled by
J. G. TAYLOR SPINK
$1.00
PUBLISHED BY The Sporting News

J.G. Taylor Spink was editor of the *Sporting News* from 1914 until his death in 1962. Mullin was a close friend of Spink and is estimated to have done more than 200 cover drawings for the *Sporting News*. Spink frequently used Mullin drawings for the covers of the *Sporting News*' specials, too. In 1958, the Dodgers moved from Brooklyn to Los Angeles. Mullin's Bum also made the transition, re-emerging as the Hollywood Bum.

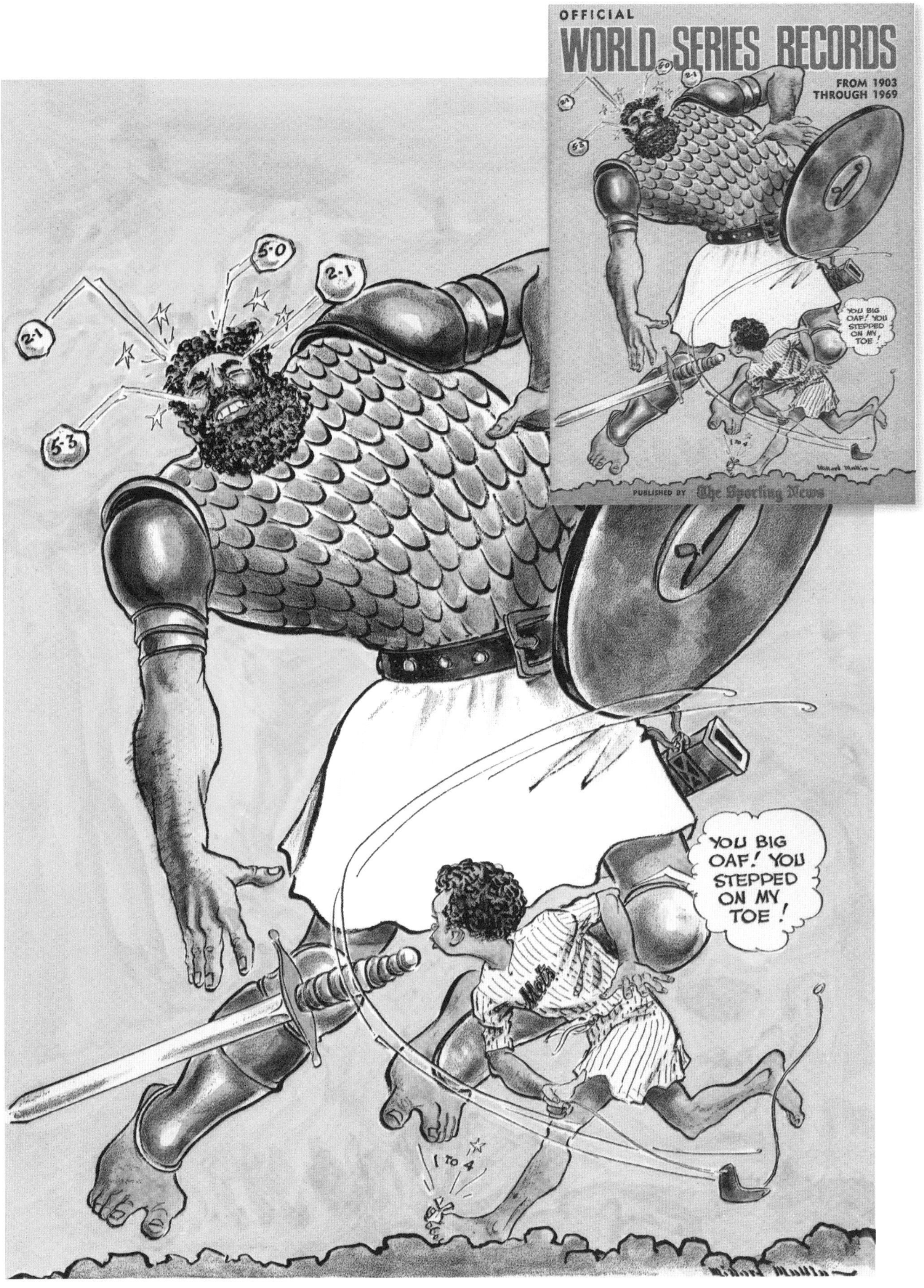
OFFICIAL
WORLD SERIES RECORDS
FROM 1903
THROUGH 1969
YOU BIG OAF! YOU STEPPED ON MY TOE!
PUBLISHED BY The Sporting News
5·0
2·1
2·1
5·3
YOU BIG OAF! YOU STEPPED ON MY TOE!
Mets
1 TO 4

In 1969, the New York Mets beat the heavily favored Baltimore Orioles to win their first World Series. This image, which was used for the cover of the 1969 edition of the Sporting News' *Official World Series Records*, displays the scores of the games the Mets won on the rocks bouncing off Goliath's head. The Orioles' sole win in the five-game series is shown as a stubbed toe.

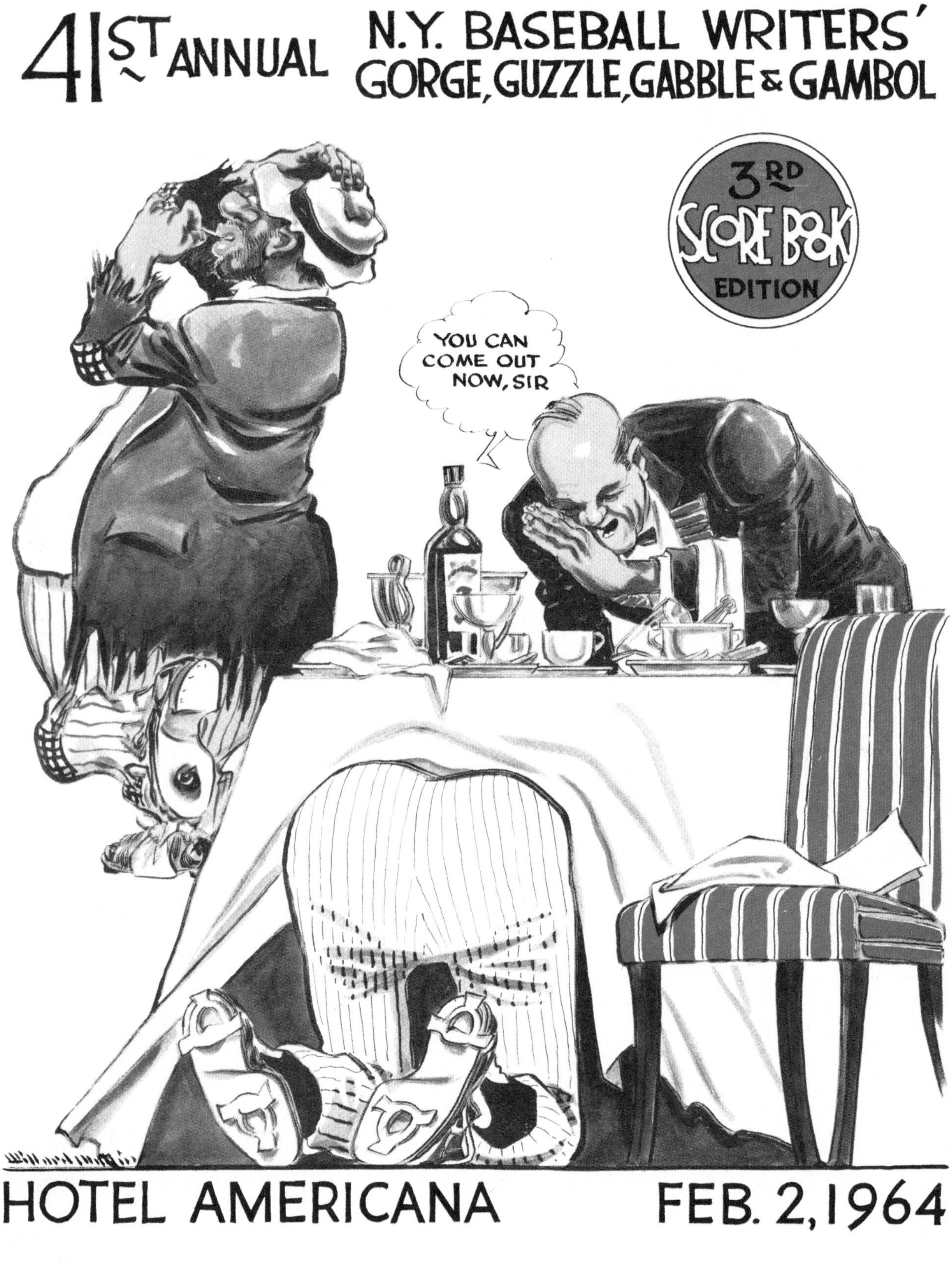
41st ANNUAL
N.Y. BASEBALL WRITERS'
GORGE, GUZZLE, GABBLE & GAMBOL
3RD
SCORE BOOK
EDITION
YOU CAN
COME OUT
NOW, SIR
HOTEL AMERICANA
FEB. 2, 1964

From 1941 to 1956, the New York Yankees played the Brooklyn Dodgers seven times in the World Series, winning six. In 1963, six years after becoming the Los Angeles Dodgers, the "Bums" gained a measure of revenge, sweeping the Yankees in four games straight to win the 1963 World Series — hence Mullin's Yankee's attempt to hide at the Baseball Writers' Dinner in January 1964.

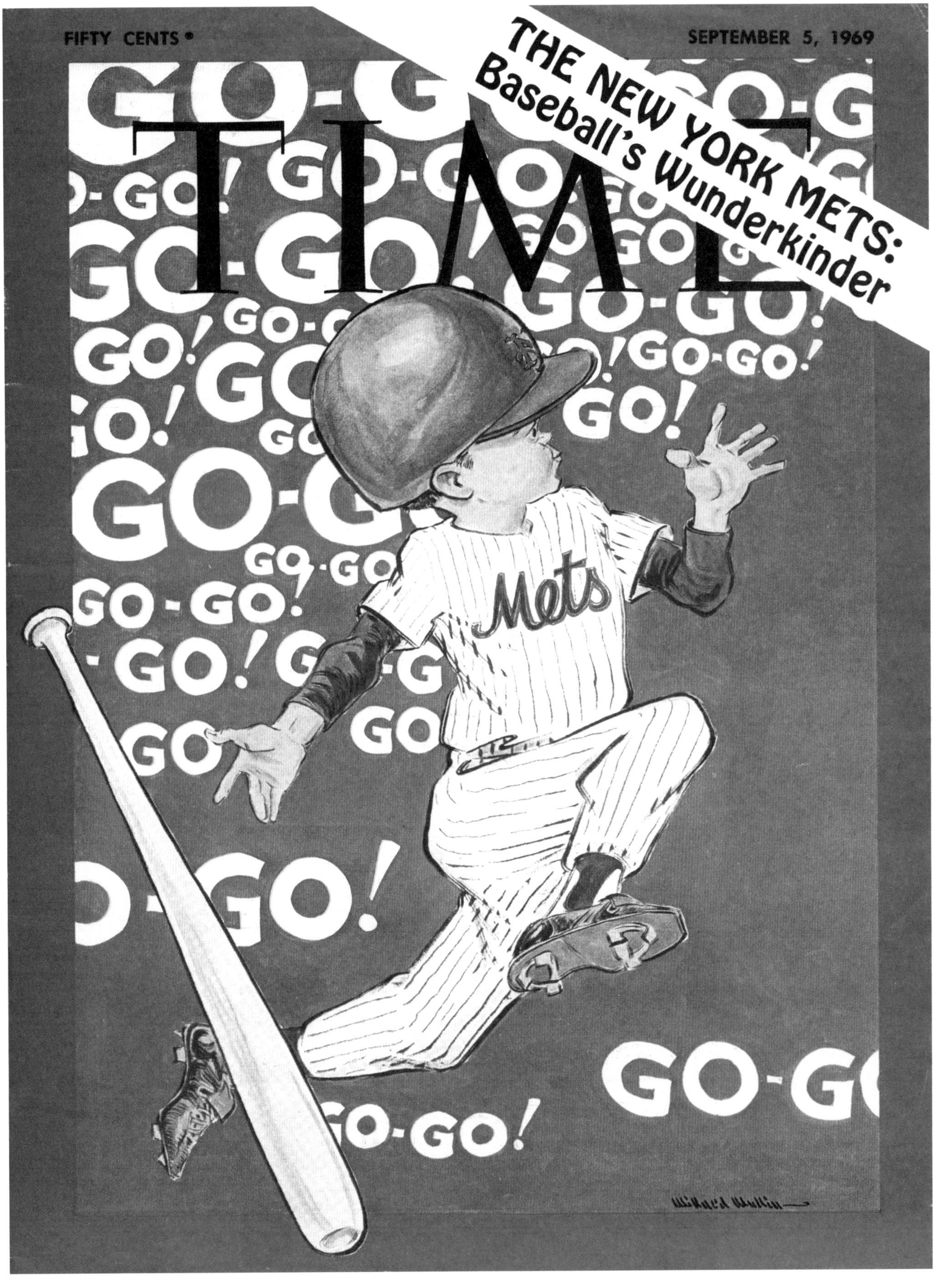
FIFTY CENTS
SEPTEMBER 5, 1969
TIME
THE NEW YORK METS:
Baseball's Wunderkinder
Mets

One of Mullin's final works before retirement was this cover for *Time* magazine, September 5, 1969.

Exaggeration

Exaggeration, as such, is not funny. A big nose, big feet or big hands do not help your cartoon unless they aid in getting over your point. But if you want to show that a shortstop has a great pair of hands and digs 'em out of the dirt, go ahead and put the dog-gonedest pair of meat hooks on him your conscience will allow you. Drawing Joe DiMaggio you'll give him a needle nose — Galento will be as wide as he is high — Hubbell's pants can drag the ground — and satchel feet are ol' Satchel Paige's trademark — but save your exaggeration for the spots where it will do some good.

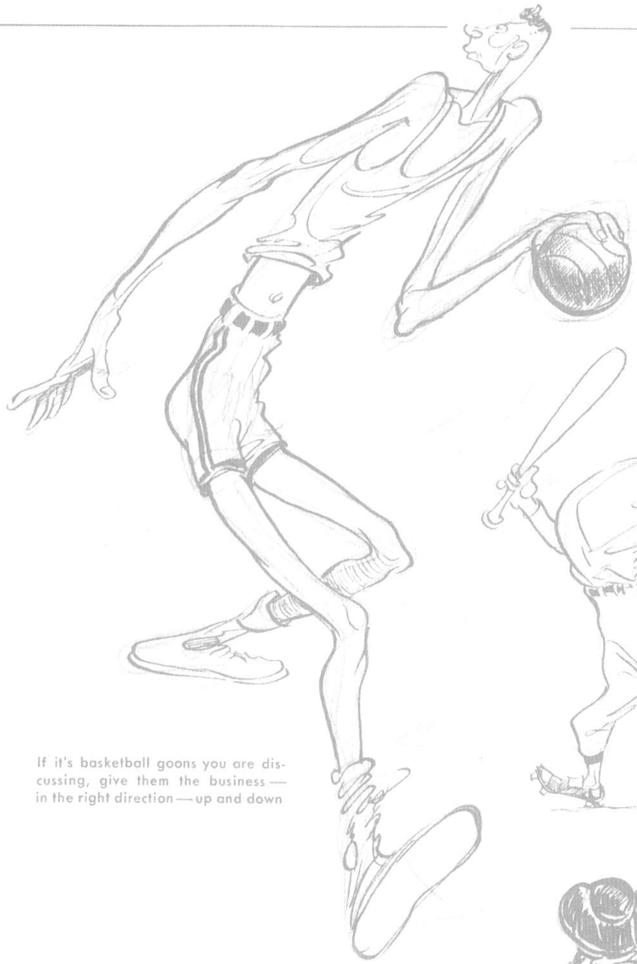

If it's basketball goons you are discussing, give them the business — in the right direction — up and down

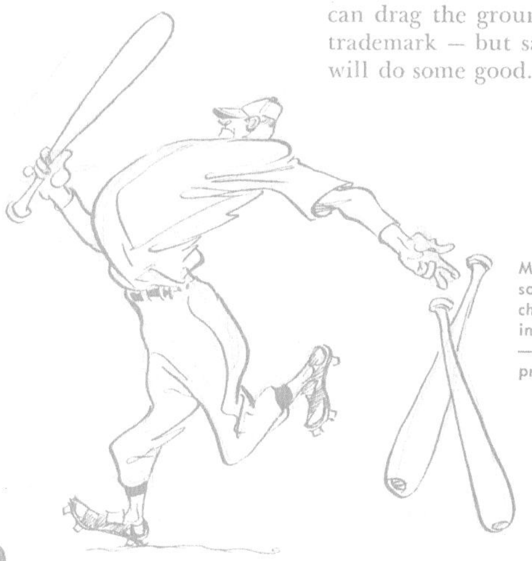

Make your little action figures mean something. Make them portray the character of the person you are talking about. If he is the clean-up man — the heavy hitter, confident and proud — let him strut

This is an example of how a gag grows. In showing exaggeration of a boxer laid flat, the question arose as to what the referee should be doing. What more natural than to have him figuring out how to scrape the guy off the floor

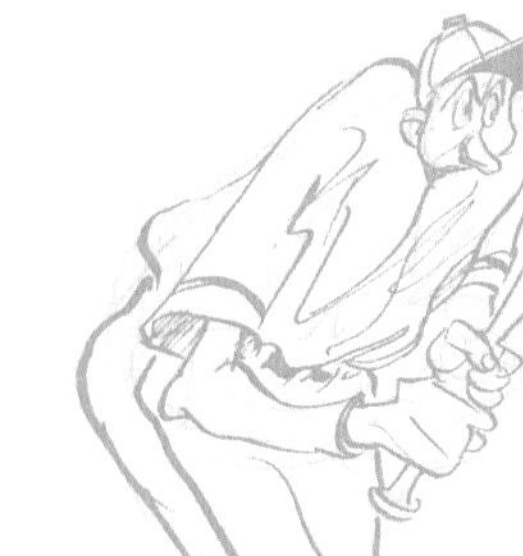

If he is the All-American out, going up there to fan, let your reader know it

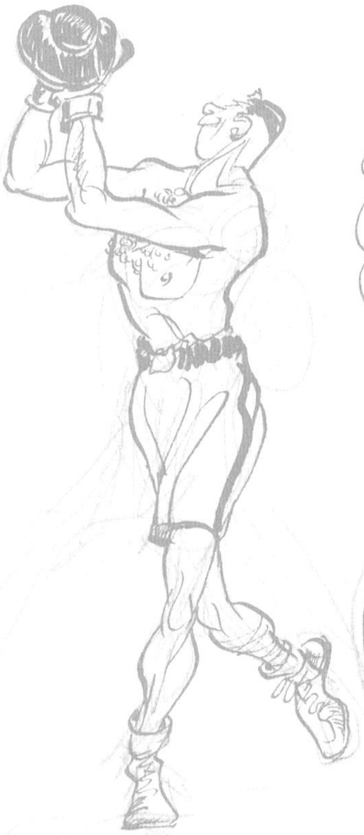

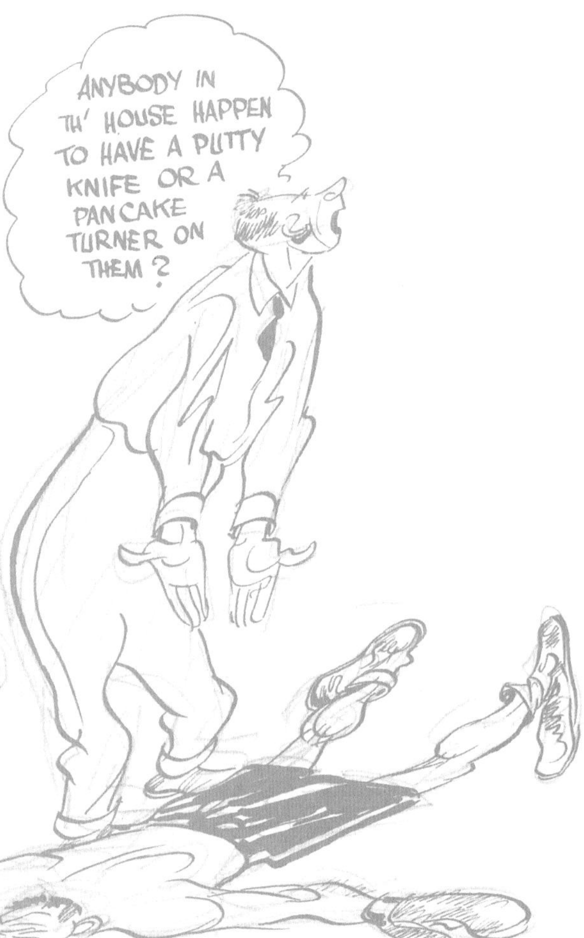
ANYBODY IN TH' HOUSE HAPPEN TO HAVE A PUTTY KNIFE OR A PANCAKE TURNER ON THEM ?

If you want to show a fighter knocked out cold and spread on the deck, you can't get him too flat

Sports Cartooning: Telling a Story in Pen and Ink

Hal Bock

IF A PHOTO IS WORTH A THOUSAND WORDS, then a cartoon is much more valuable. A photo captures an image with the lens of a camera. A cartoon tells a story through the imagination and skill of the artist.

In the early days of the 20th century, there was a pitched battle in New York journalism between two giants of the industry, Joseph Pulitzer and William Randolph Hearst. In the middle of the squabble was a silly-looking little character dressed in a full-length yellow smock. The Yellow Kid may have been the first continuing cartoon character, and even though he never showed much interest in sports, he soon had company in the pages of newspapers.

The battle between Pulitzer and Hearst led to the expansion of their papers — that expansion included the addition of sports sections and those sections were dressed up with the addition of comic strips. Among the earliest artists who created beloved comics characters were Bud Fisher (*Mutt and Jeff*), Johnny Gruelle (*Raggedy Ann and Andy*), and George Herriman (*Krazy Kat*). Each also dabbled in sports cartoons.

Mutt and Jeff were often found at the racetrack, handicapping the horses. Gruelle worked in Indianapolis and Cleveland and was syndicated by the Newspaper Enterprise Association. Herriman's work for Hearst's *New York American* often stretched the width of the page, giving him plenty of room to make his point.

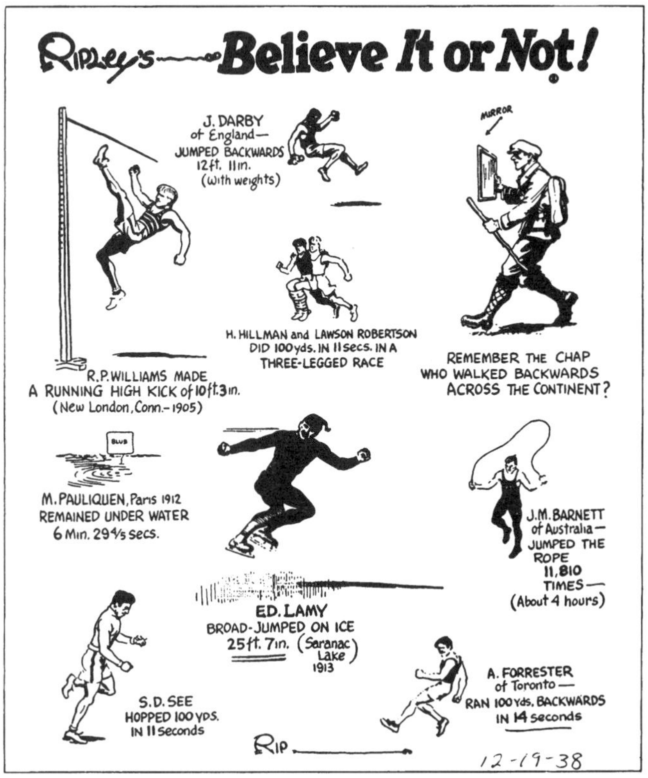
Ripley's—Believe It or Not!
J. DARBY of England— JUMPED BACKWARDS 12ft. 11in. (with weights)
MIRROR
H. HILLMAN and LAWSON ROBERTSON DID 100yds. IN 11secs. IN A THREE-LEGGED RACE
R.P. WILLIAMS MADE A RUNNING HIGH KICK of 10ft. 3in. (New London, Conn.–1905)
REMEMBER THE CHAP WHO WALKED BACKWARDS ACROSS THE CONTINENT?
M. PAULIQUEN, Paris 1912 REMAINED UNDER WATER 6 Min. 29 4/5 secs.
J.M. BARNETT of Australia— JUMPED THE ROPE 11,810 TIMES— (About 4 hours)
ED. LAMY BROAD-JUMPED ON ICE 25ft. 7in. (Saranac Lake) 1913
A. FORRESTER of Toronto— RAN 100yds. BACKWARDS IN 14 seconds
S.D. SEE HOPPED 100 YDS. IN 11 Seconds
RIP
12-19-38

In 1913, a young Californian who had done sports cartoons for the *San Francisco Bulletin* and later the *Chronicle,* sold a cartoon to the *New York Globe.* Leroy Ripley's work evolved into a regular feature and in December 1918, on a slow day, he published one called "Champs and Chumps," which strung together nine drawings that focused on obscure facts about sports. The idea caught on and a year later, the sports cartoonist changed his first name to Robert and changed his feature's title to *Believe It Or Not.*

Ripley, Fisher, and a host of others came to cartooning from California. Among that group was Rube Goldberg, who specialized in designing complicated

ABOVE: Leroy "Robert" Ripley's breakthrough came on a slow sports day.

OPPOSITE: A page Mullin did for the 1956 "Famous Artists Cartoon Course" edited by Rube Goldberg.

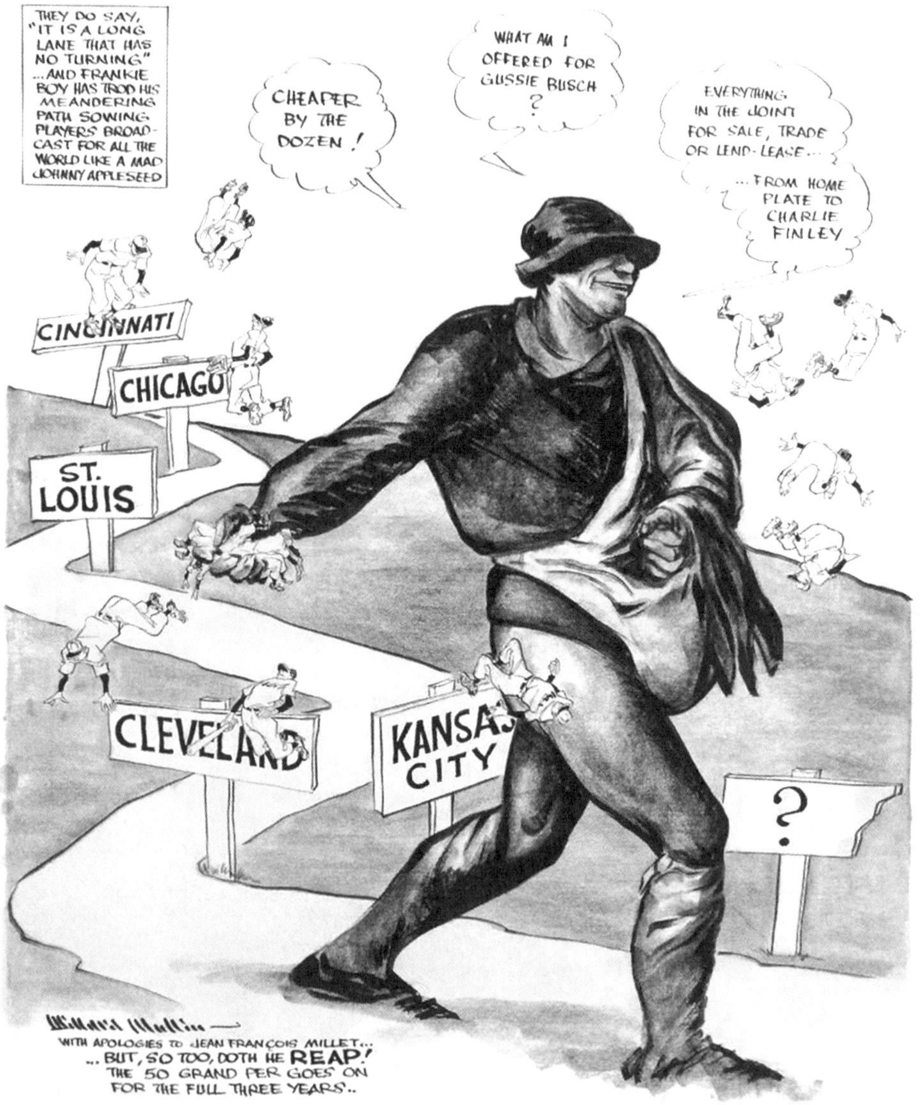
THEY DO SAY, "IT IS A LONG LANE THAT HAS NO TURNING" ...AND FRANKIE BOY HAS TROD HIS MEANDERING PATH SOWING PLAYERS BROAD-CAST FOR ALL THE WORLD LIKE A MAD JOHNNY APPLESEED
CHEAPER BY THE DOZEN!
WHAT AM I OFFERED FOR GUSSIE BUSCH ?
EVERYTHING IN THE JOINT FOR SALE, TRADE OR LEND-LEASE...
...FROM HOME PLATE TO CHARLIE FINLEY
CINCINNATI
CHICAGO
ST. LOUIS
CLEVELAND
KANSAS CITY
?
WITH APOLOGIES TO JEAN FRANCOIS MILLET...
...BUT, SO TOO, DOTH HE REAP! THE 50 GRAND PER GOES ON FOR THE FULL THREE YEARS..

ABOVE, RIGHT: Mullin studied the great artists, always seeking to improve his technique. This image is an homage to Jean-Francois Millet's *The Sower.* Mullin used the image as a metaphor for the trading propensities of the famous GM "Trader Frank" Lane. Lane, while GM of the Cardinals, once tried to trade legendary Cardinal Stan Musial for Phillies great Robin Roberts, before public outcry prompted Cardinals owner Gussie Busch to cancel the deal.

contraptions that performed simple tasks. Another was Thomas Aloysius Dorgan, who signed his work TAD. As well known as he was for his cartoons in the *New York Evening Journal,* TAD became famous for his contributions to slang as part of the English language. He originated a host of widely used phrases such as "dumbbell," "for crying out loud," "cat's meow," "cheaters," "twenty-three skidoo," and "hard boiled."

TAD's early work with the *San Francisco Chronicle* at the beginning of the century included the comic strip *Johnny Wise.* By 1905, he had moved to New York, where he produced a humor feature, *Daffydills.* He also did a single-panel series called *Indoor Sports* that evolved into his primary cartoon contribution to the craft.

Dorgan and his pal, Hype Igoe, journeyed together from San Francisco to New York and went to work for Hearst's *Evening Journal.* Igoe, who also contributed columns, was something of a dilettante. Among his skills was playing the ukulele, which he delighted doing out in the cold without benefit of an overcoat. This custom led to numerous stays in various hospitals with pneumonia. But Igoe was never deterred and even kept his ukulele in a refrigerator to improve its sound.

Sports cartoons often include acerbic commentary about players. Sometimes, the roles are reversed and the players get a platform for their own commentary. That was the case for Al Demaree, a pitcher for over eight seasons with the New York Giants, Philadelphia Phillies, Boston Braves, and Chicago Cubs. Demaree had an 80–72 lifetime record with 15 shutouts and a 2.77 earned run average. He went 13–4 in his rookie year with the Giants and 19–14 with Philadelphia when he threw complete games in both ends of a doubleheader. When the cigar-chomping Demaree retired, he turned to cartoons. His work appeared in 200 newspapers and was a staple of the *Sporting News* for 30 years.

Not all the sports cartoonists came from California. Tom Paprocki, who signed his work Pap, was a New Yorker and was working in a Brooklyn department store and going to art school at night. A friend got him a spot at the *New York American*. In 1932, he moved to The Associated Press, where his feature "Sports Slants" ran for 35 years.

Paprocki once described his craft this way: "Drawing the cartoon is more or less a mechanical process that takes four or five hours after all the materials have been gathered. It takes plenty of legwork and a lot of scratching to dig up interesting material. For the most part, it's simply a case of keeping on top of the sports news and following up leads and hunches."

Two years after Pap joined The AP, Willard Mullin arrived in New York.

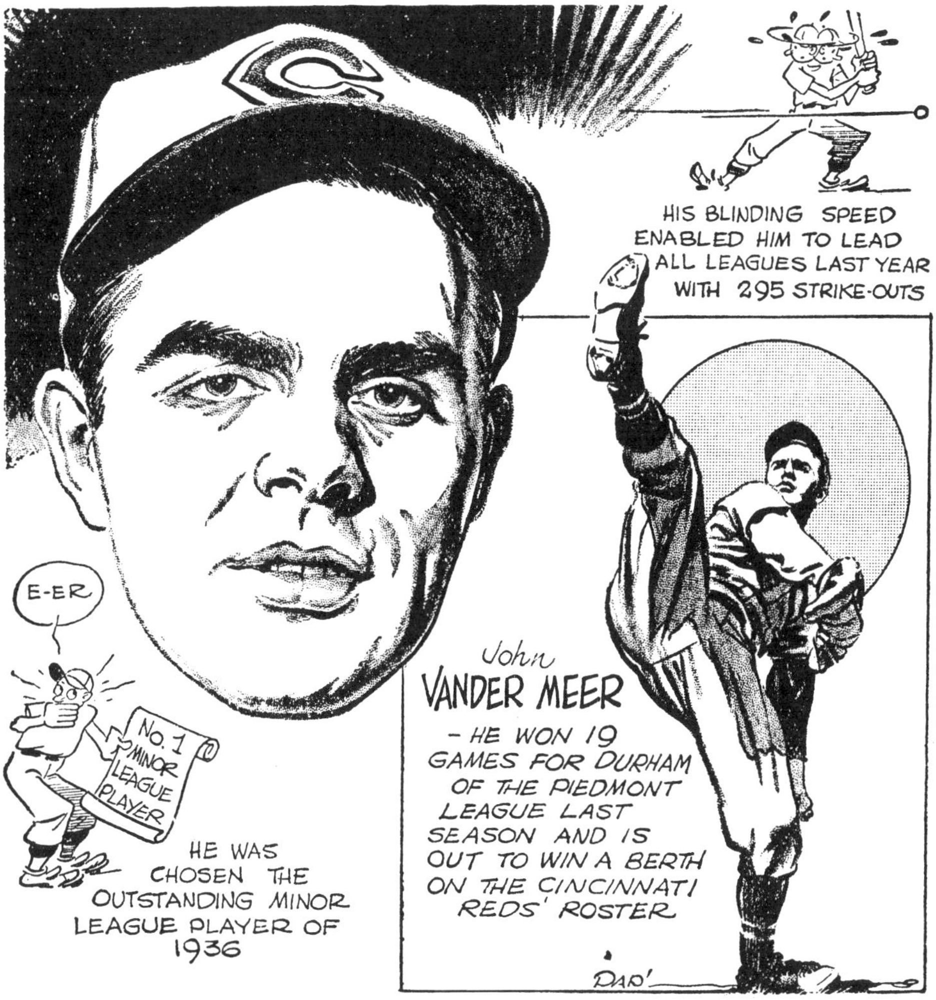
HIS BLINDING SPEED ENABLED HIM TO LEAD ALL LEAGUES LAST YEAR WITH 295 STRIKE-OUTS
E-ER
No. 1 MINOR LEAGUE PLAYER
HE WAS CHOSEN THE OUTSTANDING MINOR LEAGUE PLAYER OF 1936
John VANDER MEER
- HE WON 19 GAMES FOR DURHAM OF THE PIEDMONT LEAGUE LAST SEASON AND IS OUT TO WIN A BERTH ON THE CINCINNATI REDS' ROSTER
PAP

LEFT: This Tom "Pap" Paprocki cartoon from the spring of 1937 features rookie Johnny Vander Meer. Vander Meer would later become the only player ever to pitch back-to-back no hitters.

No Game Today—August 3, 1979

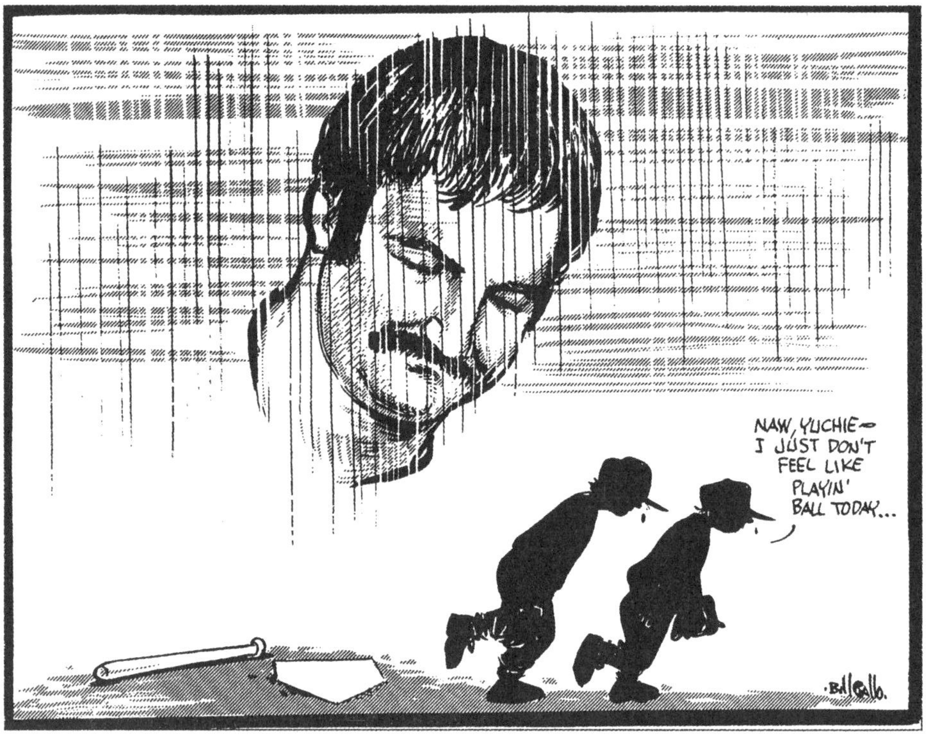
NAW, YUCHIE—
I JUST DON'T
FEEL LIKE
PLAYIN'
BALL TODAY...

Mullin had worked in Texas and California but found a home in New York, working for the *World-Telegram & Sun* and syndicated by Scripps Howard News Service. Mullin had a sense of humor, required for a cartoonist, and resided in a never-never land where bats and balls talked and players were drawn in broad strokes of pen and brush.

He also had an ability to solve problems, no matter how complicated. Once, on his way to an Army-Navy game with columnist Joe Williams, he discovered that he had left his press credential at home. No problem. When President Harry Truman's entourage entered Franklin Field, it included two extra Secret Service men at the rear — who peeled off at midfield and headed for the press box.

Mullin's work in the *World-Telegram* had plenty of company in New York over the next three decades. Burris Jenkins Jr. appeared in the *Journal-American,* John Pierotti in the *Post,* and Leo O'Melia — whose trademark was a miniature Leo the Lion and who signed his cartoons "By Leo" — in the *Daily News.*

Around the country, there were others who contributed mightily to the craft. Karl Hubenthal succeeded Mullin at the *Los Angeles Express.* Gene Mack started at the *Boston Globe* in 1915 and was famous for his renderings of Major League ballparks. At the beginning of World War II, Howard Brodie was drawing sports cartoons for the *San Francisco Chronicle.* He moved to *Yank* magazine, where he produced scores of battlefield images. Murray Olderman joined the Newspaper Enterprise Association, drawing cartoons to accompany his columns. Art was becoming a staple of the sports pages.

Jenkins, the son of a Kansas City preacher who also was editor of a local paper, called cartooning the quickest way of getting across an idea, much more effective than a column of type. His colleagues in the daily press would certainly agree with that.

ABOVE, RIGHT: The great Bill Gallo drew this iconic cartoon, which ran the day after Thurman Munson's death in a tragic plane crash in August 1979.

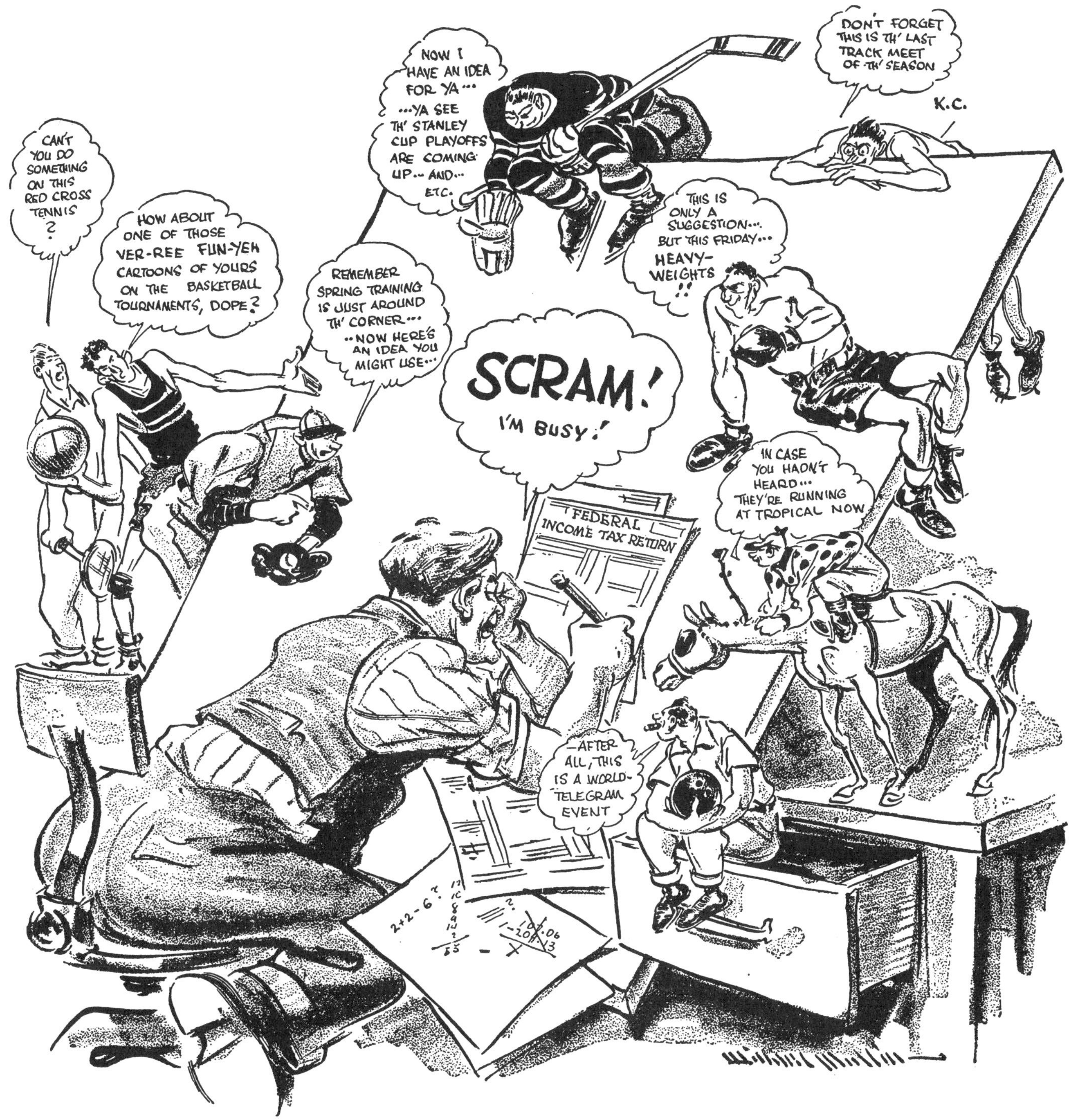
CAN'T YOU DO SOMETHING ON THIS RED CROSS TENNIS ?
HOW ABOUT ONE OF THOSE VER-REE FUN-YEH CARTOONS OF YOURS ON THE BASKETBALL TOURNAMENTS, DOPE?
NOW I HAVE AN IDEA FOR YA... ...YA SEE TH' STANLEY CUP PLAYOFFS ARE COMING UP... AND... ETC.
DON'T FORGET THIS IS TH' LAST TRACK MEET OF TH' SEASON
K.C.
REMEMBER SPRING TRAINING IS JUST AROUND TH' CORNER... ...NOW HERE'S AN IDEA YOU MIGHT USE...
THIS IS ONLY A SUGGESTION... BUT THIS FRIDAY... HEAVY-WEIGHTS !!
SCRAM! I'M BUSY!
IN CASE YOU HADN'T HEARD... THEY'RE RUNNING AT TROPICAL NOW
FEDERAL INCOME TAX RETURN
—AFTER ALL, THIS IS A WORLD-TELEGRAM EVENT
2+2-6?

Pierotti came to his craft naturally. His father was an art professor in Rome and his mother was a sculptress. He started at the *Washington Post* in 1933 and also worked for the McClure Syndicate.

Others who impressed Mullin were Billy De Beck (creator of *Barney Google* and responsible for a number of American idioms like "heebie jeebies," "balls of fire," and "hottsy-tottsy"), E.C. Segar (who created *Thimble Theater* and its star, Popeye), and Bob Edgren (whose *Miracle of Sports* cartoons were syndicated by Pulitzer's *Evening World* at the start of the 20th century).

Mullin, of course, invented the Brooklyn Bum to represent the often hapless Dodgers. Even when the Dodgers became competitive, the Bum remained their unofficial trademark. "I think of the Bum as being alive, with a personality of

ABOVE: As a general sports cartoonist, Willard Mullin had daily decisions to make about his subject matter. Mullin's boxing cartoons are as well known as his baseball cartoons.

his own," Mullin once said. "Out of his cocksureness and belligerence, the ideas come in flocks." That might explain why, of the estimated 10,000 cartoons Mullin drew for his New York audience, about 2,000 featured the Brooklyn Bum.

In 1955, when the Dodgers won the World Series for the first time, O'Melia celebrated with his own rendering of the Bum complete with bulbous nose, his mouth agape displaying a single remaining tooth, howling on the front page of the *New York Daily News*: "Who's A Bum!"

Mullin, O'Melia, and Lou Darvas of the *Cleveland Press* often occupied the front pages of the *Sporting News* when that periodical specialized in baseball.

O'Melia's successor at the *Daily News* in 1960 was Bill Gallo, a combat marine veteran who had fought at Iwo Jima and returned to become one of the most celebrated cartoonists of his time. Gallo contributed characters like Basement Bertha, who, despite all their foibles, loved the lowly New York Mets, and General Von Steingrabber, the alter ego of bombastic Yankees owner George Steinbrenner. Once, when someone asked Gallo how long it took to create a cartoon, he said, "two hours and about 40 years."

When Mullin was asked that same question, he replied with a question of his own. "Does that include the time you spend trying to outstare a piece of blank white paper, trying to hatch an idea?" he asked.

Ideas come from everywhere. Anything and everything is fodder for the sports easel. Then the cartoonist must transfer the ideas and draw well enough so that the reader understands the point the picture makes.

Once Mullin had an idea, he would set to work. He started with a sketch in pencil, first on soft paper, then on coquille paper. Then he began lettering the cartoon. Next, he used a pointed brush to begin completing the images. Black accents were then added for color and weight. After that came the final details, and then the cartoon was done.

For cartoonists, nothing is out of bounds. When Joe DiMaggio, out of character, suggested another team was crazy to think it could beat the Yankees, Mullin wheeled out a psychiatrist's couch. When Yankees owner George Steinbrenner reinvented Billy Martin for the third or fourth time, Gallo drew Martin as Gen. Douglas MacArthur returning to the Philippines during World War II. The trick is to deliver a message. Columnists use scores of words to do that. Cartoonists use pen and ink. The great ones do it every day. ❖

OPPOSITE: Willard Mullin's genius is evident in the composition of this piece. The player's entire uniform is composed of smaller line drawings of players in motion.

FOLLOWING: When the Brooklyn Dodgers won their one and only World Series title in 1955, Mullin commemorated the event by painting a full-color Bum on his drawing board and sending it to the Baseball Hall of Fame.

A LITTLE MAGIC ON THE SIDE -

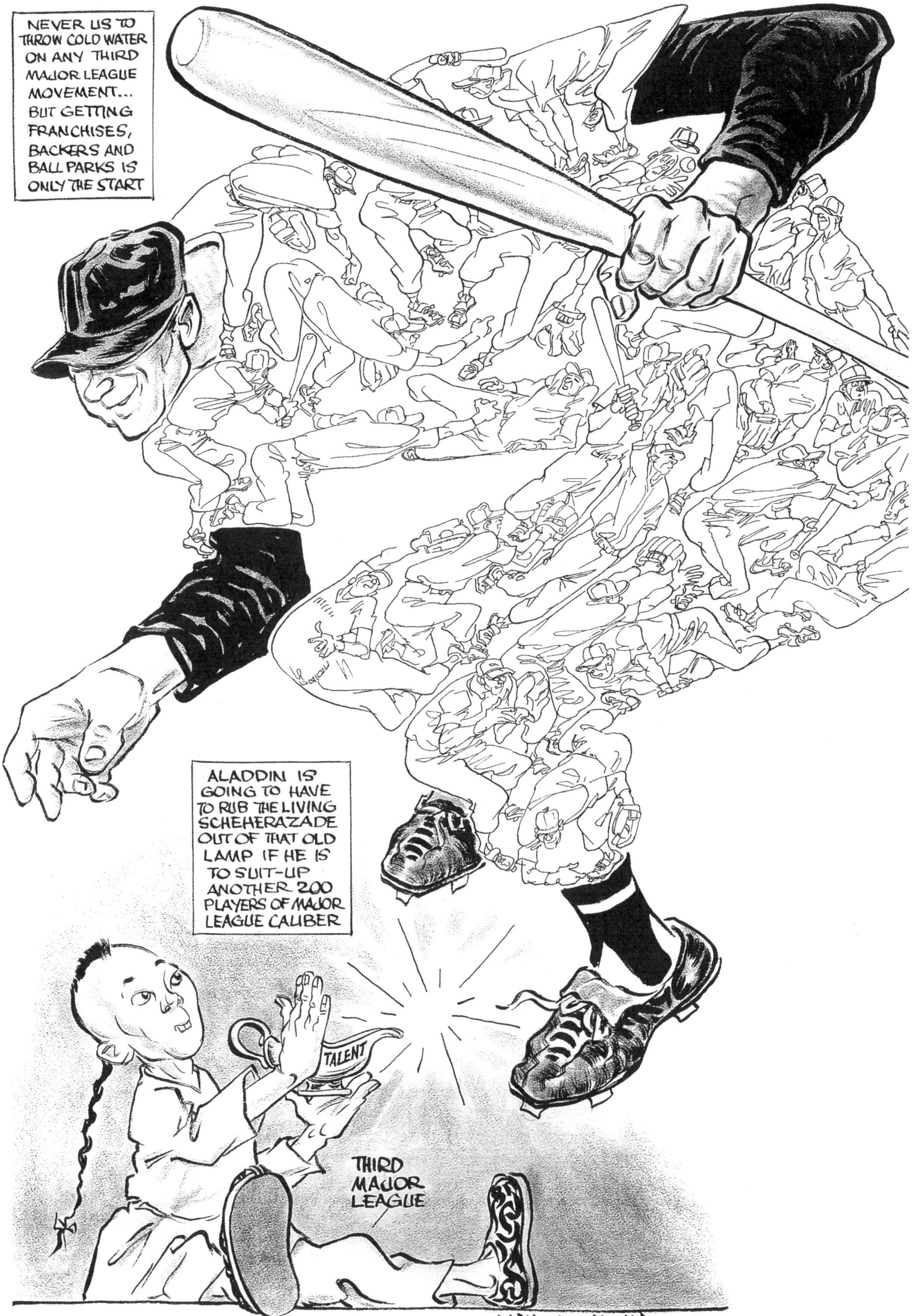
NEVER US TO THROW COLD WATER ON ANY THIRD MAJOR LEAGUE MOVEMENT... BUT GETTING FRANCHISES, BACKERS AND BALL PARKS IS ONLY THE START
ALADDIN IS GOING TO HAVE TO RUB THE LIVING SCHEHERAZADE OUT OF THAT OLD LAMP IF HE IS TO SUIT-UP ANOTHER 200 PLAYERS OF MAJOR LEAGUE CALIBER
TALENT
THIRD MAJOR LEAGUE

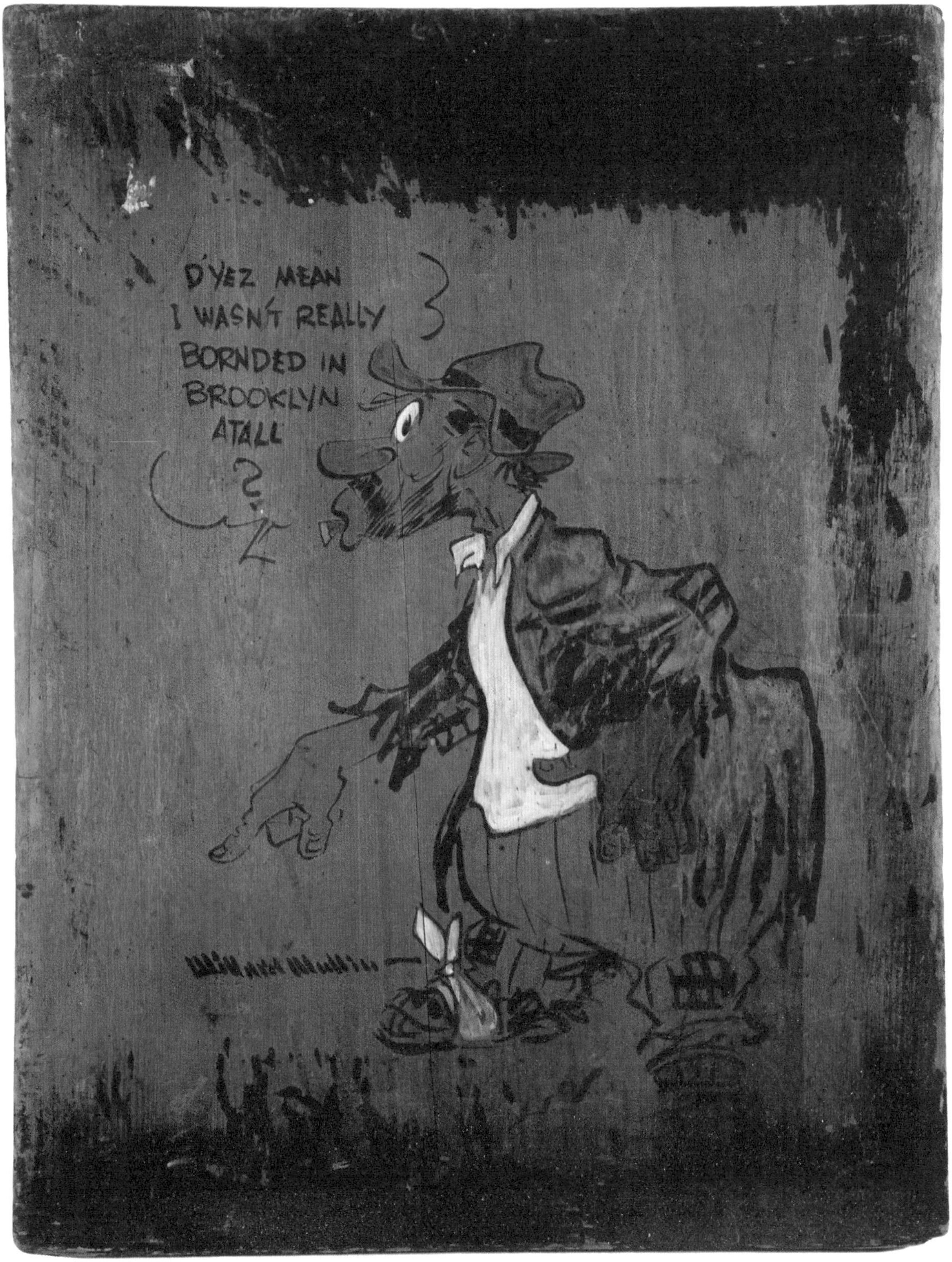
D'YEZ MEAN
I WASN'T REALLY
BORNDED IN
BROOKLYN
ATALL
?

MICHAEL POWERS is an attorney who has represented the Estate of Willard Mullin for over 15 years. During that time, he has located and catalogued over 3,000 Mullin images including all those contained in this volume. He curated the largest exhibit of Mullin's work, in 2003 at the Society of Illustrators in New York City, and the permanent Mullin exhibit at the San Francisco Giants' AT&T Park.

HAL BOCK wrote sports for 40 years at The Associated Press, covering every major event from the Kentucky Derby to the Indy 500, from Wimbledon to the Masters, from the Stanley Cup to the Davis Cup. Over his career, he covered more World Series and more Super Bowls than any other AP reporter. He has written scores of magazine articles and written or edited 13 sports books including *The Associated Press Pictorial History of Baseball* and has been Adjunct Professor of Journalism and Journalist-in-Residence at Long Island University's Brooklyn campus. He lives on Long Island with his wife, a retired psychologist, and their cat.